THE AMERICAN ASSOCIATION

O'BRIEN, St. Paul

FREEMAN, Toledo

PUTTMAN, Louisville

RITTER, Kansas City

HAYDEN, Indianapolis

HINCHMAN, Toledo

YOUNG, Minneapolis

LUNDGREN, Kansas City

CARR, Indianapolis

The
American Association

*Year-by-Year Statistics
for the Baseball Minor League,
1902 – 1952*

BY

MARSHALL D. WRIGHT

McFarland & Company, Inc., Publishers
Jefferson, North Carolina, and London

Frontipiece: Selection of T-206 baseball cards, ca. 1910, depicting
American Association players.

British Library Cataloguing-in-Publication data are available

Library of Congress Cataloguing-in-Publication Data

Wright, Marshall D.
    The American Association : year-by-year statistics for the
baseball minor league, 1902–1952 / by Marshall D. Wright.
      p.   cm.
    Includes bibliographical references (p.   ) and index. ∞
    ISBN 0-7864-0316-0 (sewn softcover : 50# alkaline paper)
    1. American Association (Baseball league)—History—Statistics.
I. Title.
    GV875.A57W75.1997
    796.357'64—dc21   96-51862
                                                   CIP

Manufactured in the United States of America

McFarland & Company, Inc., Publishers

To Dad, who watched the Millers at Nicollet, and
to Mom, who saw the Stars at Gilmore

Table of Contents

Acknowledgments

A book like this has to have a firm foundation to stand properly. To me, this foundation consists of the support and help from professional and personal sources, without which a project like this can easily crumble.

On a professional level, I would like to thank Howe Sportsdata International for letting me copy at will from their vast collection of *Spalding* and *Reach Guides*. I would also like to thank Ray Nemec for providing the hard-to-find statistics missing from the guides, as well as the photograph that appears on the cover. Thanks also to Gary Austin for supplying the statistics for a couple of missing seasons. And for the fine photography work, a special thanks to Mike and Linda Sylvester of Reflected Light Images.

On a personal level, I would like to thank Dr. Martha Gray and all my colleagues at the Health Sciences and Technology Division of the Harvard Medical School at MIT. Also, thanks to Jay Virshbo and my friends and associates at Howe Sportsdata.

Lastly, I would like to thank my family, and especially my wife Jane and my son Denny, for their unflagging support. Without them, you wouldn't be reading this today.

Introduction

Major league baseball has had its statistical story told in many different ways. Numerous tomes display the history of each and every major league player, individually and by team. However, there is a much larger group of ballplayers that have not been covered in such a glorious fashion— baseball's minor leaguers. It is the intent of this book to address this need, and to cover statistically one of baseball's top minor leagues: the American Association.

For more than ninety years, the American Association has resided squarely at the apex of the minor league baseball world, one rung below the major leagues. Together with its cohorts at the top, the International League on the East Coast and the Pacific Coast League in the West, the American Association in the center links the three to blanket the country with top minor league baseball.

Formed in 1902, the American Association was deliberately designed to be one of the top minor leagues in the land, and its teams saw the best baseball players the minors had to offer. They also participated at an early date in key innovations such as interleague and divisional play, as well as post-season playoffs, which are a key part of the minor leagues today. But the uniqueness of the Association's first fifty years lies in another direction.

During the first half of the twentieth century, minor league baseball franchises were unstable entities. In the approximately 1,000 cities and towns that boasted a minor league team between 1902 and 1950, the average duration of that franchise was under five years. The top minor leagues enjoyed more stability, although their teams averaged only seventeen years before relocation. However, the American Association did not fit this pattern for the simple reason that none of the franchises changed during the first fifty years of the league's existence. The eight cities that comprised the circuit in 1902 were the same eight cities that started the 1952 season. This 50-year run of stability for a minor league was unique and truly remarkable. In 1953, one of the original franchises was displaced by an incoming major league team, ending this remarkable run of stability.

The displacement of minor league franchises by major league expansion or relocation was not a problem unique to the American Association. Top minor leagues were vulnerable to this kind of pressure because they were generally situated in the largest cities and thus were the ripest plums to be plucked by major league owners. During the 1950s, minor league cities from coast to coast were enticed by overtures from the majors, and several succumbed. When a minor league loses a member in this fashion, something special is lost. The affected minor league generally continues, albeit in altered fashion. But a sense of innocence is lost, replaced by a sense of vulnerability; a feeling that the same thing could happen again to any league city, at any time. What is clear is that franchise usurpation serves as a clear dividing line, separating the old from the new. That is why this book deals only with the first era of the American Association, the period from 1902 to 1952.

The volume that follows is the statistical history of these first 51 years of the American Association. The statistics are arranged by year, then by team within each year. Each team includes twelve statistical categories for both batters and pitchers. For the batters the categories are games played, at bats, runs, hits, runs batted in, doubles, triples, home runs, bases on balls, strikeouts, stolen bases, and batting average. For the pitchers the statistics include wins, losses, winning percentage, games, games started, complete games, shutouts, innings pitched, hits allowed, bases on balls, strikeouts, and earned run average. On each team, the first eight batters are listed in order based upon who played the most games at the eight non-pitching positions. The rest of the batters are listed in order of most games played. The pitchers are listed in order of most wins. All individual and team leaders in any given category are in boldface type. Before each season's statistics is a short essay summing up the year.

During each year, there were several players who played for more than one Association team. Their statistics are listed in the multi-team section at the end of each year. If the multi-team player played most of the year for one team, he received a listing in the starting eight for that particular team.

The statistics used come mostly from the rich lode of information found in the *Spalding* and *Reach* baseball guides. Although fairly complete, significant omissions in the year-by-year record of the players do occur. For instance, runs batted in were not tabulated until 1920, and earned run averages were not kept until 1914. In some instances, records for some of the infrequently used pitchers were not available.

With the exception of 1902 and 1918, first names were not available for the players until 1921. In 1921, the player's first initial began to be used, followed by his full name in 1923. In some cases, the first names for the pre–1921 players were deduced from the records in 1902, 1918, or after 1921. In those instances, the index reference includes the first name. However, to remain true to the style used in the guides, first names are not listed in the body of the tables before 1921 (except 1902 and 1918). In some instances, two or more players in a particular pre–1921 season have the same last name. In those cases, a first initial is given. For some of the infrequently used players after 1921, first names are also not available.

For most of the years, the guides do not include statistics for batters who appeared in fewer than ten games or for pitchers with fewer than 45 innings pitched. However, thanks to the tireless research of Ray Nemec, the statistics for these players have been compiled. All the statistics for these less prolific players for the years 1919–1952 have been generously provided by Mr. Nemec. In addition, he has supplied complete data on the 1902 and 1918 seasons. This book is a better volume because of his help.

As you will see in the pages to come, the American Association comes alive with team and individual statistics and the stories that accompany them. This league was a truly unique institution during the first half of the twentieth century, well worthy of its place at the pinnacle of minor league baseball.

Prelude
Baseball in the Heartland

The cities of America's heartland have a rich legacy of baseball. Several cities and towns can trace their origins back to the sport's first wave of expansion westward from its East Coast beginnings, during the 1850s. When the first major leagues formed a few years later, many of these same cities (such as Chicago and St. Louis) participated as founders. Still, many midwestern cities (like Columbus, Minneapolis, St. Paul, Milwaukee, Kansas City and Toledo) enjoyed only spotty participation in the majors. Undaunted, these and other cities turned to the minor leagues.

The first two minor baseball leagues, the League Alliance and the International Association, were formed in the late 1870s. The League Alliance, which started play in 1877, included franchises from Indianapolis, Milwaukee, Minneapolis, and St. Paul. The International Association, which also started play in 1877, featured a team from Columbus. Although too loosely organized to last a long time, these organizations' importance to the Midwest is clear, for they allowed several cities to join a league for the first time.

The second minor league in the Midwest was much better organized, and was designed to cater to the region exclusively. The Northwestern League, organized in 1878, served several cities during its first few years, including Toledo, Minneapolis and St. Paul. In 1884, this circuit took an important step in legitimizing minor league play by forming a three-cornered agreement with the two major leagues, the American Association and the National League, whereby the territorial rights of each would be honored.

During the 1880s, other minor leagues such as the Western League (featuring teams in Kansas City, Denver, and Omaha) were formed. However, the strongest midwest minor league circuit to emerge from the decade was the Western Association. Organized from the Northwestern League in 1888, the Western Association featured teams in Kansas City, Minneapolis, and St. Paul. This league flourished for several years until it became part of the strongest minor league of the nineteenth century.

Late in 1891, a new minor league formed out of the Western Association incorporated several teams from the defunct major league American Association. Billed as the Western League, this league started play in 1892 with a roster of teams which included clubs in Columbus, Minneapolis, Toledo, Milwaukee, Kansas City, and Indianapolis.

After the 1893 season, the Western League came under the tutelage of a

Cincinnati sportswriter named Ban Johnson, who quickly molded it into the strongest minor league in the land. Cracking down on the rowdy and unsavory elements of the game which peppered much of nineteenth century baseball, Johnson made his Western League a model of minor league excellence which was greatly appreciated by the baseball public.

By the end of the decade, Johnson was ready for the next level. His Western League had been at the top of the minor league structure for many years, and now he felt that it could compete at the major league level. In 1900, with this in mind, he renamed his Western League the American League, and began to shift many of the franchises eastward to compete against the National League.

As a result of these changes, several midwestern cities were left without baseball. Before the 1900 season the Americans shifted the St. Paul franchise to Chicago. After the 1900 season, they dropped their Kansas City, Minneapolis and Indianapolis franchises. Following the 1901 season, the American League moved the Milwaukee team to St. Louis.

To help combat these vacancies, a new minor league was poised to take its place in the Midwest, reusing the title of the Western League. Thomas Hickey, the league's first president, organized the modest six-team circuit which began play in Kansas City, St. Paul, Omaha, St. Joseph, Des Moines, and Sioux City in 1900. For two years, this circuit enjoyed limited success, but Hickey felt that there should something more. Despite the presence of the Western League, several large cities in the Midwest were still without baseball. With that in mind, Hickey formulated a plan for a new league, a top-level minor league which would encompass these neglected Midwestern cities.

In 1901, a plan was hatched to return baseball to the forgotten cities of the heartland. Eight cities (Columbus, Indianapolis, Kansas City, Louisville, Milwaukee, Minneapolis, St. Paul, and Toledo) were to be the founding members of a new minor league in the Midwest that would begin play in 1902. This new league, borrowing a name from a major league of the past, would call itself the American Association.

1902
Territorial Dispute

Late in 1901, the American Association was formed under the guidance of Thomas Hickey. Consisting of teams in Columbus, Indianapolis, Kansas City, Louisville, Milwaukee, Minneapolis, St. Paul, and Toledo, the league was set to start in 1902, and would take the place of the Western League. To mollify Western League owners who were not included in the Association's plans, a new Western League planned to begin play in 1902.

At the same time the American Association was getting off the ground, Thomas Hickey and several other minor league presidents met and formed the National Association for Professional Baseball Leagues. This body (known as the National Association) was intended to serve as an umbrella organization over all of minor league baseball. It would govern issues such as player contracts and team territorial rights. The latter point would soon put the Western League and the American Association at loggerheads.

When the American Association listed its potential franchise sites for the 1902 season, the Western League cried foul, for in two of the Association's cities (Milwaukee and Kansas City) the Western League already had franchises. The National Association felt bound to uphold the protests from the Western League, and as a punishment banned the American Association from membership in the National Association.

Despite its tumultous beginnings and dire predictions of an early demise, the American Association enjoyed a prosperous inaugural campaign in 1902. Indianapolis outlasted a strong Louisville club to win the first flag by two games while sporting a nifty .681 winning percentage, which would prove to be third best in league annals. St. Paul, Kansas City, Columbus, Milwaukee, Minneapolis, and Toledo rounded out the standings. The first batting award went to Louisville's John Ganzel with a mark of .366, while the first home run title was garnered by Harry Lumley of St. Paul who finished with eight. Pitching honors went to Ed Dunkle of Kansas City, who won 30 and struck out 136.

The American Association's first season was considered a success, despite the territorial dispute with the Western League, which would continue to dog the new league well into the next year. But the new league was becoming firmly entrenched in its eight locations, including the two shared with the Western League. It would take a much stronger force than the Western League to dislodge any of the eight from their locations. It would also take more than fifty years to accomplish the task.

INDIANAPOLIS   1st   96-45   .681   W.H. Watkins
Indians

BATTERS	POS-GAMES	GP	AB	R	H	BI	2B	3B	HR	BB	SO	SB	BA
George Kihm	1B134,OF	134	514	99	152		36	11	5			16	.296
William Fox	2B140	142	561	91	153		10	7	1			49	.273
Peter O'Brien	SS138	141	559	95	165		19	6	3			18	.295
Charles Bass	3B49	50	188	36	56		8	5	1			10	.298
George Hogriever	OF139,2B	142	549	124	159		22	13	3			37	.290
Art Coulter	OF133	137	527	103	153		23	11	1			28	.290
Charles Kuhns	OF100,3B44,SS	142	547	79	144		18	8	3			14	.263
Mike Heydon	C111	116	384	66	99		7	11	2			14	.258
Orville Woodruff	OF40,3B40,C	96	360	57	103		12	4	1			19	.286
Win Kellum	P40,OF	50	147	24	36		5	1	0			2	.245
Jack Suthoff	P39,OF	41	120	6	39		3	1	0			3	.258
Tom Williams	P38,OF	40	132	16	29		5	1	2			5	.220
Frank Killen	P24,OF,1B	30	81	16	24		5	2	0			1	.296
Harry Matthews	C26	27	83	10	23		2	1	0			4	.277
John Grim	1B	15	58	7	20		0	1	0			0	.345
Ralph Miller	P14	14	44	2	8		0	1	0			1	.182
Sheehan	3B	4	13	1	5		1	0	0			0	.385
Charles Flick	3B,SS	2	8	1	4		1	0	0			1	.500
Seibert	3B	2	7	0	0		0	0	0			0	.000
McCormick	OF1,2B1	1	3	0	0		0	0	0			0	.000

PITCHERS		W	L	PCT	G	GS	CG	SH	IP	H	BB	SO	ERA
Win Kellum		25	10	.714	40	36	35	4	337	312	54	115	
Tom Williams		24	12	.667	38	34	31	1	315	306	80	79	
Jack Suthoff		24	13	.649	39	37	35	0	308	307	91	79	
Frank Killen		16	6	.727	24	22	20	3	190	187	39	51	
Ralph Miller		7	4	.636	14	13	9	0	107	116	39	38	

LOUISVILLE   2nd   92-45   .671   -2   William Clymer
Colonels

BATTERS	POS-GAMES	GP	AB	R	H	BI	2B	3B	HR	BB	SO	SB	BA
John Ganzel	1B73,2B55,SS	124	530	123	194		37	15	7			21	.366
Frank Bonner	2B64,SS,3B	76	339	66	97		16	14	0			10	.286
Lee Tannehill	SS72	72	295	43	98		17	6	2			7	.332
Robert Schaub	3B136,SS	139	523	70	134		21	11	1			17	.256
John Flournoy	OF125	125	499	88	142		18	20	1			34	.289
Dan Kerwin	OF102,P23	125	521	121	171		26	11	2			39	.328
William Clymer	OF79,SS33,2B	128	497	105	144		20	14	3			40	.290
Harry Spies	C72,1B	88	325	41	83		8	4	2			16	.255
Bill Gannon	1B,OF,2B	90	358	70	96		9	12	3			26	.268
William Schriver	C67,1B19	88	303	47	96		17	9	0			11	.317
Fred Odwell	OF53	56	219	49	63		6	10	1			15	.288
Pat Flaherty	P46,OF	52	168	22	49		10	2	2			0	.292
Ed Dunkle	P44	44	151	16	44		4	2	0			0	.291
Perry Coons	P37	37	126	14	37		0	2	0			1	.294
Tilford	SS,2B	15	45	7	10		0	0	0			1	.222
Larry Quinlan	SS	11	40	5	8		0	0	0			1	.200
Ollie Gfroerer	OF	8	34	7	7		0	0	0			1	.206
Dan Coogan	2B	5	23	4	7		1	0	0			1	.304
Bert Thiel	OF	5	16	0	2		0	0	0			0	.125
Roger Denzer	P3	3	10	1	3		1	0	0			0	.300
Sheehan	SS	2	8	0	1		0	0	0			0	.000
Miller	SS1	1	2	0	0		0	0	0			0	.000
Kerns	OF1	1	1	0	0		0	0	0			0	.000

PITCHERS		W	L	PCT	G	GS	CG	SH	IP	H	BB	SO	ERA
Ed Dunkle		30	10	.750	44	40	40	3	373	368	139	136	
Pat Flaherty		26	16	.619	46	42	40	3	367	351	72	91	
Perry Coons		24	9	.727	37	36	28	1	310	334	71	66	
Dan Kerwin		9	8	.529	23	17	16	1	170	179	45	21	
Roger Denzer		1	2	.333	3	3	2	0	21	30	12	5	

ST. PAUL Saints

ST. PAUL 3rd 72-67 .521 -23 Mike Kelley

BATTERS	POS-GAMES	GP	AB	R	H	BI	2B	3B	HR	BB	SO	SB	BA
Mike Kelley	1B119,OF	122	464	66	126		18	2	0			24	.272
Miller Huggins	2B124,SS,3B	130	466	82	153		18	6	1			40	.328
A. Marcan	SS56,3B	56	199	22	53		4	3	0			8	.266
Phil Geier	3B82,OF24,SS,2B,C	127	524	97	170		15	12	2			27	.324
William Shannon	OF118,2B	120	471	88	162		10	7	0			41	.344
Harry Lumley	OF113	114	452	74	135		6	14	8			14	.294
Pat Dillard	OF89,3B29,1B	123	515	84	160		23	3	2			14	.312
Jerry Hurley	C81,OF	80	273	21	58		9	7	1			2	.212
Charles Chech	P36,OF36	73	236	29	50		9	3	0			2	.212
Pierce	C62,OF	69	262	27	72		9	5	0			7	.275
Charles Ferguson	P31,1B21,3B,SS,2B,OF	69	241	32	68		9	2	0			16	.282
Dan Shay	SS39	40	155	27	47		10	3	1			19	.303
Robert Lynch	SS29	29	99	7	15		1	0	1			5	.152
Richard Cogan	P14,OF,2B	29	95	15	29		6	2	2			2	.305
Arch Stimmel	P28	28	84	5	12		1	0	0			0	.143
Edward Egan	3B20	20	71	7	16		2	0	0			1	.225
Tom Dougherty	OF17	18	65	10	10		1	1	0			4	.154
Harold Cribbins	P15	15	39	2	10		1	0	0			0	.256
Ralph Miller	P12	12	39	1	6		2	1	0			1	.154
McCann	OF	10	39	5	10		1	0	0			0	.256
Chapleskie	P4	4	14	2	5		0	0	0			1	.357
Slette	P4	4	11	0	1		0	0	0			0	.091
Harry Cook	P4	4	9	1	2		0	0	0			0	.222
Davis	P3	3	11	1	3		0	0	0			0	.273
John Bartos	P1	1	4	1	1		0	0	0			0	.250
Carney	P1	1	3	1	1		0	0	0			0	.333
Hartman	P1	1	3	0	1		0	0	0			0	.333

PITCHERS	W	L	PCT	G	GS	CG	SH	IP	H	BB	SO	ERA
Charles Ferguson	21	10	.677	31	29	29	4	267	266	32	41	
Charles Chech	15	19	.441	36	33	31	1	293	316	66	64	
Arch Stimmel	14	12	.538	28	27	25	2	228	204	75	72	
Harold Cribbins	8	3	.727	15	11	9	1	111	101	18	16	
Richard Cogan	5	7	.417	14	13	12	1	109	108	56	16	
Ralph Miller	3	6	.333	11	11	9	0	95	100	24	9	
Harry Cook	2	1	.667	4	2	2	0	23	21	12	6	
Chapleskie	1	3	.250	4	4	4	0	33	53	10	5	
Carney	1	0	1.000	1	1	0	0	7	7	3	0	
Slette	1	2	.333	4	4	2	1	29	28	14	2	
Davis	1	2	.333	3	3	2	0	25	23	15	6	
John Bartos	0	1	.000	1	1	1	0	9	9	6	1	
Hartman	0	1	.000	1	1	1	0	8	6	7	1	

KANSAS CITY Blues

KANSAS CITY 4th 69-68 .504 -25 Dale Gear

BATTERS	POS-GAMES	GP	AB	R	H	BI	2B	3B	HR	BB	SO	SB	BA
Mike Grady	1B85,3B25,2B,C	132	505	99	164		33	14	6			15	.325
Bert Thiel	2B,OF,3B	60	179	25	51		5	2	0			5	.285
Ed Lewee	SS130	138	532	72	148		22	9	0			12	.279
Tom McAndrews	3B	66	228	26	55		5	5	0			6	.241
William Nance	OF116,2B16,SS	139	485	118	144		37	14	1			20	.297
Elmer Smith	OF104,C,1B	111	412	69	127		21	7	6			7	.308
John Rothfuss	OF103,1B27	138	511	108	158		21	10	4			32	.292
Monte Beville	C129	135	522	106	161		37	3	4			12	.308
Dale Gear	OF59,P24	97	322	40	90		10	6	0			5	.280
George McBride	3B,2B	72	262	24	65		12	2	0			3	.248
Wilbert Wolfe	P39,OF,1B	47	143	22	27		9	1	0			5	.189
Jack O'Brien	2B39	42	159	29	48		7	0	1			6	.302
R. Gibson	P35,OF	36	104	15	19		1	1	0			1	.183
McDonald	P36	36	97	11	13		1	0	0			0	.134
Bill Gannon	1B,OF,P1	27	100	16	28		6	1	0			4	.280
Francis Foreman	P10,OF	16	41	4	13		3	0	0			0	.317
Gus Weyhing	P7	9	22	0	4		0	0	0			0	.182
Everhardt	C	2	8	1	2		1	0	0			0	.250
Pratt	P2	2	2	0	1		0	0	0			0	.500
Easton	P2	2	1	0	0		0	0	0			0	.000
Bill Damman	P2	2	0	0	0		0	0	0			0	----
Fred Schatzke	2B1	1	4	0	0		0	0	0			0	.000
Tate	P1	1	3	0	0		0	0	0			0	.000

KANSAS CITY (cont.)
Blues

BATTERS	POS-GAMES	GP	AB	R	H	BI	2B	3B	HR	BB	SO	SB	BA
Johnson	OF1	1	1	0	0		0	0	0			0	.000
Curtis	P1	1	0	0	0		0	0	0			0	----

PITCHERS	W	L	PCT	G	GS	CG	SH	IP	H	BB	SO	ERA
R. Gibson	19	9	.678	35	29	25	1	267	262	111	131	
Wilbert Wolfe	19	19	.500	39	35	32	2	303	336	67	105	
McDonald	16	14	.533	36	34	27	2	279	317	92	65	
Dale Gear	8	10	.444	24	19	17	0	186	227	33	42	
Gus Weyhing	3	4	.429	7	7	6	0	64	77	9	19	
Francis Foreman	3	6	.333	10	9	8	0	79	88	26	25	
Pratt	0	1	.000	2	1	0	0	10	11	5	0	
Easton	0	1	.000	2	2	0	0	8	18	3	3	
Tate	0	1	.000	1	1	1	0	8	14	2	1	
Bill Damman	0	2	.000	2	1	0	0	2	8	1	0	
Bill Gannon	0	0	----	1	0	0	0	6	9	2	0	
Curtis	0	0	----	1	0	0	0	1	1	0	1	

COLUMBUS   5th   66-74   .471   -29.5   Grim - Leonard
Senators

BATTERS	POS-GAMES	GP	AB	R	H	BI	2B	3B	HR	BB	SO	SB	BA
John Grim	1B,C	53	201	26	46		11	4	0			15	.229
Rooney Viox	2B51,3B,OF	79	286	35	67		9	3	2			10	.234
William Nattress	SS63	63	225	37	62		17	5	2			10	.276
Terrence Turner	3B111,2B	127	495	76	145		22	13	2			41	.295
Hub Knoll	OF	106	379	49	126		12	7	1			28	.332
Claude McFarland	OF	83	346	48	112		26	8	3			10	.324
James Hart	OF72,1B23,3B17,2B	123	470	85	145		11	3	3			14	.309
George Fox	C119,1B	126	455	36	107		14	2	4			9	.235
Bade Myers	1B47,C,OF,2B	74	282	36	75		14	0	0			7	.266
Pat Meaney	OF	51	211	34	66		9	1	0			16	.313
William Evans	2B48	48	184	42	50		4	6	0			5	.272
Harvey Bailey	P44,OF	46	158	11	31		5	1	2			1	.196
Dan Lally	OF	45	181	31	48		12	6	0			9	.265
Ivor Wagner	P36,OF,3B,SS	44	129	13	23		2	0	0			1	.198
William Belden	OF33	34	145	18	34		1	0	0			2	.234
William Hopke	SS33	34	126	9	17		2	2	0			1	.135
Harold O'Hagan	1B15,2B,SS	22	82	7	25		1	0	0			5	.305
Tom Thomas	P17	19	62	4	13		0	0	0			1	.210
John McMakin	P18	18	60	8	12		0	0	0			2	.200
John Hendricks	OF16	16	59	3	10		1	1	0			2	.169
Charles Fuller	C,1B,OF	14	53	7	14		3	0	0			1	.264
Charles Wagner	SS	13	50	3	9		1	0	0			0	.180
John Pfeister	P9	9	26	2	7		1	2	0			0	.269
Ed Wheeler	SS	8	30	5	8		1	0	0			1	.267
Robert Barton	SS	7	27	1	10		0	0	0			3	.370
Sam McMakin	P6	6	19	2	1		1	0	0			0	.053
Wiley Dunham	P6	6	19	0	1		0	0	0			0	.053
Cy Vorhees	P4	4	13	0	2		0	0	0			0	.154
Cliff Curtis	P4	4	8	1	3		0	0	0			0	.375
Charles Coggswell	P4	4	4	0	1		0	0	0			0	.250
Moses Vasbinder	P3	3	9	0	0		0	0	0			0	.000
William Popp	P3	3	4	0	0		0	0	0			0	.000
Fred Schaetzke	2B1	1	4	0	0		0	0	0			0	.000
Ford	P1	1	4	0	0		0	0	0			0	.000
Hutchinson	C1	1	1	0	0		0	0	0			0	.000
Brown	C1	1	0	0	0		0	0	0			0	----

PITCHERS	W	L	PCT	G	GS	CG	SH	IP	H	BB	SO	ERA
Harvey Bailey	23	19	.548	44	39	36	3	358	351	93	98	
Ivor Wagner	14	19	.424	36	35	33	3	303	283	82	60	
John McMakin	10	5	.667	18	16	14	1	145	149	30	44	
Sam McMakin	5	1	.833	6	5	4	1	49	35	6	7	
Wiley Dunham	4	2	.667	6	6	6	2	52	45	12	15	
Tom Thomas	4	13	.235	17	17	15	2	144	141	25	22	
John Pfeister	2	6	.333	9	8	7	0	65	74	27	15	
Cliff Curtis	1	0	1.000	4	2	1	0	19	17	11	4	
Charles Coggswell	1	1	.500	4	3	1	0	17	20	14	2	
Moses Vasbinder	1	1	.500	3	3	2	0	19	25	3	7	
Ford	0	1	.000	1	1	1	0	8	15	2	0	

COLUMBUS (cont.)
Senators

PITCHERS	W	L	PCT	G	GS	CG	SH	IP	H	BB	SO	ERA
William Popp	0	2	.000	3	2	1	0	12	10	7	2	
Cy Vorhees	0	4	.000	4	4	4	0	34	50	9	7	

MILWAUKEE   6th   66-75   .468   -30   Clingman - Cantillon
Brewers

BATTERS	POS-GAMES	GP	AB	R	H	BI	2B	3B	HR	BB	SO	SB	BA
Louis Runkle	1B67,3B40,2B	112	425	42	102		10	0	0			11	.240
Frank Scheibeck	2B	96	374	53	90		11	1	1			7	.241
William Clingman	SS140	141	530	84	163		20	7	3			21	.308
Tom McAndrews	3B	67	236	27	44		8	2	0			11	.186
Bill Hallman	OF141	143	587	110	190		28	6	6			30	.324
Algie McBride	OF139	141	552	75	153		27	14	1			12	.277
Sam Dungan	OF91,1B46,2B	143	569	79	158		19	4	1			13	.278
George Speer	C100	101	356	32	88		8	0	0			9	.247
Nick Altrock	P48,OF	57	181	15	33		1	1	0			1	.182
John Donohue	1B26,C16	40	139	14	30		4	1	0			4	.216
Frank Cross	C34,1B,2B	39	123	6	19		4	1	1			0	.154
George McBride	3B	38	137	16	30		3	0	2			1	.219
Claude Elliott	P37	38	97	6	20		3	2	0			1	.206
Tom Parrott	OF24	28	120	13	30		2	0	1			1	.250
Art Herman	P20	20	60	3	9		1	0	0			0	.150
Bert Thiel	2B,OF	18	68	13	18		0	0	0			5	.205
Sam McMakin	P15	15	44	3	6		1	0	0			1	.136
Frank Barber	P13,OF	15	42	2	7		2	0	0			0	.167
Henry Olmstead	P14	14	32	0	4		0	0	0			0	.125
John O'Connell	2B12	12	47	5	14		3	0	0			1	.298
Art Bourgeois	OF,2B,1B	10	44	4	6		2	0	0			0	.136
Angus Grant	2B	10	38	1	7		0	1	0			1	.184
Albert Jacobson	P6	6	19	1	4		0	0	0			0	.211
Pink Hawley	P6	6	17	1	2		0	0	0			0	.118
Tom Thomas	P5	5	15	1	3		0	0	0			0	.125
Abe Akers	OF	2	8	1	0		0	0	0			0	.000
Harry Cook	P2	2	2	0	0		0	0	0			0	.000
Griebner	SS1	1	5	0	0		0	0	0			0	.000
Hilbert	P1	1	5	0	0		0	0	0			0	.000
Peter Nolden	P1	1	4	0	0		0	0	0			0	.000
Miller	P1	1	1	1	1		0	0	0			0	1.000
George Disch	P1	1	1	0	0		0	0	0			0	.000

PITCHERS	W	L	PCT	G	GS	CG	SH	IP	H	BB	SO	ERA
Nick Altrock	28	14	.667	48	41	39	4	388	371	90	114	
Claude Elliott	11	17	.393	37	29	24	1	257	275	69	66	
Art Herman	8	10	.444	20	19	16	0	164	172	55	92	
Frank Barber	6	4	.600	13	10	10	2	93	99	29	17	
Sam McMakin	5	8	.375	15	15	11	0	113	134	19	12	
Pink Hawley	2	3	.400	6	5	5	1	50	45	10	17	
Tom Thomas	2	3	.400	5	4	3	1	38	24	13	3	
Henry Olmstead	2	4	.333	14	7	4	1	83	76	30	47	
Peter Nolden	1	0	1.000	·1	1	1	0	9	7	2	2	
Albert Jacobson	1	4	.200	6	5	3	0	44	57	18	21	
George Disch	0	1	.000	1	1	0	0	2	8	1	1	
Hilbert	0	1	.000	1	1	0	0	7	13	0	1	
Harry Cook	0	2	.000	2	2	0	0	4	12	3	0	
Miller	0	0	----	1	0	0	0	3	5	4	1	

MINNEAPOLIS   7th   54-86   .385   -41.5   Walt Wilmot
Millers

BATTERS	POS-GAMES	GP	AB	R	H	BI	2B	3B	HR	BB	SO	SB	BA
Perry Werden	1B134	138	533	64	156		26	6	2			20	.293
Angus Grant	2B,SS	104	384	37	81		10	4	0			13	.211
Lee Quillen	SS,OF	97	399	47	85		9	10	0			14	.217
William Phyle	3B84,SS	89	356	70	100		16	13	2			16	.281
Walt Wilmot	OF129	135	531	74	139		33	7	3			30	.262
Mike Lynch	OF91,3B27,2B	126	511	89	118		20	3	1			22	.231
Dan Lally	OF	87	350	61	95		14	7	1			16	.271
John Byers	C63,2B,SS,1B,3B	85	278	38	78		15	4	0			4	.281

MINNEAPOLIS (cont.)
Millers

BATTERS	POS-GAMES	GP	AB	R	H	BI	2B	3B	HR	BB	SO	SB	BA
John Zalusky	C46,OF,SS,1B	56	189	20	35		5	2	0			10	.185
Claude McFarland	OF	54	208	26	46		8	0	1			10	.221
Lefty Sporer	P39	39	115	2	22		2	1	0			0	.191
George Yeager	C31,3B	35	134	27	44		9	2	1			0	.328
Dennis Sullivan	OF31	32	116	12	26		0	1	0			6	.206
Morrissey	2B25,OF	27	109	16	26		2	0	0			3	.239
Otto Newlin	P26	26	84	4	20		0	0	0			2	.238
Harold Cribbins	P16,OF	18	66	4	15		3	0	0			2	.227
Howard Cassibone	SS	17	62	7	14		2	0	0			1	.226
William Cooley	3B15	15	54	2	12		2	0	0			1	.235
Walt Curley	SS,2B	15	54	2	10		1	0	0			1	.185
John Katoll	P14	14	38	4	11		1	0	1			2	.229
Walt Carlisle	OF	13	51	5	12		2	0	0			1	.235
Ed Bruyette	SS	12	43	4	6		1	1	0			1	.140
Fred Luther	P12	12	35	5	9		2	0	0			0	.257
Frank Figgemeier	P11	11	24	1	2		0	0	0			0	.083
Cyrus Torrence	P10	10	32	2	9		2	1	0			0	.281
Chapleskie	P9	9	20	3	5		2	0	0			0	.250
Martin	P8	8	25	0	5		1	0	0			0	.200
Dad Clarke	P7	7	16	2	2		0	0	0			0	.125
Quigley	2B	6	20	3	5		1	1	0			0	.250
Burns	2B,OF	5	15	4	6		0	0	0			0	.400
Joe Corbett	P5	5	10	3	2		0	0	0			1	.200
Mullin	P4	4	12	0	0		0	0	0			0	.000
Bracken	P3	3	5	0	2		1	0	0			0	.400
Novacek	1B,C	2	9	0	1		0	0	0			0	.111
Collett	P2	2	4	0	1		0	0	0			0	.250
Gates	OF1	1	4	1	1		1	0	0			0	.250
Murphy	3B1	1	4	0	1		0	0	0			0	.250
John Bartos	P1	1	4	0	0		0	0	0			0	.000
Smith	P1	1	3	0	1		0	0	0			0	.333

PITCHERS	W	L	PCT	G	GS	CG	SH	IP	H	BB	SO	ERA
Lefty Sporer	13	22	.371	39	35	32	0	309	327	117	85	
John Katoll	9	5	.643	14	12	12	3	113	85	35	35	
Otto Newlin	9	14	.391	26	25	22	2	203	240	58	46	
Cyrus Torrence	6	4	.600	10	8	7	0	74	90	16	19	
Harold Cribbins	4	10	.286	16	14	13	0	137	176	22	11	
Frank Figgemeier	3	2	.600	11	7	3	0	69	82	13	9	
Martin	3	4	.429	8	7	7	0	63	76	28	7	
Fred Luther	3	7	.300	12	9	7	0	92	107	21	19	
Chapleski	2	5	.286	9	6	2	0	50	73	29	13	
Joe Corbett	1	2	.333	5	5	3	0	28	37	17	7	
Dad Clarke	1	4	.200	7	6	5	0	51	66	12	15	
Collett	0	1	.000	2	1	0	0	7	6	5	3	
John Bartos	0	1	.000	1	1	1	0	9	6	9	2	
Mullin	0	3	.000	4	4	3	0	27	37	7	4	
Bracken	0	3	.000	3	2	1	0	14	28	8	2	
Smith	0	0	----	1	1	0	0	5	5	6	2	

TOLEDO   8th   43-98   .305   -53   Charles Strobel
Mud Hens

BATTERS	POS-GAMES	GP	AB	R	H	BI	2B	3B	HR	BB	SO	SB	BA
Tuck Turner	1B91,SS32	130	523	76	156		37	5	5			14	.298
John Burns	2B103,SS,OF	127	511	76	117		21	2	1			26	.229
John Kleinow	SS35,C54,1B26,2B,OF	116	422	60	124		24	5	6			11	.294
Jud Smith	3B125,1B,OF	132	504	73	135		36	3	6			10	.265
Robert Gilks	OF135,1B,OF	141	561	60	141		15	1	0			18	.251
Charles Coggswell	OF66,P8	75	276	32	86		24	2	5			1	.312
Pat Meaney	OF	61	257	43	79		13	1	0			5	.307
William Graffius	C84,OF,1B	100	336	53	82		17	0	4			6	.244
Homer Mock	P39,OF34,1B	84	292	29	72		15	6	4			2	.247
Bert Myers	SS26,2B20	47	166	18	37		9	1	1			8	.229
Harley McNeal	P38,OF	40	127	3	26		3	1	0			0	.205
Thomas Owens	SS28,3B,1B	37	144	24	45		18	0	4			5	.313
Dusty Miller	OF32,1B	33	142	20	33		4	1	0			2	.232
James Hughey	P32,OF	33	111	1	23		5	1	0			1	.207
Frank Foutz	OF,1B	18	66	6	22		6	1	1			1	.333
Julius Knoll	OF	16	65	11	17		3	0	1			3	.262
Al Pardee	P15,OF	16	51	2	4		2	0	0			0	.078
Mike Mitchell	OF	13	46	12	12		0	2	1			0	.261

TOLEDO (cont.)
Mud Hens

BATTERS	POS-GAMES	GP	AB	R	H	BI	2B	3B	HR	BB	SO	SB	BA
Harry Gorman	P10,OF	12	48	3	14		0	0	0			0	.292
Walter Salm	1B,OF,2B	12	47	1	7		0	0	0			0	.149
August Hoff	2B,1B,3B	11	45	7	10		1	0	0			0	.222
Frank Scheibeck	SS	10	42	4	10		2	0	0			2	.238
Joe Hennessy	OF	9	37	6	4		0	0	0			2	.108
John Geyer	OF	9	31	1	5		0	1	0			0	.161
James Flanagan	OF	8	30	5	6		0	0	0			0	.200
John Lundboam	P7	7	13	0	1		0	1	0			0	.077
John Keffler	SS	6	24	2	3		2	0	0			1	.125
Rooney Viox	SS	3	10	2	5		0	0	0			0	.500
Ed Frank	SS	2	6	0	1		0	0	0			0	.167
Henry Croft	2B	2	6	0	1		0	0	0			0	.167
Gus Bonno	P2	2	5	0	0		0	0	0			0	.000
Chris Heisman	P2	2	3	0	1		0	0	0			0	.333
Willis Washer	P1	1	4	1	2		0	0	0			0	.500
John Pfeister	P1	1	4	1	1		0	0	0			1	.250
Zeke Robinson	OF1	1	3	0	0		0	0	0			0	.000
Walter Gatch	P1	1	3	0	0		0	0	0			0	.000
James Jackson	3B1	1	2	1	0		0	0	0			0	.000
Foy	OF1	1	1	0	0		0	0	0			0	.000
Duval	PH	1	1	0	0		0	0	0			0	.000

PITCHERS	W	L	PCT	G	GS	CG	SH	IP	H	BB	SO	ERA
Homer Mock	14	22	.389	39	37	33	2	324	369	56	96	
Harley McNeal	11	24	.314	38	35	34	0	316	374	72	83	
James Hughey	9	21	.300	32	30	29	0	267	302	99	96	
Les German	4	6	.400	10	10	10	0	91	98	39	24	
Al Pardee	3	10	.231	15	14	10	0	130	148	47	52	
Charles Coggswell	1	3	.250	8	4	4	0	57	54	30	15	
John Lundbloam	1	6	.143	7	6	3	0	40	52	16	9	
Gus Bonno	0	1	.000	2	1	1	0	13	18	12	4	
Willis Washer	0	1	.000	1	1	1	0	9	7	7	2	
Walter Gatch	0	1	.000	1	1	1	0	9	10	1	4	
John Pfeister	0	1	.000	1	1	1	0	8	17	6	3	
Chris Heisman	0	2	.000	2	2	1	0	10	18	7	1	

TEAM BATTING

TEAMS	GP	AB	R	H	BI	2B	3B	HR	BB	SO	SB	BA
INDIANAPOLIS	142	4885	833	1372		177	84	22			222	.281
LOUISVILLE	140	5033	899	1486		211	132	24			241	.295
ST. PAUL	140	4844	707	1376		155	71	15			228	.284
KANSAS CITY	139	4643	785	1318		231	75	22			133	.284
COLUMBUS	140	4807	629	1270		180	64	19			194	.264
MILWAUKEE	143	4878	608	1231		157	40	16			130	.252
MINNEAPOLIS	142	4907	639	1203		191	62	12			176	.245
TOLEDO	142	4965	633	1282		257	34	39			119	.258
	564	38962	5733	10538		1559	562	169			1443	.270

1903
Into the Fold

In 1902, the Western League, with tacit support from the National Association, had done its best to disrupt the American Association. Before the season, the Western League boldly announced that it would honor no American Association player contracts, claiming that the Association was an "outlaw" league since it did not belong to the National Association. Other minor leagues followed suit, and several enticed American Association players to jump their contracts.

As the 1902 season progressed, the American Association weathered the storm. Once the rest of baseball saw that the new league was legitimate, and not a "Fourth of July" league (a circuit which failed mid-season), they left the American Association alone. By finishing the 1902 season successfully, the American Association had proved its worth. It only made sense, therefore, for the National Association to treat the American Association as an ally rather than an enemy and welcome the newcomers to the parent organization as soon as possible.

In 1903, the St. Paul Saints displaced Indianapolis from the throne by finishing with 88 wins, one more than Louisville. Milwaukee finished a strong third, while defending champion Indianapolis could do no better than fourth. The final four spots were represented by Kansas City, Columbus, Minneapolis, and Toledo. The champion St. Paul club was paced by batting champ Geier (.361). The home run champion came from fourth place Kansas City, whose first baseman, Grady, doubled the total of the previous champion to finish with 16. On the pitching side, Louisville's Walker finished with 26 wins, while Milwaukee's Elliott led the way with 226 strikeouts.

After the season, in October 1903, the National Association adopted a resolution allowing the American Association to compensate the aggrieved Western League owners in Milwaukee and Kansas City for encroaching on their territory. Suitably enriched, the Western League owners withdrew their objections to the new league's presence in their midst, leading the way for the Association's formal admission to the National Association.

Ironically, the whole point of contention between the Western League and American Association was soon erased. After the 1903 season, the Western League abandoned its Milwaukee and Kansas City franchises, leaving those cities to their stronger Association brethren.

ST. PAUL Saints   1st   88-46   .657   Mike Kelley

BATTERS	POS-GAMES	GP	AB	R	H	BI	2B	3B	HR	BB	SO	SB	BA
Kelley	1B67	67	252	38	78		14	1	1			9	.309
Huggins	2B124	124	444	91	137		20	4	0			48	.308
Shaffer	SS121	121	480	88	147		25	13	8			35	.306
Wheeler	3B81,3B40	121	518	68	153		30	8	6			30	.293
Shannon	OF135	135	535	**132**	165		19	7	0			41	.308
Jackson	OF135	135	520	102	160		24	12	8			42	.307
Geier	OF72,3B64	136	518	113	**187**		39	1	2			30	**.361**
J. Sullivan	C113,1B7	120	391	41	90		12	1	1			7	.232
Pierce	C32,1B25	57	183	11	39		3	0	0			6	.214
Chech	P48	48	134	22	31		7	1	0			0	.233
Ferguson	P35	35	107	9	24		4	0	1			0	.224
Stewart	P32	32	91	7	20		2	2	1			1	.218
Allemang	P31	31	94	6	19		4	1	0			8	.202
Chapleski		1	4	0	1		0	0	0			0	.250

PITCHERS		W	L	PCT	G	GS	CG	SH	IP	H	BB	SO	ERA
Chech		24	9	.727	48			2		299	75	142	
Ferguson		19	10	.655	35			4		228	36	92	
Stewart		16	10	.615	32			1		216	63	132	
Allemang		12	11	.522	31			0		293	66	60	

LOUISVILLE Colonels   2nd   87-54   .617   -4.5   William Clymer

BATTERS	POS-GAMES	GP	AB	R	H	BI	2B	3B	HR	BB	SO	SB	BA
Hart	1B60,OF42	102	407	86	127		22	9	4			22	.284
Brashear	2B102	102	502	88	129		23	5	4			28	.256
Quinlan	SS94	94	330	36	93		11	4	1			10	.281
S. Sullivan	3B136	136	533	85	165		33	12	1			34	.309
Kerwin	OF141	**141**	**703**	114	192		25	17	5			33	.273
Odwell	OF140	140	538	99	171		12	**19**	8			47	.317
Clymer	OF94	107	345	58	121		22	7	5			31	.350
Schriver	C118,1B4	132	465	49	123		27	3	4			9	.264
White	1B60,C25	85	287	31	69		15	4	0			9	.240
Walker	P58	58	170	22	37		3	0	1			0	.217
Childs	2B31,SS18	49	170	14	37		1	1	0			3	.217
Bohannon	P44	44	139	12	23		4	0	1			13	.165
Eagan	P43	43	138	13	39		4	0	0			2	.239
Schaub	3B20	20	76	6	10		3	0	2			2	.131
McCord	P19	19	54	11	8		1	1	0			0	.148
Martin		8	29	3	6		1	0	0			0	.206
Felix		1	4	1	1		0	0	0			0	.250

PITCHERS		W	L	PCT	G	GS	CG	SH	IP	H	BB	SO	ERA
Walker		**26**	7	**.788**	58			2		180	63	140	
Eagan		24	16	.600	43			2		360	84	125	
Bohannon		19	19	.500	44			1		224	132	175	
McCord		8	6	.571	19			1		124	84	50	
Eason		2	3	.400				0		55	8	23	

MILWAUKEE Brewers   3rd   77-60   .562   -12.5   Joe Cantillon

BATTERS	POS-GAMES	GP	AB	R	H	BI	2B	3B	HR	BB	SO	SB	BA
Donahue	1B123	123	524	72	179		14	7	7			20	.341
Schlafley	2B136	136	463	86	112		16	4	2			22	.241
Viox	SS			(see multi-team players)									
Unglaub	3B108,1B10	118	480	61	146		22	11	7			14	.304
Dunleavy	OF131	131	518	74	136		25	6	5			41	.262
F. Hemphill	OF116	116	408	58	113		15	1	2			2	.276
Ganley	OF			(see multi-team players)									
Wood	C98,3B12,SS11	121	481	63	156		19	6	5			9	.322
Speer	C61	61	200	12	45		8	0	0			1	.225
Dungan	OF58	58	193	38	57		4	2	1			9	.295
Meredith	P56	56	166	17	17		2	2	0			0	.102

MILWAUKEE (cont.)
Brewers

BATTERS	POS-GAMES	GP	AB	R	H	BI	2B	3B	HR	BB	SO	SB	BA
Elliott	P55	55	171	8	26		3	1	0			0	.152
Phyle	SS45	45	187	34	53		12	3	3			4	.283
Mueller	P25	28	65	2	8		2	0	0			0	.123
Peer	OF22	22	83	6	11		1	0	0			0	.132
McGill	P20	20	52	8	8		0	0	0			0	.153
Conners	OF14	14	48	3	8		2	0	0			2	.166
Hedges	P13	13	23	1	1		0	0	0			0	.043
Hale	P11	11	28	2	5		0	0	0			0	.185
Walters		4	13	0	3		0	0	0			0	.231

PITCHERS		W	L	PCT	G	GS	CG	SH	IP	H	BB	SO	ERA
Elliott		24	14	.632	55			6		270	68	226	
Meredith		21	13	.618	56			2		395	43	141	
McGill		10	5	.667	20			0		145	49	81	
Mueller		7	11	.389	25			1		164	28	68	
Hedges		5	4	.556	13			2		58	20	24	
Hale		2	5	.286	11			0		92	22	30	

INDIANAPOLIS   4th   78-61   .561   -12.5   W.H. Watkins
Indians

BATTERS	POS-GAMES	GP	AB	R	H	BI	2B	3B	HR	BB	SO	SB	BA
Kihm	1B124	124	463	93	148		28	12	3			14	.319
W. Fox	2B133	133	383	98	133		14	3	1			52	.247
Marcan	SS		(see multi-team players)										
Tamsett	3B130	130	476	68	118		15	1	0			31	.247
Coulter	OF137	137	501	73	131		23	10	2			17	.260
Hogriever	OF137	137	445	93	147		12	5	2			27	.330
Jones	OF94	94	376	63	112		20	4	6			13	.297
Heydon	C115	115	400	51	106		20	12	3			12	.265
Woodruff	C41,OF38,3B12	91	318	30	82		16	5	1			13	.257
O'Brien	SS63,OF11	74	251	31	62		11	1	0			11	.247
Kellum	P44	44	139	20	34		3	5	1			4	.244
Ford	P37	37	101	6	12		0	2	0			1	.118
Newlin	P26	26	73	9	15		1	0	0			0	.205
Williams	P23	23	65	7	12		2	0	1			1	.184
Leslie		10	28	4	9		1	0	0			0	.321
Nichols	1B7	7	23	0	7		2	0	0			1	.247
Hess		4	14	3	4		0	0	1			0	.286

PITCHERS		W	L	PCT	G	GS	CG	SH	IP	H	BB	SO	ERA
Kellum		23	10	.697	44			6		289	55	135	
Ford		17	16	.515	37			1		266	105	148	
Newlin		13	12	.520	26			1		217	76	73	
Williams		9	10	.474	23			2		175	56	43	
Crowley		3	1	.750						33	10	26	

KANSAS CITY   5th   69-66   .511   -19.5   Dale Gear
Blues

BATTERS	POS-GAMES	GP	AB	R	H	BI	2B	3B	HR	BB	SO	SB	BA
Grady	1B88,C21,3B11	120	425	89	151		32	5	16			20	.355
Nance	2B139	139	526	111	171		52	8	10			21	.325
Lewee	SS137	137	477	63	134		26	2	6			14	.280
McAndrews	3B96	96	327	32	67		19	1	1			5	.177
Rothfuss	OF139	139	586	116	167		40	9	4			31	.284
Knoll	OF128	128	476	64	131		27	9	3			19	.275
Gear	OF103,P5	103	410	65	116		31	8	4			7	.282
Butler	C		(see multi-team players)										
Maloney	C45,OF21	66	260	57	75		9	6	2			24	.288
Gibson	P54	54	155	16	24		3	0	1			1	.154
Hill	OF43	43	182	34	51		8	0	1			8	.280
Frantz	1B28	28	118	18	33		7	0	2			0	.278
Alloway	P22	22	65	9	11		0	0	0			0	.169
Hall	3B10	10	39	4	16		1	0	0			1	.410
E. Smith		5	18	5	5		0	1	1			2	.277

KANSAS CITY (cont.)
Blues

PITCHERS	W	L	PCT	G	GS	CG	SH	IP	H	BB	SO	ERA
Gibson	14	22	.389	54			1		167	105	191	
Alloway	12	7	.632	22			0		181	32	51	
Gear	3	2	.600	5			0		50	13	19	

COLUMBUS
6th   56-84   .400   -35   F.J. Leonard
Senators

BATTERS	POS-GAMES	GP	AB	R	H	BI	2B	3B	HR	BB	SO	SB	BA
Mellor	1B116	116	431	55	112		25	4	3			6	.259
Raymer	2B116	116	452	55	130		18	4	0			26	.287
Clingman	SS56	56	189	30	29		6	1	0			7	.206
T. Turner	3B114,SS12	126	503	70	156		24	9	3			23	.310
Bannon	OF131	131	505	67	130		21	5	0			25	.257
Arndt	OF130	130	517	85	144		25	13	1			18	.278
Thoney	OF47	47	175	24	51		11	4	0			9	.291
C. Fox	C87	87	309	23	74		11	2	0			0	.239
Roach	C65,OF18	83	266	33	62		15	0	0			4	.233
Gleason	SS42,OF17,2B11	70	461	43	66		15	3	0			16	.143
Wagner	P40,3B13	53	158	20	38		8	1	0			3	.240
McMakin	P24,OF11	43	119	12	25		1	0	1			0	.210
Morrissey	SS17,OF14	31	120	22	28		7	1	0			8	.216
Bridwell	SS28	28	99	14	24		1	1	0			2	.242
Smith	OF26	26	140	14	28		7	1	0			3	.200
Crabill	P24	24	77	6	21		4	2	1			0	.272
Hart	OF23	23	92	20	23		4	1	0			1	.272
Berger	P21	21	61	10	17		4	0	0			0	.278
Williams	P19	19	67	7	18		1	0	1			2	.268
Dorner	P15	15	39	4	4		0	0	0			9	.102
Slattery		7	28	5	8		1	1	0			1	.286
Wolfe		3	7	0	1		0	0	0			0	.143

PITCHERS	W	L	PCT	G	GS	CG	SH	IP	H	BB	SO	ERA
McMakin	12	12	.500	24			2		268	68	66	
Crabill	8	10	.444	24			0		193	38	50	
Dorner	7	7	.500	15			3		85	41	58	
Berger	7	8	.467	21			1		153	52	94	
Wagner	7	18	.280	40			2		241	59	74	
Williams	3	6	.333	19			2		89	28	18	

MINNEAPOLIS
7th   50-91   .355   -41.5   Wilmot-Yeager
Millers

BATTERS	POS-GAMES	GP	AB	R	H	BI	2B	3B	HR	BB	SO	SB	BA
Spooner	1B103,OF11	114	448	62	117		16	3	1			13	.261
Martin	2B125	125	563	62	100		17	2	8			19	.177
Oyler	SS139	139	519	72	137		10	5	0			14	.263
McIntyre	3B137	137	529	74	143		30	8	4			15	.270
Lally	OF134	134	543	80	156		31	4	3			10	.287
Smith	OF75	75	300	55	97		15	4	2			7	.323
McCreery	OF68	68	286	52	97		17	8	2			19	.338
Yeager	C106	106	371	60	115		19	2	6			10	.309
O. Sullivan	OF68	68	277	35	73		8	4	0			14	.270
Vasbinder	P34,1B12	46	144	8	29		6	0	0			2	.200
Ludwig	C43	43	148	14	31		5	0	0			1	.209
Maloney	OF25,C15	40	167	21	39		3	0	0			16	.233
Thomas	P38	38	124	8	28		6	0	0			0	.230
Williams	P27,OF10	37	116	11	25		4	0	1			0	.215
Katoll	P17	17	47	3	12		2	0	0			1	.255
Wilmot	OF13	13	51	8	15		5	1	1			5	.298
Hoffmeister	2B9	9	34	1	7		2	0	0			1	.205
Sporer	P7	7	16	0	4		1	0	0			0	.250
Hart	1B6	6	29	7	6		0	0	0			0	.206
Lippert		6	21	2	7		2	0	0			1	.333
Howell		3	14	3	4		0	1	0			0	.286

MINNEAPOLIS (cont.)
Millers

PITCHERS	W	L	PCT	G	GS	CG	SH	IP	H	BB	SO	ERA
Williams	11	9	.550	27			2		144	67	35	
Thomas	8	20	.286	38			0		340	92	93	
Vasbinder	7	15	.318	34			1		189	47	77	
Katoll	3	3	.500	17			0		58	10	23	
Converse	1	4	.200				0		62	23	12	
Sporer	1	5	.167	7			0		45	22	22	
St. Vrain	0	6	.000				0		61	16	24	

TOLEDO   8th   48-91   .345   -42.5   C.F. Reisling
Mud Hens

BATTERS	POS-GAMES	GP	AB	R	H	BI	2B	3B	HR	BB	SO	SB	BA
Tu. Turner	1B103	103	394	66	123		34	4	7			10	.312
Childs	2B85	85	317	42	77		12	0	0			5	.211
Owens	SS117,OF20	137	548	84	153		40	8	10			9	.279
Schaub	3B105	105	395	54	122		32	2	3			12	.306
Smith	OF130	130	542	75	133		25	4	7			24	.245
Bernard	OF110	110	431	66	133		22	3	1			14	.309
Blankenship	OF49,1B10,3B8,C6	73	279	46	81		18	1	1			15	.255
Kleinow	C115	115	403	56	129		26	3	8			11	.320
Reisling	OF23,P22,C9,SS7,3B7,1B5	73	251	31	64		10	3	6			5	.254
Cristall	P57,OF22	57	203	31	59		19	3	6			5	.290
Connors	1B35	35	124	11	31		2	0	1			8	.250
Ball		28	105	9	28		3	0	2			4	.266
German	P24	24	79	6	16		0	0	0			0	.200
Harding	OF23	23	79	17	18		4	0	1			4	.227
Altizer	3B12,SS10	22	79	5	12		1	0	0			1	.151
Coughlin	P18	18	64	1	10		1	0	0			0	.155
Flanagan	OF14	14	51	5	11		0	1	1			1	.215
Carrick	P10	10	30	1	7		0	0	0			0	.233
Hoffman		7	18	2	5		0	0	1			0	.272
Doren	P	6	15	1	1		1	0	0			0	.067
Andrews		3	13	2	3		0	0	0			0	.231

PITCHERS	W	L	PCT	G	GS	CG	SH	IP	H	BB	SO	ERA
Cristall	16	18	.471	57			2		315	134	102	
Reisling	14	11	.560	22			1		207	43	98	
German	6	15	.286	24			0		245	66	64	
Coughlin	4	12	.250	18			0		191	50	70	
Walker	3	3	.500				0		59	10	23	
Carrick	2	8	.200	10			0		114	20	30	
Doren	0	3	.000				0		55	15	14	
McGill	0	6	.000				0		64	17	21	

MULTI-TEAM PLAYERS

BATTERS	POS-GAMES	TEAMS	GP	AB	R	H	BI	2B	3B	HR	BB	SO	SB	BA
Ganley	OF124	KC-MIL	124	471	72	141		24	4	0			30	.299
Marcan	SS118	IND-SP-TOL	118	404	61	99		14	3	1			15	.245
Butler	C100	TOL-KC	100	346	59	97		24	2	1			8	.280
Viox	SS97	LOU-MIL	97	315	25	66		2	0	0			4	.209
Flournoy	OF96	TOL-SP	96	348	79	101		22	0	10			17	.290
Durham	P57	KC-IND	57	170	26	38		5	1	0			4	.223
Stimmell	P41	MIN-MIL	41	111	10	12		1	0	0			0	.114
Bailey	P35	COL-SP	35	102	11	21		3	1	0			0	.203
Coons	P26	KC-LOU	26	74	9	11		3	0	0			0	.148
McDonald	P26	KC-MIN	26	72	12	15		1	1	1			0	.208
McPartlin	P13	COL-IND	26	41	2	6		1	0	0			0	.146
Volz	P17	IND-SP	17	48	0	10		1	1	0			0	.207

PITCHERS		TEAMS	W	L	PCT	G	GS	CG	SH	IP	H	BB	SO	ERA
Durham		KC-IND	22	18	.550	57			2		365	140	169	
Stimmell		MIN-MIL	18	16	.529	41			2		287	104	126	
Bailey		COL-SP	15	15	.500	35			0		290	71	98	
Coons		KC-LOU	14	11	.560	26			0		285	59	70	
Volz		IND-SP	9	9	.500	17			1		152	100	70	

MULTI-TEAM PLAYERS (cont.)

PITCHERS	TEAMS	W	L	PCT	G	GS	CG	SH	IP	H	BB	SO	ERA
McDonald	KC-MIN	9	17	.346	26			0		297	121	79	
McPartlin	COL-IND	4	9	.308	13			0		115	33	30	
Davis	MIL-SP-MIN	2	5	.286				0		62	32	12	

TEAM BATTING

TEAMS	GP	AB	R	H	BI	2B	3B	HR	BB	SO	SB	BA
ST. PAUL	136	4825	803	**1356**		221	53	33			**267**	**.281**
LOUISVILLE	**143**	**5059**	739	1267		209	**82**	36			243	.260
MILWAUKEE	138	4710	611	1247		179	64	22			173	.266
INDIANAPOLIS	140	4726	701	1237		179	64	22			208	.261
KANSAS CITY	139	4482	**896**	1239		**294**	54	52			166	.275
COLUMBUS	141	5050	647	1300		214	54	10			143	.257
MINNEAPOLIS	142	4947	666	1274		201	43	29			148	.257
TOLEDO	141	4770	658	1297		256	32	**64**			142	.274
	560	38569	5721	10217		1753	446	268			1490	.265

1904
George Stone

Most minor league single-season batting average record holders come from the hitting heydays of the 1890s, 1920s and 1930s. The Pacific Coast record holder, Ox Eckhardt, set his mark (.414) in 1933. The International League's best totals were reached in 1897 with Dan Brouthers (.415), and in 1921 with Jack Bentley (.412). All of these totals occurred during hit-happy years when whole teams (and sometime whole leagues) batted over .300. Conversely, it comes as something of a surprise that the American Association single-season record holder, George Stone, set his mark in 1904, squarely in the middle of the dead ball era.

George Stone was a newcomer to the American Association in 1904, and he made quite an impression. While playing for the Milwaukee Brewers, he rapped out 254 hits resulting in a .405 average. His hit total was more than 50 ahead of his nearest rival, and his average was nearly the same distance over the second place finisher.

However, Stone's mark really stands out in comparison to the average of the whole American Association. For the 1904 season, the entire American Association batted only .263, thus making Stone's mark nearly 150 points better than the league average. In comparison, the Pacific Coast and International League single-season batting marks came when their league averages were in the .290s, thus making their record holders only a little more than 100 points better then their league's average.

St. Paul continued its pennant winning ways by taking a second straight title in 1904, finishing eight games ahead of Columbus. George Stone's heroics could lift Milwaukee no higher than third, while Minneapolis finished fourth. Louisville, Indianapolis, Kansas City, and Toledo rounded out the standings. Toledo finished with a particularly futile record as they topped the century mark (109) in losses while compiling a .272 win percentage, the second worst in league history. St. Paul's Jackson led the league with thirteen home runs, while his pitching teammate Chech finished with the most wins (27). Milwaukee's Curtis had the most strikeouts (210).

George Stone made the journey to the majors in 1905, landing a job with the St. Louis Browns. He stayed with the Browns until 1910, winning a batting title (.358 in 1906) along the way. He then returned to the Association for one more year, rejoining Milwaukee in 1911.

Stone's record appears to be safe. His batting title mark of .405 has never been equalled, and until this day, he remains the only American Association player to have crossed the .400 threshold.

ST. PAUL Saints

ST. PAUL   1st   95-52   .646   Mike Kelley

BATTERS	POS-GAMES	GP	AB	R	H	BI	2B	3B	HR	BB	SO	SB	BA
Kelley	1B130	130	497	79	148		36	1	4			13	.298
Marcan	2B124,SS21	145	521	70	140		33	1	1			27	.269
O'Brien	SS93,3B34	127	496	67	136		30	5	4			24	.274
Wheeler	3B114,OF29	148	612	85	181		30	9	5			26	.296
Jackson	OF147	147	579	123	194		39	3	13			59	.335
Jones	OF127	134	574	101	165		34	12	4			25	.287
Flournoy	OF71	71	262	41	64		15	5	1			18	.244
J. Sullivan	C98	108	368	36	92		13	0	0			5	.250
Pierce	C54	54	180	21	49		6	0	0			4	.272
Chech	P38,OF15	53	170	17	32		6	1	0			0	.188
Slagle	P39	47	129	13	27		0	0	0			1	.209
Sessions	P43	43	118	18	24		6	0	0			0	.203
Ferguson	P26	26	85	7	18		1	0	0			0	.211
Corbett	P26	26	59	7	23		3	0	1			1	.390
Martin	2B22	25	75	12	20		6	0	0			1	.266
Lawler	OF23	23	96	14	28		5	1	2			7	.291
Householder	OF15	19	68	8	21		2	1	1			1	.318
Kilroy	P4	4	11	3	2		0	0	0			0	.182

PITCHERS		W	L	PCT	G	GS	CG	SH	IP	H	BB	SO	ERA
Chech		27	8	.771	38			5	311	250	64	152	
Sessions		27	10	.729	43			2	294	271	86	132	
Slagle		18	13	.581	39			3	283	294	68	115	
Ferguson		14	8	.636	26			3	214	200	52	55	
Corbett		9	6	.600	26			1					
Kilroy		3	1	.750	4			1					

COLUMBUS Senators

COLUMBUS   2nd   88-61   .591   -8   William Clymer

BATTERS	POS-GAMES	GP	AB	R	H	BI	2B	3B	HR	BB	SO	SB	BA
Kihm	1B154	154	575	93	179		38	10	4			23	.311
Wrigley	2B153	153	619	89	167		38	8	2			18	.270
Bridwell	SS151	151	534	74	141		12	7	0			23	.264
Friel	3B138	144	590	94	172		18	17	5			16	.291
Martin	OF154	154	591	78	154		17	10	2			8	.260
Davis	OF148	148	600	103	165		29	22	5			25	.275
Clymer	OF139	139	536	67	120		29	5	2			17	.223
Yeager	C111	123	417	45	104		18	4	5			12	.249
Simons	C47	47	88	9	22		2	1	0			0	.250
Glendon	P33	41	112	11	25		3	1	0			0	.223
Malarkey	P35	35	111	6	20		5	1	1			0	.180
Olmstead	P34	34	94	6	15		0	1	0			0	.159
Abbott	C24	34	90	8	20		5	1	0			1	.222
Dorner	P33	33	90	5	16		2	0	0			1	.177
Hickey	P31	32	83	7	16		5	2	0			0	.192
Bowcock		10	33	3	9		1	1	0			0	.272
Berger	P10	10	28	3	6		1	0	0			2	.214

PITCHERS		W	L	PCT	G	GS	CG	SH	IP	H	BB	SO	ERA
Malarkey		24	9	.727	35			3	304	261	64	165	
Dorner		18	10	.643	33			3	263	243	71	107	
Hickey		15	10	.600	31			5	232	187	83	118	
Olmstead		13	14	.481	34			0	268	228	95	160	
Glendon		12	14	.462	33			0	236	233	81	75	
Berger		6	3	.667	10			1					

MILWAUKEE Brewers

MILWAUKEE   3rd   89-63   .585   -8.5   Joe Cantillon

BATTERS	POS-GAMES	GP	AB	R	H	BI	2B	3B	HR	BB	SO	SB	BA
Bateman	1B135,P10	149	551	73	158		22	8	9			6	.286
O'Brien	2B82,OF33	131	498	61	134		14	5	0			13	.279
Schaeffer	SS141	141	542	159	193		31	19	6			48	.356
Clark	3B134	137	554	68	141		22	5	1			28	.254
Stone	OF153	153	626	153	254		36	19	7			21	.405

MILWAUKEE (cont.)
Brewers

BATTERS	POS-GAMES	GP	AB	R	H	BI	2B	3B	HR	BB	SO	SB	BA
F. Hemphill	OF124,2B11	141	512	86	148		25	4	0			11	.288
Pennell	OF116	125	455	62	126		26	6	1			8	.276
Slattery	C102	125	429	60	113		12	7	3			5	.263
Stricklett	P40	58	130	17	34		7	1	0			6	.261
Speer	C57	57	190	16	35		4	0	0			1	.184
Curtis	P48	48	134	17	26		3	1	0			0	.194
Reitz	2B47	47	157	22	31		4	0	1			2	.197
Dougherty	P28,OF	42	126	14	19		0	3	0			3	.150
McKay	P37	40	108	9	16		1	1	0			1	.148
Wolfe	P30	30	90	10	17		5	1	0			3	.188
Baxter	2B11	11	31	3	6		0	0	0			1	.193
Manske	P11	11	24	2	5		0	0	0			0	.208
Steele	P10	10	23	0	3		1	0	0			0	.130
Meredith	P9	9	21	1	2		0	0	0			0	.095

PITCHERS		W	L	PCT	G	GS	CG	SH	IP	H	BB	SO	ERA
Curtis		24	20	.545	**48**			3	**355**	300	125	**210**	
Stricklett		20	11	.645	40			3	267	258	49	145	
McKay		19	14	.576	37			3	258	248	54	126	
Dougherty		16	9	.640	28			6	227	190	67	141	
Bateman		4	2	.667	10			2					
Meredith		3	2	.600	9			1					
Manske		2	3	.400	11								
Steele		1	3	.250	10								

MINNEAPOLIS   4th   78-67   .538   -16   W.H. Watkins
Millers

BATTERS	POS-GAMES	GP	AB	R	H	BI	2B	3B	HR	BB	SO	SB	BA
Freeman	1B79	79	304	25	72		12	2	0			4	.236
Fox	2B149	149	522	71	116		19	2	1			27	.222
Oyler	SS149	149	496	78	121		13	2	1			12	.244
McNichols	3B81,OF53	134	506	56	127		9	2	3			16	.251
Maloney	OF150	150	621	103	197		28	12	6			5	.317
Coulter	OF150	150	601	67	196		31	4	6			23	.324
D. Sullivan	OF94	94	363	62	110		15	4	2			12	.303
Weaver	C99	106	409	31	100		14	1	0			3	.244
Gremminger	3B52	52	180	26	50		15	3	2			2	.278
Leslie	1B21,C14	52	136	16	36		8	2	1			5	.264
Thomas	P42	42	128	14	11		2	1	0			2	.085
Starnagle	C23,1B14	38	143	32	32		4	0	0			1	.223
Stimmel	P38	38	106	8	18		0	0	0			1	.169
Ford	P33	33	93	8	12								.129
Morgan	P25	27	69	7	20		1	2	0			0	.304
Lally	1B24	26	93	10	22		3	1	0			0	.236
Ferry	P19	20	54	8	9		2	0	0			0	.166
O'Leary	1B14	14	41	4	9		2	0	0			0	.219
Martin	3B13	13	47	2	11		1	2	0			0	.234
Campion	1B11	11	40	4	6		0	0	0			4	.150
Bailey	P11	11	32	3	7		3	0	0			0	.218

PITCHERS		W	L	PCT	G	GS	CG	SH	IP	H	BB	SO	ERA
Thomas		21	15	.583	42			7	329	274	64	118	
Ford		17	11	.607	33			3	262	200	64	125	
Stimmel		16	14	.533	38			1	284	222	88	118	
Morgan		12	9	.571	25			2	184	148	86	88	
Ferry		6	7	.462	19			0					
Bailey		3	4	.429	11			0					

LOUISVILLE   5th   77-70   .524   -18   Charles Dexter
Colonels

BATTERS	POS-GAMES	GP	AB	R	H	BI	2B	3B	HR	BB	SO	SB	BA
White	1B74	79	274	37	65		5	1	0			10	.233
Brashear	2B148	148	532	82	149		23	8	4			29	.280
Quinlan	SS149	149	536	57	126		10	8	1			6	.235

LOUISVILLE (cont.)
Colonels

BATTERS	POS-GAMES	GP	AB	R	H	BI	2B	3B	HR	BB	SO	SB	BA
Arndt	3B125,OF11	139	544	88	168		25	5	5			13	.308
Kerwin	OF145	145	615	112	191		30	9	9			23	.310
Hallman	OF142	142	540	94	166		21	11	3			32	.307
Hart	OF73,1B30	106	419	65	135		21	11	3			16	.322
Shriver	C92,1B11	103	360	50	99		17	2	6			5	.275
Dexter	C59,1B20,OF16,3B10	108	407	59	106		11	7	2			21	.260
Campbell	P48,OF15	63	198	26	57		13	2	1			1	.288
Eagan	P44	44	131	7	28		1	0	0			2	.213
Bohannon	P33	36	87	15	28		4	3	1			0	.321
Wright	P28	29	79	11	21		1	2	0			0	.267
Reidy	P15	16	44	2	7		1	0	0			0	.159
Spangler	1B14	14	51	8	13		0	2	0			2	.254
Swormstead	P12	12	26	1	0		0	0	0			0	.000
Scott	P	8	22	4	10		3	0	0			0	.454

PITCHERS		W	L	PCT	G	GS	CG	SH	IP	H	BB	SO	ERA
Campbell		26	14	.650	48			2	338	327	83	118	
Eagan		20	20	.500	44			3	353	390	71	104	
Wright		13	9	.591	28			1	190	193	38	69	
Bohannon		8	11	.421	33			0	201	214	95	56	
Reidy		5	8	.384	15			0					
Swormstead		4	4	.500	12								
Scott		3	1	.750				1					

INDIANAPOLIS   6th   69-85   .448   -29.5   William Phillips
Indians

BATTERS	POS-GAMES	GP	AB	R	H	BI	2B	3B	HR	BB	SO	SB	BA
Dickey	1B137	137	483	68	120		12	2	0			17	.248
Martin	2B35	35	126	14	28		2	2	0			4	.222
Magoon	SS82,2B52	140	540	74	129		12	1	1			19	.239
Carey	3B149	153	583	80	178		22	7	1			24	.305
Swander	OF148	148	588	65	162		29	8	2			15	.275
McCreery	OF144	154	610	91	185		20	19	9			20	.303
Hogriever	OF86,2B37	124	482	63	121		19	4	0			18	.251
Heydon	C96,2B17	121	415	47	100		13	9	7			7	.241
Berry	C49,OF14	67	231	25	53		8	3	1			3	.229
Phillips	OF38,P23	61	193	22	47		4	1	1			2	.243
Cromley	P38	55	156	21	46		6	3	2			1	.294
Fisher	P42	42	127	14	27		4	1	0			0	.212
Allemang	P38	38	97	4	9		1	0	0			0	.093
Newlin	P35	35	93	13	15		1	2	0			0	.161
Hess	SS22	22	73	8	16		2	0	0			3	.219
DeMontreville	SS14	20	70	10	21		1	0	0			1	.300
Lynch	2B10	15	45	5	9		1	0	0			7	.200
P. O'Brien	SS11	11	44	5	7		1	0	0			0	.159
Ortleib	C10	10	28	6	5		1	0	0			2	.179
Williams	P	7	23	3	8		0	0	0			1	.356

PITCHERS		W	L	PCT	G	GS	CG	SH	IP	H	BB	SO	ERA
Fisher		16	16	.500	42			5	316	318	73	93	
Cromley		14	17	.451	38			1	258	272	42	97	
Newlin		14	19	.420	35			1	254	287	66	109	
Phillips		11	6	.647	23			1					
Allemang		10	23	.303	38			1	278	288	102	104	
Williams		3	2	.600									

KANSAS CITY   7th   60-91   .397   -37   Gear - Irwin
Blues

BATTERS	POS-GAMES	GP	AB	R	H	BI	2B	3B	HR	BB	SO	SB	BA
Massey	1B55	55	205	34	71		13	0	0			5	.346
Bonner	2B148	152	578	52	146		21	2	0			11	.252
Lewee	SS133,OF14	147	492	57	116								.236
S. Sullivan	3B84,SS11	96	354	28	83		19	1	0			7	.234
Nance	OF136	140	512	67	148		35	7	6			15	.269

KANSAS CITY (cont.)
Blues

BATTERS	POS-GAMES	GP	AB	R	H	BI	2B	3B	HR	BB	SO	SB	BA
Hill	OF132	140	567	74	148		39	5	5			21	.261
Van Buren	OF59	59	222	33	53		4	1	0			7	.238
Butler	C116	116	374	32	95		20	5	2			7	.254
Ryan	1B47,C43,3B24	127	480	58	131		30	1	0			9	.272
Rothfuss	OF35,1B20	55	206	25	44		8	4	1			6	.213
Gear	OF33,P16	53	166	17	39		7	1	0			2	.235
Isbell	P42	42	121	9	16		2	0	0			0	.132
Durham	P41	41	126	17	29		4	0	1			2	.230
Frantz	P18	32	97	8	24		2	0	0			2	.247
Barny	P29	29	87	3	15		0	0	0			0	.177
Aiken	3B15	18	68	10	15		2	0	0			2	.220
Murphy	1B18	18	65	9	16		4	0	0			0	.246
Smith	OF12	12	44	6	13		1	0	0			1	.295
Gibson	P10	10	22	0	2		0	0	0			0	.091
Eels	P8	8	20	3	5		1	0	0			0	.250

PITCHERS		W	L	PCT	G	GS	CG	SH	IP	H	BB	SO	ERA
Isbell		17	21	.448	42			1	328	300	106	122	
Barny		13	14	.481	29			1	232	242	84	63	
Durham		12	26	.315	41			1	326	357	126	159	
Frantz		7	9	.438	18			1					
Gear		6	6	.500	16			0					
Eels		3	4	.429	8			0					
Gibson		2	4	.333	10			1					

TOLEDO   8th   42-109   .272   -55   Long - Clingman
Mud Hens

BATTERS	POS-GAMES	GP	AB	R	H	BI	2B	3B	HR	BB	SO	SB	BA
Hazleton	1B42	42	151	22	42		6	0	1			6	.278
Burns	2B132	132	471	58	102		11	1	1			20	.216
Clingman	SS	(see multi-team players)											
Moriarity	3B80	83	318	20	72		11	1	0			8	.226
Frisbie	OF149	149	561	83	156		25	2	1			16	.278
Lee	OF91	100	388	38	118		26	3	8			6	.304
O'Hara	OF81,SS25	113	411	40	91		14	4	0			13	.221
Brown	C103	123	432	43	90		23	2	0			10	.208
Brouthers	3B72	72	267	32	72		22	0	1			10	.269
Reading	C30,1B27	70	231	25	71		10	1	2			7	.303
Denninger	OF42,1B21	66	254	28	60		12	4	2			10	.236
Reisling	P26	47	154	15	34		7	0	2			6	.220
Long	SS31	39	149	13	36		7	0	0			10	.241
Sweeney	SS28	36	120	11	27		7	0	1			2	.225
Cristal	P23,OF10	34	103	16	28		8	1	4			1	.271
Deering	P31	31	93	12	19		4	0	1			0	.204
Clark	C20	28	90	5	16		5	0	0			1	.177
Lundblum	P28	28	77	5	11		0	0	0			3	.143
Kemmer	1B25	25	92	8	23		4	1	0			0	.250
Donovan	OF19	23	83	8	19		0	0	0			3	.228
Wenig	P18	21	67	5	8		1	0	1			0	.119
Hannivan	OF14	17	67	6	22		5	1	0			0	.328
Martin	P9	12	33	2	6		1	0	0			1	.181
Knoll		10	31	1	8		1	0	0			0	.258
Moreton	P10	10	26	1	4		0	0	0			0	.153
German	P	5	19	2	4		1	0	0			0	.211
Stewart		5	12	0	1		0	0	0			0	.083

PITCHERS		W	L	PCT	G	GS	CG	SH	IP	H	BB	SO	ERA
Lundblum		10	13	.435	28			1	204	204	40	70	
Cristal		9	12	.429	23			1	181	214	53	76	
Deering		5	20	.250	31			1	236	271	114	72	
Wenig		4	12	.250	18			1					
Martin		3	6	.333	9			1					
German		1	4	.200									
Moreton		1	8	.111	10								

MULTI-TEAM PLAYERS

BATTERS	POS-GAMES	TEAMS	GP	AB	R	H	BI	2B	3B	HR	BB	SO	SB	BA
Montgomery	OF81,3B47	KC-LOU-IND	129	472	55	120		22	11	3			12	.275
Clingman	SS101,OF20	TOL-SP	126	454	63	114		21	7	1			22	.251
Bartes	P17	SP-TOL	34	93	5	12		1	0	0			0	.129

PITCHERS		TEAMS	W	L	PCT	G	GS	CG	SH	IP	H	BB	SO	ERA
Bartes		SP-TOL	7	7	.500	17								

TEAM BATTING

TEAMS	GP	AB	R	H	BI	2B	3B	HR	BB	SO	SB	BA
ST. PAUL	150	5183	782	1430		**270**	39	33			**237**	.276
COLUMBUS	**154**	**5263**	667	1366		236	**89**	28			157	.259
MILWAUKEE	153	5210	**785**	**1467**		217	78	29			183	.281
MINNEAPOLIS	150	5080	631	1303		183	38	22			159	.256
LOUISVILLE	150	5050	743	1435		195	75	**36**			162	**.284**
INDIANAPOLIS	**154**	5172	649	1326		232	65	22			152	.254
KANSAS CITY	**154**	5091	580	1277		241	36	15			114	.251
TOLEDO	152	5047	542	1203		223	25	27			128	.238
	609	41096	5379	10807		1797	420	212			1292	.263

1905
Concrete and Steel

Ballparks built in the 19th century were constructed as cheaply as possible, using the least expensive building material—namely wood. Building a permanent structure of more substantial materials was just not done. The expense of such an endeavor, coupled with the transient nature of most baseball franchises, made construction of a more lasting structure a risky venture to say the least. On the other hand, the wooden structures needed constant maintenance and rebuilding as many were consumed by fire. With this in mind, one American Association team decided to take a step toward a more permanent solution. This team was the Columbus Senators.

The Columbus club played in a wooden structure known as Neil Park. Located on Cleveland Avenue, the ballpark had been the home of the Columbus team since 1900. When the team turned a small profit during the 1904 season, the owners decided to redo the wooden ballpark into something else entirely. First, the team bought their previously leased stadium site. Second, they tore down the wooden grandstand. They then proceeded to build a double-decked, concrete and steel grandstand, adding bleachers made of the salvaged wood. When construction was finished, the Senators had a new, permanent stadium which could seat over 10,000.

Inspired by their new facility, the Senators cruised to their first pennant in 1905. The Milwaukee and Minneapolis teams finished in second and third, while the Louisville Colonels finished fourth. In the second division were the defending champion Saints, followed by Indianapolis, Toledo and Kansas City. Hemphill of St. Paul won the batting title with a mark of .364, while Lee of Toledo was the home run leader (13). The best pitchers came from the pennant-winning Columbus squad as Dorner posted 29 wins, while Berger struck out 200 batters.

The revamped Neil Park was a huge success. The Senators saw more than 280,000 fans go through their turnstiles during the 1905 season, almost 100,000 more than second place Minneapolis. As the next several seasons progressed, they continued to pace the league in attendance. This fact was not lost on major league team owners who knew a good idea when someone beat them to it. By the time five years had passed, the first concrete and steel stadium graced the majors.

COLUMBUS Senators

1st   100-52   .658   William Clymer

BATTERS	POS-GAMES	GP	AB	R	H	BI	2B	3B	HR	BB	SO	SB	BA
Kihm	1B143	143	508	71	145		29	6	3			15	.285
Wrigley	2B90	90	337	36	81		17	3	0			9	.240
Hulswitt	SS150	150	572	76	158		19	5	3			26	.276
Barbeau	3B151	153	524	71	129		20	6	5			25	.246
Pickering	OF153	153	**612**	92	200		28	7	3			37	.326
Congalton	OF153	153	592	88	186		36	8	2			27	.314
Davis	OF153	153	592	117	165		31	8	2			33	.278
Ryan	C85,2B17	106	392	55	112		13	4	2			2	.285
Clymer	2B46	47	164	20	40		4	3	0			11	.243
Brown	C45	45	154	15	38		6	0	0			4	.246
Berger	P44	44	122	12	17		3	0	2			0	.139
Dorner	P41	41	121	14	25		2	0	0			0	.206
Pierce	C32	38	142	15	36		5	3	0			2	.253
Veil	P38	38	101	9	16		0	1	1			0	.158
W. Hart	P19	19	62	10	14		3	0	0			2	.225
Malarkey	P16	16	53	4	10		2	4	0			0	.188

PITCHERS		W	L	PCT	G	GS	CG	SH	IP	H	BB	SO	ERA
Dorner		29	8	.784	41			6	339	242	85	132	
Berger		25	14	.641	44			9	339	285	112	**200**	
Veil		21	12	.636	38			5	283	249	80	98	
W. Hart		11	5	.688	19								
Suthoff		6	2	.750				1					
Malarkey		5	10	.333	16			0					

MILWAUKEE Brewers

2nd   91-59   .607   -8   Joe Cantillon

BATTERS	POS-GAMES	GP	AB	R	H	BI	2B	3B	HR	BB	SO	SB	BA
Ja. O'Brien	1B80,OF51	133	499	51	114		15	0	1			3	.228
McCormick	2B149	150	509	72	124		25	3	4			5	.243
Robinson	SS153	153	592	121	156		15	6	3			32	.263
Clark	3B140	143	492	79	120		22	6	2			14	.243
F. Hemphill	OF143	143	530	82	158		18	7	3			21	.298
McChesney	OF131,3B16	152	557	93	127		27	7	5			32	.228
O'Neill	OF99	99	391	65	126		24	5	6			23	.322
Beville	C123	127	450	58	116		27	1	5			3	.257
Bateman	1B74,OF34,P27	135	472	70	148		21	7	6			8	.313
Dougherty	P45	56	158	16	31		5	2	1			4	.196
Towne	C28	38	132	21	40		6	3	0			2	.303
McKay	P16	16	41	9	5		1	0	0			0	.122
Wolfe		16	36	7	9		2	1	2			1	.250
Morrison	P11	11	22	5	8		0	1	0			0	.363

PITCHERS		W	L	PCT	G	GS	CG	SH	IP	H	BB	SO	ERA
Dougherty		22	17	.564	45			3	340	280	107	156	
Bateman		13	11	.542	27			4	185	174	55	73	
McKay		6	5	.545	16			0					
Morrison		3	3	.500	11			0					

MINNEAPOLIS Millers

3rd   88-62   .578   -11   W.H. Watkins

BATTERS	POS-GAMES	GP	AB	R	H	BI	2B	3B	HR	BB	SO	SB	BA
Freeman	1B137	137	519	75	136		24	8	3			4	.262
Fox	2B150	150	521	67	112		4	3	0			30	.215
Oyler	SS142	142	510	61	145		18	0	0			12	.284
Gremminger	3B145	145	524	64	126		32	2	9			6	.240
Coulter	OF134	134	516	60	155		27	5	1			19	.300
D. Sullivan	OF133	133	491	84	145		24	6	3			28	.295
Jones	OF128	128	497	**126**	172		18	7	2			33	.346
Marshall	C78	83	306	42	96		18	6	9			7	.313
G. Graham	OF30,P21,1B11,SS10	80	283	45	76		10	2	0			3	.268
Schmidt	C69	69	246	28	55		13	3	1			12	.223
Stovall	P38	38	122	18	31		4	2	0			5	.254

MINNEAPOLIS (cont.)
Millers

BATTERS	POS-GAMES	GP	AB	R	H	BI	2B	3B	HR	BB	SO	SB	BA
Sievers	P35	35	102	17	31		5	0	0			1	.303
Thomas	P29	29	85	9	16		2	0	0			0	.188
Hynes	OF17,P10	27	100	13	26		5	2	1			0	.260
Ford	P10	10	33	1	8		1	0	0			0	.242

PITCHERS		W	L	PCT	G	GS	CG	SH	IP	H	BB	SO	ERA
Sievers		23	11	.676	35			10	273	249	46	174	
Stovall		21	15	.583	38			2	309	318	89	93	
G. Graham		12	7	.632	21			0					
Thomas		12	11	.522	29			1	216	213	57	88	
Hynes		5	3	.625	10			0					
Ford		2	4	.333	10								

LOUISVILLE   4th   76-75   .503   -23.5   Charles Dexter
Colonels

BATTERS	POS-GAMES	GP	AB	R	H	BI	2B	3B	HR	BB	SO	SB	BA
S. Sullivan	1B		(see multi-team players)										
Brashear	2B128	130	510	90	149		24	9	10			43	.292
Quinlan	SS136	136	482	37	115		13	4	0			8	.238
Woodruff	3B77,OF40	124	498	58	123		19	9	1			17	.247
Kerwin	OF152	152	603	93	184		15	17	2			29	.305
B. Hallman	OF123	123	458	72	128		11	5	0			24	.279
Clay	OF73	73	291	54	110		9	10	3			11	.378
Shaw	C96	105	365	31	98		11	11	0			7	.268
Scott	OF33,1B29,P20	82	303	30	67		8	2	1			9	.221
Dexter	1B24,C10	44	138	19	45		6	2	2			9	.326
G. Ferguson	P43	43	120	10	17		1	1	0			1	.141
Kenna	P35	35	98	9	15		2	1	0			0	.153
Dunkle	P33	33	97	8	21		2	1	1			0	.216
Schriver	C26	31	95	4	23		2	2	0			0	.242
Houser	1B27	27	96	12	22		3	3	1			1	.229
Stecher	P26	26	77	9	9		1	0	0			1	.116
Montgomery	3B17	21	74	16	23		4	5	1			3	.310
Haidt	2B18	19	60	7	14		0	1	0			5	.233
J. Hart	OF10	18	57	11	17		2	3	0			3	.298

PITCHERS		W	L	PCT	G	GS	CG	SH	IP	H	BB	SO	ERA
Dunkle		17	11	.607	33			0	239	221	75	90	
Kenna		16	13	.552	35			4	256	244	82	114	
Stecher		14	8	.636	26			2	196	207	54	86	
G. Ferguson		14	18	.438	43			4	313	329	104	127	
Scott		6	10	.375	20			1					
Campbell		2	3	.400				0					

ST. PAUL   5th   73-77   .487   -26   Mike Kelley
Saints

BATTERS	POS-GAMES	GP	AB	R	H	BI	2B	3B	HR	BB	SO	SB	BA
Kelley	1B100	101	372	39	106		18	0	0			13	.285
Marcan	2B107	111	405	51	93		13	0	0			19	.229
P. O'Brien	SS144	144	551	86	155		35	0	3			25	.281
Wheeler	3B129	139	563	76	175		34	7	2			30	.310
Ch. Hemphill	OF145	145	560	122	204		38	12	5			40	.364
Flournoy	OF135	135	493	73	140		23	3	7			23	.284
Carney	OF91,P12	103	370	52	105		13	2	1			24	.283
Ja. Sullivan	C72	79	273	29	72		4	2	0			5	.263
Geier	OF90,2B36,3B24	150	597	115	198		29	1	1			28	.333
Noonan	C52,1B38	95	356	47	105		20	6	6			15	.295
Slagle	P45	45	120	15	28		4	0	0			0	.233
Sessions	P40	40	110	5	18		5	0	0			0	.163
Ch. Ferguson	P24	32	93	8	27		4	0	0			0	.290
Evans	P30	30	64	4	6		0	0	0			0	.094
Corbett	P12	12	26	2	6		0	0	0			0	.231

ST. PAUL (cont.)
Saints

PITCHERS	W	L	PCT	G	GS	CG	SH	IP	H	BB	SO	ERA
Slagle	19	16	.543	45			3	317	**329**	70	136	
Sessions	14	18	.438	40			3	260	286	84	61	
Ch. Ferguson	9	12	.429	24			1	172	206	47	39	
Evans	8	9	.471	30			1					
Whitridge	4	1	.800				0					
Corbett	4	4	.500	12			2					
Carney	3	5	.375	12			0					
Wright	2	1	.667				1					

INDIANAPOLIS   6th   69-83   .454   -31   E.G. Barrow
Indians

BATTERS	POS-GAMES	GP	AB	R	H	BI	2B	3B	HR	BB	SO	SB	BA
Massey	1B	(see multi-team players)											
Farrell	2B77,OF45	122	425	42	105		19	4	0			16	.247
Moran	SS85	85	199	31	71		11	1	1			9	.237
Carr	3B140	140	519	52	125		12	3	2			17	.240
McCreery	OF145	148	548	83	166		19	14	3			19	.303
Thoney	OF139	147	564	73	155		12	7	6			27	.274
Bruce	OF63,2B65,P	132	492	73	124		7	3	0			19	.252
Roth	C49	52	188	18	43		7	3	1			4	.228
Osteen	SS58	61	234	22	55		7	4	0			3	.235
Cromley	P46,OF11	46	142	18	38		10	3	0			3	.267
Dickey	1B42	42	147	11	38		3	0	0			2	.258
Robertson	1B17	17	65	6	14		3	2	0			0	.215
C. Morgan	P17	17	46	4	7		1	2	0			0	.152
Swander	OF16	16	61	5	13		2	0	0			0	.211
Fisher	P16	16	34	4	7		0	1	0			1	.205
McGill	P13	13	27	1	3		0	0	0			0	.111
Schwartz		11	38	4	9		1	1	0			0	.236

PITCHERS	W	L	PCT	G	GS	CG	SH	IP	H	BB	SO	ERA
Cromley	18	13	.581	46			2	251	286	46	67	
C. Morgan	7	8	.467	17			2					
Fisher	4	5	.444	16			1					
Mattern	3	2	.600				0					
McGill	3	7	.300	13			0					
Starkell	1	2	.333				0					
Bruce	1	2	.333									

TOLEDO   7th   60-91   .397   -39.5   Finn - Grillo
Mud Hens

BATTERS	POS-GAMES	GP	AB	R	H	BI	2B	3B	HR	BB	SO	SB	BA
Boyle	1B90,C10	101	347	36	86		18	1	1			5	.244
DeMontreville	2B136,SS16	152	589	93	171		**49**	4	1			36	.290
Clingman	SS142,3B13	155	590	92	159		21	6	0			34	.269
Moriarity	3B136	136	505	73	149		37	3	3			**51**	.295
Lee	OF82,1B55,P	137	504	81	152		43	6	**13**			15	.301
Jo. Clarke	OF76	78	283	51	88		18	1	0			28	.310
Gilbert	OF	(see multi-team players)											
R. Clark	C94	94	345	36	71		12	1	1			4	.205
Durrett	OF60	60	237	30	73		14	1	0			17	.308
Camnitz	P39	40	119	7	18		7	0	0			2	.151
Doyle	1B39	39	153	15	41		10	0	0			6	.268
Minnehan	P39,OF10	39	121	14	30		6	0	1			0	.248
Fiene	P34	34	106	6	32		5	1	0			1	.301
F. O'Brien	P28	28	73	5	15		2	1	0			1	.205
Land	C22	22	70	6	12		0	0	0			2	.171
Neighbors	OF27	27	91	5	26		2	0	0			3	.285
Piatt	P16	16	47	3	11		4	0	0			0	.234

PITCHERS	W	L	PCT	G	GS	CG	SH	IP	H	BB	SO	ERA
Camnitz	17	17	.500	39			2	300	308	95	182	
Fiene	11	13	.458	34			1	233	205	64	121	
Minnehan	11	13	.458	39			2	208	190	126	109	
Piatt	9	5	.649	16								

TOLEDO (cont.)
Mud Hens

PITCHERS	W	L	PCT	G	GS	CG	SH	IP	H	BB	SO	ERA
F. O'Brien	3	19	.136	28			0	192	225	67	90	
Lee	0	3	.000									

KANSAS CITY   8th   44-102   .301   -53   Arthur Irwin
Blues

BATTERS	POS-GAMES	GP	AB	R	H	BI	2B	3B	HR	BB	SO	SB	BA
Douglas	1B47	47	176	24	48		4	1	0			7	.284
Bonner	2B116	116	414	47	115		21	2	1			7	.277
Downey	SS68	70	228	22	39		1	1	0			9	.171
Donahue	3B87,SS58	148	552	60	140		22	5	0			16	.255
Castro	OF88,3B33,1B16	146	570	81	150		28	7	7			17	.263
Nance	OF		(see multi-team players)										
Cassady	OF		(see multi-team players)										
Butler	C102	107	345	35	100		21	1	2			9	.290
Frantz	3B28,P23,OF23,2B15	92	322	40	96		21	1	1			18	.298
Rickert	OF56	56	209	25	42		12	0	1			6	.200
Hill	1B	54	197	29	58		12	5	0			10	.294
Eels	P40	41	103	5	16		4	1	0			1	.155
Durham	P20,OF11	31	99	11	25		2	1	0			1	.252
Isbell	P24	24	55	1	2		0	0	0			0	.038
Justus	P13	13	33	1	3		0	0	0			0	.087
Charles		12	37	4	6		0	0	0			3	.162
Skopec	P	11	35	4	8		3	0	0			0	.228

PITCHERS	W	L	PCT	G	GS	CG	SH	IP	H	BB	SO	ERA
Frantz	10	11	.476	23			1	174	226	28	58	
Eels	7	23	.233	40			1	279	264	**135**	148	
Durham	6	11	.353	20			0					
Isbell	4	13	.235	24			1					
Skopec	2	5	.286				0					
Justus	2	6	.250	13			0					

MULTI-TEAM PLAYERS

BATTERS	POS-GAMES	TEAMS	GP	AB	R	H	BI	2B	3B	HR	BB	SO	SB	BA
Nance	OF133,2B17	TOL-KC	152	498	65	118		30	4	3			26	.237
Massey	1B140	KC-IND	140	527	67	152		33	3	0			9	.288
Gilbert	OF138	TOL-KC	139	515	71	139		14	2	0			22	.270
S. Sullivan	1B60,3B54,SS17	KC-LOU	131	521	96	148		27	8	0			26	.284
Cassady	OF95	TOL-KC	96	348	37	87		11	3	0			11	.250
Zalusky	C58,1B14	SP-IND	73	245	24	56		10	6	1			7	.228
Friel	OF33,1B19,3B10	CO-IN-MIN	66	241	28	58		5	3	0			11	.240
Weaver	C57	MIN-IND	57	187	12	45		3	1	0			1	.240
Stoner	P48	KC-LOU	54	170	15	37		8	0	0			2	.217
Zearfoss	C42	TOL-KC	51	155	10	36		12	0	1			2	.232
Goodwin	P45	MIL-IND	45	139	14	38		8	2	1			1	.272
Hickey	P44	MIL-COL	44	114	12	16		2	0	1			1	.140
A. Morgan	P37	KC-LOU	37	87	3	15		1	0	0			1	.172
Kilroy	P35	SP-KC	35	84	7	14		2	1	0			1	.166
Curtis	P34	IND-MIL	34	103	5	24		1	0	0			0	.233
Wright	P18,OF15	LOU-KC	33	89	11	12		2	1	0			1	.134
Reidy	P32	IND-LOU	32	85	5	11		2	0	0			0	.129
Kellum	P32	TOL-MIN	32	84	8	17		4	0	0			2	.202
Murphy	OF24	LOU-KC	24	85	11	25		2	0	1			0	.294
Duff	C10	MIN-IND	22	74	4	13		3	0	0			2	.175
Martin	P22	TOL-IND	22	51	3	9		1	0	0			0	.176
Yeager	C17	SP-TOL	17	45	2	5		1	0	1			0	.111
Jaeger	P16	MIN-IND	16	39	1	4		0	1	0			0	.162
Craig	P10	MIN-IND	10	24	3	5		1	0	0			0	.208

PITCHERS		TEAMS	W	L	PCT	G	GS	CG	SH	IP	H	BB	SO	ERA
Goodwin		MIL-IND	23	12	.657	45			1	334	301	129	172	
Hickey		MIL-COL	21	12	.636	44			5	335	323	115	183	
Curtis		IND-MIL	14	19	.424	34			1	262	250	108	125	
Reidy		IND-LOU	12	17	.414	32			3	239	279	44	52	

MULTI-TEAM PLAYERS (cont.)

PITCHERS	TEAMS	W	L	PCT	G	GS	CG	SH	IP	H	BB	SO	ERA
A. Morgan	KC-LOU	11	20	.355	37			2	245	270	84	94	
Kellum	TOL-MIN	10	9	.526	32			3					
Kilroy	SP-KC	9	20	.310	35			1	252	236	94	118	
Martin	TOL-IND	5	11	.313	22			1					
Wright	LOU-KC	5	12	.294	18								
Craig	MIN-IND	4	1	.800	10								
Jaeger	MIN-IND	2	7	.222	16								

TEAM BATTING

TEAMS	GP	AB	R	H	BI	2B	3B	HR	BB	SO	SB	BA
COLUMBUS	153	5075	707	1377		218	58	23			193	.271
MILWAUKEE	153	5134	775	1336		218	51	40			150	.260
MINNEAPOLIS	153	4929	714	1343		208	46	29			161	.272
LOUISVILLE	152	5116	688	1365		164	95	23			198	.266
ST. PAUL	152	5198	748	1494		250	39	26			229	.287
INDIANAPOLIS	153	4508	501	1120		130	53	13			132	.248
TOLEDO	155	5378	694	1427		291	30	22			243	.265
KANSAS CITY	149	4741	551	1184		225	33	15			143	.249
	610	40079	5378	10646		1704	405	191			1449	.266

1906
Little World Series

The concept of a championship series between rival leagues dates back to the 1880s when the major league American Association squared off against the National League. The idea was resurrected at the beginning of the 20th century with the start of the modern World Series. The interest and money generated by these series attracted the attention of minor league magnates. Perhaps a series between rival minor leagues would be a profitable venture as well. What better place to start than at the top level of the minor leagues—the American Association vs. its East Coast rival, the Eastern League?

After the 1904 season, a brief three-game series was played between the Association pennant winners, the St. Paul Saints, and the Eastern League champions from Buffalo. After a year's hiatus, the series resumed following the 1906 season. Now dubbed the Little World Series, it pitted the Buffalo Bisons against the Columbus Senators.

The Senators won their second straight flag by outlasting Milwaukee and Minneapolis, who finished in second and third. Toledo moved up to fourth, while Kansas City, Louisville, St. Paul and Indianapolis wound up fifth through eighth. Louisville's Hallman won the batting title (.342) while Milwaukee's Green hit the most home runs (8). On the mound, it was Berger of Columbus who set the pace with 28 wins and 264 strikeouts. Berger's strikeout total would hold up as an all-time league best for almost fifty years.

The 1906 Little World Series started in Buffalo with a 4–1 win by the home team. After a tie in game two, the series resumed in Columbus where Buffalo won game three, 1–0 , while Columbus took the next, 9–2. The next two games, also in Columbus, saw another split as Buffalo prevailed 3–1, while Columbus countered 3–2. With Buffalo holding a 3–2 game lead, the rest of the series was called off. The two teams simply could not agree on division of revenue, nor on the location of the next games. With that, Buffalo was declared the winner.

Its murky ending notwithstanding, the Little World Series was considered a success, and plans were made to continue the rivalry the following year. As a result the Little World Series continued, though not every year, as a viable institution all the way until the 1970s.

COLUMBUS
Senators

1st   91-57   .615   William Clymer

BATTERS	POS-GAMES	GP	AB	R	H	BI	2B	3B	HR	BB	SO	SB	BA
Kihm	1B148	148	514	72	143		17	6	2			11	.278
Wrigley	2B150	153	580	45	132		26	7	3			27	.227
Hulswitt	SS129	129	466	43	108		14	4	1			15	.231
Friel	3B136	136	525	61	116		16	12	2			15	.221
Coulter	OF154	154	584	69	141		19	6	0			17	.241
Pickering	OF151	151	633	88	198		17	18	6			24	.317
W. Hinchman	OF107	115	442	75	139		19	8	4			19	.314
Blue	C94	94	312	27	81		13	4	0			6	.259
Ryan	C67,3B18	102	364	31	87		20	3	0			5	.241
Berger	P43	43	139	10	19		3	1	1			1	.137
Flaherty	P36	39	129	24	24		7	2	1			3	.186
Robertaille	P34	35	115	8	24		1	0	0			1	.208
Veil	P33	33	94	6	13		1	1	1			0	.138
Bruce	OF30	30	102	10	25		2	0	0			4	.245
Groth	P23	23	58	5	8		0	0	0			3	.138
Clymer	OF15	15	49	5	11		0	1	0			2	.224

PITCHERS		W	L	PCT	G	GS	CG	SH	IP	H	BB	SO	ERA
Berger		28	13	.684	43				371	260	95	264	
Flaherty		23	9	.719	36				305	278	50	86	
Veil		17	11	.607	33				203	221	85	74	
Robertaille		17	16	.515	34				298	273	85	125	
Groth		9	8	.529	23				158	164	55	66	

MILWAUKEE
Brewers

2nd   85-67   .559   -8   Joe Cantillon

BATTERS	POS-GAMES	GP	AB	R	H	BI	2B	3B	HR	BB	SO	SB	BA
Bateman	1B140	155	602	84	161		38	9	4			5	.267
McCormick	2B150	153	545	53	141		23	7	1			11	.260
Robinson	SS137	137	542	93	127		20	10	1			20	.234
H. Clark	3B125	125	450	71	115		17	8	1			21	.255
Green	OF150	150	551	119	177		34	9	8			33	.321
F. Hemphill	OF119	124	439	65	112		15	8	1			16	.255
McChesney	OF105,3B29	142	519	62	125		25	11	6			25	.241
Roth	C84	86	303	36	88		11	2	1			10	.290
Beville	C73,1B15	88	330	46	99		18	1	4			1	.300
Hynes	OF66	85	315	32	82		14	3	1			4	.260
Dougherty	P28,OF18	46	128	14	23		6	1	0			0	.179
Oberlin	P45	45	118	11	25		4	1	0			0	.212
Curtis	P44	44	123	10	20		1	0	0			2	.164
Goodwin	P33	33	93	12	20		3	1	2			0	.215
Sage	P15	15	41	4	7		1	1	0			0	.171

PITCHERS		W	L	PCT	G	GS	CG	SH	IP	H	BB	SO	ERA
Curtis		22	14	.611	44				323	283	80	158	
Oberlin		18	16	.529	45				306	259	109	180	
Goodwin		16	12	.571	33				246	226	114	107	
Dougherty		11	13	.458	28				194	194	79	76	

MINNEAPOLIS
Millers

3rd   79-66   .545   -11.5   Mike Kelley

BATTERS	POS-GAMES	GP	AB	R	H	BI	2B	3B	HR	BB	SO	SB	BA
Freeman	1B101	101	363	37	84		12	4	0			14	.231
Fox	2B131	131	441	33	89		3	4	0			18	.202
Oyler	SS132	132	455	52	119		7	4	0			14	.261
Gremminger	3B142	144	538	76	163		29	9	2			13	.305
Davis	OF149	149	612	112	204		34	10	3			47	.333
D. Sullivan	OF138	138	526	73	164		21	7	2			29	.311
Hart	OF94,1B52	146	542	69	134		16	11	6			20	.249
Yeager	C77	78	265	17	51		10	2	0			5	.192
G. Graham	OF52,2B24,SS21,C19	122	451	48	110		14	4	2			18	.244
Shannon	C61	61	191	13	34		8	1	0			1	.178
Gehring	P31,OF22	53	163	15	30		8	3	2			2	.184

MINNEAPOLIS (cont.)
Millers

BATTERS	POS-GAMES	GP	AB	R	H	BI	2B	3B	HR	BB	SO	SB	BA
Thomas	P42	42	122	6	21		4	0	0			0	.172
Ford	P38	38	108	4	11		2	0	0			0	.102
Cadwallader	P38	38	96	1	5		1	2	0			0	.052
Kilroy	P26	26	72	8	13		0	0	0			2	.181

PITCHERS		W	L	PCT	G	GS	CG	SH	IP	H	BB	SO	ERA
Ford		21	13	.618	38				296	276	86	101	
Thomas		18	15	.545	42				318	311	56	148	
Cadwallader		16	13	.552	38				261	240	105	79	
Kilroy		12	12	.500	26				210	178	77	85	
Gehring		12	13	.486	31				222	194	66	108	

TOLEDO   4th   79-69   .534   -13   J. Ed Grillo
Mud Hens

BATTERS	POS-GAMES	GP	AB	R	H	BI	2B	3B	HR	BB	SO	SB	BA
W.J. Clark	1B152	152	509	60	140		28	3	1			19	.275
Knabe	2B149	149	532	64	150		23	4	1			21	.282
DeMontreville	SS80,OF40	133	524	67	148		29	5	3			33	.282
Krueger	3B153	153	551	72	141		36	3	1			19	.256
Jo. Clarke	OF124	124	473	65	132		26	5	2			23	.279
Nance	OF106	107	364	61	100		20	7	2			17	.274
Jude	OF71	72	279	43	88		18	6	1			16	.315
Abbott	C105	112	382	44	110		21	4	3			16	.288
Clingman	SS73	75	308	43	75		10	1	0			11	.243
Odwell	OF69	69	252	43	77		13	3	5			15	.305
Land	C55	61	212	23	55		3	2	0			3	.259
Cannell	OF48	48	188	28	49		11	1	1			9	.260
Camnitz	P43	43	128	8	19		2	0	0			5	.148
Minnehan	P34	34	99	6	15		0	0	1			1	.152
Suthoff	P33	33	86	7	17		0	1	1			2	.200
Piatt	P26	26	59	12	17		7	0	0			0	.288
Chech	P23	23	57	3	7		2	0	0			0	.123

PITCHERS		W	L	PCT	G	GS	CG	SH	IP	H	BB	SO	ERA
Camnitz		22	17	.564	43				342	304	100	217	
Minnehan		15	12	.556	34				261	225	124	120	
Suthoff		15	15	.500	33				240	213	73	83	
Piatt		9	10	.474	26				170	179	48	60	
Chech		9	11	.450	23				180	164	26	63	

LOUISVILLE   5th   71-79   .473   -22   S. Sullivan
Colonels

BATTERS	POS-GAMES	GP	AB	R	H	BI	2B	3B	HR	BB	SO	SB	BA
Su. Sullivan	1B130,3B20	155	630	74	180		29	10	2			28	.285
Brashear	2B155	155	576	72	164		18	19	3			34	.284
Quinlan	SS149	149	543	44	138		18	9	0			4	.254
Woodruff	3B137	151	599	60	174		17	9	2			40	.290
Hallman	OF147	147	572	81	196		22	11	1			54	.342
Kerwin	OF144	144	562	79	172		25	11	0			20	.306
Stovall	OF		(see multi-team players)										
Shaw	C105	108	362	35	79		13	5	1			1	.218
Stoner	C62	62	196	11	36		4	3	0			3	.183
Kenna	P43	55	166	20	54		3	8	0			3	.325
Puttmann	P37	41	136	9	30		5	4	2			0	.220
Dunkle	P38	41	130	7	31		5	1	1			0	.238
Murpy	OF33	33	135	11	43		2	6	0			3	.318
Elliott	P31	33	92	2	13		0	1	0			0	.141
Stecher	P25	25	50	4	7		0	0	0			0	.140

PITCHERS		W	L	PCT	G	GS	CG	SH	IP	H	BB	SO	ERA
Puttmann		18	17	.514	37				297	263	96	149	
Dunkle		16	19	.457	38				302	350	81	89	
Kenna		12	21	.364	43				305	308	139	95	

LOUISVILLE (cont.)
Colonels

PITCHERS	W	L	PCT	G	GS	CG	SH	IP	H	BB	SO	ERA
Elliott	11	14	.440	31				236	218	58	80	
Stecher	9	7	.563	25				144	180	49	47	

KANSAS CITY   6th   69-79   .466   -23   James Burke
Blues

BATTERS	POS-GAMES	GP	AB	R	H	BI	2B	3B	HR	BB	SO	SB	BA
Frantz	1B54,P31	110	385	35	92		17	4	2			12	.233
Phyle	2B53,OF17	72	275	34	81		19	5	2			10	.295
Perrine	SS92,2B54	153	577	106	178		39	10	3			41	.308
Burke	3B152	152	539	77	153		16	3	2			50	.284
Hill	OF152	156	598	83	170		35	10	3			32	.284
Cassaday	OF133	133	480	70	131		23	6	2			15	.273
Waldron	OF114	114	423	47	117		10	6	0			16	.276
Leahy	C90	104	350	35	99		17	4	0			11	.283
Ja. Sullivan	C69,1B17	88	277	14	45		12	0	0			5	.162
McBride	SS59	59	232	24	56		14	2	0			4	.241
Bohannan	OF31,P16	51	160	12	43		5	2	2			1	.269
Slattery	1B47	47	176	18	35		5	2	0			6	.198
Swann	P39	42	127	6	16		2	1	0			1	.126
Durham	P40	40	109	7	15		1	1	0			0	.137
Whitney	1B36	36	141	16	36		7	2	1			6	.255
Donohue	2B35	35	125	15	26		2	0	0			3	.208
Crutcher	P17	26	70	6	10		1	0	0			1	.143
Egan	P16	16	37	3	4		0	0	0			1	.108

PITCHERS	W	L	PCT	G	GS	CG	SH	IP	H	BB	SO	ERA
Swann	22	13	.629	39				327	292	73	114	
Frantz	14	15	.483	31				257	238	70	79	
Durham	14	18	.438	40				300	298	111	117	

ST. PAUL   7th   66-80   .452   -25   Richard Padden
Saints

BATTERS	POS-GAMES	GP	AB	R	H	BI	2B	3B	HR	BB	SO	SB	BA
Sugden	1B127,C15	142	538	67	144		16	4	1			15	.267
Padden	2B140	140	480	77	138		27	3	3			19	.287
Rockenfield	SS63	63	206	41	58		15	2	2			12	.285
Wheeler	3B143	151	585	63	154		29	8	2			19	.263
Frisk	OF127	127	485	85	155		36	11	6			13	.321
Van Zandt	OF114	128	508	69	145		24	5	6			12	.285
Geier	OF76,SS64	154	619	97	188		29	4	2			23	.303
Drill	C124	124	400	46	109		15	2	1			9	.272
Coy	OF65,P27	92	301	34	81		18	8	0			5	.267
Myers	OF35	49	170	20	49		3	0	0			7	.288
Morgan	P39	41	125	10	22		3	0	1			1	.176
Slagle	P28	36	93	13	12		4	1	0			0	.129
Pruitt	P20	25	79	9	15		0	0	0			3	.190
Parkins	P24	24	58	6	14		2	0	0			0	.241
Buchanan	P22	22	50	3	5		1	0	0			0	.100
Pierce	C19	19	74	3	23		4	0	0			0	.310

PITCHERS	W	L	PCT	G	GS	CG	SH	IP	H	BB	SO	ERA
Morgan	22	12	.647	39				308	274	97	154	
Coy	12	10	.545	27				194	208	40	32	
Pruitt	11	8	.578	20				164	150	41	88	
Slagle	6	11	.353	28				184	198	86	56	
Parkins	5	8	.385	24				137	164	37	33	
Buchanan	4	12	.250	22				148	150	58	52	

INDIANAPOLIS   8th   53-96   .356   -38.5   C.C. Carr
Indians

BATTERS	POS-GAMES	GP	AB	R	H	BI	2B	3B	HR	BB	SO	SB	BA
C. Carr	1B109	110	439	44	137		28	10	4			11	.312
Marcan	2B		(see multi-team players)										
Williams	SS80	83	310	31	71		8	2	1			22	.229
Atherton	3B89	89	319	32	70		8	5	2			10	.219
Dunleavy	OF129	129	513	59	135		18	6	2			17	.263
Perry	OF115	115	418	40	86		5	3	0			17	.205
Himes	OF78,1B34	114	442	54	112		8	7	2			21	.253
Holmes	C88	88	305	21	50		3	1	0			6	.164
Kahoe	C51	78	288	17	79		8	2	0			5	.274
J. Carr	SS53	69	257	38	69		5	6	0			13	.268
James	3B47,1B22	66	225	28	55		4	2	0			4	.244
Kellum	P38	52	169	11	32		3	1	0			3	.189
Thielman	P23,OF20	43	132	11	27		5	3	0			0	.205
Rothgeb	OF41	41	165	22	45		4	0	0			12	.272
Fisher	P36	36	103	10	26		4	2	1			1	.252
Cromley	P22	32	108	7	22		1	0	0			2	.204
Vinson	OF23	23	84	17	23		0	3	1			5	.273
Kelly	2B20	22	83	7	20		3	0	0			2	.241
Weaver	C20	20	72	5	18		1	0	0			0	.250
Farrell	2B15	15	61	6	19		1	1	0			3	.311

PITCHERS		W	L	PCT	G	GS	CG	SH	IP	H	BB	SO	ERA
Kellum		16	19	.457	38				319	299	60	102	
Thielman		11	10	.524	23				199	194	56	86	
Fisher		10	22	.313	36				276	275	92	91	
Cromley		9	12	.429	22				182	173	24	56	

MULTI-TEAM PLAYERS

BATTERS	POS-GAMES	TEAMS	GP	AB	R	H	BI	2B	3B	HR	BB	SO	SB	BA
Marcan	2B115,SS31	SP-IND	146	513	34	81		7	2	1			11	.158
Stovall	OF116	LOU-SP	133	521	56	137		19	3	2			24	.263
Hickey	P28	MIL-IND	30	80	3	16		0	1	0			1	.200

PITCHERS		TEAMS	W	L	PCT	G	GS	CG	SH	IP	H	BB	SO	ERA
Hickey		MIL-IND	7	19	.269	28				209	229	96	68	

TEAM BATTING

TEAMS	GP	AB	R	H	BI	2B	3B	HR	BB	SO	SB	BA
COLUMBUS	155	5106	579	1269		175	73	21			153	.248
MILWAUKEE	154	5131	714	1330		223	72	30			148	.259
MINNEAPOLIS	153	4945	564	1232		169	61	17			183	.249
TOLEDO	156	5003	649	1340		249	45	22			210	.267
LOUISVILLE	156	5270	565	1454		180	100	14			210	.276
KANSAS CITY	156	5111	611	1310		226	58	17			215	.256
ST. PAUL	155	4882	654	1336		232	49	25			141	.274
INDIANAPOLIS	155	5188	506	1213		128	59	14			169	.234
	620	40636	4842	10484		1582	517	160			1429	.258

1907
Columbus Senators

The first dynasty in the American Association was built in central Ohio. Here the Columbus Senators became the first team in the league to win three flags in a row. The Senators finished fifth, sixth and second during their first three years in theAssociation. Building on their second place finish in 1904, Columbus took their first pennant in 1905. They then won a second the next year. The Senators' champion clubs were built around a nucleus of pitching and defense. This was easy to see in 1906, as Columbus finished second from the bottom in hitting with a lackluster .248 mark, but first in fielding with a crisp .965 average. Also, the Senator pitching staff allowed their opponents the fewest hits.

As the summer of 1907 progressed, a stubborn Toledo club clung to the Senators' heels before Columbus prevailed by a slim two-game margin. The 1907 version differed somewhat from its light hitting predecessors, finishing second in hitting. Outfielder Gessler (.325), shortstop Hulswitt (.296), first baseman Kihm (.288), and third baseman Friel (.285) led the surge of the Columbus batting up to the .270 mark. The pitching remained strong as the squad boasted of two twenty-game winners, Upp (27-10) and Robertaille (21-14).

In the rest of the league, Minneapolis and Kansas City rounded out the first division, while Louisville, Indianapolis, Milwaukee, and St. Paul finished on the final four rungs. Beckley of Kansas City ended up as the top batter with a total of .365, while Freeman of Minneapolis set a new home run record (18). The aforementioned Upp of the pennant winning Columbus squad pitched the most victories (27), while Puttman of Louisville had 174 strikeouts.

After its trifecta of champions, Columbus would go through a drought of nearly thirty years before its next triumph during the 1930s. There the team would enter a time of prosperity which would see it dominate post-season play like no other, past or future. But these later triumphs should not diminish the accomplishments of the Senators during the first decade of this century. To win a championship three times in a row was a difficult feat—a feat that only would be accomplished by two other teams during the first fifty years of the Association's existence.

COLUMBUS Senators   1st   90-64   .584   William Clymer

BATTERS	POS-GAMES	GP	AB	R	H	BI	2B	3B	HR	BB	SO	SB	BA
Kihm	1B158	158	573	81	165		17	10	0			22	.288
Wrigley	2B152	152	560	61	139		21	3	0			19	.248
Hulswitt	SS159	159	631	90	187		35	14	2			36	.296
Friel	3B159	159	662	104	189		34	9	1			21	.285
Jude	OF142	142	531	83	146		21	6	1			13	.275
Gessler	OF135	135	470	84	153		35	12	6			36	.325
Reilley	OF74	74	284	42	64		4	3	0			14	.225
Blue	C99	99	348	24	82		12	2	0			1	.235
Fohl	C67	71	238	33	66		11	4	1			4	.279
Servatius	OF46	46	182	27	47		9	4	2			3	.258
Upp	P41	42	122	11	29		3	2	0			0	.238
Wicker	P29	39	122	10	23		3	0	0			3	.189
Robertaille	P38	38	118	11	25		2	1	0			0	.212
McCreery	OF37	37	132	24	41		7	1	0			6	.311
Geyer	P32	32	95	3	21		1	1	0			2	.223
Townsend	P26	26	68	4	11		1	0	1			2	.168
Jackson	OF24	24	79	5	19		2	0	0			3	.240
Hall	P16	17	42	5	14		2	1	0			0	.333

PITCHERS		W	L	PCT	G	GS	CG	SH	IP	H	BB	SO	ERA
Upp		27	10	.730	41				327	253	70	142	
Robertaille		21	14	.600	38				297	292	50	111	
Wicker		14	12	.538	29				246	218	56	113	
Geyer		12	10	.545	32				233	236	70	98	
Townsend		7	11	.389	26				188	180	67	56	

TOLEDO Mud Hens   2nd   88-66   .571   -2   William Armour

BATTERS	POS-GAMES	GP	AB	R	H	BI	2B	3B	HR	BB	SO	SB	BA
W. Clarke	1B152	152	530	49	133		20	1	0			15	.251
Pokorney	2B58,3B26	84	309	50	91		18	4	0			9	.294
Barbeau	SS125	125	458	93	135		35	7	4			28	.295
Perring	3B135	135	499	78	150		22	3	9			27	.301
Jo. Clarke	OF154	154	557	94	179		29	4	0			54	.321
Smoot	OF141	141	541	84	169		36	3	1			14	.312
Armbruster	OF133	133	500	88	161		34	8	5			18	.322
Abbott	C87	95	330	37	84		23	0	1			15	.255
Land	C75	77	270	35	69		13	2	0			8	.256
Reagan	OF47,2B17	69	236	26	62		6	3	0			11	.263
Chech	P39	39	118	25	25		9	1	0			2	.211
Lattimore	P31	32	98	8	23		6	0	0			1	.238
West	P31	31	90	5	17		3	0	0			0	.189
Gillen	P29	29	66	6	10		3	0	0			1	.152
DeMontreville	2B27	28	107	10	20		6	0	0			3	.187
Suthoff	P26	26	69	10	12		1	0	1			0	.174
Eels	P24	24	59	6	15		2	0	1			1	.254
Diehl	SS22	22	84	14	34		6	0	3			3	.393

PITCHERS		W	L	PCT	G	GS	CG	SH	IP	H	BB	SO	ERA
Chech		25	11	.694	39				314	286	67	134	
West		17	9	.654	31				231	233	52	140	
Suthoff		15	8	.652	26				193	173	54	62	
Lattimore		13	8	.619	31				239	203	36	82	
Gillen		11	11	.500	29				196	189	63	75	
Eels		6	12	.333	24				171	196	65	58	

MINNEAPOLIS Millers   3rd   80-74   .520   -10   M.E. Cantillon

BATTERS	POS-GAMES	GP	AB	R	H	BI	2B	3B	HR	BB	SO	SB	BA
Je. Freeman	1B151	153	484	64	175		25	10	4			21	.335
Dundon	2B121	127	455	66	87		9	1	1			16	.191
Oyler	SS133	133	452	46	107		14	4	0			4	.237
Greminger	3B147	147	536	55	140		25	4	3			9	.261
O'Neill	OF146	146	591	96	169		24	11	1			39	.286

MINNEAPOLIS (cont.)
Millers

BATTERS	POS-GAMES	GP	AB	R	H	BI	2B	3B	HR	BB	SO	SB	BA
Jo. Freeman	OF142	142	528	80	177		38	10	18			21	.335
Mertes	OF111	115	425	76	119		29	10	5			34	.280
G. Graham	C73,OF18	103	338	36	77		11	4	0			9	.228
Perrine	OF33,2B18	70	255	35	54		7	2	0			8	.212
Shannon	C41	41	132	8	16		3	1	0			0	.121
Kilroy	P35	35	104	10	19		0	0	0			1	.183
J. Freeman	P35	35	75	4	9		0	0	0			1	.120
Thomas	P31	31	96	6	19		1	0	0			0	.198
Ford	P31	31	81	0	8		1	0	0			1	.099
Manske	P25	27	60	8	15		2	0	0			0	.250
Towne	C24	26	94	9	23		4	1	0			0	.245
Buelow	C25	25	78	3	16		0	1	0			2	.205

PITCHERS		W	L	PCT	G	GS	CG	SH	IP	H	BB	SO	ERA
Kilroy		19	10	.655	35				269	278	68	105	
Thomas		14	16	.467	31				241	243	45	89	
Manske		12	6	.667	25				157	145	78	67	
J. Freeman		12	14	.462	35				247	215	68	165	
Ford		12	15	.444	31				232	237	63	80	

KANSAS CITY   4th   78-76   .510   -12   James Burke
Blues

BATTERS	POS-GAMES	GP	AB	R	H	BI	2B	3B	HR	BB	SO	SB	BA
Beckley	1B100	100	378	65	138		10	4	1			12	.365
O. Krueger	2B152	156	552	82	137		18	6	0			26	.248
McBride	SS151	151	550	67	148		24	5	2			29	.269
Burke	3B154	154	555	63	148		21	2	1			16	.267
Hill	OF152	152	604	80	161		29	8	7			30	.266
Huelsman	OF149	149	566	91	168		37	14	5			24	.297
Kerwin	OF	(see multi-team players)											
J. Sullivan	C119	121	390	27	87		11	0	0			12	.223
McCarthy	OF49	49	177	23	60		9	1	0			11	.339
Leahy	C36	46	145	17	35		2	0	0			4	.241
Swann	P45	45	112	10	23		1	1	0			4	.205
Case	P40	40	83	6	8		0	0	0			2	.096
Egan	P37	37	94	11	20		0	2	0			3	.202
Crutcher	P20	22	62	9	11		2	0	0			1	.177
Brandom	P18	18	44	2	2		0	0	0			0	.045

PITCHERS		W	L	PCT	G	GS	CG	SH	IP	H	BB	SO	ERA
Swann		21	19	.525	45				326	320	64	109	
Egan		14	15	.483	37				279	284	75	65	
Case		14	16	.467	40				272	270	76	86	
Crutcher		7	5	.583	20				144	129	59	32	

LOUISVILLE   5th   77-77   .500   -13   Richard Cooley
Colonels

BATTERS	POS-GAMES	GP	AB	R	H	BI	2B	3B	HR	BB	SO	SB	BA
Cooley	1B87,OF33	120	466	60	122		20	11	1			14	.262
Brashear	2B158	158	600	81	157		18	7	0			42	.262
Quinlan	SS156	156	583	65	140		17	4	2			10	.240
S. Sullivan	3B93,1B58	154	588	67	160		21	7	0			20	.272
Stanley	OF154	154	589	84	142		19	7	4			24	.242
Stovall	OF97	99	417	57	128		17	2	1			16	.307
Woodruff	OF92,3B65	158	580	81	149		17	5	0			39	.257
Pietz	C85	101	348	35	84		8	1	1			6	.241
Hughes	C80	89	289	38	64		8	7	1			7	.221
Puttmann	P45	49	155	14	36		5	3	3			0	.232
Gnadinger	OF49	49	154	14	31		3	1	1			2	.201
J. Durham	P38	38	115	12	16		2	0	0			0	.139
L. Durham	P37	37	107	9	20		2	1	0			2	.187
Neal	OF30	35	129	14	42		4	2	0			8	.325
Kenna	P17	17	42	5	6		1	1	0			0	.143

LOUISVILLE (cont.)
Colonels

PITCHERS	W	L	PCT	G	GS	CG	SH	IP	H	BB	SO	ERA
Puttmann	21	20	.512	45				358	338	108	**174**	
J. Durham	18	15	.545	38				292	284	75	97	
L. Durham	16	18	.471	37				280	273	110	68	

INDIANAPOLIS   6th   73-81   .473   -17   C.C. Carr
Indians

BATTERS	POS-GAMES	GP	AB	R	H	BI	2B	3B	HR	BB	SO	SB	BA
C. Carr	1B137	137	521	64	164		25	10	3			14	.315
Krug	2B70,SS28	98	361	29	96		12	1	1			9	.266
O. Williams	SS128	128	501	54	109		12	4	0			21	.217
Hopke	3B155	155	534	43	135		15	10	3			6	.253
Coulter	OF155	155	567	85	162		17	11	5			25	.286
Seigle	OF116,2B16	132	467	46	113		18	7	3			11	.242
Himes	OF90,1B21	111	403	47	110		13	12	2			15	.273
Livingstone	C112	112	365	37	93		14	6	1	·		12	.255
Cook	OF80	81	304	49	77		6	4	0			25	.253
Howley	C51	62	204	17	50		6	1	0			8	.245
Kellum	P34	42	118	9	27		3	1	1			1	.229
Slagle	P36	41	113	5	20		3	1	0			1	.177
Summers	P36	36	107	5	18		0	0	0			0	.169
Briggs	P33	33	91	3	16		1	1	0			0	.176
Chenault	P18	18	30	0	2		0	0	0			0	.067

PITCHERS	W	L	PCT	G	GS	CG	SH	IP	H	BB	SO	ERA
Briggs	16	14	.533	33				268	233	96	122	
Kellum	15	16	.484	34				257	258	63	87	
Slagle	15	16	.484	36				283	273	63	128	
Summers	14	16	.467	36				295	257	96	130	

MILWAUKEE   7th   71-83   .461   -19   Jack Doyle
Brewers

BATTERS	POS-GAMES	GP	AB	R	H	BI	2B	3B	HR	BB	SO	SB	BA
Connors	1B88	90	364	62	106		18	8	1			15	.291
McCormick	2B150	150	538	54	135		17	3	1			21	.251
Robinson	SS154	154	606	82	148		28	4	2			23	.244
H. Clark	3B136	136	450	55	88		9	3	3			16	.196
Green	OF150	150	562	107	143		30	4	3			24	.254
McChesney	OF105	114	418	66	105		18	9	5			29	.251
Dougherty	OF61,P24	96	341	32	78		13	6	1			8	.229
Roth	C86	88	334	51	107		12	5	2			23	.320
Beville	C70,1B32	102	393	32	104		17	2	1			8	.265
Goodwin	P46	47	145	10	23		2	1	0			6	.158
Curtis	P42	42	123	7	26		0	0	0			0	.211
McCann	OF30	36	131	10	24		4	1	0			3	.183
Schneiberg	P35	36	105	7	12		0	0	0			0	.114
Mahoney	OF33	33	132	12	23		1	2	1			4	.174
Stevens	OF30	30	95	15	27		3	1	0			10	.284
F. Hemphill	OF27	28	94	11	26		5	0	0			7	.277
Wilson	P28	28	60	2	7		1	0	0			0	.117
Bateman	1B23	25	91	6	16		3	0	0			0	.177

PITCHERS	W	L	PCT	G	GS	CG	SH	IP	H	BB	SO	ERA
Goodwin	21	**23**	.477	46				**376**	351	**115**	173	
Curtis	18	21	.462	42				337	312	95	153	
Schneiberg	13	16	.448	35				274	226	90	135	
Dougherty	10	10	.500	24				191	156	77	109	
Wilson	9	11	.450	28				176	149	77	83	

ST. PAUL 8th 59-95 .383 -31 Ed Ashenbach
Saints

BATTERS	POS-GAMES	GP	AB	R	H	BI	2B	3B	HR	BB	SO	SB	BA
Nordyke	1B150	150	543	72	142		26	4	4			19	.261
Flood	2B69	70	264	40	84		19	2	4			16	.318
Geier	SS		(see multi-team players)										
Tiemeyer	3B132	141	520	55	136		25	10	4			7	.262
Dunleavy	OF149	149	599	72	159		25	3	1			29	.264
Frisk	OF147	147	568	89	162		33	8	8			18	.286
Koehler	OF133	148	517	55	117		17	5	0			26	.226
Sugden	C80	85	277	23	72		9	1	0			3	.260
Laughlin	C65	65	228	12	56		8	1	0			0	.246
Criss	P27,OF18	53	164	13	46		11	1	2			0	.281
Padden	2B52	52	179	24	40		5	1	0			10	.223
LeRoy	P40	40	120	5	23		0	0	0			2	.192
Farris	P34	40	111	8	21		3	2	0			0	.189
Hartzell	SS25	39	156	19	42		8	3	0			4	.269
Essick	P19	22	62	6	11		1	0	0			0	.178
Minnehan	P16	16	53	3	15		3	0	0			0	.283

PITCHERS		W	L	PCT	G	GS	CG	SH	IP	H	BB	SO	ERA
LeRoy		14	22	.389	40				302	327	80	133	
Farris		13	18	.419	34				265	263	94	102	
Criss		11	10	.524	27				175	162	59	108	

MULTI-TEAM PLAYERS

BATTERS	POS-GAMES	TEAMS	GP	AB	R	H	BI	2B	3B	HR	BB	SO	SB	BA
Geier	SS101,OF30	SP-MIL	139	529	71	152		18	4	0			29	.287
Lindsay	2B69,1B55	KC-IND	124	465	71	125		14	2	1			28	.269
Kerwin	OF114	LOU-KC	114	445	75	117		17	3	2			18	.263
Williams	2B67,3B15	SP-TOL	95	336	49	79		11	2	1			13	.235
Frantz	P31	KC-LOU	43	122	17	24		3	0	0			3	.197
Cromley	P18	IND-KC	23	66	12	18		4	0	0			1	.273

PITCHERS		TEAMS	W	L	PCT	G	GS	CG	SH	IP	H	BB	SO	ERA
Frantz		KC-LOU	13	15	.464	31				214	236	65	84	

TEAM BATTING

TEAMS	GP	AB	R	H	BI	2B	3B	HR	BB	SO	SB	BA
COLUMBUS	**159**	5257	702	1421		220	**73**	14			185	.270
TOLEDO	156	5257	**767**	**1468**		**283**	38	26			**223**	**.279**
MINNEAPOLIS	153	4884	602	1230		193	59	**32**			159	.251
KANSAS CITY	156	4899	641	1295		181	45	17			215	.264
LOUISVILLE	**159**	**5607**	711	1414		179	62	16			208	.252
INDIANAPOLIS	156	4752	505	1210		149	69	19			149	.254
MILWAUKEE	154	4982	621	1198		181	49	20			197	.240
ST. PAUL	157	4890	567	1278		211	45	23			163	.261
	625	40528	5116	10514		1597	440	167			1499	.259

1908
Dead Ball

In 1902, the American Association as a league batted .270. During the next few years, the league average slid down to .265 in 1903, .263 in 1904, .266 in 1905, .258 in 1906, and .259 in 1907. However, during the next year this already modest level would take a ten-point tumble. The dead ball era was in full flower.

The term "dead ball" was coined at a later date to describe baseball during the early part of the century. During any given game, only one ball was used, and by the time the later innings arrived, the spheroid was discolored, lumpy, and mushy. In no uncertain terms the ball was "dead." As a result, it was very difficult to get hits and runs, and batting averages and scoring fell across the board in all baseball leagues. The American Association was not exempt from this practice. When the 1908 season's results were tallied, only four qualifiers for the batting championship managed to cross the .300 barrier. Three of the eight teams ended up with batting averages under .240, as the league as a whole could only manage a paltry .246. Ironically, the St. Paul Saints, in last place, featured the best hitting as they finished with a league best .265 average.

While batters suffered, pitchers rejoiced, for the dead ball era was a boon to them. Association hurlers took advantage of weak batting in 1908 by tossing seven no-hitters during the course of the season.

Indianapolis, after a six-year absence, returned to the top spot by besting Louisville by four games. Defending champion Columbus dropped to third, while Toledo slid by Minneapolis into fourth. The last three spots were taken by Milwaukee, Kansas City, and St. Paul. The batting title was won by Indianapolis' Hayden (.316), while James of Columbus, and Freeman of Minneapolis tied for the home run title with a total of ten. Pitching honors went to Marquard of Indianapolis (28-19), who also tossed one of the previously mentioned seven no-hitters and struck out a league best 250 batters.

The dead ball era continued for a few more years until the governors of baseball decided to make a change. Tired of the lack of hitting, baseball rule makers decided to improve the quality of balls used in the game, thus bolstering the hitting. After experimentation, baseballs with a rubber-coated cork center were introduced into the game. The result was a much better ball—a ball that felt much more alive.

INDIANAPOLIS Indians

| | | 1st | 92-61 | .601 | | | | | | C. C. Carr | | |

BATTERS	POS-GAMES	GP	AB	R	H	BI	2B	3B	HR	BB	SO	SB	BA
C. Carr	1B133	133	522	56	157		31	8	8			12	.301
O. Williams	2B141	143	504	44	127		20	2	2			**38**	.252
Bush	SS153	153	562	**99**	139		10	7	2			28	.247
Hopke	3B155	155	493	39	99		9	4	2			17	.201
Hayden	OF154	154	588	86	**186**		30	18	3			27	**.316**
Coulter	OF119	119	412	53	89		14	1	1			17	.229
Davidson	OF118	118	405	48	106		8	5	0			20	.262
Livingston	C118	119	388	26	89		11	5	3			16	.229
Cook	OF79	79	269	37	56		6	1	0			13	.208
Marquard	P47	47	130	10	22		1	0	0			1	.169
Howley	C36	44	123	4	30		3	5	0			1	.244
Slagle	P35	35	95	3	19		0	0	0			3	.200
Lindsay	2B18,1B15	33	135	8	39		4	3	0			5	.289
Druhot	P26	26	51	7	13		2	0	0			0	.255
Sievers	P24	24	58	3	20		1	2	0			1	.345
Eubanks	P15	15	37	1	4		0	0	0			0	.108

PITCHERS	W	L	PCT	G	GS	CG	SH	IP	H	BB	SO	ERA
Marquard	28	19	.596	47				367	234	135	**250**	
Slagle	20	14	.588	35				279	221	63	100	
Sievers	13	7	.650	24				165	156	30	77	
Druhot	6	6	.500	26				154	135	52	43	

LOUISVILLE Colonels

| | | 2nd | 88-65 | .575 | | -4 | | | | James Burke | | |

BATTERS	POS-GAMES	GP	AB	R	H	BI	2B	3B	HR	BB	SO	SB	BA
S. Sullivan	1B116	127	467	50	115		10	3	0			19	.246
Perrine	2B147	147	540	61	124		14	5	3			32	.230
Quinlan	SS150	150	518	43	118		12	8	0			6	.228
Burke	3B128	128	450	54	113		12	1	2			32	.251
Stanley	OF153	153	563	91	157		24	9	5			27	.279
Woodruff	OF130,3B17	147	553	76	146		30	1	2			30	.264
Stovall	OF98	106	387	43	90		8	0	1			32	.233
Hughes	C81	81	249	29	59		8	1	6			12	.237
Harley	OF65,1B15	80	269	37	61		11	1	0			19	.227
Pietz	C73	78	244	17	59		12	2	1			9	.242
Halla	P42	42	121	5	21		4	2	0			1	.173
Puttmann	P41	41	125	10	31		6	2	1			0	.248
Adams	P41	41	107	14	19		3	1	0			0	.178
Swacina	1B23	26	89	10	23		5	2	0			3	.258
Poole	P21	21	48	3	5		0	1	0			0	.104
J. Durham	P17	17	39	1	8		0	1	0			0	.205
Landreth	OF16	16	53	6	20		0	0	1			8	.377

PITCHERS	W	L	PCT	G	GS	CG	SH	IP	H	BB	SO	ERA
Puttmann	26	12	.684	41				329	275	81	144	
Halla	23	16	.599	42				336	275	53	118	
Adams	22	12	.647	41				312	262	40	118	
J. Durham	5	8	.385	17								
Poole	4	9	.308	21				117	127	46	42	

COLUMBUS Senators

| | | 3rd | 86-68 | .558 | | -6.5 | | | | William Clymer | | |

BATTERS	POS-GAMES	GP	AB	R	H	BI	2B	3B	HR	BB	SO	SB	BA
Kihm	1B154	154	533	60	128		17	5	0			16	.240
Wrigley	2B155	155	533	49	116		14	3	0			14	.218
Raidy	SS144	144	518	58	121		13	2	1			36	.234
Friel	3B150	150	603	79	148		18	6	0			26	.245
Congalton	OF151	152	594	76	179		**41**	4	3			18	.301
Odwell	OF143	144	568	82	141		22	9	2			32	.248
A. Krueger	OF124	124	497	71	124		18	8	0			36	.249
James	C88	88	304	48	83		15	8	**10**			4	.273
Fohl	C69	69	235	21	52		3	2	0			6	.221

COLUMBUS (cont.)
Senators

BATTERS	POS-GAMES	GP	AB	R	H	BI	2B	3B	HR	BB	SO	SB	BA
Jackson	OF50	50	183	22	41		8	1	0			6	.224
Geyer	P44	44	122	11	25		3	2	0			0	.205
Taylor	P38	39	91	8	26		6	1	0			2	.286
Rogers	P24	24	50	1	2		0	0	0			0	.040
Kahl		18	61	9	12		3	1	0			2	.197
Upp	P15	17	38	1	5		0	0	0			0	.132

PITCHERS		W	L	PCT	G	GS	CG	SH	IP	H	BB	SO	ERA
Geyer		20	20	.500	44				342	289	119	145	
Taylor		18	14	.563	38				245	242	79	71	
Hess		9	4	.692									
Rogers		9	5	.643	24				142	124	41	65	

TOLEDO   4th   81-72   .530   -11   William Armour
Mud Hens

BATTERS	POS-GAMES	GP	AB	R	H	BI	2B	3B	HR	BB	SO	SB	BA
Lister	1B117	117	397	41	92		14	0	4			16	.232
H. Hinchman	2B154	154	602	82	158		22	4	3			24	.262
Barbeau	SS137	137	546	84	154		27	5	6			32	.280
Elwert	3B96	98	334	31	80		16	3	0			9	.239
Armbruster	OF148	148	545	73	148		37	5	1			37	.272
Smoot	OF131	131	501	66	151		35	5	3			18	.301
Hopkins	OF64	64	193	29	51		7	1	6			10	.264
Land	C87	98	355	38	88		14	0	0			12	.248
McCarthy	OF54,3B51	111	386	43	98		25	1	0			13	.254
Abbott	C63,1B15	79	272	36	90		17	1	1			13	.331
Hickman	OF46	47	181	26	74		16	5	2			1	.409
West	P36	36	91	6	18		4	0	0			1	.198
Gillen	P32	33	83	6	21		3	2	1			1	.253
Nagle	P33	33	73	5	12		3	0	0			0	.164
C. Williams		28	88	7	13		4	1	0			9	.148
Steen	P26	26	64	10	10		2	0	0			0	.156
Lattimore	P21	22	70	7	18		1	0	0			1	.257
Asher	P18	18	32	3	7		1	0	0			1	.218

PITCHERS		W	L	PCT	G	GS	CG	SH	IP	H	BB	SO	ERA
West		18	9	.667	35				259	212	70	115	
Gillen		14	9	.607	31				215	222	77	86	
Steen		12	10	.545	26				190	151	80	71	
Nagle		12	11	.522	33				201	196	62	102	
Lattimore		10	7	.588	21								
Asher		3	8	.273	18								

MINNEAPOLIS   5th   77-77   .500   -15.5   M.E. Cantillon
Millers

BATTERS	POS-GAMES	GP	AB	R	H	BI	2B	3B	HR	BB	SO	SB	BA
W. Clarke	1B130	130	431	31	93		7	2	0			12	.217
O'Brien	2B		(see multi-team players)										
Oyler	SS116	116	442	70	120		12	4	0			26	.271
Smith	3B86,SS29	115	361	38	69		11	5	0			16	.191
O'Neill	OF151	151	610	72	166		35	10	0			22	.272
Welday	OF115	115	462	49	123		15	9	2			31	.266
Freeman	OF84	92	325	32	71		11	5	10			9	.218
Block	C115	116	442	70	120		17	1	1			6	.267
Quillen	3B70,OF28	121	437	47	89		10	2	5			20	.204
Fiene	P38,OF28	66	226	25	56		7	1	0			5	.248
Buelow	C46	59	185	10	34		2	0	0			1	.184
Patterson	P44	51	123	11	29		3	0	0			1	.236
Oberlin	P36	37	103	8	21		4	0	1			0	.204
Wilson	P36	36	77	3	4		0	0	0			1	.052
O. Graham	P20	20	39	10	13		4	0	4			2	.333
Biersdorfer	P19	19	27	1	1		0	0	0			0	.037

MINNEAPOLIS (cont.)
Millers

PITCHERS	W	L	PCT	G	GS	CG	SH	IP	H	BB	SO	ERA
Patterson	22	11	.667	44				306	258	49	86	
Fiene	20	13	.606	38				309	223	85	127	
Wilson	14	17	.453	36				236	169	85	103	
Oberlin	9	16	.360	36				253	224	76	160	
O. Graham	8	5	.615	20				111	104	33	53	

MILWAUKEE   6th   71-83   .461   -21.5   Barry McCormick
Brewers

BATTERS	POS-GAMES	GP	AB	R	H	BI	2B	3B	HR	BB	SO	SB	BA
A. Brown	1B150	150	516	43	99		15	4	3			20	.192
McCormick	2B154	154	512	61	121		25	1	3			12	.236
Robinson	SS151	151	580	67	163		38	8	1			21	.281
H. Clark	3B112	112	374	54	95		16	6	5			12	.254
Randall	OF121	121	431	56	109		19	5	5			24	.253
McChesney	OF90	90	348	44	84		14	4	1			18	.241
Bateman	OF62,P19	78	272	24	66		9	2	2			6	.243
Beville	C80	80	272	21	65		7	1	1			6	.239
Flynn	OF50,3B35	92	330	44	76		19	3	2			24	.230
Roth	C75	76	291	38	84		17	3	1			15	.289
Green	OF50	50	176	15	28		6	1	0			5	.159
Curtis	P40	48	138	12	32		5	1	0			0	.233
Dougherty	P26	40	121	16	26		6	2	0			4	.215
Manske	P37	37	106	7	15		1	0	0			1	.113
Schneiberg	P34	34	96	7	9		1	0	1			0	.094
Manusch	OF27	27	105	14	22		2	2	0			4	.210
Kutina	OF24	24	87	6	18		3	1	1			2	.207
McGilvray	OF20	20	67	9	14		1	0	0			4	.209
Pape	P20	20	56	5	3		0	1	0			1	.053

PITCHERS	W	L	PCT	G	GS	CG	SH	IP	H	BB	SO	ERA
Curtis	15	19	.441	40				297	247	92	110	
Schneiberg	14	19	.424	34				287	235	90	145	
Pape	13	5	.722	20				172	132	44	80	
Manske	13	20	.394	37				286	220	**146**	176	
Dougherty	9	12	.429	26				194	168	75	89	
Bateman	7	8	.467	19								

KANSAS CITY   7th   70-83   .456   -22   Monte Cross
Blues

BATTERS	POS-GAMES	GP	AB	R	H	BI	2B	3B	HR	BB	SO	SB	BA
Beckley	1B136	136	496	66	134		19	5	1			13	.270
Brashear	2B156	156	555	73	164		32	8	3			30	.295
Cross	SS146	146	438	63	98		20	3	0			35	.224
Downey	3B113	114	387	27	77		10	1	0			9	.202
Hallman	OF144	144	505	62	110		15	5	0			32	.218
Neighbors	OF122	122	452	66	128		18	2	1			26	.283
Carlisle	OF95	95	318	38	71		24	1	1			17	.223
J. Sullivan	C90	90	285	22	60		3	1	0			7	.211
D. Brown	C20,1B16	53	174	17	37		3	1	1			4	.213
O. Krueger	3B41	48	160	17	33		8	1	0			7	.206
Crisp	C39	39	120	3	17		2	1	0			4	.142
Hill	OF23	33	119	6	27		3	3	1			1	.227
Brandom	P33	33	90	7	14		0	0	0			2	.155
Wood	P24	32	77	3	12		2	0	0			2	.156
Swann	P28	30	86	7	15		0	1	0			5	.174
Carter	P26	26	73	7	14		3	0	0			3	.192
Egan	P23	23	59	3	7		0	0	0			0	.119
Murphy	OF21	21	78	7	18		2	0	0			1	.231

PITCHERS	W	L	PCT	G	GS	CG	SH	IP	H	BB	SO	ERA
Brandom	17	13	.567	33				252	212	68	124	
Swann	14	11	.560	28				246	231	58	83	
Carter	10	13	.435	26				208	195	57	80	
Egan	7	9	.438	23				176	178	37	41	
Wood	7	12	.368	24				178	118	60	116	

ST. PAUL 8th   48-104   .316   -43.5   Flood - Kelley
Saints

BATTERS	POS-GAMES	GP	AB	R	H	BI	2B	3B	HR	BB	SO	SB	BA
Wheeler	1B57,2B37,SS18	125	499	44	140		29	3	2			24	.281
Flood	2B107	108	402	55	104		26	3	5			13	.259
Nee	SS101	101	343	40	93		12	3	0			15	.271
Tiemeyer	3B148	148	512	61	143		30	5	4			3	.279
Geier	OF140	147	591	79	157		33	2	1			21	.266
Davis	OF140	140	541	76	155		25	8	1			19	.287
B. Meyers	OF90	90	332	40	90		9	1	0			21	.271
J. Meyers	C86	88	329	45	96		19	1	1			4	.292
Dunleavy	OF60	69	210	24	45		4	0	0			8	.214
Laughlin	C56	63	221	22	56		4	2	0			2	.253
Gehring	P29,OF24	53	181	11	51		13	1	2			5	.282
LeRoy	P49	51	124	9	29		5	0	0			3	.234
Noonan	1B33	45	157	21	45		11	2	2			2	.287
Rowan	1B41	41	141	13	33		5	0	0			5	.234
McKune	SS25	31	101	15	24		1	0	0			4	.238
Teal	P25	25	53	3	7		1	0	0			1	.132
Farris	P17	18	34	0	6		1	0	0			0	.176

PITCHERS	W	L	PCT	G	GS	CG	SH	IP	H	BB	SO	ERA
LeRoy	16	21	.432	49				332	321	69	144	
Gehring	12	14	.462	29				227	214	74	112	
Teal	6	12	.333	25				149	162	56	79	
Farris	1	8	.111	17								

MULTI-TEAM PLAYERS

BATTERS	POS-GAMES	TEAMS	GP	AB	R	H	BI	2B	3B	HR	BB	SO	SB	BA
O'Brien	2B137	MIN-SP	148	510	55	118		15	3	0			10	.231
Kerwin	OF102	KC-MIL	102	363	51	91		13	3	0			22	.251
Hall	P39,1B20	SP-COL	63	181	11	36		8	0	0			2	.204
Essick	P34	KC-SP	36	82	11	17		0	0	0			3	.207
L. Durham	P35	IND-LOU	35	96	7	26		5	1	0			1	.271
Goodwin	P34	COL-KC	34	108	14	33		9	4	1			1	.306
Suthoff	P23	TOL-LOU	23	56	1	3		0	0	0			0	.054
Wakefield	1B15	TOL-IND	22	80	10	22		4	2	0			1	.275
Leahy	C19	IND-KC	19	62	5	12		1	0	0			1	.194

PITCHERS		TEAMS	W	L	PCT	G	GS	CG	SH	IP	H	BB	SO	ERA
L. Durham		IND-LOU	19	7	.731	35				261	211	81	78	
Goodwin		COL-KC	13	13	.500	34				248	259	77	77	
Essick		KC-SP	13	16	.448	34				237	207	75	95	
Hall		SP-COL	8	21	.276	39				243	245	122	115	
Suthoff		TOL-LOU	7	13	.350	23				170	154	48	39	

TEAM BATTING

TEAMS	GP	AB	R	H	BI	2B	3B	HR	BB	SO	SB	BA
INDIANAPOLIS	155	4930	536	1233		156	62	21			200	.250
LOUISVILLE	153	4822	550	1169		159	40	22			230	.242
COLUMBUS	155	5038	610	1236		190	56	16			199	.245
TOLEDO	154	4949	604	1308		252	35	27			199	.264
MINNEAPOLIS	156	4789	504	1122		153	42	23			162	.234
MILWAUKEE	154	4878	543	1129		204	45	26			169	.231
KANSAS CITY	156	4917	556	1144		177	36	8			223	.233
ST. PAUL	154	4952	569	1310		236	31	18			152	.265
	619	39275	4472	9651		1527	347	161			1534	.246

1909
Stoney McGlynn

The dead ball era featured many feats in which pitchers performed as men of iron, rather than flesh and blood. Pitchers all across baseball dazzled foe and fan alike with 60-game, 300-inning seasons. In the American Association one particular iron man hurler deserves special mention for his feats in 1909. His name was Ulysses Simpson Grant McGlynn, but he went by the nickname of Stoney.

Stoney McGlynn started his baseball career in 1902 in his native Pennsylvania, pitching for the Lancaster entry in the Pennsylvania State League. In 1904, he moved on to the York team of the Tri-State League, where he remained for three years. During his three-year stay in Lancaster, he rang up more than ninety wins, which got him noticed by the major leagues, and late in the 1906 season, he was sold to the St. Louis Cardinals. After three so-so years in St. Louis (he led the National League in losses with 25 in 1907) McGlynn joined the Milwaukee Brewers for the start of the 1909 campaign. He then put on a display of pitching strength and durability that has never been topped. During the course of the year, Stoney McGlynn pitched in 64 games, throwing an unheard of 446 innings. He led the league with 27 victories, 14 via the shutout route. Conversely, he also led the league with 21 defeats. In addition, McGlynn bested the league with 183 strikeouts. In all, McGlynn had a hand in nearly 30 percent of Milwaukee's wins and losses during 1909.

Playing an expanded 168-game schedule, Louisville captured its first Association flag, finishing two and one-half games over Milwaukee and four and one-half over Minneapolis. Not far behind was the rest of the pack, which consisted of Indianapolis, St. Paul, Toledo, Columbus, and Kansas City. Even the last place team finished within 20 games of the leaders, which would prove to be the closest eighth place finish ever. The batting malaise kept its grip on the league as not one batting qualifier finished over .300. Minneapolis outfielder O'Neill won the title with an all-time low mark of .296. Likewise, James of Columbus hit the lowest total of home runs ever to lead the Association: seven.

Stoney McGlynn pitched two more years for Milwaukee, posting similar but not spectacular numbers. After a one-year suspension, he drifted out of the American Association to finish his career in the low minors in Utah and New Mexico. Although he did not pitch long in the Association, Stoney McGlynn set single season records that are not likely to be broken. Two records in particular—446 innings and 14 shutouts in a season—should stand the test of time.

LOUISVILLE Colonels   1st   93-75   .554   Henry Peitz

BATTERS	POS-GAMES	GP	AB	R	H	BI	2B	3B	HR	BB	SO	SB	BA
Salm	1B60	60	195	17	44		4	2	0			5	.225
Olson	2B167	170	633	62	151		22	7	1			34	.238
Quinlan	SS		(see multi-team players)										
Su. Sullivan	3B87,1B43	137	495	40	114		19	4	0			12	.230
F. Delahanty	OF134	134	503	53	119		22	3	3			31	.236
Dunleavy	OF126	126	467	63	114		14	2	0			34	.244
Woodruff	OF87,3B65	156	583	66	135		17	7	1			32	.231
J. Hughes	C107	108	326	34	70		8	2	2			15	.214
Peitz	C72,1B18	90	257	21	52		8	0	3			4	.202
Tate	1B54,OF25	79	266	26	65		10	4	0			6	.244
Landreth	OF43	43	159	12	40		7	2	0			3	.251
Reilly	OF21,3B19	43	152	10	28		0	0	0			7	.184
Selby	P41	41	90	11	18		0	0	0			2	.200
Packard	P39	40	91	8	17		0	0	1			2	.187
Fenlon	OF39	39	144	15	36		5	4	0			4	.250
Halla	P36	39	106	9	26		4	1	0			1	.245
Thielman	P20,OF17	37	105	13	28		5	0	1			1	.267
Hogg	P37	37	100	3	21		2	1	0			1	.210
Puttmann	P16	24	62	3	16		2	1	0			1	.258
Diehl	OF20	20	62	8	14		2	1	1			3	.226

PITCHERS		W	L	PCT	G	GS	CG	SH	IP	H	BB	SO	ERA
Selby		20	13	.606	41				305	258	106	78	
Halla		17	12	.586	36				272	247	49	68	
Hogg		17	14	.548	37				295	238	104	125	
Packard		14	17	.453	39				250	216	81	90	
Thielman		10	7	.588	20				149	137	29	45	

MILWAUKEE Brewers   2nd   90-77   .539   -2.5   J.J. McCloskey

BATTERS	POS-GAMES	GP	AB	R	H	BI	2B	3B	HR	BB	SO	SB	BA
McGann	1B160	160	559	65	137		19	6	3			22	.245
McCormick	2B173	**173**	602	57	133		23	2	3			14	.221
C. Robinson	SS144	144	541	60	123		20	2	0			18	.227
Ha. Clark	3B173	**173**	548	78	141		25	8	4			28	.257
Randall	OF167	167	620	**91**	173		20	7	3			35	.279
Barry	OF139	150	584	67	137		18	0	0			29	.236
Strunk	OF112	112	434	47	106		10	6	3			14	.244
Hostetler	C80	80	277	18	69		8	0	2			3	.249
Moran	C60	77	246	24	51		12	0	1			5	.207
Barrett	OF44,SS30	76	255	29	61		11	5	2			5	.239
Dougherty	P45,OF23	68	182	14	36		7	0	0			6	.198
McGlynn	P64	64	158	5	25		4	0	0			1	.158
Ed. Collins	OF38	38	115	17	24		5	2	0			12	.208
Schneiberg	P30	30	69	6	12		1	0	0			1	.174
Curtis	P27	27	66	3	11		2	0	0			0	.167
Wacker	P25	25	61	3	7		1	0	0			0	.115
Manske	P24	24	63	2	6		1	1	0			0	.099
Warner	C23	23	72	6	14		1	0	0			0	.194

PITCHERS		W	L	PCT	G	GS	CG	SH	IP	H	BB	SO	ERA
McGlynn		**27**	21	.563	**64**			14	446	304	114	**183**	
Dougherty		21	11	.656	45				298	224	78	120	
Schneiberg		13	13	.500	30				202	164	64	81	
Manske		11	10	.550	24				168	115	77	87	
Wacker		7	7	.500	25				153	140	36	65	
Curtis		7	11	.389	27				185	125	64	75	

MINNEAPOLIS Millers   3rd   88-79   .527   -4.5   James Collins

BATTERS	POS-GAMES	GP	AB	R	H	BI	2B	3B	HR	BB	SO	SB	BA
Gill	1B138	138	470	45	114		15	2	0			**41**	.242
Downs	2B167	167	652	67	177		44	11	2			32	.271
Oyler	SS140	140	518	49	110		6	4	0			20	.212

MINNEAPOLIS (cont.)
Millers

BATTERS	POS-GAMES	GP	AB	R	H	BI	2B	3B	HR	BB	SO	SB	BA
J. Collins	3B152	153	556	61	152		21	3	2			13	.273
O'Neill	OF144	144	548	65	162		23	10	2			19	**.296**
Cravath	OF125	125	413	60	120		23	7	4			21	.290
Quillen	OF77,SS31	123	386	50	72		16	4	0			13	.186
Block	C146	147	464	46	109		16	9	3			7	.235
Pickering	OF70	70	244	23	52		5	1	0			6	.213
Young	P46	46	111	11	17		2	0	1			0	.153
Olmstead	P41	42	121	12	30		5	1	1			1	.248
O. Collins	OF31	37	137	18	34		2	4	0			2	.248
Patterson	P29	31	74	4	10		2	0	0			2	.135
Altrock	P22	30	70	5	11		0	0	0			3	.157
Rapp	C28	28	78	4	17		2	1	0			0	.218
Edmondson	OF27	27	97	7	22		4	1	0			6	.227
Wheeler	1B19	25	90	8	20		3	1	0			3	.222
Oberlin	P23	23	58	1	11		0	0	0			1	.190
Wilson	P23	23	44	1	4		0	0	0			0	.088
O. Clymer	OF20	22	82	9	14		2	1	0			5	.172

PITCHERS	W	L	PCT	G	GS	CG	SH	IP	H	BB	SO	ERA
Olmstead	24	12	.667	41				304	240	53	131	
Young	23	18	.561	46				335	259	61	158	
Patterson	10	12	.455	29				208	168	36	70	
Altrock	9	7	.563	22				140	117	18	49	
Wilson	7	8	.467	23				124	110	42	54	
Oberlin	6	7	.462	23				153	128	43	75	
T. Hughes	5	6	.455									

INDIANAPOLIS   4th   83-85   .494   -10   C.C. Carr
Indians

BATTERS	POS-GAMES	GP	AB	R	H	BI	2B	3B	HR	BB	SO	SB	BA
C. Carr	1B155	155	595	67	166		37	6	5			14	.279
O. Williams	2B154	154	540	42	121		15	4	0			20	.224
Hopke	SS104,3B30	134	440	37	91		16	1	0			6	.207
Burke	3B139	139	509	54	125		14	3	0			27	.246
Hayden	OF168	168	651	71	178		39	9	1			19	.273
Chadbourne	OF127	127	484	79	119		8	6	0			20	.248
McChesney	OF75	75	268	34	67		10	4	2			11	.250
Howley	C135	135	466	41	103		16	6	0			15	.221
Davidson	OF73	74	268	27	58		3	1	0			13	.216
Glaze	P40	40	98	3	21		0	2	0			2	.214
O. Graham	P40	40	93	12	19		3	0	2			1	.204
Slagle	P39	40	93	8	15		0	0	0			3	.161
Cheney	P39	39	88	9	19		1	1	0			1	.216
J. O'Rourke	2B17	26	95	10	18		4	0	0			2	.189
Shaw	C22	22	74	6	18		3	0	0			1	.243
Smith	OF21	21	76	11	21		7	0	0			3	.276
Jones	P20	21	46	5	9		0	0	0			1	.195
Kuepper	P20	20	28	2	6		0	0	0			0	.214
Wakefield		17	59	7	14		1	0	0			1	.237
Lindaman	P16	16	42	4	5		1	0	0			1	.119

PITCHERS	W	L	PCT	G	GS	CG	SH	IP	H	BB	SO	ERA
Cheney	19	10	.655	39				272	195	99	149	
Glaze	17	17	.500	40				296	229	59	152	
O. Graham	15	15	.500	40				254	218	93	118	
Slagle	12	20	.375	39				286	267	75	91	
Lindaman	9	5	.643	16								
Jones	7	10	.412	20				149	129	43	53	
Kuepper	3	4	.429	20				75	79	29	29	

ST. PAUL   5th   80-83   .491   -10.5   Mike Kelley
Saints

BATTERS	POS-GAMES	GP	AB	R	H	BI	2B	3B	HR	BB	SO	SB	BA
Flynn	1B110	119	452	61	120		26	3	4			29	.265

ST. PAUL (cont.)
Saints

BATTERS	POS-GAMES	GP	AB	R	H	BI	2B	3B	HR	BB	SO	SB	BA
Wrigley	2B		(see multi-team players)										
Boucher	SS64	67	252	32	60		7	4	3			18	.238
Cockman	3B99	111	361	25	74		14	2	0			12	.205
Davis	OF139	139	540	65	123		26	4	2			18	.228
Armbruster	OF118,1B30	148	545	64	154		33	2	2			19	.282
Liese	OF109	120	426	41	108		17	4	2			13	.253
Carisch	C101,1B17	118	374	32	96		14	4	1			10	.257
O'Brien	SS57,3B34,2B20	111	396	34	84		10	1	1			2	.212
Murray	OF103	103	376	39	92		16	9	5			10	.245
LeRoy	P57	57	125	6	22		0	0	1			1	.176
Gehring	P36	45	151	10	32		9	0	3			1	.212
E. Spencer	C34	34	112	8	37		6	0	0			0	.330
Yeager	C34	34	103	7	24		2	0	0			4	.233
Kilroy	P31	31	62	3	4		1	0	0			1	.064
Hall	P26	28	80	6	18		6	0	0			2	.225
Hoey	OF25	25	89	7	26		3	0	1			0	.292
Breen	3B22	23	80	9	16		4	0	1			2	.200
Perrine	SS16	19	58	8	8		0	0	0			2	.138
Steele	P18	18	51	4	12		1	1	0			1	.235
Chech	P16	16	37	3	6		1	0	0			0	.162
Karger	P	15	47	1	4		1	0	0			0	.081

PITCHERS	W	L	PCT	G	GS	CG	SH	IP	H	BB	SO	ERA
LeRoy	20	17	.541	57				372	291	72	179	
Kilroy	14	10	.583	31				207	175	70	79	
Gehring	14	17	.453	36				256	232	88	106	
Steele	10	6	.625	18								
Karger	7	3	.700									
Chech	5	9	.357	16								
Hall	4	13	.235	26				172	138	72	120	

TOLEDO   6th   80-86   .482   -12   Abbott - Seybold
Mud Hens

BATTERS	POS-GAMES	GP	AB	R	H	BI	2B	3B	HR	BB	SO	SB	BA
Freeman	1B127	127	456	55	127		16	1	1			16	.278
H. Hinchman	2B162	162	608	90	162		14	8	1			39	.266
Lynch	SS72	72	213	22	39		4	1	0			5	.183
Elwert	3B146	146	519	54	132		21	10	2			25	.254
Hickman	OF165	167	644	70	183		49	7	5			21	.284
Smoot	OF137	137	504	60	136		17	9	3			15	.270
McCarthy	OF76,SS38	128	507	58	112		19	5	3			14	.221
Abbott	C87	93	348	32	86		19	0	3			12	.247
Land	C67	83	292	22	62		6	3	0			9	.212
Nill	SS59	73	254	30	50		8	1	0			5	.197
Raftery	OF48	48	174	32	44		5	1	1			17	.253
Seybold	OF43	43	144	24	32		2	1	1			4	.222
West	P44	45	122	12	20		4	3	0			3	.164
Ka. Robinson	P39	39	89	5	16		1	0	0			0	.180
McSurdy	P42	42	91	5	13		2	1	0			0	.142
Daubert	1B35	35	129	16	24		6	0	0			6	.186
F.M. Owen	P32	33	85	11	18		3	0	0			0	.212
Nally	OF30	30	107	10	19		0	0	1			5	.177
W. Clarke	C20	20	58	3	17		1	0	0			1	.293
Lattimore	P15	20	58	3	10		3	0	0			0	.171

PITCHERS	W	L	PCT	G	GS	CG	SH	IP	H	BB	SO	ERA
West	18	14	.563	44				327	279	72	143	
K. Robinson	17	12	.586	39				259	222	81	103	
F.M. Owen	14	13	.519	32				243	197	69	76	
McSurdy	13	14	.481	42				258	241	92	86	
Wright	6	5	.545									
Lattimore	6	8	.429	15								

COLUMBUS Senators   7th   80-87   .479   -12.5   William Clymer

BATTERS	POS-GAMES	GP	AB	R	H	BI	2B	3B	HR	BB	SO	SB	BA
Odwell	1B147	158	618	82	154		25	7	2			38	.249
Ja. O'Rourke	2B116	129	464	66	123		12	9	0			15	.265
Moriarity	SS	(see multi-team players)											
Friel	3B134	134	470	38	110		10	3	1			12	.234
A. Krueger	OF168	168	670	82	194		24	6	0			27	.289
Congalton	OF168	168	669	63	183		26	7	2			11	.274
Jo. Clarke	OF156	157	588	83	154		16	12	2			37	.262
James	C117	117	408	55	112		23	16	7			10	.274
Schreckengost	C45,1B15	60	222	16	45		16	1	0			1	.203
Goodwin	P45	45	113	9	25		7	0	0			0	.221
Linke	P42	42	98	9	17		3	0	0			0	.173
Wratton	3B28	41	134	18	28		3	2	0			4	.209
Geyer	P41	41	116	7	21		1	2	0			0	.181
LaRhue	SS16	21	74	4	18		5	0	1			2	.243
Upp	P20	21	48	3	9		1	0	0			0	.187

PITCHERS		W	L	PCT	G	GS	CG	SH	IP	H	BB	SO	ERA
Link		22	12	.647	42				299	235	119	140	
Geyer		20	17	.541	41				317	256	100	153	
Goodwin		18	18	.500	45				304	271	107	75	
Upp		5	9	.357	20				118	110	41	37	

KANSAS CITY Blues   8th   71-93   .432   -20   Cross - Buckley - Shay

BATTERS	POS-GAMES	GP	AB	R	H	BI	2B	3B	HR	BB	SO	SB	BA
Beckley	1B113	113	428	41	120		16	3	1			12	.280
Brashear	2B155	159	529	53	115		20	4	1			15	.211
Love	SS94,OF22	138	491	59	135		21	4	1			37	.275
Hetling	3B143	143	493	48	120		25	3	0			12	.244
Shannon	OF162	162	601	81	126		13	4	0			31	.210
Hallman	OF153	153	546	71	144		19	4	1			22	.264
Carlisle	OF127	127	427	49	110		14	7	4			19	.258
Ritter	C81	81	239	23	42		4	2	0			10	.176
Jo. Sullivan	C68,1B24	92	292	13	64		9	0	0			1	.219
Shay	SS47	47	171	17	29		3	0	1			9	.169
Boles	OF19	44	135	15	25		3	1	0			5	.185
Swann	P39	39	101	6	19		0	1	0			2	.188
Essick	P38	38	90	5	14		3	1	0			1	.155
Flaherty	P31	33	103	12	20		5	1	2			3	.194
Dorner	P33	33	88	5	15		3	1	0			0	.170
Carter	P32	32	91	3	14		3	1	0			2	.154
Rapps	1B22	22	71	4	18		1	1	0			3	.253
Neighbors	OF20	20	84	8	21		3	0	1			2	.250
Moore	3B19	19	66	1	14		0	0	0			2	.212
Frambes	C15	15	47	2	6		0	0	0			1	.127

PITCHERS		W	L	PCT	G	GS	CG	SH	IP	H	BB	SO	ERA
Carter		15	12	.556	32				229	196	45	81	
Swann		15	18	.455	39				304	284	58	85	
Flaherty		14	13	.519	31				244	236	62	29	
Essick		14	16	.467	38				268	224	93	109	
Dorner		9	18	.333	33				246	212	87	68	

MULTI-TEAM PLAYERS

BATTERS	POS-GAMES	TEAMS	GP	AB	R	H	BI	2B	3B	HR	BB	SO	SB	BA
Wrigley	2B139	COL-SP	153	526	35	112		20	5	0			12	.213
Quinlan	SS145	LOU-COL	145	501	37	129		18	1	0			5	.257
Moriarity	SS127	COL-LOU	127	453	59	110		12	2	0			16	.243
Cross	SS75	KC-IND	77	239	24	40		5	1	0			7	.167
Nee	2B27	SP-COL	40	133	10	21		7	0	0			2	.158
Nelson	P27	SP-COL	27	53	5	11		4	1	0			0	.207

MULTI-TEAM PLAYERS (cont.)

PITCHERS	TEAMS	W	L	PCT	G	GS	CG	SH	IP	H	BB	SO	ERA
Nelson	SP-COL	5	12	.294	27				153	161	53	73	

TEAM BATTING

TEAMS	GP	AB	R	H	BI	2B	3B	HR	BB	SO	SB	BA
LOUISVILLE	170	5297	511	1237		169	42	13			203	.233
MILWAUKEE	174	5452	592	1266		188	39	21			193	.232
MINNEAPOLIS	167	5213	546	1258		191	60	15			195	.241
INDIANAPOLIS	169	5423	578	1279		185	45	10			183	.236
ST. PAUL	165	4717	465	1120		197	34	26			145	.237
TOLEDO	170	5402	614	1302		200	51	21			197	.241
COLUMBUS	168	5857	644	1447		205	73	15			187	.247
KANSAS CITY	167	5093	516	1171		165	38	12			189	.230
	675	42454	4466	10080		1500	382	133			1492	.237

1910
Tom Hughes

During the history of the American Association, pitchers have reached the 20 victory plateau about 100 times. Going to the next level of accomplishment, 25 wins, has ocurred in fewer than 30 instances. Only three times has the Association seen a thirty-game winner. Of these three, one finished at 30, while two finished at the pinnacle of 31. The first to accomplish this feat was Tom Hughes.

Tom Hughes joined the major league Chicago Cubs in 1900 at the age of 22. After a spectacularly unsuccessful season in 1901, where he finished with 23 losses, Hughes bounced to the American League where he stayed for the next seven years. While in the junior circuit, he toiled for four teams, winning twenty once and losing twenty again, spending the most time with the Washington Senators. After a mediocre beginning in the majors in 1909, Tom Hughes joined the Minneapolis Millers midway through the season, where he posted a modest 5–6 record. However, his feats the next year were anything but average. Tom Hughes won consistently and often during the 1910 season, and when the dust settled, he had finished the campaign with a league record 31 wins, countered by only 12 defeats, thus bettering Dunkle's 1902 record by one.

Not surprisingly, Hughes led his Minneapolis Millers to their first American Association pennant. The race wasn't very close, as the Millers dusted the second place Mud Hens of Toledo by 15 games. Columbus, St. Paul, and Kansas City all finished over .500, while Milwaukee, Indianapolis, and defending champion Louisville brought up the rear. Minneapolis outfielder Cravath led the circuit in both batting average (.326) and home runs (14) to become the first double winner in league annals. In addition to his wins leadership, Tom Hughes struck out 222 to pace the league.

After his phenomenal year in the American Association, Tom Hughes returned to the Washington Senators for three more years before leaving the majors for good. However, in that space of three years, he didn't win as many games as he did in that one memorable season in Minneapolis. Although his stay in the Association was a mere bump in his pitching career, Tom Hughes' gem of a season in 1910 will sparkle for a long time.

MINNEAPOLIS   1st   107-61   .637   Joe Cantillon
Millers

BATTERS	POS-GAMES	GP	AB	R	H	BI	2B	3B	HR	BB	SO	SB	BA
Gill	1B161	162	551	83	139		13	7	0			37	.252
J. Williams	2B148	149	549	83	173		37	9	4			16	.315
Altizer	SS156	163	580	**111**	174		18	10	2			**65**	.300
Ferris	3B125	129	499	55	133		19	7	4			11	.267
Cravath	OF164	164	612	106	**200**		41	13	14			25	**.326**
Clymer	OF139	139	582	109	179		30	7	3			38	.308
Rossman	OF		(see multi-team players)										
F. Owens	C99	100	328	27	62		7	2	0			3	.189
W. Smith	C73	79	224	33	52		3	2	3			9	.232
Altrock	P51	52	112	11	23		3	2	0			3	.205
T. Hughes	P43	45	119	18	27		6	2	2			5	.227
Patterson	P45	45	112	10	23		1	1	0			1	.205
Fiene	P26	30	71	7	15		3	0	0			4	.211
Lelivelt	P24	24	55	7	14		1	0	1			0	.255
Dawson		24	42	8	13		3	1	1			1	.309
Sage	P21	22	46	2	13		2	0	0			0	.283
Tannehill		22	44	7	8		1	1	0			0	.182

PITCHERS		W	L	PCT	G	GS	CG	SH	IP	H	BB	SO	ERA
T. Hughes		**31**	12	**.721**	43				326	234	**129**	**222**	
Patterson		22	12	.636	45				318	257	76	118	
Altrock		19	13	.594	51				300	273	54	82	
Fiene		15	6	.714	26				188	173	63	91	
Lelivelt		8	7	.533	24				159	130	45	53	
Sage		7	7	.500	21				108	96	72	49	

TOLEDO   2nd   91-75   .548   -15   Holmes - Hinchman
Mud Hens

BATTERS	POS-GAMES	GP	AB	R	H	BI	2B	3B	HR	BB	SO	SB	BA
Freeman	1B169	169	601	65	156		12	7	2			16	.260
H. Hinchman	2B170	171	659	99	175		20	9	0			20	.265
Butler	SS151	152	564	55	133		13	7	3			42	.236
Elwert	3B130	131	418	36	95		8	8	2			12	.227
Hickman	OF162	167	598	64	190		25	15	4			12	.317
D. Sullivan	OF137	137	504	71	130		18	6	3			17	.258
Hallman	OF		(see multi-team players)										
Land	C83	88	305	19	66		7	1	0			8	.226
J. McCarthy	3B38,OF36	92	274	28	62		10	2	2			8	.226
Abbott	C71	90	259	28	61		8	3	1			8	.235
Yingling	P40	53	114	15	23		3	0	0			1	.202
West	P46	47	114	8	29		5	4	1			5	.254
K. Robinson	P39	39	79	7	9		0	1	0			3	.114
Baskette	P32	32	50	2	7		0	1	0			1	.140
J. Bailey	OF21	24	64	7	11		3	1	0			1	.172
Hartley	C19	19	54	7	14		4	0	0			0	.259
Zinn	OF16	19	53	7	13		0	0	0			0	.245
Boice	P19	19	27	1	7		0	1	0			0	.259
Burns	OF18	18	69	9	19		0	1	0			2	.275
D. Callahan	OF14	15	46	6	8		5	0	0			3	.174

PITCHERS		W	L	PCT	G	GS	CG	SH	IP	H	BB	SO	ERA
Yingling		22	9	.710	40				287	231	74	112	
West		19	18	.514	46				319	267	95	120	
K. Robinson		16	12	.571	39				248	185	92	114	
Baskette		7	9	.437	32				168	130	64	78	

COLUMBUS   3rd   88-77   .533   -17.5   William Friel
Senators

BATTERS	POS-GAMES	GP	AB	R	H	BI	2B	3B	HR	BB	SO	SB	BA
Odwell	1B100,OF62	162	596	65	135		16	9	0			39	.227
Downs	2B159	159	613	91	188		34	12	1			25	.307
Quinlan	SS77	77	251	19	49		6	1	0			3	.195
O'Rourke	3B79	87	336	52	86		10	0	1			18	.256
W. Hinchman	OF150,1B14	167	581	102	150		30	**13**	2			24	.258

COLUMBUS (cont.)
Senators

BATTERS	POS-GAMES	GP	AB	R	H	BI	2B	3B	HR	BB	SO	SB	BA
Congalton	OF137	144	543	58	158		29	2	1			16	.291
Reilley	OF121	124	472	43	108		13	3	1			22	.229
Carisch	C86	90	268	32	57		8	5	0			3	.213
Arbogast	C82	89	266	21	52		8	6	0			3	.195
Perring	3B30,1B22,SS20	74	280	59	76		13	4	1			8	.271
Wratton	3B54,SS17	71	210	25	43		3	2	0			16	.205
Mahling	SS57	60	204	15	46		8	2	0			7	.226
Packard	P42	48	96	16	22		2	0	0			1	.229
Liebhardt	P45	45	112	7	18		3	1	0			1	.160
Sitton	P39	39	78	4	11		1	0	1			2	.141
Kaler	P23	23	67	7	13		2	2	0			0	.194
Friel		23	58	5	10		2	0	0			1	.172
Stremmel	P20	20	47	2	8		3	0	0			0	.170
Nelson	P15	15	26	1	1		0	0	0			0	.038

PITCHERS		W	L	PCT	G	GS	CG	SH	IP	H	BB	SO	ERA
Liebhardt		23	16	.590	44				320	260	93	115	
Sitton		16	10	.615	39				245	199	100	81	
Packard		13	11	.542	40				248	202	65	102	
Kaler		11	8	.579	23				184	146	71	104	
Nelson		5	5	.500	15								
Stremmel		3	7	.300	20								

ST. PAUL   4th   88-80   .524   -19   Mike Kelley
Saints

BATTERS	POS-GAMES	GP	AB	R	H	BI	2B	3B	HR	BB	SO	SB	BA
Autry	1B164	164	570	61	146		21	3	2			23	.256
Wrigley	2B101	101	354	31	80		6	6	3			9	.226
M. McCormick	SS160	160	577	75	151		22	9	2			24	.262
Boucher	3B151	156	582	69	129		18	8	6			38	.222
Jones	OF165	168	641	93	158		18	13	5			52	.246
Murray	OF139	140	507	73	131		18	10	11			37	.258
Clarke	OF128	131	485	81	142		18	9	2			29	.293
E. Spencer	C78	81	274	22	68		5	8	0			4	.248
Liese	OF46,P15	80	207	27	60		7	2	2			7	.289
W. Kelly	C61	63	189	24	50		4	2	1			5	.265
Gehring	P54	60	131	14	28		5	2	1			0	.213
Chech	P49	60	113	14	13		4	1	0			2	.115
LeRoy	P46	46	95	9	14		5	0	1			2	.147
Ryan	P31	42	79	9	21		3	2	0			0	.266
Pierce	C40	40	115	9	20		4	1	0			1	.174
Brain	2B26	39	131	18	27		1	3	0			4	.207
Baker	2B30	30	96	6	19		1	0	0			3	.198
Steiger		25	59	6	14		0	2	0			3	.236
Kilroy	P22	24	44	1	7		1	0	0			1	.159
Reiger	P22	22	39	2	4		0	0	0			1	.102

PITCHERS		W	L	PCT	G	GS	CG	SH	IP	H	BB	SO	ERA
Chech		19	15	.559	49				299	295	77	99	
Gehring		18	20	.474	54				343	300	95	137	
Ryan		17	7	.708	31				211	149	50	103	
LeRoy		14	16	.467	46				268	221	53	89	
Reiger		9	5	.643	22				117	104	18	50	
Kilroy		5	8	.385	22				126	113	68	56	

KANSAS CITY   5th   85-81   .512   -21   Dan Shay
Blues

BATTERS	POS-GAMES	GP	AB	R	H	BI	2B	3B	HR	BB	SO	SB	BA
Hunter	1B162	162	589	103	174		27	9	2			38	.295
Love	2B128	157	577	79	152		22	7	5			31	.263
Barbeau	SS60,3B64	125	434	59	111		22	1	3			29	.256
Downey	3B75,SS78	164	551	46	125		18	2	0			12	.227
Shannon	OF169	169	620	101	153		12	6	2			36	.246
Raftery	OF147	151	539	66	137		18	6	1			32	.254

KANSAS CITY (cont.)
Blues

BATTERS	POS-GAMES	GP	AB	R	H	BI	2B	3B	HR	BB	SO	SB	BA
Cocash	OF59	88	255	32	59		9	3	1			8	.231
James	C		(see multi-team players)										
Ritter	C66	67	175	15	46		6	2	0			10	.263
Brandom	P54	54	109	5	12		0	1	0			0	.110
Rhoades	P45	47	112	6	17		1	1	2			0	.152
Campbell	P37	47	107	8	22		8	2	0			0	.206
Shay	2B24,SS15	45	112	13	28		3	1	0			7	.250
Swann	P36	36	77	6	10		0	1	0			1	.130
J. Sullivan	C26	28	78	4	7		1	0	0			0	.090
Moran	OF24	24	83	15	21		2	0	0			5	.253
Yohe	3B21	23	80	11	21		5	0	0			2	.263
Powell	P20	22	57	6	15		0	1	1			0	.263
Cranston	2B17	18	49	6	10		2	0	0			0	.205
Carter	P16	16	18	1	3		1	0	0			0	.167

PITCHERS	W	L	PCT	G	GS	CG	SH	IP	H	BB	SO	ERA
Rhoades	21	15	.583	45				308	286	81	114	
Brandom	20	15	.571	54				337	271	89	134	
Campbell	12	14	.462	37				227	262	59	51	
Swann	11	13	.458	35				224	211	57	58	
Powell	9	7	.563	20								

MILWAUKEE   6th   76-91   .455   -30.5   J.J. McCloskey
Brewers

BATTERS	POS-GAMES	GP	AB	R	H	BI	2B	3B	HR	BB	SO	SB	BA
D. McGann	1B150	151	520	65	117		15	5	1			22	.225
Charles	2B124	124	470	59	112		12	3	2			12	.238
Lewis	SS		(see multi-team players)										
H. Clark	3B164	164	525	69	131		22	7	4			20	.250
Randall	OF146	146	565	71	153		30	10	5			20	.271
Barry	OF92,1B23	130	420	36	106		11	3	0			7	.252
DeGroff	OF54	54	190	36	54		7	4	2			6	.284
Marshall	C87	89	276	17	62		3	8	5			1	.224
Breen	SS42,OF21,C18	106	310	27	60		6	4	0			6	.194
Ludwig	C79	85	233	23	47		7	3	1			4	.202
McGlynn	P63	63	138	4	15		3	0	0			0	.109
Dougherty	P33	53	128	12	28		2	3	0			0	.219
Barrett	OF51	51	173	34	61		7	3	3			13	.353
Cutting	P43	44	77	2	6		0	0	0			0	.078
Schardt	P42	43	119	10	18		2	5	0			0	.151
R. Bailey	OF28	31	92	6	17		2	1	0			0	.185
Cantwell	P20	24	37	4	9		1	0	0			0	.243
Gilligan	P22	22	52	3	11		1	1	0			0	.212
Bartliff		20	42	2	5		1	0	0			0	.119

PITCHERS	W	L	PCT	G	GS	CG	SH	IP	H	BB	SO	ERA
Schardt	21	16	.568	42				326	260	89	147	
McGlynn	16	21	.432	63				392	337	129	160	
Dougherty	14	12	.538	33				249	214	99	92	
Cutting	11	18	.378	43				238	221	69	80	
Gilligan	8	9	.470	22				153	136	76	52	
Cantwell	3	7	.300	20				72	77	36	17	

INDIANAPOLIS   7th   69-96   .418   -36.5   Carr - Burke
Indians

BATTERS	POS-GAMES	GP	AB	R	H	BI	2B	3B	HR	BB	SO	SB	BA
C. Carr	1B154	157	584	63	153		18	5	4			11	.262
O. Williams	2B130	133	485	45	116		6	1	0			26	.239
Coffey	SS90	93	301	29	68		6	4	0			16	.226
Murch	3B143	143	496	49	114		16	2	1			7	.230
Hayden	OF143	143	547	52	152		25	10	1			11	.278
Chadbourne	OF106	110	405	51	102		10	4	0			22	.252
Delahanty	OF100	100	391	47	90		5	9	3			26	.230
Bowerman	C79	91	278	23	77		6	0	0			6	.277

INDIANAPOLIS (cont.)
Indians

BATTERS	POS-GAMES	GP	AB	R	H	BI	2B	3B	HR	BB	SO	SB	BA
Milligan	OF40,2B37	94	296	28	75		3	0	0			11	.253
Howley	C54	57	181	9	33		6	0	0			4	.182
O'Day	OF41	41	162	27	44		4	3	0			2	.271
Hardgrove	P39	39	93	5	14		2	0	0			0	.150
Orth	P22	35	56	2	15		1	1	1			0	.267
Cheney	P34	34	43	5	8		0	0	0			1	.186
Glaze	P29	30	57	1	5		0	0	0			1	.088
Keene	3B17	28	97	11	12		0	3	0			1	.124
Kerns	P21	28	76	3	17		2	1	0			0	.224
Kendall	OF25	25	90	6	23		2	0	0			3	.257
Higgins	P20	21	63	6	11		3	1	0			0	.175
Lindaman	P21	21	37	3	5		1	0	0			0	.135
Lemon		17	40	6	7		2	0	0			1	.175

PITCHERS		W	L	PCT	G	GS	CG	SH	IP	H	BB	SO	ERA
Hardgrove		16	16	.500	39				277	259	74	103	
Cheney		10	12	.455	34				173	157	90	94	
Glaze		7	9	.437	30				167	138	60	80	
Orth		4	8	.333	22								
Lindaman		4	11	.267	21				119	122	45	46	

LOUISVILLE   8th   60-103   .368   -44.5   Henry Peitz
Colonels

BATTERS	POS-GAMES	GP	AB	R	H	BI	2B	3B	HR	BB	SO	SB	BA
D. Howard	1B98	104	343	39	82		11	5	4			10	.239
Magee	2B115,SS17	132	442	45	95		11	6	0			31	.215
C. Robinson	SS	(see multi-team players)											
Ja. Doyle	3B76,OF15	92	315	34	80		8	9	0			18	.254
Stanley	OF156	162	614	74	156		21	12	4			33	.253
Dunleavy	OF51	53	195	28	42		6	4	0			11	.215
Pickering	OF	(see multi-team players)											
J. Hughes	C76	108	329	30	93		4	3	1			11	.283
Halla	P41	74	144	9	31		2	0	0			1	.215
Schreckengost	C54	71	188	11	39		1	2	0			1	.207
R. Myers	1B54	54	208	24	50		5	0	0			20	.240
Flournoy	OF49	53	169	13	41		4	0	0			3	.243
S. Sullivan	3B25	50	168	12	43		3	1	0			3	.256
Richter	P49	49	75	2	7		1	0	0			0	.093
Moriarity	SS24	35	111	12	24		2	0	0			5	.216
Allen	C28	30	97	5	22		1	1	0			2	.227
Weaver	P30	30	72	1	8		2	0	0			0	.111
Fisher	OF25	26	79	8	16		1	1	0			3	.202
Peitz	C15	23	39	6	12		2	0	0			0	.309
Higginbotham	P18	21	42	3	11		2	0	0			1	.262
Decanniere	P21	21	31	3	5		0	0	0			0	.160
Konnick		20	75	5	24		4	0	0			3	.320
Bohannon		20	71	7	21		2	1	1			2	.296
Reilly	C15	18	53	10	15		2	2	0			3	.283
Burke	OF16	16	56	4	8		1	1	0			0	.143
Schwenk		14	24	0	8		1	0	0			0	.333

PITCHERS		W	L	PCT	G	GS	CG	SH	IP	H	BB	SO	ERA
Halla		10	**23**	.303	41				279	281	48	97	
Weaver		9	14	.391	30				207	157	67	145	
Richter		7	14	.333	49				217	165	80	130	
Higginbotham		6	6	.500	18								
Decanniere		5	12	.294	21				111	110	52	58	

MULTI-TEAM PLAYERS

BATTERS	POS-GAMES	TEAMS	GP	AB	R	H	BI	2B	3B	HR	BB	SO	SB	BA
Pickering	OF160	MIN-LOU	160	544	61	131		12	9	2			22	.241
Rossman	OF118,1B32	COL-MIN	155	583	56	162		20	8	2			8	.278
Lewis	SS155	IND-MIL	155	561	54	142		17	5	0			9	.253
Hallman	OF146	KC-TOL	148	542	84	151		13	3	0			24	.279

MULTI-TEAM PLAYERS (cont.)

BATTERS	POS-GAMES	TEAMS	GP	AB	R	H	BI	2B	3B	HR	BB	SO	SB	BA
C. Robinson	SS144	MIL-LOU	147	553	59	136		9	13	3			18	.246
A. Spencer	OF143	IND-MIL	144	484	51	114		10	4	2			32	.236
Smoot	OF125	LOU-KC	130	484	46	114		14	0	1			17	.236
Woodruff	2B56,OF35,3B23	LOU-SP	115	437	45	103		8	8	3			24	.236
James	C101	COL-KC	108	370	39	92		19	4	9			1	.248
B. McCormick	2B60,3B37	MIL-MIN	105	341	29	77		8	1	2			6	.226
O'Neill	OF54	LOU-MIN	63	201	23	47		7	1	0			4	.234
F.M. Owen	P31	KC-TOL	31	84	8	13		3	0	0			1	.155
Slagle	P29	IND-LOU	31	66	7	15		2	2	0			2	.227
O. Graham	P27	IND-MIL	27	55	8	14		3	0	1			1	.255
Essick	P23	KC-TOL	24	47	4	5		0	0	0			0	.106

PITCHERS	TEAMS	W	L	PCT	G	GS	CG	SH	IP	H	BB	SO	ERA
Slagle	IND-LOU	13	11	.542	29				203	212	69	68	
F. Owen	KC-TOL	11	14	.440	31				235	200	92	58	
Essick	KC-TOL	10	7	.588	23				136	125	50	51	
O. Graham	IND-MIL	8	10	.444	27				156	124	52	55	

TEAM BATTING

TEAMS	GP	AB	R	H	BI	2B	3B	HR	BB	SO	SB	BA
MINNEAPOLIS	167	5558	802	1514		225	79	39			237	.272
TOLEDO	171	5571	631	1385		158	68	18			186	.249
COLUMBUS	168	5479	655	1311		191	59	10			190	.239
ST. PAUL	172	5596	672	1339		164	90	34			267	.239
KANSAS CITY	169	5478	667	1317		192	45	26			229	.240
MILWAUKEE	169	5341	575	1241		157	65	29			242	.232
INDIANAPOLIS	166	5404	527	1273		133	45	10			165	.235
LOUISVILLE	167	5312	526	1269		118	67	13			203	.239
	675	43739	5055	10649		1338	518	179			1719	.243

1911
Minneapolis Millers

In the pitching-rich era of pre–World War I baseball, a power hitting dynasty broke forth in the American Association: the Minneapolis Millers. And unlike their counterparts in Columbus who five years before had used pitching and defense to garner their successes, the Millers relied on hitting, and surprisingly the long ball, to achieve their victories.

The Millers had achieved modest success during the Association's first decade by finishing third four times. Minneapolis management then put together a winning team, not with talented yet untested youngsters, but with proven major league veterans. Players like Tom Hughes, Rube Waddell, Jimmy Williams, Dave Altizer, Roy Patterson, Otis Clymer, and others were proven winners who knew how to play the game. This combination proved to be the ticket as the Millers cruised easily to the 1910 pennant, winning a record 107 games along the way.

Impressive as 1910 was, the 1911 version of the Minneapolis Miller pennant machine would surpass it to secure a place among the best teams in Association history. This squad was the first Association team to bat over .300. This feat was impressive because no other team in 1911 could hit higher than .279, and the league as whole batted only .268. The team was led by one of the few members of the club to have minimal major league experience, Gavvy Cravath. Cravath obliterated the home run record by blasting 29 circuit clouts, while winning the batting title (.363) to boot. Other strong hitters on the club included Rossman (.356), Clymer (.342), Altizer (.335), Williams (.332), and Ferris (.303) who also poled 14 home runs. Pitching was not too shabby as Patterson (24-10) and Waddell (20-17) both excelled.

The Millers did not run away with the pennant in 1911, as they had done in 1910. Kansas City hung on strong to finish only four and one-half games back, with Columbus in third. The rest of the league wound up under .500 in the following order: St. Paul, Milwaukee, Toledo, Indianapolis, and Louisville. The aforementioned Cravath won the batting honors, while his teammate Patterson pitched the most victories. The highest strikeout total was rung up by O'Toole of St. Paul (199).

In 1912, Minneapolis became the second team in the Association to capture three pennants in a row as they won the flag yet again. As the years progressed, the Millers enjoyed one more pennant during the teens, before seeing hard times which ended with more pennant successes during the 1930s. But those later championships pale when compared to the Minneapolis Millers of 1911, a team whose hitting dominated the league in ways not seen before or since.

MINNEAPOLIS Millers

| | | 1st | 99-66 | .600 | | | | | | Joe Cantillon |

BATTERS	POS-GAMES	GP	AB	R	H	BI	2B	3B	HR	BB	SO	SB	BA
Gill	1B162	162	572	109	144		20	6	1			**55**	.252
J. Williams	2B161	162	647	110	215		43	6	7			20	.332
Altizer	SS73	73	284	64	95		13	3	1			30	.335
Ferris	3B154	154	598	73	181		34	8	14			6	.303
Cravath	OF167	167	608	147	**221**		53	13	**29**			33	**.363**
Rossman	OF155	155	596	93	212		31	9	4			17	.356
Clymer	OF147	147	632	**149**	216		48	10	3			51	.342
F. Owens	C119	126	439	55	120		25	5	5			7	.273
Killifer	SS63,OF27	122	366	58	106		24	3	4			18	.290
W. Smith	C52	68	178	27	40		4	1	0			4	.225
Waddell	P54	56	93	7	19		2	0	0			1	.204
Patterson	P39	39	109	12	26		3	0	0			1	.239
Cavet	P34	34	57	8	12		1	0	0			0	.212
Dawson		32	70	8	14		3	0	0			0	.200
Leever	P24	26	46	6	8		1	0	0			1	.174
Loudell	P25	26	38	5	10		0	0	0			2	.263
Leverette	P19	22	42	8	8		0	0	0			0	.190
Peters	P17	17	44	1	9		2	0	0			0	.205
Peaster	P17	17	13	0	0		0	0	0			1	.000

PITCHERS		W	L	PCT	G	GS	CG	SH	IP	H	BB	SO	ERA
Patterson		**24**	10	**.706**	39				293	268	48	115	
Waddell		20	17	.541	54				300	262	96	185	
Cavet		14	6	.700	34				158	182	64	59	
Peters		11	3	.786	17								
Leever		7	4	.636	24				125	139	39	39	
Leverette		6	4	.600	19								
Loudell		5	6	.455	25				110	109	32	37	
Peaster		4	2	.667	17								

KANSAS CITY Blues

| | | 2nd | 94-70 | .573 | -4.5 | | | | | Dan Shay |

BATTERS	POS-GAMES	GP	AB	R	H	BI	2B	3B	HR	BB	SO	SB	BA
Bowerman	1B79	81	293	33	75		9	0	0			0	.256
Downey	2B100,SS36	151	500	81	134		16	5	3			11	.268
Corriden	SS129	137	433	72	107		22	10	4			17	.247
Barbeau	3B152	154	564	136	167		33	6	9			33	.296
Love	OF129,1B28	159	641	88	179		38	4	4			23	.279
Hyatt	OF119,1B47	166	643	**159**	210		31	13	14			20	.326
D. Sullivan	OF98	109	397	64	123		17	7	1			11	.310
O'Connor	C102	108	302	32	79		16	3	0			3	.262
A. James	C82	94	241	34	82		15	5	9			4	.340
Gardner	OF55	59	191	28	48		7	4	0			4	.251
Maddox	P54	59	130	11	30		8	1	0			0	.231
Rhoades	P52	53	114	14	24		6	0	1			0	.210
Rockenfield	2B49	52	164	17	40		9	0	1			6	.244
Shannon	OF48	52	162	35	35		3	1	0			7	.216
Powell	P44	48	107	17	33		5	0	0			0	.308
Brandom	P48	48	72	2	7		2	0	0			0	.097
Smoot	OF36	44	116	21	44		8	2	2			2	.379
Schaller	OF36	36	124	26	38		4	0	2			15	.306
F.M. Owen	P21	22	32	4	10		2	0	1			0	.313
Siebert	P14	22	17	5	3		1	0	0			1	.176

PITCHERS		W	L	PCT	G	GS	CG	SH	IP	H	BB	SO	ERA
Maddox		22	13	.629	54				331	350	109	98	
Rhoades		20	16	.555	52				314	321	68	125	
Powell		19	12	.613	44				249	263	113	144	
Brandom		11	14	.440	48				210	230	62	66	
F.M. Owen		5	5	.500	21				79	93	29	18	
Siebert		0	2	.000	14								

COLUMBUS Senators
3rd   87-78   .527   -12   William Friel

BATTERS	POS-GAMES	GP	AB	R	H	BI	2B	3B	HR	BB	SO	SB	BA
Perring	1B109,3B46	156	577	90	185		36	10	2			18	.321
Downs	2B115,2B48	163	641	95	193		25	10	4			33	.301
Mahling	SS145	145	553	74	150		19	8	0			10	.271
O'Rourke	3B114,2B33	147	545	88	133		16	8	0			27	.244
Congalton	OF165	165	669	99	211		49	5	3			0	.315
W. Hinchman	OF159	166	628	122	185		43	9	8			28	.295
Odwell	OF139	141	501	55	130		20	7	0			25	.259
Rapp	C		(see multi-team players)										
Packard	P40	54	131	19	36		1	3	2			1	.275
Liebhardt	P52	53	105	6	25		4	0	0			2	.238
Lattimore	2B24	49	130	19	26		3	3	0			3	.200
Bemis	C47	47	162	17	40		7	2	1			1	.247
Cook	P39	39	90	10	19		2	0	0			1	.211
Lessard	P34	34	90	3	10		2	1	1			0	.111
Berger	P23	23	45	4	3		2	0	0			0	.067
Bonin		18	44	12	17		3	4	0			0	.386
McQuillan	P17	17	36	2	4		0	0	0			0	.111

PITCHERS		W	L	PCT	G	GS	CG	SH	IP	H	BB	SO	ERA
Liebhardt		19	15	.559	52				290	303		126	
Cook		18	12	.600	39				252	249	102	90	
Packard		18	13	.581	40				287	271	111	133	
Lessard		16	12	.572	34				242	220	86	66	
Berger		7	10	.412	23				142	125	41	72	
McQuillan		5	8	.385	17								
Sitton		2	0	1.000									

ST. PAUL Saints
4th   79-85   .481   -19.5   Mike Kelley

BATTERS	POS-GAMES	GP	AB	R	H	BI	2B	3B	HR	BB	SO	SB	BA
Autry	1B160	160	575	75	169		24	9	3			21	.294
Howell	2B		(see multi-team players)										
A. Butler	SS91,3B24	115	409	66	106		14	7	2			29	.259
M. McCormick	3B89,SS78	168	626	95	172		28	9	6			28	.274
F. Delahanty	OF143	147	576	74	159		23	7	3			46	.276
C. Jones	OF117	122	443	70	116		14	12	8			25	.262
J. Clarke	OF112	113	407	64	106		13	5	1			16	.260
W. Kelly	C72	74	276	37	79		10	6	3			25	.286
Beaumont	OF54	74	233	35	58		5	5	2			8	.249
Land	C61	61	203	16	50		4	1	0			10	.246
LeRoy	P60	60	92	7	20		0	0	0			2	.217
Chech	P46	56	86	7	10		1	1	0			1	.116
Steiger	P	48	78	12	17		1	2	0			3	.218
E. Spencer	C38	41	137	16	42		3	1	0			3	.307
Gehring	P36	38	78	6	15		1	0	0			0	.193
Decanniere	P36	36	65	8	14		0	0	0			2	.215
Kohl	3B33	35	117	13	23		2	2	1			4	.197
P. Howard	2B21	34	112	18	24		3	1	2			7	.214
Rieger	P31	32	56	5	9		2	0	0			1	.161
O'Toole	P30	31	84	5	14		3	1	1			0	.167

PITCHERS		W	L	PCT	G	GS	CG	SH	IP	H	BB	SO	ERA
LeRoy		18	**23**	.439	**60**				300	315	80	131	
O'Toole		15	11	.577	30				204	162	84	**199**	
Decanniere		13	11	.542	36				203	181	84	135	
Chech		11	13	.458	46				234	262	60	69	
Gehring		10	12	.455	36				226	233	51	55	
Reiger		8	9	.471	31				166	188	35	51	
Steiger		2	3	.400									

MILWAUKEE Brewers
5th   79-87   .476   -20.5   James Barrett

BATTERS	POS-GAMES	GP	AB	R	H	BI	2B	3B	HR	BB	SO	SB	BA
T. Jones	1B122	122	454	62	129		25	3	2			16	.284

MILWAUKEE (cont.)
Brewers

BATTERS	POS-GAMES	GP	AB	R	H	BI	2B	3B	HR	BB	SO	SB	BA
Charles	2B149	149	596	84	146		17	10	5			23	.245
Lewis	SS161	161	582	65	175		31	6	1			13	.301
H. Clark	3B162	162	540	82	141		20	7	6			14	.261
Randall	OF144	148	570	76	170		42	8	6			16	.298
Stone	OF114	114	433	61	122		14	9	3			16	.282
Liebold	OF81	88	288	40	51		9	5	0			7	.178
Marshall	C124	131	405	46	100		17	5	6			7	.247
Breen	2B22,C22	82	263	33	80		12	2	0			10	.304
Barrett	OF52	79	201	24	45		4	2	1			0	.224
McGlynn	P55	55	96	4	11		4	0	0			0	.115
Dougherty	P40	54	138	13	32		4	2	2			0	.232
Nicholson	P47	47	71	1	10		1	0	0			0	.141
Cutting	P41	41	68	3	7		0	1	0			0	.103
Schalk	C28	31	76	9	18		2	1	0			2	.228
Maloney	OF28	30	103	9	23		3	2	0			5	.223
Marion	P30	30	49	6	7		0	1	0			0	.143
DeGroff	OF29	29	91	11	18		2	1	2			5	.198
Dolan		20	71	10	18		2	1	0			2	.253

PITCHERS	W	L	PCT	G	GS	CG	SH	IP	H	BB	SO	ERA
McGlynn	22	15	.595	55				287	281	81	115	
Dougherty	19	15	.559	40				310	271	147	117	
Nicholson	11	19	.367	47				222	209	65	69	
Cutting	10	10	.500	41				228	200	50	80	
Marion	4	8	.333	29				129	103	71	57	
Short	0	4	.000									

TOLEDO   6th   78-86   .476   -20.5   Harry Hinchman
Mud Hens

BATTERS	POS-GAMES	GP	AB	R	H	BI	2B	3B	HR	BB	SO	SB	BA
Hornhorst	1B127	131	497	73	150		20	8	1			43	.302
H. Hinchman	2B159	159	615	94	189		21	7	2			25	.307
W. Butler	SS116	123	417	54	111		19	2	0			26	.268
Bronkie	3B120,SS34	154	535	55	148		14	3	2			41	.277
Burns	OF152	161	535	66	131		20	15	1			11	.245
Niles	OF111,3B47	171	678	108	188		18	10	1			29	.277
Flick	OF83	84	313	63	102		13	7	3			10	.326
Carisch	C		(see multi-team players)										
Baskette	P40	47	117	6	22		2	2	0			1	.189
Clynes	OF39	40	139	9	28		2	0	2			4	.201
Yingling	P35	40	87	9	20		4	0	0			0	.230
L. James	P36	38	79	7	7		1	1	0			1	.089
Derrick	1B33	37	123	17	31		1	1	1			6	.252
Swann	P28	30	63	7	16		0	0	0			2	.254
Donahue	C21	23	69	2	11		1	1	0			1	.159
Griggs		21	52	8	15		4	0	0			5	.288
Meloan	OF18	18	62	9	20		1	2	1			5	.323
West	P16	17	28	2	5		1	0	0			0	.179
Chapman	SS16	16	62	8	23		4	2	0			1	.371
Hauger	OF15	15	47	6	11		0	0	0			4	.235

PITCHERS	W	L	PCT	G	GS	CG	SH	IP	H	BB	SO	ERA
Baskette	23	16	.590	46				330	297	96	152	
Yingling	18	11	.621	36				246	227	51	92	
Swann	10	8	.526	28				196	213	45	53	
L. James	8	12	.400	36				237	233	78	67	
West	4	5	.444	16								
K. Robinson	3	3	.500									
W. James	2	6	.250	13								

INDIANAPOLIS   7th   78-88   .470   -21.5   James T. Burke
Indians

BATTERS	POS-GAMES	GP	AB	R	H	BI	2B	3B	HR	BB	SO	SB	BA
Houser	1B124	126	447	61	148		18	9	1			16	.331

INDIANAPOLIS (cont.)
Indians

BATTERS	POS-GAMES	GP	AB	R	H	BI	2B	3B	HR	BB	SO	SB	BA
O. Williams	2B166	166	586	60	163		14	6	0			14	.278
Mowe	SS158	158	483	38	96		4	3	0			13	.199
Getz	3B116	118	459	45	127		21	1	0			18	.277
Woodruff	OF159	162	644	98	179		28	9	0			21	.278
Hoffman	OF118	118	447	86	111		13	12	4			19	.248
B. Hallman	OF	(see multi-team players)											
Ritter	C	(see multi-team players)											
Schlitzer	P49	49	100	10	15		0	0	1			3	.150
Link	P44	45	107	8	23		2	0	0			3	.215
Merz	P41	41	67	6	8		1	0	0			0	.119
W. Robertson	P30	31	67	6	12		0	1	1			0	.167
Webb	P31	31	64	3	7		0	0	0			0	.109
Channell	P26	27	104	12	24		1	3	0			1	.231
Freeman	1B22	24	81	11	21		2	2	0			2	.260
Niehoff	3B19	23	63	4	9		2	1	0			4	.143
Hunter	1B20	20	68	7	20		3	0	2			2	.294
Wentz		15	41	3	12		1	0	0			2	.293

PITCHERS		W	L	PCT	G	GS	CG	SH	IP	H	BB	SO	ERA
Link		21	16	.568	44				306	287	100	145	
Schlitzer		18	18	.500	49				327	336	66	141	
Merz		11	11	.500	41				215	218	59	90	
W. Robertson		11	12	.478	30				179	172	46	48	
Webb		7	17	.292	31				186	212	40	69	
Dowd		4	4	.500									
Kimball		3	1	.750									
White		2	2	.500									

LOUISVILLE   8th   67-101   .398   -33.5   Del Howard
Colonels

BATTERS	POS-GAMES	GP	AB	R	H	BI	2B	3B	HR	BB	SO	SB	BA
D. Howard	1B128	150	517	79	156		33	13	3			12	.302
Hulswitt	2B84	90	320	40	100		9	8	0			17	.313
C. Robinson	SS113	119	474	60	114		18	6	2			14	.241
Stansbury	3B80,OF36,2B33	152	569	78	161		23	10	3			21	.283
Stanley	OF168	168	609	83	141		24	3	5			31	.232
Hayden	OF143	143	542	71	156		18	10	6			13	.288
Fisher	OF82	93	290	32	64		7	4	1			15	.221
Hughes	C110	119	354	38	90		20	6	3			9	.254
Grimshaw	1B50,OF44	97	372	62	135		14	14	3			5	.363
Lennox	3B71	75	278	38	92		22	4	2			10	.331
E. Baker		41	115	11	28		4	1	0			11	.243
Boucher	SS35	35	129	15	35		8	3	1			4	.271
Emerson	OF28	29	96	7	20		3	1	0			2	.208
Miller	C21	29	72	4	20		2	0	0			3	.278
Slagle	P25	25	48	6	12		3	1	0			0	.250
Pfeister	P23	23	54	1	4		0	0	0			1	.074
Hearn	P22	23	44	2	5		0	0	0			0	.113
Long	P16	16	40	3	4		0	0	0			0	.100
Hafford		15	51	8	16		7	1	0			2	.314

PITCHERS		W	L	PCT	G	GS	CG	SH	IP	H	BB	SO	ERA
Pfeister		7	12	.370	23				150	175	37	50	
Slagle		6	10	.375	25				140	149	47	35	
Long		4	10	.286	16								
E.W. Baker		2	3	.400	10								
Kroh		2	4	.333	10								
Hearn		2	11	.154	22				124	146	38	52	

MULTI-TEAM PLAYERS

BATTERS	POS-GAMES	TEAMS	GP	AB	R	H	BI	2B	3B	HR	BB	SO	SB	BA
B. Hallman	OF131	TOL-IND	136	500	80	153		19	7	4			19	.306

MULTI-TEAM PLAYERS (cont.)

BATTERS	POS-GAMES	TEAMS	GP	AB	R	H	BI	2B	3B	HR	BB	SO	SB	BA
Ritter	C134	IND-KC	135	465	53	112		12	6	0			13	.241
Carisch	C109,OF16	IND-TOL	131	436	49	117		16	3	0			8	.268
B. McCormick	2B64,SS40	MIN-SP	122	402	37	90		18	3	0			7	.224
Ralston	OF93	SP-CO-MIL	101	337	45	70		8	8	6			30	.208
J. McCarthy	3B33,OF33	IND-TOL	98	298	45	80		10	3	2			9	.268
Howell	2B89	LOU-SP	96	335	38	87		14	8	2			5	.260
H. Baker	2B45	LOU-KC	92	204	28	51		7	4	0			6	.250
Hickman	OF65	TOL-MIL	88	307	36	106		23	6	1			11	.345
J. McCarty	OF31,C20	IND-TOL	75	174	22	51		6	5	0			4	.295
Orendorff	1B37,C24	LOU-MIL	74	246	35	58		8	3	2			5	.236
Rapp	C65	TOL-COL	67	194	12	36		7	0	0			5	.186
J. Walsh	C62	COL-IND	67	182	20	34		4	0	0			3	.187
Ludwig	C52	LO-MIL-CO	64	154	19	35		8	2	0			3	.227
Higginbotham	P52	TOL-LOU	62	135	17	39		2	5	0			3	.289
Cheney	P42	IND-TOL	42	90	6	15		3	4	0			0	.167
Gilligan	P27	MIL-MIN	31	64	6	16		0	1	0			0	.250
Altrock	P30	MIN-KC	31	54	7	10		4	0	0			2	.185
Fiene	P23	TO-KC-MIN	28	56	7	20		3	1	0			1	.363
Flynn		SP-KC	20	62	11	20		2	1	1			5	.323
Brady	P	IND-TOL	17	34	5	6		0	0	0			0	.176

PITCHERS		TEAMS	W	L	PCT	G	GS	CG	SH	IP	H	BB	SO	ERA
Cheney		IND-TOL	19	11	.633	42				282	215	116	137	
Higginbotham		TOL-LOU	19	22	.463	52				340	360	109	111	
Altrock		MIN-KC	12	4	.750	30				149	173	26	37	
Gilligan		MIL-MIN	8	11	.421	27				164	178	62	74	
Brady		IND-TOL	6	3	.667									
Fiene		TO-KC-MIN	5	10	.333	23				126	129	55	52	

TEAM BATTING

TEAMS	GP	AB	R	H	BI	2B	3B	HR	BB	SO	SB	BA
MINNEAPOLIS	167	5747	969	1727		306	74	68			248	.301
KANSAS CITY	165	5546	878	1549		267	62	52			168	.279
COLUMBUS	165	5573	774	1488		249	74	20			166	.267
ST. PAUL	166	5484	727	1390		176	86	39			268	.253
MILWAUKEE	167	5544	693	1399		329	67	33			139	.252
TOLEDO	169	5611	719	1501		194	72	17			251	.268
INDIANAPOLIS	169	5504	671	1419		159	70	16			169	.258
LOUISVILLE	170	5694	738	1520		231	103	30			175	.267
	669	44703	6169	11993		1911	608	275			1584	.268

1912
Harry Clark

Most American Association record holders were men who could recite a list of impressive feats of domination. However, some record holders were honored for more pedestrian, yet no less important achievements. Such a man was third baseman Harry Clark. His legacy in the American Association didn't come from his flashy play, but from his longevity. In 1912 Harry Clark played his ninth straight year in the Association, and when his career ended a few years later he held a record unlikely to be matched. In all the years of the American Association, no one has played in more games than Harry Clark, for he participated in an astounding 1,834 games. Even more remarkably, they were all for the same team.

After starting his career with Dallas in the Texas League, Harry Clark joined the Chicago White Sox for a brief 15-game stint at the end of the 1903 season. Though he batted a respectable .308 in his major league trial, Clark began the 1904 season with the Association's Milwaukee Brewers, a team which he never left. During his first few years in Milwaukee, he played a solid, average game. His batting average stayed between .244 and .261 (with the exception of an unexpected dip to .196 in 1907). He never hit many homers, reaching a career best total of six in 1911.

In 1912, Clark reached a new level of hitting, attaining a career best .292, accompanied by 13 triples. But he could lift his team no higher than fifth as thrice-in-a-row champion Minneapolis, followed by Toledo, Columbus, and Kansas City, finished ahead of Milwaukee. St. Paul placed sixth, and the Louisville Colonels climbed out of the cellar to seventh, while Indianapolis replaced them in eighth. Butler of St. Paul won the batting title (.329) while James of Kansas City finished with the most home runs (10) for a third time. Minneapolis hurler Olmstead finished as the best pitcher with a 28-10 mark, while the most strikeouts (174) were chalked up by Powell of Kansas City.

Harry Clark went on to play four more years as the Brewers' regular third baseman, crossing the .300 threshold once along the way. At the beginning of the 1913 season, the owners honored his steady perserverance by making him the team's manager as well—a position he held, off and on, for more than a decade, long after his 1,834 games and 15 years in the field were behind him.

MINNEAPOLIS Millers

MINNEAPOLIS   1st   105-60   .636   Joe Cantillon

BATTERS	POS-GAMES	GP	AB	R	H	BI	2B	3B	HR	BB	SO	SB	BA
Gill	1B122	123	376	59	99		11	5	1			24	.263
J. Williams	2B139	139	523	94	155		32	6	2			18	.296
Altizer	SS162	162	625	125	184		21	4	6			**68**	.294
Killifer	3B149	161	594	97	171		24	1	0			45	.288
Rossman	OF163	166	581	80	187		32	8	5			13	.322
Clymer	OF157	157	651	**127**	**200**		37	5	4			61	.307
F. Delahanty	OF146	146	511	75	136		11	5	0			36	.266
Owens	C136	136	438	52	105		17	6	3			8	.240
Ferris	OF32,2B27,3B16	91	286	35	79		16	7	5			4	.276
Unglaub	1B29	67	182	20	38		5	2	1			5	.209
Olmstead	P45	51	133	15	33		4	0	0			1	.248
Young	P51	51	92	6	14		1	1	0			1	.152
Comstock	P36	37	41	3	4		0	0	0			0	.098
Patterson	P35	35	89	10	14		1	2	0			0	.157
W. Smith	C34	34	80	18	23		4	3	1			2	.288
Waddell	P33	33	47	4	13		1	0	0			0	.277
Allen	C31	31	86	13	22		1	0	0			2	.256
J. Delahanty	1B22	27	96	18	43		7	2	0			1	.448
Burns	P14	15	27	3	4		0	0	0			0	.148

PITCHERS		W	L	PCT	G	GS	CG	SH	IP	H	BB	SO	ERA
Olmstead		**28**	10	.737	45				316	279	82	131	
Patterson		21	9	.700	35				282	227	46	83	
Young		16	14	.533	**51**				275	263	73	142	
Waddell		12	6	.667	33				151	138	59	113	
Lelivelt		7	1	.875	10								
Burns		6	2	.750	14								
Comstock		6	5	.545	36				125	122	63	51	

TOLEDO Mud Hens

TOLEDO   2nd   98-66   .598   -6.5   T.F. Hartsel

BATTERS	POS-GAMES	GP	AB	R	H	BI	2B	3B	HR	BB	SO	SB	BA
Derrick	1B142	143	497	49	120		21	5	1			26	.241
H. Hinchman	2B	(see multi-team players)											
Chapman	SS140	140	513	101	159		22	13	2			49	.310
Bronkie	3B135	135	500	69	135		25	7	0			35	.270
Burns	OF165	165	572	69	147		24	7	1			12	.257
Flick	OF115	115	382	60	100		16	5	2			28	.262
Niles	OF113,3B25	140	548	92	161		23	8	1			18	.298
Land	C110	110	377	35	87		11	3	1			4	.231
Carisch	C58	58	181	17	45		3	4	0			2	.249
E. Gardner	2B54	54	194	33	50		8	3	0			13	.258
Falkenberg	P38	38	115	7	13		1	0	0			2	.113
Brady	2B24	36	127	18	23		5	1	0			8	.181
Collamore	P33	34	65	6	11		1	2	0			1	.169
L. James	P33	33	79	5	7		0	0	0			0	.089
W. James	P30	30	76	3	12		1	1	0			0	.158
Krause	P22	23	64	4	18		2	0	0			1	.281
J. Reilly	OF22	22	82	17	21		1	4	1			4	.256
West	P21	21	42	6	5		0	3	0			0	.119
George	P18	18	47	2	10		2	0	0			0	.213

PITCHERS		W	L	PCT	G	GS	CG	SH	IP	H	BB	SO	ERA
Falkenberg		25	8	.758	38				309	257	89	113	
L. James		17	13	.567	33				260	210	93	122	
Krause		13	4	**.760**	22				169	145	53	86	
W. James		13	13	.500	30				211	175	82	108	
George		10	7	.588	18								
West		9	6	.600	21				107	131	36	29	
Collamore		8	7	.533	33				160	148	69	67	

COLUMBUS
Senators
3rd   98-68   .590   -7.5   William Friel

BATTERS	POS-GAMES	GP	AB	R	H	BI	2B	3B	HR	BB	SO	SB	BA
A. Miller	1B168	168	598	93	177		31	10	9			7	.296
O'Rourke	2B136	136	457	74	122		12	3	1			22	.267
Gerber	SS166	166	599	63	140		19	11	1			6	.234
Perring	3B159	164	610	100	190		36	9	5			10	.311
Shelton	OF167	167	659	122	164		30	12	5			52	.249
W. Hinchman	OF161	161	606	120	187		29	20	6			22	.309
Congalton	OF		(see multi-team players)										
Smith	C155	155	539	47	152		16	9	0			3	.282
Johns	OF45	55	202	23	51		8	3	3			3	.252
McQuillan	P49	49	101	5	14		4	1	0			0	.140
Packard	P43	45	112	18	28		3	1	1			1	.250
Cook	P41	41	95	7	11		1	0	0			0	.116
Cooper	P31	31	84	10	18		2	1	0			0	.214
Murphy	C27	27	59	8	10		1	0	0			2	.169
Brock	P25	25	43	4	4		0	0	0			0	.093
Farrell	OF20	20	72	7	14		1	0	0			5	.194

PITCHERS	W	L	PCT	G	GS	CG	SH	IP	H	BB	SO	ERA
Packard	24	8	.750	43				292	259	89	171	
Cook	17	15	.531	41				278	241	99	84	
McQuillan	17	18	.486	49				307	289	71	140	
Cooper	16	9	.640	31				219	184	107	117	
Brock	8	5	.615	25				124	127	58	35	
McConnaghey	5	2	.714	12								

KANSAS CITY
Blues
4th   85-82   .509   -21   C.C. Carr

BATTERS	POS-GAMES	GP	AB	R	H	BI	2B	3B	HR	BB	SO	SB	BA
C. Carr	1B148	148	556	72	178		41	4	3			13	.320
Downey	2B134,3B15	151	544	69	151		23	2	4			3	.284
Corriden	SS119	121	424	69	135		28	12	4			30	.318
Barbeau	3B135	137	477	102	117		36	4	3			31	.245
Coulson	OF133	133	501	79	121		19	9	3			27	.242
Schaller	OF89	89	338	61	105		23	6	6			14	.311
Love	OF79	83	299	46	73		11	2	1			18	.244
O'Connor	C110	110	355	42	84		16	4	0			7	.237
Fiene	OF72,1B25,P12	124	380	39	108		23	2	4			3	.284
James	C91	91	259	45	74		12	2	10			2	.286
Tannehill	SS44	49	159	16	39		9	0	0			4	.245
Powell	P45	47	136	10	37		5	1	0			0	.272
Rhoades	P40	40	110	9	20		3	0	1			3	.182
Baxter	OF35	35	97	18	22		3	0	0			8	.227
Rockenfield	2B28	29	90	12	18		3	0	0			4	.200
Drake	OF27	27	102	21	35		10	1	0			3	.343
Walker	OF27	27	97	15	30		6	1	0			2	.286
Clarke	OF25	25	84	14	16		2	3	0			3	.190
Gallia	P23	23	32	3	2		0	0	0			0	.063
Altrock	P19	19	40	4	10		0	0	0			0	.250
Shaw	OF16	16	65	3	17		0	0	0			0	.262

PITCHERS	W	L	PCT	G	GS	CG	SH	IP	H	BB	SO	ERA
Powell	27	12	.692	45				340	297	166	174	
Rhoades	21	15	.583	40				306	286	68	100	
Gallia	5	7	.417	23				107	86	49	46	
Altrock	5	9	.357	19								
Dessau	1	2	.333	12								
Fiene	1	2	.333	12								

MILWAUKEE
Brewers
5th   78-85   .479   -26   Hugh Duffy

BATTERS	POS-GAMES	GP	AB	R	H	BI	2B	3B	HR	BB	SO	SB	BA
T. Jones	1B150	150	547	72	150		21	3	1			24	.274
Charles	2B104,3B25	134	522	77	125		10	8	2			21	.239

MILWAUKEE (cont.)
Brewers

BATTERS	POS-GAMES	GP	AB	R	H	BI	2B	3B	HR	BB	SO	SB	BA
P. Lewis	SS132,2B18	150	537	53	135		17	2	1			10	.251
H. Clark	3B138	138	473	74	138		24	13	4			17	.292
Randall	OF160	161	630	86	183		38	3	3			30	.290
Chappelle	OF131	131	482	66	132		10	17	5			10	.274
Leibold	OF128,2B26	158	622	92	177		18	9	3			19	.285
Hughes	C81	81	213	23	63		11	2	1			6	.296
Schalk	C80	80	266	19	72		8	4	3			6	.271
Slapnicka	P44	44	90	8	15		3	0	0			2	.167
Hovlik	P44	44	72	3	6		0	0	0			0	.083
Nicholson	P42	42	89	5	12		0	0	0			0	.135
Marion	P36	36	53	2	14		0	1	0			1	.264
Cutting	P34	34	62	4	3		1	0	0			0	.048
Blackburn	SS19	31	105	14	30		1	1	0			5	.286
Dougherty	P23	31	73	6	8		2	0	0			1	.110
Breen	2B15	28	76	15	14		4	1	0			2	.184
Block	C25	25	68	5	15		2	1	0			0	.221

PITCHERS		W	L	PCT	G	GS	CG	SH	IP	H	BB	SO	ERA
Nicholson		20	12	.625	42				244	235	64	81	
Cutting		13	12	.520	34				184	166	31	84	
Slapnicka		12	13	.480	44				255	225	108	109	
Hovlik		12	15	.444	44				244	203	78	147	
Marion		8	4	.667	36				155	153	68	55	
Dougherty		6	14	.300	23				171	156	78	52	
Noel		3	6	.333	17								

ST. PAUL   6th   77-90   .461   -29   Mike Kelley
Saints

BATTERS	POS-GAMES	GP	AB	R	H	BI	2B	3B	HR	BB	SO	SB	BA
Autry	1B157	157	544	67	148		23	9	0			15	.272
J. Lewis	2B	(see multi-team players)											
Butler	SS84,OF33	125	513	86	169		19	9	2			37	**.329**
Rehg	3B79	86	300	41	92		7	16	2			24	.307
Hoffman	OF129	129	426	64	110		17	4	3			23	.258
Flynn	OF111	117	418	53	99		21	6	2			15	.237
Ralston	OF81	81	271	36	67		8	6	6			11	.247
Marshall	C	(see multi-team players)											
Riggert	OF80	80	267	39	64		8	6	2			10	.239
Goodman	3B72	72	263	26	53		14	3	2			5	.202
Karger	P46	57	120	10	31		7	2	2			0	.258
D. Howard	OF55	55	200	23	60		8	2	1			2	.300
Dauss	P51	51	94	12	17		2	1	2			0	.181
Murray	C49	49	147	20	33		4	2	0			3	.224
Block	C45	45	117	18	35		4	2	0			1	.299
LeRoy	P44	44	94	6	15		2	0	0			0	.160
McKechnie	SS41	41	158	22	37		7	3	1			9	.234
Decanniere	P38	38	52	3	6		0	1	0			0	.115
H. Gardner	P31	31	57	5	10		3	0	0			0	.175
Rieger	P25	25	46	12	8		0	0	0			2	.174
Walsh	1B20	21	52	8	12		1	1	2			1	.231
F. Thomas	P20	20	34	2	4		1	0	0			0	.118
R. Thomas	OF16	16	33	8	8		1	1	0			4	.242

PITCHERS		W	L	PCT	G	GS	CG	SH	IP	H	BB	SO	ERA
LeRoy		20	10	.667	44				277	**297**	51	117	
H. Gardner		12	10	.545	31				181	203	84	81	
Dauss		12	19	.387	**51**				271	277	120	156	
Rieger		11	6	.647	25				161	165	35	48	
Karger		11	22	.333	46				276	281	99	125	
Decanniere		7	13	.350	38				181	195	94	104	
F. Thomas		2	8	.200	20				99	118	26	37	

LOUISVILLE Colonels

7th   66-101   .395   -40   Jack Tighe

BATTERS	POS-GAMES	GP	AB	R	H	BI	2B	3B	HR	BB	SO	SB	BA
Fisher	1B107	107	357	27	94		13	6	0			4	.263
Hulswitt	2B	(see multi-team players)											
Beaumiller	SS163	163	556	66	141		14	14	1			16	.254
Burke	3B91,2B35	141	483	57	117		16	5	1			7	.242
Burch	OF170	170	648	103	166		14	8	1			33	.256
Stansbury	OF116,3B16	142	529	49	159		25	7	0			13	.301
Hayden	OF95	95	308	24	76		13	5	0			9	.247
Schlei	C83	83	257	34	61		7	1	1			4	.237
Bell	2B50	50	184	13	34		5	1	0			2	.185
Bransfield	1B47	47	192	14	46		12	2	0			1	.240
G. Lowdermilk	P43	43	93	7	13		2	0	0			0	.140
Moskiman	P24	43	73	10	18		2	0	0			1	.247
Richter	P41	41	59	5	9		1	2	0			0	.153
Stanley	OF32	32	112	12	29		7	0	1			0	.259
Northrop	P36	36	74	8	11		1	0	0			1	.143
Ludwig	C32	32	72	3	12		1	0	0			1	.167
Spencer	C31	31	98	2	19		5	0	0			0	.194
Toney	P29	29	58	1	4		0	1	0			0	.069
Criss	P14	25	55	3	12		5	0	1			0	.218
Davis	1B23	23	60	3	17		0	1	0			1	.283
Madden	C15	15	31	7	9		1	0	0			1	.290

PITCHERS	W	L	PCT	G	GS	CG	SH	IP	H	BB	SO	ERA
G. Lowdermilk	17	16	.515	43				271	229	141	155	
Northrop	12	15	.444	36				221	214	68	91	
Toney	10	11	.476	29				177	121	78	95	
Moskiman	5	6	.455	24				125	129	25	26	
Richter	5	14	.263	41				188	196	88	86	
Snyder	3	3	.500	11								
R. Clemons	3	6	.333	12								
Vallandingham	2	2	.500	14								
Criss	1	6	.143	14								
Kroh	1	6	.143	10								

INDIANAPOLIS Indians

8th   56-111   .335   -50   Burke - O'Leary - O'Day

BATTERS	POS-GAMES	GP	AB	R	H	BI	2B	3B	HR	BB	SO	SB	BA
Hunter	1B138	138	452	69	121		16	10	1			19	.268
O. Williams	2B145	145	508	52	123		12	2	0			23	.242
O'Leary	SS84,2B16	109	395	39	85		5	2	0			10	.215
Ingerton	3B135	143	511	62	154		27	12	1			8	.301
Woodruff	OF138	150	578	76	145		15	2	0			27	.251
McCarty	OF90,C19	113	388	46	97		11	4	3			8	.250
Veach	OF70	70	253	37	72		13	3	4			15	.285
Clarke	C92	92	278	30	74		12	1	0			2	.266
Gagnier	SS70,OF22	92	318	23	71		10	4	0			8	.223
Hixon	P43	58	122	15	30		5	3	0			1	.246
Kaiser	OF56	56	198	25	53		6	3	0			10	.268
Merz	P44	44	95	3	10		1	1	0			1	.105
Keene	1B31	41	138	9	23		3	2	1			3	.167
E. Williams	OF35	35	135	13	32		3	4	0			7	.237
Reilley	OF35	35	134	14	38		2	2	0			15	.284
Link	P34	34	80	6	12		0	1	0			0	.150
McKee	C27	27	69	6	16		5	0	1			2	.232
Robertson ·	P22	22	58	7	9		1	0	0			0	.155
Wentz	SS17	21	65	6	10		2	0	0			2	.154
Ashenfelder	P21	21	43	2	8		0	0	0			0	.186
Wisterzil	3B19	19	68	8	14		1	2	0			0	.206

PITCHERS	W	L	PCT	G	GS	CG	SH	IP	H	BB	SO	ERA
Hixon	15	20	.429	43				279	281	103	129	
Link	12	17	.414	34				224	210	76	95	
Robertson	9	8	.529	22				164	166	31	50	
Merz	9	25	.265	44				280	274	81	95	
Ashenfelder	5	5	.500	21				121	103	76	49	

MULTI-TEAM PLAYERS

BATTERS	POS-GAMES	TEAMS	GP	AB	R	H	BI	2B	3B	HR	BB	SO	SB	BA
H. Hinchman	2B164	TOL-SP	164	644	98	166		22	6	0			27	.258
Congalton	OF143	COL-TOL	143	550	75	154		27	4	2			9	.280
Meloan	OF120	TOL-LOU	120	397	54	103		11	2	1			20	.259
Hulswitt	2B104	COL-LOU	117	400	49	121		13	7	4			14	.303
McCormick	SS60,3B28,2B19	SP-TOL	107	336	62	83		10	2	1			14	.247
Lennox	3B86	LOU-KC	98	315	37	82		16	7	3			6	.260
J. Lewis	2B72,SS19	SP-MIL	93	296	36	61		7	3	3			9	.206
Capron	OF88	MIL-SP	88	304	48	84		4	8	2			22	.276
Marshall	C85	MIL-SP	85	237	31	56		9	2	1			2	.236
Casey	C66	IND-SP	66	197	10	42		9	1	0			3	.213
Hallman	OF48	IND-LOU	48	172	27	38		2	3	0			8	.221
Liebhardt	P37	COL-MIN	39	76	9	16		2	0	0			0	.211
Pearce	C35	IND-LOU	35	103	7	24		4	1	0			1	.233
Maddox	P34	KC-LOU	34	58	3	15		1	0	0			0	.259
Schlitzer	P33	IND-KC	33	77	4	10		0	0	0			0	.130
D. Sullivan	OF30	KC-IND	30	101	15	25		5	0	1			0	.248
Kimball	P27	IND-COL	28	60	1	8		1	0	0			0	.133
Hohnhurst	1B20	TOL-IND	20	63	5	13		3	0	0			3	.206
Cann	P18	TOL-KC	18	19	0	2		0	0	0			0	.105

PITCHERS	TEAMS	W	L	PCT	G	GS	CG	SH	IP	H	BB	SO	ERA
Liebhardt	COL-MIN	10	11	.476	37				212	204	73	111	
Maddox	KC-LOU	10	13	.435	34				179	192	82	59	
Schlitzer	IND-KC	8	16	.333	33				235	261	51	93	
Kimball	IND-KC	6	14	.300	27				158	150	67	56	
Cann	TOL-KC	2	2	.500	18								

TEAM BATTING

TEAMS	GP	AB	R	H	BI	2B	3B	HR	BB	SO	SB	BA
MINNEAPOLIS	168	5570	**865**	**1549**		227	57	29			**292**	**.278**
TOLEDO	165	5408	715	1368		207	72	11			233	.253
COLUMBUS	168	**5587**	805	1462		215	87	33			138	.262
KANSAS CITY	168	5533	794	1477		**282**	56	**41**			184	.267
MILWAUKEE	163	5435	676	1380		182	70	27			169	.254
ST. PAUL	168	5503	739	1394		188	**99**	32			205	.253
LOUISVILLE	**170**	5458	591	1358		179	68	11			132	.249
INDIANAPOLIS	168	5464	604	1314		163	64	12			173	.240
	669	43958	5789	11302		1643	573	196			1526	.257

1913
Federal Threat

Early in 1913, a new baseball league was formed in the Midwest. Rising from the ashes of a failed venture known as the Columbian League, the reborn league posed a direct threat to the American Association. Christened the Federal League, the new organization was considered an outlaw league, existing and operating outside the aegis of the National Association, minor league baseball's governing body.

When the curtain opened on the 1913 season, the Feds had placed a team in one Association city, Indianapolis. The Indianapolis Federal franchise played in a facility across the city from the Indians' Association ballpark. When the Covington (Kentucky) Federal franchise folded in mid-season, it was transferred to Kansas City, where the Packers of the Federal League shared the Blues' Association digs. Both teams were seriously inconvenienced by the new upstarts.

The Milwaukee Brewers broke the three-year chokehold of Minneapolis, as they held off the Millers to win their first pennant by three games. Louisville made a startling jump to third, while Columbus rose to fourth. St. Paul, Toledo, Kansas City, and Indianapolis finished in the second division. Reilley of the last place Indians came in first in batting (.337) while Riggert of St. Paul hit the most home runs (12). Pitcher Slapnicka of the Brewers garnered top pitching honors as he compiled a 25-14 record, while Lowdermilk of Louisville won the strikeout crown (197).

The next threat posed by the Feds would be felt in Toledo. The Toledo Association franchise was owned by Charles Somers, a wealthy Cleveland businessman. Somers was also the owner of the American League's Cleveland entry. When the Federals started encroaching on the availability of Cleveland's League Park for the 1914 season, Somers got alarmed. (The Cleveland Federal team had played in Luna Park, which was considered inadequate, in 1913.) He had no desire to see a competing team in Cleveland, yet his American League club could not hope to occupy League Park 100 percent of the time. Somer's solution was simple. He transferred his Toledo team to Cleveland, where they would play in League Park when his American League was on the road. This was deemed a temporary measure, only to keep the Federals at bay. With no place to play, the Federals soon abandoned the idea of keeping their team in Cleveland and turned their attention elsewhere. It was ironic that the biggest impact of the Federals felt in the American Association was in a city not even threatened by a rival team. Although Indianapolis and Kansas City had to share their cities with other teams, Toledo had to share its team with another city, leaving Toledo with no team at all for the duration of the Federal League conflict.

MILWAUKEE Brewers

	1st	100-67	.599	Harry Clark

BATTERS	POS-GAMES	GP	AB	R	H	BI	2B	3B	HR	BB	SO	SB	BA
T. Jones	1B150	150	536	71	146		19	5	1			21	.272
Lewis	2B138	148	541	79	135		14	7	0			25	.250
Blackburne	SS163	165	580	80	153		21	7	1			31	.266
Clark	3B165	165	556	85	159		16	19	3			25	.286
Gilbert	OF149	155	557	89	157		21	6	10			43	.282
Randall	OF140	140	548	94	158		21	14	4			15	.288
Chapelle	OF85	85	350	60	122		15	11	5			12	.349
Hughes	C143	148	470	48	121		22	5	3			20	.257
Beall	OF78	79	279	50	70		7	11	1			19	.251
Berg	2B32	68	175	25	39		2	1	1			6	.223
Slapnicka	P47	51	112	13	27		1	0	0			2	.241
Marshall	C39	50	126	10	32		5	3	0			3	.254
Cutting	P39	39	93	6	15		0	0	0			1	.161
Dougherty	P35	35	96	11	26		7	1	0			0	.271
Braun	P35	35	55	8	7		1	0	0			1	.127
Hovlik	P27	27	50	2	5		0	0	0			1	.100
Felsch	OF23	26	71	4	13		4	1	2			2	.183
Watson	P17	17	20	1	5		0	2	0			1	.250
J. Nicholson	P15	15	25	2	2		0	0	0			0	.080

PITCHERS		W	L	PCT	G	GS	CG	SH	IP	H	BB	SO	ERA
Slapnicka		25	14	.641	47				321	311	113	129	
Cutting		21	9	.700	39				273	229	67	128	
Dougherty		14	9	.609	35				231	247	75	97	
Hovlik		11	9	.550	27				151	118	51	89	
Braun		10	7	.588	35				162	143	50	60	
Watson		5	3	.625	17				77	88	38	31	
J. Nicholson		3	7	.300	15								

MINNEAPOLIS Millers

	2nd	97-70	.581	-3	Joe Cantillon

BATTERS	POS-GAMES	GP	AB	R	H	BI	2B	3B	HR	BB	SO	SB	BA
J. Delahanty	1B107,OF45	157	610	81	181		25	4	4			5	.297
J. Williams	2B171	172	637	94	157		38	2	4			19	.246
Altizer	SS166	166	640	141	187		37	6	4			45	.293
Tannehill	3B	(see multi-team players)											
Rossman	OF143	155	549	72	166		24	5	4			14	.302
F. Delahanty	OF128	136	442	70	106		10	4	1			31	.240
Killifer	OF117,3B37	161	556	86	149		22	8	0			42	.268
Owens	C116	122	384	41	95		18	16	1			8	.247
Hunter	1B70,OF14	97	249	38	63		16	2	5			16	.253
W. Smith	C62	67	184	19	40		7	3	0			5	.217
Clymer	OF40	40	166	25	44		6	1	0			4	.265
Browne	OF29	38	111	21	31		7	1	1			5	.279
Olmstead	P37	38	85	8	20		5	0	0			1	.236
Patterson	P37	37	100	7	22		3	0	0			1	.220
Mogridge	P36	36	69	4	11		1	0	0			1	.159
Burns	P30	32	77	4	20		3	0	0			0	.260
Gilligan	P30	30	63	8	10		0	1	0			1	.157
Rondeau	C16	19	45	8	17		4	1	0			1	.378
Comstock	P18	18	51	5	5		1	0	0			0	.098

PITCHERS		W	L	PCT	G	GS	CG	SH	IP	H	BB	SO	ERA
Patterson		17	12	.583	37				288	267	38	131	
Olmstead		15	8	.652	37				202	213	56	86	
Mogridge		13	10	.565	36				202	214	49	72	
Burns		12	9	.571	30				203	218	36	62	
Gilligan		11	7	.611	30				162	152	64	75	
Comstock		10	5	.667	18								
Lake		5	3	.625	10								

LOUISVILLE Colonels   3rd   94-72   .566   -5.5   Jack Hayden

BATTERS	POS-GAMES	GP	AB	R	H	BI	2B	3B	HR	BB	SO	SB	BA
Weinberg	1B169	169	604	71	144		21	13	6			12	.238
Hulswitt	2B127	135	473	55	121		17	17	0			20	.256
Beaumiller	SS165	165	583	73	147		20	12	1			23	.252
Niehoff	3B170	170	581	89	172		31	14	6			48	.296
Osborn	OF171	171	668	101	214		17	20	2			12	.320
Burch	OF155	158	615	96	158		10	11	2			22	.257
Stansbury	OF145,2B24	169	638	78	145		18	9	0			23	.227
V. Clemons	C112	112	315	35	90		11	8	0			3	.286
Severeid	C80	92	273	30	76		14	7	2			10	.278
Lowdermilk	P51	51	107	7	21		6	2	0			0	.196
Northrop	P48	48	94	12	14		1	1	0			0	.149
J. Powell	P41	41	83	7	15		3	0	0			1	.181
Woodburn	P39	39	75	8	16		3	1	0			0	.213
Boyle	SS12	38	61	7	14		0	1	0			2	.230
O. Nicholson	OF29	32	107	21	28		3	1	2			2	.262
Toney	P24	24	61	3	11		1	4	0			0	.180
R. Clemons	P23	23	32	1	2		0	0	0			1	.063
F. Roth	C10	20	45	3	14		2	0	0			0	.311
Smith	P19	19	35	3	8		0	1	0			0	.229

PITCHERS		W	L	PCT	G	GS	CG	SH	IP	H	BB	SO	ERA
Lowdermilk		20	14	.588	51				304	235	137	197	
Northrop		17	10	.630	48				268	232	61	118	
J. Powell		17	13	.567	41				240	238	56	76	
Woodburn		15	10	.600	39				214	179	105	119	
Toney		13	8	.619	27				172	143	41	93	
R. Clemons		7	3	.700	23				102	99	31	33	
Smith		5	3	.625	19								
Ellis		0	5	.000	21								

COLUMBUS Senators   4th   93-74   .557   -7   William Hinchman

BATTERS	POS-GAMES	GP	AB	R	H	BI	2B	3B	HR	BB	SO	SB	BA
R. Miller	1B166	166	604	77	188		31	8	7			15	.311
Benson	2B164	164	625	85	147		22	10	5			7	.235
Gerber	SS167	167	592	63	154		15	10	3			10	.260
Perring	3B147	161	607	90	162		29	5	4			9	.267
W. Hinchman	OF167	167	593	120	176		43	12	9			19	.290
Shelton	OF144	144	592	115	160		25	13	2			26	.270
J. Jones	OF76	81	281	30	79		13	3	1			3	.281
S. Smith	C133	133	483	31	137		23	1	1			4	.284
Johns	OF23,3B23	54	184	18	35		7	1	0			3	.190
Cole	P46	46	123	8	18		2	2	0			1	.146
F. Davis	P44	44	100	5	22		5	0	0			0	.220
Cook	P43	43	85	4	12		0	0	0			0	.141
Murphy	C32	40	92	10	28		5	1	0			3	.304
Bonin	OF30	32	101	20	29		7	2	1			1	.287
Ferry	P27	27	83	7	19		4	0	0			0	.229
Eayrs	P16	27	59	15	22		3	1	0			0	.373
McQuillan	P21	21	44	3	7		1	0	0			0	.159
Kommers	OF20	20	70	7	15		2	3	0			1	.214

PITCHERS		W	L	PCT	G	GS	CG	SH	IP	H	BB	SO	ERA
Cole		23	11	.676	46				342	286	118	140	
F. Davis		17	16	.515	44				273	247	134	96	
Ferry		14	12	.538	27				225	203	57	66	
Cook		13	18	.419	43				268	262	101	80	
McQuillan		12	4	.750	21				129	102	26	38	
Eayrs		9	4	.692	16								
Turner		2	1	.667	14								

ST. PAUL Saints

ST. PAUL Saints	5th	75-87	.463	-22.5	William Friel			

BATTERS	POS-GAMES	GP	AB	R	H	BI	2B	3B	HR	BB	SO	SB	BA
Autry	1B169	169	617	64	161		15	5	1			9	.261
H. Hinchman	2B157	159	641	94	166		21	7	1			20	.263
Scott	SS168	168	620	72	167		20	6	1			26	.269
O'Rourke	3B130	141	537	91	127		9	7	0			14	.236
Riggert	OF165	165	614	95	179		19	23	12			24	.293
Rehg	OF120	122	474	55	141		15	18	2			14	.297
Hemphill	OF107	107	428	60	122		13	6	0			9	.285
A. James	C105	110	336	38	106		25	9	6			4	.315
Miller	C79	86	247	26	64		11	5	3			1	.259
Ferris	3B37,OF10	74	194	23	56		11	5	0			1	.288
E. Walker	P50	50	113	10	28		4	2	0			1	.248
H. Gardner	P44	44	89	10	21		2	1	0			0	.236
Rieger	P44	44	86	12	6		0	0	0			4	.070
Booe	OF40	43	141	21	42		7	4	0			12	.298
Karger	P40	43	124	15	25		7	4	1			0	.202
Schreiber	OF42	42	160	15	38		3	5	0			1	.238
McKechnie	3B22	32	110	11	27		0	6	0			6	.245
Brandt	P25	25	65	1	9		1	0	0			0	.138

PITCHERS	W	L	PCT	G	GS	CG	SH	IP	H	BB	SO	ERA
E. Walker	18	15	.545	50				290	282	98	153	
Karger	18	17	.514	40				292	292	80	104	
Rieger	15	16	.484	44				276	323	40	56	
H. Gardner	11	11	.500	44				245	233	91	98	
Brandt	8	10	.444	25				175	148	83	111	

KANSAS CITY Blues

KANSAS CITY Blues	6th (T)	69-98	.413	-31	William Armour			

BATTERS	POS-GAMES	GP	AB	R	H	BI	2B	3B	HR	BB	SO	SB	BA
C. Carr	1B72	77	256	26	68		20	0	3			2	.266
O. Williams	2B95	95	320	33	73		8	3	0			19	.228
Breton	SS65	66	233	30	55		5	5	1			10	.236
Barbeau	3B144	144	534	97	137		27	2	11			25	.257
Drake	OF131,1B32	154	611	61	163		40	4	4			17	.267
Walker	OF131	131	532	89	163		36	21	6			24	.307
Downey	OF45,2B34,SS33,3B14	134	457	65	116		23	5	2			8	.254
O'Connor	C104	115	353	32	83		8	8	0			4	.235
Roth	3B22,OF14	54	153	25	36		6	5	0			3	.236
Kritchell	C40	47	142	18	39		8	2	0			3	.275
Mattick	OF42	42	155	12	43		11	4	0			4	.278
Vaughn	P42	42	82	5	16		2	2	0			1	.195
Moore	C33	41	109	15	19		2	2	1			1	.174
Rath	2B39	39	144	24	42		5	2	0			6	.292
Rhoades	P38	38	76	6	18		3	2	1			0	.237
Brief	1B37	37	120	7	29		3	2	0			0	.225
Compton	OF36	36	130	15	34		4	4	4			7	.261
Gessler	OF33	35	112	10	32		6	2	1			1	.286
Covington	P35	35	65	4	10		1	0	0			0	.154
Baxter	OF22	31	77	17	19		2	1	0			10	.247
Morgan	P29	29	70	4	8		0	0	1			0	.114
Payne	OF24	25	100	5	22		1	0	2			1	.220
Coulson	OF19	20	75	7	21		2	2	0			1	.280
Harper	OF11	16	37	4	11		2	1	0			0	.297

PITCHERS	W	L	PCT	G	GS	CG	SH	IP	H	BB	SO	ERA
Morgan	15	8	.652	29				200	147	100	108	
Vaughn	14	13	.519	42				255	195	149	176	
Rhoades	11	16	.407	38				234	261	50	85	
Covington	5	15	.250	35				192	182	107	76	
Allison	4	5	.444	10								
Riley	1	4	.200	11								
Daniels	1	5	.167	11								

TOLEDO   6th (T)   69-98   .413   -31   Hartsel - Bronkie
Mud Hens

BATTERS	POS-GAMES	GP	AB	R	H	BI	2B	3B	HR	BB	SO	SB	BA
Bluhm	1B132	132	478	58	105		17	6	1			17	.220
E. Gardner	2B130	130	496	57	118		22	3	2			20	.238
Stumpf	SS83	88	292	25	59		10	3	1			6	.202
Bronkie	3B151,SS11	162	587	78	158		22	13	1			25	.269
Burns	OF131	133	475	50	122		18	10	1			7	.257
Kirke	OF91,1B30.3B16	136	525	56	168		26	9	8			15	.320
D. Jones	OF83	85	298	57	92		6	2	0			12	.309
DeVogt	C68	72	193	27	42		3	4	0			2	.218
Brady	SS72,2B30	104	369	56	94		8	10	2			18	.255
C. Jones	OF53	55	199	38	65		15	4	2			5	.327
Kruger	C41	44	145	16	37		6	1	0			4	.255
Collamore	P43	43	112	11	26		1	2	1			3	.232
George	P40	42	112	13	32		4	2	2			0	.286
Baskette	P31	39	98	14	22		2	3	1			0	.225
Southworth	OF37	37	117	10	26		6	0	1			4	.222
L.J. James	P30	30	78	6	10		0	0	0			1	.128
E. Smith	OF26	26	74	8	17		3	1	0			1	.230
Land	C25	25	78	5	15		1	0	0			2	.193
Hauger	OF22	22	73	7	16		2	0	0			4	.219
Warren	OF13	15	57	7	20		5	1	0			0	.351

PITCHERS		W	L	PCT	G	GS	CG	SH	IP	H	BB	SO	ERA
Collamore		18	15	.545	43				288	256	133	133	
George		16	20	.444	40				288	281	109	110	
L.J. James		14	15	.483	30				227	187	83	89	
Baskette		12	15	.444	31				213	200	61	74	
R. Walker		1	1	.500	11								
Dashner		1	3	.250	11								
Benn		1	4	.200	16								
Brenton		1	8	.111	10								
Stevenson		0	2	.000	11								

INDIANAPOLIS   8th   68-99   .407   -32   Mike Kelley
Indians

BATTERS	POS-GAMES	GP	AB	R	H	BI	2B	3B	HR	BB	SO	SB	BA
Metz	1B146	146	526	62	155		23	12	6			14	.295
Downs	2B58	59	226	30	57		10	7	1			6	.252
Crandall	SS88,2B66	154	525	65	129		24	4	1			24	.246
Krug	3B72,OF32,SS32	140	503	52	119		12	13	2			20	.237
Reilley	OF154	156	466	83	157		16	10	0			47	**.337**
Niles	OF74,3B67	144	544	85	141		9	8	3			18	.259
Gettman	OF59	61	237	33	54		7	4	1			8	.228
Casey	C72	73	220	15	52		5	2	0			3	.236
Galloway	3B30,OF23,2B19	84	249	22	65		7	2	3			8	.261
Livingston	C69	82	234	21	60		9	5	2			3	.260
Merz	P53	53	89	6	16		2	1	0			0	.180
Schardt	P51	51	84	5	11		3	1	0			0	.131
Harrington	P44	44	69	6	11		0	3	0			1	.159
Cotter	C38	40	109	12	19		3	0	0			4	.174
Works	P39	39	70	4	8		0	0	0			0	.114
Kelliher	SS36	36	115	13	26		0	1	0			3	.226
Clarke	C27	28	78	10	22		6	0	0			4	.278
Kaiserling	P27	27	35	4	5		2	0	0			0	.143
Willis	P23	23	60	5	7		0	0	0			0	.117
Stewart	OF16	18	55	4	15		1	1	0			4	.272
Wheeler	OF17	17	64	6	11		2	1	0			2	.171
McCarty	1B15	15	55	6	7		1	1	0			1	.127

PITCHERS		W	L	PCT	G	GS	CG	SH	IP	H	BB	SO	ERA
Merz		15	14	.517	**53**				272	258	90	108	
Schardt		12	17	.414	51				275	255	98	103	
Willis		10	10	.500	23				174	163	49	59	
Works		8	18	.308	39				209	209	91	82	
Harrington		7	17	.292	44				209	184	137	110	
Kaiserling		5	7	.417	27				109	121	38	39	
Burk		5	9	.357	15								
Wetzel		1	2	.333	11								

MULTI-TEAM PLAYERS

BATTERS	POS-GAMES	TEAMS	GP	AB	R	H	BI	2B	3B	HR	BB	SO	SB	BA
Tannehill	3B92,SS62	KC-MIN	162	552	59	121		20	1	1			7	.219
Flynn	OF92,1B17	SP-IND	122	419	48	104		19	8	1			18	.248
Eddington	OF100	COL-TOL	106	336	50	84		7	10	3			6	.250
Woodruff	OF79	IND-MIL	86	299	29	67		6	2	0			6	.224
Fiene	1B38,OF22,P11	KC-MIN	85	266	34	78		17	2	1			4	.293
T. Downey	2B49	IND-LOU	71	223	23	48		9	3	1			15	.215
Whelan	OF31,3B26	IND-MIN	70	223	26	48		2	3	0			9	.215
LeRoy	P44	SP-IND	44	80	5	12		1	0	0			0	.150
Young	P41	MIN-MIL	41	66	7	9		0	0	0			1	.136
W. Powell	P33	KC-MIL	33	59	1	9		2	0	0			0	.153
Schlitzer	P29	KC-TOL	29	43	2	8		0	0	0			1	.186
Ingerton	OF16	IND-LOU	23	73	12	22		6	1	0			3	.301

PITCHERS		TEAMS	W	L	PCT	G	GS	CG	SH	IP	H	BB	SO	ERA
Young		MIN-MIL	15	10	.600	41				226	214	45	112	
LeRoy		SP-IND	11	20	.355	44				235	251	50	90	
Fiene		KC-MIN	7	2	.778	11								
W. Powell		KC-MIL	7	15	.318	33				182	211	92	68	
Schlitzer		KC-TOL	6	8	.429	29				138	167	27	44	
Zabel		KC-LOU	1	4	.200	11								

TEAM BATTING

TEAMS	GP	AB	R	H	BI	2B	3B	HR	BB	SO	SB	BA
MILWAUKEE	170	5530	764	1443		183	91	31			227	.261
MINNEAPOLIS	173	5739	818	1489		253	58	25			202	.259
LOUISVILLE	171	5634	725	1458		176	131	20			189	.259
COLUMBUS	170	5686	655	1489		239	75	31			111	.262
ST. PAUL	169	5735	739	1521		185	112	26			151	.265
KANSAS CITY	169	5595	690	1411		250	78	40			154	.253
TOLEDO	168	5525	677	1381		199	86	26			160	.250
INDIANAPOLIS	172	5593	601	1386		195	83	22			185	.248
	681	45037	5669	11578		1680	714	221			1379	.257

1914
Jake Northrop

Of all the great pitchers to play in the American Association, only one managed to win over 200 games during his Association career. This pitcher played for fourteen seasons for four different teams during his record breaking career. His name was George Howard Northrop, but he was more commonly known as Jake.

Born in Pennsylvania, Jake Northrop started his baseball career for Trenton in the Tri-State League in 1909. After two mediocre seasons and one astonishingly good one (27-4) in the Tri-State, he was acquired by the Association's Louisville Colonels for the start of the 1912 campaign. Two decent seasons, a 12–15 record for a seventh place team in 1913 and a 17–10 record for a third place team in 1914, left Northrop primed for a stellar season in 1915.

Playing for a true flag contender for the first time, Jake Northrop responded in kind. He pitched Louisville into second place with 26 wins, with only 10 losses, while throwing a stalwart 329 innings. This proved to be his best season.

Finishing just four games ahead of Louisville was Milwaukee, which won its second championship in a row. Five and one-half games behind the Colonels, in third, rested Indianapolis, who made a dramatic rise from the cellar. Following these three were Columbus, the transposed Toledo squad in Cleveland, Kansas City, Minneapolis, and St. Paul. Batting laurels went to Hinchman of Columbus (.366), while Milwaukee's Felsch swatted the most home runs (19). On the pitching side, under the new earned run average statistic, the first winner was Toledo/Cleveland's James who finished with a mark of 2.35. Northrop's teammate, Lowdermilk struck out the most batters (254). Gallia of Kansas City shared the League lead with Northrop with 26 wins.

After his fine 1914 season, Jake Northrop pitched two more seasons in Louisville before jumping to Indianapolis. After a short stay with the Indians, Northrop joined the Boston Braves of the National League for an even briefer stay. Following his six victory major league career, he rejoined the American Association, this time with Milwaukee. He finished his Association career pitching for a dreadful Columbus team during the 1920's. For each of his first three Association teams, Northrop managed at least one twenty-win season. Toiling for Columbus, he lost nearly twenty in four of the five seasons he spent there. That is why in addition to his record of most Association wins (222), he also unfortunately holds the record for the most losses (189).

MILWAUKEE Brewers
1st   98-68   .590   Harry Clark

BATTERS	POS-GAMES	GP	AB	R	H	BI	2B	3B	HR	BB	SO	SB	BA
T. Jones	1B163	163	589	69	146		22	3	2	39	23	17	.248
Lewis	2B156	160	617	91	182		23	11	4	63	15	27	.295
Berg	SS113,2B18,3B16	148	582	101	142		22	5	2	78	60	23	.244
Clark	3B142	150	478	108	144		25	4	4	**143**	37	16	.301
Beall	OF169	169	603	92	188		28	19	10	94	87	27	.312
Randall	OF168	168	651	110	209		27	11	6	77	43	29	.321
Felsch	OF145	151	576	99	175		41	11	**19**	30	**114**	19	.304
Hughes	C151	153	493	63	132		18	6	2	59	60	15	.268
Barbeau	SS46	68	201	40	56		10	3	2	52	20	15	.279
McGraw	C32	48	111	8	22		9	0	0	8	24	1	.198
Hovlik	P47	47	115	12	18		3	0	0	10	27	0	.157
Young	P47	47	108	5	18		0	1	0	3	36	2	.167
Cutting	P30	30	55	2	5		0	0	0	2	15	0	.091
Dougherty	P25	29	67	10	14		3	1	0	6	7	1	.119
Slapnicka	P28	29	58	8	6		0	1	0	9	15	0	.103
Braun	P29	29	50	4	12		2	2	0	8	17	2	.240
Shackelford	P23	23	48	5	10		0	0	0	3	15	0	.208
W. Powell	P22	22	33	4	10		1	1	0	3	4	0	.303
Sheehan		16	36	8	10		0	2	0	4	5	0	.278

PITCHERS	W	L	PCT	G	GS	CG	SH	IP	H	BB	SO	ERA
Hovlik	24	14	.632	47				323	278	134	216	2.54
Young	20	16	.556	47				304	292	66	111	2.87
Dougherty	14	4	**.778**	25				163	174	81	53	3.60
Shackelford	11	2	.846	23				135	137	49	54	2.87
Cutting	9	8	.529	30				167	165	45	82	2.91
Slapnicka	8	9	.471	28				157	155	82	62	3.84
Braun	6	5	.545	29				136	140	48	73	3.31
W. Powell	5	9	.357	22				99	112	54	37	4.00

LOUISVILLE Colonels
2nd   95-73   .565   -4   Jack Hayden

BATTERS	POS-GAMES	GP	AB	R	H	BI	2B	3B	HR	BB	SO	SB	BA
Weinberg	1B151	154	535	75	142		20	13	2	73	78	4	.265
McLarry	2B155	157	529	93	167		36	9	11	88	52	21	.316
Beaumiller	SS130	130	453	86	108		13	7	1	79	59	9	.238
Dodge	3B82	84	274	34	55		8	8	0	46	37	16	.201
Osborn	OF170	170	656	94	174		16	16	3	74	24	21	.265
Ingerton	OF120,1B26	153	558	66	142		33	5	2	10	66	54	.254
Stansbury	OF109,3B36	160	655	96	182		26	11	1	64	26	17	.278
Severeid	C125	143	515	88	163		24	10	6	61	24	14	.317
Burch	OF92	107	324	60	93		10	3	0	66	27	8	.287
V. Clemons	C54,P12	91	216	30	72		17	7	0	22	17	4	.333
Midkiff	3B55	69	266	38	72		9	3	2	32	22	10	.271
Toney	P49	49	115	3	21		2	0	0	4	21	1	.183
Northrop	P46	46	114	6	17		1	2	0	9	27	2	.149
Lowdermilk	P42	42	106	6	24		2	3	1	3	26	2	.227
Clothier	SS28	33	104	10	26		4	0	0	21	14	0	.250
Ellis	P33	33	49	4	8		0	1	0	1	13	0	.163
Perry	P21	21	28	2	3		1	0	0	4	11	0	.107
Calahan	OF19	19	60	11	18		1	1	0	3	5	1	.300
Leverette	P19	19	28	4	9		1	0	0	0	6	0	.321

PITCHERS	W	L	PCT	G	GS	CG	SH	IP	H	BB	SO	ERA
Northrop	**26**	10	.722	46				329	329	87	114	3.18
Toney	21	15	.583	49				311	304	96	152	3.21
Lowdermilk	18	16	.529	42				284	224	159	**254**	2.85
Ellis	9	6	.600	33				147	152	35	52	3.25
Danforth	6	5	.545	13				89	80	48	74	3.84
Perry	4	1	.800	21				84	101	42	28	4.82
W. Taylor	4	1	.800	7				44	32	22	20	2.25
Leverette	2	5	.286	19				73	88	59	32	8.14
Baker	1	3	.250	11				48	49	17	22	3.19
V. Clemons	1	3	.250	12				45	58	18	25	4.20
Woodburn	1	3	.250	6				30	26	32	16	4.50

INDIANAPOLIS Indians

3rd	88-77	.533	-9.5	J.C. Hendricks

BATTERS	POS-GAMES	GP	AB	R	H	BI	2B	3B	HR	BB	SO	SB	BA
Metz	1B169	169	621	99	184		19	9	4	95	44	24	.296
Crandall	2B143	146	505	76	135		18	11	2	71	38	21	.267
Kelleher	SS100	115	353	42	73		6	8	2	29	42	13	.207
Bronkie	3B157	157	600	93	158		20	9	1	68	67	35	.263
Cole	OF154	155	548	91	142		24	12	1	100	56	30	.259
Griffith	OF136	136	500	79	170		26	18	3	57	29	24	.340
Reilley	OF135	137	536	94	140		24	6	0	70	54	32	.261
Livingston	C109	124	376	62	120		23	11	2	46	17	9	.319
Galloway	SS80,2B27	132	427	56	124		18	15	4	33	46	4	.290
Merz	P48	48	111	10	19		3	1	2	4	38	1	.171
J. Willis	P46	46	107	8	24		1	0	1	3	14	1	.224
Blackburn	C38	45	127	25	33		9	3	1	21	26	0	.260
LeRoy	P44	44	73	5	19		2	1	0	6	16	2	.260
McCarthy	OF27	41	106	16	27		6	3	0	10	19	1	.255
Gossett	C34	40	115	6	25		4	0	0	7	17	2	.217
Burk	P35	35	63	1	9		0	0	0	1	16	0	.143
Schardt	P34	34	81	9	17		2	0	0	11	26	0	.210
Adams	P26	26	61	6	7		2	1	0	9	30	0	.115
Allen	OF22	25	81	12	15		2	1	0	19	22	5	.185

PITCHERS	W	L	PCT	G	GS	CG	SH	IP	H	BB	SO	ERA
Merz	20	19	.513	48				314	311	88	78	3.83
J. Willis	19	13	.594	46				291	277	90	142	2.57
Adams	13	8	.619	26				176	164	77	83	3.47
Schardt	13	12	.520	34				234	236	69	73	2.93
LeRoy	12	5	.706	44				201	226	50	54	3.27
Burk	7	14	.333	35				195	197	100	70	3.10
Harrington	2	2	.500	6				18	25	10	7	6.00
O'Brien	2	4	.333	8				50	60	33	26	5.58

COLUMBUS Senators

4th	86-77	.528	-10.5	William Hinchman

BATTERS	POS-GAMES	GP	AB	R	H	BI	2B	3B	HR	BB	SO	SB	BA
R. Miller	1B142	155	555	91	177		2	10	8	85	32	12	.319
Benson	2B91	93	345	50	83		19	5	1	29	31	5	.241
Gerber	SS161	161	619	96	160		17	7	1	57	37	14	.259
Johns	3B151	152	573	92	167		27	6	6	51	26	11	.291
W. Hinchman	OF163	163	620	**139**	**227**		57	21	9	87	39	21	**.366**
Shelton	OF131	132	514	116	129		14	12	4	92	61	30	.251
Dell	OF81	81	299	52	82		8	3	2	42	17	20	.275
S. Smith	C146	148	549	44	157		27	3	0	36	18	5	.286
Daley	2B61,3B15	95	312	47	82		9	5	1	32	54	5	.263
Earys	P28,OF16	81	164	18	37		7	2	0	16	9	3	.226
Davis	P44	44	94	6	22		2	0	0	6	10	0	.234
Cook	P37	37	94	13	23		4	1	0	5	20	0	.245
Scheneberg	P35	35	86	8	16		2	1	0	2	21	0	.186
Thompson	1B24	29	100	8	18		4	0	0	3	15	1	.180
Robertson	C27	29	81	8	18		4	2	0	4	21	1	.222
Ferry	P23	23	52	4	9		0	0	0	3	13	0	.173
Shovlin	2B15	17	57	10	13		2	1	2	4	7	1	.228

PITCHERS	W	L	PCT	G	GS	CG	SH	IP	H	BB	SO	ERA
Cook	18	11	.621	37				242	233	103	77	3.65
Scheneberg	16	10	.610	35				232	193	156	78	3.41
Davis	15	10	.600	44				247	252	127	107	3.65
Earys	11	9	.550	28				182	165	117	87	4.00
Ferry	8	8	.500	23				139	160	40	33	3.82
Goshorn	4	3	.571	8				48	45	25	9	3.19
Boothby	3	2	.600	9				40	41	20	16	3.15
McVaugh	2	2	.500	9				34	43	23	8	5.56
Green	2	3	.400	8				54	52	27	20	3.00
Humphrey	2	5	.286	12				63	68	27	20	4.00
B. Taylor	1	4	.200	12				66	79	30	15	6.68

TOLEDO (CLEVELAND)   5th   82-81   .503   -14.5   James Sheckard
Mud Hens

BATTERS	POS-GAMES	GP	AB	R	H	BI	2B	3B	HR	BB	SO	SB	BA
Lelivelt	1B92	92	369	56	109		11	7	3	18	20	8	.295
E. Gardner	2B112	118	456	64	131		17	7	0	33	30	20	.287
Knight	SS132	135	530	75	163		26	13	3	46	55	13	.308
Stumpf	3B62,2B52,SS15	132	478	54	137		16	7	0	47	48	21	.287
Southworth	OF138	139	483	78	123		12	11	1	87	29	22	.255
Wilie	OF122	122	468	95	148		21	14	3	72	52	30	.316
Sheckard	OF115	119	371	58	94		21	3	0	90	46	8	.253
DeVogt	C111	114	373	35	91		14	4	0	49	49	4	.249
Kirke	1B46,OF24	74	307	44	107		17	6	3	6	21	6	.349
Bates	3B62	72	262	35	76		10	6	1	11	18	9	.290
Hillyard	OF60	66	214	31	60		15	5	2	19	35	7	.280
T. Reilly	3B38	57	194	25	45		7	4	0	19	32	6	.232
Billings	C43	47	145	13	33		5	0	0	7	17	3	.228
George	P40	44	126	14	38		6	2	0	4	16	0	.302
Kahler	P38	38	84	5	11		3	0	0	3	33	0	.131
Brenton	P32	32	79	7	15		2	0	0	7	18	0	.190
Lush	P10	25	52	3	12		3	0	0	5	7	2	.230
E. Smith	OF23	23	90	4	28		4	4	0	3	3	1	.311
S. Jones	P23	23	43	3	4		1	0	0	7	18	0	.093
Paulette	1B22	22	76	9	18		4	1	0	3	7	1	.237
W. James	P19	19	51	1	6		1	1	0	4	7	0	.118
Neale	OF17	18	48	8	11		1	0	1	4	8	1	.229
Spellman		15	41	5	11		1	2	0	6	6	0	.268

PITCHERS		W	L	PCT	G	GS	CG	SH	IP	H	BB	SO	ERA
Kahler		15	11	.577	38				238	236	104	108	3.06
Brenton		14	11	.560	32				212	187	105	112	3.39
George		13	18	.419	40				275	266	119	94	3.90
S. Jones		10	4	.714	23				129	112	64	50	2.44
W. James		9	6	.600	19				134	105	65	83	**2.35**
Collamore		5	4	.556	9				77	69	37	37	3.63
Lush		3	5	.375	10				67	88	20	26	5.24
Benn		2	5	.286	14				66	56	50	23	4.23
Bowman		2	5	.286	9				57	54	48	20	3.31
Hoffer		1	0	1.000	7				28	21	23	7	2.89
Beck		1	3	.250	7				35	27	31	9	5.40
Haggerty		0	1	.000	5				17	17	10	6	3.71
Frost		0	0	----	6				21	29	11	11	4.29

KANSAS CITY   6th   84-84   .500   -15   William Armour
Blues

BATTERS	POS-GAMES	GP	AB	R	H	BI	2B	3B	HR	BB	SO	SB	BA
Brief	1B169	169	645	117	205		51	16	12	77	70	38	.318
Rath	2B155	167	669	122	226		23	6	0	77	26	36	.338
Wortman	SS141,3B28	169	627	76	146		13	8	2	49	65	42	.233
Downey	3B112,2B15	137	493	54	114		17	4	0	71	47	7	.231
Compton	OF164	166	607	89	197		33	13	11	63	59	58	.325
Mattick	OF127	137	500	73	137		30	4	0	49	29	17	.274
Roth	OF114	123	464	91	136		28	19	12	52	102	29	.293
Geibel	C103	109	354	37	86		5	4	0	41	33	4	.233
Titus	OF96	98	315	62	108		10	7	7	70	26	11	.343
Moore	C70	80	248	31	66		10	6	1	30	30	3	.266
Delhi	P32,OF20	61	167	21	41		5	2	0	6	27	2	.246
Gallia	P51	51	17	6	14		2	0	0	6	40	0	.120
Allison	P35	35	73	4	10		1	0	0	2	17	0	.137
Pfeffer	SS32	32	113	21	20		3	0	0	27	18	2	.177
Regan	P29	29	72	15	14		2	0	0	7	13	0	.194
Morgan	P22	22	40	1	8		1	0	0	1	10	0	.200
Richie	P21	21	41	1	2		0	0	0	5	11	0	.049

PITCHERS		W	L	PCT	G	GS	CG	SH	IP	H	BB	SO	ERA
Gallia		**26**	12	.684	**51**				326	279	109	164	2.65
Regan		13	9	.591	29				192	229	90	82	5.20
Delhi		12	11	.522	32				196	219	54	62	4.18
Allison		8	17	.320	35				210	248	71	38	4.50
Richie		6	7	.462	21				132	149	42	25	4.37
Morgan		6	10	.375	22				112	101	90	42	5.06
McCoy		1	4	.200	13				72	86	37	27	5.00

MINNEAPOLIS Millers

MINNEAPOLIS Millers   7th   75-93   .446   -24   Joe Cantillon

BATTERS	POS-GAMES	GP	AB	R	H	BI	2B	3B	HR	BB	SO	SB	BA
Hunter	1B141	141	485	72	116		19	6	2	57	79	25	.239
J. Williams	2B143	146	551	66	158		25	7	3	48	49	6	.287
Altizer	SS170	170	635	132	210		37	9	14	99	24	32	.331
Tannehill	3B170	170	609	52	167		21	6	1	39	41	7	.274
Killifer	OF103,2B15	118	430	102	148		31	11	0	59	21	42	.344
Rossman	OF94	101	377	41	95		15	3	1	38	22	3	.252
Rondeau	OF82,C64	150	510	78	157		37	5	2	49	37	15	.308
W. Smith	C105	109	360	37	79		14	2	0	35	40	8	.219
Fiene	OF51,P26,1B23	124	388	49	112		21	4	2	23	42	2	.288
Lake	P37,OF29	86	231	32	78		15	1	5	6	36	0	.338
Whelan	OF68	79	251	38	57		9	1	0	49	38	6	.227
Uhler	OF70	70	270	32	72		11	3	0	28	29	8	.267
Hogue	P48	48	88	11	16		3	0	0	16	27	0	.182
Clymer	OF25	26	101	18	23		4	1	0	12	9	2	.228
Gharrity	C18	21	57	4	13		1	2	1	4	13	0	.228
Patterson	P20	21	56	3	8		0	0	0	6	8	0	.143
Gilligan	P20	21	49	4	13		2	0	0	2	10	1	.265

PITCHERS		W	L	PCT	G	GS	CG	SH	IP	H	BB	SO	ERA
Lake		16	13	.552	37				273	304	69	102	3.56
Fiene		13	10	.565	26				196	197	54	46	3.72
Hogue		12	17	.414	48				237	240	118	85	4.37
Patterson		9	9	.500	21				162	170	42	55	3.50
Gilligan		6	9	.400	20				138	154	61	52	3.98
Dumont		3	3	.500	9				59	72	28	17	5.64
Nelson		2	2	.500	9				33	30	22	6	3.82
Duval		2	3	.400	5				20	25	19	6	4.50
Drucke		1	5	.167	10				40	49	38	20	6.92
Case		0	2	.000	5				31	36	21	9	7.29

ST. PAUL Saints

ST. PAUL Saints   8th   56-111   .335   -42.5   William Friel

BATTERS	POS-GAMES	GP	AB	R	H	BI	2B	3B	HR	BB	SO	SB	BA
Autry	1B168	168	584	59	139		25	4	0	60	42	6	.238
H. Hinchman	2B164	164	652	75	174		22	11	0	39	48	15	.267
McNally	SS110	110	402	51	105		7	7	1	35	30	16	.261
O'Rourke	3B119	143	510	78	113		12	8	4	87	48	14	.222
Paddock	OF117	122	487	71	139		24	8	5	45	32	8	.285
Murray	OF74	74	281	42	74		12	5	7	23	41	9	.263
Niles	OF		(see multi-team players)										
Glenn	C92	104	337	29	90		7	4	0	40	22	5	.267
James	C80	104	275	33	77		17	2	10	52	40	2	.280
Hall	OF52,P37	99	315	47	93		9	5	4	10	35	5	.295
McCormick	OF59	63	229	21	64		15	2	0	13	28	2	.279
E. Walker	P50	50	141	13	25		2	1	0	9	29	0	.177
Johnson	3B36	45	160	31	38		8	2	0	20	23	0	.238
Karger	P33	45	132	10	30		7	1	0	0	14	1	.227
H. Gardner	P42	42	90	4	17		2	0	0	2	21	0	.186
Hopper	P37	37	86	3	15		2	0	0	1	17	0	.174
Hemphill	OF30	31	101	7	28		3	0	0	10	6	4	.277
Nifnecker	SS21	21	85	15	20		1	1	0	6	10	7	.236

PITCHERS		W	L	PCT	G	GS	CG	SH	IP	H	BB	SO	ERA
E. Walker		18	19	.486	50				335	340	164	189	4.00
Hall		12	17	.414	37				258	296	125	106	4.08
Hopper		9	16	.360	37				228	235	86	75	3.87
Karger		7	23	.233	33				235	265	86	85	4.67
H. Gardner		6	25	.194	42				265	276	102	116	4.21
Larsen		2	3	.400	5				41	46	19	16	6.14
Works		1	2	.333	9				30	30	24	8	6.30
Boardman		0	2	.000	9				31	59	20	14	8.71

MULTI-TEAM PLAYERS

BATTERS	POS-GAMES	TEAMS	GP	AB	R	H	BI	2B	3B	HR	BB	SO	SB	BA
Niles	OF100,SS31	IND-SP	147	594	84	178		27	6	2	53	42	14	.300
J. Jones	OF54	COL-MIL	65	206	31	47		9	1	0	18	12	5	.228
Bailey	OF61	SP-COL	63	224	44	65		12	4	3	59	33	11	.290
Capron	OF40	MIL-SP	49	142	14	30		2	1	0	9	20	2	.211
Burns	P47	MIN-LOU	47	87	6	13		2	0	0	9	19	1	.149
Baskette	P44	T/C-KC	44	95	10	26		5	1	1	4	16	1	.274
Eddington	OF27	COL-IND	28	102	12	25		0	0	1	20	9	10	.245
Ingersoll	P26	COL-MIN	26	61	3	8		0	1	0	2	19	1	.131
Covington	P15	T/C-KC	16	33	4	8		1	0	0	4	8	1	.242

PITCHERS	TEAMS	W	L	PCT	G	GS	CG	SH	IP	H	BB	SO	ERA
Baskette	T/C-KC	13	15	.464	44				239	246	107	103	4.52
Burns	MIN-LOU	10	18	.357	47				263	306	61	104	3.73
Ingersoll	COL-MIN	7	11	.389	26				168	155	81	42	3.75
Covington	T/C-KC	6	5	.545	15				96	42	64	48	3.10

TEAM BATTING

TEAMS	GP	AB	R	H	BI	2B	3B	HR	BB	SO	SB	BA
MILWAUKEE	169	5607	855	1527		236	83	**51**	705	657	189	.272
LOUISVILLE	170	5726	816	1530		226	100	30	**732**	587	140	.267
INDIANAPOLIS	169	5511	811	1472		207	**109**	24	684	642	212	.267
COLUMBUS	165	5628	**874**	1533		247	86	36	631	534	136	.272
TOLEDO (CLEV.)	166	5623	741	1535		225	98	17	569	638	161	.273
KANSAS CITY	169	**5734**	849	**1578**		238	89	46	652	**666**	**239**	**.275**
MINNEAPOLIS	170	5719	791	1572		**271**	61	33	603	597	154	.275
ST. PAUL	168	5720	692	1471		207	70	34	534	575	109	.257
	673	45268	5699	12218		1857	696	271	5110	4896	1340	.270

1915
Twin Cities

The eight cities comprising the original American Association were all located in the Midwest, and the distance between some of the cities was several hundred miles. However, for two league cities this was not the case, for they were located within spitting distance of each other, with their ballparks less than ten miles apart.

In the other two top minor leagues, the International League and the Pacific Coast League, adjacent city rivalries were also present. In the International League, two New Jersey cities, Newark and Jersey City, were near neighbors. In the Pacific Coast League, two pairs of cities in California (Oakland and San Francisco, as well as Los Angeles and Hollywood) coexisted peaceably. In the Association, the two nearby franchises were located in the twin cities of Minnesota, Minneapolis and St. Paul.

From the outset of organized baseball leagues in the 19th century, Minneapolis and St. Paul had been natural adversaries. For example, both cities fielded teams in the Northwestern League (1886-87), the Western Association (1888–90), and the Western League (1892–99). It was a natural continuation of their rivalry to include both cities in the American Association when it was formed in 1902.

In 1915, the competition between the twin cities reached a fever pitch, as the two spent the summer battling for the pennant. At the beginning of June, matters looked bleak for both teams as St. Paul resided in fourth place, while Minneapolis sat in the cellar. The Saints made their move late in June, and by mid–July had reached first. The Millers, with a lot farther to go, waited a little longer before starting their rise through the standings. By September, thanks to an 18-game winning streak, the Millers had caught and passed the Saints. The two battled through the month before the Millers finally prevailed by a slender one and one-half game margin.

Indianapolis, which had led the pack for most of the season, had to settle for third, while Louisville finished fourth. Farther back were Kansas City, Milwaukee, Cleveland/Toledo, and Columbus. The league's best hitter was Lelivelt from Kansas City (.346), while Riggert of St. Paul had the most home runs (9). The twin cities boasted all the pitching leaders as Minneapolis had win leader Williams (29) and earned run average leader Yingling (2.17), while St. Paul enjoyed the services of strikeout leader Steele (183). Also of note was the 16-game winning streak by Saint pitcher Hall, the longest streak in Association history. The 1915 pennant race was special in more than one way. Not only was it a spirited contest between two natural opponents, it was also one of only two times that the Millers and the Saints finished in first and second, thus giving a special flavor to their rivalry.

MINNEAPOLIS   1st   92-62   .597   Joe Cantillon
Millers

BATTERS	POS-GAMES	GP	AB	R	H	BI	2B	3B	HR	BB	SO	SB	BA
Autry	1B137	138	486	50	140		22	9	1	35	25	2	.288
Holland	2B97	107	407	58	99		7	2	0	56	22	11	.243
Jennings	SS119	127	476	69	146		24	6	0	44	34	7	.307
W. Smith	3B154	154	550	95	173		31	10	4	71	36	15	.315
R. Massey	OF149	151	575	103	168		28	11	1	86	42	19	.292
Rondeau	OF128	129	496	97	165		27	7	2	53	42	23	.333
Altizer	OF114,SS35	149	582	**118**	176		26	11	8	72	26	19	.302
Sullivan	C104	105	339	28	73		11	4	0	20	48	3	.215
Cashion	OF40,1B36	98	297	40	97		21	13	3	19	30	5	.327
J. Williams	2B63	91	287	39	76		7	2	1	32	18	2	.265
Gharrity	C70	86	227	38	70		22	3	1	23	34	5	.308
D.C. Williams	P64	64	161	17	26		4	1	0	13	63	0	.161
Yingling	P47	50	131	15	33		5	0	0	11	12	2	.252
Ingersoll	P28	28	41	1	8		2	0	0	0	13	1	.195
Hopper	P22	22	73	9	13		2	0	0	0	16	0	.179
Harper	P21	21	55	2	10		0	0	0	1	14	0	.182
Bentley	P14	16	42	9	10		1	2	0	1	3	1	.239

PITCHERS		W	L	PCT	G	GS	CG	SH	IP	H	BB	SO	ERA
D.C. Williams		**29**	16	.644	**64**				**441**	392	164	180	2.53
Yingling		19	13	.594	47				291	258	96	109	**2.17**
Hopper		18	3	**.857**	22				177	177	45	17	2.59
Bentley		7	4	.636	14				85	79	49	32	3.18
Harper		7	9	.438	21				154	99	127	148	2.81
Engel		5	3	.625	15				64	72	61	24	6.47
Ingersoll		5	11	.313	28				131	135	63	36	3.71
Hogue		2	2	.500	6								
Willey		0	1	.000	2								

ST. PAUL   2nd   90-63   .588   -1.5   Mike Kelley
Saints

BATTERS	POS-GAMES	GP	AB	R	H	BI	2B	3B	HR	BB	SO	SB	BA
Dressen	1B133	135	438	67	109		18	1	2	59	41	42	.249
O'Leary	2B84	87	302	31	78		11	0	0	22	20	9	.258
Martin	SS145	145	510	67	118		19	4	0	76	45	20	.231
Dyer	3B107,P3	119	397	44	93		19	11	4	58	**82**	4	.234
Riggert	OF144	145	542	102	153		20	16	**9**	53	67	24	.282
Cruise	OF128	134	473	82	139		16	14	6	61	56	16	.294
Paddock	OF112	117	418	65	116		18	10	7	59	43	11	.277
Johnson	C103	107	350	45	93		16	3	2	20	28	1	.266
Niles	OF59,2B58,3B37	**156**	613	87	171		22	13	6	83	48	19	.279
Glenn	C59	63	189	30	56		4	2	1	20	10	7	.296
Hall	P42	57	137	11	29		9	1	1	10	19	2	.211
R. Steele	P54	54	113	3	19		1	1	0	4	23	2	.168
Leifield	P41	41	83	9	16		3	1	0	18	14	0	.193
Karger	P25	30	59	4	18		5	2	0	3	4	0	.305
R. Williams	P27	27	54	3	7		1	0	0	8	12	0	.130
Marshall	C16	17	43	8	11		0	1	1	9	9	1	.255

PITCHERS		W	L	PCT	G	GS	CG	SH	IP	H	BB	SO	ERA
Hall		24	10	.706	42				299	253	98	108	2.62
R. Steele		20	16	.556	54				316	265	142	**183**	2.48
Leifield		17	14	.548	41				273	247	92	107	2.40
R. Williams		15	6	.714	27				161	157	49	43	2.18
Karger		4	10	.286	25				122	132	46	43	3.76
LeRoy		3	2	.600	11				57	52	16	24	3.00
Gipe		1	0	1.000	4								
North		1	0	1.000	3								
Dyer		0	1	.000	3								

INDIANAPOLIS Indians

3rd	81-70	.536	-9.5	J.C. Hendricks

BATTERS	POS-GAMES	GP	AB	R	H	BI	2B	3B	HR	BB	SO	SB	BA
Metz	1B155	155	551	72	164		22	5	3	82	42	19	.298
Crandall	2B139	140	494	74	138		21	3	2	53	45	23	.279
McMillan	SS154	155	623	93	167		18	10	0	72	32	13	.268
Bronkie	3B153	153	575	89	156		19	7	0	51	37	39	.271
Reilley	OF152	154	545	85	157		17	8	1	73	33	47	.288
Kelly	OF145	147	550	107	165		20	5	1	54	26	61	.300
Butcher	OF112	123	421	51	118		18	7	3	28	42	16	.281
Gossett	C83	92	260	35	61		10	3	1	32	36	6	.235
Cole	OF61,2B20	102	292	40	80		14	2	0	33	17	7	.274
Blackburn	C76	81	235	39	56		9	4	1	40	26	6	.238
Willis	P47	47	104	5	22		2	1	0	6	12	0	.212
Schardt	P44	44	104	5	25		5	0	0	8	19	0	.240
Merz	P35	35	53	4	10		0	0	0	4	13	1	.189
Tipple	P32	32	66	7	12		0	3	0	3	21	1	.182
Burk	P24	24	64	7	16		2	1	0	2	16	1	.250

PITCHERS	W	L	PCT	G	GS	CG	SH	IP	H	BB	SO	ERA
Schardt	21	22	.656	44				289	309	78	85	2.77
Burk	14	6	.700	24				179	165	79	84	3.37
Willis	14	18	.438	47				275	289	87	89	2.78
Tipple	12	9	.571	32				183	140	140	88	3.79
Merz	6	10	.375	35				164	164	62	47	3.35
Dawson	4	3	.571	11				66	55	25	24	2.46
Conzelman	4	4	.500	10				75	56	42	37	2.04
Leverenz	3	3	.500	7				54	41	35	20	2.33
Aldridge	2	2	.500	6								
Cantwell	1	1	.500	6								
F. Regan	0	3	.000	3								

LOUISVILLE Colonels

4th	78-72	.520	-12	Hayden - Midkiff

BATTERS	POS-GAMES	GP	AB	R	H	BI	2B	3B	HR	BB	SO	SB	BA
E. Miller	1B74,2B72	148	523	85	137		26	7	2	65	52	35	.262
Corriden	2B63,3B33	99	346	71	110		19	12	5	37	16	12	.318
Derrick	SS142	143	493	70	126		18	6	2	51	44	12	.256
Midkiff	3B75	81	278	31	79		8	5	0	14	19	10	.284
Osborn	OF150	151	567	82	150		17	8	0	63	16	11	.264
Daniels	OF146	150	598	112	179		24	28	1	67	45	30	.299
Platte	OF77	79	302	56	97		13	12	2	38	36	15	.321
Clemons	C100	110	332	50	102		21	4	3	74	29	4	.307
Stansbury	OF43,3B37,2B31,SS15	130	469	57	127		18	10	0	38	13	11	.271
Crossin	C62	83	248	23	63		5	1	1	13	12	3	.254
Callahan	1B32	57	148	24	38		3	4	1	28	17	10	.257
Northrop	P48	49	130	12	26		4	2	1	9	25	4	.200
Weinberg	1B44	44	154	19	33		7	3	1	19	13	3	.214
Middleton	P44	44	102	8	25		0	1	0	2	9	1	.245
Ellis	P41	41	64	4	11		0	0	0	4	8	1	.172
Dell	OF38	39	106	13	27		5	2	0	12	10	11	.255
Danforth	P33	33	65	1	4		0	0	0	4	25	1	.062
W. Taylor	P28	28	52	5	11		0	0	0	2	14	0	.212
Earys	OF18,P5	26	75	13	18		4	0	0	12	4	0	.240

PITCHERS	W	L	PCT	G	GS	CG	SH	IP	H	BB	SO	ERA
Northrop	25	15	.625	48				335	308	98	97	2.82
Danforth	12	8	.600	33				189	150	91	172	3.00
Middleton	12	14	.462	44				258	265	76	99	3.11
Ellis	11	9	.550	41				187	205	44	32	3.47
W. Taylor	6	7	.462	28				138	139	68	35	3.52
Hoch	5	6	.455	13				85	77	39	19	3.87
Reynolds	3	8	.273	15				76	87	52	23	5.56
Marks	2	1	.667	10								
Scanlon	1	2	.333	8								
Perry	1	2	.333	5								
Earys	0	3	.000	5								

KANSAS CITY   5th   71-79   .473   -19   Dan Shay
Blues

BATTERS	POS-GAMES	GP	AB	R	H	BI	2B	3B	HR	BB	SO	SB	BA
Lelivelt	1B151	152	575	85	**199**		**41**	9	7	56	24	16	**.346**
Hinchman	2B136	136	559	88	182		20	9	3	41	33	14	.326
Wortman	SS153	153	593	82	130		15	2	0	90	52	31	.219
Leonard	3B	(see multi-team players)											
Mattick	OF149	153	550	72	134		24	3	2	65	40	19	.244
Compton	OF104	104	414	83	142		19	9	**9**	39	26	19	.343
Titus	OF59	59	209	34	55		15	3	4	34	13	4	.263
Geibel	C69	77	201	22	46		3	1	0	29	15	2	.229
Regan	P39,OF38	92	241	23	55		5	2	3	19	45	4	.228
Delhi	P47	73	166	16	36		6	0	0	7	24	2	.219
Alexander	C69	70	234	26	67		14	4	2	41	31	6	.286
Sanders	P38	49	102	11	21		1	2	2	1	15	0	.206
Burns	OF46	46	164	17	34		7	0	1	25	11	5	.207
Rath	3B39	40	159	31	47		7	1	0	20	7	6	.296
Faye	OF23	33	124	11	36		4	1	0	4	11	6	.290
Allison	P24	24	40	8	11		0	0	0	3	9	0	.275
George	P22	22	44	2	10		2	0	0	2	5	1	.227
Crisp	C16	21	54	6	11		2	0	0	8	11	0	.204
Mayer	OF17	17	61	7	22		2	1	0	1	7	0	.361
Moore	C15	15	45	1	7		1	0	0	3	5	0	.156

PITCHERS		W	L	PCT	G	GS	CG	SH	IP	H	BB	SO	ERA
Delhi		21	15	.583	47				325	353	82	85	2.60
Regan		14	15	.483	39				212	241	55	69	3.69
Sanders		9	10	.474	38				194	203	71	72	3.43
Allison		5	11	.313	24				117	134	18	24	3.69
George		3	6	.333	22				102	111	53	31	3.71
Carroll		2	1	.667	5								
Pennybacker		0	1	.000	1								

MILWAUKEE   6th   67-81   .453   -22   Harry Clark
Brewers

BATTERS	POS-GAMES	GP	AB	R	H	BI	2B	3B	HR	BB	SO	SB	BA
Lewis	1B93,2B34,SS21	151	571	74	141		10	8	3	54	20	16	.247
Barbeau	2B90,3B15	121	414	76	121		24	5	2	78	36	25	.292
Berg	SS87,2B25,3B19	131	513	77	129		11	2	2	73	37	27	.251
Clark	3B117	130	358	59	97		13	6	1	**104**	33	12	.271
J. Beall	OF149	154	557	111	186		33	13	7	95	51	29	.334
Randall	OF142	144	550	83	153		14	8	3	85	36	19	.278
Chappelle	OF139	139	498	64	154		20	9	7	51	41	18	.309
Brannan	C108	115	356	35	74		17	0	0	33	24	7	.208
Hughes	C67	81	206	22	44		5	2	0	37	28	6	.214
Dougherty	P36	49	125	11	32		3	2	1	10	27	6	.256
Young	P49	49	105	9	15		2	0	1	6	35	0	.143
Slapnicka	P45	45	112	16	20		3	1	0	16	24	4	.179
Fiene	1B29,P1	42	126	17	31		5	1	2	7	7	1	.246
Shackelford	P38	38	95	11	14		2	0	0	4	21	0	.147
Stutz	SS34	36	140	14	36		3	1	0	12	12	10	.257
Jones	1B30	33	112	17	21		3	0	0	4	4	0	.188
Rhoades	P22	22	53	1	10		2	0	0	4	22	0	.189

PITCHERS		W	L	PCT	G	GS	CG	SH	IP	H	BB	SO	ERA
Young		20	18	.526	49				292	304	74	75	2.62
Slapnicka		14	15	.483	45				309	335	110	115	3.29
Shackelford		14	15	.483	38				258	255	80	69	2.79
Dougherty		8	15	.348	36				212	210	79	75	3.48
Rhoades		7	9	.438	22				158	143	65	64	2.57
Faeth		2	2	.500	5								
Fiene		1	0	1.000	1								
E. Walker		1	2	.333	7								
Hovlik		1	4	.200	7								
Seaman		0	1	.000	2								

TOLEDO (CLEVELAND)   7th   67-82   .450   -22.5   J.W. Knight
Mud Hens

BATTERS	POS-GAMES	GP	AB	R	H	BI	2B	3B	HR	BB	SO	SB	BA
G. Beall	1B69	69	219	17	39		4	2	0	26	32	4	.178
E. Gardner	2B122	123	475	65	143		16	0	0	48	20	13	.301
Knight	SS100,2B15	131	440	61	124		26	5	4	64	40	12	.282
Hofman	3B58	63	225	24	52		11	4	0	18	55	6	.231
Nixon	OF146	148	557	88	163		26	16	0	59	27	47	.293
Wilie	OF93	93	338	67	105		14	5	3	58	16	21	.311
Wood	OF64,1B22	89	333	52	96		11	6	1	19	22	32	.288
DeVogt	C79	90	275	29	56		11	1	0	27	41	3	.204
M. Massey	SS37,3B21,OF15	88	313	46	82		8	4	0	20	41	11	.262
Kirke	1B51	68	266	28	76		19	3	1	17	11	9	.286
Billings	C53	68	234	43	67		13	6	0	18	22	19	.286
Evans	3B47	55	197	28	51		4	2	1	24	17	8	.259
Eschen	OF48	48	200	24	55		7	5	1	16	21	6	.275
W. James	P46	46	92	9	11		1	0	0	9	17	0	.119
Carter	P33	43	113	13	26		1	4	0	3	17	0	.230
Southworth	OF39	40	152	33	51		7	7	1	32	14	4	.336
Brenton	P28	31	80	6	20		2	0	0	2	15	2	.250
Collamore	P31	31	70	6	11		3	0	0	5	17	0	.157
Bassler	C20	29	71	10	13		0	1	0	16	4	4	.183
McColl	P21	21	33	0	3		1	0	0	4	10	0	.091
Bowman	P20	20	54	8	14		3	1	0	3	8	0	.259

PITCHERS		W	L	PCT	G	GS	CG	SH	IP	H	BB	SO	ERA
W. James		19	13	.594	46				271	273	148	125	3.29
Carter		13	14	.481	33				243	236	83	75	3.08
Brenton		11	11	.500	28				201	183	104	79	3.18
Collamore		10	13	.435	31				196	216	92	73	3.58
Bowman		9	7	.563	20				138	126	92	45	3.60
Vaiden		2	4	.333	9				60	86	35	13	6.00
A. Osborne		1	1	.500	2								
McColl		1	11	.083	21				107	109	36	24	3.79
Dillinger		0	1	.000	5								
Benn		0	1	.000	3								
Kahler		0	3	.000	5								
Hill		0	3	.000	6								

COLUMBUS   8th   54-91   .372   -33.5   Rudy Hulswitt
Senators

BATTERS	POS-GAMES	GP	AB	R	H	BI	2B	3B	HR	BB	SO	SB	BA
R. Miller	1B110	113	395	51	114		17	2	5	52	19	8	.289
Benson	2B143	145	534	62	127		16	8	4	46	43	8	.238
Shovlin	SS72,3B60	138	432	50	106		15	12	1	54	55	6	.245
Johns	3B54,SS46	110	411	51	112		19	5	1	31	32	9	.273
Burch	OF132	137	515	69	114		8	2	0	70	46	16	.221
Shelton	OF119	122	416	60	106		14	4	1	46	40	37	.255
Wright	OF69	69	246	28	66		9	4	1	28	17	7	.268
Coleman	C125	131	440	36	116		14	1	0	48	49	9	.263
Robertson	OF27,C27,1B19	81	255	30	40		8	3	0	21	40	6	.157
Hulswitt	OF23	67	163	13	45		4	1	0	17	3	7	.276
Scheneberg	P47	47	96	1	7		1	0	0	0	26	0	.073
O'Toole	P35	40	109	9	22		4	0	0	1	18	2	.202
Davis	P37	37	84	7	14		3	0	0	5	8	0	.167
Curtis	P30	30	75	2	12		1	0	0	1	16	1	.160
Steil	SS27	27	88	11	24		7	1	0	9	8	0	.273
Bratschi	OF25	25	90	17	30		3	6	0	15	7	7	.333
Ferry	P23	23	61	3	14		3	0	0	3	7	1	.230

PITCHERS		W	L	PCT	G	GS	CG	SH	IP	H	BB	SO	ERA
Davis		16	14	.533	37				254	226	157	116	2.98
O'Toole		14	15	.483	35				235	250	105	90	3.72
Scheneberg		12	24	.333	47				287	287	150	86	3.89
Ferry		7	11	.389	23				158	162	53	21	2.67
Curtis		5	18	.217	30				207	205	111	47	3.56
Bennett		0	1	.000	10								
Turner		0	1	.000	6								
Boothby		0	2	.000	6								
Bacon		0	2	.000	2								

MULTI-TEAM PLAYERS

BATTERS	POS-GAMES	TEAMS	GP	AB	R	H	BI	2B	3B	HR	BB	SO	SB	BA
Leonard	3B125	COL-KC	127	398	60	112		19	6	3	73	53	16	.281
Lathrop	OF23,P24	KC-SP	59	171	21	40		12	3	0	8	31	4	.234
H. Gardner	P38	SP-KC	48	84	7	13		2	0	0	4	10	0	.155
C. Miller	OF34	SP-KC	37	137	19	25		6	1	0	14	21	4	.182

PITCHERS		TEAMS	W	L	PCT	G	GS	CG	SH	IP	H	BB	SO	ERA
H. Gardner		SP-KC	13	14	.481	48				246	282	62	94	3.66
Lathrop		KC-SP	7	4	.636	24				144	127	56	52	3.00
Larsen		SP-KC	2	6	.250	16				83	100	42	24	4.55

TEAM BATTING

TEAMS	GP	AB	R	H	BI	2B	3B	HR	BB	SO	SB	BA
MINNEAPOLIS	155	**5327**	**805**	**1504**		**246**	78	22	550	499	113	**.282**
ST. PAUL	**156**	5108	704	1307		195	87	**39**	603	**581**	162	.256
INDIANAPOLIS	155	5043	725	1363		175	60	12	566	448	**237**	.270
LOUISVILLE	155	5077	727	1357		188	**106**	19	559	430	173	.267
KANSAS CITY	154	5164	711	1394		215	55	37	570	481	147	.270
MILWAUKEE	154	5032	714	1305		166	60	29	**687**	494	180	.259
TOLEDO (CLEV.)	151	4960	672	1301		187	77	12	496	509	206	.262
COLUMBUS	148	4782	532	1154		164	49	13	490	495	129	.241
	614	40493	5590	10685		1536	572	183	4521	3937	1347	.264

1916
Paul Carter

Paul Carter, a pitcher, played only a few seasons in the American Association, but during one of them he set an all-time best standard. When the results of this campaign were tallied, Paul Carter had the record for the lowest earned run average for a single season. This new statistical category was unveiled in the Association for the first time in 1914. The statistic endeavored to rate the pitchers on the number of runs per game for which they were personally responsible (via opponent's hits, etc.), excluding runs scored against them over which they had no control (runs scored on fielding errors and catcher's miscues). The new statistic was coined "earned run average," and it soon became one of the most important categories by which to judge a pitcher's performance.

Paul Carter pitched several years in the American Association for Kansas City beginning in 1908. He entered the major leagues for the first time in 1914, playing in five games for the Cleveland Indians. In 1915 he spent time with both the Indians and the Mud Hens. This was easily accomplished because both teams were owned by the same man and temporarily resided in the same city.

In 1916, Carter joined the Indianapolis Indians. Pitching in just 23 games, he compiled a 15-4 record and a league best .789 win percentage. Good as that was, he also only allowed 37 earned runs in his 202 innings pitched. This translated to a 1.65 earned run average which not only was good enough to lead the league, but stands as the all-time best in Association history.

After a seven-year absence, Louisville returned to the top spot followed closely by Paul Carter's Indianapolis squad. Minneapolis and St. Paul slipped two notches and finished in third and fourth. The rest of the pack consisted of Kansas City, Toledo, Columbus, and Milwaukee. (Note: with the Federal League in tatters after the 1915 season, the Mud Hens were shipped back to Toledo for 1916 and subsequent seasons.) The season's best batter on two fronts was Becker of Kansas City who had the best average (.343) and the most home runs (15). Minneapolis hurler Yingling posted the most victories (24), while Paul Carter's teammate in Indianapolis, Falkenberg, struck out the most batters (178).

Paul Carter spent part of the season in the major leagues with the Chicago Cubs. After five years in the majors, mostly spent as a relief pitcher, Carter returned to the Association in the 1920s, pitching three years for the Kansas City Blues. Though his record for lowest earned run average has been threatened, it has never been topped, and Paul Carter remains the American Association's earned run average king.

LOUISVILLE
Colonels

1st   101-66   .605   William Clymer

BATTERS	POS-GAMES	GP	AB	R	H	BI	2B	3B	HR	BB	SO	SB	BA
Kirke	1B		(see multi-team players)										
McCarthy	2B168	168	618	55	160		28	10	1	33	64	20	.259
Roach	SS168	168	587	62	159		22	10	3	47	56	21	.269
Corriden	3B168	168	582	85	161		26	18	2	71	28	27	.277
Whiteman	OF120	125	450	63	123		20	11	3	44	26	10	.273
Platte	OF108	129	382	72	106		15	13	2	74	53	12	.277
Compton	OF70	73	278	42	81		12	5	3	28	26	9	.291
LaLonge	C		(see multi-team players)										
Barney	OF52	60	188	24	46		5	4	1	28	21	4	.245
Killifer	OF58	59	202	31	52		10	0	1	20	8	9	.257
Daniels	OF49	52	182	28	57		10	4	1	24	23	13	.313
Luque	P48	51	76	9	22		5	0	0	1	16	2	.289
Billings	C47	49	145	18	34		7	0	3	16	19	14	.234
Farmer	OF38	48	146	21	37		8	5	0	21	26	4	.253
Middleton	P38	38	96	8	20		2	1	0	0	9	0	.208
Northrop	P34	36	81	7	10		0	0	0	0	21	0	.123
Palmero	P34	36	53	4	11		0	1	0	11	12	1	.208
James	P33	33	38	9	4		1	0	0	7	16	0	.105
Perdue	P30	30	75	3	6		0	0	0	2	16	2	.080
Zinn	OF18	21	68	8	15		6	0	2	8	10	1	.221
Schauer	P18	19	27	4	7		0	1	0	1	8	1	.259
Wendell		16	24	2	5		1	0	0	1	6	0	.208

PITCHERS		W	L	PCT	G	GS	CG	SH	IP	H	BB	SO	ERA
Middleton		21	9	.700	38				278	221	66	137	2.01
Northrop		16	13	.552	34				222	194	49	81	3.08
Perdue		14	9	.609	30				222	209	37	108	2.35
Luque		13	8	.619	38				167	147	68	100	2.64
Palmero		11	6	.647	34				153	120	73	112	2.83
Stroud		8	3	.727	13				95	83	23	48	2.18
James		8	7	.533	33				136	136	62	53	3.91
Schauer		6	3	.667	18				87	85	35	62	2.58
Ring		1	0	1.000	2								
Lear		1	1	.500	7								
McGraynor		1	1	.500	3								

INDIANAPOLIS
Indians

2nd   95-71   .572   -5.5   J.C. Hendricks

BATTERS	POS-GAMES	GP	AB	R	H	BI	2B	3B	HR	BB	SO	SB	BA
Leary	1B167	170	686	86	195		32	11	3	16	54	19	.284
Crandall	2B168	169	571	72	142		19	8	2	96	65	17	.248
Derrick	SS160	162	551	72	148		22	7	0	52	46	20	.268
Bronkie	3B162	162	613	101	178		22	13	0	54	61	45	.290
Wickland	OF152	156	590	96	153		20	14	4	81	71	16	.259
Reilley	OF120	127	449	48	131		13	5	2	39	31	37	.292
Dolan	OF115	142	476	93	135		27	14	3	86	66	35	.284
Schang	C119	122	367	49	84		9	5	3	58	52	10	.229
Zwilling	OF79	80	270	39	66		13	5	2	26	33	10	.244
Gossett	C49	53	167	19	40		6	2	0	10	24	0	.241
Dawson	P43	43	12	10	27		4	1	0	3	20	3	.241
Falkenberg	P39	39	94	6	15		3	0	0	5	33	5	.159
Rogge	P37	37	94	7	25		1	1	0	4	18	0	.266
Kelly	OF33	35	121	15	36		4	2	1	7	7	8	.298
Aldridge	P35	35	94	8	25		2	1	0	1	15	0	.266
Cole	OF17	25	69	9	17		2	0	0	7	7	7	.247
Carter	P23	24	82	5	19		2	1	0	2	6	0	.232
Willis	P21	21	20	1	3		1	0	0	1	4	0	.150

PITCHERS		W	L	PCT	G	GS	CG	SH	IP	H	BB	SO	ERA
Dawson		20	14	.588	43				291	256	113	113	2.75
Falkenberg		19	14	.576	39				291	230	62	178	1.83
Aldridge		16	14	.533	35				263	225	103	121	2.39
Carter		15	4	.789	23				202	141	58	79	1.65
Rogge		15	13	.536	37				256	225	87	117	2.78
Seaton		6	2	.750	10				81	60	28	49	1.22
Dale		2	2	.500	6								
Willis		2	7	.222	21				63	83	19	31	4.43

MINNEAPOLIS   3rd   88-76   .537   -11.5   Joe Cantillon
Millers

BATTERS	POS-GAMES	GP	AB	R	H	BI	2B	3B	HR	BB	SO	SB	BA
Knight	1B123,2B32	164	592	89	151		27	9	1	72	64	22	.255
Holland	2B132,3B33	165	624	93	157		29	2	0	87	61	14	.252
Jennings	SS157	159	574	83	164		24	3	3	41	51	17	.286
W. Smith	3B68	68	244	30	57		5	3	1	27	13	6	.234
Massey	OF138	143	549	84	155		27	6	1	45	49	11	.282
Acosta	OF122	122	470	72	120		15	4	3	67	38	25	.255
Menosky	OF110	115	405	65	108		10	13	11	40	64	20	.267
Owens	C130	135	416	45	105		15	4	2	18	40	3	.252
Altizer	OF73,3B55,1B25	164	597	108	178		22	9	8	98	31	17	.299
Cashion	OF37,P21,1B20	97	299	42	81		11	6	2	11	46	9	.271
Yingling	P42	66	158	20	41		7	1	0	14	24	0	.259
Burk	P45	47	132	12	23		4	0	0	5	36	1	.174
Williams	P43	43	96	6	14		4	0	0	8	30	0	.146
Bentley	P19	36	78	11	24		6	2	0	2	11	3	.308
Dumont	P22	22	56	6	11		1	0	0	1	26	0	.196
Hopper	P16	18	26	0	7		0	0	0	0	7	0	.269
Rondeau	OF15	16	55	12	21		4	0	0	9	2	2	.382

PITCHERS		W	L	PCT	G	GS	CG	SH	IP	H	BB	SO	ERA
Yingling		24	13	.649	42				323	307	82	137	2.67
Burk		21	16	.568	45				333	321	143	140	3.73
Williams		15	15	.500	43				278	270	94	87	3.11
Dumont		11	6	.647	22				146	144	54	88	3.76
Bentley		8	6	.571	21				117	126	43	38	4.16
Hopper		4	7	.364	16				71	90	42	30	6.21
Cashion		4	8	.333	21				124	108	73	39	4.14
Coffey		1	2	.333	10				46	63	23	14	6.45

ST. PAUL   4th   86-79   .521   -14   Mike Kelley
Saints

BATTERS	POS-GAMES	GP	AB	R	H	BI	2B	3B	HR	BB	SO	SB	BA
Dressen	1B147	147	504	69	122		16	4	4	53	47	32	.242
Malone	2B118	118	400	51	100		8	6	6	33	59	13	.250
Berghammer	SS124,2B15	140	510	73	135		17	8	4	56	39	11	.265
F. Smith	3B149	160	546	68	145		23	7	5	66	60	24	.265
Riggert	OF155	158	601	91	168		25	19	9	46	70	34	.279
Cruise	OF134	140	520	70	153		25	6	7	57	60	15	.294
Paddock	OF115	130	465	70	126		16	7	5	53	47	12	.271
Clemons	C93	110	304	44	99		17	4	2	33	27	9	.326
Walsh	SS47,2B19	80	254	31	54		5	2	0	25	19	6	.213
Glenn	C40	54	111	7	26		5	0	0	15	8	3	.234
Upham	P50	53	89	6	20		4	2	0	6	16	2	.225
Griner	P46	46	85	10	17		5	0	1	8	28	0	.200
Niehaus	P42	44	83	6	15		2	0	0	6	23	0	.181
Leifield	P39	40	92	4	19		2	1	0	6	18	0	.207
Douglas	P37	37	70	2	13		2	0	0	6	20	0	.186
Finneran	P28	32	57	6	11		1	0	1	6	9	0	.193
Duncan	OF27	27	93	16	26		3	1	1	14	4	6	.279
O'Leary		20	52	4	9		0	0	0	9	2	2	.173

PITCHERS		W	L	PCT	G	GS	CG	SH	IP	H	BB	SO	ERA
Leifield		19	14	.576	39				263	229	95	111	2.81
Griner		17	14	.548	46				256	250	71	108	3.45
Upham		14	16	.467	50				263	269	59	112	3.32
Finneran		12	8	.600	28				165	154	59	61	3.33
Douglas		12	11	.522	37				226	185	72	134	2.11
Niehaus		10	11	.476	42				236	210	65	131	3.05
Martina		2	4	.333	8				50	42	21	18	3.60

KANSAS CITY   5th   86-81   .515   -15   Shay - Phelan
Blues

BATTERS	POS-GAMES	GP	AB	R	H	BI	2B	3B	HR	BB	SO	SB	BA
Lewis	1B108,2B21	145	505	45	150		21	6	0	33	16	10	.297
Phelan	2B150	155	500	80	119		24	1	0	70	68	19	.213

KANSAS CITY (cont.)
Blues

BATTERS	POS-GAMES	GP	AB	R	H	BI	2B	3B	HR	BB	SO	SB	BA
Wortman	SS89	89	358	47	99		20	6	0	20	35	12	.277
Deal	3B117	118	436	64	138		22	4	3	24	12	20	.316
Gilbert	OF168	168	629	100	173		27	6	8	80	91	35	.275
Becker	OF152	153	508	91	174		33	2	15	61	66	20	.343
Lelivelt	OF97,1B57	154	517	80	158		28	12	3	58	48	14	.306
Berry	C117	122	324	28	68		14	2	2	48	41	3	.210
Hargrave	C83	105	243	22	77		15	6	0	18	32	5	.317
Regan	P53	73	145	19	33		8	0	0	6	24	2	.228
Sanders	P54	63	123	11	39		5	1	1	3	24	0	.317
Mulligan	SS54	55	189	20	45		10	0	0	18	24	6	.238
Tierney	SS19,OF17	55	136	10	26		4	1	0	5	14	4	.191
Crutcher	P48	50	101	9	21		2	0	0	5	24	0	.208
Humphries	P48	48	81	6	14		4	0	0	6	19	0	.173
Lathrop	P16	32	58	4	16		3	0	0	2	7	0	.276
Cocreham	P22	30	42	4	6		0	1	1	1	13	0	.143
Beck	1B18	20	58	6	12		1	0	0	3	3	1	.207
Handford		17	40	3	8		1	0	0	7	8	0	.200

PITCHERS	W	L	PCT	G	GS	CG	SH	IP	H	BB	SO	ERA
Regan	22	17	.564	53				340	317	73	132	2.78
Sanders	20	18	.526	54				302	300	124	177	4.77
Crutcher	16	15	.516	48				279	248	109	139	3.13
Humphries	15	12	.556	48				254	278	60	76	3.65
Cocreham	7	11	.389	22				133	133	66	81	3.73
Lathrop	2	2	.500	16				72	80	18	27	4.38
Hemming	1	0	1.000	4								

TOLEDO   6th   78-86   .476   -21.5   Roger Bresnahan
Mud Hens

BATTERS	POS-GAMES	GP	AB	R	H	BI	2B	3B	HR	BB	SO	SB	BA
Stovall	1B141	150	550	63	156		16	14	0	28	36	12	.284
E. Gardner	2B159	159	603	87	159		21	8	1	45	60	32	.264
Rawlings	SS169	169	596	82	149		12	13	3	68	52	30	.250
Perring	3B134	156	548	65	146		32	11	2	61	35	8	.266
Evans	OF159	162	591	101	176		33	16	10	63	71	20	.298
Wood	OF143	148	566	69	146		28	12	0	27	54	32	.258
Scheer	OF98	105	390	53	97		21	9	1	52	37	13	.249
Sweeney	C127	129	382	44	93		7	1	0	48	24	13	.243
Shaw	OF49	70	190	23	42		6	3	4	29	27	5	.221
Strand	OF27,P24	61	135	17	29		2	1	0	4	20	2	.215
Wells	C47	50	119	15	34		4	1	0	27	15	5	.286
Wise	3B30	46	141	16	41		5	1	0	5	23	8	.291
Bresnahan	OF24,C12	44	120	19	29		6	1	2	20	11	4	.242
Bailey	P44	44	77	6	12		1	1	1	15	18	1	.156
Kaiserling	P36	38	80	5	11		3	1	0	11	35	1	.138
Pierce	P36	36	65	6	10		2	0	0	6	21	0	.154
Adams	P33	35	63	6	10		2	0	0	1	25	0	.157
DeVogt	C17	31	39	6	9		1	1	0	6	9	0	.231
Main	P21	24	53	1	8		3	1	0	3	19	0	.151
G. Beall	1B16	17	59	12	17		4	2	0	7	7	6	.288
Hulswitt		16	21	2	3		0	0	0	2	4	0	.143

PITCHERS	W	L	PCT	G	GS	CG	SH	IP	H	BB	SO	ERA
Bedient	16	18	.471	49				305	298	64	149	3.10
Pierce	14	11	.560	36				202	184	73	109	2.81
Bailey	14	16	.467	44				245	240	107	89	3.64
Kaiserling	10	13	.435	36				240	239	76	87	3.49
Strand	8	5	.615	24				124	107	46	46	3.20
Adams	8	10	.444	33				181	183	79	57	4.48
Main	7	9	.438	21				148	130	42	62	2.67
McColl	1	1	.500	4								

COLUMBUS
Senators
7th   71-90   .441   -27   Hulswitt - Johnson

BATTERS	POS-GAMES	GP	AB	R	H	BI	2B	3B	HR	BB	SO	SB	BA
H. Bradley	1B145	146	543	69	136		18	9	2	38	30	14	.250
Johns	2B105,OF20	130	482	36	115		17	6	1	23	28	18	.239
Gerber	SS159	159	561	64	133		18	9	0	36	34	15	.237
Leonard	3B98	99	386	62	104		10	8	4	49	40	12	.269
Demmitt	OF151	152	577	78	178		36	14	11	44	43	15	.309
Chappelle	OF116	116	415	67	132		17	10	4	41	36	13	.318
McCarty	OF110,1B18	136	478	57	119		23	6	4	27	37	18	.249
Coleman	C70	74	237	16	55		12	3	0	17	26	1	.232
Steil	2B44	57	181	18	32		6	3	0	15	25	3	.177
Bratschi	OF54	55	195	30	38		9	3	2	30	47	8	.195
Pratt	C45	54	131	13	19		4	2	1	18	23	2	.145
Davis	P42	42	88	5	18		2	0	0	1	7	0	.205
George	P34	34	91	7	12		1	3	1	4	14	0	.132
Wright	OF25	33	104	9	25		3	1	0	7	14	1	.240
Curtis	P33	33	63	4	10		1	0	0	3	11	1	.157
Blodgett	P31	31	59	5	5		1	0	0	1	13	0	.085
Murphy	C21	27	59	8	16		2	2	0	7	8	2	.271
Brady	P27	27	54	3	12		1	1	0	3	14	0	.226
Bruck	P20	20	41	2	4		0	1	0	6	12	0	.097
Pieh	P16	16	22	1	5		1	1	0	1	5	0	.227
Vance	P14	15	14	2	1		0	0	0	1	2	0	.071

PITCHERS		W	L	PCT	G	GS	CG	SH	IP	H	BB	SO	ERA
Curtis		13	14	.481	33				213	210	71	68	3.43
Davis		13	15	.464	42				237	218	114	121	3.27
George		12	15	.444	34				252	252	90	85	3.29
Brady		10	11	.476	27				153	138	88	53	3.47
Blodgett		7	10	.412	31				164	157	42	72	2.85
Bruck		4	7	.364	20				118	100	42	56	3.82
Dickerson		3	2	.600	10				63	43	41	27	2.47
Pieh		3	6	.333	16				73	69	36	34	3.46
Lingrel		2	1	.667	7								
Vance		2	2	.500	14								
Fillingim		2	5	.286	10				59	60	27	21	4.43

MILWAUKEE
Brewers
8th   54-110   .329   -45.5   Clark - Martin

BATTERS	POS-GAMES	GP	AB	R	H	BI	2B	3B	HR	BB	SO	SB	BA
Kraft	1B	(see multi-team players)											
Benson	2B152	154	535	50	127		27	12	1	47	87	16	.237
Martin	SS146	147	523	65	115		15	3	2	60	50	21	.220
Clark	3B84	89	243	36	50		6	3	1	60	24	10	.205
Thorpe	OF141	143	573	85	157		25	14	10	31	117	48	.274
J. Beall	OF130	136	465	62	143		18	13	8	70	57	28	.308
McHenry	OF72	72	258	28	62		4	6	2	14	45	9	.240
Mayer	C	(see multi-team players)											
Stutz	3B53,SS16	83	242	21	51		10	4	1	15	32	9	.211
Critchlow	OF55	65	208	20	52		5	2	1	14	29	7	.250
Dilhoefer	C46	50	154	15	45		4	1	1	15	16	9	.292
Devore	OF46	46	160	23	39		8	2	0	13	23	5	.244
Spellman	C21	41	84	9	16		0	1	1	7	17	1	.190
Faeth	P41	41	72	4	14		1	0	0	3	19	0	.194
Comstock	P38	38	80	3	9		0	0	0	2	19	1	.113
Shackelford	P36	36	86	4	15		2	0	0	3	23	2	.174
Slapnicka	P36	36	78	4	13		1	0	0	10	23	1	.167
Block		28	77	3	15		1	0	1	0	1	3	.195
Williams	OF23	23	82	4	14		0	0	1	8	14	2	.171
Heatley	OF21	21	83	11	21		2	2	0	3	9	1	.253
Stumpf	C21	21	56	3	6		1	0	0	6	12	2	.107
Young	P16	16	17	2	3		0	0	0	0	5	0	.176

PITCHERS		W	L	PCT	G	GS	CG	SH	IP	H	BB	SO	ERA
Comstock		15	19	.441	38				244	242	74	121	3.13
Shackelford		10	16	.385	36				240	221	90	79	2.92
Slapnicka		9	12	.429	36				235	216	104	92	3.29
Faeth		8	19	.296	41				218	216	90	96	3.26
R. Aitchison		2	1	.667	7								
Sherdell		2	5	.286	9				67	72	14	23	3.36

MILWAUKEE (cont.)
Brewers

PITCHERS	W	L	PCT	G	GS	CG	SH	IP	H	BB	SO	ERA
Bluejacket	1	2	.333	3								
Reed	1	3	.250	6								
Young	0	3	.000	16					50	70	22	11	4.50

MULTI-TEAM PLAYERS

BATTERS	POS-GAMES	TEAMS	GP	AB	R	H	BI	2B	3B	HR	BB	SO	SB	BA
Kirke	1B160	MIL-LOU	168	633	78	192		40	5	5	48	39	14	.303
Kraft	1B150	LOU-MIL	154	560	81	144		25	10	8	45	78	23	.257
Bues	3B108	KC-COL	137	484	62	132		24	7	8	28	42	13	.273
Niles	OF94,2B18	KC-SP	131	412	42	87		8	6	1	48	34	8	.211
Mayer	C93	MIL-SP	104	328	33	69		9	0	2	21	53	12	.210
Land	C88	SP-MIN	96	274	20	71		18	1	0	14	14	1	.259
LaLonge	C92	LOU-COL	95	260	29	64		11	1	0	36	43	2	.246
Faye	OF64	IND-KC	83	191	28	48		8	1	1	16	25	8	.251
Moran	P34	LOU-MIL	36	65	4	11		2	0	0	1	12	0	.192
Walsh	3B34	LOU-MIL	34	93	9	19		4	0	1	9	8	5	.204
J. Hovlik	P32	MIL-KC	32	62	2	8		0	0	0	2	19	0	.129

PITCHERS		TEAMS	W	L	PCT	G	GS	CG	SH	IP	H	BB	SO	ERA
Moran		LOU-MIL	6	15	.286	34				171	184	72	74	4.37
J. Hovlik		MIL-KC	4	18	.182	32				190	219	75	94	4.60

TEAM BATTING

TEAMS	GP	AB	R	H	BI	2B	3B	HR	BB	SO	SB	BA
LOUISVILLE	168	5376	694	1392		229	95	31	547	599	157	.259
INDIANAPOLIS	170	5499	744	1459		200	88	20	548	628	228	.265
MINNEAPOLIS	166	5588	800	1470		224	65	32	558	611	148	.263
ST. PAUL	168	5471	695	1392		193	69	46	564	625	184	.254
KANSAS CITY	168	5521	711	1478		259	49	36	511	639	158	.268
TOLEDO	169	5545	706	1401		209	97	24	545	668	190	.253
COLUMBUS	163	5380	630	1329		205	87	37	412	555	136	.247
MILWAUKEE	164	5254	564	1218		159	75	36	484	826	207	.232
	668	43634	5544	11139		1678	625	262	4169	5151	1408	.255

1917
Interlocking

For the 1917 season, the American Association and International (née Eastern) League proposed a new idea. Their plan would expand on the benefits of post league play between the leagues, to make play between the leagues part of the regular season. In short, what the two leagues were suggesting was an interlocking schedule.

The plan was outlined as follows. From the beginning of the season in April until August 5, both leagues would play a normal 112-game schedule. From August 6 until the end of the season on September 22, the two leagues would play an additional 48 games against the other league. From August 6 to 29, the American Association teams would visit International League sites, and from August 31 to September 22, the International League would return the favor.

This was an exciting new idea, and if circumstances had been different, it probably would have worked. But with a war raging in Europe, and with the United States entering the conflict in April, the American Association pulled out of the interlocking plan and instituted a shortened 154-game schedule for itself alone.

After several lean years, Indianapolis won the pennant in 1917 with an impressive wire-to-wire performance in which the team never resided lower than first. Within a few games were the next three teams: St. Paul, Louisville, and Columbus. The lower quartet, Milwaukee, Minneapolis, Kansas City, and Toledo, finished quite a few games back. Becker of Kansas City won his second successive double crown as he finished with a fine .323 batting average and fifteen home runs. Lowdermilk of Columbus did him one better by winning the pitching triple crown, finishing with the most wins (25), best earned run average (1.70), and most strikeouts (250). Louisville's Davis managed to win 25 games as well.

As a compromise, the American Association and the International League reinstated the Little World Series after the 1917 season following a decade-long layoff. Indianapolis, continuing on their impressive regular season dominance, dusted off the International League champion Toronto club four games to one in their best of seven series.

Although events doomed the interlocking schedule in 1917, the concept remained a glowing ember in the minds of minor league executives. It took over 70 years, but the idea reignited and then became reality in the late 1980s, when the American Association and International League, for a period of several years, decided to share their schedules with one another.

INDIANAPOLIS 1st   90-63   .588   J.C. Hendricks
Indians

BATTERS	POS-GAMES	GP	AB	R	H	BI	2B	3B	HR	BB	SO	SB	BA
Leary	1B150	151	584	63	142		23	10	1	21	44	11	.243
Yerkes	2B136	152	549	65	155		28	11	1	34	33	6	.282
Derrick	SS144	144	500	55	119		15	6	1	42	39	17	.238
Bronkie	3B138	138	525	69	139		12	9	0	46	47	20	.265
Reilley	OF137	141	512	54	126		16	10	3	29	34	28	.246
Wickland	OF124	126	455	79	118		25	17	9	87	47	13	.259
Zwilling	OF93	102	329	36	87		13	5	5	31	46	6	.264
Gossett	C85	96	294	36	65		10	2	3	31	46	3	.221
Dolan	OF87,3B17	127	417	72	112		13	13	7	79	43	37	.269
Schang	C82	86	227	27	51		4	3	2	38	27	6	.225
Dawson	P36	42	98	7	18		2	1	0	5	24	0	.184
Fillingim	P35	40	99	11	21		0	1	0	8	20	0	.212
Kantlehner	P37	39	96	10	22		3	0	0	10	18	1	.229
Northrop	P31	34	98	9	24		1	0	0	7	21	0	.245
Rogge	P22	24	35	4	6		0	0	0	1	3	0	.171
Dale	P11	23	46	11	17		2	5	0	5	11	1	.370
Falkenberg	P20	20	56	1	6		1	0	0	2	20	1	.107
Oakes	OF14	14	49	5	7		0	0	0	4	5	0	.143

PITCHERS	W	L	PCT	G	GS	CG	SH	IP	H	BB	SO	ERA
Fillingim	20	9	.690	35			2	261	226	85	128	2.35
Northrop	20	10	.667	31			1	253	241	68	110	2.53
Dawson	15	14	.517	36			1	256	243	69	99	2.71
Kantlehner	14	14	.500	37			3	257	243	88	97	3.08
Falkenberg	11	6	.647	20			1	163	133	42	106	1.99
Rogge	6	6	.500	22			3	99	102	45	43	3.64
Dale	4	3	.571	11			1	65	55	23	19	3.04
Nabors	0	1	.000	1								

ST. PAUL 2nd (T)   88-66   .571   -2.5   Mike Kelley
Saints

BATTERS	POS-GAMES	GP	AB	R	H	BI	2B	3B	HR	BB	SO	SB	BA
Dressen	1B153	153	587	118	171		26	4	4	88	27	55	.291
Ellison	2B97,OF36	139	528	72	147		15	22	5	39	66	19	.278
McMillan	SS105	135	426	51	105		12	6	1	35	31	12	.246
Smith	3B69	71	235	22	46		6	2	2	19	31	7	.196
Riggert	OF155	155	604	73	173		27	12	8	42	56	27	.286
Duncan	OF133	137	464	52	128		19	6	2	61	36	15	.276
Nicholson	OF113	113	415	61	118		22	16	7	37	43	12	.284
Glenn	C81	96	259	25	73		10	7	0	18	13	2	.282
Berghammer	SS38,2B21	63	189	24	40		6	1	2	30	20	7	.211
Land	C49	53	149	11	32		6	1	0	4	9	7	.215
Griner	P45	53	102	11	18		5	1	0	10	35	0	.177
R. Williams	P51	52	96	12	28		1	1	0	6	18	0	.291
DeFate	SS21,OF13	49	134	23	35		9	3	2	22	25	7	.261
Finneman	P37	45	96	8	22		2	1	0	6	17	1	.229
Hofman	C36	40	131	8	24		3	2	0	7	24	1	.183
Hagerman	P40	40	67	5	11		1	1	1	1	30	0	.164
Niehaus	P28	30	55	6	11		1	0	0	10	18	0	.200
Upham	P21	23	47	5	9		4	0	0	3	15	0	.191
Malone	2B20	22	66	4	13		0	0	0	3	12	7	.197
Leifield	P16	16	30	0	3		0	0	0	4	9	0	.100

PITCHERS	W	L	PCT	G	GS	CG	SH	IP	H	BB	SO	ERA
R. Williams	22	14	.611	51			4	265	258	80	78	2.82
Finneman	18	11	.621	37			3	241	230	61	93	2.80
Griner	15	11	.577	45			7	261	235	81	121	2.86
Hagerman	14	10	.583	40			2	209	166	126	118	2.93
Niehaus	9	5	.643	28			0	162	132	74	90	1.94
Upham	7	4	.636	21			2	121	102	31	26	2.38
Leifield	3	11	.214	16			2	103	96	27	33	2.71

LOUISVILLE Colonels

2nd (T) 88-66 .571 -2.5 William Clymer

BATTERS	POS-GAMES	GP	AB	R	H	BI	2B	3B	HR	BB	SO	SB	BA
Kirke	1B102,OF38	148	550	70	175		**37**	8	2	37	30	16	.318
McCarthy	2B143	143	510	64	141		31	6	2	48	65	8	.276
Roach	SS155	**155**	530	54	133		27	6	3	43	41	8	.251
Corriden	3B104,OF34	151	529	66	146		19	14	2	69	33	17	.276
G. Williams	OF148	148	577	93	161		29	**24**	7	52	**84**	28	.279
Daniels	OF137	137	535	66	136		18	12	0	39	60	11	.254
Compton	OF60	61	215	30	48		6	3	1	21	19	5	.223
Clemons	C90	103	315	29	90		22	3	0	38	33	6	.286
Luque	3B47,P19	91	262	28	59		11	6	0	24	34	3	.225
Kocher	C67	81	250	30	64		12	4	1	12	30	9	.256
Brief	1B43	48	156	23	45		8	2	1	16	32	1	.288
Davis	P44	44	103	12	29		4	1	0	9	12	1	.281
Beebe	P36	38	82	5	9		5	1	0	0	13	0	.110
Stroud	P35	35	76	6	16		2	1	2	3	16	0	.211
Main	P33	33	81	7	14		2	1	1	2	22	1	.173
Cooper	OF28	28	101	13	22		0	0	1	12	16	4	.218
Platte	OF17	22	58	12	12		3	0	0	12	11	0	.207
Palmero	P12	14	19	3	6		1	0	0	1	2	0	.316

PITCHERS		W	L	PCT	G	GS	CG	SH	IP	H	BB	SO	ERA
Davis		25	11	.694	44			5	292	238	131	136	2.34
Stroud		16	10	.615	35			4	236	222	41	96	2.37
Beebe		16	13	.552	36			4	226	196	51	95	2.43
Main		15	9	.625	33			3	218	187	77	80	2.48
Comstock		2	0	1.000	11			0					
Perdue		2	1	.667	3			0					
Luque		2	4	.333	19			0	79	71	38	49	2.39
Middleton		2	4	.333	13			1	45	42	15	24	2.60
Palmero		1	6	.143	12			0					

COLUMBUS Senators

4th 84-69 .549 -6 J. B. Tinker

BATTERS	POS-GAMES	GP	AB	R	H	BI	2B	3B	HR	BB	SO	SB	BA
Hasbrook	1B78	83	305	25	63		14	1	0	18	4	11	.207
Johns	2B137	144	532	58	127		16	12	1	21	35	15	.239
Gerber	SS148	148	561	74	149		23	4	1	43	38	22	.266
Shovlin	3B119,2B19	139	446	59	120		26	7	0	45	58	13	.269
Demmitt	OF132	133	483	74	154		34	9	7	46	40	16	.319
Chappelle	OF129	132	495	69	129		24	11	4	48	24	22	.261
McCarty	OF75,1B78	153	591	66	142		25	8	9	38	61	21	.240
Coleman	C101	114	318	28	77		13	1	1	45	25	4	.242
Kelly	OF64	64	246	46	61		9	3	1	21	27	13	.248
George	P55	59	109	12	20		3	0	1	4	21	1	.183
Blackburn	C47	56	137	25	48		8	5	1	22	7	1	.350
Witter	OF45	52	165	27	41		3	1	1	25	9	3	.248
Lowdermilk	P50	51	122	5	18		2	0	0	6	34	0	.148
M. Brown	P30	31	62	4	14		0	0	0	7	14	0	.226
Curtis	P30	30	56	1	12		0	0	0	0	10	0	.214
Dilhoefer		29	71	5	21		4	2	0	6	5	4	.296
Knetzer	P22	23	48	5	8		0	0	0	1	19	0	.167
Tinker	3B14	22	51	5	6		1	1	0	2	10	4	.118
Barney	OF11	21	44	6	8		0	1	0	7	5	1	.182
Caveney	3B13	20	78	16	23		3	1	0	7	10	2	.295
Bues		14	29	1	7		0	1	0	0	3	1	.179

PITCHERS		W	L	PCT	G	GS	CG	SH	IP	H	BB	SO	ERA
Lowdermilk		25	14	.641	50			7	355	254	128	**250**	**1.70**
George		19	14	.576	55			2	262	263	89	89	2.67
Curtis		10	7	.588	30			1	167	170	60	31	3.18
Brown		10	12	.455	30			2	185	167	51	61	2.77
Knetzer		6	6	.500	22			0	138	146	45	47	3.85
Carter		5	5	.500	13			2	85	74	21	31	1.69
Erhardt		2	1	.667	5			0					
E. Hamilton		2	3	.400	6			0					
Willis		1	0	1.000	1			0					
Hoffman		1	1	.500	3			0					
A. Carlo		0	1	.000	1			0					
James		0	2	.000	2			0					

MILWAUKEE   5th   71-81   .467   -18.5   Shay - Friel -
Brewers   Livingstone

BATTERS	POS-GAMES	GP	AB	R	H	BI	2B	3B	HR	BB	SO	SB	BA
Barry	1B129	135	488	51	136		12	6	1	49	21	14	.279
Bohne	2B	(see multi-team players)											
Martin	SS151	151	517	45	118		15	4	0	59	40	19	.233
Beck	3B113,1B19	135	490	60	131		23	10	3	22	33	22	.267
Beall	OF147	147	539	76	155		22	11	7	59	58	18	.288
Anderson	OF140	146	543	80	167		17	6	2	69	34	21	.308
McHenry	OF100	102	373	46	87		14	6	4	30	69	13	.233
Murphy	C84	90	288	31	78		8	1	0	37	28	4	.271
Barbeau	2B55,3B31	104	326	39	83		20	7	0	41	35	12	.255
Bescher	OF64	64	232	44	67		5	7	2	46	14	17	.289
Kerr	P41	57	129	8	27		6	2	0	9	14	3	.209
Slapnicka	P34	55	122	8	24		5	1	0	11	24	0	.196
DeBerry	C40	46	129	8	26		5	3	0	11	9	0	.202
Sherdel	P44	45	90	9	17		1	1	2	4	20	0	.189
Livingston	C32	35	95	12	22		2	0	0	12	2	1	.232
Goodwin	P27	28	48	2	9		2	0	0	4	6	0	.188
North	P19	22	55	6	9		2	0	0	1	11	0	.164
Barbare	2B21	21	80	6	13		4	0	0	7	4	1	.162
Harding	P15	15	24	1	2		0	0	0	0	7	0	.083

PITCHERS	W	L	PCT	G	GS	CG	SH	IP	H	BB	SO	ERA
Sherdell	19	16	.543	44			1	262	258	71	94	3.18
Kerr	14	19	.424	41			4	277	273	97	94	3.25
Slapnicka	10	10	.500	34			1	197	190	83	67	4.09
North	9	8	.529	19			0	137	146	68	65	4.20
Goodwin	8	9	.471	27			2	170	133	47	78	1.91
Shellenback	3	3	.500	8			1	62	68	31	32	4.64
Harding	3	5	.375	15			1	74	79	24	22	4.13
Reed	1	3	.250	6			0					
Dickerson	1	4	.200	9			0	49	55	36	19	4.59

MINNEAPOLIS   6th   68-86   .442   -22.5   Joe Cantillon
Millers

BATTERS	POS-GAMES	GP	AB	R	H	BI	2B	3B	HR	BB	SO	SB	BA
Knight	1B103,3B48	151	563	75	154		32	8	6	68	62	16	.274
Sawyer	2B154	155	562	78	137		27	10	5	51	66	23	.244
Jennings	SS137	145	511	59	127		20	5	1	56	44	15	.249
Holland	3B45	53	171	14	29		4	2	0	25	20	2	.170
Massey	OF150	150	591	105	169		26	3	3	91	42	24	.286
Rondeau	OF135	145	545	70	151		20	5	5	49	55	15	.277
Altizer	OF125,3B20	149	525	85	169		20	4	7	90	26	18	.322
Owens	C114	117	391	40	107		23	2	4	22	37	5	.274
C. Thomas	P62	63	129	8	15		3	0	0	9	45	1	.116
Crane	3B30,SS20	53	193	18	64		10	3	0	8	24	4	.332
Milan	OF44	52	139	9	33		6	2	0	16	15	3	.237
Tiffany	1B48	50	176	19	44		12	0	0	15	21	2	.250
Bachant	C38	44	133	13	28		3	1	0	6	17	2	.210
Stevenson	P21	43	107	8	22		4	1	0	11	20	2	.206
D.C. Williams	P41	41	81	2	7		3	0	0	3	30	0	.086
Boardman	P24	32	75	9	18		2	0	1	2	20	0	.240
Burk	P27	31	71	6	17		3	0	0	2	14	0	.239
C. Humphrey	P30	30	48	3	5		0	0	0	2	21	0	.104
Cashion	OF10	30	46	3	11		3	0	1	1	5	0	.239
Harper	OF18	26	58	9	20		1	0	3	9	7	1	.345

PITCHERS	W	L	PCT	G	GS	CG	SH	IP	H	BB	SO	ERA
C. Thomas	20	24	.455	62			4	374	338	113	108	2.69
D.C. Williams	9	13	.409	41			1	227	216	68	112	3.55
Stevenson	8	7	.533	21			0	121	135	35	38	3.55
C. Humphrey	8	11	.421	30			1	161	184	57	53	3.64
Boardman	7	10	.412	24			2	168	151	86	84	3.54
Burk	6	16	.273	27			1	175	187	56	62	3.49
Patterson	5	3	.625	8			0	72	63	9	23	1.50
Rose	3	1	.750	8			0					
Thielman	2	1	.667	5			0					

KANSAS CITY Blues

7th 66-86 .434 -23.5 John Ganzel

BATTERS	POS-GAMES	GP	AB	R	H	BI	2B	3B	HR	BB	SO	SB	BA
Mollwitz	1B123	123	468	81	142		18	6	1	36	22	35	.303
Viox	2B94	96	330	55	104		19	5	1	57	20	7	.315
Mulligan	SS98	100	348	35	88		7	3	2	20	54	15	.253
Phelan	3B113,2B23	150	532	74	134		21	8	3	60	47	12	.252
Becker	OF151	151	551	84	**178**		21	11	**15**	75	54	24	**.323**
Lelivelt	OF98	102	343	40	101		15	7	6	39	28	4	.294
Leach	OF79,3B30	117	386	57	94		22	7	1	57	47	8	.243
Berry	C117	117	363	22	82		13	1	0	38	34	4	.226
Hargrave	C49,OF16	86	231	23	51		10	3	2	12	21	0	.221
Good	OF74	75	300	51	89		20	4	0	19	17	16	.297
Sanders	P45	63	138	19	30		5	0	2	6	25	1	.217
Tierney	2B38	52	186	11	47		5	3	2	13	27	6	.253
Wagner	SS46	50	177	18	41		4	1	0	19	19	3	.231
McQuillan	P43	43	88	4	12		1	0	0	14	27	0	.136
Altenberg	OF40	40	151	18	33		3	0	1	20	14	6	.218
B. Humphries	P35	35	65	4	11		4	0	0	2	27	0	.169
McConnell	P30	32	76	5	20		6	1	0	2	7	0	.263
Miller	1B31	31	106	12	30		6	1	0	18	5	2	.283
Pierce	P28	28	63	5	13		2	1	0	7	25	0	.206
Simmons		15	13	2	4		1	0	0	1	2	0	.308
Smith	P12	13	34	3	10		1	1	1	0	5	0	.294

PITCHERS		W	L	PCT	G	GS	CG	SH	IP	H	BB	SO	ERA
Sanders		18	16	.529	45			2	277	276	114	133	3.80
McQuillan		14	19	.424	43			4	286	301	52	91	3.21
B. Humphries		11	9	.550	35			2	179	175	30	54	3.30
McConnell		9	14	.391	30			1	203	198	75	83	3.32
Pierce		7	13	.350	28			1	187	201	78	93	3.78
Smith		4	3	.571	12			0	74	82	35	32	4.37
Chalmers		2	2	.500	7			0					
Cocreham		1	2	.333	9			0					
Flaherty		0	2	.000	2			0					
Crutcher		0	3	.000	8			0					

TOLEDO Mud Hens

8th 57-95 .375 -32.5 Roger Bresnahan

BATTERS	POS-GAMES	GP	AB	R	H	BI	2B	3B	HR	BB	SO	SB	BA
Mullen	1B106	144	509	55	118		14	6	0	39	29	19	.232
Boone	2B78,3B20	111	395	39	93		6	6	0	33	29	25	.235
Fabrique	SS84	84	324	34	97		4	6	2	32	28	14	.299
Hamilton	3B52	56	184	19	37		2	2	0	18	37	3	.201
Evans	OF132	136	492	55	139		18	7	1	43	62	8	.282
Fluhrer	OF114	124	395	44	94		10	5	0	33	31	14	.238
Wise	OF85,3B52	141	509	61	146		6	4	2	16	58	16	.287
Sweeney	C113	114	352	39	97		14	0	2	50	33	6	.276
Knaupp	SS62,2B49	113	425	40	100		13	3	0	42	27	8	.235
Keating	P41,1B21	64	177	20	33		4	2	0	5	35	0	.186
Hartzell	3B23,OF21	57	178	20	43		3	2	0	20	17	7	.242
Bowman	P26	51	93	10	26		3	0	0	0	13	3	.279
Brady	P46	46	97	6	16		1	0	0	4	24	1	.165
Aragon	3B18	42	144	19	28		2	2	0	11	10	7	.194
Schultz	P40	40	89	7	13		2	0	0	2	13	0	.146
Bresnahan	C20	40	80	10	22		5	0	0	12	8	1	.275
Piercy	P28	29	57	3	12		1	0	0	1	14	2	.212
Bankston	OF16	17	62	6	16		2	0	0	8	7	3	.258
Vance	P15	16	25	3	3		0	1	0	2	5	0	.120
Bailey	P16	16	24	0	4		0	0	0	6	11	1	.167

PITCHERS		W	L	PCT	G	GS	CG	SH	IP	H	BB	SO	ERA
Keating		15	17	.469	41			4	259	231	115	141	3.27
Schulz		13	19	.406	40			1	260	283	108	109	3.71
Brady		9	20	.310	46			3	268	275	108	82	3.29
Bowman		8	9	.471	26			2	165	147	81	79	3.55
Piercy		6	16	.273	28			2	172	173	110	74	3.72
Bailey		2	4	.333	16			1	83	93	35	20	3.36
Vance		2	6	.250	15			0	71	63	25	30	2.28
Bedient		1	2	.333	6			0					
Ford		1	2	.333	5			0					

MULTI-TEAM PLAYERS

BATTERS	POS-GAMES	TEAMS	GP	AB	R	H	BI	2B	3B	HR	BB	SO	SB	BA
Bohne	SS71,2B70	SP-MIL	145	561	101	154		27	7	4	40	44	38	.275
Bates	OF78	LOU-TOL	79	274	47	78		16	3	1	57	22	5	.285
Shackelford	P36	MIL-LOU	36	79	4	13		1	0	0	2	14	0	.165
Crossin	C15	LOU-TOL	20	47	4	14		2	0	0	1	8	0	.298
Kahler	P20	COL-MIL	20	32	0	6		0	0	0	0	10	0	.188

PITCHERS		TEAMS	W	L	PCT	G	GS	CG	SH	IP	H	BB	SO	ERA
Shackelford		MIL-LOU	10	11	.476	36			3	213	200	57	62	2.57
Kahler		COL-MIL	3	4	.429	21			0	106	110	44	32	4.08

TEAM BATTING

TEAMS	GP	AB	R	H	BI	2B	3B	HR	BB	SO	SB	BA
INDIANAPOLIS	154	4999	619	1242		169	**93**	30	482	530	147	.248
ST. PAUL	155	5026	**652**	1307		191	89	38	504	590	**204**	.260
LOUISVILLE	155	5077	620	**1329**		**236**	89	23	457	584	122	.262
COLUMBUS	155	5124	637	1297		212	68	32	429	533	156	.253
MILWAUKEE	154	5004	598	1278		177	71	25	505	483	159	.255
MINNEAPOLIS	**156**	5163	632	1326		221	47	32	**538**	**607**	157	.257
KANSAS CITY	154	5008	626	1326		207	66	**39**	523	547	140	**.265**
TOLEDO	155	5043	563	1252		133	50	8	451	561	146	.248
	619	40444	4947	10357		1546	573	227	3889	4435	1231	.256

1918
Half a Loaf

With the entry of the United States into World War I in April 1917, nonessential activities such as baseball were shunted aside. To keep the war effort going kept much of America's most valuable resource—manpower—occupied. There just wasn't time for baseball as many ballplayers entered the service or various war related industries.

In 1918, with this in mind, the American Association decided to trim its schedule to 140 games and delay the start of the season until May 1. To further complicate the business of baseball, the United States Government issued a "work or fight" bill, which stated that people engaged in non–war related work would be eligible for the draft.

It was no great surprise then in late July, at a special meeting, that the league adopted a resolution cancelling the rest of the season. For the American Association, the season was over, even though only just over half of the scheduled games had been played.

Kansas City was declared the winner, on the strength of its three and one-half game bulge over Columbus and Indianapolis, which finished tied for second. Louisville, Milwaukee, St. Paul, Minneapolis, and Toledo finished in the last five spots. The batting title was garnered by Johnston of Milwaukee (.374), while home run laurels went St. Paul's Riggert (6). Pitching honors went to Kerr of Milwaukee for his 17 wins and 99 strikeouts. The earned run average title was shared by Merritt (St. Paul) and Dale (Indianapolis) with a mark of 1.50. (Note: although these earned run averages rank lower than Paul Carter's 1.65 mark in 1916, Carter is still considered the record holder because Merritt and Dale pitched in so few innings in 1918.)

The American Association was not the only league to feel the pinch of the war effort. Of the more than 20 minor leagues that played in 1917, only 10 even started the season in 1918. Of these 10, only one (International League) managed to complete its season; the other nine, like the Association, ended their seasons in May, June, or July. While it is true that American Association followers saw only half a season in 1918, nevertheless, it was better than having no season at all.

KANSAS CITY
Blues

| | 1st | 44-30 | .595 | | | John Ganzel |

BATTERS	POS-GAMES	GP	AB	R	H	BI	2B	3B	HR	BB	SO	SB	BA
Bunny Brief	1B73	74	260	32	68		6	2	4	25	26	3	.261
Alex McCarthy	2B68	74	263	35	73		11	6	0	17	9	6	.278
Jim McAuley	SS66	66	225	31	46		10	0	0	41	25	3	.204
George Cochran	3B62	67	261	36	74		10	4	1	25	14	11	.284
Beals Becker	OF73	74	245	36	68		14	3	5	46	24	13	.278
Wilbur Good	OF73	73	271	44	87		10	4	1	23	13	13	.321
Joe Schultz	OF42	62	209	22	64		8	1	0	16	9	11	.306
John Onslow	C58	67	179	23	47		9	1	1	19	12	0	.263
James Viox	OF35	50	146	14	31		8	0	0	23	6	5	.212
Earl Blackburn	C19	25	75	5	21		2	0	0	8	6	1	.280
Roy Johnson	P22	23	33	5	9		2	0	1	1	5	0	.273
Charles Adams	P19	19	63	1	16		1	0	0	3	5	1	.254
Chester Hoff	P17	18	36	2	12		1	0	0	3	1	0	.333
Herb Hall	P16	16	37	4	6		1	0	0	0	13	0	.162
Jesse Winters	P13	13	23	0	3		0	0	0	0	3	0	.130
Carmen Hill	P5	6	11	1	1		0	0	0	0	4	1	.091
John Peters	C	5	6	1	2		0	0	0	0	0	0	.333
Red Smith	P2,C	4	5	1	1		0	0	0	0	1	0	.200
Dick Crutcher	P2	2	3	0	0		0	0	0	0	0	0	.000
Peter Henning	P1	1	4	1	2		0	0	0	0	0	0	.500
John Ganzel	1B1	1	1	0	0		0	0	0	0	0	0	.000

PITCHERS	W	L	PCT	G	GS	CG	SH	IP	H	BB	SO	ERA
Charles Adams	14	3	.824	19				167	122	29	79	1.67
Herb Hall	7	4	.636	17				113	84	46	43	1.51
Roy Johnson	6	7	.462	22				97	107	49	49	2.88
Chester Hoff	5	7	.417	17				99	93	40	34	2.73
Carmen Hill	3	1	.750	5				33	25	8	10	1.91
Jesse Winters	3	2	.600	13				67	64	23	18	2.42
Red Smith	2	0	1.000	2				4	7	7	6	15.75
Peter Henning	1	0	1.000	1				6	2	3	0	1.50
Dick Crutcher	0	0	----	2				10	13	3	0	1.80

COLUMBUS
Senators

| | 2nd (T) | 41-34 | .547 | -3.5 | | J.B. Tinker |

BATTERS	POS-GAMES	GP	AB	R	H	BI	2B	3B	HR	BB	SO	SB	BA
John McCarty	1B54,OF15	70	263	34	67		8	3	1	18	16	7	.255
John Shovlin	2B65	65	217	22	49		10	0	2	19	20	4	.226
James Caveney	SS72	72	251	23	51		6	4	0	19	22	5	.203
Charles Pechous	3B67	68	226	19	42		5	3	2	19	29	3	.186
Harry Harper	OF70	71	263	35	72		6	3	0	26	24	12	.274
John Collins	OF63	64	249	36	63		5	5	1	29	21	5	.253
Robert Taggart	OF59	59	225	32	73		2	4	0	14	18	17	.324
William Wagner	C46	50	144	13	43		12	2	1	19	12	0	.299
Grover Hartley	C,1B16	57	172	21	54		2	1	0	18	11	4	.314
Tom George	P28	32	66	8	13		1	0	0	4	15	0	.197
Paul Sherman	P18	18	41	0	7		0	0	0	6	11	0	.171
Findley Yardley	OF	14	31	2	8		1	0	0	6	3	3	.258
Mordecai Brown	P12	13	16	1	1		0	0	0	2	5	0	.063
George McQuillan	P12	12	27	1	4		1	0	0	3	7	0	.148
James Park	P11	11	23	1	4		0	0	0	2	4	0	.174
Joe Willis	P8	8	17	1	1		0	0	0	0	3	0	.059
William Jackson	1B	7	19	2	1		0	0	0	1	1	0	.053
James Rumler	OF	7	16	1	2		0	0	0	0	1	1	.125
Ray Brubaker	3B	5	18	3	4		0	0	0	1	1	1	.222
Cliff Curtis	P3	3	4	0	0		0	0	0	0	1	0	.000
Clyde Barfoot	P3	3	4	0	0		0	0	0	0	1	0	.000
Jim Bluejacket	P3	3	3	0	2		0	0	0	0	0	0	.667

PITCHERS	W	L	PCT	G	GS	CG	SH	IP	H	BB	SO	ERA
Tom George	11	9	.550	28				148	122	53	52	2.12
Paul Sherman	8	6	.571	18				132	99	52	29	1.85
George McQuillan	5	6	.455	12				81	93	22	20	2.89
James Park	4	3	.571	11				73	56	33	19	2.71
Mordecai Brown	3	2	.600	12				50	49	9	13	2.70
Joe Willis	3	2	.600	8				45	42	13	16	2.40
Clyde Barfoot	1	0	1.000	3				11	5	5	2	0.00
Cliff Curtis	1	1	.500	3				19	11	5	1	0.95

COLUMBUS (cont.)
Senators

PITCHERS	W	L	PCT	G	GS	CG	SH	IP	H	BB	SO	ERA
Jim Bluejacket	0	1	.000	3				10	20	2	0	8.10

INDIANAPOLIS   2nd (T)   41-34   .547   -3.5   Nap Lajoie
Indians

BATTERS	POS-GAMES	GP	AB	R	H	BI	2B	3B	HR	BB	SO	SB	BA
Nap Lajoie	1B56,2B22	78	291	39	82		12	2	2	27	7	10	.282
Robert Gill	2B30,OF31,SS13	76	303	33	75		9	3	0	18	35	2	.248
Sam Crane	SS40	40	158	17	33		5	3	0	20	15	11	.209
Herman Bronkie	3B72	78	307	35	82		2	1	0	27	23	13	.267
Dutch Zwilling	OF78	78	243	45	68		14	5	2	61	36	12	.280
Henry Butcher	OF57	58	205	15	46		9	0	1	16	15	7	.224
Fred Bratschi	OF17	17	56	7	8		0	3	0	6	7	1	.143
Robert Schang	C50	52	150	18	34		2	1	1	26	15	11	.227
John Gossett	C31,OF13	50	155	13	40		6	1	0	11	19	4	.258
C. Covington	1B22	22	80	12	18		1	1	0	17	6	0	.225
Cy Falkenberg	P20	20	54	3	7		1	1	0	0	11	1	.130
Jake Northrop	P18	19	63	4	12		3	0	0	3	12	0	.190
Bruno Betzel	SS14	18	71	12	26		2	1	1	2	3	5	.366
Gus Williams	OF16	17	68	13	19		4	3	0	5	4	1	.279
Calvin Crum	P17	17	41	2	4		1	0	0	3	12	0	.097
Clint Rogge	P16	16	39	4	11		0	0	0	3	3	1	.282
Roy Ellam	2B12	12	37	9	11		2	0	0	14	6	1	.297
John Lewis	SS11	11	43	7	11		3	0	0	0	3	0	.255
Gene Dale	P9	10	19	1	3		0	1	0	0	2	0	.158
Andy Lotshaw	OF	9	20	1	2		0	0	0	2	5	0	.100
Eddie McDonald	3B	8	26	5	9		1	0	0	2	3	0	.346
Tiller Cavet	P7	8	25	4	4		1	0	0	0	1	0	.160
Charles French	2B	7	28	2	4		0	0	0	0	1	0	.143
Elmer Koestner	P1	1	4	0	1		0	0	0	0	1	0	.250
Farrell	P1	1	2	0	0		0	0	0	0	0	0	.000
John Nabors	P1	1	2	0	0		0	0	0	0	2	0	.000

PITCHERS	W	L	PCT	G	GS	CG	SH	IP	H	BB	SO	ERA
Jake Northrop	13	3	.812	18				161	141	34	36	1.95
Cy Falkenberg	10	10	.500	20				161	150	39	77	2.63
Clint Rogge	5	8	.385	16				112	96	37	37	2.66
Tiller Cavet	4	2	.667	7				54	41	9	24	2.00
Calvin Crum	4	7	.364	17				119	101	36	33	2.49
Gene Dale	2	2	.500	9				42	37	22	16	1.50
Elmer Koestner	1	0	1.000	1				9	10	4	2	2.00
John Nabors	0	0	----	1				6	4	3	3	0.00
Farrell	0	0	----	1				5	10	8	1	12.60

LOUISVILLE   4th   43-36   .544   -3.5   William Clymer
Colonels

BATTERS	POS-GAMES	GP	AB	R	H	BI	2B	3B	HR	BB	SO	SB	BA
Jay Kirke	1B38,OF36	75	257	30	78		10	7	0	13	25	5	.304
Joe McCarthy	2B75	75	274	26	59		6	1	1	15	17	3	.215
Roxy Roach	SS37	37	145	12	36		6	1	0	3	5	1	.248
Art Kores	3B47,SS23	71	257	30	78		10	7	0	13	25	5	.304
Bob Bescher	OF68	68	257	48	66		12	5	1	25	14	20	.257
Duke Reilley	OF41	41	167	31	39		5	3	0	11	7	11	.233
John Lelivelt	OF36,1B36	72	265	30	86		11	11	1	22	9	10	.325
Brad Kocher	C44	47	165	19	43		5	5	1	12	13	1	.261
Bill Meyer	C31	38	103	11	28		0	1	0	3	0	0	.271
Albert Tyson	OF19,P13	35	92	11	19		2	3	1	4	12	3	.207
Dolf Luque	P20,3B10	33	92	9	21		2	2	1	3	9	2	.228
Art Bues	3B23	23	89	12	21		1	3	0	5	5	2	.236
Ralph Stroud	P19	20	45	1	7		0	0	0	1	7	0	.156
Al Humphries	P18	18	42	6	9		0	1	0	2	5	0	.214
Pete Compton	OF15	15	59	14	23		1	2	1	2	4	5	.390
Fred Beebe	P15	15	28	1	5		2	0	0	1	8	0	.179
Peter Knisley	OF13	13	49	9	14		4	2	1	4	3	1	.286
Cy Barger	P4,OF	12	31	4	11		1	0	0	1	1	1	.355
Joe Berger	SS10	10	32	5	6		1	1	0	5	1	2	.188

LOUISVILLE (cont.)
Colonels

BATTERS	POS-GAMES	GP	AB	R	H	BI	2B	3B	HR	BB	SO	SB	BA
Joe Bennett	P2	2	3	0	0		0	0	0	1	0	0	.000
Earl Yingling	P1	1	4	1	1		0	0	0	0	0	0	.250
Jim Parnham	P1	1	2	0	0		0	0	0	0	0	0	.000

PITCHERS		W	L	PCT	G	GS	CG	SH	IP	H	BB	SO	ERA
Dolf Luque		11	2	.847	18				117	97	39	64	2.00
Al Humphries		8	7	.533	18				128	116	26	45	2.67
Ralph Stroud		7	5	.583	19				127	103	28	50	2.76
Albert Tyson		4	3	.571	13				71	53	24	17	2.15
Fred Beebe		4	6	.400	16				88	81	26	40	2.97
Earl Yingling		1	0	1.000	1				9	4	7	5	2.00
Cy Barger		1	2	.333	4				24	22	1	7	2.25
Joe Bennett		0	1	.000	2				9	7	6	8	5.00
Jim Parnham		0	0	----	1				3	2	0	0	0.00

MILWAUKEE   5th   38-35   .521   -5.5   J.J. Egan
Brewers

BATTERS	POS-GAMES	GP	AB	R	H	BI	2B	3B	HR	BB	SO	SB	BA
Doc Johnston	1B30	31	115	30	43		11	0	4	19	5	16	.374
Jess Rumser	2B27	37	100	9	14		1	1	1	14	29	2	.140
John Martin	SS66	67	242	27	51		7	2	0	22	15	8	.211
Jap Barbeau	3B		(see multi-team players)										
George Anderson	OF73	73	274	42	69		10	6	3	35	22	18	.252
John Beall	OF48	48	171	26	47		12	7	2	21	14	3	.275
Austin McHenry	OF44	44	170	26	52		14	3	5	10	17	9	.306
Leo Murphy	C46	50	161	17	38		3	5	0	6	11	6	.236
Cosy Dolan	1B22,OF22	62	199	30	49		8	1	0	30	14	11	.248
Emil Huhn	C33,1B14	53	167	18	45		4	3	0	9	11	4	.269
Marty Kavanaugh	3B13,1B10	30	113	12	38		4	4	0	13	11	10	.336
Dickie Kerr	P28	28	73	6	12		2	0	0	5	8	0	.164
James Smyth	2B21	27	102	17	35		1	0	0	13	11	16	.343
George Distell	OF12	20	74	6	18		1	2	0	6	10	4	.243
Reese Williams	P18	20	52	3	12		1	0	0	5	5	0	.230
Moran	OF15	15	64	4	12		1	0	0	2	4	2	.187
Donohue	2B13	14	44	6	6		3	0	0	5	3	5	.136
Rankin Johnson	P13	13	30	5	8		1	0	0	1	3	0	.267
Tony Faeth	P12	12	25	0	6		0	1	0	1	2	0	.240
Earl Howard	P8	8	15	0	3		0	0	0	1	4	0	.200
Jack Kotzeknick	P5	5	11	0	1		0	0	0	0	0	1	.091
Tim Murchison	P5	5	9	0	1		0	0	0	0	1	0	.000
G. Johnson	OF	4	12	1	1		0	0	0	2	1	1	.083
Oscar Johnson	P2	2	2	1	1		0	0	0	0	0	0	.500
Robert Trentman	P2	2	3	0	0		0	0	0	0	1	0	.000
Lou North	P1	1	6	1	2		0	1	0	0	1	0	.333
Orville Weaver	P1	1	4	0	1		0	1	0	0	0	0	.250
Clifton Marr	3B1	1	2	0	0		0	0	0	0	0	0	.000

PITCHERS		W	L	PCT	G	GS	CG	SH	IP	H	BB	SO	ERA
Dickie Kerr		17	7	.708	28				207	183	48	99	2.04
Rankin Johnson		6	4	.600	11				71	75	28	23	3.82
Tony Faeth		5	3	.625	12				77	59	31	22	3.16
Reese Williams		4	10	.286	18				135	157	37	29	3.66
Earl Howard		2	2	.500	8				40	27	15	7	1.80
Lou North		1	0	1.000	1				9	8	6	7	4.00
Orville Weaver		1	0	1.000	1				9	4	7	5	2.00
Jack Kotzeknick		1	3	.250	5				34	29	17	13	3.44
Robert Trentman		0	1	.000	2				7	9	2	1	7.71
Tim Murchison		0	2	.000	5				29	25	16	11	2.17
Oscar Johnson		0	0	----	2				4	2	5	1	4.50

ST. PAUL   6th   39-38   .506   -6.5   Mike Kelley
Saints

BATTERS	POS-GAMES	GP	AB	R	H	BI	2B	3B	HR	BB	SO	SB	BA
Gus Gleichman	1B36	41	137	10	39		0	0	0	9	11	5	.285

ST. PAUL (cont.)
Saints

BATTERS	POS-GAMES	GP	AB	R	H	BI	2B	3B	HR	BB	SO	SB	BA
Art Butler	2B43,OF13	61	204	33	48		7	1	0	33	11	20	.235
Marty Berghammer	SS51	57	208	30	53		7	1	1	28	14	8	.255
Bobby Byrne	3B33	35	108	17	25		7	0	0	12	7	4	.231
Joe Riggert	OF78	**78**	**311**	**48**	**101**		**16**	7	6	16	26	20	.325
Lou Blue	OF59,1B12	71	258	33	59		6	4	3	26	51	5	.229
John Corriden	OF47,SS11	66	219	27	59		7	3	4	19	10	9	.269
Harry Glenn	C46	50	145	20	41		6	0	0	25	11	3	.283
Ray Keating	P17	38	120	6	24		5	2	0	4	18	0	.200
Charles Hall	P25	36	96	7	19		3	2	0	5	15	1	.177
Graff	SS18	25	81	16	22		4	1	0	13	7	1	.272
BubblesHargrave	C15	23	83	10	25		3	4	0	3	4	3	.301
Glenn Cook	C18	20	55	4	9		1	0	0	2	2	0	.164
H. Rook	P19	19	34	1	4		0	0	0	0	6	0	.118
Bill Piercy	P18	18	31	5	9		0	1	0	0	10	0	.290
Zeriah Hagerman	P18	18	20	3	4		0	0	0	1	7	0	.200
Hardin Herndon	OF10	16	54	3	4		1	0	0	7	3	2	.074
George Harper	OF15	15	60	6	16		2	1	0	3	1	0	.267
Oscar Dugey	2B13	15	51	4	7		1	1	0	3	3	0	.137
D. Williams	1B14	14	46	3	10		2	0	0	3	4	2	.217
Clyde DeFate	SS	12	47	5	12		2	1	0	5	1	0	.255
Bob McMenemy	OF,C	12	32	4	8		1	0	1	2	6	0	.250
John Bates	3B11	11	36	3	7		0	0	0	0	3	1	.194
Joe Cobb	C	11	32	3	7		1	1	1	3	8	1	.219
Howard Merritt	P10	10	22	0	2		0	0	0	1	4	0	.090
Eddie Foster	P6	6	6	0	0		0	0	0	0	1	0	.000
Yockley	OF	4	11	1	2		0	0	0	0	2	0	.182
Lutzke	OF	4	8	0	0		0	0	0	0	3	1	.000
Harry Jasper	P4	4	4	0	1		0	0	0	0	2	1	.250
Louis LeRoy	P3	3	7	0	1		0	0	0	0	4	1	.143
Fred Schliebner	1B1,OF1	2	3	1	0		0	0	0	0	0	1	.000
Richard Niehaus	P1	1	0	0	0		0	0	0	0	0	0	----

PITCHERS		W	L	PCT	G	GS	CG	SH	IP	H	BB	SO	ERA
Charles Hall		15	8	.652	25				189	159	38	69	1.85
Ray Keating		9	7	.563	17				137	115	73	62	2.95
Howard Merritt		6	3	.667	10				66	60	13	30	**1.50**
Bill Piercy		6	6	.500	18				92	77	64	34	2.84
H. Rook		3	2	.600	19				96	84	56	30	3.47
Harry Jasper		0	1	.000	4				15	17	8	7	3.00
Richard Niehaus		0	1	.000	1				0	4	0	0	108.00
Louis LeRoy		0	2	.000	3				19	23	8	8	3.79
Eddie Foster		0	3	.000	6				20	12	15	12	3.11
Zeriah Hagerman		0	5	.000	18				67	70	46	48	4.56

MINNEAPOLIS   7th   34-42   .447   -11   Joe Cantillon
Millers

BATTERS	POS-GAMES	GP	AB	R	H	BI	2B	3B	HR	BB	SO	SB	BA
Wallace Smith	1B42	47	146	21	39		3	3	1	15	9	9	.267
Carl Sawyer	2B75	76	310	38	95		12	5	0	11	26	12	.306
Morely Jennings	SS52	52	185	15	44		9	6	0	16	20	4	.238
William Weidell	3B60,SS11	76	286	28	75		10	1	1	25	23	7	.262
Henry Rondeau	OF76	76	289	25	67		9	4	0	17	29	6	.232
Carl Cashion	OF51	52	211	20	73		16	5	5	12	25	3	.346
Dave Altizer	OF36	52	174	16	42		2	1	1	15	5	5	.241
Frank Owens	C41	46	145	10	43		10	1	1	6	7	1	.297
Tony Burgwald	OF31	41	139	17	26		4	1	0	13	23	1	.187
John Knight	1B27	27	107	6	30		6	0	0	8	10	5	.280
Dolly Gray	C17	27	65	11	17		2	2	2	4	7	1	.262
D.C. Williams	P27	27	53	3	8		0	0	0	0	18	0	.151
Charles Jackson	OF22	22	86	11	16		1	0	0	9	13	4	.186
Tom Hughes	P20	22	42	5	8		0	0	1	1	7	0	.190
Frank Kitchens	C15	17	47	7	9		2	1	0	7	6	0	.191
Emilio Palmero	P9	17	31	2	6		0	0	0	3	5	0	.194
Roy Patterson	P14	14	30	7	3		0	0	0	6	6	0	.100
William Lindberg	P14	14	29	2	1		0	0	0	0	15	0	.035
Charles Robertson	P9	10	20	0	2		0	0	0	2	3	0	.100
Robert Coleman	C	9	25	2	6		0	0	0	2	5	0	.240
Robert Hewitt	P9	9	18	3	3		1	1	0	3	4	0	.167
Claude Thomas	P8	8	8	1	1		0	0	0	2	5	0	.125

MINNEAPOLIS (cont.)
Millers

BATTERS	POS-GAMES	GP	AB	R	H	BI	2B	3B	HR	BB	SO	SB	BA
William Patterson	SS	7	21	4	5		1	1	0	3	4	0	.238
Hub Perdue	P6	6	13	0	3		0	0	0	2	3	0	.231
Harry Wolfe	SS	4	13	1	1		0	0	0	2	1	0	.077
Charles Humphrey	P4	4	3	1	0		0	0	0	2	3	0	.000
Frank Shellenback	P3	3	8	0	1		0	0	0	0	1	0	.125
Horace Leverette	P3	3	1	0	0		0	0	0	2	0	0	.000
Neis	3B1	1	2	0	0		0	0	0	0	1	0	.000
Sumner	P1	1	1	0	0		0	0	0	0	0	0	.000

PITCHERS		W	L	PCT	G	GS	CG	SH	IP	H	BB	SO	ERA
Tom Hughes		8	6	.571	20				116	104	41	48	2.95
R.C. Williams		8	11	.421	27				151	144	46	57	2.29
Roy Patterson		5	3	.625	14				98	99	24	19	2.30
Emilo Palmero		3	1	.750	9				49	39	18	23	2.02
William Lindberg		3	5	.375	14				80	56	30	26	2.03
Hub Perdue		2	2	.500	6				35	37	10	11	2.57
Charles Robertson		2	7	.222	9				65	52	22	24	1.93
Charles Humphrey		1	0	1.000	4				15	17	8	7	3.00
Frank Shellenback		1	2	.333	3				21	14	7	9	0.86
Horace Leverette		0	1	.000	3				7	8	4	3	6.43
Robert Hewitt		0	1	.000	1				4	8	3	1	4.50
Claude Thomas		0	3	.000	8				29	48	14	7	7.45
Sumner		0	0	----	1				2	4	4	2	

TOLEDO   8th   23-54   .299   -22.5   Roger Bresnahan
Mud Hens

BATTERS	POS-GAMES	GP	AB	R	H	BI	2B	3B	HR	BB	SO	SB	BA
Tom DeNoville	1B36	39	140	7	33		2	1	0	9	7	1	.236
Lute Boone	2B76	76	278	27	72		6	4	0	29	12	9	.259
William Purtell	SS38	40	143	12	25		0	0	0	16	15	5	.175
Harold Wise	3B40,OF27	68	244	23	60		4	4	0	20	12	6	.246
Al Schweitzer	OF56	60	211	22	39		5	1	1	25	25	4	.185
Halman Brokaw	OF51	52	180	17	46		2	1	0	12	8	7	.256
Bill Lamar	OF36	36	128	15	37		3	4	1	4	6	4	.289
Bernard Kelly	C52	53	170	13	37		3	0	1	17	3	5	.217
Walt Alexander	1B34,C10	50	152	10	38		1	2	0	18	12	2	.250
Charles Bauman	3B31	32	118	14	28		2	1	0	12	3	4	.237
Alvah Bauman	P24	30	67	5	9		0	0	0	4	5	1	.134
Alex McColl	P25	26	50	4	11		2	0	0	0	8	1	.220
Roy Sanders	P22	23	46	3	4		1	0	0	6	22	0	.087
Angel Aragon	SS22	22	71	7	20		3	2	1	5	3	0	.282
Neal Brady	P21	22	49	4	9		1	0	1	0	8	0	.184
Cecil Coombs	OF18	19	62	3	13		2	0	0	6	4	0	.210
Stan Hubbard	SS17	19	62	2	10		2	0	0	0	10	0	.161
Roger Bresnahan	OF14	19	52	4	12		2	0	1	4	5	0	.230
Williams	OF14	14	45	1	6		1	0	0	4	4	0	.133
Louis Cally	OF11	13	38	2	5		0	0	0	0	7	0	.132
Charles Boardman	P11	12	20	2	3		0	0	0	1	7	0	.150
George Carey	1B	6	14	2	3		1	0	0	0	0	4	.214
Al Schultz	P5	5	8	0	0		0	0	0	0	4	0	.000
Paul Carpenter	P4	4	5	1	2		0	0	0	0	0	0	.400
Joe Birmingham	OF	3	8	0	0		0	0	0	0	1	0	.000
George Runge	1B	2	6	1	3		1	0	1	0	0	0	.500
John Meeks	OF1	1	2	0	0		0	0	0	0	0	0	.000

PITCHERS		W	L	PCT	G	GS	CG	SH	IP	H	BB	SO	ERA
Neal Brady		8	8	.500	21				132	130	44	38	3.07
Alex McColl		6	8	.429	25				148	157	40	26	3.16
Alvah Bauman		5	17	.227	24				175	157	80	60	3.24
Roy Sanders		4	13	.235	22				147	123	63	43	2.64
Charles Boardman		2	5	.286	11				55	42	26	24	2.12
Paul Carpenter		0	2	.000	4				15	18	6	0	6.60
Al Schultz		0	4	.000	5				29	37	16	6	6.21

MULTI-TEAM PLAYERS

BATTERS	POS-GAMES	TEAMS	GP	AB	R	H	BI	2B	3B	HR	BB	SO	SB	BA
Jap Barbeau	3B58,2B10	MIL-SP	68	216	37	50		5	3	0	51	24	8	.231
Joe Devine	C19	TOL-MIN	24	79	8	19		2	0	0	7	5	1	.241
Charles Wheatley	P17	KC-MIL	17	20	2	3		1	0	0	1	7	1	.150
Red Shackelford	P16	LOU-IND	16	30	1	2		0	0	0	1	4	1	.067
Paul Zahniser	P10	COL-TOL	10	19	1	1		0	0	0	4	6	0	.053
Frank Caporal	P5	KC-MIL	5	14	1	4		0	0	0	0	0	0	.286

PITCHERS		TEAMS	W	L	PCT	G	GS	CG	SH	IP	H	BB	SO	ERA
Red Shackelford		LOU-IND	7	5	.583	16				89	90	33	19	3.44
Paul Zahniser		COL-TOL	4	3	.571	10				62	63	24	12	3.48
Charles Wheatley		KC-MIL	3	4	.429	17				59	70	22	25	4.28
Frank Caporal		KC-MIL	2	2	.500	5				32	27	8	4	3.10

TEAM BATTING

TEAMS	GP	AB	R	H	BI	2B	3B	HR	BB	SO	SB	BA
KANSAS CITY	74	2375	299	634		93	22	13	256	181	72	.267
COLUMBUS	75	2363	270	578		62	25	8	225	231	60	.245
INDIANAPOLIS	78	2537	307	621		78	25	7	284	247	85	.245
LOUISVILLE	77	2558	314	660		83	54	9	203	194	79	.258
MILWAUKEE	73	2414	314	604		92	37	15	270	241	137	.250
ST. PAUL	78	2555	304	617		82	30	17	246	256	84	.241
MINNEAPOLIS	77	2538	267	626		93	32	12	185	295	60	.247
TOLEDO	78	2394	205	530		46	20	7	212	214	50	.221
	305	19734	2280	4870		629	245	88	1881	1859	627	.247

1919
A Journey West

The Little World Series, instituted in 1904, had seen spotty scheduling. Only four times since its creation (1904, 1906, 1907, and 1917) had it even taken place. So when the American Association champion St. Paul Saints were approached about a special challenge series to be held after the 1919 season, they were intrigued.

The champions of the Pacific Coast League in 1919 were the Vernon Tigers, who were located in a suburb of Los Angeles. Following the season, the Tigers issued a challenge to the Association champions. They proposed a championship series between St. Paul and themselves. The only catch was that all of the games would be played in California, in the Tigers' home park.

The St. Paul Saints won the 1919 pennant easily over second place Kansas City, the defending champions. Louisville and Indianapolis finished in a near tie for third, while Minneapolis, Columbus, Toledo, and Milwaukee finished in the second division. Hendryx of Louisville was the loop's best hitter (.368), while E. Miller of St. Paul clubbed the most home runs (15). On the mound, Indianapolis pitcher Cavet finished with the most wins (28), while Columbus thrower Wilkinson had the best earned run average (2.09), and Louisville hurler Davis struck out the most batters (165).

The championship series between St. Paul and Vernon opened in California on October 14., with the visiting Association club prevailing 5-0. The next two games were split, with Vernon taking the first 6–2 and St. Paul prevailing in the next 3–1. Vernon won the next two (2–1 and 7–1) before St. Paul posted another shutout (5-0). The same pattern held true for the next three games of the series as Vernon won twice (2–1 and 12–2) before St. Paul's victory (2–1) in game nine. With Vernon leading at this point, five games to four, trouble reared its ugly head. St. Paul accused Vernon of using an ineligible player in the series. (Note: Brooks, a catcher for Vernon who played in the series, does not appear on their roster of players for the regular season.) Also, the Saints felt themselves poorly treated by their hosts. However valid or invalid, these issues were enough to insure that the series ended at this point.

Despite the cloudy ending, this championship series was successful enough that it would be played twice more in the next six years before being permanently tabled. The concept for this series was sound, but perhaps the physical distance kept a championship series between the Pacific Coast League and the American Association from becoming a permanent fixture.

ST. PAUL Saints

1st   94-60   .610   Mike Kelley

BATTERS	POS-GAMES	GP	AB	R	H	BI	2B	3B	HR	BB	SO	SB	BA
Dressen	1B154	154	610	113	166		17	4	3	94	29	46	.272
Berghammer	2B57,SS31	94	273	40	76		9	3	1	39	22	29	.279
Martin	SS71	71	238	30	55		11	2	2	24	19	4	.231
F. Smith	3B108	108	340	32	73		3	1	1	28	30	7	.215
E. Miller	OF154	154	608	100	191		34	16	15	49	48	24	.314
Duncan	OF147	149	541	87	151		28	6	1	59	22	29	.279
Corriden	OF72	80	284	43	73		13	3	1	37	15	11	.257
Hargrave	C142	146	511	71	155		35	5	11	49	47	16	.303
Boone	SS58,2B35,3B22	115	362	39	94		16	2	1	33	19	13	.260
Riggert	OF68	68	261	51	80		11	9	3	33	22	16	.306
C. Hall	P45	64	130	14	30		5	1	1	7	20	1	.231
Griner	P50	58	124	6	26		4	0	1	13	26	0	.210
Niehaus	P50	56	114	13	27		5	1	0	14	16	1	.237
Merritt	P42	42	91	7	13		1	0	0	9	23	1	.142
Halas	OF18	39	84	15	23		2	1	0	14	12	6	.273
McMenemy	C28	36	79	11	22		6	0	1	8	17	0	.278
McDonald	3B20	20	74	9	22		3	1	0	9	3	5	.297

PITCHERS		W	L	PCT	G	GS	CG	SH	IP	H	BB	SO	ERA
Niehaus		23	13	.639	50				307	267	119	156	2.87
Griner		21	14	.600	50				321	297	76	100	3.14
Merritt		19	9	.679	42				258	245	59	113	2.62
C. Hall		17	13	.567	45				279	231	63	122	2.29
Browne		4	1	.800	14				58	47	36	15	1.55
Monroe		2	3	.400	12				46	60	19	18	5.28
Foster		1	1	.500	2								

KANSAS CITY Blues

2nd   86-65   .570   -6.5   John Ganzel

BATTERS	POS-GAMES	GP	AB	R	H	BI	2B	3B	HR	BB	SO	SB	BA
Brief	1B149	152	564	89	183		30	11	13	54	67	13	.324
A. McCarthy	2B126	138	482	51	130		22	3	0	30	21	5	.270
McAuley	SS137	140	525	88	144		21	6	0	75	57	18	.274
Cochran	3B120	126	486	69	151		27	6	3	33	42	16	.311
W. Miller	OF148	148	556	116	177		21	16	2	82	27	20	.318
Becker	OF145	148	545	106	181		31	4	14	63	28	25	.332
Good	OF140	140	586	91	204		31	12	7	26	33	23	.349
LaLonge	C121	132	424	47	100		17	1	0	34	44	2	.236
Halt	2B55,SS16	87	291	28	74		14	2	4	21	36	5	.254
H. Hall	P49	52	112	11	16		2	1	1	8	28	1	.143
Johnson	P47	48	70	6	13		6	0	0	2	16	0	.186
Monroe	C27	34	65	1	11		0	0	0	1	6	0	.169
Evans	P28	31	78	8	16		1	1	1	2	10	0	.205
Haines	P28	31	77	6	15		0	0	0	2	13	0	.186
J. Brock	C22	27	81	5	13		4	0	0	8	7	1	.160
Warner		27	64	9	16		6	0	0	5	6	1	.250
Allen	P22	22	23	2	3		0	0	0	2	6	0	.130
Shackelford	P9	9	18	2	3		1	0	0	3	5	0	.167
A. Brock	3B	8	18	3	2		1	0	0	5	5	0	.111
Ragan	P8	8	12	0	0		0	0	0	0	6	0	.000
Hoffman	P8	8	11	0	1		0	0	0	0	2	0	.091
Henning	P7	7	5	2	0		0	0	0	0	0	0	.000
Slattery	P6	6	6	0	1		0	0	0	0	1	0	.167
Beedle	P2	5	3	0	1		0	0	0	0	1	0	.333
Hitt	P4	4	3	0	0		0	0	0	0	3	0	.000
Tierney	2B	3	11	1	2		0	0	0	1	3	1	.182
V. Barnes	P2	2	0	0	0		0	0	0	0	0	0	----

PITCHERS		W	L	PCT	G	GS	CG	SH	IP	H	BB	SO	ERA
Haines		21	5	.808	28				213	199	52	66	2.12
H. Hall		21	16	.568	49				296	298	141	86	3.77
Evans		16	8	.667	28				195	182	72	89	2.26
Johnson		6	7	.462	47				197	173	84	59	4.25
Shackelford		2	2	.500	9				50	56	13	5	3.60
Henning		2	2	.500	7								
Allen		2	3	.400	12				46	60	19	18	5.28
Hoffman		1	2	.333	8								
Beedle		0	1	.000	2								

KANSAS CITY (cont.)
Blues

PITCHERS	W	L	PCT	G	GS	CG	SH	IP	H	BB	SO	ERA
Ragan	0	2	.000	8								
Slattery	0	3	.000	6								

LOUISVILLE 3rd 86-67 .562 -7.5 Flaherty - McCarthy
Colonels

BATTERS	POS-GAMES	GP	AB	R	H	BI	2B	3B	HR	BB	SO	SB	BA
Kirke	1B144	145	524	67	158		24	15	4	36	19	19	.302
J. McCarthy	2B140	147	550	60	130		28	8	3	23	28	11	.236
Wortman	SS150	150	541	51	109		12	8	3	29	32	17	.201
Betzel	3B110,2B18	141	547	72	157		20	11	0	52	44	26	.287
Acosta	OF154	154	563	87	146		16	6	0	74	26	36	.259
Hendryx	OF118,3B25	143	514	83	189		31	5	3	66	38	30	.368
Bescher	OF110	111	408	78	104		15	5	2	77	26	41	.255
Meyer	C87	103	314	33	88		14	3	0	24	15	6	.280
Wolfe	3B48,OF44	97	382	54	96		18	3	0	32	45	13	.251
Kocher	C77	90	276	23	64		7	2	2	15	23	2	.232
Stewart	OF34,P32	70	171	12	30		3	0	0	8	24	1	.175
Davis	P48	58	149	8	29		4	2	0	6	17	2	.195
Tincup	P24	51	114	9	29		6	2	1	8	15	3	.254
Long	P41	41	99	10	15		3	0	0	4	20	2	.152
Cinesi	SS22	22	72	7	13		2	0	0	6	2	0	.181
Corey	P10	12	22	0	3		0	0	0	1	5	0	.136
Friday	P6	6	7	1	1		1	0	0	1	2	0	.143
Fisher	OF	4	11	2	1		0	0	0	2	2	1	.091
Moore	C1	1	3	0	0		0	0	0	1	2	0	.000
Nies	P1	1	2	0	0		0	0	0	0	1	0	.000
Ballenger	2B	1	0	0	0		0	0	0	0	0	0	----

PITCHERS	W	L	PCT	G	GS	CG	SH	IP	H	BB	SO	ERA
Long	23	13	.639	41				292	256	105	112	2.47
Davis	22	20	.524	48				372	306	161	165	2.42
Stewart	13	11	.542	32				216	207	58	32	2.71
Tincup	11	8	.579	24				183	183	46	72	2.85
Anderson	6	1	.857	13				72	55	22	17	2.88
Corey	2	3	.400	10				57	62	26	16	2.68
Friday	1	4	.200	6								

INDIANAPOLIS 4th 85-68 .565 -8.5 J.C. Hendricks
Indians

BATTERS	POS-GAMES	GP	AB	R	H	BI	2B	3B	HR	BB	SO	SB	BA
C. Covington	1B147	148	534	70	161		22	13	6	72	41	15	.301
Yerkes	2B131	131	483	69	155		30	11	1	32	13	8	.321
Crane	SS148	149	578	85	146		15	9	2	36	42	36	.253
O'Mara	3B138	138	544	71	185		25	9	1	16	26	23	.340
Zwilling	OF143	144	542	90	149		26	12	9	72	48	13	.275
Reilley	OF141	142	548	67	138		12	6	1	37	33	44	.252
Rehg	OF135	138	545	88	155		33	9	4	50	26	26	.284
Leary	C82	99	331	32	100		14	5	1	10	21	4	.302
Gossett	C61	71	214	14	53		7	5	0	17	25	2	.248
Cavet	P60	69	161	17	37		8	2	1	8	32	3	.230
Wolf	2B26	66	179	16	47		5	1	0	17	19	0	.263
Rogge	P41	43	107	6	26		1	4	0	3	18	0	.243
Crum	P43	43	96	8	13		1	0	0	1	24	1	.135
Steele	P27	33	69	6	17		0	0	0	5	16	2	.247
Devore	OF21	28	71	12	22		2	1	0	4	4	2	.310
C. Hill	P26	26	62	6	7		0	0	0	6	21	0	.113
Henline	C18	18	54	4	11		2	0	1	6	11	1	.204
Orcutt	OF	8	26	1	4		1	0	0	1	2	0	.154
Hemingway	OF	7	24	4	3		1	0	0	2	3	1	.125
M. Brown	P6	7	13	1	3		0	0	0	1	6	0	.231
Voyles	P7	7	10	1	0		0	0	0	0	5	0	.000
Dale	P2	6	15	1	2		0	1	0	1	6	1	.133
Sweeney		1	4	2	4		0	1	0	0	0	0	1.000
Dawson	P1	1	3	0	1		0	0	0	0	0	0	.333

INDIANAPOLIS (cont.)
Indians

PITCHERS	W	L	PCT	G	GS	CG	SH	IP	H	BB	SO	ERA
Cavet	28	16	.636	60				359	357	50	127	2.26
Crum	20	14	.588	43				286	285	82	90	3.11
Rogge	16	14	.533	41				289	265	100	86	2.96
C. Hill	14	9	.609	26				182	188	52	64	2.92
Steele	6	9	.400	27				181	185	63	100	3.55
Voyles	1	0	1.000	7								
Dawson	0	1	.000	1								
Dale	0	2	.000	2								
M. Brown	0	3	.000	6								

MINNEAPOLIS   5th   72-82   .468   -22   J.J. Egan
Millers

BATTERS	POS-GAMES	GP	AB	R	H	BI	2B	3B	HR	BB	SO	SB	BA
Jourdan	1B142	143	526	78	159		30	10	4	45	48	11	.302
Sawyer	2B130	132	508	81	150		29	4	4	52	48	18	.295
Jennings	SS78	96	313	36	84		13	7	4	24	18	3	.268
Davis	3B86,SS15	107	365	62	94		11	4	0	62	36	11	.258
Rondeau	OF149	151	577	85	163		32	14	3	56	55	12	.282
Lelivelt	OF134,1B18	153	600	75	172		34	7	3	51	26	21	.287
Russell	OF92,P1	92	364	51	97		13	4	9	10	35	2	.267
Owens	C110	120	393	41	131		17	5	4	23	29	4	.333
Weidell	SS47,3B38,2B25	119	403	49	89		12	6	0	38	40	9	.221
J. Henry	C53	68	187	19	45		8	5	0	22	23	2	.241
Schauer	P56	66	141	17	43		3	1	1	9	32	2	.305
Roberson	P31	33	81	5	17		2	0	0	3	13	0	.210
Hovlik	P32	32	78	6	17		2	1	0	4	30	0	.218
Craft	P18	26	55	3	13		1	2	1	1	9	0	.236
Whitehouse	P26	26	55	0	4		0	0	0	1	17	0	.073
Milan	OF25	25	94	7	19		2	0	0	7	9	2	.202
Shellenback	P20	23	37	0	4		0	0	0	6	10	0	.108
Jackson	OF21	21	84	11	13		3	0	0	10	7	0	.155
Lindsey	SS	12	37	6	5		0	0	0	3	8	1	.135
D.C. Williams	P11	11	22	1	3		0	0	0	3	8	0	.136
Gomez	C	7	18	2	5		0	0	0	2	2	2	.278
Patterson	P4	4	6	0	0		0	0	0	0	2	0	.000
Burk	P4	4	5	0	2		0	0	0	0	1	0	.400
Lindberg	P4	4	4	0	0		0	0	0	0	2	0	.000
Humphrey	P2	2	4	0	0		0	0	0	0	2	0	.000
Dean	3B	1	2	0	0		0	0	0	0	1	0	.000
Fisher	P1	1	2	0	0		0	0	0	0	0	0	.000
E.A. Miller	P1	1	1	0	0		0	0	0	1	1	0	.000

PITCHERS	W	L	PCT	G	GS	CG	SH	IP	H	BB	SO	ERA
Schauer	21	17	.553	56				351	324	99	102	2.64
Roberson	11	13	.458	31				212	206	60	97	3.10
Hovlik	10	18	.357	32				208	202	96	91	3.65
Shellenback	7	3	.700	20				109	114	25	39	3.22
Whitehouse	7	11	.389	26				167	141	55	62	2.58
Craft	6	7	.462	18				118	95	65	51	2.51
D.C. Williams	4	3	.571	11				59	58	12	18	2.75
Burk	2	1	.667	4								
Russell	1	0	1.000	1								
Patterson	1	1	.500	4								
Humphrey	0	2	.000	2								

COLUMBUS   6th   70-84   .455   -24   Grover Hartley
Senators

BATTERS	POS-GAMES	GP	AB	R	H	BI	2B	3B	HR	BB	SO	SB	BA
McCarty	1B90,OF25	120	434	52	115		24	5	4	11	7	12	.265
Shovlin	2B136	136	470	69	138		25	13	2	28	13	22	.293
Roach	SS93	104	385	42	90		14	4	1	12	14	8	.234
Pechous	3B142	155	537	63	116		12	11	2	24	29	7	.216
Taggart	OF151	151	588	97	172		25	16	2	18	11	35	.293
Massey	OF108,3B13	124	475	67	128		14	8	1	17	13	13	.269
Sloan	OF71	71	277	30	79		7	5	2	7	3	10	.285
Wagner	C119	141	480	63	127		23	7	4	27	22	8	.265

COLUMBUS (cont.)
Senators

BATTERS	POS-GAMES	GP	AB	R	H	BI	2B	3B	HR	BB	SO	SB	BA
Stumpf	C65	80	235	8	46		4	2	0	9	21	3	.196
George	P41,OF14	72	206	23	62		11	3	1	1	7	0	.301
Bailey	OF63	68	230	30	64		9	3	2	13	11	5	.278
Hartley	1B35	51	183	21	52		3	2	0	4	2	12	.284
Wilkinson	P43	48	111	9	25		5	3	0	1	6	1	.225
Sherman	P42	42	94	2	11		1	0	0	2	8	0	.117
Wolfer	OF28	28	112	12	34		4	2	0	4	3	3	.304
Robertson	SS21	24	96	14	27		4	1	1	1	3	2	.281
R. Walker	P21	21	48	3	8		1	1	0	1	6	0	.167
Horstman	P18	18	33	2	3		0	0	0	0	6	0	.091
Lambeth	P15	15	33	1	6		0	0	0	1	1	0	.182
Lukenovic	P11	12	26	2	1		1	0	0	1	6	0	.038
Leyme	P6	9	19	4	4		0	0	0	0	0	0	.211
Collins	OF	8	22	2	8		1	0	0	3	0	0	.364
Loney	2B	7	25	2	7		1	1	0	0	2	0	..280
Herzog	1B	2	6	0	2		0	0	0	0	0	0	.333
Thornton	P2	2	5	0	2		1	.0	0	0	3	0	.400

PITCHERS		W	L	PCT	G	GS	CG	SH	IP	H	BB	SO	ERA
George		20	15	.571	41				278	270	90	77	2.46
Wilkinson		17	15	.531	43				208	269	89	106	**2.09**
R. Walker		10	7	.588	21				140	140	67	95	3.21
Sherman		10	18	.357	42				253	232	111	85	3.17
Lambeth		4	7	.364	15				94	97	37	31	3.43
Horstman		2	5	.286	18				97	94	49	33	3.25
Leyme		1	4	.200	6								
Lukenovic		1	5	.167	11				63	72	45	32	4.57

TOLEDO   7th   59-91   .393   -33   Zeider - Bresnahan
Mud Hens

BATTERS	POS-GAMES	GP	AB	R	H	BI	2B	3B	HR	BB	SO	SB	BA
Hyatt	1B125	149	515	85	169		**36**	9	9	**97**	32	9	.328
Getz	2B86,3B55	150	568	47	129		12	3	0	13	18	16	.227
J. Jones	SS51	51	211	20	50		2	5	1	4	12	8	.237
Wise	3B97,OF21	122	431	57	109		11	5	0	33	31	10	.253
Camp	OF120	123	481	56	121		16	8	1	26	33	13	.252
J.H. Kelly	OF119	128	505	71	127		18	9	2	38	34	23	.251
Knisely	OF106	110	411	47	113		16	6	0	42	18	8	.275
D. Murphy	C92	196	318	21	72		9	2	0	19	20	4	.227
M. Kelly	C70	99	248	25	52		5	1	0	25	6	4	.210
Shea	SS45,2B24	77	277	21	53		4	1	0	17	22	3	.191
Brady	P40	57	146	5	24		3	1	0	9	25	0	.164
Zeider	2B24,SS23	49	185	26	43		3	0	0	29	10	12	.233
Miljus	P27,OF15	47	119	9	25		3	2	0	3	10	0	.210
Sanders	P47	47	100	3	11		2	0	0	8	49	0	.110
A. Ferguson	P37	39	69	4	7		0	0	0	5	25	0	.101
McColl	P31	33	74	2	13		0	1	0	2	11	0	.176
Kane	OF26	32	92	5	13		0	0	0	5	10	4	.141
K. Adams	P26	26	43	0	7		0	0	0	1	13	0	.163
W. Adams	1B24	25	84	9	21		1	0	0	9	10	3	.250
Murray	SS24	24	89	6	16		0	0	0	13	7	1	.180
McCarthy	OF	3	10	4	4		2	0	0			0	.400
Durning	P	3	1	0	0		0	0	0			0	.000
Zahniser	P	3	1	0	0		0	0	0			0	.000
Turner	P2	2	3	0	1		0	0	0			0	.333
Bell	P1	1	2	0	0		0	0	0			0	.000
Lobmiller	P1	1	2	0	0		0	0	0			0	.000
Collamore	P1	1	1	0	0		0	0	0			0	.000

PITCHERS		W	L	PCT	G	GS	CG	SH	IP	H	BB	SO	ERA
Brady		13	**21**	.382	40				306	345	101	70	3.38
A. Ferguson		12	16	.428	37				212	218	80	82	3.36
Sanders		12	19	.387	47				294	270	137	103	2.97
McColl		10	11	.476	31				200	183	36	45	2.12
Miljus		9	8	.529	27				165	182	47	41	3.25
K. Adams		3	10	.231	26				132	146	48	22	4.16
Turner		0	1	.000	2								
Lobmiller		0	1	.000	1								
Bell		0	1	.000	1								

MILWAUKEE Brewers

8th	58-93	.384	-34.5	Clarence Rowland

BATTERS	POS-GAMES	GP	AB	R	H	BI	2B	3B	HR	BB	SO	SB	BA
Barry	1B56	57	198	19	45		7	2	0	13	18	4	.227
Butler	2B116	131	446	71	117		10	5	1	49	26	33	.262
Darringer	SS111	123	411	53	102		13	2	0	57	23	15	.248
Smyth	3B76,2B59	148	534	70	160		14	9	1	57	24	37	.300
Anderson	OF132	134	519	61	131		18	4	2	56	42	13	.252
Haas	OF124	129	459	76	135		20	8	7	24	45	13	.294
Kirkham	OF92	94	335	43	91		17	6	3	34	22	5	.271
Huhn	C85,1B23	117	344	39	97		16	9	3	40	27	9	.282
Mostil	OF85,2B34	132	500	70	134		12	14	2	37	48	12	.268
Conroy	3B36,2B17	73	238	18	52		5	1	0	26	31	3	.219
Brainard	1B26,3B24	58	211	23	58		7	1	3	7	35	9	.275
F. Henry	1B43	46	160	27	46		5	3	0	15	25	13	.288
Howard	P44	45	88	9	9		0	2	0	8	31	0	.102
Lees	C39	40	127	12	31		3	1	2	9	21	2	.244
Northrop	P25	36	75	2	16		1	0	0	2	12	4	.213
Faeth	P35	36	74	0	13		1	1	0	3	17	0	.176
Hansan	P28	33	61	1	9		1	1	0	3	13	0	.148
Hargrove	SS21	22	82	9	13		3	1	0	8	26	3	.159
Enzmann	P18	19	51	5	10		2	0	0	2	10	0	.196
Phillips	P14	15	40	6	9		1	0	0	1	8	0	.225
Marshall	OF	14	57	1	16		1	1	0	1	5	3	.281
Walsh	P4	14	20	3	2		0	1	0	0	2	1	.100
Pickup	OF	12	40	5	10		1	0	0	3	6	0	.250
Bues	3B	8	26	3	5		1	0	0	1	0	1	.192
Wolfgang	P	8	8	1	2		0	0	0	1	0	0	.250
Runge	1B	5	21	0	2		0	0	0	1	2	0	.095
Jasper	P5	5	6	2	1		0	0	0	1	2	1	.167
Kotzeknick	P5	5	3	0	0		0	0	0	1	2	0	.000
B. Stumpf	C	4	14	0	2		0	0	0	1	0	0	.143
McWeeny	P4	4	8	0	0		0	0	0	0	8	0	.000
Berger		3	5	0	1		0	1	0	0	2	0	.200
Petty	P3	3	4	0	0		0	0	0	0	2	0	.000
Huber	C1	1	3	0	2		0	0	0	0	0	0	.667
Murchison	P2	1	2	0	0		0	0	0	0	0	0	.000
North	P1	1	1	0	0		0	0	0	0	0	0	.000
Latina	C1	1	1	0	0		0	0	0	0	1	0	.000
Keerin	C1	1	1	0	0		0	0	0	0	0	0	.000

PITCHERS	W	L	PCT	G	GS	CG	SH	IP	H	BB	SO	ERA
Howard	12	20	.375	44				265	276	81	122	3.74
Faeth	11	13	.458	35				214	197	70	85	3.24
Northrop	10	11	.476	25				164	194	32	65	3.84
Hansan	6	7	.462	28				142	137	41	53	3.32
Enzmann	6	11	.353	18				141	161	46	36	3.90
Phillips	3	7	.300	14				94	92	48	37	4.98
Walsh	2	2	.500	4								
McWeeny	1	2	.333	4								
Kotzeknick	0	1	.000	5								
Petty	0	1	.000	3								
Murchison	0	1	.000	1								
North	0	1	.000	1								
Jasper	0	2	.000	5								

MULTI-TEAM PLAYERS

BATTERS	POS-GAMES	TEAMS	GP	AB	R	H	BI	2B	3B	HR	BB	SO	SB	BA
R. Williams	P44	MIL-SP	48	102	7	20		1	1	0	6	14	0	.196
Palmero	P25	MIN-LOU	41	97	8	20		3	1	0	8	15	2	.206
Graham	P39	KC-LOU	39	84	5	16		2	0	0	5	22	0	.190
Bennett	P21	COL-LOU	28	60	3	9		0	0	0	6	5	0	.150
Park	P23	COL-KC	24	29	2	5		1	0	0	4	1	0	.172

PITCHERS		TEAMS	W	L	PCT	G	GS	CG	SH	IP	H	BB	SO	ERA
Graham		KC-LOU	16	13	.552	39				224	233	60	66	3.13
R. Williams		MIL-SP	15	18	.455	44				281	310	47	78	2.98
Park		COL-KC	5	10	.333	23				102	88	47	26	2.47
Palmero		MIN-LOU	4	11	.267	25				130	133	46	35	3.35
Bennett		COL-LOU	3	5	.375	21				79	107	35	35	5.92
Durning		LOU-TOL	0	1	.000	5								

TEAM BATTING

TEAMS	GP	AB	R	H	BI	2B	3B	HR	BB	SO	SB	BA
ST. PAUL	**155**	5151	**739**	1380		215	57	43	**581**	454	**216**	.268
KANSAS CITY	152	5175	**739**	**1469**		**238**	63	**46**	473	520	134	**.284**
LOUISVILLE	154	5087	624	1316		187	69	19	485	383	203	.259
INDIANAPOLIS	**155**	5233	669	1441		204	**90**	27	419	454	169	.275
MINNEAPOLIS	**155**	**5259**	671	1402		225	72	33	456	**555**	108	.267
COLUMBUS	**155**	5175	630	1325		191	88	21	426	495	144	.256
TOLEDO	150	4999	522	1181		143	53	13	408	431	119	.236
MILWAUKEE	152	5036	584	1275		156	69	23	458	551	167	.253
	614	41115	5178	10789		1559	561	225	3706	3843	1260	.262

1920
St. Paul Saints

After World War I, another dynasty took shape in the American Association. This team would garner four flags in the space of six years, while setting an all-time record in the process. The team was the St. Paul Saints.

St. Paul had achieved moderate success during the first 20 years of the Association. They won two pennants (1903 and 1904) while finishing in the first division five other times. In 1919, the team won its first pennant in 15 years, but that was a mere prelude to the colossus that rose the following year.

Playing an expanded 168 game schedule, the Saints won more than 70 percent of their games, finishing with 115 wins. St. Paul's record was sparked by a strong hitting club which batted over .300 as a team. Their best hitters included: batting champion third baseman Rapp (.335); catcher Hargrave (.335); outfielders E. Miller (.333), Duncan (.313), and Haas (.307); and secondbaseman Berghammer (.304). (Note: Rapp prevailed in the closest batting race in Association history as five other players finished within two percentage points.) The team also enjoyed a trio of 20-game winners with a fourth pitcher missing the mark by a whisker. Hall led his team (as well as the league) with 27 wins, followed by Merritt (21), Williams (20), and Coumbe (19). Hall also had the circuit's best earned run average (2.06).

The Saints battered the second place Louisville Colonels by a record 28 1/2 game margin. Among the rest of the teams, Toledo, Minneapolis, and Indianapolis finished at .500 or better. Milwaukee, Columbus and Kansas City finished on the bottom three rungs, averaging almost fifty games behind the leaders. Last place Kansas City's roster included Brief, who led the league in home runs (23) and the new statistic of runs batted in (120). Columbus pitcher Danforth had the best strikeout mark, finishing with a total of 188.

The runs batted in statistic was first calculated in the American Association in 1920. Originally called "runs responsible for," the statistic was designed to measure a batter's worth by counting how many other players could score because of his hits. A true team statistic, the runs batted in category soon became one of the basic measures of a batter's ability.

St. Paul went on to win two more firsts and one second during the next four years. After that, the team won two pennants during the 1930s, and one during the 1940s. However, this 1920 Saints club is the one to be remembered, for it set two records that haven't been topped. St. Paul's 115 wins and its resulting .701 win percentage stand as the American Association's best, unlikely to be bettered for a long time to come.

ST. PAUL Saints

ST. PAUL Saints	1st	115-49	.701			Mike Kelley

BATTERS	POS-GAMES	GP	AB	R	H	BI	2B	3B	HR	BB	SO	SB	BA
Dressen	1B153	154	625	**131**	184	78	16	16	4	88	36	**50**	.294
Berghammer	2B158	158	517	93	157	75	23	8	2	78	30	21	.304
Boone	SS153	153	552	80	164	68	33	8	2	28	35	29	.297
Rapp	3B144	155	558	93	187	83	37	9	0	45	21	49	**.335**
E. Miller	OF159	159	618	108	206	104	46	8	8	45	37	24	.333
Riggert	OF132	137	514	89	147	71	15	17	9	35	42	12	.286
Haas	OF106,P1	130	446	73	137	64	24	5	11	27	46	12	.307
B. Hargrave	C136	142	496	115	166	109	36	12	22	59	27	13	.335
Duncan	OF103	118	402	72	126	64	18	6	2	40	25	6	.313
McMenemy	C49	58	126	18	31	24	4	4	2	22	36	3	.246
Brazill	3B18	52	135	34	51	17	5	3	2	11	12	5	.378
C. Hall	P48	50	108	10	21	8	5	1	0	4	23	0	.194
Williams	P46	48	90	3	25	6	1	0	0	7	20	0	.277
Merritt	P47	47	101	7	9	9	1	0	0	2	21	0	.089
Griner	P44	44	75	5	13	5	4	2	0	13	27	1	.173
Coumbe	P32	40	93	15	27	18	9	3	1	4	4	0	.290
Browne	P23	23	22	1	3	0	1	0	0	0	3	0	.136
Foster	P9	10	22	2	4	0	0	0	0	0	7	0	.182
Shauley	SS	8	26	5	7	3	0	1	0	3	2	1	.269
Cole	OF	6	19	3	7	2	0	1	0	2	2	0	.368
W. Hargrave	3B	4	14	1	4	2	2	0	0	2	0	1	.286

PITCHERS	W	L	PCT	G	GS	CG	SH	IP	H	BB	SO	ERA
C. Hall	27	8	**.771**	48				327	233	88	133	**2.06**
Merritt	21	10	.677	47				291	285	81	106	2.63
Williams	20	6	.769	46				256	263	50	69	3.34
Coumbe	19	7	.731	32				218	198	62	79	3.14
Griner	16	13	.552	44				232	255	46	62	3.61
Foster	5	3	.625	9				52	50	66	65	3.11
Overlook	4	1	.800	8				31	28	11	15	2.90
Browne	2	1	.667	23				73	81	35	16	3.89
Haas	1	0	1.000	1				8	6	4	1	2.25

LOUISVILLE Colonels

LOUISVILLE Colonels	2nd	88-79	.527	-28.5		Joe McCarthy

BATTERS	POS-GAMES	GP	AB	R	H	BI	2B	3B	HR	BB	SO	SB	BA
Kirke	1B157	161	634	84	209	114	32	6	8	20	17	19	.330
Betzel	2B145	157	606	89	174	72	27	14	5	40	44	28	.287
Wortman	SS166	166	579	62	136	57	20	8	1	39	34	17	.235
Schepner	3B160	160	591	80	149	52	16	7	0	47	37	13	.252
Acosta	OF165,P1	165	607	87	140	53	16	12	1	89	37	18	.231
Massey	OF151	158	574	81	172	69	36	6	0	52	36	18	.300
Lamar	OF89	89	361	51	114	58	17	7	4	10	19	11	.316
Kocher	C101	125	400	30	103	40	12	6	2	26	52	5	.258
Tincup	OF66,P34	124	360	75	119	53	16	16	8	27	43	14	.331
Meyer	C76	93	281	26	75	27	9	4	0	16	6	6	.267
J. McCarthy	2B23,OF20	58	175	17	44	21	12	2	0	19	17	3	.251
W.B. Wright	P52	55	103	8	26	12	8	1	0	10	28	0	.252
Long	P41	45	78	11	17	8	2	1	0	7	21	1	.218
Koob	P42	43	75	8	9	3	0	0	0	13	29	0	.120
Graham	P39	39	78	5	16	4	1	1	0	5	18	0	.205
Decatur	P22	22	35	3	7	1	1	0	0	4	9	0	.200
Ballenger	OF	14	30	7	11	4	1	0	0	2	1	2	.367
Ellis	OF	12	43	7	16	3	3	0	0	1	0	4	.372
Meeks	OF	8	18	2	1	0	0	0	0	0	6	0	.056
Tatum	P8	8	9	2	2	1	0	0	0	0	2	0	.222

PITCHERS	W	L	PCT	G	GS	CG	SH	IP	H	BB	SO	ERA
Long	18	13	.581	41				243	229	114	88	3.29
Koob	17	17	.500	42				251	244	101	85	4.05
Tincup	15	12	.556	34				238	222	67	71	2.83
W.B. Wright	15	15	.500	52				280	295	85	100	3.05
Graham	11	10	.524	39				230	270	75	48	4.62
Decatur	7	8	.468	22				122	129	23	47	3.02
Estell	3	1	.750	7				39	42	12	16	3.00
Tatum	0	0	----	8				24	29	21	11	8.25
Lee	0	0	----	4				7	19	8	2	15.43
H. Miller	0	0	----	4				6	12	7	2	15.00
Acosta	0	0	----	1				5	8	7	1	12.60

TOLEDO   3rd   87-79   .524   -29.5   Roger Bresnahan
Mud Hens

BATTERS	POS-GAMES	GP	AB	R	H	BI	2B	3B	HR	BB	SO	SB	BA
Hyatt	1B138	152	530	96	168	93	34	11	9	112	29	13	.317
J. Jones	2B96,SS44	143	541	64	133	66	17	7	1	26	33	12	.246
Derrick	SS55	58	194	29	55	33	7	2	0	24	17	4	.283
Dyer	3B57,2B61,SS49	167	632	94	170	82	36	12	2	65	92	23	.269
J.H. Kelly	OF165	166	695	100	207	92	25	10	1	50	42	29	.298
Wickland	OF116	120	455	81	152	65	24	15	4	72	35	9	.334
Wilhoit	OF101	104	390	53	117	39	13	3	0	37	16	11	.300
McNeill	C69	85	242	17	58	31	2	4	0	16	9	6	.240
Dubuc	3B45,OF23,P21	102	305	46	89	50	10	5	1	31	19	3	.292
Fox	OF58,SS21	99	324	54	84	17	10	2	0	42	35	8	.259
D. Murphy	C69	73	231	24	49	28	10	2	0	16	22	0	.212
Brady	P48	53	131	17	36	15	7	0	2	4	19	0	.275
Middleton	P46	48	130	10	34	19	3	1	0	2	15	1	.261
McColl	P43	44	103	8	10	7	0	1	0	7	24	0	.097
Woodall	C40	40	153	17	40	20	6	5	0	6	11	0	.261
Hill	OF34	34	134	25	49	14	2	2	0	22	11	2	.366
Nelson	P34	34	55	12	12	3	1	2	0	5	10	0	.218
Okrie	P15	16	36	1	8	1	0	0	0	1	9	0	.222
Richbourg	1B	12	22	5	7	5	0	1	0	4	4	0	.318
Thompson	3B	10	28	2	7	4	0	0	0	5	7	0	.250
Clayton	3B	7	12	1	3	1	0	0	0	0	0	2	.250
Mead	P4	4	5	2	1	0	0	0	0	1	2	0	.200
Furman	P2	2	1	0	0	0	0	0	0	0	1	0	.000
Frost	PH	1	1	0	0	0	0	0	0	0	0	0	.000

PITCHERS	W	L	PCT	G	GS	CG	SH	IP	H	BB	SO	ERA
Middleton	26	14	.650	46				332	337	66	123	2.93
McColl	19	13	.594	43				275	302	70	57	3.89
Brady	14	20	.412	48				313	347	98	84	3.59
Nelson	9	4	.690	34				148	187	53	46	5.17
Dubuc	9	7	.563	21				126	117	28	46	2.72
Okrie	4	9	.308	15				105	100	47	45	3.51
Mead	0	0	----	4				21	15	10	9	3.00
Furman	0	0	----	2				4	0	12	1	6.75

MINNEAPOLIS   4th   85-79   .518   -30   Joe Cantillon
Millers

BATTERS	POS-GAMES	GP	AB	R	H	BI	2B	3B	HR	BB	SO	SB	BA
W. H. Smith	1B133	138	498	52	143	61	27	0	2	41	27	9	.287
Sawyer	2B165	166	599	74	169	70	50	1	7	40	53	31	.282
Jennings	SS97	97	381	40	111	63	9	2	0	25	24	8	.291
Davis	3B143,SS19	163	620	90	180	48	34	6	0	56	57	24	.290
Jackson	OF140	147	534	88	126	32	15	4	4	79	65	19	.236
Wade	OF136,SS23	159	620	80	196	87	29	7	8	43	60	14	.316
Rondeau	OF101	101	393	74	131	59	26	4	1	31	20	10	.333
Mayer	C151	152	468	55	127	59	19	2	6	81	62	6	.271
McDonald	SS25,OF23,3B21	87	297	42	80	27	16	2	2	15	46	6	.269
Russell	OF80,P3	85	298	46	101	41	22	8	6	9	24	5	.339
Carlisle	OF69	76	236	40	69	22	14	2	3	32	21	3	.292
James	P45	56	126	10	36	13	6	0	3	4	15	0	.286
Owens	C21	53	83	3	16	9	5	1	0	4	9	0	.193
C. Robertson	P45	48	122	6	27	5	2	1	0	6	13	2	.221
Bowman	1B16	38	102	15	19	14	4	0	3	10	23	1	.186
A. Schauer	P33	37	85	7	21	8	1	0	0	2	8	0	.247
Craft	P22	37	84	9	21	8	6	0	1	0	16	2	.250
Lowdermilk	P31	32	86	9	17	7	4	1	1	4	21	0	.198
Hovlik	P28	29	39	4	4	5	0	0	0	3	8	0	.102
R. Murphy	OF21	21	82	13	24	9	3	0	1	11	6	2	.293
Mokan	OF	13	45	5	12	4	3	0	0	7	3	2	.267
Fisher	P2	4	7	1	1	1	1	0	0	0	3	0	.143
Nufer	2B	3	9	1	2	1	1	0	0	0	0	0	.222
Cullop	P3	3	8	2	3	1	0	1	0	0	1	0	.375
Eberhardt	P3	3	8	2	1	1	0	0	0	0	3	0	.125
Thompson	P2	2	5	0	0	0	0	0	0	0	4	0	.000
Brundage	P1	1	3	0	0	0	0	0	0	0	0	0	.000
Packard	P1	1	1	0	0	0	0	0	0	0	1	0	.000

MINNEAPOLIS (cont.)
Millers

PITCHERS	W	L	PCT	G	GS	CG	SH	IP	H	BB	SO	ERA
James	21	17	.553	45				299	359	110	149	3.22
C. Robertson	18	16	.529	45				322	305	86	144	2.82
Loudermilk	14	12	.538	31				223	184	151	119	2.99
A. Schauer	12	12	.500	33				203	204	66	65	3.11
Craft	7	6	.538	22				144	134	68	61	3.19
Hovlik	4	5	.444	28				128	107	75	50	3.17
Fisher	1	0	1.000	2				12	10	3	1	3.00
Eberhardt	1	1	.500	3				19	22	5	4	2.84
Cullop	1	2	.333	3				16	17	16	12	6.75
Hanson	1	2	.333	3				11	17	6	2	12.38
Russell	0	1	.000	3				15	16	3	5	2.40
Brundage	0	1	.000	1				8	15	5	2	13.50
Thompson	0	2	.000	2				12	19	5	5	12.75
Jackson	0	0	----	1				3	1	3	0	0.00
Packard	0	0	----	1				2	3	5	0	18.00
Schwab	0	0	----	1				2	2	1	1	0.00

INDIANAPOLIS   5th   83-83   .500   -33   J.C. Hendricks
Indians

BATTERS	POS-GAMES	GP	AB	R	H	BI	2B	3B	HR	BB	SO	SB	BA
Covington	1B161	165	585	103	173	82	35	15	6	92	23	9	.296
J. Smith	2B125,SS18	146	537	71	130	50	20	13	5	27	77	12	.242
Schreiber	SS153	164	615	56	156	67	20	9	1	19	43	27	.254
Kores	3B		(see multi-team players)										
Rehg	OF151	165	634	104	200	83	36	14	1	54	34	16	.315
Zwilling	OF135	144	451	60	126	84	15	6	12	90	40	6	.279
Reilley	OF111	111	459	72	125	28	17	6	0	37	23	32	.272
Henline	C111	131	388	48	114	58	21	5	4	31	38	10	.294
Wolf	3B52,2B46	98	285	28	49	12	2	4	0	33	34	5	.172
Gossett	C69	79	241	21	56	29	8	4	3	11	26	2	.232
Cavet	P50	55	121	13	33	14	6	3	2	11	31	0	.273
Rogge	P43	43	112	4	17	1	0	0	0	1	19	0	.152
J.P. Jones	P40	40	111	1	25	11	3	1	0	1	21	2	.225
Petty	P33	33	82	2	10	6	0	1	0	2	34	0	.122
O'Mara	3B32	32	134	20	51	7	7	1	0	2	1	7	.380
Emerich	OF	16	22	2	2	2	1	0	0	1	4	0	.091
Gaw	P14	14	18	2	5	1	0	1	0	3	0	0	.278
Hunter	OF,IF	13	36	5	10	6	1	1	0	6	1	1	.278
Flaherty	P5	5	9	1	4	0	0	0	0	0	2	0	.444
Crum	P3	3	5	1	2	1	0	0	0	1	0	0	.400
Turner	P2	2	2	0	0	0	0	0	0	0	0	0	.000
Adams	P1	1	1	0	0	0	0	0	0	0	0	0	.000
Goldsmith	P1	1	0	0	0	0	0	0	0	0	0	0	----
Lynch	P1	1	0	0	0	0	0	0	0	0	0	0	----

PITCHERS	W	L	PCT	G	GS	CG	SH	IP	H	BB	SO	ERA
J.P. Jones	20	13	.606	40				286	253	92	126	2.52
Rogge	17	18	.486	43				302	322	96	110	3.55
Petty	14	14	.500	33				230	232	50	95	3.17
Cavet	14	17	.452	50				317	348	65	82	3.10
Gaw	3	5	.375	14				70	80	16	12	3.21
Flaherty	1	2	.333	5				22	24	13	5	7.36
Murray	1	3	.250	8				29	36	25	7	5.28
Crum	0	2	.000	5				18	14	10	9	2.00
Turner	0	0	----	2				5	8	5	1	5.40
Adams	0	0	----	1				5	4	3	0	0.00
Goldsmith	0	0	----	1				1	2	1	0	18.00
Lynch	0	0	----	1				1	4	2	0	18.00

MILWAUKEE   6th   78-88   .470   -38   J.J. Egan
Brewers

BATTERS	POS-GAMES	GP	AB	R	H	BI	2B	3B	HR	BB	SO	SB	BA
Huhn	1B119,C26	151	546	89	161	75	37	12	5	45	57	8	.295
Butler	2B145	146	546	104	163	84	26	9	4	60	27	34	.299
J. Cooney	SS142	145	541	79	142	57	10	6	2	32	24	12	.262
Lutzke	3B96,SS29,P1	148	523	46	119	50	12	9	4	35	58	7	.228

MILWAUKEE (cont.)
Brewers

BATTERS	POS-GAMES	GP	AB	R	H	BI	2B	3B	HR	BB	SO	SB	BA
Hauser	OF155,P1	156	549	94	156	79	22	16	15	91	86	7	.284
Mostil	OF151	155	597	125	190	49	29	12	4	67	55	27	.318
Gearin	OF88,P21	112	352	32	97	46	12	8	3	43	35	2	.276
Gaston	C110	111	374	40	112	56	22	6	7	24	46	4	.299
Bues	3B68	68	265	35	72	21	14	5	2	18	7	4	.272
Northrop	P39	49	147	11	29	9	5	2	0	7	27	0	.197
Kirkham	OF42	48	171	22	50	29	7	5	4	5	7	4	.292
Reinhart	P30	44	105	13	28	6	2	2	0	8	16	0	.267
P.S. Smith	OF38	43	147	12	37	17	6	2	1	11	15	5	.252
Ulrich	C24	38	112	10	31	8	4	3	0	5	11	0	.277
McWeeny	P38	38	76	1	2	0	0	0	0	4	41	0	.026
Gainer	1B28	37	127	25	49	29	6	2	5	23	3	9	.386
Trentman	P25	29	71	5	11	0	1	0	0	6	22	0	.155
Cozington	OF26	26	87	6	12	4	1	0	0	4	16	1	.138
Forsythe	2B20	22	66	5	13	1	1	0	0	6	8	2	.197
Staylor	C20,P1	20	65	6	14	6	3	2	1	2	22	1	.215
Burgwald	OF,3B	14	51	5	13	5	0	0	0	7	11	2	.255
Mueller	OF	13	47	6	9	4	0	1	0	1	6	1	.191
Schulz	P13	13	21	1	3	0	0	0	0	1	5	0	.143
Brielmaner	OF	7	12	0	0	0	0	0	0	2	4	0	.000
Glockson	1B,C	6	23	0	4	2	1	0	0	0	5	0	.174
Brandt	OF	5	13	0	1	2	0	0	0	1	2	2	.077
Gill	IF	4	12	2	2	3	0	0	0	1	4	0	.167
Stumpf	C	3	9	0	1	0	0	0	0	1	0	0	.111
Glenn	P3	3	7	1	1	0	0	0	0	0	0	0	.143
Bergerino	SS	2	7	1	0	0	0	0	0	0	1	0	.000
Stack	3B1	1	4	0	2	0	0	0	0	0	0	0	.500
Aaron	3B1,OF1	1	3	0	0	0	0	0	0	0	1	0	.000
Haines	C1	1	1	0	0	0	0	0	0	0	1	0	.000
Kevenow	PH	1	1	0	0	0	0	0	0	0	0	0	.000
Armstrong	P1	1	1	0	0	0	0	0	0	0	0	0	.000
Petke	1B1	1	0	0	0	0	0	0	0	0	0	0	----

PITCHERS		W	L	PCT	G	GS	CG	SH	IP	H	BB	SO	ERA
Northrop		20	17	.541	39				339	373	48	127	3.53
McWeeny		15	14	.517	38				243	233	87	155	3.53
Reinhart		10	13	.435	30				193	213	56	65	3.50
North		7	4	.636	11				100	98	28	45	3.06
Gearin		7	9	.437	21				161	167	56	60	3.80
Trentman		6	9	.400	25				167	205	35	46	4.74
Schulz		3	4	.429	13				65	75	24	19	4.43
Howard		2	7	.222	11				57	73	17	26	5.53
Glenn		0	1	.000	3				15	22	4	7	6.00
Lutzke		0	0	----	1				5	7	5	2	1.80
Armstrong		0	0	----	1				3	2	5	0	6.00
Hauser		0	0	----	1				2	5	2	0	9.00
Staylor		0	0	----	1				1	4	6	1	45.00

COLUMBUS
Senators
7th   66-99   .400   -49.5   William Clymer

BATTERS	POS-GAMES	GP	AB	R	H	BI	2B	3B	HR	BB	SO	SB	BA
F. Henry	1B133	137	516	73	147	75	32	8	4	29	57	16	.285
Robertson	2B64,SS22	86	333	37	88	30	10	2	0	20	20	4	.264
Pechous	SS123,3B22,P2	149	502	62	120	65	21	9	2	39	62	7	.239
Brainard	3B114,OF34	163	612	81	170	86	33	17	4	32	73	18	.278
Bescher	OF140	141	531	82	142	50	27	10	3	86	40	21	.267
Taggart	OF139	140	545	95	155	78	17	11	11	35	34	22	.284
Magee	OF80,1B26	113	392	58	120	49	28	4	4	50	31	13	.306
Hartley	C74	80	276	38	97	41	18	4	1	14	7	3	.351
Wolfer	OF54	68	221	22	61	21	7	1	1	18	8	8	.276
Krueger	2B64	64	247	22	60	27	13	4	0	14	27	5	.243
Mulrennan	P44	44	92	6	17	1	1	0	0	3	15	0	.185
Barger	P26	41	72	6	17	8	1	0	0	1	3	2	.236
Sherman	P40	41	66	5	14	8	2	1	1	3	12	1	.212
Danforth	P29	29	79	8	13	5	0	1	0	11	14	1	.165
Lyons	P28	29	60	5	15	5	2	0	0	3	6	0	.250
Brown	3B22	28	87	11	19	14	3	1	1	10	14	1	.218
McQuillan	P28	28	46	5	8	4	1	0	0	6	13	0	.174
Wagner	C21	25	82	9	25	13	7	2	1	8	12	0	.305

COLUMBUS (cont.)
Senators

BATTERS	POS-GAMES	GP	AB	R	H	BI	2B	3B	HR	BB	SO	SB	BA
Thompson	OF23	24	85	15	30	7	3	3	1	15	7	5	.353
DeFate		22	76	9	16	11	2	1	1	12	0	3	.211
Turner	2B18	19	66	8	14	1	2	0	0	7	4	1	.212
Gaffney	OF15	17	53	9	14	4	0	1	0	5	7	1	.264
Devfel	C	13	39	4	11	5	1	1	1	6	4	1	.282
Coltryn	SS	8	28	4	9	1	1	0	0	1	2	1	.321
Eldridge	P7	7	11	2	1	0	0	0	0	2	2	1	.091
Connolly	C	6	8	0	2	2	0	0	0	0	1	0	.250
Nesser	OF	4	11	2	0	0	0	0	0	0	1	0	.000
Gross	P4	4	7	1	0	1	0	0	0	0	2	0	.000
Willis	P4	4	6	0	2	0	0	0	0	0	0	0	.333
Farley	P2	2	2	0	1	0	0	0	0	0	1	0	.500
Sully	OF1	1	4	0	0	0	0	0	0	0	0	0	.000
Ackerman	OF1	1	4	1	0	0	0	0	0	0	1	0	.000
Solomon	PH	1	1	0	0	0	0	0	0	0	1	0	.000
Griffith	C1	1	1	0	0	0	0	0	0	0	0	0	.000
Bennett	P1	1	0	0	0	0	0	0	0	1	0	0	----

PITCHERS	W	L	PCT	G	GS	CG	SH	IP	H	BB	SO	ERA
Danforth	13	12	.520	29				228	198	68	188	2.57
Mulrennan	11	16	.407	44				259	282	118	96	3.79
McQuillan	8	11	.421	28				138	163	24	47	3.26
Sherman	7	13	.350	40				183	199	109	62	4.43
Lyons	6	14	.300	28				172	206	42	46	3.93
Eldridge	4	2	.667	7				45	50	16	13	4.80
Gross	3	1	.750	4				31	37	19	21	4.06
Barger	3	9	.250	26				123	159	30	27	4.75
Bennett	1	0	1.000	1				3	6	4	1	12.00
Newkirk	1	1	.500	2				5	8	4	0	9.00
Willis	0	1	.000	4				14	18	6	6	3.38
Farley	0	1	.000	2				10	11	16	4	5.40
Pechous	0	0	----	2				6	9	1	2	7.50

KANSAS CITY   8th   60-106   .361   -56   Alex McCarthy
Blues

BATTERS	POS-GAMES	GP	AB	R	H	BI	2B	3B	HR	BB	SO	SB	BA
Brief	1B117,2B30,OF15	165	615	99	196	120	41	9	23	69	87	15	.319
A.G. McCarthy	2B112,SS39	157	601	78	158	56	23	3	1	43	17	6	.263
Hartford	SS79	83	284	25	64	24	6	2	0	18	19	3	.225
E.Y. Wright	3B96	108	403	41	108	39	12	8	1	27	16	12	.268
Good	OF166	166	686	110	229	119	37	15	11	32	31	26	.334
W. Miller	OF124	134	499	95	137	44	16	9	1	74	45	15	.275
Letter	OF54,P12	74	231	24	66	22	11	3	0	15	25	6	.286
J. Brock	C88	99	289	29	69	32	13	3	1	36	32	6	.239
Sweeney	OF,C36,1B31	130	396	26	116	53	16	2	0	47	16	9	.293
Stucker	3B54	54	166	18	54	16	7	4	0	10	14	3	.325
Roche	OF19,3B17	53	165	10	33	15	6	3	0	7	13	5	.200
Horstman	P39	40	78	6	9	2	2	0	0	4	20	1	.115
Ames	P39	39	84	8	14	7	4	0	0	3	25	1	.167
Bolden	P25	29	52	4	13	4	0	0	0	1	2	0	.250
Fabrique	SS25	25	94	18	26	10	2	1	0	13	8	0	.277
Scott		24	59	10	9	2	2	0	0	6	13	1	.153
Weaver	P20	22	43	2	9	2	0	0	0	0	7	1	.209
Foster	SS17	21	57	2	11	7	5	0	0	7	9	0	.193
Ross	P13	19	35	3	7	4	1	1	0	2	12	0	.200
Tuero	P19	19	30	2	5	1	0	0	0	3	3	0	.167
J. Smith	OF18	18	46	9	9	1	0	0	0	12	9	0	.196
Reynolds	P17	17	38	2	6	1	2	0	0	2	13	0	.158
D. Branom	1B15	15	60	4	18	4	4	2	0	2	4	0	.300
L. Williams	P6	15	34	2	6	3	1	0	0	2	4	0	.176
Woodward	P14	14	34	3	5	3	0	1	0	2	9	0	.147
Songer	P14	14	13	0	0	1	0	0	0	0	5	0	.000
Platte	OF	10	35	4	9	3	1	0	1	2	1	0	.257
McDougal	OF	8	27	3	9	6	2	0	0	2	6	0	.333
Lamb	C	8	18	0	4	5	1	1	0	1	4	0	.222
T. Connolly	C	7	5	1	2	2	1	1	0	2	1	0	.400
Watkins	3B	6	19	2	4	0	0	0	1	0	1	7	.211
Meadows	P4	4	8	0	2	0	0	0	0	0	1	0	.250
Campbell	P4	4	7	0	0	0	0	0	0	0	3	0	.000
Alexander	P4	4	5	0	0	0	0	0	0	0	0	0	.000

KANSAS CITY (cont.)
Blues

BATTERS	POS-GAMES	GP	AB	R	H	BI	2B	3B	HR	BB	SO	SB	BA
Brown	P4	4	1	0	0	0	0	0	0	0	1	0	.000
Schorr	P2	2	1	0	0	0	0	0	0	0	1	0	.000
Reynolds	P1	1	3	0	0	0	0	0	0	0	0	0	.000
Deere	P1	1	1	0	0	0	0	0	0	0	0	0	.000
Knabe	PH	1	1	0	0	0	0	0	0	0	0	0	.000
Saunders	P1	1	0	0	0	0	0	0	0	0	0	0	----
Sheppard	P1	1	0	0	0	0	0	0	0	0	0	0	----
Burnett	P1	1	0	0	0	0	0	0	0	0	0	0	----

PITCHERS	W	L	PCT	G	GS	CG	SH	IP	H	BB	SO	ERA
Ames	16	17	.485	39				249	296	50	73	4.34
Horstman	9	16	.360	39				240	274	90	92	3.72
Weaver	8	9	.471	20				102	119	49	38	4.68
Reynolds	4	3	.571	17				104	120	32	30	3.90
Bolden	4	13	.235	25				130	167	45	46	6.09
Songer	3	2	.600	14				40	47	22	13	5.63
Woodward	3	6	.333	14				97	91	43	36	3.16
Lambert	3	7	.300	11				56	63	32	27	4.34
L. Williams	2	1	.667	6				45	45	18	21	3.00
Evans	2	5	.286	8				64	57	22	14	2.81
Ross	2	7	.222	13				83	95	31	32	4.66
Tuero	2	8	.200	19				103	111	38	41	5.16
Alexander	1	1	.500	4				13	15	4	2	10.39
Johnson	1	2	.333	4				9	14	8	2	11.00
Brown	0	1	.000	5				10	17	6	1	7.50
Campbell	0	1	.000	4				19	19	8	5	4.26
Meadows	0	3	.000	4				18	26	11	4	9.00
Letter	0	4	.000	12				54	70	19	15	6.34
Beedle	0	0	----	3				10	12	11	6	9.00
Schultz	0	0	----	2				6	14	3	3	9.00
Saunders	0	0	----	1				3	5	1	0	6.75
Deere	0	0	----	1				2	4	1	2	9.00
Sheppard	0	0	----	1				0	2	2	0	inf.
Burnett	0	0	----	1				1	0	2	1	9.00

MULTI-TEAM PLAYERS

BATTERS	POS-GAMES	TEAMS	GP	AB	R	H	BI	2B	3B	HR	BB	SO	SB	BA
Kores	3B131	TOL-IND	139	487	63	123	54	20	5	1	43	48	6	.253
M. Kelly	C55,1B37	TOL-COL	108	345	59	103	33	13	3	0	33	11	14	.299
George	P44	COL-MIN	55	121	11	27	10	4	4	0	4	16	0	.223
Whitehouse	P37	MIN-IND	39	92	8	14	11	0	2	0	5	25	0	.152
E.A. Miller	P36	MIL-LOU	36	73	4	10	1	1	0	0	1	24	0	.137
Stryker	P30	TOL-IND	30	58	2	11	4	1	1	1	2	12	0	.190
J. Henry		COL-MIN	17	42	3	15	5	2	1	0	4	12	0	.357

PITCHERS		TEAMS	W	L	PCT	G	GS	CG	SH	IP	H	BB	SO	ERA
Whitehouse		MIN-IND	15	10	.600	37				256	249	87	75	3.38
George		COL-MIN	12	19	.387	44				260	279	83	89	3.77
E.A. Miller		MIL-LOU	10	13	.435	36				203	216	88	74	4.00
Stryker		TOL-IND	6	12	.333	30				176	188	56	80	4.19

TEAM BATTING

TEAMS	GP	AB	R	H	BI	2B	3B	HR	BB	SO	SB	BA
ST. PAUL	165	5575	961	1679	803	287	102	66	538	504	229	.301
LOUISVILLE	168	5682	748	1543	644	232	91	29	433	474	154	.272
TOLEDO	168	5769	819	1594	675	225	88	23	585	516	135	.276
MINNEAPOLIS	166	5615	728	1569	647	289	37	46	475	578	137	.280
INDIANAPOLIS	169	5656	702	1477	562	215	96	37	456	555	165	.261
MILWAUKEE	170	5696	777	1504	626	214	101	58	520	672	128	.264
COLUMBUS	166	5551	735	1493	603	245	91	35	458	505	148	.269
KANSAS CITY	166	5640	697	1516	588	236	69	43	505	539	115	.269
	669	45184	6167	12375	5148	1943	675	337	3970	4343	1211	.274

1921
Upset

The 1921 American Association champion Louisville Colonels were set to face the International League champion Baltimore Orioles in the Little World Series. Few gave the Colonels any chance of victory. The Orioles juggernaut had just won its third pennant in a row, posting 119 victories along the way. Louisville could only manage 98 victories. However, results of these post-season matchups are unpredictable.

Although seemingly overmatched, Louisville was a strong team in its own right. Finishing with their first pennant in five years, the Colonels beat back second place Minneapolis by showcasing a strong hitting club of their own. Louisville first baseman Jay Kirke won the batting title with a robust .386 mark as he stroked 282 hits, the league's all-time best. In addition, six other players hit over .300. Also, pitcher Ben Tincup finished with a perfect 9-0 record.

Behind Minneapolis, Kansas City rose from the cellar to finish third, followed by Indianapolis in fourth. The second division was comprised of Milwaukee, defending champion St. Paul, Toledo, and Columbus. Bunny Brief of Kansas City continued to dominate the slugging categories as he set records for most home runs (42) and runs batted in (191) in a single season. On the pitching front, Dave Danforth won the triple crown as he topped the earned run average (2.66), strikeout (204), and wins (25) categories, sharing the latter with Gus Bono of Kansas City. Danforth's feat was amazing considering he pitched for last place Columbus.

The Little World Series opened in Louisville on October 5 with quite a surprise. Behind a 19-hit attack, Louisville pasted the highly favored Orioles 16-1. Baltimore evened the score with a 2-1 victory the next day, before Louisville once again shelled the vaunted Oriole pitching staff 14-8. In game four, on October 9, Baltimore was cruising with a 12-4 lead when, with two outs in the top of the ninth, unruly Louisville fans rushed onto the field causing the game to be forfeited. The series venue switched to Baltimore on October 13, and the Orioles responded with a 10-5 victory. However, this would be Baltimore's last taste of triumph, as Louisville won the next three games (3-0, 7-6, and 11-5) to wrap up the series five games to three. Despite being heavy favorites, the mighty Orioles had fallen to the underdog Colonels, in what some have called the greatest upset in minor league baseball.

Though beaten, the Orioles were not down long, as they returned to the Little World Series the next four years in a row. In the fourth of those years, they would once again face Louisville for the championship. And this time, Louisville fans, not those of Baltimore, would be the ones upset.

LOUISVILLE Colonels

1st 98-70 .583 Joe McCarthy

BATTERS	POS-GAMES	GP	AB	R	H	BI	2B	3B	HR	BB	SO	SB	BA
J. Kirke	1B168	**168**	**730**	125	**282**	157	43	17	21	29	29	13	**.386**
B. Betzel	2B113	113	485	88	152	70	15	20	4	45	32	15	.313
P. Ballenger	SS151	156	590	107	167	86	30	13	1	15	33	15	.283
J. Schepner	3B168	**168**	653	108	207	109	27	15	2	51	19	12	.317
R. Massey	OF166	168	664	134	210	98	35	7	2	24	49	21	.316
B. Acosta	OF146	152	588	135	206	86	36	10	4	116	35	21	.350
G. Ellis	OF139	139	556	98	187	100	27	12	2	34	32	6	.336
B. Meyer	C95	114	365	57	114	57	10	5	1	25	8	4	.312
B. Tincup	OF62,P26	102	299	50	85	58	16	7	3	29	38	14	.284
B. Kocher	C81	92	299	34	81	43	13	4	4	15	31	10	.271
R. Sanders	P51	51	93	6	11	3	1	0	0	12	41	0	.118
E. Koob	P50	50	96	6	10	5	0	0	0	8	48	0	.104
W.B. Wright	P48	48	65	7	11	4	1	0	0	3	18	0	.169
T. Long	P41	46	74	13	13	4	2	0	0	8	28	0	.176
T. Estell	P45	45	65	9	16	4	1	1	0	10	2	0	.246
N. Cullop	P38	38	87	5	15	5	0	0	0	7	14	0	.172
R. Miller		26	59	8	14	4	1	0	0	5	3	1	.236
T. Gaffney	SS14	22	50	6	12	5	2	1	0	2	7	1	.240
J. McCarthy	SS,2B	13	18	1	5	7	0	0	1	0	1	0	.278
H. Miller	P3	3	3	0	0	0	0	0	0	0	0	0	.000
S. King	P2	2	0	0	0	0	0	0	0	0	0	0	----
W. Dean	P1	1	1	1	1	0	0	0	0	0	0	0	1.000

PITCHERS		W	L	PCT	G	GS	CG	SH	IP	H	BB	SO	ERA
E. Koob		22	9	.710	50			1	270	313	119	93	5.07
R. Sanders		18	11	.621	51			0	262	315	146	91	4.98
N. Cullop		14	10	.583	38			1	252	300	56	70	3.61
W.B. Wright		13	15	.464	48			2	196	210	97	52	4.68
T. Estell		11	12	.478	45			0	199	242	88	45	4.25
T. Long		11	12	.478	41			1	215	265	128	73	4.98
B. Tincup		9	0	1.000	26			0	105	101	31	43	2.84
H. Miller		0	1	.000	3				11	15	2	1	6.55
S. King		0	0	----	2				4	2	2	4	0.00
W. Dean		0	0	----	1				2	4	2	0	13.50

MINNEAPOLIS Millers

2nd 92-73 .558 -4.5 Joe Cantillon

BATTERS	POS-GAMES	GP	AB	R	H	BI	2B	3B	HR	BB	SO	SB	BA
W. Conroy	1B129,3B11	149	562	89	174	85	37	4	3	55	4	14	.310
G. Fisher	2B164	164	706	131	248	96	40	11	14	29	26	16	.351
M. Jennings	SS111	111	435	66	125	70	28	11	3	31	19	4	.287
W. McKechnie	3B153	156	661	140	212	65	31	7	8	64	31	10	.321
R. Wade	OF150	152	596	124	195	126	37	7	31	50	55	8	.327
A. Russell	OF141,P5	146	549	118	202	132	35	18	33	41	47	9	.368
H. Rondeau	OF116	126	452	50	119	73	28	3	3	29	47	3	.263
W. Mayer	C110	112	339	53	94	54	15	2	6	70	60	0	.277
S. Magee	OF91,1B25	137	444	90	150	93	39	6	13	72	37	8	.338
T. George	P42	50	72	8	23	14	4	1	0	1	11	0	.319
G. Shestak	C35	45	102	9	24	13	6	1	0	5	19	0	.235
C. Robertson	P44	44	100	0	20	4	4	0	0	3	5	1	.200
S. Mokan	OF33	41	107	18	36	21	8	2	0	7	7	3	.336
A. Schauer	P37	41	60	7	13	9	0	1	1	4	11	0	.216
W. James	P39	39	70	6	16	3	1	0	0	3	23	0	.228
Crosby	C35	36	130	11	34	10	3	2	0	6	12	0	.261
W. Smallwood	P35	36	56	4	7	3	2	0	0	0	14	0	.125
E. Yingling	P19	29	49	8	19	5	1	0	0	1	6	0	.388
G. Lowdermilk	P25	25	63	7	18	1	2	0	0	1	13	0	.286
Connelly	SS24	24	88	13	18	4	1	0	0	4	4	3	.205
W. Smith		21	42	3	8	4	1	0	0	2	4	0	.190
J. Stevenson	SS18	19	76	12	21	9	3	0	1	2	8	3	.276
H. McLaughlin	P15	15	24	3	4	1	0	0	1	1	5	0	.167
L. Mangum	P12	12	30	5	10	1	0	0	0	0	2	0	.333
W. Perritt	P12	12	11	3	3	4	0	0	1	0	1	0	.273
H. Allen	IF	8	19	2	6	2	0	0	2	0	0	0	.316
J. Weinecke	P8	8	16	1	3	0	0	0	0	0	5	0	.188
D. Williams	P8	8	9	1	3	1	0	0	0	0	2	0	.333
D. Mulrennan	P8	8	7	0	1	0	0	0	0	0	0	0	.143
J. Grabowski	C	7	9	1	4	2	1	0	0	0	2	0	.444
C. Grover	P4	4	2	0	1	0	1	0	0	0	0	0	.500
R. Birkenstock	P3	3	0	0	0	0	0	0	0	0	0	0	----

MINNEAPOLIS (cont.)
Millers

BATTERS	POS-GAMES	GP	AB	R	H	BI	2B	3B	HR	BB	SO	SB	BA
Barrett	P1	1	2	0	0	0	0	0	0	0	2	0	.000

PITCHERS		W	L	PCT	G	GS	CG	SH	IP	H	BB	SO	ERA
C. Robertson		17	15	.531	44			2	300	312	116	175	3.48
W. Smallwood		12	8	.600	36			0	173	180	47	76	3.91
G. Loudermilk		11	9	.550	25			0	166	149	117	128	4.18
T. George		10	8	.556	42			0	156	173	61	67	4.04
W. James		10	16	.385	39			0	195	211	104	95	5.45
L. Mangum		8	1	.889	12			0	70	71	29	22	3.21
E. Yingling		6	3	.667	19			0	97	113	38	43	4.82
A. Schauer		6	6	.500	37			0	135	172	54	55	5.46
W. Perritt		3	1	.750	12				35	41	25	12	5.14
J. Weinecke		3	2	.600	8				38	35	14	14	4.03
D. Williams		2	0	1.000	8				21	26	11	5	4.71
D. Mulrennan		2	1	.667	8				19	24	17	8	8.05
A. Russell		1	0	1.000	5				11	4	2	3	1.64
H. McLaughlin		1	2	.333	15			0	61	88	35	18	5.31
C. Grover		0	1	.000	4				9	10	13	2	8.00
R. Birkenstock		0	0	----	3				4	7	1	1	7.20

KANSAS CITY   3rd   84-80   .512   -12   Otto Knabe
Blues

BATTERS	POS-GAMES	GP	AB	R	H	BI	2B	3B	HR	BB	SO	SB	BA
B. Brief	1B156	164	615	166	222	191	51	11	42	117	98	12	.361
A. Butler	2B115	122	457	130	168	62	35	11	4	84	18	18	.367
H. Leathers	SS101	107	345	60	91	49	11	6	1	56	35	4	.264
G. Cochran	3B90,SS25	120	466	85	148	65	30	5	4	52	35	9	.322
W. Good	OF164	164	711	165	248	157	38	9	23	46	35	25	.349
D. Zwilling	OF140	145	480	102	156	120	35	4	23	115	61	8	.325
G. Paskert	OF93	102	373	79	113	38	17	2	2	58	34	13	.303
L. McCarthy	C101	103	357	44	101	65	28	2	1	33	33	4	.283
B. Friberg	OF87,2B31	124	464	77	134	61	27	6	4	58	47	10	.289
W. Lutzke	3B67,SS33	107	368	62	109	47	16	14	3	37	45	11	.296
F. Scott	2B26,C17	87	212	38	69	30	16	2	3	14	35	8	.325
P. Carter	P46	51	127	17	33	13	9	0	0	3	7	0	.260
B. Skiff	C45	50	148	19	42	32	4	2	0	2	8	2	.284
G. Bono	P44	49	122	21	32	17	3	1	0	4	17	2	.262
O. Fuhr	P39	39	54	11	10	4	2	2	0	8	16	0	.185
L. Ames	P36	36	94	14	21	13	5	0	0	10	35	0	.223
O. Horstman	P33	33	37	4	10	5	0	0	0	2	10	0	.270
D. Brannon	1B11	31	58	9	16	7	2	3	1	1	6	0	.276
D. Lambert	P27	28	29	3	4	1	0	0	0	3	9	0	.138
F. Blackwell	C24	24	56	9	15	5	3	0	0	5	5	0	.272
O. Strucker	3B10	23	56	12	15	6	4	1	0	5	9	0	.267
S. Baumgartner	P14	16	40	6	15	7	2	1	0	3	4	0	.375
A. Holtzhauser	P16	16	20	0	3	1	2	0	0	0	7	0	.150
F. Murphy	SS13	15	54	13	15	6	2	0	0	9	10	6	.278
F. Cady	C	10	22	1	4	2	0	0	0	2	2	0	.182
C. Williams	P10	10	15	5	8	5	1	1	0	0	2	0	.533
G. Wright	SS	6	18	4	5	4	0	1	1	2	3	0	.278
J. Brock	C	5	11	3	1	0	0	0	0	4	2	1	.091
J. Reynolds	P5	5	7	1	2	0	0	0	0	0	1	0	.286
G. Felix	OF	4	12	1	4	0	1	0	0	1	2	0	.333
Johnson	P4	4	1	0	0	0	0	0	0	0	0	0	.000
T. Connolly	C	3	5	1	1	1	0	0	0	0	3	0	.200
O. Knabe	PH	3	3	0	0	1	0	0	0	0	1	0	.000
J. Gross	P2	2	1	0	0	0	0	0	0	0	0	0	.000
D. Songer	P2	2	0	0	0	0	0	0	0	0	0	0	----
F. Watts	P1	1	1	0	0	0	0	0	0	0	0	0	.000

PITCHERS		W	L	PCT	G	GS	CG	SH	IP	H	BB	SO	ERA
G. Bono		25	11	.694	44			0	300	321	167	146	4.68
P. Carter		19	19	.500	46			1	303	395	94	82	4.78
L. Ames		17	15	.531	36			1	256	321	78	79	5.17
S. Baumgartner		7	6	.538	14			0	85	115	21	31	6.35
O. Fuhr		5	14	.263	39			1	174	242	70	64	6.21
O. Horstman		4	6	.400	33			0	106	128	59	32	5.70
C. Williams		2	1	.667	10				32	47	20	6	8.72
D. Lambert		2	6	.250	27			0	97	124	58	27	6.59

KANSAS CITY (cont.)
Blues

PITCHERS	W	L	PCT	G	GS	CG	SH	IP	H	BB	SO	ERA
J. Scheneberg	1	0	1.000	7				10	15	12	2	11.70
F. Watts	1	0	1.000	1				4	4	3	2	11.25
A. Holtzhauser	1	1	.500	16			0	51	73	37	34	8.65
J. Reynolds	0	1	.000	5				14	19	7	4	7.07
D. Songer	0	1	.000	2				1	0	1	0	9.00
Johnson	0	0	----	4				5	6	6	4	7.20
J. Gross	0	0	----	2				3	5	5	2	9.00

INDIANAPOLIS   4th   83-85   .494   -15   J.C. Hendricks
Indians

BATTERS	POS-GAMES	GP	AB	R	H	BI	2B	3B	HR	BB	SO	SB	BA
C. Covington	1B157	158	569	99	185	104	31	14	10	98	31	15	.325
E. Sicking	2B147,SS20	167	590	82	168	82	29	3	2	72	40	22	.285
H. Schreiber	SS153	153	614	80	194	102	26	21	6	21	54	18	.316
D. Baird	3B158	160	617	119	191	68	28	14	3	13	39	72	.310
R. Shinners	OF163	164	683	138	236	94	50	26	13	28	46	52	.347
W. Rehg	OF140,2B16	164	637	100	206	117	34	14	2	40	32	27	.323
R. Kinsella	OF132	143	505	71	146	59	21	13	6	48	69	7	.289
L. Dixon	C115	117	376	31	76	26	12	5	0	16	77	3	.202
E. Morrison	OF81	99	282	40	72	40	14	4	5	29	34	4	.255
W. Henline	C50	54	163	16	44	18	8	4	2	11	14	0	.269
T. Cavet	P48	54	126	12	29	18	6	1	4	10	34	0	.230
L. Bartlett	P41	41	73	16	11	8	1	5	1	7	12	0	.151
J. Petty	P40	40	92	4	10	6	1	0	0	0	39	0	.109
S. Stryker	P35	37	50	4	11	4	2	1	0	1	6	0	.220
H. Weaver	P34	36	76	7	12	3	1	1	0	1	12	0	.158
C. Rogge	P31	33	94	12	28	7	1	0	0	3	12	0	.298
J. Enzmann	P12	13	21	2	1	3	0	0	0	2	4	0	.048
F. Watson	C	9	14	4	4	3	1	0	1	3	3	0	.286
R. Attreau	1B	7	20	3	10	8	4	0	0	0	5	0	.500
Sewell	C	5	7	1	2	0	0	0	0	0	3	0	.286
C. Whitehouse	P4	4	8	0	1	1	0	0	0	0	3	0	.125
J. Jones	P4	4	5	0	2	0	0	1	0	0	0	0	.400
L. Seifert	P1	1	2	0	1	0	0	0	0	0	0	0	.500
S. Van Dyke	OF1	1	2	0	0	0	0	0	0	0	0	0	.000
W. Zink	P1	1	1	0	0	0	0	0	0	0	0	0	.000
Hinkle	2B1	1	1	0	0	0	0	0	0	0	0	0	.000
S. King	P1	1	0	0	0	0	0	0	0	0	0	0	----

PITCHERS	W	L	PCT	G	GS	CG	SH	IP	H	BB	SO	ERA
T. Cavet	23	16	.590	48			3	331	363	69	93	3.29
J. Petty	15	17	.469	40			0	275	326	80	112	3.80
C. Rogge	14	13	.519	31			1	227	250	86	67	3.92
H. Weaver	13	12	.520	34			2	208	220	102	81	4.16
L. Bartlett	9	13	.409	41			0	196	229	69	64	5.09
J. Enzmann	5	2	.714	12			0	62	65	13	19	4.06
S. Stryker	3	10	.231	35			0	137	175	56	27	5.12
J. Jones	1	1	.500	4				13	14	4	2	4.85
C. Whitehouse	0	1	.000	4				22	35	11	5	8.59
L. Seifert	0	0	----	1				2	7	1	1	13.50
W. Zink	0	0	----	1				2	5	0	0	13.50

MILWAUKEE   5th   81-86   .485   -16.5   J.J. Egan
Brewers

BATTERS	POS-GAMES	GP	AB	R	H	BI	2B	3B	HR	BB	SO	SB	BA
J. Hauser	1B167	167	632	126	200	110	26	9	20	93	103	12	.316
F. Lear	2B153	153	534	138	191	112	43	4	13	116	70	24	.358
J. Cooney	SS162	164	665	130	196	74	31	11	5	63	18	18	.295
A. McCarthy	3B141	146	572	64	162	88	25	4	4	37	27	7	.283
E. Lober	OF138	144	544	96	149	52	22	12	2	75	33	5	.274
D. Gainer	OF134	135	529	107	180	124	32	16	9	50	44	24	.340
W. Matthews	OF94	95	364	65	123	47	17	7	0	36	21	13	.338
G. Clark	C72	75	256	25	65	42	10	3	0	22	19	2	.254
K. Kirkham	OF85	111	348	55	101	52	22	5	5	26	12	2	.290
D. Gearin	OF46,P35	100	277	39	85	38	17	0	2	36	17	6	.307

MILWAUKEE (cont.)
Brewers

BATTERS	POS-GAMES	GP	AB	R	H	BI	2B	3B	HR	BB	SO	SB	BA
J. Gossett	C51	59	173	16	48	34	10	0	2	17	25	1	.277
C. Forsythe	3B24,2B17	51	124	17	22	14	3	0	0	18	21	3	.177
F. Sengstock	C43	46	148	5	42	16	9	1	0	6	15	0	.284
E. Schaack	P40	40	98	10	22	12	3	2	1	9	26	2	.225
V. Barnes	P36	36	97	1	19	4	3	1	0	3	23	0	.196
R. Lingrel	P32	34	63	7	8	4	1	0	0	3	26	0	.127
R. Trentman	P24	24	34	4	4	2	0	0	0	4	13	0	.118
J. Ebert	OF18	19	60	6	14	4	2	0	0	2	11	4	.233
G. Gaw	P19	19	38	1	8	4	0	0	0	4	5	0	.211
J. Kiefer	P17	17	35	2	3	3	0	0	0	2	6	0	.086
Lewis	C	9	28	5	3	3	1	0	0	3	3	0	.107
J. Burke	3B	6	25	3	6	3	0	0	1	2	2	0	.240
M. Staylor	C	6	21	3	7	4	0	1	0	2	2	1	.333
E. Donaher	OF	6	13	1	1	0	0	0	0	2	3	0	.077
M. Collins	OF	5	17	6	4	8	0	1	2	1	3	0	.235
A. Dunn	C	5	15	1	2	3	0	0	0	1	4	0	.133
Gregory	C	4	10	2	3	0	0	0	0	0	2	0	.300
C. Slaughter	P4	4	9	0	1	3	0	0	0	0	1	0	.111
Gerstner	P4	4	7	0	1	0	0	0	0	0	4	0	.143
G. Richardson	P1	2	2	0	0	0	0	0	0	0	0	0	.000
Brewster	P1	1	2	0	1	0	0	0	0	0	0	0	.000
Dobratz	3B1	1	2	0	0	0	0	0	0	0	0	0	.000
Glahn	P1	1	0	0	0	0	0	0	0	0	0	0	----

PITCHERS	W	L	PCT	G	GS	CG	SH	IP	H	BB	SO	ERA
E. Schaack	18	14	.563	40			1	253	305	61	56	4.52
V. Barnes	17	15	.531	36			4	259	273	98	117	4.24
D. Gearin	14	11	.560	35			1	215	267	93	89	5.02
R. Lingrel	6	8	.429	32			0	150	202	56	31	5.76
J. Keifer	5	4	.556	17			1	95	111	38	28	4.55
R. Trentman	5	7	.417	24			0	99	146	20	32	6.27
G. Gaw	5	9	.357	19			0	104	137	43	20	4.93
C. Slaughter	0	1	.000	4				15	39	5	3	15.00
Gerstner	0	3	.000	4				19	29	2	3	8.53
Richter	0	0	----	2				7	13	3	0	9.00
Brewster	0	0	----	1				4	7	1	2	6.75
Roth	0	0	----	1				3	6	1	1	12.00
G. Richardson	0	0	----	1				3	6	3	0	18.00
Glahn	0	0	----	1				0	2	0	0	inf.

ST. PAUL   6th   80-87   .479   -17.5   Mike Kelley
Saints

BATTERS	POS-GAMES	GP	AB	R	H	BI	2B	3B	HR	BB	SO	SB	BA
L. Dressen	1B144,3B14	147	579	103	158	35	17	5	2	85	26	40	.273
M. Berghammer	2B81,SS40	123	457	61	144	57	25	9	1	43	27	11	.315
L. Boone	SS125	129	469	71	135	76	28	4	2	41	42	19	.288
G. Armstrong	3B137	144	515	85	167	82	30	10	9	41	23	9	.324
J. Riggert	OF149	162	596	107	185	93	28	20	13	61	52	17	.310
B. Haas	OF111,2B19	144	527	100	171	72	27	7	6	36	37	14	.324
E. Miller	OF102	102	402	77	126	96	30	4	18	40	33	12	.313
N. Allen	C120	128	401	48	127	55	24	5	3	20	56	4	.317
V. Duncan	OF85	114	358	51	109	44	9	6	2	38	20	2	.304
T. Whelan	2B64,1B28	105	336	60	104	44	12	8	4	60	25	9	.310
B. McMenemy	C71	85	214	38	60	34	13	2	4	21	42	4	.280
C. Hall	P5	56	110	10	32	19	6	1	1	10	21	0	.291
T. Hendryx	OF52	54	194	38	64	39	8	1	3	30	11	6	.330
R. Williams	P47	49	68	3	14	6	0	1	0	7	9	1	.206
H. Merritt	P48	48	94	5	18	10	2	2	0	3	16	0	.191
E. Foster	P38	38	56	7	19	7	2	1	1	5	12	0	.336
R. Kelly	P30	30	33	4	8	4	2	1	0	0	8	0	.242
P. Shea	P27	27	42	7	9	6	1	0	0	4	11	0	.214
D. Reilley	OF14	23	46	8	9	5	2	0	0	13	6	1	.196
J. Jones	3B16	22	59	5	9	6	2	0	0	2	2	2	.153
T. Sheehan	P20	20	40	3	7	2	0	2	0	0	1	0	.175
J. Benton	P15	15	38	5	10	4	0	0	0	0	7	0	.263
E. Hanson	P15	15	17	3	6	1	1	0	0	1	4	0	.353
L. Cole	OF	9	16	0	3	1	1	0	1	1	4	0	.188
J. Pierce	C	9	11	0	0	0	0	0	0	0	2	0	.000
D. Griner	P9	9	8	2	3	2	0	0	0	2	1	0	.375
T. Stanley	2B	7	22	1	8	4	2	0	0	2	2	0	.364

ST. PAUL (cont.)
Saints

BATTERS	POS-GAMES	GP	AB	R	H	BI	2B	3B	HR	BB	SO	SB	BA
B. Marquardt		6	8	0	1	1	0	0	0	0	5	0	.125
C. Schlee	C	4	7	3	1	0	0	0	0	0	0	0	.143
M. Koenig	OF	4	4	0	0	0	0	0	0	0	0	0	.000
C. Schmehl	2B	3	3	0	0	0	0	0	0	0	2	0	.000
T. Connolly	PH	3	3	0	0	0	0	0	0	0	2	0	.000
Finch	P1	1	0	0	0	0	0	0	0	0	0	0	----

PITCHERS		W	L	PCT	G	GS	CG	SH	IP	H	BB	SO	ERA
C. Hall		20	14	.588	54			0	306	354	108	105	4.36
H. Merritt		19	14	.576	48			4	287	290	117	115	3.76
P. Shea		9	10	.474	27			1	141	148	49	53	3.96
E. Foster		7	5	.583	38			0	161	211	74	56	5.36
T. Sheehan		7	9	.437	20			0	110	120	43	44	3.19
J. Benton		6	7	.462	15			1	92	111	26	32	4.70
R. Williams		6	14	.300	47			2	202	254	42	68	5.17
R. Kelly		3	7	.300	30			0	83	88	62	32	6.40
B. Marquardt		1	0	1.000	7				22	26	14	6	7.27
D. Griner		1	3	.250	9				26	34	9	5	6.58
E. Hanson		1	4	.200	15			0	46	52	33	22	5.28
Finch		0	0	----	1				4	4	3	3	6.75

TOLEDO
Mud Hens

7th   80-88   .476   -18   Clymer - Luderus

BATTERS	POS-GAMES	GP	AB	R	H	BI	2B	3B	HR	BB	SO	SB	BA
F. Luderus	1B144	144	603	80	195	106	29	20	2	76	27	7	.323
Roy Grimes	2B145	157	626	122	186	93	35	16	12	57	54	10	.297
C. Derrick	SS82	89	302	31	91	42	14	2	0	27	25	6	.301
C. Bauman	3B90,2B12	126	432	60	121	55	21	7	3	36	14	15	.280
A. Wickland	OF156	156	609	128	175	57	34	11	5	105	50	7	.288
J. Thorpe	OF123	133	505	79	181	112	36	13	9	22	22	34	.358
A. Hill	OF127	137	512	89	163	68	24	10	6	42	18	8	.318
A. Schauffle	C93	94	272	33	69	25	9	2	0	53	37	2	.254
H. Manush	OF39	89	195	37	57	14	9	1	2	11	7	5	.292
C. Huber	3B65,SS19	87	322	30	84	34	6	7	2	21	15	15	.261
B. Lamar	OF59	74	247	43	86	37	16	3	6	13	14	5	.348
B. Dyer	SS26,2B15	51	184	27	45	26	8	1	2	22	31	10	.244
R. Wright	P46	46	105	13	18	6	1	1	0	8	28	0	.171
H. Bedient	P42	42	95	13	20	3	2	0	1	15	34	1	.211
P. McCullough	P41	41	86	15	18	7	2	0	1	15	34	1	.211
K. Grimes	SS32	34	113	11	27	9	5	2	0	8	12	2	.239
C. Morgan	C31	34	80	9	20	10	3	1	0	1	8	0	.250
Y. Ayres	P33	33	81	8	18	7	2	0	0	2	6	0	.222
B. Morrisette	P28	32	48	8	15	6	3	2	0	2	9	2	.313
C. Manion	C23	23	76	10	18	9	4	1	0	8	2	1	.237
A. McColl	P16	16	18	3	4	0	1	0	0	2	4	0	.222
Laabs	C15	15	36	2	4	4	1	0	0	5	3	0	.111
F. Okrie	P11	13	13	3	3	0	0	0	0	0	4	0	.231
H. Mead	P11	11	18	1	3	1	0	0	0	1	8	0	.167
A. Stokes	P9	9	9	2	3	3	0	0	0	2	3	0	.333
C. Decker	SS,C	7	26	0	7	5	0	0	0	1	3	0	.269
J. Haines	C	7	15	2	3	2	1	0	0	0	1	0	.200
D. Claire	SS	6	18	2	5	2	0	0	0	2	2	1	.278
B. O'Neill	P6	6	13	1	2	2	0	0	0	0	3	0	.154
W. Hammond	C	5	17	4	3	1	1	0	0	2	3	0	.176
R. Bresnahan	C	5	12	0	5	2	0	0	0	3	0	2	.417
J. Curtin	C	4	10	1	3	0	0	0	0	0	2	0	.300
E. Bowen	2B	4	5	0	0	0	0	0	0	1	1	0	.000
T. Gullman	P4	4	2	0	0	0	0	0	0	0	2	0	.000
R. Shoberg	2B	3	4	0	0	0	0	0	0	1	1	0	.000
S. Vick	OF1	1	4	0	0	0	0	0	0	0	0	0	.000
W. Sandquist	SS1	1	2	0	0	0	0	0	0	1	2	0	.000
Gehring	C1	1	1	1	0	0	0	0	0	0	0	0	.000
R. Collins	P1	1	1	0	0	0	0	0	0	0	1	0	.000
C. Goszdowski	C1	1	1	0	0	0	0	0	0	0	1	0	.000
W. Alexander	P1	1	1	0	0	0	0	0	0	0	0	0	.000
J. Walsh	P1	1	1	0	0	0	0	0	0	0	0	0	.000

PITCHERS		W	L	PCT	G	GS	CG	SH	IP	H	BB	SO	ERA
H. Bedient		20	13	.606	42			2	274	327	52	75	4.11

TOLEDO (cont.)
Mud Hens

PITCHERS	W	L	PCT	G	GS	CG	SH	IP	H	BB	SO	ERA
Y. Ayres	15	11	.577	33			1	219	235	63	82	4.40
R. Wright	15	20	.429	46			0	300	340	68	86	3.75
P. McCullough	13	7	.650	31			0	233	242	97	101	3.94
B. Morrissette	5	8	.385	28			0	106	132	68	38	5.52
F. Okrie	3	4	.429	11			0	33	48	21	15	6.09
H. Mead	1	1	.500	11			0	53	54	30	15	4.08
A. Stokes	1	2	.333	9			0	32	34	16	14	4.78
B. O'Neill	1	4	.200	6			0	39	47	16	16	5.54
A. McColl	1	5	.167	16			0	59	87	26	10	6.56
J. Walsh	0	1	.000	1			0	2	5	1	0	18.00
T. Gullman	0	0	----	4				8	11	5	1	6.75
W. Alexander	0	0	----	1				2	4	3	0	13.50
R. Collins	0	0	----	1				2	4	2	2	27.00

COLUMBUS   8th   67-96   .411   -28.5   Clarence Rowland
Senators

BATTERS	POS-GAMES	GP	AB	R	H	BI	2B	3B	HR	BB	SO	SB	BA
M. Burrus	1B159	161	643	105	201	84	29	3	14	39	59	10	.313
C. Herzog	2B	(see multi-team players)											
C. Pechous	SS135	143	444	54	124	58	17	9	2	47	40	10	.279
J. Swetonic	3B93	108	294	38	63	32	9	3	2	52	41	7	.214
C. High	OF134	140	505	97	167	75	31	12	13	58	43	17	.331
J. Shannon	OF118	132	430	66	128	64	26	7	2	39	25	11	.298
E. Murphy	OF117	117	484	77	142	49	15	11	2	61	19	16	.293
A. Wilson	C83	93	280	28	76	28	11	1	1	36	12	3	.271
F. Brainard	3B65,2B23,SS22,OF21	142	526	88	155	28	32	16	13	35	62	27	.295
R. Taggart	OF108	128	406	65	122	47	14	5	4	39	30	23	.301
G. Hartley	C78	105	290	33	98	57	15	6	0	22	5	13	.338
J. Thompson	OF21	62	107	10	26	1	2	2	0	1	2	5	.243
H. Haid	P51	52	86	7	13	5	2	0	0	8	27	0	.151
D. Danforth	P44	44	118	13	22	4	3	2	0	8	29	1	.187
W. Wilson	P33	37	69	8	19	7	3	1	0	2	9	0	.275
R. Clark	P33	33	57	4	8	6	2	0	0	7	17	0	.119
W. Gleason	2B30	30	117	24	32	11	2	6	0	14	3	4	.278
P. Martin	P28	30	36	3	12	4	2	1	0	1	2	0	.333
C. DeFate	SS20	25	56	6	10	6	2	0	0	4	11	1	.179
T. Odenwald	P21	21	29	1	1	0	0	0	0	1	14	0	.035
L. Sewell	C16	17	52	11	17	8	4	1	0	5	0	1	.327
W. Campbell	3B	14	47	8	11	7	0	0	0	4	4	0	.234
H. Rush	P10	10	16	0	3	2	0	0	0	0	5	0	.188
E. Ambrose	P4	4	10	2	2	1	1	0	0	0	1	0	.200
L. Jacoby	P4	4	2	0	1	0	1	0	0	0	0	0	.500
Costello	P2	2	0	0	0	0	0	0	0	0	0	0	----
Ray Grimes	2B1	1	4	0	1	0	1	0	0	0	0	0	.250
F. Bowman	P1	1	0	0	0	0	0	0	0	0	0	0	----
Van Natta	P1	1	0	0	0	0	0	0	0	0	0	0	----

PITCHERS	W	L	PCT	G	GS	CG	SH	IP	H	BB	SO	ERA
D. Danforth	25	16	.610	44			4	329	292	114	204	2.66
R. Clark	12	13	.480	33			1	184	226	77	42	5.14
H. Haid	8	15	.348	51			0	265	272	112	111	4.65
W. Wilson	6	11	.353	33			0	172	198	75	46	4.61
P. Martin	4	12	.250	28			0	120	174	69	39	5.63
H. Rush	2	5	.286	10			0	50	66	30	22	5.40
E. Ambrose	1	2	.333	3				25	35	7	4	5.76
L. Jacoby	0	1	.000	4				11	22	11	4	9.00
Van Atta	0	0	----	1				1	0	1	0	9.00
Costello	0	0	----	1				1	2	2	0	27.00

MULTI-TEAM PLAYERS

BATTERS	POS-GAMES	TEAMS	GP	AB	R	H	BI	2B	3B	HR	BB	SO	SB	BA
C. Herzog	2B158	COL-LOU	160	610	112	177	76	22	11	1	69	24	20	.295
N. Brady	P23,OF10	TOL-MIL	49	108	12	27	12	3	1	1	7	33	0	.250
J. Northrop	P40	MIL-COL	44	104	9	29	11	5	5	0	7	15	1	.279
P. Sherman	P39	COL-MIL	39	39	2	8	3	0	0	0	2	9	0	.205
W. Schirmer	SS,2B	SP-IND	4	7	1	1	0	0	0	0	0	0	0	.143

MULTI-TEAM PLAYERS (cont.)

PITCHERS	TEAMS	W	L	PCT	G	GS	CG	SH	IP	H	BB	SO	ERA
J. Northrop	MIL-COL	16	16	.500	40			0	276	332	62	85	4.40
N. Brady	TOL-MIL	5	14	.263	31			1	168	228	62	48	5.73
P. Sherman	COL-MIL	3	7	.300	39			0	130	139	67	47	5.68

TEAM BATTING

TEAMS	GP	AB	R	H	BI	2B	3B	HR	BB	SO	SB	BA
LOUISVILLE	168	**6029**	1042	**1864**		273	112	44	561	457	137	.309
MINNEAPOLIS	165	5889	991	1815		333	75	**120**	505	501	82	.308
KANSAS CITY	165	5786	**1148**	1809		**342**	81	112	**739**	**715**	132	**.313**
INDIANAPOLIS	168	5729	850	1648		272	**128**	57	490	576	**222**	.288
MILWAUKEE	167	5802	934	1675		278	81	65	657	542	115	.289
ST. PAUL	168	5788	918	1721		277	89	68	562	520	153	.297
TOLEDO	**169**	5860	888	1695		273	100	52	580	528	140	.289
COLUMBUS	164	5594	813	1588		245	92	53	558	548	165	.284
	665	46477	7584	13815		2293	758	571	4652	4387	1146	.297

1922
Bunny Brief

There were many great hitters in the American Association who starred during the hit-happy decade of the 1920s. But one man dominated the decade in two statistical categories, winning five home run and five runs batted in titles. The man's name was Anthony Vincent Brief, but most called him Bunny.

Born Antonio Bordetski, Bunny Brief started his baseball career in 1910 for Traverse City, a Michigan State League team. After a three-year apprenticeship, which included two home run titles, Brief made the jump to the big leagues with the St. Louis Browns of the American League late in the 1912 season. Following a brief sojourn, Brief was sent to Kansas City of the American Association where he stayed for two years. His 1914 season with the Blues won him another promotion to the majors, this time with the Chicago American League entry. After one year here, Brief jumped to Salt Lake City of the Pacific Coast League, where he enjoyed a fine season in 1916, winning another home run title. This led to another major league callup, this time with the Pittsburgh Pirates of the National League. After half a season, he was sent to the Association again, this time for good.

After half a season with Louisville, Bunny Brief rejoined the Kansas City Blues at the beginning of the 1918 season. This is the place where he garnered most of his glory. After two solid years, Bunny exploded in 1920 with 23 home runs and 120 runs batted in, winning honors in both. The next year he did the same, this time with a league record 42 home runs and 191 runs batted in. The latter record stands as the all-time best mark for a single season. Brief's 1922 campaign was a virtual carbon copy of the previous two, as he won his third consecutive home run (40) and runs batted in (151) titles. He complemented this team well, as Kansas City finished a strong third. Ahead of the Blues resided St. Paul in first and Minneapolis in second. Behind Kansas City trailed Indianapolis, Milwaukee, Louisville, Toledo, and Columbus. The batting title was won by Glen Myatt of Milwaukee with a .370 mark, while pitching laurels went to Tom Sheehan of St. Paul for wins (26) and earned run average (3.01), and to Joe Giard of Toledo for most strikeouts (141).

Bunny Brief went on to win two more home run and runs batted in titles during his career, some with his new team, the Milwaukee Brewers, which he joined in 1925. When his career was over many career records belonged to him. Not only did he have the most home runs (276), and runs batted in (1,451) in Association history, he held the mark for the most runs (1,342), hits (2,196), and doubles (458). His was a truly remarkable career, one not likely to be surpassed.

ST. PAUL Saints

| | 1st | 107-60 | .641 | | Mike Kelley |

BATTERS	POS-GAMES	GP	AB	R	H	BI	2B	3B	HR	BB	SO	SB	BA
Golvin	1B141	143	553	91	141	53	18	15	4	69	40	6	.255
M. Berghammer	2B157	158	563	95	162	86	24	15	2	83	35	25	.288
L. Boone	SS166	167	630	104	181	115	36	6	8	56	51	20	.287
C. Dressen	3B117	131	411	64	125	59	17	10	2	50	38	16	.304
W. Christensen	OF150	154	572	117	166	54	30	4	2	97	38	20	.290
B. Haas	OF126,1B11	146	547	105	181	90	35	14	8	55	50	24	.331
J. Riggert	OF122	137	475	95	150	77	27	14	3	40	42	3	.316
M. Gonzalez	C131	134	433	61	129	70	24	5	2	56	27	14	.298
T. Hendryx	OF87	108	302	58	103	64	18	6	3	66	17	7	.341
Armstrong	3B53,OF11	73	232	32	63	46	13	4	4	21	14	2	.272
Allen	C54	61	167	14	41	17	3	1	1	9	26	1	.246
T. Sheehan	P53	53	116	11	24	13	2	0	2	11	12	1	.207
C. Hall	P43	45	92	7	21	12	3	0	0	7	14	0	.228
Rogers	P41	44	84	10	21	10	6	0	1	1	15	1	.250
Benton	P42	42	102	4	17	7	2	1	0	4	16	0	.167
E. Martin	P40	41	70	7	13	3	1	1	1	3	17	1	.186
H. Merritt	P38	38	57	6	12	5	2	2	0	2	7	0	.212
Weiss	OF12	27	45	9	13	9	4	0	0	10	4	1	.289
H. Morse	2B10	13	47	6	6	7	0	0	1	4	3	4	.128
McGee	OF	10	22	5	9	5	0	1	0	2	2	7	.409
M. Koenig	3B	7	17	2	7	1	1	0	0	0	3	1	.412
W. Dougan	C	6	14	2	2	0	0	0	0	1	1	0	.143
J. Martin	SS	5	14	1	5	1	0	0	0	2	1	0	.357
Hill	P5	5	10	1	2	2	0	0	0	0	2	0	.200
R. Williams	P4	4	4	0	1	0	0	0	0	0	0	0	.250
Brooks	OF	3	1	0	1	0	0	0	0	0	0	0	1.000

PITCHERS		W	L	PCT	G	GS	CG	SH	IP	H	BB	SO	ERA
T. Sheehan		26	12	.684	53				332	295	132	121	3.01
C. Hall		22	8	.733	43				271	274	109	91	3.65
Benton		22	11	.667	42				283	271	96	105	3.24
Rogers		13	8	.619	41				218	237	62	76	3.72
E. Martin		13	10	.565	40				211	240	92	99	5.03
H. Merritt		9	9	.500	38				164	177	87	72	5.05
Hill		2	2	.500	5				31	29	5	8	2.03
R. Williams		0	0	----	4				11	14	2	0	6.55

MINNEAPOLIS Millers

| | 2nd | 92-75 | .551 | -15 | Joe Cantillon |

BATTERS	POS-GAMES	GP	AB	R	H	BI	2B	3B	HR	BB	SO	SB	BA
T. Jourdan	1B157	159	599	124	187	98	48	11	15	92	54	6	.312
Fisher	2B150	156	624	102	191	78	38	8	6	30	29	6	.306
DeFate	SS66,2B17	83	289	51	82	42	20	5	4	51	23	3	.284
Conroy	3B71,1B11	86	323	54	96	47	28	6	3	45	42	4	.297
R. Wade	OF164	165	684	131	213	119	32	10	22	53	41	10	.311
Rondeau	OF156	159	575	84	162	96	33	8	8	61	36	4	.282
A. Russell	OF75	77	245	53	81	63	17	8	17	41	21	3	.331
Mayer	C163	164	527	105	167	114	31	3	19	111	26	4	.317
S. Magee	OF64,3B10	106	257	66	92	63	21	4	12	46	13	7	.358
M. Jennings	3B44,SS33,OF10	87	325	36	87	33	6	2	0	29	10	1	.268
R. Browne	SS59,3B21	80	253	32	58	16	10	3	0	29	11	0	.229
Cravath	OF25	52	90	14	25	19	3	0	4	10	14	1	.277
E. Smith	OF54	48	196	44	62	25	10	3	6	19	15	1	.316
E. Yingling	P41	48	67	6	17	3	1	0	1	7	5	0	.253
O. Bluege	3B33,SS11	44	168	30	53	15	9	1	1	26	17	2	.315
B. McGraw	P41	43	84	15	20	8	2	5	0	13	27	0	.239
H. Thormahlen	P33	39	56	13	17	9	6	1	2	6	16	1	.304
W. Smallwood	P38	38	46	5	11	4	1	2	0	2	7	0	.239
A. Schauer	P33	35	68	7	17	12	2	0	1	2	8	1	.250
L. Mangum	P24	25	37	4	8	6	0	0	0	1	3	0	.216
F. Owens	C19	24	42	0	5	0	0	0	0	2	3	0	.119
T. Phillips	P21	21	58	5	8	6	2	0	0	2	19	0	.138
H. Haid	P21	21	25	4	4	0	0	0	0	5	9	0	.160
A. McColl	P20	20	37	4	6	3	2	0	0	1	14	0	.162
Hollingsworth	P14	14	30	1	5	3	1	0	0	4	16	0	.167
D. Williams	P11	12	10	1	2	4	0	0	0	2	0	0	.200
Shaw	P10	10	13	1	4	1	1	0	0	2	4	0	.308
H. McLaughlin	P1	1	2	0	0	0	0	0	0	0	0	0	.000

MINNEAPOLIS (cont.)
Millers

PITCHERS	W	L	PCT	G	GS	CG	SH	IP	H	BB	SO	ERA
B. McGraw	16	11	.593	41				248	252	121	117	4.21
H. Thormahlen	13	6	.674	33				148	193	51	49	4.62
E. Yingling	12	11	.522	41				173	196	59	69	4.11
T. Phillips	9	7	.563	21				143	156	51	47	4.47
A. Schauer	9	8	.529	33				161	180	62	7	3.86
W. Smallwood	7	7	.500	38				132	182	46	45	5.72
A. McColl	7	7	.500	20				106	121	46	21	4.58
Mangum	5	5	.500	24				103	131	42	37	5.16
Hollingsworth	5	5	.500	14				86	83	55	73	3.55
H. Haid	4	5	.444	21				97	108	53	44	4.91
D. Williams	2	0	1.000	11				25	29	16	9	6.12
Shaw	2	0	1.000	10				37	41	15	10	3.65
H. McLaughlin	0	1	.000	1				3	8	5	0	15.00
Hennings	0	0	----	1				1	0	0	1	0.00

KANSAS CITY   3rd   92-76   .548   -15.5   Knabe - Good
Blues

BATTERS	POS-GAMES	GP	AB	R	H	BI	2B	3B	HR	BB	SO	SB	BA
B. Brief	1B120	139	519	133	176	151	40	7	40	85	76	7	.339
W. Hammond	2B73	76	293	60	94	30	17	2	0	25	25	12	.321
G. Wright	SS92,2B47	142	515	64	154	94	26	4	10	25	57	3	.299
W. Lutzke	3B159	159	582	101	189	131	46	8	11	76	58	3	.325
W. Good	OF165	165	707	149	249	97	31	3	6	57	38	13	.352
B. Becker	OF155	158	621	137	228	138	40	8	26	78	48	3	.367
D. Zwilling	OF118	128	410	84	128	61	19	7	14	84	56	1	.312
McCarty	C69	72	238	40	69	31	20	3	2	18	23	2	.290
F. Scott	OF56	97	276	47	91	31	22	5	2	40	27	7	.330
B. Skiff	C68	80	225	24	78	32	13	2	0	7	5	4	.347
F. Luderus	1B54	72	199	32	60	34	14	3	1	25	6	0	.302
Caldwell	P38	46	118	12	26	9	3	1	0	3	13	1	.220
G. Bono	P45	45	76	8	12	9	2	0	0	4	12	0	.158
E. Shinault	C40	41	128	20	34	19	3	2	1	18	17	1	.266
Dowd	2B39	39	149	39	40	8	10	3	1	25	28	1	.268
P. Carter	P34	39	74	11	18	1	2	0	0	5	5	0	.243
R. Wilkinson	P36	36	87	7	15	8	5	0	0	5	22	0	.172
J. Zinn	P27	29	86	11	27	12	7	1	1	4	5	0	.314
J. Dawson	P26	28	70	9	13	9	2	1	0	3	9	0	.186
Acosta	P10	10	2	0	0	0	0	0	0	0	2	0	.000
J. Russell	P9	9	13	1	2	0	0	0	0	1	4	0	.154
D. Branom	1B	8	20	4	8	3	1	0	0	1	3	1	.400
Morris	P8	8	13	2	5	3	3	0	0	1	2	0	.385
Ames	P8	8	6	0	0	0	0	0	0	0	0	0	.000
F. Schupp	P7	7	20	6	5	4	2	0	0	6	4	0	.250
Boardman	P7	7	8	1	2	0	1	0	0	0	0	0	.250
Boyd	P3	3	2	0	0	0	0	0	0	0	2	0	.000
Campbell	P2	2	7	1	1	2	0	1	0	0	1	0	.143
E. Smith	SS,2B	2	3	2	2	0	0	0	0	0	0	0	.667
D. Songer	P2	2	3	0	0	0	0	0	0	0	0	0	.000
Jenkins	PH	2	2	0	0	0	0	0	0	0	0	0	.000
Lee	P2	2	0	0	0	0	0	0	0	0	0	0	----
A. Holtzhauser	P1	1	3	0	0	0	0	0	0	0	0	0	.000
Patterson	OF1	1	3	0	0	0	0	0	0	0	0	0	.000
Lamb	C1	1	3	0	0	0	0	0	0	0	0	0	.000
Cashion	1B1	1	2	0	0	0	0	0	0	0	0	0	.000
Anderson	P1	1	0	0	0	0	0	0	0	0	0	0	----
Butler	2B1	1	0	0	0	0	0	0	0	1	0	0	----

PITCHERS	W	L	PCT	G	GS	CG	SH	IP	H	BB	SO	ERA
Caldwell	22	12	.647	38				263	269	62	85	3.59
J. Zinn	18	5	.783	27				217	250	71	82	3.98
J. Dawson	11	8	.579	26				148	157	82	63	4.13
P. Carter	11	12	.478	34				201	230	64	44	3.90
R. Wilkinson	10	11	.476	36				222	257	81	92	4.79
G. Bono	9	15	.375	45				218	255	19	79	4.91
F. Schupp	5	1	.833	7				61	54	44	49	4.57
Ames	2	0	1.000	8				18	26	4	3	4.00
Morris	2	4	.333	8				39	56	22	15	7.15
A. Holtzhauser	1	0	1.000	1				9	8	3	5	2.00
Campbell	1	1	.500	2				18	14	8	2	3.00
Boardman	1	2	.333	7				26	37	17	17	6.92
Acosta	0	2	.000	10				14	37	3	8	10.93

KANSAS CITY (cont.)
Blues

PITCHERS	W	L	PCT	G	GS	CG	SH	IP	H	BB	SO	ERA
J. Russell	0	5	.000	9				39	70	22	15	8.54
Boyd	0	0	----	3				5	9	1	1	10.80
D. Songer	0	0	---	2				7	13	5	2	10.29
Lee	0	0	----	2				3	3	1	0	6.00
Anderson	0	0	----	1				1	1	1	1	0.00

INDIANAPOLIS   4th   87-80   .521   -20   J.C. Hendricks
Indians

BATTERS	POS-GAMES	GP	AB	R	H	BI	2B	3B	HR	BB	SO	SB	BA
C. Covington	1B162	163	618	93	180	102	26	9	9	64	25	3	.291
E. Sicking	2B148,SS21	169	656	110	190	87	14	4	4	62	39	14	.290
H. Schreiber	SS147	149	575	67	163	93	26	16	7	21	54	14	.283
Baird	3B149	160	615	107	167	68	20	16	5	88	44	29	.271
E. Brown	OF157	161	633	110	214	133	44	16	12	28	35	4	.338
W. Rehg	OF149	149	570	99	160	67	21	16	4	40	26	13	.281
H. Purcell	OF72	97	266	40	87	31	10	7	3	16	36	4	.327
E. Krueger	C151	152	527	70	169	99	32	12	17	50	34	11	.321
T. Whelan	OF49,1B43	106	309	47	79	32	16	8	0	52	28	1	.256
T. Cavet	P47	49	97	16	25	17	3	3	1	3	20	1	.258
S, Yerkes	2B21,3B19	48	154	18	46	21	9	2	0	6	9	1	.299
J. Petty	P45	46	80	5	15	2	1	2	0	0	20	0	.187
Weaver	P43	43	109	8	17	6	5	1	0	3	17	1	.156
C. Seib	P33	40	64	4	19	7	2	1	0	2	9	0	.297
C. Hill	P35	35	77	9	19	7	1	0	2	2	14	0	.247
L. Dixon	C31	31	94	10	20	5	2	1	0	7	18	0	.213
Bartlett	P29	29	32	3	10	2	0	0	0	2	2	0	.313
Hammill	OF25	25	93	14	31	7	3	3	1	5	12	2	.333
Causey	P11	11	27	2	5	0	0	0	0	0	5	0	.185
Jonnard	P9	9	27	2	4	0	0	1	0	1	9	0	.148
F. Fitzsimmons	P7	7	24	6	5	1	2	1	0	0	1	0	.208
P. Shea	P7	7	13	1	2	0	0	0	0	1	2	0	.154
Spencer	OF	4	14	1	3	1	1	0	0	1	0	0	.214
Attreau	1B	2	1	0	0	0	0	0	0	1	0	0	.000
A. Lotshaw	OF1	1	1	0	0	0	0	0	0	0	0	0	.000
Berry	PH	1	1	0	0	0	0	0	0	0	0	0	.000
Heine	PH	1	0	0	0	0	0	0	0	0	0	0	----

PITCHERS	W	L	PCT	G	GS	CG	SH	IP	H	BB	SO	ERA
Weaver	20	16	.556	43				308	281	173	104	3.51
C. Hill	15	12	.556	35				210	214	66	93	3.36
T. Cavet	14	11	.560	47				256	308	41	66	3.17
J. Petty	11	12	.478	45				212	251	62	94	4.37
C. Seib	9	7	.563	33				153	143	82	82	3.94
Jonnard	7	1	.875	9				75	63	24	41	2.16
F. Fitzsimmons	3	4	.429	7				48	48	20	16	3.19
Causey	3	7	.300	11				78	92	20	25	4.27
P. Shea	2	2	.500	7				34	35	18	3	5.56
Bartlett	1	6	.143	29				88	92	27	18	4.19

MILWAUKEE   5th   85-83   .506   -22.5   Harry Clark
Brewers

BATTERS	POS-GAMES	GP	AB	R	H	BI	2B	3B	HR	BB	SO	SB	BA
I. Griffin	1B168	168	673	107	204	92	31	13	11	30	34	8	.303
E. Lear	2B126	126	483	85	171	100	42	15	1	69	39	5	.354
J. Cooney	SS163	163	652	103	190	85	28	12	1	38	21	24	.291
A. McCarthy	3B140,2B22	168	666	92	198	97	27	6	7	38	21	24	.291
P. Johnson	OF166	166	652	95	205	108	30	15	14	44	67	2	.314
E. Lober	OF148	151	563	108	159	66	23	7	9	78	46	6	.282
W. Matthews	OF120	123	451	72	150	62	17	2	1	42	14	21	.333
G. Myatt	C111	121	370	85	137	77	18	16	10	52	36	3	.370
O. Mellilo	OF82	98	311	48	87	44	9	6	5	25	28	3	.280
J. Gossett	C72	83	219	36	74	33	11	3	7	17	25	0	.338
D. Gearin	P31,OF10	66	117	19	41	14	6	3	1	16	7	0	.350
Schultz	3B27	51	116	18	30	13	7	3	0	3	9	2	.259
R. Clarke	P40	50	62	5	21	7	5	2	2	7	11	0	.339

MILWAUKEE (cont.)
Brewers

BATTERS	POS-GAMES	GP	AB	R	H	BI	2B	3B	HR	BB	SO	SB	BA
Bigbee	P33	46	84	17	30	19	7	2	1	11	5	0	.357
R. Lingrel	P39	44	99	15	26	14	6	1	0	7	18	0	.262
E. Schaack	P25	35	69	7	20	12	6	0	0	4	11	0	.289
N. Pott	P34	34	77	4	11	8	2	0	1	1	16	0	.143
Riviere	P32	32	44	4	8	2	1	1	0	3	7	0	.182
A. Simmons	OF12	19	50	9	11	7	2	1	1	2	6	0	.220
Rose	P17	17	17	2	3	0	1	0	0	3	3	0	.176
Stannert	2B13	14	46	6	13	8	3	0	1	3	5	0	.283
F. Sengstock	C	10	19	2	5	1	0	0	0	1	2	0	.263
D. Keefe	P9	9	19	3	4	3	0	0	0	2	4	0	.211
P. Sherman	P5	5	8	0	0	0	0	0	0	0	0	0	.000
Clark	3B	5	13	2	2	1	0	0	0	4	1	0	.154
Brady	P3	3	4	0	1	1	0	0	0	0	0	0	.250
Schneider	P3	3	3	1	1	1	0	0	0	0	0	0	.333
Dietrich	P2	2	3	0	0	0	0	0	0	0	1	0	.000
Drumme	3B	2	2	0	0	0	0	0	0	0	0	0	.000
Kempling	P2	2	0	0	0	0	0	0	0	0	0	0	----
Hartman	C1	1	2	1	1	0	0	0	0	0	0	0	.500
Higgins	P1	1	2	0	0	0	0	0	0	0	0	0	.000
Patterson	P1	1	1	0	0	0	0	0	0	0	0	0	.000
Meiser	P1	1	0	0	0	0	0	0	0	0	0	0	----

PITCHERS	W	L	PCT	G	GS	CG	SH	IP	H	BB	SO	ERA
N. Pott	15	10	.600	34				216	241	52	72	4.25
R. Lingrel	12	14	.462	39				263	322	76	65	4.45
Bigbee	11	11	.500	33				186	201	147	92	4.93
D. Gearin	11	12	.478	31				177	197	68	76	4.27
Riviere	10	10	.500	32				142	159	87	45	5.00
R. Clarke	9	5	.643	40				157	183	83	45	5.90
E. Schaack	9	10	.474	25				160	175	65	40	3.77
Rose	3	3	.500	17				53	71	19	17	6.45
P. Sherman	2	1	.667	5				26	28	16	8	3.46
Keefe	2	5	.286	9				57	68	28	19	6.00
Schneider	1	0	1.000	3				9	9	3	2	4.00
Brady	0	1	.000	3				11	14	8	2	4.09
Higgins	0	1	.000	1				6	8	5	3	10.50
Dietrich	0	0	----	2				5	8	3	0	7.20
Kempling	0	0	----	2				3	6	0	0	9.00
Patterson	0	0	----	1				4	8	1	0	9.00
Meiser	0	0	----	1				3	3	3	0	6.00

LOUISVILLE   6th   77-91   .458   -30.5   Joe McCarthy
Colonels

BATTERS	POS-GAMES	GP	AB	R	H	BI	2B	3B	HR	BB	SO	SB	BA
J. Kirke	1B168	168	664	112	236	123	38	16	9	57	40	8	.355
B. Betzel	2B161	164	655	86	176	88	29	6	4	43	55	6	.269
P. Ballenger	SS122,2B11,OF10	145	507	66	119	53	21	12	1	61	33	8	.235
J. Schepner	3B170	170	620	86	159	64	21	9	3	60	30	14	.256
G. Ellis	OF161	163	643	89	194	118	32	14	7	40	43	3	.308
B. Acosta	OF146	146	579	103	172	57	23	15	0	88	40	21	.297
E. Combs	OF117	130	485	86	167	55	21	18	4	42	39	9	.344
B. Meyer	C109	128	408	49	123	49	15	2	1	42	16	5	.301
Massey	OF86	97	313	53	90	36	11	4	0	61	22	3	.288
B. Tincup	P46	86	149	22	46	17	5	3	0	14	18	1	.308
Brottem	C70	83	255	30	60	31	20	2	3	25	42	2	.235
T. Gaffney	SS66	71	210	18	43	21	8	2	0	10	25	4	.205
DeBerry	P52	52	94	6	17	8	3	0	0	0	12	0	.180
Estell	P46	48	71	5	17	11	3	1	0	7	8	0	.239
E. Koob	P46	46	74	4	3	0	0	0	0	6	37	0	.041
T. Long	P41	45	43	10	9	1	1	0	0	4	12	1	.209
N. Cullop	P44	44	81	7	12	5	2	0	0	2	14	0	.148
W. Dean	P11	11	32	4	5	4	1	1	0	1	8	0	.156
S. King	P11	11	4	0	0	0	0	0	0	0	2	0	.000
E. Holley	P5	5	11	2	1	2	0	0	0	0	6	0	.091
Baylin	P6	6	2	0	0	0	0	0	0	0	2	0	.000
L. Lamb	PH	1	1	0	0	0	0	0	0	0	0	0	.000

PITCHERS	W	L	PCT	G	GS	CG	SH	IP	H	BB	SO	ERA
B. Tincup	20	14	.588	46				279	297	111	91	4.19

LOUISVILLE (cont.)
Colonels

PITCHERS	W	L	PCT	G	GS	CG	SH	IP	H	BB	SO	ERA
N. Cullop	16	13	.552	44				219	267	55	63	3.99
E. Koob	12	17	.414	46				240	288	105	87	4.80
DeBerry	9	15	.375	52				276	295	69	75	4.24
Estell	8	13	.381	46				212	277	81	50	5.39
T. Long	7	9	.438	41				152	177	69	53	4.80
W. Dean	3	5	.375	11				72	85	30	22	4.67
E. Holley	2	3	.400	5				35	43	12	16	4.63
S. King	0	1	.000	11				17	37	8	7	11.12
Baylin	0	0	----	6				10	22	9	3	16.20

TOLEDO   7th   65-101   .392   -41.5   Luderus - Whitted
Mud Hens

BATTERS	POS-GAMES	GP	AB	R	H	BI	2B	3B	HR	BB	SO	SB	BA
E. Konetchy	1B114	133	458	67	142	81	25	11	11	35	13	5	.310
Roy Grimes	2B		(see multi-team players)										
W. Black	SS116,2B14	132	492	55	127	59	25	8	6	34	51	7	.258
G. Whitted	3B107	112	400	52	109	47	13	4	1	33	32	14	.273
B. Lamar	OF166	168	667	118	235	90	32	**18**	10	37	33	26	.352
A. Hill	OF149	152	594	88	176	56	29	16	5	24	28	16	.296
A. Wickland	OF88	93	335	53	105	21	21	8	2	51	31	4	.313
B. Kocher	C143	146	486	38	118	58	22	4	1	27	48	9	.243
Terry	1B48,P26	88	235	41	79	61	11	4	14	30	32	2	.336
L. King	OF50	58	203	26	57	21	12	3	4	18	21	3	.281
J. Giard	P50	50	76	2	6	0	0	0	0	2	41	0	.079
P. McCullough	P49	49	67	7	14	7	3	1	1	4	13	0	.209
H. Bedient	P43	43	87	11	17	7	2	2	0	6	26	0	.195
R. Wright	P39	39	90	7	14	3	4	0	0	6	23	0	.155
Ayres	P35	36	79	7	16	5	1	0	0	4	9	0	.202
J. Murphy	C30	34	79	1	17	8	4	0	0	9	7	0	.215
R. Shinners	OF26	28	82	12	27	8	5	3	1	14	9	6	.329
I. Boone	OF24	26	88	9	24	13	5	1	0	8	10	0	.273
Mee	3B12,SS10	22	71	6	14	2	1	0	0	6	3	1	.197
C. Huber	3B17	21	72	6	15	6	2	2	0	4	6	2	.208
F. Lindstrom	3B10	18	23	3	7	1	2	0	0	0	1	0	.304
Buffington	3B16	16	59	6	14	8	1	0	0	3	6	0	.236
Wolgamot		15	29	3	4	1	0	1	0	0	3	0	.138
Sallee	P12	12	30	3	7	2	2	0	0	2	8	0	.233
Yaryan	C	9	24	3	4	3	0	0	1	2	3	0	.167
A. Schauffle	C	8	10	2	3	1	0	1	0	5	1	0	.300
Kapshaw	C	7	12	0	2	0	0	0	0	0	1	1	.167
D. Claire	SS	6	7	2	0	1	0	0	0	2	1	0	.000
Wilson	C	4	8	0	0	0	0	0	0	0	4	0	.000
Shoup	P5	5	2	0	0	0	0	0	0	0	1	0	.000
Parks	P5	5	2	0	0	0	0	0	0	1	0	0	.000
Baker	SS	4	11	0	1	0	0	0	0	4	2	1	.091
Scherbath	3B	3	5	1	1	0	0	0	0	0	2	1	.200
A. Seydler	P3	3	5	0	1	0	0	0	0	0	1	0	.200
B. O'Neill	P3	3	4	0	0	0	0	0	0	0	1	0	.000
P. Malone	P3	3	3	0	1	0	0	0	0	0	0	0	.333
Herbst	P2	2	0	0	0	0	0	0	0	0	0	0	----
Merrick	P1	1	1	0	0	0	0	0	0	0	0	0	.000
Poeppleman	P1	1	0	0	0	0	0	0	0	0	0	0	----

PITCHERS	W	L	PCT	G	GS	CG	SH	IP	H	BB	SO	ERA
H. Bedient	15	18	.455	43				271	316	63	80	3.59
Ayres	12	13	.480	35				229	229	51	92	3.38
R. Wright	12	16	.429	39				226	271	83	72	4.26
B. Terry	9	9	.500	26				127	147	59	35	4.26
J. Giard	9	18	.333	50				232	240	161	**141**	4.54
P. McCullough	4	12	.250	49				214	250	97	68	5.08
Sallee	2	9	.182	12				87	117	15	22	4.35
P. Malone	1	0	1.000	3				8	14	8	5	7.20
B. O'Neill	1	2	.333	3				13	18	4	4	6.23
Shoup	0	1	.000	5				13	18	4	4	6.23
Parks	0	3	.000	5				12	21	7	8	9.75
A. Seydler	0	0	----	3				9	17	0	3	5.00
Herbst	0	0	----	2				3	3	0	0	0.00
Merrick	0	0	----	1				2	0	2	0	0.00
Poeppleman	0	0	----	1				1	2	2	0	18.00

COLUMBUS   8th   63-102   .382   -43   Clarence Rowland
Senators

BATTERS	POS-GAMES	GP	AB	R	H	BI	2B	3B	HR	BB	SO	SB	BA
Burrus	1B134	139	513	61	157	75	34	4	6	34	21	7	.306
W. Gleason	2B128	137	476	75	117	46	20	9	1	42	35	9	.246
M. Shannon	SS94,2B30,3B19	147	497	45	136	70	24	11	4	63	55	7	.274
Davis	3B137	141	525	69	133	47	19	10	1	41	36	17	.253
J. Shannon	OF142	144	514	71	144	71	33	8	5	40	57	3	.280
E. Murphy	OF138	140	543	98	172	58	27	11	4	62	23	10	.317
J. Sullivan	OF83	93	316	52	94	50	23	7	3	29	27	3	.297
G. Hartley	C131	138	464	55	155	55	28	9	1	49	9	17	.334
G. Paskert	OF80,1B13	125	357	53	109	49	16	7	1	46	29	6	.305
P. Todt	OF79	85	267	35	73	39	10	0	12	26	38	5	.273
Lees	C47	55	148	13	31	13	3	1	0	21	21	2	.209
E. Palmero	P42	50	100	17	20	9	6	1	0	22	17	0	.200
B. Burwell	P48	49	107	10	18	5	4	0	0	3	3	0	.169
B. Snyder	P46	46	64	5	8	1	0	0	0	2	16	0	.125
J. Northrop	P39	42	92	7	19	10	3	0	0	6	21	0	.207
Lee	SS27	38	108	14	20	5	2	1	1	17	15	0	.185
Collins	OF16	24	52	2	8	7	1	1	0	10	10	0	.153
R. Sanders	P24	24	48	4	9	7	4	1	0	4	21	1	.188
J. Gleason	P21	21	54	9	12	6	3	2	0	5	13	0	.222
Wilson	C,1B	7	13	1	2	1	0	0	1	1	2	0	.154
Glaser	P5	5	2	3	0	0	0	0	0	3	0	1	.000
Hudson	OF	4	11	2	3	0	0	0	0	0	3	0	.273
L. Jacoby	P1	1	2	0	0	0	0	0	0	0	1	0	.000

PITCHERS	W	L	PCT	G	GS	CG	SH	IP	H	BB	SO	ERA
E. Palmero	15	17	.469	42				276	296	99	87	3.82
B. Burwell	14	23	.378	48				304	364	66	55	4.47
J. Northrop	11	19	.367	39				256	293	73	66	3.87
R. Sanders	9	8	.529	24				133	147	45	58	3.65
B. Snyder	7	11	.389	46				184	205	84	59	4.20
J. Gleason	6	12	.333	21				148	162	72	27	4.08
G. Lowdermilk	0	2	.000	7				29	23	27	15	
Glaser	0	0	----	5				18	25	6	3	7.50
L. Jacoby	0	0	----	1				5	5	5	1	5.40

MULTI-TEAM PLAYERS

BATTERS	POS-GAMES	TEAMS	GP	AB	R	H	BI	2B	3B	HR	BB	SO	SB	BA
Morrison	OF102	IND-SP	115	357	55	88	36	14	13	6	38	51	7	.246
F. Murphy	2B84	KC-TOL	110	369	55	96	27	10	3	2	26	30	16	.260
Blackburne	SS85,3B10	TOL-KC	106	366	70	110	42	16	4	0	41	25	11	.301
Roy Grimes	2B87	TOL-COL	98	365	52	107	42	15	11	5	31	30	9	.293
Pechous	SS72,3B12	COL-TOL	87	311	28	63	17	4	1	1	25	48	6	.203
C. Rogge	P26	IND-COL	26	40	5	9	5	1	1	0	2	5	0	.225

PITCHERS		TEAMS	W	L	PCT	G	GS	CG	SH	IP	H	BB	SO	ERA
C. Rogge		IND-COL	3	12	.200	26				126	163	47	32	6.08

TEAM BATTING

TEAMS	GP	AB	R	H	BI	2B	3B	HR	BB	SO	SB	BA
ST. PAUL	170	5767	937	1657		274	103	48	683	509	161	.287
MINNEAPOLIS	167	5730	991	1680		329	79	119	677	547	53	.293
KANSAS CITY	170	5906	1090	1861		355	78	115	666	603	76	.315
INDIANAPOLIS	169	5775	866	1669		239	128	70	469	597	105	.289
MILWAUKEE	168	5894	945	1797		286	103	82	524	447	79	.305
LOUISVILLE	170	5796	838	1648		257	103	31	560	496	85	.284
TOLEDO	168	5671	732	1551		244	101	62	432	566	127	.273
COLUMBUS	166	5598	724	1508		267	83	40	584	501	107	.269
	674	46137	7123	13371		2251	778	567	4595	4266	793	.290

1923
Tom Sheehan

In 1910, a Minneapolis pitcher reached the pinnacle of pitching success by winning 31 games. This record wasn't in serious jeopardy until a St. Paul pitcher made a serious run at the record in 1923. His name was Tom Sheehan.

Born in Illinois, Tom Sheehan began his baseball career with the Streator team of the Illinois-Missouri League in 1913. After a 1915 stint with Peoria in the Three I League, his contract was purchased by the majors, and Sheehan joined the Philadelphia Athletics of the American League. Pitching for one of the worst teams in major league annals, Sheehan compiled a woeful 1–15 mark in 1916. The next year he joined Atlanta of the Southern League, staying for three seasons. After winning 26 in 1920, Tom Sheehan returned to the American League, this time with the Yankees. Following a brief stay in the big leagues in 1921, Sheehan made his debut in the American Association for St. Paul. He came into his own the following year as he won 26 and claimed the earned run average title (3.01) for the pennant winning Saints.

In 1923, as the Saints were battling the Kansas City Blues for the flag, Sheehan racked up win after win. Through no fault of his own, in the end St. Paul finished second, as Tom Sheehan tied Tom Hughes' 13-year-old record of 31 wins in a season. Sheehan finished with only nine defeats and won the earned run title (2.90) for the second consecutive year.

The Kansas City Blues won their first flag in five years by nosing out the Saints by a scant two-game margin, though St. Paul finished with the Association's best ever second place record. Third place Louisville was the only other team over the .500 mark, as the rest of the league (Columbus, Milwaukee, Minneapolis, Indianapolis, and Toledo) finished far behind. Bill Lamar of last place Toledo won the batting title with a near record .391, as Minneapolis batter Carl East clubbed the most home runs (31) and Bunny Brief of Kansas City won his fourth straight runs batted in title (164). Tom Sheehan's St. Paul teammate, pitcher Cliff Markle, finished with the most strikeouts (184).

After his record-tying performance, Tom Sheehan joined the Cincinnati Reds of the National League for the 1924 season. After three so-so years in the majors, Sheehan returned to the American Association for the Kansas City club. He would post several fine years for the Blues (including a 26-win season) before ending his career in the International and Pacific Coast leagues. Of all the records set in the American Association, the record for most wins is unique, as it is the only one that is mutually held. It is shared by two fine pitchers, Tom Hughes and Tom Sheehan.

KANSAS CITY Blues

| | | 1st | 112-54 | | .675 | | | | | Wilbur Good | | |

BATTERS	POS-GAMES	GP	AB	R	H	BI	2B	3B	HR	BB	SO	SB	BA
Dud Branom	1B95	120	379	71	132	76	18	14	9	29	23	2	.348
Walter Hammond	2B121	121	446	66	134	72	20	7	3	36	38	13	.300
Glenn Wright	SS152	153	600	109	188	122	34	9	15	60	50	8	.313
R. Blackburne	3B72,2B51,SS15	138	493	73	149	76	29	10	2	53	39	4	.302
Wilbur Good	OF155	155	662	136	232	91	40	15	11	64	44	17	.350
Beals Becker	OF135	143	499	101	150	93	29	13	13	88	46	12	.301
Bobby Roth	OF	(see multi-team players)											
Bill Skiff	C117	121	400	51	134	71	31	6	4	27	22	1	.335
Bunny Brief	1B76,OF60,3B30	166	640	**161**	230	**164**	47	15	29	101	70	9	.359
Floyd Scott	OF47	76	238	46	74	36	15	3	5	19	34	6	.311
Dutch Zwilling	OF31	57	110	30	33	22	4	2	5	21	9	2	.300
James Zinn	P43	52	130	29	46	22	8	1	3	6	20	2	.354
Lew McCarty	C49	51	170	23	48	22	17	1	1	11	20	0	.282
R. Caldwell	P40	42	87	13	23	9	3	1	0	3	9	0	.264
Ferd Schupp	P37	37	98	21	21	12	0	3	1	13	27	0	.214
Roy Wilkinson	P37	37	45	8	7	4	0	0	0	4	10	0	.156
Joe Dawson	P31	31	54	5	16	8	2	2	0	0	7	0	.296
Herb Thormahlen	P24	24	58	4	7	3	2	0	0	4	23	1	.121
John Saladna	P23	23	53	4	5	4	0	0	0	3	19	0	.094
Paul Carter	P21	22	19	1	4	2	1	0	0	0	5	0	.211
Fuhrman	C	6	9	1	3	1	0	0	0	0	0	0	.333
Forrest	C	4	8	1	2	2	1	1	0	0	1	0	.250
Ted Menze	OF	2	7	3	2	0	0	0	2	0	1	0	.286
Ernest Smith	SS1	1	5	1	3	2	0	2	0	0	0	0	.600
E. Reginald	P1	1	3	0	1	2	0	1	0	0	0	0	.333

PITCHERS		W	L	PCT	G	GS	CG	SH	IP	H	BB	SO	ERA
James Zinn		27	6	.818	43				297	342	60	99	3.94
Ferd Schupp		19	10	.655	37				268	256	142	173	4.23
Roy Wilkinson		18	6	.750	37				143	170	38	52	4.60
R. Caldwell		16	10	.615	40				238	273	73	95	4.47
John Saladna		11	4	.733	23				148	134	28	43	3.71
Herb Thormahlen		10	9	.526	24				167	197	47	62	4.15
Joe Dawson		7	7	.500	31				135	122	64	50	3.73
Paul Carter		3	2	.600	21				68	82	20	13	3.84
E. Reginald		0	0	----	1				5	6	1	5	

ST. PAUL Saints

| | | 2nd | 111-57 | | .661 | | -2 | | | Mike Kelley | | |

BATTERS	POS-GAMES	GP	AB	R	H	BI	2B	3B	HR	BB	SO	SB	BA
Fred Beck	1B80	80	275	39	74	48	9	3	6	30	11	1	.269
Hap Morse	2B88	122	396	72	106	62	25	3	5	63	36	15	.268
Lute Boone	SS162	162	636	124	196	98	42	4	10	55	32	32	.308
Charles Dressen	3B158	161	588	102	179	99	50	9	12	73	47	18	.304
W. Christensen	OF158	162	636	130	188	64	32	5	4	**102**	46	33	.296
Bruno Haas	OF145	156	554	112	186	111	37	15	14	73	51	22	.336
Joe Riggert	OF125	133	495	86	143	91	26	10	11	49	41	16	.289
Mike Gonzalez	C106,1B35	146	482	79	146	84	26	14	7	49	29	17	.303
Marty Berghammer	2B87	105	313	57	90	49	10	4	1	57	25	19	.288
Nick Allen	C79	82	261	39	78	40	16	3	2	18	24	4	.299
Tom Sheehan	P54	56	124	16	31	17	5	3	2	4	12	0	.250
E. Morrison	OF49	55	128	22	32	17	8	4	1	21	22	2	.250
Cliff Markle	P54	54	109	11	17	11	1	0	1	9	26	0	.156
Howard Merritt	P51	52	119	8	31	17	8	1	1	1	20	0	.261
Charles Hall	P46	47	113	17	35	23	4	1	3	11	11	2	.310
Nelson Hawks	1B30	32	110	29	30	14	6	6	0	22	14	6	.273
S. Napier	P25	25	31	3	6	3	1	1	1	3	6	0	.194
A. Holtzhauser	P25	25	29	1	5	4	2	0	0	0	8	0	.172
Cooper	1B	11	25	5	8	1	2	0	1	0	0	0	.320
Tom Rogers	P10	10	14	4	3	4	1	0	1	0	4	0	.214
Eddie Foster	P5	5	9	2	2	0	0	0	0	0	0	0	.222
Horan	OF	4	4	0	1	0	0	0	0	0	0	0	.250
W. Dougan	C	3	6	0	0	0	0	0	0	0	0	0	.000
M. Koenig	2B	2	6	2	1	0	0	1	0	0	0	0	.167
McGee	OF	2	3	0	0	0	0	0	0	0	0	1	.000
D. Williams	P1	1	2	0	0	0	0	0	0	0	0	0	.000
Hoke Floyd	OF1	1	1	0	0	0	0	0	0	0	0	0	.000
Gus Ketchum	P1	1	0	0	0	0	0	0	0	0	0	0	----

ST. PAUL (cont.)
Saints

PITCHERS	W	L	PCT	G	GS	CG	SH	IP	H	BB	SO	ERA
Tom Sheehan	**31**	9	.775	**54**				335	337	116	89	**2.90**
Cliff Markle	25	12	.676	**54**				319	302	117	**184**	3.36
Charles Hall	24	13	.649	46				298	322	77	66	3.50
Howard Merritt	20	11	.645	51				310	318	94	120	3.37
A. Holtzhauser	5	4	.556	25				102	110	50	41	4.76
S. Napier	3	6	.333	25				104	117	42	26	4.67
Tom Rogers	2	0	1.000	8				24	43	4	13	
Eddie Foster	1	1	.500	5				21	25	6	7	
D. Williams	0	1	.000	1				5	10	0	0	
Gus Ketchum	0	0	----	1				2	5	1	0	

LOUISVILLE
Colonels

3rd   94-77   .550   -21   Joe McCarthy

BATTERS	POS-GAMES	GP	AB	R	H	BI	2B	3B	HR	BB	SO	SB	BA
C. Covington	1B153	158	560	86	145	85	32	12	10	60	42	8	.259
Bruno Betzel	2B159	161	663	108	194	78	42	7	3	40	50	18	.293
Maurice Shannon	SS171	**171**	620	99	183	90	30	12	4	63	52	13	.295
Joe Schepner	3B154	159	556	60	154	59	13	5	1	49	13	14	.277
Earl Combs	OF166	166	634	127	**241**	145	46	15	14	64	38	42	.380
P. Ballenger	OF94,3B15	131	487	76	138	56	25	7	5	45	42	20	.283
Joe Hamel	OF89	98	289	41	63	32	8	9	1	37	47	4	.218
Bill Meyer	C97	113	329	51	90	43	8	3	1	39	16	12	.274
Tony Brottem	C82	90	263	34	71	35	11	7	1	35	38	1	.270
Sammy Mayer	OF56,1B17	74	299	43	93	38	15	6	3	15	17	6	.311
Ben Tincup	P43	73	129	20	39	17	4	5	1	5	9	4	.302
Baldomero Acosta	OF54	54	209	39	54	29	12	5	1	39	17	7	.258
Joe DeBerry	P45	46	86	7	22	8	4	1	0	3	9	0	.256
Wayland Dean	P36	38	90	11	17	6	4	0	0	9	24	1	.189
Ernie Koob	P37	38	74	6	12	7	1	1	0	5	36	1	.162
Nick Cullop	P38	38	86	11	13	10	0	1	1	3	13	0	.151
Tom Estell	P31	32	32	2	5	1	0	0	0	0	3	0	.156
James Viox	OF24	31	100	24	33	13	7	0	1	13	7	3	.330
Allen Sothoron	P26	27	32	2	5	3	0	1	0	2	4	0	.156
Armando Marsans	OF16	24	69	9	22	3	1	0	0	5	4	0	.319
Edgar Holley	P16	16	20	5	7	3	1	1	0	2	5	0	.350
Stanley	3B	2	6	0	1	0	0	0	0	0	0	0	.167
Miller	1B	2	5	1	1	0	0	0	0	1	1	0	.200
Martin Baylin	P2	2	5	0	1	0	0	0	0	0	1	0	.200
S. King	P2	2	2	1	1	0	0	0	0	0	1	0	.500
Martin	OF1	1	0	1	0	0	0	0	0	0	0	0	----
A. Weldon	P1	1	1	0	0	0	0	0	0	0	0	0	.000
Campbell	OF1	1	0	0	0	0	0	0	0	0	0	0	----

PITCHERS	W	L	PCT	G	GS	CG	SH	IP	H	BB	SO	ERA
Wayland Dean	21	8	.724	36				259	251	113	107	3.27
Nick Cullop	17	14	.548	38				242	272	65	68	3.64
Ben Tincup	17	16	.515	43				252	260	81	98	4.03
Joe DeBerry	14	9	.609	45				236	256	63	81	4.08
Ernie Koob	9	12	.429	37				216	249	88	71	4.42
Allen Sothoron	6	9	.400	26				108	112	57	73	4.66
Tom Estell	4	5	.444	31				97	140	41	18	7.06
Edgar Holley	3	3	.500	16				72	84	28	22	5.63
Martin Baylin	0	1	.000	2				10	10	5	4	
S. King	0	0	----	2				5	15	1	3	
A. Weldon	0	0	----	1				3	8	6	5	

COLUMBUS
Senators

4th   79-89   .470   -34   Carleton Molesworth

BATTERS	POS-GAMES	GP	AB	R	H	BI	2B	3B	HR	BB	SO	SB	BA
M. Burrus	1B106	120	398	62	123	67	25	7	14	42	13	8	.309
Bill Kenworthy	2B127	131	463	63	141	70	32	5	2	35	20	7	.305
H. Schreiber	SS157	159	629	93	198	106	38	11	4	30	46	12	.315
I. Davis	3B169	169	687	139	216	69	43	13	3	78	59	31	.314
E. Murphy	OF152	154	595	116	209	94	39	8	13	68	18	42	.351
John Brooks	OF143	145	534	58	146	58	25	7	2	23	48	12	.273
John Sullivan	OF113	122	399	55	114	61	26	6	4	44	28	7	.286

COLUMBUS (cont.)
Senators

BATTERS	POS-GAMES	GP	AB	R	H	BI	2B	3B	HR	BB	SO	SB	BA
Grover Hartley	C101	108	373	60	110	54	17	2	1	40	10	9	.295
George Paskert	OF100	109	344	66	103	55	24	5	3	57	40	8	.299
Roy Grimes	1B74	96	285	57	89	40	17	3	5	35	17	7	.312
Douglas Baird	2B44,3B18	89	242	46	74	35	12	3	3	19	22	17	.306
Harold Elliott	C68	71	236	24	72	38	19	2	3	14	7	2	.305
Roy Sanders	P52	52	103	7	11	9	7	0	1	4	53	0	.107
Emelio Palmero	P44	44	94	13	11	3	0	0	0	6	13	0	.117
Harry Weaver	P44	44	64	3	10	4	1	0	0	1	19	0	.156
Jake Northrop	P40	40	93	5	19	5	5	1	0	3	17	0	.204
Elmer Ambrose	P36	36	77	4	17	2	3	0	0	3	16	0	.221
William Gleason	P33	33	45	4	9	2	1	0	0	3	8	0	.200
Alan Hill	OF18	23	54	8	11	11	4	2	0	4	1	0	.204
Bill Snyder	P16	16	19	2	4	3	1	0	1	0	11	0	.211
Al Demaree	P10	10	16	0	3	1	0	0	0	0	2	0	.188
Albert Cooper	C	6	17	4	8	0	2	0	0	0	0	0	.471
Roy Luther	P6	6	8	0	0	0	0	0	0	0	0	0	.000
Clint Rogge	P2	2	1	0	0	0	0	0	0	0	0	0	.000
Brown	P1	1	2	1	1	0	0	0	0	0	1	0	.500

PITCHERS	W	L	PCT	G	GS	CG	SH	IP	H	BB	SO	ERA
Roy Sanders	18	20	.474	52				297	330	107	88	4.52
Jake Northrop	15	13	.536	40				249	280	70	70	4.34
Emelio Palmero	15	15	.500	44				266	310	114	71	4.60
Elmer Ambrose	13	10	.565	36				217	219	86	81	4.10
Harry Weaver	10	14	.417	44				186	213	95	50	5.56
William Gleason	4	7	.364	33				127	147	62	24	5.25
Al Demaree	3	6	.333	10				53	52	13	9	3.91
Bill Snyder	1	1	.500	16				51	69	29	7	6.35
Roy Luther	0	1	.000	6				26	32	13	9	
Clint Rogge	0	1	.000	2				6	7	5	0	
Brown	0	1	.000	1				8	8	1	0	

MILWAUKEE   5th   75-91   .452   -37   Harry Clark
Brewers

BATTERS	POS-GAMES	GP	AB	R	H	BI	2B	3B	HR	BB	SO	SB	BA
Ivy Griffin	1B166	166	660	98	239	112	33	15	9	48	36	18	.362
Oscar Melillo	2B74,OF15	102	360	51	101	35	17	6	3	22	43	6	.280
James Cooney	SS155	155	600	98	185	92	19	10	2	40	26	60	.308
Alex McCarthy	3B150	161	581	75	171	72	16	10	3	56	17	12	.294
Elmer Lober	OF163	162	630	118	176	70	25	17	4	76	52	10	.279
Pat McNulty	OF126	128	480	92	150	75	20	8	4	68	37	24	.313
Paul Johnson	OF123	131	495	81	146	66	17	13	3	40	46	0	.295
Enoch Shinault	C134	135	455	71	135	68	20	12	7	51	39	8	.297
Ed Schaack	P37	53	121	18	31	17	1	3	3	9	13	0	.256
Nelson Pott	P47	52	110	11	28	13	5	4	0	3	9	0	.255
Fred Lear	2B48	51	165	30	49	25	9	3	2	34	20	9	.297
Sherry Magee	OF47	48	190	30	63	41	8	3	7	14	12	1	.332
Russ Young	C43	47	137	14	30	12	3	3	1	7	23	0	.219
Dennis Gearin	P20	44	92	14	31	12	3	2	1	8	4	0	.337
Ray Lingrel	P31	38	93	7	27	17	2	2	2	7	12	0	.290
David Keefe	P35	35	75	11	22	7	2	0	0	6	8	0	.293
Charles Palmer	P13	35	72	12	22	8	2	2	0	7	10	1	.306
Jim Lindsay	P26	26	51	1	6	0	1	0	0	1	14	0	.118
Harry Strohm	2B25	25	104	15	30	8	2	2	2	5	7	2	.288
Al Simmons	OF24	24	98	20	39	16	2	3	0	13	9	5	.398
Fred Baldowsky		19	54	5	9	5	2	2	0	5	13	1	.167
John Gossett		18	35	3	7	6	3	0	0	6	7	0	.200
Herb Herbstreith	P1	17	38	5	12	9	2	1	0	1	3	0	.316
Heilberger	OF	13	27	5	6	1	2	0	0	2	4	0	.222
Tom Meek	P9	9	13	1	3	0	0	0	0	0	0	0	.231
Charles Shaney	P8	8	18	2	1	0	0	0	0	0	0	0	.056
Harry Clark	3B	5	11	2	2	0	1	0	0	0	0	0	.182
Bergerino	2B	4	13	1	1	0	0	0	0	0	0	0	.077
Linehan	OF	3	11	1	2	0	1	0	0	0	0	0	.182
Willis	OF	3	11	0	1	0	0	0	0	0	0	0	.091
Zeiser	3B	2	6	0	1	0	1	0	0	0	0	0	.167
Nichols	C2	2	2	1	1	0	0	0	0	0	0	0	.500
James Robertson	P2	2	0	0	0	0	0	0	0	0	0	0	----
Seigel	PH	1	1	0	0	0	0	0	0	0	0	0	.000

MILWAUKEE (cont.)
Brewers

BATTERS	POS-GAMES	GP	AB	R	H	BI	2B	3B	HR	BB	SO	SB	BA
Funke	P1	1	0	0	0	0	0	0	0	0	0	0	----
Harold Gill	P1	1	0	0	0	0	0	0	0	0	0	0	----
Stewart	P1	1	0	0	0	0	0	0	0	0	0	0	----

PITCHERS	W	L	PCT	G	GS	CG	SH	IP	H	BB	SO	ERA
Ed Schaack	17	15	.531	37				278	300	88	67	4.46
Nelson Pott	13	17	.433	47				265	350	59	88	5.09
Dennis Gearin	12	5	.706	20				153	148	66	70	3.76
Ray Lingrel	8	12	.400	31				207	272	62	48	5.65
Jim Lindsay	8	12	.400	26				142	172	39	55	4.79
David Keefe	8	20	.286	35				218	302	83	71	6.03
Charles Shaney	4	2	.667	8				47	63	11	9	4.21
Tom Meek	2	3	.400	9				35	55	7	12	
Charles Palmer	1	1	.500	13				48	54	24	15	5.25
Harold Gill	0	1	.000	1				2	2	2	0	
Herb Herbstreith	0	0	----	1				2	2	3	0	
James Robertson	0	0	----	1				0	0	3	0	
Funke	0	0	----	1				0	3	3	0	
Stewart	0	0	----	1				1	1	2	0	

MINNEAPOLIS   6th   74-92   .446   -38   Joe Cantillon
Millers

BATTERS	POS-GAMES	GP	AB	R	H	BI	2B	3B	HR	BB	SO	SB	BA
Ted Jourdan	1B144	150	568	102	160	73	33	6	4	76	46	7	.282
Hugh Critz	2B69,SS84	154	628	115	205	73	34	13	9	31	36	15	.327
Laster Fisher	SS67	69	242	22	66	28	10	2	3	13	22	2	.273
E. O'Shaughnessy	3B73	77	271	18	75	39	9	3	1	17	27	1	.277
Carl East	OF155	157	595	118	223	151	43	12	31	87	29	4	.375
Henry Rondeau	OF110	126	439	79	137	59	24	6	5	44	34	9	.312
Earl Smith	OF107,3B26	139	487	86	154	82	34	9	11	28	38	12	.316
Walter Mayer	C99	111	343	44	96	59	13	2	4	60	41	3	.279
Roy Massey	OF69,3B18	114	370	60	102	40	18	4	2	47	39	3	.276
Clyde Milan	OF77	101	314	43	93	25	12	4	3	23	14	2	.296
John Grabowski	C75	98	316	49	100	55	25	5	3	19	26	2	.316
Robert Fisher	2B52,3B15	87	279	39	78	40	16	1	2	13	13	3	.280
Y. Ayres	P47	47	64	9	12	2	1	0	0	3	6	0	.187
Bill Hollahan	2B38	46	148	15	35	17	5	4	2	18	28	1	.236
Bob McGraw	P40	46	89	11	18	10	1	0	3	10	28	0	.203
E. Erickson	P43	45	82	8	11	4	0	0	0	7	24	0	.134
Dan Tipple	P39	41	74	12	13	7	3	0	1	9	25	0	.176
Bill Morrissette	P36	40	68	11	21	12	2	0	3	6	16	0	.309
A. Schauer	P21	25	32	3	10	4	2	1	0	3	5	0	.313
Gilbert	3B21	21	82	11	25	12	4	0	1	5	3	1	.305
Walt Nufer		15	49	8	12	3	1	0	0	4	5	1	.245
Tom Phillips	P12	12	28	2	3	4	0	0	0	2	5	0	.107
Leo Mangum	P11	11	18	2	2	0	0	0	0	1	0	0	.111
R. Browne	SS	10	25	3	3	2	0	0	0	2	1	0	.120
Frank Brinzda	P10	10	24	3	4	0	2	0	0	0	1	0	.167
Carl Eng	P8	8	13	2	2	2	2	0	0	0	0	0	.154
Earl Yingling	P7	7	12	1	1	0	0	0	0	0	1	0	.083
Frank Owens	C	3	3	0	1	0	0	0	0	0	0	0	.333
Clarence Griffin	P6	6	6	0	0	0	0	0	0	0	2	0	.000
William Lindberg	P2	2	0	0	0	0	0	0	0	0	0	0	----
Jan Hammond	P1	1	1	0	0	0	0	0	0	0	0	0	.000

PITCHERS	W	L	PCT	G	GS	CG	SH	IP	H	BB	SO	ERA
Dan Tipple	16	17	.485	39				240	233	170	141	4.57
Bob McGraw	15	12	.556	40				226	244	94	90	4.38
Y. Ayres	10	12	.455	47				199	247	98	94	5.20
Bill Morrissette	8	5	.615	36				168	192	84	71	4.66
E. Erickson	7	25	.219	43				246	299	104	148	5.30
Leo Mangum	4	2	.667	11				51	48	19	17	4.41
Tom Phillips	4	4	.500	12				73	82	33	24	5.06
Carl Eng	3	3	.500	7				41	43	14	8	
Earl Yingling	2	0	1.000	6				29	36	9	7	
Frank Brinzda	2	5	.286	10				63	101	32	11	9.43
A. Schauer	2	6	.250	21				68	108	24	28	7.42
Clarence Griffin	1	1	.500	6				17	27	13	8	
William Lindberg	0	0	----	2				2	0	3	0	
Jan Hammond	0	0	----	1				3	9	1	1	

INDIANAPOLIS
Indians

INDIANAPOLIS   7th   72-94   .434   -40   Jack Hendricks

BATTERS	POS-GAMES	GP	AB	R	H	BI	2B	3B	HR	BB	SO	SB	BA
Jay Kirke	1B122	128	468	50	117	74	19	5	4	23	20	4	.250
Ed Sicking	2B113,SS49	162	638	101	185	61	20	12	3	50	35	28	.290
Hal Janvrin	SS73,2B37	111	394	42	120	52	16	4	2	33	27	6	.305
Bill Campbell	3B156	156	551	87	167	64	20	8	1	37	34	25	.303
Walter Rehg	OF164	164	657	98	197	90	32	12	1	47	25	28	.300
Ed Brown	OF156	156	620	96	224	104	37	19	8	50	30	6	.361
Lloyd Christenbury	OF145	154	634	131	195	68	33	12	7	72	31	13	.308
Ernie Krueger	C96,1B16	131	434	66	127	66	34	8	17	37	40	7	.293
Tom Whelan	SS46,1B29,OF28	111	344	55	106	53	24	6	3	64	28	4	.308
Leo Dixon	C73	73	235	30	56	18	8	1	1	28	20	4	.250
Bill Burwell	P46	55	141	18	37	12	2	1	3	10	14	0	.262
Jesse Petty	P47	47	111	11	21	3	2	1	0	1	28	0	.189
Carmen Hill	P44	44	99	13	30	16	5	2	1	9	15	0	.303
Tiller Cavet	P40	41	77	8	23	15	2	0	5	0	12	0	.299
Fred Fitzsimmons	P33	37	77	8	23	6	2	0	1	4	10	0	.299
Stephen Yerkes	2B18	32	87	5	16	11	6	0	0	12	4	1	.184
Harry Purcell		17	39	5	6	1	1	2	0	4	6	2	.154
Clyde Seib	P8	8	8	3	4	1	0	0	0	0	0	0	.500
Payne	OF	6	13	2	3	0	1	0	0	2	0	0	.231
Calvin Crum	P4	4	1	0	0	0	0	0	0	0	0	0	.000
Francis	P3	3	6	0	0	0	0	0	0	0	3	0	.000
Schmutte	P2	2	7	1	1	0	0	0	0	1	3	0	.143
Schott	1B1	1	3	0	0	0	0	0	0	0	1	0	.000
Minton	C1	1	1	0	0	0	0	0	0	0	0	0	.000

PITCHERS	W	L	PCT	G	GS	CG	SH	IP	H	BB	SO	ERA
Jesse Petty	19	18	.514	47				302	337	81	115	4.05
Bill Burwell	18	21	.462	46				342	411	77	64	3.58
Carmen Hill	12	21	.364	44				263	331	72	100	4.93
Fred Fitzsimmons	9	4	.692	33				173	185	49	58	4.53
Tiller Cavet	7	15	.318	40				180	265	44	44	5.35
Schmutte	1	0	1.000	2				15	13	22	3	
Clyde Seib	0	1	.000	4				8	7	5	4	
Francis	0	2	.000	3				19	18	17	4	
Calvin Crum	0	0	----	4				7	9	4	0	

TOLEDO
Mud Hens

TOLEDO   8th   54-114   .321   -59   Whitted - Terry

BATTERS	POS-GAMES	GP	AB	R	H	BI	2B	3B	HR	BB	SO	SB	BA
Bill Terry	1B107	109	427	73	161	82	22	11	15	45	37	2	.377
Fred Lindstrom	2B147	147	581	77	157	39	21	7	1	28	24	19	.270
Charles Pechous	SS171	171	667	53	149	67	20	14	4	41	102	4	.245
Walter Barbare	3B160	161	618	80	178	72	39	8	4	26	30	9	.288
Fred Nicholson	OF164	167	650	104	199	86	36	22	4	61	35	12	.306
Bill Lamar	OF117	126	489	94	191	78	37	15	10	34	23	8	.391
Paul Danielly	OF105	105	427	65	114	40	14	6	2	51	51	8	.267
Zeke Smith	C89	115	331	37	111	47	14	0	1	28	7	7	.335
Owen Kelly	OF73,3B16	119	381	50	116	38	21	9	0	21	27	8	.304
John Anderson	C85	95	307	40	95	32	8	4	0	32	16	5	.309
Lee Dempsey	1B48	50	167	17	48	16	7	2	1	2	15	3	.287
Bill McGloughlin	P23	44	63	5	17	2	2	0	1	1	6	0	.270
Pat Malone	P42	42	90	9	13	5	2	0	1	4	30	0	.144
George Whitted	1B19,OF15	41	115	21	29	14	6	2	1	11	5	2	.252
Joe Giard	P41	41	86	5	12	4	4	0	0	6	30	0	.140
Joe Shannon	OF37	39	137	22	36	14	8	1	1	14	14	3	.263
Hugh Bedient	P39	39	74	7	11	4	1	0	1	14	23	0	.149
Joe Finneran	P25	26	46	1	12	4	4	1	0	2	3	0	.261
R. Wright	P22	22	61	7	14	3	2	1	0	6	12	1	.230
Fred Johnson	P19	19	42	5	8	5	0	0	0	0	9	0	.190
William Black	2B16	16	59	5	17	5	4	2	0	2	5	1	.288
Joe Bradshaw	P15	16	42	2	9	4	1	0	1	0	6	0	.214
Bill O'Neill	P9	13	6	2	1	0	0	0	0	2	4	1	.167
Herman Vigerust	C	12	25	3	4	1	0	0	0	2	3	1	.120
Ernest Woolfolk	P12	12	13	0	2	0	0	0	0	0	1	0	.154
Robert Shanklin	P10	10	6	0	1	0	0	0	0	0	5	0	.167
Art Seydler	P7	8	4	1	1	0	0	0	0	0	0	0	.250
Lamb	C	6	22	4	5	0	2	0	0	3	2	1	.227
Tom Davies	OF	6	13	2	4	0	0	1	0	0	0	0	.308
Mack Allison	P6	6	12	1	5	1	2	0	0	2	2	0	.417

TOLEDO (cont.)
Mud Hens

BATTERS	POS-GAMES	GP	AB	R	H	BI	2B	3B	HR	BB	SO	SB	BA
Figner	OF	4	9	2	1	0	0	0	0	3	1	0	.111
Daniels	P2	2	2	0	1	0	0	0	0	0	0	0	.500
Ben Frey	P2	2	0	0	0	0	0	0	0	0	0	0	----
Lefty Burr	P1	1	0	0	0	0	0	0	0	0	0	0	----
Causey	PR	1	0	0	0	0	0	0	0	0	0	0	----

PITCHERS	W	L	PCT	G	GS	CG	SH	IP	H	BB	SO	ERA
Joe Giard	11	16	.407	42				242	263	153	109	4.73
Hugh Bedient	10	21	.323	39				238	304	72	55	5.37
Pat Malone	9	21	.300	42				241	285	120	103	5.64
R. Wright	8	9	.471	22				182	188	56	44	3.61
Joe Bradshaw	5	7	.417	15				105	108	54	46	5.31
Fred Johnson	4	11	.267	19				117	140	37	26	5.64
Joe Finnernan	3	7	.300	25				113	161	45	19	6.93
Mack Allison	2	3	.400	6				33	56	6	1	
Bill O'Neill	1	4	.200	9				32	38	18	6	
Bill McGloughlin	1	13	.071	23				104	130	59	27	5.71
Bob Shanklin	0	1	.000	10				22	27	13	10	
Art Seydler	0	1	.000	7				15	12	9	2	
Ernest Woolfolk	0	0	----	12				37	13	12	6	
Lefty Burr	0	0	----	1				1	1	4	0	
Daniels	0	0	----	2				5	8	1	1	

MULTI-TEAM PLAYERS

BATTERS	POS-GAMES	TEAMS	GP	AB	R	H	BI	2B	3B	HR	BB	SO	SB	BA
Bobby Roth	OF131	KC-SP	133	518	110	168	97	32	8	12	74	52	19	.324
G. Armstrong	3B58,1B19	SP-KC	95	326	60	100	45	18	3	4	39	17	6	.307
Lyle Bigbee	OF31,P19	MIL-LOU	70	151	20	45	19	6	4	0	23	22	2	.298
Gus Bono	P34	KC-IND	34	60	8	15	5	4	1	0	2	3	0	.250
P. Regan	3B23	KC-MIN	28	79	18	23	9	5	1	0	13	16	2	.291

PITCHERS	TEAMS	W	L	PCT	G	GS	CG	SH	IP	H	BB	SO	ERA
Gus Bono	KC-IND	7	12	.368	34				163	169	111	59	5.41
Lyle Bigbee	MIL-LOU	2	3	.400	19				91	126	31	38	7.32

TEAM BATTING

TEAMS	GP	AB	R	H	BI	2B	3B	HR	BB	SO	SB	BA
KANSAS CITY	167	5843	**1083**	**1844**		347	110	**109**	637	**586**	97	.316
ST. PAUL	170	5747	1026	1676		328	93	88	**661**	525	**190**	.292
LOUISVILLE	**171**	5738	871	1627		266	98	46	565	492	147	.283
COLUMBUS	169	5776	887	1695		327	75	59	532	464	157	.293
MILWAUKEE	168	5887	902	1741		216	**121**	53	544	499	145	.296
MINNEAPOLIS	166	5705	882	1670		293	73	87	529	548	61	.293
INDIANAPOLIS	166	5700	831	1671		268	93	57	509	394	126	.293
TOLEDO	**171**	**5903**	793	1724		276	104	48	461	554	95	.292
	674	46299	7275	13648		2321	767	547	4438	4062	1018	.295

1924
Double Duty

In baseball, generally one is a batter or a pitcher. Normally, batters are not asked to pitch, and pitchers are forgiven their feeble efforts at the plate. However, in the 1920s and 1930s in the American Association there were a handful of players who excelled in both facets of the game. During the two decades, perhaps a dozen players participated in this practice. Of these few, none was better than Ben Tincup and James Zinn.

After a journey through the lower minors and a four-year stay with the major league Philadelphia Phillies, Ben Tincup, a full-blooded Cherokee Indian, joined the roster of the Louisville Colonels in 1919. In a decade-long stay with the Colonels, Tincup's pitching high points included his perfect 9–0 mark in 1921 and his 24 wins in 1924. During the times he was not used on the mound, Tincup played around 30 games a year in the field, batting nearly .300 in the process. His best years at the plate included 1920 (.331 and 16 triples), 1922 (.308), and 1929 (.325).

James Zinn joined the American Association's Kansas City club in 1922 after several seasons in the Texas League and a four-year stay in the big leagues. Zinn posted several fine seasons for the Blues, winning twenty games three times, topped by a twenty-seven win season in 1923. When not pitching, Zinn played 20 to 30 games a year in the outfield, or at first base. Here, his hitting prowess was demonstrated by his six .300 seasons, led by a .366 mark in 1926.

St. Paul returned to the top rung in 1924, after a year's absence, while Indianapolis moved up to second and Louisville finished third. Milwaukee, Toledo, Minneapolis, Columbus, and Kansas City, who went from first to last, completed the the standings. Milwaukee's Lester Bell won the batting title (.365), while Charles Dressen of St. Paul knocked in the most runs (151) and Louisville's Elmer Smith hit the most home runs (28). Pitching laurels went to Jesse Petty of Indianapolis, who won 29 games with a 2.83 earned run average, leading the league in both categories. George Walberg of Milwaukee struck out the most batters (175).

By the time World War II came, the number of double duty players in the American Association dwindled almost to nothing. Today they are nonexistent in the high minors. But for a period of time these double duty players served as examples of complete ballplayers, perhaps the most athletic ever to play. They mastered both batting and pitching, which requires not one, but two distinct skills.

ST. PAUL   1st   95-70   .576   Nick Allen
Saints

BATTERS	POS-GAMES	GP	AB	R	H	BI	2B	3B	HR	BB	SO	SB	BA
John Neun	1B162	162	629	136	222	100	38	18	5	57	46	**55**	.353
Hap Morse	2B108	136	422	65	115	52	17	7	3	80	35	13	.273
Lute Boone	SS134	134	549	79	142	65	31	2	4	42	34	26	.259
Charles Dressen	3B164	164	612	110	212	**151**	41	10	18	73	27	25	.347
W. Christensen	OF147	150	593	**145**	186	73	35	9	8	74	24	31	.314
Bruno Haas	OF141,P3	155	536	85	157	100	22	13	11	35	57	24	.293
Joe Riggert	OF101	110	327	52	96	53	13	8	9	35	39	10	.294
Leo Dixon	C148	149	452	75	123	67	27	7	10	67	**73**	5	.272
R. Wade	OF72	76	227	32	66	30	9	5	4	25	29	7	.291
Mark Koenig	SS25,2B18	68	165	16	44	16	7	2	0	7	17	2	.267
Marty Berghammer	2B49,P1	62	176	24	40	15	4	1	0	24	13	10	.227
Cliff Lee	OF51	55	191	21	73	36	8	4	3	14	21	6	.382
Howard Merritt	P47	47	101	7	14	6	2	2	0	5	22	1	.139
Paul Fittery	P41	47	72	10	10	2	0	0	0	9	14	4	.139
Nick Allen	C31	42	92	8	22	12	3	2	0	7	8	1	.239
Tony Faeth	P39	41	71	9	11	6	1	0	0	8	14	1	.155
H. McQuaid	P39	41	39	4	9	2	3	1	0	2	6	0	.231
Cliff Markle	P40	40	89	4	20	9	5	1	0	2	27	1	.225
A. Holtzhauser	P39	39	62	5	12	2	2	0	0	1	11	0	.194
Hoke Floyd	OF26	38	82	9	20	13	7	1	0	9	11	2	.244
Oscar Roettger	P23	27	58	8	16	6	1	2	1	1	5	1	.276
S. Napier	P16	16	10	0	1	0	0	0	0	1	2	0	.100
McGee	OF	5	8	1	0	1	0	0	0	0	0	0	.000
Julian Wera	3B	4	11	0	2	0	0	0	0	0	3	0	.182
Ryder	OF	2	10	2	5	0	1	1	0	0	0	0	.500
Reilly	2B1	1	1	1	1	0	1	0	0	0	0	1	1.000

PITCHERS		W	L	PCT	G	GS	CG	SH	IP	H	BB	SO	ERA
Cliff Markle		19	9	.679	40				254	233	110	128	3.02
Howard Merritt		19	17	.528	47				277	333	86	99	4.68
Paul Fittery		16	10	.615	41				214	246	97	64	4.37
Tony Faeth		15	4	**.789**	39				219	216	62	64	3.46
A. Holtzhauser		10	14	.417	39				185	174	102	61	5.69
Oscar Roettger		8	4	.667	23				139	133	78	81	4.79
H. McQuaid		7	9	.438	39				137	168	72	49	5.12
S. Napier		1	2	.333	16				42	59	17	15	
Bruno Haas		0	0	----	3				8	12	4	2	
Marty Berghammer		0	0	----	1				2	1	2	0	0.00

INDIANAPOLIS   2nd   92-73   .558   -3   Donie Bush
Indians

BATTERS	POS-GAMES	GP	AB	R	H	BI	2B	3B	HR	BB	SO	SB	BA
Ray Schmandt	1B163	163	604	88	173	96	28	10	2	60	36	4	.286
Ed Sicking	2B125,SS45	167	653	115	209	63	32	10	1	57	23	12	.320
John Jones	SS80	82	286	28	86	37	19	6	2	13	14	5	.301
Bill Campbell	3B110	119	411	66	99	32	19	3	0	45	27	9	.241
Lloyd Christenbury	OF154	156	575	109	189	71	34	13	6	74	21	11	.329
Horace Allen	OF120	130	450	87	149	77	29	11	14	44	52	10	.331
Walter Rehg	OF93	105	349	68	117	53	16	5	0	26	15	16	.335
Ernie Krueger	C160	164	593	113	201	128	45	7	17	56	39	16	.339
Tom Whelan	3B31,OF26,SS19	110	297	48	80	46	16	8	2	43	30	2	.269
Johnny Hodapp	3B38,2B29,SS26	100	318	49	109	64	15	6	4	27	24	3	.343
E. Bailey	OF93	96	330	66	87	27	15	1	0	40	28	14	.264
Jesse Petty	P47	47	123	4	15	11	1	0	0	1	33	0	.122
Carmen Hill	P45	46	84	6	14	7	5	1	0	1	13	1	.167
Fred Fitzsimmons	P39	44	106	12	30	14	3	2	0	4	12	0	.283
Bill Burwell	P33	43	97	12	24	11	4	2	1	7	5	0	.247
Otto Miller	C19	43	69	8	26	15	4	0	4	1	7	2	.377
George Smith	P43	43	26	1	2	3	0	0	0	3	12	0	.077
Ed Brown	OF40	40	171	23	56	32	9	2	3	7	9	2	.328
S. Niles	P32	32	50	5	8	2	0	1	0	1	11	2	.160
Hod Eller	P31	32	33	2	9	4	0	0	0	1	11	1	.273
Robert Blessing		24	69	9	18	4	3	0	0	1	9	0	.261
Begley		15	60	9	13	5	1	1	0	2	10	0	.216
Donie Bush		6	7	2	0	0	0	0	0	0	0	0	.000
Ropiequet	P4	4	1	0	0	0	0	0	0	0	0	0	.000
Turner	C	3	5	0	0	0	0	0	0	0	0	0	.000

INDIANAPOLIS (cont.)
Indians

PITCHERS	W	L	PCT	G	GS	CG	SH	IP	H	BB	SO	ERA
Jesse Petty	29	8	.784	47				328	297	91	149	2.83
Bill Burwell	17	10	.630	33				237	275	52	47	4.10
Carmen Hill	17	14	.548	45				213	235	56	66	3.97
Fred Fitzsimmons	14	17	.452	39				279	313	74	100	4.54
S. Niles	6	11	.353	32				173	197	61	30	3.85
George Smith	3	5	.375	43				112	143	37	26	4.34
Hod Eller	3	6	.333	31				108	126	43	33	3.33
Ropiequet	0	0	----	4				6	5	7	3	

LOUISVILLE   3rd   90-75   .545   -5   Joe McCarthy
Colonels

BATTERS	POS-GAMES	GP	AB	R	H	BI	2B	3B	HR	BB	SO	SB	BA
C. Covington	1B147	148	517	92	150	88	27	6	5	84	35	7	.290
BrunoBetzel	2B169	169	668	106	208	108	32	12	7	54	44	11	.311
Maurice Shannon	SS169	169	653	113	222	107	35	11	4	57	46	12	.340
Joe Schepner	3B76	83	278	27	76	37	9	1	2	20	10	2	.273
Elmer Smith	OF169	169	646	132	216	132	45	17	28	82	56	24	.334
Albert Tyson	OF168,P1	169	685	127	227	106	37	19	8	34	46	24	.331
Baldomero Acosta	OF69	79	260	39	66	35	14	8	2	31	8	3	.254
Tony Brottem	C72	78	230	29	66	30	8	0	3	41	34	1	.287
P. Ballenger	3B64,OF38	126	453	102	146	62	29	8	1	65	35	11	.322
Ben Tincup	P49	75	149	24	40	20	5	2	1	7	18	6	.268
Henry Haines	OF53	55	224	45	59	24	11	4	0	20	20	9	.263
W. Meyer	C51	54	163	20	42	16	8	2	0	19	8	1	.258
T. Gaffney	3B34	50	128	16	34	11	4	3	0	4	17	1	.266
Joe DeBerry	P44	44	76	13	20	10	4	0	0	10	7	0	.263
Henry Vick	C38	43	144	16	45	17	7	0	1	12	5	3	.313
Nick Cullop	P43	43	74	5	6	3	1	0	1	4	14	0	.081
Ed Holley	P41	42	76	9	21	7	3	1	1	4	15	0	.276
Ernie Koob	P41	41	84	7	10	4	0	0	0	8	43	0	.119
Tom Estell	P37	40	62	7	12	5	1	0	0	2	4	0	.194
Sam Mayer		17	37	5	8	2	1	0	0	8	3	1	.216
Martin Baylin	P16	16	14	0	2	0	0	0	0	0	1	0	.143
John Anderson	OF15	15	58	13	16	11	3	2	2	8	9	2	.276
James Viox	OF	10	41	7	13	5	1	0	0	3	2	1	.317
Schmidt	C	6	18	2	5	0	1	0	0	1	1	0	.278
Hungling	C	5	5	0	0	0	0	0	0	0	0	0	.000
Dorsey Carroll	PH	4	4	0	0	0	0	0	0	0	0	0	.000
Green	P4	4	2	0	1	0	0	0	0	0	0	0	.500

PITCHERS	W	L	PCT	G	GS	CG	SH	IP	H	BB	SO	ERA
Ben Tincup	24	17	.585	49				293	338	98	109	3.96
Joe DeBerry	17	10	.630	44				246	277	45	84	3.81
Nick Cullop	16	12	.571	43				230	269	60	81	4.16
Ernie Koob	13	12	.520	41				242	290	94	68	4.35
Ed Holley	10	12	.455	41				223	250	85	79	3.87
Tom Estell	8	9	.471	37				166	188	48	30	5.31
M. Baylin	0	1	.000	16				42	73	18	16	
Green	0	0	----	4				8	15	7	1	
Albert Tyson	0	0	----	1				1	0	0	0	0.00

MILWAUKEE   4th   83-83   .500   -12.5   Harry Clark
Brewers

BATTERS	POS-GAMES	GP	AB	R	H	BI	2B	3B	HR	BB	SO	SB	BA
Ivy Griffin	1B137	138	550	72	168	64	25	7	2	34	28	7	.305
Oscar Melillo	2B135	146	541	92	154	79	15	13	7	42	48	11	.284
Lester Bell	SS141	154	630	145	230	114	53	16	18	62	46	12	.365
Alex McCarthy	3B95	113	425	67	130	57	14	3	1	30	10	4	.306
Frank McGowan	OF140	147	490	72	142	80	17	10	14	82	59	11	.290
Lance Richbourg	OF120	123	502	82	161	56	33	11	6	52	48	10	.321
Paul Johnson	OF109	121	429	55	118	70	15	4	7	45	44	2	.275
Russ Young	C78	82	258	34	77	31	7	7	2	17	32	1	.298
Elmer Lober	OF90	109	342	60	97	48	12	6	8	40	29	1	.284
Harry Strohm	3B60,2B31	101	335	53	97	47	15	5	1	26	17	7	.290
Enoch Shinault	C75	84	249	36	71	42	18	5	7	35	29	3	.285

MILWAUKEE (cont.)
Brewers

BATTERS	POS-GAMES	GP	AB	R	H	BI	2B	3B	HR	BB	SO	SB	BA
Sherry Magee	OF37	83	196	38	62	35	6	4	6	29	17	1	.316
Ed Schaack	P36	58	85	14	20	10	2	0	0	7	19	0	.236
Nelson Pott	P44	46	96	9	29	10	2	1	1	2	13	0	.302
G. Winn	P41	44	48	8	8	6	0	0	0	12	8	0	.167
Ray Lingrel	P31	39	78	11	19	11	0	2	1	6	14	0	.244
J. Walker	P36	37	74	9	14	6	1	0	0	8	21	1	.189
George Walberg	P36	36	89	7	22	12	4	0	1	2	19	0	.247
Wid Matthews	OF26	26	106	16	34	4	6	2	0	8	7	6	.321
Charles Shaney	P24	24	24	4	7	4	3	1	0	5	9	0	.292
James Cooney	SS17	17	67	7	11	10	2	0	1	2	2	2	.164
H. Scheer	2B15	16	49	8	13	2	0	1	0	3	3	2	.265
Dave Keefe	P11	11	15	1	6	0	0	0	0	1	3	0	.400
Pritchard	P11	11	14	3	3	0	1	0	0	0	0	0	.214
Claude Willoughby	P5	5	11	0	1	0	0	0	0	0	0	0	.091
Herb Herbstreith		3	6	0	2	0	0	0	0	0	0	0	.333
Fred Schulte	OF	2	11	2	3	0	0	0	0	0	0	0	.273
Tom Meek	P1	1	2	0	0	0	0	0	0	0	0	0	.000
Fox	3B1	1	2	0	0	0	0	0	0	0	0	0	.000
Stokes	C1	1	2	0	0	0	0	0	0	0	0	0	.000
Bryant	P1	1	1	0	0	0	0	0	0	0	0	0	.000
Stanley Ross	P1	1	0	0	0	0	0	0	0	0	0	0	----

PITCHERS	W	L	PCT	G	GS	CG	SH	IP	H	BB	SO	ERA
George Walberg	18	14	.563	36				245	239	82	175	3.78
Ed Schaack	13	12	.520	36				182	201	70	44	5.24
Ray Lingrel	12	7	.632	31				178	209	49	49	4.91
Nelson Pott	10	10	.500	44				245	335	68	90	5.77
G. Winn	8	9	.471	41				147	189	67	34	6.43
Dennis Gearin	5	1	.833	6				53	59	18	17	2.89
Joe Edelman	5	2	.714	9				64	69	10	15	3.52
J. Walker	5	13	.278	36				186	238	77	88	5.95
Dave Keefe	3	4	.429	11				51	64	13	18	5.12
Charles Shaney	2	6	.250	24				85	113	26	25	5.51
Claude Willoughby	1	3	.250	6				42	41	28	18	
Bryant	0	0	----	1				3	4	3	2	
Tom Meek	0	0	----	1				2	4	0	1	
Stanley Ross	0	0	----	1				1	1	1	0	0.00

TOLEDO   5th   82-83   .497   -13   Jimmy Burke
Mud Hens

BATTERS	POS-GAMES	GP	AB	R	H	BI	2B	3B	HR	BB	SO	SB	BA
Fred Schleibner	1B146	146	537	92	158	87	32	8	9	75	52	9	.294
Fred Maguire	2B96	111	417	50	129	54	13	4	2	16	33	2	.309
B. Helgeth	SS111	111	380	65	99	38	16	11	1	66	59	7	.261
Joe Rapp	3B145	145	613	96	199	69	30	8	0	48	32	19	.325
Ralph Shinners	OF142	148	614	116	184	78	36	16	9	29	49	25	.300
Paul Strand	OF101	101	409	68	132	71	20	18	6	40	23	14	.323
Fred Nicholson	OF99,2B37,1B16	153	614	112	188	101	28	20	4	48	55	12	.306
Alex Gaston	C92	99	339	34	95	29	18	6	1	26	39	3	.280
John Scott	P52	82	163	23	44	28	11	2	3	9	12	1	.269
Owen Kelly	2B41,3B15	78	220	25	50	22	11	3	0	25	23	4	.227
Bill Lamar	OF65	65	269	48	96	39	12	8	2	18	8	3	.357
Joe Giard	P49	50	111	15	17	8	5	2	0	15	36	0	.153
Joe Shannon	OF31	37	124	12	28	16	6	1	0	4	12	1	.226
Joe Bradshaw	P35	35	71	10	17	12	1	1	0	2	11	0	.239
Paul McCullough	P34	35	49	7	11	7	2	0	1	2	11	0	.224
Robert Kinsella	OF17	24	62	14	23	10	4	2	0	10	7	1	.371
Herman Vigerust	C16	23	44	2	14	6	1	1	0	3	5	0	.318
R. Naylor	P22	22	43	6	11	5	0	1	0	3	11	0	.255
Fred Johnson	P21	21	29	3	9	1	0	1	0	0	6	0	.310
Earl Webb	OF17	17	69	11	23	10	3	3	0	4	10	0	.334
Howard Baldwin	P16	16	42	5	12	8	3	0	0	0	5	0	.286
Clint Blume	P15	15	22	1	1	0	0	0	0	0	3	0	.045
Ben Frey	P14	14	17	1	1	0	0	0	0	1	6	0	.158
Charles Ward	SS	11	23	3	5	3	0	0	0	4	1	0	.217
Gus Ketchum	P11	11	10	0	2	0	0	0	0	0	1	0	.200
Leonard Page	SS	8	7	1	1	1	0	0	0	1	3	0	.143
Moses Solomon	1B	5	21	0	3	1	0	1	0	0	1	0	.143
Harold Elliott	C	5	15	1	3	0	0	0	0	0	2	0	.200
Hugh Canavan	P4	4	16	1	5	2	0	0	0	0	0	0	.313

TOLEDO (cont.)
Mud Hens

BATTERS	POS-GAMES	GP	AB	R	H	BI	2B	3B	HR	BB	SO	SB	BA
Frank McCullough	3B	3	9	0	3	2	0	0	0	1	1	0	.333
McMillan	1B	3	3	0	0	0	0	0	0	0	1	0	.000
Walter Barbare	3B	2	4	0	0	0	0	0	0	0	0	0	.000
Bert Lewis	P2	2	2	0	1	1	1	0	0	0	0	0	.500
Thomas	2B1	1	1	0	0	1	0	0	0	0	1	0	.000
Robert Shanklin	P2	2	0	0	0	0	0	0	0	0	0	0	----
Herb Herschler	P1	1	0	0	0	0	0	0	0	0	0	0	----
Art Seydler	P1	1	0	0	0	0	0	0	0	0	0	0	----

PITCHERS	W	L	PCT	G	GS	CG	SH	IP	H	BB	SO	ERA
Joe Giard	20	17	.541	49				328	359	143	111	3.62
John Scott	20	20	.500	52				341	354	91	129	3.25
Paul McCullough	9	5	.643	34				136	126	84	85	4.17
Joe Bradshaw	9	10	.474	35				185	206	122	72	4.87
Howard Baldwin	7	6	.538	16				110	106	29	34	3.02
Hugh Canavan	4	0	1.000	4				28	33	9	9	4.82
Fred Johnson	4	5	.444	21				79	89	31	20	4.79
R. Naylor	4	10	.286	22				124	151	40	18	5.16
Clint Blume	2	2	.500	15				55	63	20	10	5.24
Bert Lewis	1	1	.500	2				7	4	7	0	3.86
Ben Frey	1	2	.333	14				55	64	20	13	4.58
Gus Ketchum	1	5	.167	11				39	41	14	10	5.08
Robert Shanklin	0	0	----	2				2	2	0	0	0.00
Art Seydler	0	0	----	1				2	1	0	1	0.00
Herb Herschler	0	0	----	1				1	0	1	0	0.00

MINNEAPOLIS   6th   77-89   .464   -18.5   Mike Kelley
Millers

BATTERS	POS-GAMES	GP	AB	R	H	BI	2B	3B	HR	BB	SO	SB	BA
Jay Kirke	1B92,OF40	151	521	70	170	97	45	2	14	32	27	8	.326
Mike Gazella	2B61,3B84	151	512	92	139	53	29	11	12	107	72	19	.272
John Mitchell	SS97	97	405	56	98	33	14	2	1	49	20	13	.242
Morris Berg	3B			(see multi-team players)									
Earl Smith	OF154	158	641	139	226	127	64	4	23	56	37	25	.353
George Fisher	OF106	112	398	58	123	72	27	7	10	39	45	12	.309
Henry Rondeau	OF86	95	318	54	96	33	19	3	4	31	16	9	.302
Walter Mayer	C71	96	211	35	56	26	12	2	4	58	33	5	.265
Charles See	OF50,P29	104	287	62	91	40	18	4	9	13	22	5	.317
C. Walker	OF51	70	211	41	66	34	14	1	8	21	15	3	.313
William Black	2B46	69	223	35	68	34	12	2	2	19	27	10	.305
Ray French	SS67	67	272	46	67	28	14	2	0	23	33	6	.246
Elwood Wirts	C58	67	177	30	48	27	11	1	4	40	25	1	.271
Joe Klugman	2B33,OF20	55	213	26	80	34	20	1	1	14	12	3	.376
John Grabowski	C46	50	166	21	53	27	7	0	4	16	17	0	.319
W. Harris	P47	49	82	3	19	13	2	0	0	2	14	0	.232
Earl Hamilton	P32	36	43	8	7	4	0	0	0	5	11	0	.163
Hugh Critz	2B35	35	134	24	44	22	12	1	4	11	9	6	.328
Leo Mangum	P31	32	70	8	16	4	4	0	0	2	4	0	.228
Richard Niehaus	P27	31	42	4	8	5	1	1	0	2	5	0	.190
Doug McWeeney	P26	26	40	5	5	3	0	0	0	3	18	0	.125
Adrian Lynch	P26	26	28	1	0	2	0	0	0	1	12	0	.000
Bob McGraw	P25	25	36	8	8	6	0	1	2	2	12	1	.222
G. Edmondson	P21	21	32	1	4	1	0	0	0	0	14	0	.125
Pat Malone	P20	20	23	1	6	4	0	0	0	0	7	0	.261
G. Burger	P13	15	18	5	5	5	0	0	1	0	6	0	.278
Ray Moore	P1	12	9	1	2	0	0	0	0	0	2	0	.222
F. Sengstock	C	9	29	4	8	3	2	0	0	1	0	0	.276
Carl Eng	P9	9	11	1	1	0	0	0	0	0	7	0	.111
Lum Davenport	P6	8	10	1	1	0	0	0	0	1	3	1	.100
Chick Shorten	OF	7	20	5	6	4	2	0	0	1	0	0	.300
Clarence Griffin	P7	7	4	0	0	0	0	0	0	0	0	0	.000
Godfrey Brogan	P1	5	2	0	0	0	0	0	0	0	0	0	.000
E. Erickson	P4	4	1	0	0	0	0	0	0	0	0	0	.000
Jan Hammond	P3	3	9	1	1	1	0	0	0	0	2	0	.111
George Dumont	P3	3	7	1	1	0	1	0	0	0	2	0	.143
McCue	3B	2	6	1	0	1	0	0	0	0	2	0	.000
O'Shea		2	3	1	2	0	1	0	0	1	0	0	.667
Parenti	2B	2	2	0	0	0	0	0	0	0	1	0	.000

MINNEAPOLIS (cont.)
Millers

PITCHERS	W	L	PCT	G	GS	CG	SH	IP	H	BB	SO	ERA
Leo Mangum	14	7	.667	31				182	170	53	57	3.56
W. Harris	10	13	.435	47				219	286	92	118	5.06
Charles See	7	7	.500	29				147	155	79	89	4.28
Richard Niehaus	7	7	.500	27				105	123	57	38	4.72
G. Edmondsen	6	3	.667	21				100	109	28	37	3.69
Bob McGraw	6	6	.500	25				110	125	49	54	3.84
Doug McWeeny	6	9	.400	26				121	136	53	77	5.58
Earl Hamilton	6	10	.375	32				144	209	48	60	5.63
Adrian Lynch	3	9	.250	26				104	130	49	36	6.49
Carl Eng	2	1	.667	9				35	50	14	5	6.69
Lum Davenport	2	1	.667	6				32	27	13	21	2.53
George Dumont	2	1	.667	3				24	19	8	20	2.25
Jan Hammond	2	1	.667	3				22	27	6	10	4.09
G. Burger	2	4	.333	13				52	74	15	19	6.23
Pat Malone	2	9	.182	20				77	96	56	27	8.30
Roy Moore	0	1	.000	1				0	3	0	0	108.00
Clarence Griffin	0	0	----	7				19	30	13	9	6.63
E. Erickson	0	0	----	4				5	5	5	3	1.80
Godfrey Brogan	0	0	----	1				0	0	3	0	27.00

COLUMBUS 7th 75-92 .448 -21 Carleton Molesworth
Senators

BATTERS	POS-GAMES	GP	AB	R	H	BI	2B	3B	HR	BB	SO	SB	BA
Roy Grimes	1B134	137	534	94	173	92	34	11	9	44	36	13	.324
Douglas Baird	2B73,3B38	129	420	54	118	67	18	6	4	44	32	11	.281
H. Schreiber	SS133	134	526	62	132	73	24	8	6	30	42	12	.251
I. Davis	3B125	139	548	106	155	56	30	6	2	80	35	17	.283
E. Murphy	OF143	146	568	106	199	71	30	12	5	67	14	18	.350
John Brooks	OF138	145	571	110	195	95	37	14	7	40	37	10	.342
A. Russell	OF107,1B35	150	531	105	180	116	36	16	25	63	47	4	.339
Grover Hartley	C101	118	382	43	122	63	24	9	1	19	7	9	.319
Hugh High	OF105	125	405	70	124	57	20	8	6	43	26	3	.306
Jose Lopez	2B30,OF28	89	214	44	55	27	14	4	0	48	25	3	.257
Martin McGaffigan	2B59	82	222	30	51	29	5	1	1	31	27	8	.230
Roy Sanders	P53	53	75	4	19	9	0	1	0	4	24	0	.253
L. Urban	C45	49	163	14	40	23	5	4	0	15	5	0	.245
Elmer Ambrose	P44	44	76	8	18	5	4	2	0	4	14	0	.237
Emilio Palmero	P41	43	75	17	17	7	2	1	0	11	10	1	.227
Jake Northrop	P38	38	80	7	12	3	1	0	0	5	15	1	.150
D. Foulk	P38	38	67	4	15	4	1	0	0	4	17	0	.224
C. Ketchum	P37	37	50	5	11	6	2	0	0	4	14	0	.220
George McQuillan	P35	35	67	4	15	4	1	0	0	4	17	0	.224
Forest Cady	C18	19	64	4	12	3	4	0	0	1	6	0	.187
Fred Nicolai	SS16	16	57	10	16	1	0	0	0	7	9	1	.281
R. Williamson	P4	4	15	1	3	0	0	0	0	0	10	0	.200
Art Miner	C	2	4	1	0	0	0	0	0	1	0	0	.000
Layne	OF1	1	1	0	0	0	0	0	0	0	0	0	.000
Roy Luther	P1	1	0	0	0	0	0	0	0	0	0	0	----

PITCHERS	W	L	PCT	G	GS	CG	SH	IP	H	BB	SO	ERA
Jake Northrop	13	18	.419	38				227	279	65	62	4.52
Emilio Palmero	12	16	.429	41				224	247	94	70	4.82
Elmer Ambrose	11	9	.550	44				201	248	67	64	5.01
George McQuillan	11	10	.524	35				193	263	51	33	4.62
D. Foulk	10	10	.500	38				196	243	112	69	5.00
Roy Sanders	10	17	.370	53				225	286	72	55	4.92
C. Ketchum	6	8	.429	37				140	157	62	47	4.69
R. Williamson	2	2	.500	4				35	37	10	6	3.06
Al Demaree	0	3	.000	13				32	48	16	11	8.16
Roy Luther	0	0	----	1				2	1	1	0	4.50

KANSAS CITY 8th 68-96 .415 -26.5 Good - Lavan
Blues

BATTERS	POS-GAMES	GP	AB	R	H	BI	2B	3B	HR	BB	SO	SB	BA
Dud Branom	1B163	164	629	98	200	105	37	22	11	31	23	9	.318
R. Blackburne	2B72,SS44	116	391	48	105	48	13	5	4	38	31	7	.269

KANSAS CITY (cont.)
Blues

BATTERS	POS-GAMES	GP	AB	R	H	BI	2B	3B	HR	BB	SO	SB	BA
Doc Lavan	SS57,3B17,2B16	90	326	49	91	29	18	3	1	21	17	8	.279
George Armstrong	3B138	140	574	83	182	61	39	8	6	31	32	3	.317
Bunny Brief	OF143,2B15	159	601	106	203	104	58	12	17	81	51	5	.338
Floyd Scott	OF72	76	288	55	92	40	20	4	6	32	29	9	.319
Wilbur Good	OF70	71	292	50	77	18	19	8	2	25	21	8	.264
Bill Skiff	C95	101	348	37	95	46	8	3	3	10	21	6	.273
James Zinn	P37,OF20	87	197	34	64	33	16	5	4	16	19	2	.325
James Sweeney	OF63	64	255	48	72	22	8	10	1	27	44	7	.282
John Billings	C58	59	201	20	54	26	8	1	0	8	23	0	.269
Harold Gagnon	SS56	58	196	13	52	11	4	3	0	5	16	3	.265
Bert Griffith	OF45	56	197	22	64	27	19	2	4	13	7	2	.325
Beals Becker	OF46	56	179	27	54	23	10	4	3	10	21	5	.302
Roy Wilkinson	P47	47	88	4	12	4	0	0	0	6	32	0	.136
Hal Janvrin	2B39	44	154	13	36	9	5	1	0	14	13	2	.234
Ray Caldwell	P31	34	78	6	19	4	3	1	0	3	15	0	.244
Ferd Schupp	P33	33	81	7	15	8	0	2	0	8	21	0	.185
Ben Ahman	P26	30	50	6	12	8	3	0	0	1	17	0	.240
Ernest Smith		21	62	15	23	11	7	1	0	4	7	0	.371
John Saladna	P20	20	23	0	1	1	0	0	0	1	13	0	.043
P. Regan		17	60	5	19	8	0	2	1	3	5	2	.317
Bevo LeBourveau	OF15	15	62	6	19	7	3	1	1	4	4	4	.306
Shoots	OF	14	56	5	16	5	2	1	0	0	6	0	.286
Jim Lindsey	P14	14	20	2	2	1	0	0	0	2	2	0	.100
Kaufman	C	13	34	0	9	2	1	0	0	1	8	0	.265
Shaner	OF	13	28	3	4	2	0	0	0	4	5	0	.143
James Moore	OF	11	48	7	10	0	2	2	0	0	0	1	.208
Ed Pick	OF	11	40	9	15	5	4	2	0	4	7	0	.375
William Walker	P10	11	13	0	0	0	0	0	0	0	7	0	.000
Freeman	1B	10	19	2	8	0	2	0	0	0	0	0	.421
Brauchle	2B	9	32	1	7	2	1	2	0	2	9	0	.219
Inman	SS	9	26	1	7	0	0	0	0	2	4	0	.269
Wells	C	7	14	1	4	0	1	0	0	0	0	0	.286
Herb Thormahlen	P5	6	9	0	2	2	1	0	0	1	1	0	.222
James Sullivan	P5	5	13	1	2	0	0	0	0	0	4	0	.154
McCollister	2B	5	10	1	1	0	1	0	0	0	0	0	.100
Anderson	P5	5	5	0	1	0	0	0	0	0	1	1	.200
Zeigler	P5	5	4	0	0	0	0	0	0	0	0	0	.000
Virgil Cheeves	P3	3	5	0	0	0	0	0	0	0	0	0	.000
Connally	P2	2	3	1	2	0	0	0	0	0	1	0	.667
Hargraves	PH	2	2	2	2	1	0	1	0	0	0	0	1.000
Peterson	P2	2	1	1	0	0	0	0	0	0	0	0	.500
Wyatt	OF1	1	5	0	0	0	0	0	0	0	0	0	.000
Lamb	C1	1	3	0	0	0	0	0	0	0	2	0	.000
Ted Menze	OF1	1	1	0	0	0	0	0	0	0	0	0	.000

PITCHERS	W	L	PCT	G	GS	CG	SH	IP	H	BB	SO	ERA
Roy Wilkinson	14	16	.467	47				265	271	96	77	3.60
James Zinn	14	16	.467	37				255	296	70	78	3.71
Ferd Schupp	12	15	.444	33				236	236	112	149	4.16
Ray Caldwell	9	14	.391	31				198	210	44	86	3.95
Ben Ahman	7	6	.538	26				119	114	55	28	3.93
Jim Lindsey	3	4	.429	14				60	76	19	19	5.70
James Sullivan	2	2	.500	5				33	35	15	16	3.27
John Saladna	2	5	.286	20				71	91	31	24	7.10
Zeigler	0	1	.000	5				15	11	5	7	3.00
Herb Thormahlen	0	1	.000	5				25	41	7	10	5.40
Virgil Cheeves	0	2	.000	3				14	23	11	3	10.93
William Walker	0	4	.000	10				42	54	31	27	
Anderson	0	0	----	5				17	23	11	4	5.82
Connally	0	0	----	2				8	18	2	4	9.00
Peterson	0	0	----	2				5	7	9	3	9.00

MULTI-TEAM PLAYERS

BATTERS	POS-GAMES	TEAMS	GP	AB	R	H	BI	2B	3B	HR	BB	SO	SB	BA
Morris Berg	3B71,SS43	MIN-TOL	118	417	45	110	65	16	0	1	13	27	6	.264
John Schulte	C82,OF17	TOL-LOU	109	331	65	86	62	18	4	4	73	28	6	.260
Ted Jourdan	1B99	MIL-MIN	100	356	68	99	48	17	5	8	54	29	8	.278
Bob McMenemy	C44	SP-MIL	52	142	20	42	20	3	3	7	13	39	0	.296
Joe Dawson	P36	KC-LOU	41	54	6	13	8	3	0	0	1	3	0	.241

MULTI-TEAM PLAYERS (cont.)

BATTERS	POS-GAMES	TEAMS	GP	AB	R	H	BI	2B	3B	HR	BB	SO	SB	BA
Guy Morton	P27	KC-IND	27	38	1	10	3	1	0	0	0	9	0	.263

PITCHERS		TEAMS	W	L	PCT	G	GS	CG	SH	IP	H	BB	SO	ERA
Joe Dawson		KC-LOU	6	10	.375	36				125	147	82	67	5.40
Guy Morton		KC-IND	5	6	.455	27				105	118	48	43	4.89
T. Pritchard		MIL-SP	2	3	.400	11				41	49	25	15	

TEAM BATTING

TEAMS	GP	AB	R	H	BI	2B	3B	HR	BB	SO	SB	BA
ST. PAUL	168	5624	920	1620		292	95	75	580	567	**223**	.288
INDIANAPOLIS	170	5792	930	1715		298	87	56	529	457	120	.296
LOUISVILLE	169	5820	**979**	1728		295	90	65	606	501	124	.297
MILWAUKEE	**171**	**6008**	953	**1796**		259	110	90	597	**611**	85	**.299**
TOLEDO	167	5839	893	1678		286	**121**	44	530	571	126	.287
MINNEAPOLIS	168	5850	952	1700		**354**	60	**113**	**621**	577	134	.291
COLUMBUS	169	5847	920	1714		293	96	67	576	503	117	.293
KANSAS CITY	168	5891	810	1685		311	107	66	432	578	81	.286
	675	46671	7357	13636		2388	766	576	4471	4365	1010	.292

1925
Louisville Colonels

By the middle of the 1920s, the St. Paul Saints had a several year monopoly on winning the pennant, by finishing first in 1919, 1920, 1922, and 1924. Finally, one team was able to break the Saints' perch on the top rung in convincing fashion. This team was the Louisville Colonels.

Louisville won its first Association pennant in 1909. After dropping to last for the next two years, the team rebounded with several first division finishes culminated by another pennant in 1916. After a fourth, two thirds, and a second, the Colonels won their third pennant in 1921, then went on to upset the International League Baltimore Orioles in the Little World Series. Next followed a sixth and two more thirds, before the Colonels would contend again.

The Louisville club came out of the gate strongly in 1925. They won 26 of 28 games in June, including fourteen in a row, winning the pennant convincingly by 13 1/2 games. The team positively bristled with .300 hitters led by batting champion Joe Guyon (.363, 106 RBI), Albert Tyson (.352, 132 RBI), Harvey Cotter (.326, 129 RBI), John Anderson (.314), Bruno Betzel (.312, 101 RBI), and Baldomero Acosta (.310). The pitching was also strong as a bevy of 20-game winners, Norman Cullop (22–8), Ed Holley (20–7), and Joe DeBerry (20–8) graced the team.

Second place Indianapolis finished just ahead of defending champ St. Paul, which ended in third. Minneapolis, Kansas City, Milwaukee, Toledo, and Columbus rounded out the standings. The home run and runs batted in titles were won again by Bunny Brief, this time with the Milwaukee club. He won his fourth Association home run title with a total of 37, and his fifth runs batted in title with a total of 175. Pitcher Bill Burwell of Indianapolis won the most games (24) and finished with the best earned run average (2.73), while Bob McGraw of Minneapolis struck out the most batters (141).

Louisville went on to capture its second straight flag in 1926, with another following four years later. After a pair of unlikely playoff triumphs around 1940, the Colonels captured their next first place finish after World War II. It was, however, these 1920s versions of the team which stand as Louisville's strongest Association entries. Not only did they capture two pennants in a row, they finished with over 210 wins during the two-year span. Over a similar period, no other Association team has won more.

LOUISVILLE Colonels

LOUISVILLE   1st   106-61   .635   Joe McCarthy

BATTERS	POS-GAMES	GP	AB	R	H	BI	2B	3B	HR	BB	SO	SB	BA
Harvey Cotter	1B166	166	598	108	195	129	33	24	7	86	49	10	.326
Bruno Betzel	2B161	161	593	83	185	101	24	17	6	64	39	14	.312
Maurice Shannon	SS163	**169**	649	109	191	98	30	14	5	64	45	6	.294
P. Ballenger	3B136	143	561	115	163	78	36	8	5	76	43	16	.291
Albert Tyson	OF167	167	644	126	227	132	45	20	8	74	38	29	.352
Joe Guyon	OF157	157	628	**152**	**228**	106	38	17	9	68	53	18	**.363**
Baldomero Acosta	OF105	118	377	84	117	78	23	5	5	67	25	1	.310
Bill Meyer	C99	102	328	50	94	50	17	2	1	44	24	2	.287
John Anderson	OF90	107	356	76	112	62	30	8	6	36	37	4	.314
Redman	C76	81	234	17	50	18	11	0	0	28	24	1	.214
Ben Tincup	P36	65	114	20	33	27	9	3	0	13	14	3	.289
T. Gaffney	3B42	62	180	24	45	21	10	3	0	18	27	2	.250
Ed Holley	P45	45	94	13	21	12	5	0	0	5	18	0	.223
Norman Cullop	P45	45	89	12	21	13	3	1	0	5	19	0	.236
Joe DeBerry	P37	39	87	12	15	9	1	0	0	7	15	0	.172
Ernie Koob	P38	39	52	5	10	5	2	0	0	5	18	0	.192
Joe Dawson	P33	34	71	4	11	5	2	0	0	3	11	0	.155
Tony Brottem		16	40	3	6	3	3	0	0	3	7	0	.150

PITCHERS	W	L	PCT	G	GS	CG	SH	IP	H	BB	SO	ERA
Norman Cullop	22	8	.733	45				237	277	52	69	3.57
Ed Holley	20	7	**.741**	45				260	270	109	117	4.05
Joe DeBerry	20	8	.714	37				235	246	45	79	3.37
Ben Tincup	14	16	.483	37				243	261	99	108	4.07
Joe Dawson	11	8	.579	33				187	189	76	89	3.75
Ernie Koob	9	9	.500	39				153	186	70	49	6.00
Martin Baylin	1	0	1.000	1				6	9	4	4	
Joe Bradshaw	1	2	.333	11				48	53	31	22	5.06
Tom Estell	0	1	.000	5				14	19	4	2	
Wayland Dean	0	0	----	2				5	7	3	1	

INDIANAPOLIS Indians

INDIANAPOLIS   2nd   92-74   .554   -13.5   Donie Bush

BATTERS	POS-GAMES	GP	AB	R	H	BI	2B	3B	HR	BB	SO	SB	BA
Ray Schmandt	1B160	160	565	75	156	85	25	13	5	51	48	7	.276
Ed Sicking	2B116	120	469	73	148	43	27	4	1	48	23	16	.316
H. Schreiber	SS166	166	632	78	191	103	27	13	4	20	59	15	.301
Johnny Hodapp	3B99	110	448	62	125	72	19	2	4	22	23	2	.279
Walter Rehg	OF127	129	499	74	154	85	18	12	4	24	17	7	.309
Wid Matthews	OF104	104	419	84	130	39	11	9	2	37	16	30	.310
Horace Allen	OF90	101	340	55	87	43	18	4	17	33	25	8	.256
Charles Robertson	C98	107	305	36	87	40	19	8	0	37	17	2	.285
Elmer Yoter	3B57,2B41,OF33	141	484	86	148	63	18	11	2	49	32	26	.306
Lloyd Christenbury	OF54	67	201	31	51	16	12	2	0	29	11	9	.254
Paul Florence	C51	55	137	22	43	14	5	2	0	11	7	3	.314
Clarke	OF47	53	150	19	31	17	5	2	0	9	6	2	.207
Bill Burwell	P41	47	118	15	30	14	5	1	2	5	5	0	.254
Frank Henry	P35	46	99	15	34	18	6	4	0	7	11	1	.343
Ernie Krueger	C38	44	147	20	41	15	7	3	5	17	12	1	.279
Ernie Maun	P40	43	114	19	27	9	1	1	1	3	6	0	.237
Carmen Hill	P37	42	92	11	15	11	4	1	0	7	14	2	.163
Schemanske	P34	35	48	6	14	4	1	0	0	3	8	0	.292
Fred Fitzsimmons	P27	28	70	5	14	8	4	1	0	4	10	0	.200
Joe Klugman		21	80	12	21	9	3	0	1	4	7	1	.263
J. Thompson	P21	21	34	0	8	0	0	0	0	1	9	0	.235

PITCHERS	W	L	PCT	G	GS	CG	SH	IP	H	BB	SO	ERA
Bill Burwell	**24**	9	.727	41				303	282	40	92	**2.73**
Ernie Maun	19	14	.576	40				276	308	74	89	3.95
Carmen Hill	16	15	.516	37				251	237	61	100	3.91
Fred Fitzsimmons	14	6	.700	27				184	189	50	55	3.77
Frank Henry	12	14	.462	35				222	256	67	88	4.13
Schemanske	6	9	.400	34				127	150	69	26	5.34
J. Thompson	1	3	.250	21				94	106	36	33	4.50

ST. PAUL
Saints

3rd	91-75	.548	-14.5	Nick Allen

BATTERS	POS-GAMES	GP	AB	R	H	BI	2B	3B	HR	BB	SO	SB	BA
Fritz Mollwitz	1B163	163	568	74	161	87	33	8	2	47	31	22	.283
Norm McMillan	2B75	94	366	60	105	43	13	3	7	15	30	9	.287
Mark Koenig	SS123	126	496	78	153	76	35	7	11	34	29	13	.308
Hap Morse	3B88,2B20	118	323	55	96	41	20	0	1	68	25	7	.297
Cedric Durst	OF159	168	653	131	227	105	59	25	7	72	36	23	.348
Walt Christensen	OF151	151	597	126	194	56	39	7	5	94	28	49	.325
Bruno Haas	OF105,P1	117	419	70	133	78	24	6	10	26	29	18	.317
Pat Collins	C126	132	418	87	132	100	22	0	19	86	71	5	.316
Lute Boone	2B63,3B50,SS36	149	589	90	156	75	34	8	5	33	35	31	.265
R. Wade	OF88	127	334	55	98	68	19	9	5	33	21	5	.293
Fred Hofmann	C56	75	200	33	61	40	10	4	5	20	22	3	.305
Oscar Roettger	P33,OF26	75	170	28	61	31	6	1	4	5	16	2	.359
Curtis Fullerton	P43	57	103	9	34	14	6	1	0	6	11	0	.330
Ray Kolp	P53	55	107	11	17	5	2	1	0	2	14	0	.159
Heinie Odom	3B29	48	144	19	36	19	5	1	2	3	16	6	.250
Howard Merritt	P47	47	50	1	11	5	1	0	0	2	8	1	.220
Cliff Markle	P40	41	86	5	17	4	3	2	0	6	17	0	.198
H. McQuaid	P37	37	60	4	14	5	1	0	0	1	12	0	.233
Marty Berghammer	2B26	36	81	15	24	6	1	2	0	11	5	3	.296
Walter Beall	P24	25	52	3	7	3	0	0	0	7	17	0	.135

PITCHERS		W	L	PCT	G	GS	CG	SH	IP	H	BB	SO	ERA
Ray Kolp		22	13	.629	53				302	306	82	122	3.78
Curtis Fullerton		15	8	.652	46				213	253	89	92	5.62
H. McQuaid		14	5	.737	37				177	185	52	60	3.81
Cliff Markle		13	18	.419	40				262	282	111	121	4.84
Oscar Roettger		12	8	.600	33				170	174	106	80	4.98
Walter Beall		7	8	.467	25				166	137	105	117	3.63
Howard Merritt		6	13	.316	47				160	196	60	42	4.78
A. Holtzhauser		1	1	.500	5				20	27	8	5	4.95
Haas		0	1	.000	1				7	22	1	1	20.57
Tony Faeth		0	0	----	6				12	18	13	8	
Gore		0	0	----	6				12	18	14	9	
Thomas		0	0	----	1				1	2	1	0	
Farquhar		0	0	----	1				1	1	0	0	

MINNEAPOLIS
Millers

4th	86-80	.518	-19.5	Mike Kelley

BATTERS	POS-GAMES	GP	AB	R	H	BI	2B	3B	HR	BB	SO	SB	BA
Ted Jourdan	1B141	144	560	124	177	63	31	9	12	100	45	6	.316
William Black	2B101	111	370	58	106	69	22	1	12	39	28	6	.286
John Butler	SS81,3B44,1B22	147	601	122	204	82	33	6	9	51	35	23	.339
Joe Fowler	3B85	100	385	74	121	51	17	7	3	38	38	15	.314
Earl Smith	OF164	164	665	132	208	156	54	11	31	63	40	11	.313
Pat Duncan	OF163	163	631	128	218	139	49	9	27	75	44	12	.345
George Fisher	OF119	123	431	83	151	96	23	6	19	45	37	15	.350
Ed Ainsmith	C93	107	298	40	99	55	17	2	10	43	32	2	.332
C. Schmehl	SS44,2B33,OF23	123	397	75	114	53	23	4	2	47	38	12	.287
Charles See	OF22,P11	80	116	17	37	24	6	2	3	8	5	5	.319
Parenti	2B47	63	137	24	37	18	4	5	0	9	20	1	.270
F. Sengstock	C58	61	152	15	32	11	1	2	0	9	17	2	.210
Elwood Wirts	C47	60	159	23	35	16	7	0	2	25	28	1	.220
W. Harris	P54	56	104	13	29	9	1	0	1	2	3	1	.279
Jim Middleton	P49	51	68	13	20	2	3	1	0	2	10	0	.294
Bob McGraw	P49	49	106	14	21	20	2	1	4	9	46	0	.198
Dumont	P41	41	86	6	17	9	3	0	1	3	28	0	.198
Francis	P25	34	69	10	15	4	3	1	0	0	17	0	.217
Gross	SS27	31	94	12	24	12	5	1	1	10	11	3	.256
C. Walker	OF20	30	74	10	21	6	3	0	3	7	9	2	.284
Brovold	3B15	29	91	10	22	9	8	0	0	9	18	4	.242
Earl Hamilton	P22	23	25	4	7	2	2	0	0	2	7	0	.280
Greene	P18	19	35	1	6	1	0	0	0	5	8	0	.171
Swenson		18	46	9	8	1	0	0	0	2	8	1	.174
Watson	P16	17	16	0	2	1	0	0	0	0	6	0	.125
Charles Hall	P14	16	24	2	4	3	1	0	0	2	6	0	.167

PITCHERS		W	L	PCT	G	GS	CG	SH	IP	H	BB	SO	ERA
Bob McGraw		22	13	.629	49				282	286	113	141	4.40

MINNEAPOLIS (cont.)
Millers

PITCHERS	W	L	PCT	G	GS	CG	SH	IP	H	BB	SO	ERA
W. Harris	18	15	.545	54				263	279	101	140	4.45
Dumont	15	13	.530	41				223	228	82	92	4.32
Jim Middleton	12	7	.632	49				193	211	80	73	3.96
Greene	6	5	.545	18				97	124	31	27	4.27
Francis	6	6	.500	25				146	179	40	47	2.96
Charles Hall	3	4	.429	14				54	63	23	19	4.83
Earl Hamilton	3	5	.375	22				73	91	25	18	5.18
Pat Shea	1	1	.500	8				16	19	9	0	6.75
G. Edmondson	0	1	.000	11				28	31	11	9	7.07
Charles See	0	1	.000	11				21	31	20	14	10.71
Lum Davenport	0	1	.000	2				3	3	3	1	0.00
Jan Hammond	0	1	.000	2				6	9	4	3	9.00
W. Hubbell	0	1	.000	1				8	8	2	2	4.50
Wilson	0	1	.000	1				7	9	0	0	3.86
Pat Malone	0	2	.000	4				18	26	11	6	9.50
Watson	0	3	.000	16				48	67	25	15	7.50

KANSAS CITY   5th   80-87   .479   -26   Doc Lavan
Blues

BATTERS	POS-GAMES	GP	AB	R	H	BI	2B	3B	HR	BB	SO	SB	BA
Dud Branom	1B137	138	514	66	151	99	20	9	7	33	25	3	.294
Fresco Thompson	2B113	113	469	76	135	54	12	22	1	25	28	19	.288
Rick	SS81,OF45	148	538	110	175	104	23	24	10	73	59	15	.325
Frank Ellerbe	3B108	109	437	69	128	39	18	7	1	35	22	7	.293
Frank McGowan	OF141	144	500	65	133	85	25	11	10	63	48	7	.266
Bevo LeBourveau	OF114	117	441	86	159	84	19	19	8	47	38	25	.361
Floyd Scott	OF102	119	389	70	122	61	16	6	4	65	49	16	.314
Enoch Shinault	C99	113	358	51	105	55	27	6	2	40	36	3	.293
Frank Snyder	C63,3B36	115	380	43	107	54	17	5	5	44	35	2	.282
Robert Murray	SS67,2B32	104	396	67	102	30	17	4	0	65	21	12	.258
James Zinn	P39	60	122	20	40	20	8	4	2	9	19	1	.328
Kelleher	1B25,SS15	50	204	38	65	30	16	0	3	15	12	6	.319
Ed Schaack	P35	42	82	9	18	13	5	0	0	5	13	0	.220
Andy Messenger	P39	39	80	7	19	9	1	0	0	4	13	0	.238
James Moore	OF35	37	134	27	52	34	11	3	8	15	12	4	.388
Peterson	P29	29	25	1	4	2	0	1	0	2	6	0	.160
Ferd Schupp	P28	28	66	9	10	6	2	0	1	9	20	0	.152
Keenan	P27	27	22	0	2	0	0	0	0	2	11	0	.090

PITCHERS	W	L	PCT	G	GS	CG	SH	IP	H	BB	SO	ERA
Andy Messenger	19	13	.594	40				224	242	72	87	4.74
James Zinn	16	16	.500	39				274	326	69	122	4.80
Ferd Schupp	14	9	.609	28				198	186	110	100	3.82
Schaack	11	15	.423	35				195	230	59	52	5.54
Keenan	2	4	.333	28				70	88	52	22	5.40
Bill Hargrove	1	0	1.000	3				20	23	3	9	6.75
Evans	1	1	.500	4				10	9	4	6	2.70
Olsen	1	2	.333	5				32	27	10	15	2.53
Peterson	1	3	.250	29				86	94	46	27	5.65
Ahman	1	3	.250	6				23	29	11	3	6.26
Koupal	1	4	.200	12				55	65	21	21	4.10
McGrew	0	1	.000	2				0	4	5	5	245.00
Wayneburg	0	0	----	8				17	24	7	6	
Bonnelly	0	0	----	5				7	13	6	2	
Houck	0	0	----	3				8	16	1	2	
Patterson	0	0	----	3				4	5	2	1	
Youngblood	0	0	----	2				5	7	1	2	
Lorbeer	0	0	----	1				1	2	0	0	

TOLEDO   6th   77-90   .461   -29   Jimmy Burke
Mud Hens

BATTERS	POS-GAMES	GP	AB	R	H	BI	2B	3B	HR	BB	SO	SB	BA
Fred Schleibner	1B164	164	593	98	189	82	27	9	5	79	52	23	.319
Fred Maguire	2B138	138	581	92	173	67	28	10	3	31	40	12	.298
Woody English	SS129	131	459	48	101	32	4	8	0	39	43	3	.220
Mack Hillis	3B132	153	578	85	146	60	27	9	6	58	85	14	.253

TOLEDO (cont.)
Mud Hens

BATTERS	POS-GAMES	GP	AB	R	H	BI	2B	3B	HR	BB	SO	SB	BA
Fred Nicholson	OF152	164	615	102	190	109	25	14	6	72	65	12	.309
Paul Strand	OF133	141	527	85	158	86	30	8	11	44	23	8	.300
Earl Webb	OF113	114	422	77	139	66	22	9	11	52	63	3	.329
Alex Gaston	C99	104	332	32	96	34	16	0	2	34	36	4	.289
John Schulte	C76	102	256	36	80	52	11	0	6	55	22	5	.312
Kelly	3B45,2B16	73	216	26	55	30	8	0	1	24	17	0	.255
Hugh Canavan	P43	66	96	11	31	13	3	3	0	20	10	1	.323
S. Napier	OF29	60	136	20	33	8	5	0	0	10	16	4	.243
Fred Johnson	P58	59	56	3	8	5	1	0	0	2	3	0	.143
Hack Wilson	OF55	55	210	42	72	36	15	6	4	24	16	8	.343
Claude Jonnard	P47	49	116	9	15	3	2	0	0	7	63	1	.129
Robert Kinsella	OF29	41	127	30	40	10	9	1	0	18	15	4	.315
George Lyons	P38	38	80	3	15	7	4	0	1	2	20	0	.187
Tunney	P28	28	46	6	8	7	1	0	0	1	7	0	.174
Grant	P21	21	45	5	5	3	0	0	0	4	16	0	.111
Dom Torpe	P20	20	32	1	2	1	0	0	0	4	6	0	.063
Ben Frey	P19	19	12	1	2	1	0	0	0	0	3	0	.167
William Bayne	P15	15	11	1	1	2	0	0	0	2	3	0	.091

PITCHERS	W	L	PCT	G	GS	CG	SH	IP	H	BB	SO	ERA
Claude Jonnard	22	19	.537	47				333	319	126	127	3.38
George Lyons	14	16	.467	38				230	288	84	73	4.70
Hugh Canavan	13	12	.520	43				210	227	94	66	4.97
Tunney	8	6	.571	30				139	148	47	34	4.73
Johnson	7	8	.467	57				168	197	57	47	4.71
Grant	5	12	.294	21				137	176	48	46	5.39
Dom Torpe	4	6	.400	20				103	116	45	20	5.07
Ben Frey	2	2	.500	18				42	48	20	9	4.07
William Bayne	1	4	.200	15				48	70	13	27	7.88
Howard Baldwin	1	4	.200	7				35	49	12	9	7.71
R. Naylor	0	1	.000	3				11	20	7	2	10.64
Meis	0	0	----	3				7	6	1	2	
Jacobs	0	0	----	3				7	7	9	4	
Ernest Woolfolk	0	0	----	1				1	0	0	1	0.00

MILWAUKEE
Brewers

	7th	74-94	.440	-32.5	Harry Clark

BATTERS	POS-GAMES	GP	AB	R	H	BI	2B	3B	HR	BB	SO	SB	BA
Ivy Griffin	1B159	161	632	112	212	92	35	10	6	67	29	20	.335
Oscar Melillo	2B152	152	609	86	179	118	27	6	13	36	47	16	.294
Otis Miller	SS99	99	389	43	121	59	15	2	3	16	24	3	.311
Alex McCarthy	3B113,SS17	139	538	67	134	65	21	3	4	31	26	11	.249
Bunny Brief	OF158	167	618	134	221	175	45	13	37	105	80	2	.358
Lance Richbourg	OF111	124	468	86	146	56	17	15	7	32	30	24	.312
Frank Luce	OF100	123	384	88	121	69	20	14	14	27	58	8	.315
Bill Skiff	C99	101	353	51	100	43	9	1	4	18	7	9	.283
Taylor Douthit	OF92	92	376	90	140	46	25	10	10	40	29	26	.372
Dennis Gearin	P44	78	154	29	49	17	11	2	1	17	14	2	.318
Fred Schulte	OF62	74	244	38	67	33	8	4	2	16	18	4	.275
George Armstrong	3B54	72	252	45	65	41	11	3	4	23	27	3	.258
Ovid McCracken	P46	56	57	6	15	3	0	0	0	6	11	0	.263
Herman Bell	P50	50	116	9	17	0	0	1	0	5	28	0	.146
Roy Sanders	P50	50	99	9	14	4	2	1	1	4	41	0	.141
Connally	SS43	46	159	26	48	21	6	2	0	16	10	5	.302
Joe Eddleman	P37	37	72	9	8	6	0	0	0	1	14	0	.111
Sherry Magee		22	28	7	13	9	2	1	0	5	5	0	.464
Reitz	P15	15	16	2	3	1	1	0	0	1	5	0	.187

PITCHERS	W	L	PCT	G	GS	CG	SH	IP	H	BB	SO	ERA
Dennis Gearin	20	13	.606	44				309	383	144	110	5.50
Herman Bell	18	19	.486	50				323	380	72	124	3.90
Roy Sanders	15	16	.484	50				266	330	110	92	5.82
Joe Eddleman	10	15	.400	37				192	230	61	48	4.92
Ovid McCracken	4	11	.267	46				171	212	92	74	5.21
Stuart	2	5	.286	11				64	62	47	32	4.22
Earl Howard	1	0	1.000	4				8	14	10	1	9.00
Mack	1	2	.333	5				31	27	35	10	4.65
Burke	1	4	.200	5				16	28	12	6	10.69

MILWAUKEE (cont.)
Brewers

PITCHERS	W	L	PCT	G	GS	CG	SH	IP	H	BB	SO	ERA
Reitz	1	5	.167	15				48	58	35	11	6.19
Smith	0	1	.000	2				5	10	1	0	7.20
Claude Willoughby	0	0	----	9				20	31	22	6	
Ropp	0	0	----	3				11	27	7	6	
Lindstrom	0	0	----	2				8	19	4	4	
Joe Finneran	0	0	----	2				3	6	5	1	
Schneider	0	0	----	2				2	0	0	0	
Schramm	0	0	----	1				6	7	10	1	
Bryant	0	0	----	1				4	7	4	0	
Bruno	0	0	----	1				1	0	1	0	

COLUMBUS   8th   61-106   .365   -45   Carleton Molesworth
Senators

BATTERS	POS-GAMES	GP	AB	R	H	BI	2B	3B	HR	BB	SO	SB	BA
Roy Grimes	1B160	161	607	128	201	122	36	16	22	63	58	11	.331
P. Regan	2B142	149	548	71	163	88	33	10	12	38	56	9	.298
Fred Nicolai	SS112,2B28	142	535	72	139	44	16	10	1	65	49	5	.260
Doug Baird	3B87	117	370	55	111	41	10	9	0	30	18	10	.300
Albert Russell	OF129	146	493	109	157	131	22	13	30	69	39	6	.318
E. Murphy	OF100	100	390	82	155	71	21	5	3	39	25	16	.397
Paul Johnson	OF	(see multi-team players)											
L. Urban	C88	101	306	36	79	55	14	5	2	36	18	5	.258
Campbell	3B50,SS47	103	337	38	81	28	7	7	2	29	27	8	.240
Joe Bird	C74	84	242	33	74	43	8	3	2	39	18	2	.306
James Horn	OF62	62	239	39	62	21	12	4	1	35	26	3	.259
Quintana	3B27,SS27	61	176	22	43	12	7	0	0	13	17	0	.244
Emilio Palmero	P40	43	88	11	21	6	1	0	1	14	7	1	.239
Bob Bescher	OF29	40	95	15	28	11	6	1	1	11	8	0	.295
Gorham Leverett	P38	38	84	11	19	7	1	2	1	2	26	1	.226
Jake Northrop	P35	35	79	10	15	7	2	0	1	6	21	0	.190
George Stueland	P33	35	73	4	17	9	3	2	1	1	24	1	.233
John Brooks	OF27	28	118	20	39	21	9	5	0	2	11	0	.331
George McQuillan	P28	28	46	6	1	0	0	0	0	6	15	0	.022
Robert Blessing	3B16	27	94	9	30	13	7	0	0	4	12	2	.319
Werre	P26	26	23	2	3	0	0	0	0	0	5	0	.130
Folk	P18	18	28	2	9	4	0	0	1	2	4	0	.321
Harry Layne	OF16	17	67	10	10	7	2	1	1	5	8	0	.149

PITCHERS	W	L	PCT	G	GS	CG	SH	IP	H	BB	SO	ERA
Emilio Palmero	18	10	.643	41				242	274	106	101	4.72
Gorham Leverett	13	18	.419	38				225	271	71	92	4.76
George McQuillan	9	12	.429	28				151	205	41	28	4.29
Jake Northrop	8	19	.296	35				216	275	70	54	5.00
Foulk	3	5	.375	18				69	72	53	17	6.52
Werre	3	6	.333	26				86	124	38	23	6.91
Stueland	3	18	.143	33				197	263	97	61	5.94
Reno	1	2	.333	12								
Harry Fishbaugh	1	2	.333	7				33	43	9	4	5.73
McGraynor	0	1	.000	5				15	19	2	1	8.40
Ketchum	0	1	.000	1				8	13	3	0	7.88
Metevier	0	2	.000	9				27	39	12	5	6.33
Morbitzer	0	0	----	1				2	6	1	0	

MULTI-TEAM PLAYERS

BATTERS	POS-GAMES	TEAMS	GP	AB	R	H	BI	2B	3B	HR	BB	SO	SB	BA
Paul Johnson	OF134,P5	COL-KC	140	543	94	166	92	22	6	20	29	50	5	.306
Riggs Stephenson	OF113	KC-IND	118	456	97	148	89	34	10	8	46	28	5	.325
Bob McMenemy	C85	SP-MIL	96	281	34	67	36	9	8	6	33	53	4	.238
Roy Wilkinson	P46	KC-LOU	46	37	7	9	9	1	0	0	11	12	0	.243
Ray Lingrel	P31	MIL-KC	45	69	12	20	6	1	2	0	5	12	0	.289
Nelson Pott	P35	COL-KC	35	55	6	12	5	2	0	0	1	7	0	.218
Leonard Metz	SS30	KC-TOL	34	106	10	19	9	1	1	0	14	16	3	.179
S. Niles	P22	IND-COL	22	33	2	8	1	0	0	0	0	4	0	.242
Wells		KC-MIN	17	39	7	17	7	3	1	0	5	3	1	.436

MULTI-TEAM PLAYERS (cont.)

PITCHERS	TEAMS	W	L	PCT	G	GS	CG	SH	IP	H	BB	SO	ERA
Roy Wilkinson	KC-LOU	8	6	.571	46				131	156	58	59	4.60
Ray Lingrel	MIL-KC	7	7	.500	31				159	195	72	37	5.43
Nelson Pott	COL-KC	7	9	.437	35				162	175	39	45	4.22
S. Niles	IND-KC	1	9	.100	22				100	116	44	15	6.53
P. Johnson	COL-KC	0	0	----	5				12	17	8	4	

TEAM BATTING

TEAMS	GP	AB	R	H	BI	2B	3B	HR	BB	SO	SB	BA
LOUISVILLE	169	5792	1021	1732		324	117	51	**660**	465	94	.299
INDIANAPOLIS	166	5643	845	1635		249	95	53	446	375	132	.290
ST. PAUL	168	5844	950	1733		**333**	82	81	569	501	**204**	.297
MINNEAPOLIS	169	5876	**1040**	1775		324	70	104	619	597	117	**.302**
KANSAS CITY	168	5811	912	1719		270	**127**	64	603	538	116	.296
MILWAUKEE	**170**	**6078**	1012	**1797**		271	96	**112**	532	596	161	.296
TOLEDO	168	5677	828	1583		233	77	56	594	**661**	103	.279
COLUMBUS	168	5760	886	1644		238	96	101	534	563	85	.285
	673	46481	7494	13618		2242	760	622	4557	4296	1012	.293

1926
Scraping the Bottom

By the 1926 season, some two dozen American Association teams had finished their seasons with a winning percentage under .400. Two teams had even checked in at under .300. But never before had a team plumbed the depths as the poor Columbus Senators would this year, setting a mark for futility that has yet to be matched.

During the 1920s, Columbus had been a perennial second division finisher, ending in the cellar on three occasions. In all three instances, they finished with over 100 losses. Bad as this was, it was only a taste of the year to come in 1926. As the season started, Columbus quickly dropped into the cellar. The Senators pumped player after player (57 in all) into their lineup to try to stem the bleeding, but the losses kept mounting. At season's end, the record showed the Senators posting 125 losses versus only 39 victories, for a measly winning percentage of .238. All three figures serve as Association benchmarks of mediocrity. In addition, the team also gave up a whopping total of 1,229 runs, nearly seven and one-half per game.

On the flip side, Louisville won its second straight flag in solid fashion, besting second place Indianapolis by ten games. Milwaukee and Toledo finished in the final two spots of the first division, while the last four places were taken by Kansas City, St. Paul, Minneapolis, and aforementioned Columbus. Toledo enjoyed the talents of Bevo LeBourveau, who won the batting title (.377), while Bunny Brief of Milwaukee won his fifth and final home run title (26). Pat Duncan of Minneapolis finished with the most runs batted in (123). Two pitching honors went to George Pipgras of St. Paul as he won 22 games and finished with 156 strikeouts. The third honor fell to Ernie Maun of Toledo, as he pitched his way to a 2.71 earned run average.

As bleak as Columbus' fortunes seemed after the 1926 season, success was not too far away. In a few years' time, the team would be revamped under a whole new operating system which would garner it distinction. This in turn would do much to rub away the stigma of the Senators' cellar dwelling forays of the 1920s, as they replaced last place finishes with pennants.

LOUISVILLE Colonels   1st   105-62   .629   Bill Meyer

BATTERS	POS-GAMES	GP	AB	R	H	BI	2B	3B	HR	BB	SO	SB	BA
Harvey Cotter	1B163	163	594	99	162	94	27	15	2	97	51	17	.273
Bruno Betzel	2B146	147	546	85	176	83	21	10	1	46	28	11	.322
Clarke Pittenger	SS162	162	674	127	210	73	39	3	2	36	26	25	.312
Howard Shanks	3B148	150	515	79	147	81	20	10	5	61	30	3	.285
Joe Guyon	OF153	154	609	132	209	86	36	13	2	65	60	21	.343
Earl Webb	OF126	130	474	96	158	111	32	8	18	67	41	8	.333
John Anderson	OF112	116	433	90	134	84	24	8	9	41	28	8	.310
Al DeVormer	C106	115	400	53	147	71	28	8	7	25	28	13	.368
G. Ellis	OF62	84	270	55	95	41	19	7	1	16	16	8	.352
Bill Meyer	C72	78	258	36	79	33	9	3	1	15	19	2	.306
Baldomero Acosta	OF66	76	239	45	51	28	7	2	4	41	15	2	.213
Ben Tincup	P34	62	117	17	30	12	2	2	1	11	12	3	.256
T. Gaffney	2B20,3B19	46	135	18	37	18	7	6	2	8	16	5	.274
Joe DeBerry	P37	39	99	15	30	9	2	0	0	9	4	0	.303
Ed Holley	P37	38	74	14	23	13	2	1	4	6	16	0	.310
Roy Wilkinson	P38	38	35	2	11	3	1	0	0	2	5	0	.315
Norman Cullop	P37	37	100	13	23	12	3	1	0	2	22	0	.230
Joe Dawson	P30	31	82	8	25	11	3	0	1	2	5	0	.305
Ernie Koob	P31	31	68	6	18	2	2	1	0	2	25	0	.265
Mulvey	OF12	14	45	7	16	4	1	1	0	4	0	2	.356
Otis Wicker	P6	6	6	1	1		0	0	0			0	.167
Cross	1B	3	8	1	1		1	0	0			0	.125
Dan Rutherford	SS1	1	2	0	2		0	0	0			0	1.000
Martin Baylin	P1	1	1	0	1		0	0	0			0	1.000

PITCHERS	W	L	PCT	G	GS	CG	SH	IP	H	BB	SO	ERA
Norman Cullop	20	8	.714	37				261	269	55	102	3.62
Ben Tincup	18	7	.720	34				242	246	57	95	3.09
Joe Dawson	17	7	.708	30				215	213	81	94	3.26
Joe DeBerry	17	13	.567	37				276	321	57	65	4.14
Ernie Koob	14	10	.583	31				187	221	58	54	4.81
Roy Wilkinson	10	5	.667	38				108	105	36	48	3.42
Ed Holley	8	10	.444	37				192	263	70	75	5.72
Otis Wicker	1	2	.333	6				20	31	4	4	
Martin Baylin	0	0	----	1				3	4	3	1	

INDIANAPOLIS Indians   2nd   94-71   .570   -10   Donie Bush

BATTERS	POS-GAMES	GP	AB	R	H	BI	2B	3B	HR	BB	SO	SB	BA
Walter Holke	1B143	145	541	70	167	97	18	8	4	34	22	7	.309
Ed Sicking	2B137,SS23	162	617	97	185	50	27	7	1	55	25	17	.300
H. Schreiber	SS64	66	225	30	59	35	10	3	3	7	22	2	.262
Elmer Yoter	3B167	167	605	87	171	65	25	12	4	64	25	15	.283
Wid Matthews	OF151	153	622	104	191	42	16	5	1	61	23	23	.307
Albert Russell	OF92,1B18	119	376	79	121	61	16	10	14	51	35	4	.322
Walter Rehg	OF91	98	319	51	93	52	15	4	1	18	16	0	.292
Grover Hartley	C86	96	298	38	86	36	20	5	0	13	13	4	.289
Ed Ainsmith	C73	76	194	13	39	10	4	0	0	18	10	2	.201
Frank Henry	P38	71	142	5	37	17	9	1	2	6	14	0	.260
Riggs Stephenson	OF51	51	195	34	75	40	12	4	4	23	8	4	.385
Bill Burwell	P43	45	102	10	29	13	4	0	1	9	5	0	.285
Carmen Hill	P39	42	99	14	21	8	2	2	1	2	16	1	.212
Byron Speece	P36	36	74	7	14	5	4	0	1	2	18	0	.189
Wisner	P33	34	72	5	15	3	0	0	0	1	2	0	.208
Maurice Shannon	SS28	33	112	15	32	21	7	3	1	6	4	0	.286
Paul Florence	C30	30	106	16	39	18	4	2	2	3	4	0	.368
Munson	OF22	25	72	11	23	10	8	0	1	8	5	0	.319
Joe Klugman	2B10	21	39	7	8	1	2	0	0	0	1	0	.205
S. Niles	P14	15	14	0	6	4	1	0	0	2	2	0	.429
J. Thompson	P15	15	14	0	2	1	0	0	0	0	3	0	.143
Reynolds	P5	10	9	2	2	2	0	1	0	0	0	0	.222
Morrison	P7	7	4	1	2		0	0	0			0	.500
C. Boone	P4	4	7	2	2		0	0	0			0	.286
Harry Weaver	P4	4	5	1	1		1	0	0			0	.200
Sindlinger	P4	4	3	0	0		0	0	0			0	.000
Carter	2B	3	3	2	0		0	0	0			0	.000
Ray	P3	3	1	0	0		0	0	0			0	.000
Stanton	P2	2	0	0	0		0	0	0			0	----
Donie Bush	SS1	1	2	1	1		1	0	0			0	.500

INDIANAPOLIS (cont.)
Indians

BATTERS	POS-GAMES	GP	AB	R	H	BI	2B	3B	HR	BB	SO	SB	BA
Woodward	P1	1	1	0	1	0	0	0				0	.500

PITCHERS		W	L	PCT	G	GS	CG	SH	IP	H	BB	SO	ERA
Carmen Hill		21	7	.750	39				264	274	59	106	3.24
Bill Burwell		21	14	.600	43				294	311	63	75	3.28
Byron Speece		17	10	.630	36				204	234	47	93	4.06
Frank Henry		17	18	.486	38				290	318	73	106	3.63
Wisner		11	8	.579	33				222	223	55	63	3.16
S. Niles		3	2	.600	14				41	60	15	7	
C. Boone		2	1	.667	3				27	21	4	12	
J. Thompson		0	1	.000	15				40	45	18	16	
Reynolds		0	1	.000	5				20	25	7	9	
Sindlinger		0	1	.000	4				13	16	2	1	
Weaver		0	1	.000	4				11	19	8	2	
Ray		0	2	.000	3				3	6	5	1	
Morrison		0	0	----	6				17	14	10	2	
Stanton		0	0	----	2				3	9	3	0	
Woodward		0	0	----	1				4	10	3	2	

MILWAUKEE   3rd   93-71   .567   -10.5   Jack Lelivelt
Brewers

BATTERS	POS-GAMES	GP	AB	R	H	BI	2B	3B	HR	BB	SO	SB	BA
Ivy Griffin	1B147	149	612	103	205	105	28	9	9	49	26	19	.335
Harry Strohm	2B63,3B79	153	601	83	181	119	27	10	6	28	27	22	.301
Flippin	SS121	121	381	54	88	34	9	3	1	51	21	13	.231
Syl Simon	3B94	107	357	57	110	59	19	7	5	27	39	14	.308
Lance Richbourg	OF164	164	714	151	247	84	38	28	3	49	48	48	.346
Bunny Brief	OF140,1B20	161	583	130	205	122	38	10	26	94	89	9	.352
Fred Schulte	OF131,2B19	150	596	142	207	104	30	14	13	73	37	31	.347
Bob McMenemy	C101	113	342	62	120	50	22	7	3	42	44	2	.351
Oswald Orwoll	P33,OF26	78	181	28	52	42	5	3	3	11	26	6	.287
Frank Luce	OF38	70	161	39	58	22	12	2	5	14	14	3	.360
LaMotte	SS31,2B28	69	237	26	64	35	12	2	3	16	17	7	.270
Russ Young	C55	65	198	23	53	24	13	1	1	10	18	1	.268
Clyde Beck	2B55	55	195	28	55	36	9	3	1	28	20	2	.282
Roy Sanders	P46	46	64	6	9	2	1	0	0	5	24	0	.141
Dave Danforth	P43	43	93	12	18	4	2	1	0	7	21	0	.194
Joe Eddleman	P41	41	81	5	7	3	1	2	0	3	11	0	.086
Dennis Gearin	P34	37	76	7	15	8	2	1	0	9	5	0	.198
Claude Jonnard	P22	22	52	2	3	1	0	1	0	3	23	0	.058
Charles Robertson	P18	18	50	4	4	3	1	0	0	3	4	0	.080
Ray Thompson	C14	17	45	5	11	3	3	1	0	6	4	1	.244
Stauffer	P11	11	12	0	1	0	0	0	0	0	0	0	.083
William Coggin	P7	7	4	0	1		1	0	0			0	.250
Al Reitz	P6	6	0	1	0		0	0	0			0	.000
Ovid McCracken	P6	6	0	0	0		0	0	0			0	----
Costello	SS	5	3	0	1		0	0	0			0	.333
Burke	P5	5	0	0	0		0	0	0			0	----
Goff	P4	4	1	0	0		0	0	0			0	.000
Childer	OF1	1	5	1	1		0	0	0			0	.200
Klug	P1	1	0	0	0		0	0	0			0	----
Campbell	P1	1	0	0	0		0	0	0			0	----

PITCHERS		W	L	PCT	G	GS	CG	SH	IP	H	BB	SO	ERA
Joe Eddleman		17	10	.630	41				238	282	54	51	4.58
Dave Danforth		17	15	.531	43				273	294	74	123	3.92
Roy Sanders		14	11	.560	46				183	220	66	65	4.38
Oswald Orwoll		12	4	.750	33				168	189	78	93	4.07
Charles Robertson		12	5	.706	18				146	148	43	81	3.38
Dennis Gearin		10	12	.455	34				202	243	79	70	4.50
Claude Jonnard		9	9	.500	22				163	160	67	71	3.53
Coggin		1	1	.500	7				17	26	0	10	
Stauffer		1	4	.200	11				36	51	24	6	
Ovid McCracken		0	0	----	6				7	16	3	2	
Burke		0	0	----	5				6	9	7	4	
Goff		0	0	----	4				7	11	4	1	
Al Reitz		0	0	----	3				5	14	5	1	
Campbell		0	0	----	1				1	2	0	0	
Klug		0	0	----	1				1	2	1	0	

TOLEDO Mud Hens
4th 87-77 .530 -16.5 Casey Stengel

BATTERS	POS-GAMES	GP	AB	R	H	BI	2B	3B	HR	BB	SO	SB	BA
Fred Schleibner	1B	(see multi-team players)											
Fred Maguire	2B161	162	639	105	198	78	35	7	2	32	52	22	.310
Woody English	SS162	162	551	68	166	69	17	15	4	40	48	7	.301
Heinie Groh	3B103	104	382	72	116	27	22	4	1	53	23	4	.304
Bobby Veach	OF155	156	588	113	213	105	43	14	9	60	24	38	.362
Bevo LeBourveau	OF146	149	584	124	220	117	33	12	17	42	47	45	.377
Horace Koehler	OF132	153	553	70	157	44	18	4	2	29	23	20	.284
John Heving	C118	121	436	51	125	69	14	4	0	23	24	5	.287
Casey Stengel	OF56	88	201	40	66	27	14	2	0	23	12	10	.328
Ray Grimes	1B45	61	158	18	45	25	5	0	1	30	9	3	.285
L. Urban	C50	60	184	16	57	17	3	2	0	11	10	2	.310
Pete Cote	3B40	43	167	23	46	13	6	4	0	7	18	7	.275
Paul McCullough	P41	41	71	4	8	6	1	0	2	2	11	0	.113
Tim McNamara	P36	36	77	6	10	3	1	0	0	5	18	0	.130
Myers	OF23	35	91	20	31	13	4	0	1	5	6	7	.341
Ernest Woolfolk	P34	35	32	3	7	1	1	0	0	3	12	0	.219
Wilfred Ryan	P32	33	48	5	9	2	1	0	0	5	13	0	.188
Clarkson	P29	29	54	8	17	13	3	4	0	4	9	0	.315
Ed Pfeffer	P24	24	48	2	7	1	1	0	0	5	18	0	.130
Ernie Maun	P22	24	66	6	15	4	3	0	0	0	6	0	.227
Fred Johnson	P16	16	9	0	1	1	0	0	0	0	1	0	.111
Hugh Canavan	P11	15	17	1	1	2	1	0	0	1	2	0	.059
Ben Frey	P14	14	10	0	1	0	0	0	0	0	3	0	.100
Cooper	P9	10	22	3	4	0	1	0	0	0	0	0	.182
Thomas	P10	10	15	3	4	2	1	0	0	0	4	0	.267
Tunney	P10	10	12	0	3	0	0	0	0	0	3	0	.250
Frank Parkinson	SS-3B	9	11	2	2	2	0	0	1	2	1	0	.182
Robert Caffrey	P8	9	5	1	3		0	0	0			1	.600
Albert Herman	P8	8	5	0	0		0	0	0			0	.000
White Chambers	P6	6	3	0	0		0	0	0			0	.000
Dom Torpe	P3	3	1	0	0		0	0	0			0	.000
Oliver Klee	OF	2	5	0	1		0	0	0			0	.200
Hawkins	SS1	1	0	0	0		0	0	0			0	----

PITCHERS	W	L	PCT	G	GS	CG	SH	IP	H	BB	SO	ERA
Tim McNamara	14	11	.560	36				220	216	48	56	4.08
Paul McCullough	13	11	.542	41				215	232	92	71	3.60
Clarkson	12	5	.706	29				146	140	68	43	4.10
Ed Pfeffer	11	8	.579	24				143	145	30	43	3.71
Wilfred Ryan	8	6	.571	32				147	142	53	80	3.40
Ernie Maun	8	10	.444	22				156	158	33	34	2.71
Ernest Woolfolk	6	7	.462	34				112	120	56	36	3.78
Fred Johnson	3	2	.600	16				40	53	13	6	
Tunney	3	2	.600	10				35	39	18	7	
Ben Frey	3	4	.429	14				33	39	11	9	
Cooper	2	5	.286	9				55	75	9	25	
Thomas	1	1	.500	10				38	36	28		
Hugh Canavan	1	3	.250	11				36	51	14	8	
Robert Caffrey	0	0	----	8				15	16	7	6	
Albert Herman	0	0	----	8				15	10	11	1	
White Chambers	0	0	----	6				9	12	3	4	
Dom Torpe	0	0	----	3				6	12	0	0	

KANSAS CITY Blues
5th 87-78 .527 -17 Spencer Abbott

BATTERS	POS-GAMES	GP	AB	R	H	BI	2B	3B	HR	BB	SO	SB	BA
Dud Branom	1B163	163	632	98	222	116	34	7	10	33	21	10	.351
Ernest Smith	2B87,SS58,3B11	156	631	94	197	77	36	11	3	53	49	17	.312
Robert Murray	SS90,2B14	116	427	83	130	41	12	6	0	54	17	10	.304
Ed Pick	3B55,OF102	161	580	109	194	109	33	17	14	100	54	18	.334
Denver Grigsby	OF142	142	527	91	152	71	33	8	7	65	35	15	.288
Fred Nicholson	OF128	135	472	88	151	69	28	12	4	48	37	13	.320
James Moore	OF122	131	473	88	135	44	25	5	7	35	24	10	.285
Enoch Shinault	C87	93	285	33	80	50	9	5	5	38	22	3	.281
Frank Snyder	C67	71	220	33	55	30	8	2	7	18	18	0	.250
Philbin	2B46,3B15	65	260	32	60	14	13	2	1	15	13	4	.231
James Zinn	P35	54	112	15	41	19	8	4	1	9	12	1	.366
Heinie Meine	P36	43	132	19	37	17	7	5	0	1	16	0	.280
Andy Messenger	P33	33	65	1	16	4	1	0	0	3	8	0	.246

KANSAS CITY (cont.)
Blues

BATTERS	POS-GAMES	GP	AB	R	H	BI	2B	3B	HR	BB	SO	SB	BA
Ralph Michaels	3B21	28	74	10	26	13	7	1	0	8	4	0	.351
Tom Sheehan	P24	24	60	3	15	5	3	0	0	2	3	0	.250
Olsen	P24	24	37	3	5	0	0	0	0	1	12	0	.135
Evans	P22	22	43	7	12	7	0	5	0	3	2	0	.279
Bill Hargrove	P22	22	30	4	6	4	1	1	0	1	1	0	.200
Dumovich	P20	20	27	6	7	3	1	1	0	2	5	0	.259
Ed Schaack	P11	12	23	4	4	0	0	0	0	1	5	0	.174
Oldham	P13	13	30	4	11	6	1	1	0	6	7	0	.367
W. Warmoth	P9	9	12	1	2		0	0	0			0	.167
Frank McGowan	OF	8	18	2	3		0	1	0			1	.167
Albert Cowell	SS,1B	3	3	1	1		0	0	0			0	.333
Joe Kuhel	1B	2	2	0	0		0	0	0			0	.000
Lynn Nelson	P1	1	2	0	0		0	0	0			0	.000
Joe Brown	P1	1	3	0	0		0	0	0			0	.000
Alfred Feigert	P1	1	1	0	1		0	0	0			0	1.000
Howell	2B1	1	1	0	0		0	0	0			0	.000
Ray Lingrel	P1	1	0	0	0		0	0	0			0	----
Gilligan	SS1	1	0	0	0		0	0	0			0	----
Alvin Montgomery	P1	1	0	0	0		0	0	0			0	----

PITCHERS	W	L	PCT	G	GS	CG	SH	IP	H	BB	SO	ERA
Heinie Meine	17	14	.548	36				275	281	88	74	3.27
James Zinn	16	13	.552	35				258	286	65	67	3.76
Evans	10	6	.625	22				114	136	31	30	4.66
Tom Sheehan	9	11	.450	24				162	177	43	49	3.89
Olsen	8	4	.667	24				105	119	34	38	4.03
Oldham	7	5	.583	13				93	87	25	23	3.00
Andy Messenger	7	13	.350	33				184	207	30	66	3.47
Dumovich	5	4	.556	20				83	114	44	26	6.83
Ed Schaack	4	0	1.000	11				58	62	8	17	2.64
W. Warmoth	3	2	.600	9				36	39	11	20	
Bill Hargrove	1	4	.200	22				82	96	28	26	5.38
Joe Brown	0	1	.000	1				8	6	5	2	
Lynn Nelson	0	0	----	1				5	6	1	3	
Alfred Feigert	0	0	----	1				4	6	0	2	
Ray Lingrel	0	0	----	1				1	4	2	0	
Alvin Montgomery	0	0	----	1				0	3	0	0	inf.

ST. PAUL　　6th　　82-81　　.503　　-21　　Nick Allen
Saints

BATTERS	POS-GAMES	GP	AB	R	H	BI	2B	3B	HR	BB	SO	SB	BA
Stuvengen	1B147	147	576	78	169	93	32	8	9	33	28	5	.293
Norm McMillan	2B154	154	640	108	185	71	25	18	7	30	37	21	.289
Paul Wanninger	SS162	162	683	97	216	59	21	8	4	29	12	12	.316
Julian Wera	3B110	116	392	50	116	49	20	7	4	18	24	6	.298
Bruno Haas	OF158	158	590	75	194	76	51	8	8	50	43	20	.329
Harold Anderson	OF124	127	473	72	144	46	18	9	3	25	21	12	.304
Nick Cullop	OF119	125	449	92	141	68	22	7	22	40	67	32	.314
Fred Hofmann	C139	141	454	64	137	66	20	3	13	56	53	1	.302
R. Wade	OF103	122	397	56	125	46	18	10	9	28	30	6	.315
Deeby Foss	3B46,1B15	76	229	30	69	46	12	7	0	18	22	14	.302
Oscar Roettger	P21	54	106	21	39	12	10	3	5	3	4	2	.368
George Pipgras	P50	50	114	11	23	5	3	0	0	4	21	1	.202
Heinie Odom	3B18,2B14	49	128	23	34	5	3	1	0	3	11	6	.266
L. McCarthy	C36	45	114	7	19	6	2	2	0	4	9	1	.167
Ray Kolp	P41	41	98	9	29	13	2	0	1	2	9	0	.296
H. Johnson	P35	35	65	9	14	5	2	1	1	2	8	0	.215
Meade	P22	22	57	3	8	4	0	0	2	1	19	0	.140
Farquhar	P16	17	21	2	5	1	0	0	0	1	4	0	.238
Walter Betts	P12	15	36	5	15	8	1	1	0	1	3	0	.417
Carl Thomas	P7	7	8	0	2		1	0	0			0	.250
A. Holtzhauser	P7	7	7	1	2		0	0	0			0	.286
Wernke	P7	7	4	0	0		0	0	0			0	.000
Watts	P6	6	1	0	0		0	0	0			0	.000
Nick Allen	C	3	3	0	1		1	0	0			0	.333
Hesner	C	2	4	1	1		0	0	0			0	.250

PITCHERS	W	L	PCT	G	GS	CG	SH	IP	H	BB	SO	ERA
George Pipgras	22	19	.537	50				312	300	113	156	3.86

ST. PAUL (cont.)
Saints

PITCHERS	W	L	PCT	G	GS	CG	SH	IP	H	BB	SO	ERA
Ray Kolp	18	11	.621	41				276	294	66	76	3.62
Ed Meade	12	7	.632	22				156	182	53	49	3.40
Oscar Roettger	7	5	.583	21				140	169	61	40	4.95
H. Johnson	6	15	.286	35				186	185	111	89	4.31
Walter Betts	5	3	.625	12				88	84	20	25	3.89
Farquhar	2	2	.500	16				57	88	41	22	6.63
A. Holtzhauser	1	1	.500	7				21	23	11	9	
Wernke	1	3	.250	7				16	28	6	2	
Thomas	0	1	.000	7				28	36	9	2	
Watts	0	0	----	6				5	10	2	0	

MINNEAPOLIS   7th   72-94   .434   -32.5   Mike Kelley
Millers

BATTERS	POS-GAMES	GP	AB	R	H	BI	2B	3B	HR	BB	SO	SB	BA
Ted Jourdan	1B95	95	385	66	110	32	24	3	3	43	25	6	.285
William Black	2B121	138	475	72	141	86	25	9	14	26	37	8	.297
Hod Ford	SS71,2B19	90	302	39	87	54	27	1	5	35	30	3	.288
Joe Fowler	3B126	129	493	69	150	42	18	10	0	23	39	8	.304
Earl Smith	OF154	159	642	103	194	94	47	8	15	34	65	17	.302
Pat Duncan	OF151	153	562	110	197	**123**	30	6	23	82	49	14	.351
John Brooks	OF76	84	294	47	87	35	9	3	8	18	34	13	.296
Ernie Krueger	C62	87	249	28	66	32	17	1	3	16	13	3	.265
Richard Loftus	OF57,1B42	119	429	48	126	24	21	8	0	24	16	9	.294
Jim McAuley	SS42,2B22	80	230	31	47	15	6	0	3	24	29	6	.204
Frank Emmer	SS59	59	225	24	54	20	11	2	6	21	33	5	.240
Byler	C54	57	149	8	33	10	4	0	0	9	15	1	.221
Jim Middleton	P53	56	102	14	26	14	7	0	0	4	15	0	.254
Hollingsworth	P50	53	85	5	7	1	1	0	0	10	35	1	.082
W. Hubbell	P51	51	73	4	13	4	1	0	0	5	17	0	.179
Wilson	P39	41	54	5	14	1	3	0	0	1	10	0	.259
J. Benton	P39	39	77	3	13	2	1	0	0	2	13	0	.169
Dumont	P29	35	55	3	10	6	1	0	1	2	24	0	.182
Hudgens	1B32	32	119	12	39	20	7	2	3	3	14	1	.328
Schultz	OF12	20	49	7	13	7	3	1	1	5	4	0	.265
Greene	P16	16	12	3	5	1	0	0	0	0	1	0	.417
Francis	P14	15	7	1	2	2	0	0	0	1	2	0	.286
Clyde Sukeforth	C	9	22	4	4		1	0	0			0	.182
Leo Moon	P6	7	1	0	0		0	0	0			0	.000
Ed Kenna	C	5	19	3	4		0	1	0			0	.211
McCann	P5	5	16	0	1		0	0	0			0	.063
Pete Kilduff	2B	4	7	0	1		1	0	0			0	.143
Hurt	SS1	1	2	0	0		0	0	0			0	.000

PITCHERS	W	L	PCT	G	GS	CG	SH	IP	H	BB	SO	ERA
Jim Middleton	20	15	.571	53				273	315	100	87	4.18
W. Hubbell	14	16	.467	51				237	270	83	75	4.52
Benton	12	16	.429	39				232	276	63	53	3.76
Hollingsworth	11	18	.379	50				271	278	**164**	146	4.48
Dumont	7	10	.412	29				159	172	72	60	3.91
Wilson	6	10	.375	39				161	189	53	49	5.14
Francis	1	2	.333	14				31	54	7	13	
Greene	1	4	.200	16				37	51	10	12	
William Harris	0	1	.000	9				26	34	22	6	
McCann	0	2	.000	5				35	41	16	9	
Leo Moon	0	0	----	6				10	10	3	2	

COLUMBUS   8th   39-125   .238   -64.5   Gowdy - McQuillan
Senators

BATTERS	POS-GAMES	GP	AB	R	H	BI	2B	3B	HR	BB	SO	SB	BA
Roy Grimes	1B		(see multi-team players)										
EmmettMcCann	2B102	104	413	65	139	59	19	8	1	19	16	23	.337
Otis Miller	SS		(see multi-team players)										
Jim Geygan	3B53,SS15	78	284	49	79	31	17	4	2	11	18	3	.278
Harry Leibold	OF122	141	498	82	160	40	27	5	2	65	32	9	.321
Kenzie Kirkham	OF76	80	280	30	77	37	14	3	4	18	11	3	.275
Mike Menosky	OF62	65	212	43	53	27	14	3	5	33	19	4	.250

COLUMBUS (cont.)
Senators

BATTERS	POS-GAMES	GP	AB	R	H	BI	2B	3B	HR	BB	SO	SB	BA
Meuter	C61	69	202	18	42	18	8	3	1	14	35	0	.208
Langford	OF59	60	230	22	66	23	13	2	2	19	10	6	.287
Leonard	OF42	60	156	15	34	14	4	0	0	6	12	2	.218
Pete Harris	P45	55	86	10	15	7	1	0	0	2	10	3	.174
Paul Strand	OF43	47	173	27	58	25	10	4	1	13	13	9	.335
P. Ballenger	3B37	41	146	29	45	12	11	0	1	23	15	6	.308
Emory Zumbro	P35	39	73	5	14	5	1	1	0	2	11	0	.192
P. Regan	2B34	38	148	27	47	24	12	0	3	11	5	5	.317
Rudy Sommers	P31	37	75	7	21	8	3	1	0	2	10	1	.280
Ray Hayworth	C32	32	103	14	22	8	0	1	0	6	17	0	.214
Lucas	OF23	28	95	12	25	9	4	1	0	3	10	2	.263
Biemiller	P25	27	29	2	3	1	0	0	0	2	7	0	.103
Dover	3B10,SS10	25	90	9	27	6	3	2	0	2	9	0	.300
Joe Bird	C14	25	64	3	22	10	2	0	0	9	4	0	.344
Pratt	SS23	23	77	5	13	4	0	1	0	6	13	0	.169
McCarren		22	62	6	18	2	1	0	0	3	2	0	.290
White	C10	18	46	5	7	3	0	0	0	0	2	0	.152
Sam Withem	P16	18	32	4	7	0	0	1	0	0	10	0	.219
George Picard	P16	18	26	1	3	0	0	0	0	0	4	0	.115
Fred Nicolai	SS17	17	66	6	14	2	3	0	0	5	4	0	.212
George McQuillan	P15	15	35	1	0	0	0	0	0	1	9	0	.000
John Doljack	3B14	14	53	10	17	3	2	1	0	3	4	1	.321
Lackey	C14	14	44	1	9	1	1	0	0	1	11	1	.205
James Horn	OF13	13	53	4	18	5	1	1	0	1	2	2	.340
Burke		10	14	4	5	0	1	2	0	0	2	0	.357
Thelan	OF	9	39	1	4		0	0	0			0	.103
Harry Layne	OF	9	21	1	6		0	0	0			0	.286
Emilio Palmero	P9	9	17	0	4		0	0	0			0	.235
Neubauer	P8	8	10	0	1		0	0	0			0	.100
Harry Fishbaugh	P7	7	9	0	1		0	0	0			0	.111
Pat Shea	P7	7	4	1	1		1	0	0			0	.250
Dougherty	1B	6	21	3	5		0	0	0			0	.238
Dundon	C	5	15	2	3		0	0	0			0	.200
Richard Ferrell	C	5	14	4	4		1	0	0			0	.286
George Stueland	P4	5	5	0	1		1	0	0			0	.200
Jack Slappey	P5	5	2	1	2		0	0	0			0	1.000
Happ	SS	4	15	0	0		0	0	0			0	.000
Charles Ketchum	P4	4	5	1	1		1	0	0			0	.200
Reis	P3	3	3	0	0		0	0	0			0	.000
Ussati	SS	2	10	0	0		0	0	0			0	.000
Baker	SS	2	6	0	1		0	0	0			0	.167
E. Johnson	P2	2	4	1	2		0	1	0			0	.500
Hal Sullivan	OF	2	2	0	0		0	0	0			0	.000
Gruber	P2	2	2	0	0		0	0	0			0	.000
Joe Bradshaw	P2	2	1	0	0		0	0	0			0	.000
E. Murphy	OF1	1	2	1	2		0	0	0			0	1.000
Rapp	C1	1	2	0	0		0	0	0			0	.000
Walker	OF1	1	2	0	0		0	0	0			0	.000
Mulby	C1	1	0	0	0		0	0	0			0	----
Kelly	P1	1	0	0	0		0	0	0			0	----

PITCHERS	W	L	PCT	G	GS	CG	SH	IP	H	BB	SO	ERA
Rudy Sommers	10	14	.417	31				186	209	75	41	4.64
Emory Zumbro	5	12	.294	35				193	242	44	32	4.84
Pete Harris	4	21	.160	45				216	331	63	41	6.75
Harry Fishbaugh	2	1	.667	7				16	28	11	6	
Biemiller	2	8	.200	25				90	146	43	18	8.40
George McQuillan	2	9	.182	15				102	132	22	22	4.41
Sam Withem	1	4	.200	16				75	118	23	18	5.54
Burke	1	5	.167	8				44	34	10	3	
Emilio Palmero	1	6	.143	9				56	66	28	17	4.34
Slappey	0	1	.000	5				7	19	11	3	
Charles Ketchum	0	1	.000	4				14	22	6	3	
Reis	0	1	.000	3				8	6	10	3	
Gruber	0	1	.000	2				5	2	8	0	
Joe Bradshaw	0	1	.000	2				1	1	4	0	
Pat Shea	0	3	.000	7				21	29	12	6	
Stueland	0	3	.000	4				11	21	7	4	
Neubauer	0	4	.000	8				32	34	8	0	
George Picard	0	6	.000	16				74	103	23	18	4.86
E. Johnson	0	0	----	2				7	22	5	3	

MULTI-TEAM PLAYERS

BATTERS	POS-GAMES	TEAMS	GP	AB	R	H	BI	2B	3B	HR	BB	SO	SB	BA
Roy Grimes	1B156	COL-TOL	160	587	106	191	111	28	9	14	78	57	8	.325
Otis Miller	SS81,2B36	COL-IND	140	498	55	135	58	25	8	3	20	17	7	.271
George Fisher	OF128	MIN-IND	139	484	101	159	89	29	8	14	47	37	19	.328
Fred Schleibner	1B117	TOL-COL	135	430	61	130	49	17	3	2	50	40	8	.302
Wyatt	OF95,3B23	IND-COL	131	439	63	135	73	26	7	7	33	35	7	.308
M. Connolly	SS69,3B33,2B22	TOL-COL	129	461	79	141	62	23	4	2	48	20	15	.306
Lute Boone	3B60,SS30,2B13	KC-LOU	108	382	60	103	53	18	4	0	25	19	7	.270
Tierney	2B46,3B62	MIN-KC	103	333	61	96	56	22	3	8	34	30	8	.288
Hank Gowdy	C66	COL-MIN	78	210	30	71	28	9	0	6	44	15	1	.338
Hruska	C34	TOL-COL-TOL	40	88	10	21	5	7	1	0	5	8	2	.239
Ferd Schupp	P36	SP-IND	37	62	5	7	6	1	0	1	12	18	0	.113
George Lyons	P33	TOL-COL	33	68	6	15	4	2	2	0	3	18	0	.221
Wells	C28	KC-MIL	30	79	12	26	5	2	2	0	9	5	3	.329
Tony Faeth	P29	COL-IND	29	51	3	10	2	0	0	0	2	7	0	.196
Youngblood	P5	KC-COL	5	5	0	0		0	0	0			0	.000

PITCHERS		TEAMS	W	L	PCT	G	GS	CG	SH	IP	H	BB	SO	ERA
Ferd Schupp		SP-IND	11	16	.407	36				206	224	132	104	5.20
George Lyons		TOL-COL	10	11	.476	33				186	225	70	50	4.93
Tony Faeth		COL-IND	4	15	.211	29				147	207	61	34	5.81
Youngblood		KC-COL	0	2	.000	5				16	28	11	6	

TEAM BATTING

TEAMS	GP	AB	R	H	BI	2B	3B	HR	BB	SO	SB	BA
LOUISVILLE	**169**	**5867**	**1012**	**1805**		285	101	60	571	467	130	**.308**
INDIANAPOLIS	167	5659	814	1655		239	79	54	488	359	93	.292
MILWAUKEE	165	5652	970	1719		273	**102**	79	570	554	176	.304
TOLEDO	164	5654	869	1717		260	78	47	463	464	**184**	.304
KANSAS CITY	166	5686	910	1701		285	99	60	**587**	422	116	.299
ST. PAUL	164	5700	822	1694		264	94	86	392	482	139	.297
MINNEAPOLIS	167	5754	825	1639		**304**	63	**106**	480	**599**	121	.285
COLUMBUS	164	5637	757	1560		253	65	36	508	565	109	.277
	663	45609	6979	13490		2163	681	528	4059	3912	1068	.296

1927
Toledo Mud Hens

All the teams of the American Association had tasted of success save one. This team had breathed the heady air of the first division a mere handful of times, because their most common finishing place was seventh or eighth, one of which they had occupied a dozen times since 1902. These were the Toledo Mud Hens.

The Mud Hens had never won an Association pennant as their three second place finishes (1907, 1910, and 1912) served as their high point to date. In the mid–1920s, however, the tide of mediocrity began to turn. In 1926, Toledo hired an eccentric and unique former New York Giants ballplayer to be their next manager. That year the new manager, Casey Stengel, led the Mud Hens to a respectable fourth place finish, their highest in six years.

In 1927, everything clicked into place, as Toledo proved itself to be a contending team. The Mud Hens led the league for most of the season until Kansas City caught them in August, pursued closely by Milwaukee. During the final month of the season, Toledo's hopes seemed bleak until they reeled off a ten-game win streak to pull themselves back into the thick of the chase. When Toledo swept a doubleheader from Indianapolis on the season's final day, the pennant was won, the team's first in 25 years.

The 1927 Mud Hens won their laurels via their potent hitting attack. In a lineup studded with hitting stars, a quintet of players stood out: Roy Grimes (.368, 122 RBI), Bobby Veach (.363, 145 RBI), Bevo LeBourveau (.346), Joe Kelly (.328), and Fred Maguire (.326). Veach's runs batted in total led the league, as the Mud Hens ended up batting .312 as a team.

Both Milwaukee and Kansas City ended two games back in one of the most exciting pennant races in league history. St. Paul and Minneapolis finished in fourth and fifth, while the sixth through eighth slots were occupied by Indianapolis, Louisville, and Columbus. Albert Russell of Indianapolis ended up as the top batter (.385), while Frank Emmer of Minneapolis won home run honors (32). Tom Sheehan of Kansas City won the most games (26) while his teammate, James Zinn, had the lowest earned run average (3.08). Minneapolis pitcher Pat Malone had the most strikeouts, finishing with 214.

Toledo would see-saw between the first and second divisions for the next few years before returning to its initial residence in the lower half of the standings. Thus, 1927 remains a high point for the Mud Hens team, because it marked the one and only time Toledo won the pennant during its first fifty years in the American Association.

TOLEDO   1st   101-67   .601   Casey Stengel
Mud Hens

BATTERS	POS-GAMES	GP	AB	R	H	BI	2B	3B	HR	BB	SO	SB	BA
Roy Grimes	1B170	170	650	128	239	122	50	6	16	71	53	15	.368
Fred Maguire	2B171	171	720	130	235	94	42	13	5	40	52	18	.326
Pete Cote	SS127,3B17	145	573	95	150	39	19	7	1	25	50	6	.262
William Marriott	3B98	107	358	68	96	37	14	7	3	28	25	23	.268
Bobby Veach	OF163	164	623	133	226	145	45	10	12	45	27	22	.363
Bevo LeBourveau	OF153	159	618	130	214	88	40	17	12	55	54	28	.346
Joe Kelly	OF93	116	341	62	112	55	17	6	4	20	14	2	.328
George O'Neil	C81	81	261	22	72	41	13	3	1	18	24	2	.276
Horace Koehler	OF88,3B42	137	465	49	134	85	27	7	3	31	27	7	.288
John Heving	C74	89	250	28	89	45	15	4	0	11	7	2	.356
Wilfred Ryan	P49	51	62	8	19	6	5	0	1	2	2	0	.306
Emil Meusel	OF41	47	158	27	56	28	12	2	3	8	9	1	.354
L. Urban	C39	45	130	14	42	17	8	2	0	15	2	6	.323
George Milstead	P44	44	81	9	19	6	3	1	1	1	21	0	.235
Paul McCullough	P38	38	50	0	8	6	1	0	0	1	11	0	.160
Walt Huntzinger	P36	36	66	7	18	8	0	1	0	1	9	0	.273
Scott	SS33	33	124	20	39	12	9	0	1	2	3	3	.315
Emilio Palmero	P31	31	63	11	13	4	2	0	0	9	13	0	.206
Ed Pfeffer	P29	29	60	5	14	7	1	0	0	4	12	0	.233
Ernie Maun	P18	18	31	2	6	3	2	0	0	0	1	0	.194
Casey Stengel		18	17	3	3	3	0	0	1	1	2	0	.176
Joe Bush	P6	13	28	2	6	5	1	0	0	1	3	0	.214
Jack Smith	1B	9	13	3	2		1	0	0			0	.154
Jesse Barnes	P7	7	16	2	2		0	0	0			0	.125
Ernest Woolfolk	P4	4	2	0	0		0	0	0			0	.000
Charles Dalbock	PH	4	1	0	0		0	0	0			0	.000
LeRoy Parmelee	P3	3	3	0	1		0	0	0			0	.333
Carl Lind	SS1	1	3	0	0		0	0	0			0	.000
John Chambers	OF1	1	2	0	0		0	0	0			0	.000
White Chambers	P1	1	1	0	0		0	0	0			0	.000
Robert Caffrey	P1	1	0	0	0		0	0	0			0	----
Ben Frey	P1	1	0	0	0		0	0	0			0	----

PITCHERS	W	L	PCT	G	GS	CG	SH	IP	H	BB	SO	ERA
George Milstead	16	11	.593	44				215	247	69	64	3.81
Wilfred Ryan	15	9	.625	49				152	168	53	59	4.17
Emilio Palmero	14	5	.737	31				195	196	64	63	3.60
Walt Huntzinger	13	5	.722	36				179	219	66	45	5.53
Ed Pfeffer	9	9	.500	29				187	219	45	48	4.67
Paul McCullough	7	4	.636	38				141	156	25	52	3.70
Ernie Maun	6	5	.545	18				89	130	27	17	7.08
Joe Bush	4	2	.667	6				51	45	17	20	2.65
Jesse Barnes	3	2	.600	7				48	52	10	13	3.19
LeRoy Parmelee	1	0	1.000	3				13	18	4	3	
Ernest Woolfolk	0	0	----	4				6	10	2	4	
James Baxter	0	0	----	3				3	5	2	0	3.00
White Chambers	0	0	----	1				4	7	1	2	6.75
Robert Caffrey	0	0	----	1				0	0	0	2	54.00
Ben Frey	0	0	----	1				0	2	0	0	27.00

KANSAS CITY   2nd (T)   99-69   .589   -2   Dutch Zwilling
Blues

BATTERS	POS-GAMES	GP	AB	R	H	BI	2B	3B	HR	BB	SO	SB	BA
Joe Hauser	1B169	169	617	145	218	134	49	22	20	96	74	25	.353
Bill Wambsganss	2B155	155	567	114	174	68	30	14	0	70	33	13	.307
Ernest Smith	SS147	157	568	83	156	99	24	6	1	50	38	14	.275
Howard Freigau	3B97	97	394	71	120	53	17	6	3	22	21	11	.305
Fred Nicholson	OF167	167	635	100	203	113	34	17	5	46	51	20	.320
Denver Grigsby	OF122	136	447	90	146	77	25	11	2	65	22	7	.327
James Moore	OF110	114	439	85	146	51	20	11	4	39	27	8	.333
Enoch Shinault	C100	107	308	46	82	46	16	11	4	33	38	6	.266
Ralph Michaels	3B38,2B25,SS23,OF12	108	322	44	89	50	13	4	1	37	32	8	.276
Frank McGowan	OF102	102	357	55	117	74	19	6	3	54	29	11	.328
John Peters	C85	95	285	34	94	46	16	5	0	14	17	3	.330
James Zinn	P45	81	152	28	47	32	11	5	4	8	16	1	.309
Tom Sheehan	P43	43	126	19	38	17	7	0	0	2	3	1	.302
Ed Pick	3B37	39	142	29	51	29	6	4	2	26	9	3	.359
Ed Schaack	P33	37	55	10	15	7	4	0	0	3	6	0	.272
W. Warmoth	P26	32	24	4	3	3	1	1	0	6	6	0	.125
Murray	P28	28	49	5	13	5	2	0	0	0	10	0	.265

KANSAS CITY (cont.)
Blues

BATTERS	POS-GAMES	GP	AB	R	H	BI	2B	3B	HR	BB	SO	SB	BA
Charles Chatham		28	41	10	15	1	1	0	0	3	8	5	.366
Roy	P23	23	47	7	12	8	0	1	1	4	14	1	.255
Davis	P22	22	46	3	9	8	0	1	0	7	12	0	.196
Oldham	P20	21	30	2	9	5	2	0	0	4	2	0	.300
Witt	OF15	19	53	8	20	5	3	1	0	3	3	1	.377
Elwood Wirts	C	9	14	1	4		0	0	0			0	.286
Andy Messenger	P8	8	11	0	1		0	0	0			0	.091
Bill Hargrove	P8	8	3	1	0		0	0	0			0	.000
Lynn Nelson	P6	6	7	2	3		0	1	0			0	.429
Belve Bean	P2	2	2	1	1		0	0	1			0	.500
Joe Kuhel	PH	2	1	0	0		0	0	0			0	.000
Hubbell	P2	2	0	0	0		0	0	0			0	----

PITCHERS		W	L	PCT	G	GS	CG	SH	IP	H	BB	SO	ERA
Tom Sheehan		26	13	.667	43				331	346	98	108	3.62
James Zinn		24	12	.667	45				330	250	55	83	3.08
Davis		12	7	.632	22				140	124	59	51	3.60
Ed Schaack		12	10	.545	33				160	189	35	27	4.17
Roy		7	7	.500	23				137	155	73	41	5.12
Murray		6	5	.545	28				143	168	39	46	4.59
W. Warmoth		6	5	.545	26				81	90	41	35	5.22
Oldham		3	4	.429	20				81	125	28	27	7.66
Olsen		2	3	.400	20				50	62	25	15	4.86
Nelson		1	0	1.000	6				18	14	9	9	
Andy Messenger		0	1	.000	8				23	32	7	13	
Bill Hargrove		0	2	.000	8				14	24	6	6	
Belve Bean		0	0	----	2				4	8	3	2	
Hubbell		0	0	----	2				0	4	0	0	

MILWAUKEE
Brewers

2nd (T)   99-69   .589   -2   Jack Lelivelt

BATTERS	POS-GAMES	GP	AB	R	H	BI	2B	3B	HR	BB	SO	SB	BA
Ivy Griffin	1B133	138	566	90	183	88	28	8	4	23	26	11	.323
Fred Lear	2B114	132	448	86	148	102	27	6	11	65	35	6	.330
Harry Riconda	SS105,2B62	168	722	141	255	102	57	18	11	48	49	13	.353
Harry Strohm	3B170	170	685	102	214	111	46	12	5	31	35	20	.312
Frank Wilson	OF139	145	572	121	193	53	41	15	7	70	56	12	.337
Frank Luce	OF128	135	475	105	154	98	21	17	11	59	57	6	.324
George Gerken	OF104	104	333	78	99	62	20	3	12	38	41	16	.297
Bob McMenemy	C113	117	385	64	112	65	28	10	6	45	43	5	.291
Bunny Brief	OF86,1B33	126	432	89	133	86	27	4	14	55	56	3	.308
Oswald Orwoll	OF40,P33	99	230	49	85	31	7	8	2	16	22	5	.370
Russ Young	C65	77	242	35	75	54	16	6	9	17	15	0	.310
Flippin	SS66	67	197	27	52	19	8	3	3	14	16	1	.264
H. Johnson	P39	55	132	19	43	26	3	3	3	7	15	0	.326
Elsh	OF45	54	157	25	44	17	10	7	0	4	16	6	.280
Roy Sanders	P50	50	59	2	8	3	2	0	0	5	22	0	.136
Claude Jonnard	P44	44	110	12	20	15	3	1	2	13	48	0	.182
Joe Eddleman	P42	42	98	10	17	6	2	1	0	1	17	1	.173
Dennis Gearin	P28	36	72	6	20	11	3	2	1	5	4	0	.278
Robert Murray	SS13	21	52	9	12	8	1	0	0	8	4	2	.230
Dennison	P11	11	9	0	2	1	0	0	0	0	3	0	.222
Ray Thompson	C	9	15	2	4		2	0	0			0	.267
Charles Willis	P7	7	15	2	4		0	0	0			0	.267
Dave Danforth	P7	7	6	1	0		0	0	0			0	.000
George Humber	P6	6	5	2	3		0	0	0			0	.600
Ray Caldwell	P5	5	6	0	2		0	0	0			0	.333
Walter Beck	P5	5	4	1	1		0	0	1			0	.250
Neil Baker	P3	3	4	0	1		0	0	0			0	.250

PITCHERS		W	L	PCT	G	GS	CG	SH	IP	H	BB	SO	ERA
Claude Jonnard		22	14	.611	44				282	297	136	176	4.18
Joe Eddleman		21	10	.677	42				266	333	56	57	4.23
H. Johnson		18	10	.643	39				249	240	116	147	4.41
Oswald Orwoll		17	6	.739	33				212	210	83	108	3.99
Roy Sanders		10	12	.455	50				176	222	66	58	4.75
Dennis Gearin		8	9	.471	28				159	190	75	42	5.32
Dennison		1	1	.500	11				32	35	22	13	

MILWAUKEE (cont.)
Brewers

PITCHERS	W	L	PCT	G	GS	CG	SH	IP	H	BB	SO	ERA
Dave Danforth	1	1	.500	7				25	40	13	7	
Charles Willis	1	2	.333	7				36	44	11	10	
Walter Beck	0	1	.000	5				15	15	9	4	
Ray Caldwell	0	3	.000	7				26	30	8	7	
George Humber	0	0	----	6				15	21	9	6	
Neil Baker	0	0	----	3				9	20	2	0	

ST. PAUL   4th   90-78   .536   -11   Nick Allen
Saints

BATTERS	POS-GAMES	GP	AB	R	H	BI	2B	3B	HR	BB	SO	SB	BA
Oscar Roettger	1B106,OF12,P1	124	474	86	159	114	29	7	19	26	48	6	.335
Norm McMillan	2B161	164	607	107	185	97	33	8	11	54	46	43	.305
Leo Durocher	SS171	171	594	60	150	78	27	10	7	52	82	9	.253
Gene Robertson	3B148	153	587	103	163	65	32	10	5	69	17	5	.278
Russ Scarritt	OF150	158	609	93	203	101	30	13	9	44	39	10	.333
Liz Funk	OF143	151	592	110	184	58	31	20	4	58	38	15	.311
Bruno Haas	OF115	115	440	64	147	63	32	5	6	31	28	24	.334
Alex Gaston	C122	122	384	43	117	43	16	3	7	50	31	0	.305
Harold Anderson	OF99	110	384	56	116	39	22	6	1	21	23	20	.302
Seimer	C78	78	190	26	56	38	10	0	0	12	5	0	.295
Stuvengen	1B61	70	244	32	68	26	12	0	4	9	12	5	.279
Deeby Foss	3B20,2B13	67	169	33	48	17	7	2	4	10	8	4	.284
Al Shealy	P46	49	108	9	25	14	2	0	1	6	11	0	.231
Fred Heimach	P40	44	106	12	30	11	3	3	0	4	15	0	.283
Walter Betts	P38	44	97	9	19	6	6	0	0	1	15	0	.196
Paul Zahniser	P40	40	112	9	11	5	1	0	0	4	32	0	.098
H. McQuaid	P39	39	65	10	13	2	3	0	0	3	12	0	.200
Paul Wanninger	SS12	26	25	2	7	0	1	0	0	0	4	0	.280
George Kirsch	P16	16	24	7	5	2	1	0	0	3	6	0	.208
Maley	P12	12	23	3	3	0	0	0	0	0	0	0	.130
Lewis		12	23	1	2	2	1	0	0	1	0	0	.087
Walter Beall	P9	9	17	1	2	3	0	0	0	3	5	0	.118
Ted Pillette	P9	9	8	1	2		0	0	0			0	.250
Ed Meade	P3	3	8	0	1		1	0	0			0	.125
Heine Odom	SS2	2	3	1	1		0	0	0			0	.333
Tony Faeth	P2	2	2	1	1		0	0	0			0	.500

PITCHERS	W	L	PCT	G	GS	CG	SH	IP	H	BB	SO	ERA
Paul Zahniser	20	15	.571	40				313	379	79	72	4.14
Walter Betts	18	13	.581	38				241	254	69	56	3.35
Al Shealy	17	18	.486	46				292	297	93	119	3.48
Fred Heimach	16	12	.571	40				270	333	61	75	3.64
H. McQuaid	9	11	.450	39				184	188	64	36	3.86
George Kirsch	3	1	.750	16				60	65	17	35	4.65
Maley	3	3	.500	12				72	82	22	24	3.37
Walter Beall	2	2	.500	9				50	34	56	42	4.68
Meade	1	1	.500	3				14	21	11	4	6.23
Ted Pillette	1	2	.333	8				22	28	9	3	
Tony Faeth	0	0	----	2				6	13	2	3	
Oscar Roettger	0	0	----	1				3	4	3	1	

MINNEAPOLIS   5th   88-80   .524   -13   Mike Kelley
Millers

BATTERS	POS-GAMES	GP	AB	R	H	BI	2B	3B	HR	BB	SO	SB	BA
Richard Loftus	1B71,OF59	141	543	103	164	47	26	2	3	49	14	12	.302
Jim McAuley	2B50	64	188	36	59	28	14	0	2	26	8	4	.314
Frank Emmer	SS164	164	645	154	213	116	34	15	32	31	79	12	.330
Sam Bohne	3B98,2B38	143	512	89	143	63	26	7	11	62	42	23	.279
Earl Smith	OF161	161	658	132	225	135	49	11	25	53	33	16	.342
Pat Duncan	OF147	152	591	80	208	110	26	3	10	46	27	12	.352
Ollie Tucker	OF123	123	457	92	156	100	19	7	24	75	33	12	.341
Ed Kenna	C82	93	285	46	97	49	24	4	10	44	17	5	.340
Ezzell	3B58,2B27	101	302	45	79	29	11	5	1	13	24	12	.262
Ernie Krueger	C53	72	191	24	48	20	8	4	5	21	14	4	.251
Hank Gowdy	C41	64	142	10	40	15	6	0	1	23	10	0	.282

MINNEAPOLIS (cont.)
Millers

BATTERS	POS-GAMES	GP	AB	R	H	BI	2B	3B	HR	BB	SO	SB	BA
Pat Malone	P53	56	122	13	25	11	4	0	2	7	26	2	.204
Leo Moon	P55	56	85	7	16	9	1	0	3	0	27	1	.188
Kelley	1B48	52	187	26	43	24	5	0	10	21	30	0	.230
Ellison	1B31	52	149	20	37	29	5	0	4	14	11	2	.248
W. Hubbell	P52	52	70	8	17	3	3	0	0	4	9	0	.243
J. Benton	P46	46	94	11	24	13	3	1	0	6	17	1	.256
Jim Middleton	P41	41	77	9	21	7	2	0	1	3	8	0	.272
G. Wilson	P37	40	73	13	17	8	4	0	1	5	16	0	.233
Poole	1B31	32	118	17	30	15	9	1	4	13	8	1	.254
R. Wade		18	33	6	8	2	2	0	2	3	6	0	.242
George Redfern	3B15	16	55	1	10	2	1	2	0	1	7	0	.182
Hurt		16	36	3	11	2	4	0	0	5	1	0	.306
Joe Sprinz	C11	11	34	3	10	6	0	2	1	2	4	0	.294
Owens	P10	10	4	1	1	0	0	0	0	1	0	0	.250
Frank Wetzel	OF	7	20	0	5	4	0	0	0	4	1	0	.250
George Fisher	OF	3	9	0	1	2	0	0	0	2	1	0	.111
Claude Davenport	P3	3	3	0	0	0	0	0	0	0	0	0	.000

PITCHERS	W	L	PCT	G	GS	CG	SH	IP	H	BB	SO	ERA
Pat Malone	20	18	.526	53				319	325	126	**214**	3.98
J. Benton	18	13	.581	46				256	326	68	81	4.64
Leo Moon	16	22	.421	55				260	298	91	98	4.36
Jim Middleton	12	7	.632	41				207	238	73	64	4.35
G. Wilson	12	9	.571	37				203	263	56	77	5.10
W. Hubbell	9	9	.500	52				216	256	68	55	4.33
Owens	1	1	.500	10				26	29	3	8	
Claude Davenport	0	1	.000	3				8	2	3	4	

INDIANAPOLIS   6th   70-98   .417   -31   Bruno Betzel
Indians

BATTERS	POS-GAMES	GP	AB	R	H	BI	2B	3B	HR	BB	SO	SB	BA
Walter Holke	1B167	167	640	78	198	98	20	13	8	35	37	12	.309
Bruno Betzel	2B113	119	407	49	115	48	18	7	2	40	29	5	.283
Otis Miller	SS62,2B33	119	415	40	118	50	10	5	1	17	21	10	.284
Elmer Yoter	3B114	114	452	89	140	60	22	10	6	46	30	13	.310
Wid Matthews	OF159	161	601	100	173	52	26	11	2	77	35	35	.288
Albert Russell	OF118	128	431	80	166	96	34	4	10	43	23	8	.385
Herman Layne	OF114	123	440	81	143	86	25	10	10	41	35	20	.325
Paul Florence	C88	97	297	47	88	51	11	0	14	24	22	1	.296
Frank Snyder	C75	83	255	30	67	35	7	2	3	25	33	1	.263
John Anderson	OF49	55	187	25	54	21	8	3	2	15	7	4	.289
Bill Burwell	P37	54	121	13	31	7	4	1	0	4	7	1	.256
Fred Haney	3B50	50	190	34	63	16	7	3	2	23	20	7	.332
Kopf	SS20,2B14	46	135	13	26	11	2	3	0	11	9	1	.193
Koupal	P40	43	92	10	27	9	1	2	0	0	7	2	.293
S. Swetonic	P33	40	44	9	9	4	0	1	0	7	4	1	.205
Gorham Leverett	P38	38	103	14	25	12	4	0	2	6	27	0	.243
Schemanske	P36	37	37	4	4	1	0	0	0	2	9	0	.108
Ferd Schupp	P31	32	70	10	11	4	2	1	0	13	24	0	.157
Carl Boone	P29	32	55	10	16	13	2	0	2	5	6	1	.291
Fred Brickell	OF27	28	93	15	26	14	1	1	4	12	9	3	.279
Wyatt	OF19	25	70	11	23	16	3	3	1	5	5	2	.329
Rabbit Warstler	SS18	23	67	6	14	6	3	0	1	5	5	0	.209
Walsh		16	38	6	11	6	1	0	1	4	4	0	.289
Ray Carl	3B	5	10	2	2		0	0	0			0	.200
James Houston	1B	2	6	1	1		0	0	0			0	.167
Hal Meyers	P2	2	6	0	1		0	0	0			0	.167
Elmer Ambrose	P2	2	0	0	0		0	0	0			0	----
Wally Hurt	P1	1	3	0	0		0	0	0			0	.000
Wilson	1B1	1	1	0	0		0	0	0			0	.000
Paul Gants	P1	1	1	0	0		0	0	0			0	.000
Lloyd Christenbury	PR	1	0	0	0		0	0	0			0	----

PITCHERS	W	L	PCT	G	GS	CG	SH	IP	H	BB	SO	ERA
Gorham Leverett	15	12	.556	38				278	268	92	118	3.98
Bill Burwell	14	20	.412	37				254	296	50	56	5.10
Koupal	13	14	.481	40				232	276	92	71	4.58
Ferd Schupp	8	17	.320	31				215	208	99	114	3.93
Schemanske	5	7	.417	36				101	136	49	29	6.60

INDIANAPOLIS (cont.)
Indians

PITCHERS	W	L	PCT	G	GS	CG	SH	IP	H	BB	SO	ERA
Carl Boone	5	10	.333	29				140	178	58	50	5.21
S. Swetonic	3	8	.273	33				140	167	52	38	4.69
Hurt	0	1	.000	1				9	11	5	5	
Gants	0	1	.000	1				3	9	0	1	
Hall Meyers	0	2	.000	2				14	13	5	1	
Elmer Ambrose	0	0	----	2				2	3	0	1	5.42

LOUISVILLE   7th   65-103   .387   -36   Bill Meyer
Colonels

BATTERS	POS-GAMES	GP	AB	R	H	BI	2B	3B	HR	BB	SO	SB	BA
Harvey Cotter	1B90	90	304	37	66	31	10	2	1	39	29	6	.217
Ed Sicking	2B		(see multi-team players)										
Maurice Shannon	SS95,3B68	169	657	69	191	89	24	8	1	45	27	15	.291
Howard Shanks	3B44	45	159	18	35	14	4	0	0	11	9	1	.220
Joe Guyon	OF124	129	506	93	181	62	20	9	3	41	36	12	.358
Lewan	OF79,1B28	124	412	51	119	69	16	13	6	25	38	6	.289
Simon Rosenthal	OF69	76	246	36	68	36	12	5	6	35	25	5	.277
Hugh McMullen	C120	131	386	48	104	52	20	5	4	30	52	8	.269
G. Ellis	OF65,1B18	102	296	40	100	49	22	2	5	17	24	3	.338
Dan Rutherford	3B40,SS27,OF24	93	340	46	92	42	18	5	3	25	35	6	.271
Bill Meyer	C68	79	214	21	57	21	7	0	0	17	9	3	.267
Ben Tincup	P38	72	127	14	31	13	6	2	1	11	10	3	.244
John Riffe	OF68	69	271	52	74	22	9	4	2	22	49	8	.273
T. Gaffney	2B44,SS14	65	221	21	57	20	10	2	0	13	17	6	.258
John Brooks	OF56	59	202	28	55	18	8	1	3	15	16	4	.272
Lute Boone	SS38,2B14	55	188	20	51	18	5	2	1	15	8	3	.271
Cross	1B43	48	164	16	48	28	8	2	6	4	42	0	.293
Roy Wilkinson	P43	45	55	6	15	12	6	1	1	5	11	0	.272
Friday	P41	41	34	2	1	1	0	0	0	6	14	0	.029
Joe DeBerry	P36	38	87	11	19	3	3	0	1	1	9	1	.218
Baldomero Acosta	OF35	35	119	26	34	11	9	0	2	25	6	3	.286
Ernie Koob	P29	29	46	2	2	2	0	0	0	0	12	0	.043
Ed Holley	P26	28	62	3	14	7	4	1	0	2	10	0	.226
Norman Cullop	P28	28	49	3	6	4	0	0	0	1	16	0	.122
Clarence Nachand	OF23	23	80	9	21	16	6	0	1	7	16	1	.263
Malcolm Moss	P17	18	51	2	8	2	2	0	0	1	4	0	.157
Otis Wicker	P15	15	22	3	6	1	0	0	0	2	1	0	.273
Art Funk	3B14	14	48	7	15	8	0	2	0	2	2	0	.313
Joe Dawson	P10	10	21	2	4	1	0	1	0	0	3	0	.190
Joe Olivares	SS	6	22	1	4		0	0	0	1	6	0	.182
Leon Austin	P3	3	7	0	0		0	0	0	0	1	0	.000
Ewarts	SS1	1	1	0	0		0	0	0	0	0	0	.000

PITCHERS	W	L	PCT	G	GS	CG	SH	IP	H	BB	SO	ERA
Ben Tincup	16	15	.516	38				265	289	89	121	4.27
Ernie Koob	9	10	.474	29				158	188	58	48	4.67
Joe DeBerry	8	17	.320	36				231	309	45	54	5.10
Roy Wilkinson	7	13	.350	43				145	164	66	51	3.97
Ed Holley	6	11	.353	26				144	173	63	65	6.00
Joe Dawson	5	3	.625	10				60	60	25	16	4.35
Malcolm Moss	4	9	.308	17				136	147	57	44	4.56
Norm Cullop	4	10	.286	28				142	164	45	21	3.73
Friday	3	12	.200	41				149	190	46	62	5.31
Leon Austin	2	1	.667	3				24	26	12	10	
Otis Wicker	1	2	.333	15				58	81	30	9	4.81

COLUMBUS   8th   60-108   .357   -41   Ivy Wingo
Senators

BATTERS	POS-GAMES	GP	AB	R	H	BI	2B	3B	HR	BB	SO	SB	BA
Fred Schleibner	1B140	140	502	69	129	61	17	8	3	55	42	8	.257
Emmett McCann	2B102	109	425	64	133	69	25	7	1	14	17	11	.313
Fred Nicolai	SS165	165	643	112	203	70	29	7	3	65	40	11	.316
Joe Stripp	3B125	130	496	95	156	99	46	7	7	33	41	16	.315
Harry Leibold	OF126	130	514	95	158	51	26	5	3	72	24	12	.307
James Horn	OF121	126	408	72	116	54	26	10	4	43	44	10	.285
Hal Sullivan	OF110	126	458	69	139	68	14	7	8	31	28	13	.304

COLUMBUS (cont.)
Senators

BATTERS	POS-GAMES	GP	AB	R	H	BI	2B	3B	HR	BB	SO	SB	BA
Richard Ferrell	C103	104	345	42	86	44	14	4	2	34	17	2	.249
Jim Geygan	2B46,3B39,1B19	115	387	51	109	57	28	4	4	27	24	8	.282
Walter Rehg	OF94	112	397	52	136	54	27	3	3	19	21	6	.343
Kenzie Kirkham	OF35	82	168	16	61	34	9	0	2	11	9	1	.363
Joe Bird	C52	58	160	13	36	20	4	1	2	19	8	1	.225
Emory Zumbro	P44	47	97	4	18	7	2	1	0	6	12	0	.186
Roy Meeker	P43	43	112	15	29	6	6	2	0	7	17	0	.259
Walt Christensen	OF421	42	159	30	44	24	9	4	0	25	9	2	.277
Pete Harris	P41	42	81	6	27	6	2	0	0	4	6	0	.333
Biemiller	P35	37	45	5	10	1	0	1	0	1	11	0	.222
J. Morris	P35	36	42	3	5	6	0	0	0	1	4	0	.119
Harry Fishbaugh	P34	34	63	6	12	0	0	0	0	2	8	0	.190
Ivy Wingo	C19	24	66	4	17	4	1	0	0	6	5	1	.258
George Lyons	P22	22	61	2	8	1	0	0	1	0	9	0	.131
Ray Wolf	1B17	17	63	4	15	11	5	2	0	3	10	0	.238
Sidney Dyer	P9	10	10	0	1	1	0	0	0	0	3	0	.100
Sam Withem	P9	9	9	0	2		0	0	0			0	.222
John Doljack		8	15	4	3		1	1	1			0	.200
Julius Solters	C	7	20	1	5		0	0	0			0	.250
Hack Ennis	C	5	5	1	1		0	0	0			0	.200
George Picard	P5	5	5	1	1		0	0	0			0	.200
Ed Mancuso	SS	3	8	0	2		0	0	0			0	.250
Fred Hasselman	PR	2	0	1	0		0	0	0			0	----

PITCHERS		W	L	PCT	G	GS	CG	SH	IP	H	BB	SO	ERA
Roy Meeker		15	23	.395	43				323	394	109	99	4.43
Emory Zumbro		13	17	.433	44				267	326	61	28	4.72
Harry Fishbaugh		8	9	.471	34				171	224	25	29	4.28
Pete Harris		8	11	.421	41				215	326	40	40	5.19
J. Morris		6	11	.353	35				139	173	68	31	5.96
George Lyons		6	14	.300	22				167	200	60	40	4.53
Biemiller		3	16	.158	35				140	228	71	32	6.94
Sidney Dyer		2	6	.250	9				30	35	14	17	
George Picard		0	1	.000	5				13	25	5	3	
Sam Withem		0	0	----	9				27	39	10	9	

MULTI-TEAM PLAYERS

BATTERS	POS-GAMES	TEAMS	GP	AB	R	H	BI	2B	3B	HR	BB	SO	SB	BA
M. Connolly	SS84,3B26,2B17	TOL-IND	132	474	67	130	48	28	7	2	55	30	18	.274
Ed. Sicking	2B108,SS10	IND-LOU	118	459	81	139	41	25	5	1	50	23	12	.302
John Rawlings	2B73	COL-MIN	81	279	51	81	21	11	3	1	23	24	5	.290
Byron Speece	P41	IND-TOL	41	56	3	7	2	1	0	0	2	12	1	.125
Enger	OF34	SP-IND	38	116	14	36	11	2	2	0	8	8	1	.310
Wisner	P35	IND-TOL	35	60	3	12	4	0	0	0	1	4	0	.200
Bernard Tesmer	C28	SP-IND	30	83	12	14	12	3	0	1	5	18	0	.169

PITCHERS		TEAMS	W	L	PCT	G	GS	CG	SH	IP	H	BB	SO	ERA
Byron Speece		IND-TOL	12	10	.545	41				174	185	60	59	4.14
Wisner		IND-TOL	9	11	.450	35				168	182	51	45	3.48

TEAM BATTING

TEAMS	GP	AB	R	H	BI	2B	3B	HR	BB	SO	SB	BA
TOLEDO	171	6028	986	1882		340	89	63	435	449	140	.312
KANSAS CITY	170	5757	1000	1787		298	127	52	604	475	139	.310
MILWAUKEE	171	6035	1079	1890		351	124	101	542	597	105	.313
ST.PAUL	171	5914	875	1718		300	88	78	469	504	141	.290
MINNEAPOLIS	169	5881	954	1769		293	67	154	552	505	121	.301
INDIANAPOLIS	171	5835	853	1692		236	85	74	510	468	139	.290
LOUISVILLE	169	5813	767	1608		249	72	48	475	556	106	.277
COLUMBUS	168	5844	857	1685		293	75	44	505	438	104	.288
	680	47107	7371	14031		2360	727	614	4092	3992	995	.298

1928
Bevo LeBourveau

One of the American Association's best batters ever had a short career in the league, playing in only five full seasons and parts of four others. During this short space of time, this hitter won two batting titles, narrowly missing a third. When he retired, he owned the record for the highest career batting average in Association history. His name was DeWitt Wiley LeBourveau, also known as Bevo.

Bevo LeBourveau's baseball career started on the West Coast in 1918 for the Seattle club of the Pacific Coast International League. After one season in Peoria, in the Three I league, LeBourveau joined the National League Philadelphia Phillies late in the 1919 season. Here he stayed for four years before playing a two-year stint in the Southern League for Little Rock and Nashville. Bevo then first joined the American Association during the 1924 season, landing with the Kansas City Blues.

Bevo LeBourveau's first three full years in the Association saw him hit the ball at a terrific clip. In 1925, he batted .361, in 1926 (now with Toledo) he won his first batting title with a mark of .377, and in 1927 he batted .346.

Le Bourveau started the 1928 season in Portland of the Pacific Coast League. After 100 games, he jumped ship and returned to the Association, this time with the Milwaukee Brewers. In the partial season left him, he hit his highest average yet, flirting with the .400 barrier before settling for .399. Unfortunately, he did not have enough plate appearances to qualify for the batting title.

In 1928, Indianapolis broke an 11-year pennant drought, landing in first. Minneapolis finished a close second, while Milwaukee, St. Paul, and Kansas City rounded out the first division. The defending champion Toledo Mud Hens tumbled to sixth, with Columbus and Louisville bringing up the rear. Batting honors fell to Bobby Veach of Toledo (.382), and the home run title was won by Spence Harris of Minneapolis, who poked 32. Louisville's Dud Branom knocked in the most runs, finishing with a total of 128. Milwaukee pitchers Ernie Wingard won the most games (24), and Claude Jonnard finished with the most strikeouts (150) while Fred Heimach of St. Paul took the earned run average crown (2.76).

Bevo LeBourveau went on to play five more years in the American Association, picking up another batting title for Toledo along the way. Though his stay in the league was relatively short, and his stints with his five different Association teams even shorter, Bevo LeBourveau is remembered as one of the top hitters in league annals. When his career was at an end, he owned a .360 career batting average in the American Association, a record that has never been bested.

INDIANAPOLIS 1st 99-68 .593 Bruno Betzel
Indians

BATTERS	POS-GAMES	GP	AB	R	H	BI	2B	3B	HR	BB	SO	SB	BA
Walter Holke	1B113,P1	116	397	51	116	62	20	9	4	28	27	8	.292
M. Connolly	2B138	147	525	65	153	62	29	8	1	35	20	7	.291
Rabbit Warstler	SS167	167	630	99	178	88	20	15	7	53	49	7	.283
Fred Haney	3B160	162	623	115	208	78	38	16	3	44	25	43	.334
Wid Matthews	OF150	151	585	103	189	58	28	16	4	46	20	14	.323
Herman Layne	OF113	115	412	68	143	65	25	7	7	23	47	16	.347
Adam Comorosky	OF89	89	333	49	119	62	14	12	8	26	20	12	.357
Ray Spencer	C138	140	467	68	138	59	19	7	4	37	21	4	.296
Albert Russell	OF88,1B11	109	328	60	102	55	21	3	17	34	27	2	.311
Emil Yde	P39	64	143	24	53		9	2	0			1	.371
Paul Florence	C33	48	105	9	24		3	2	3			0	.229
S. Swetonic	P40	47	82	8	16		3	0	0			1	.195
Maurice Burrus	1B42	43	150	23	46		8	1	0			2	.307
Bruno Betzel	2B37	39	116	8	28		3	1	0			2	.241
Ferd Schupp	P37	37	83	5	11		2	0	0			0	.132
Gorham Leverett	P34	34	79	7	16		2	1	0			0	.202
Bill Burwell	P30	32	83	11	26		4	0	0			0	.313
Carl Boone	P32	32	65	4	8		2	0	1			0	.123
Byron Speece	P28	28	24	3	7		1	0	2			0	.292
Ralph Miller	1B12	27	72	6	17		1	0	0			2	.238
John Anderson	OF23	25	82	9	23		3	1	3			2	.280
Vern Blenkiron	OF21	21	87	20	30		5	1	2			9	.345
Walt Mueller	OF15	19	41	7	9		1	0	0			1	.219
Len Koenecke	OF17	17	71	17	28		6	2	4			0	.397
John Riddle	C10	11	34	4	11		2	0	0			0	.324
Erv Brame	P6	9	22	3	6	4	1	0	0	1	2	0	.273
Worth	OF	7	19	2	3		1	1	0			0	.176
Ed Onslow	1B	4	3	0	0		0	0	0			0	.000
Clyde Barnhart	PH	2	2	0	0		0	0	0			0	.000
Herman Meyers	P2	2	1	0	0		0	0	0			0	.000
Walter Wolf	P1	1	0	0	0		0	0	0			0	----

PITCHERS		W	L	PCT	G	GS	CG	SH	IP	H	BB	SO	ERA
S. Swetonic		20	8	.714	40				234	224	55	87	3.00
Emil Yde		19	12	.613	39				280	295	88	115	3.54
Gorham Leverett		19	12	.613	34				232	254	54	83	3.65
Bill Burwell		13	10	.565	30				219	230	50	47	3.17
Ferd Schupp		12	14	.462	37				221	241	105	128	4.16
Carl Boone		11	6	.647	32				167	164	56	54	3.07
Erv Brame		4	1	.800	6				51	54	14	17	2.30
Byron Speece		1	4	.200	28				83	109	26	37	5.20
Hal Meyers		0	1	.000	2				2	8	3	1	36.00
Walter Wolf		0	0	----	1				2	1	1	1	
Walter Holke		0	0	----	1				2	3	1	1	

MINNEAPOLIS 2nd 97-71 .577 -2.5 Mike Kelley
Millers

BATTERS	POS-GAMES	GP	AB	R	H	BI	2B	3B	HR	BB	SO	SB	BA
Harvey Cotter	1B	(see multi-team players)											
Minter Hayes	2B57	57	235	42	78	32	17	2	5	17	20	5	.332
Grant Gillis	SS98,2B21	120	456	69	138	41	18	8	1	30	35	14	.303
Elmer Yoter	3B117,SS26	143	566	112	182	45	32	13	2	60	20	13	.322
Spence Harris	OF169	169	669	133	219	127	41	4	32	87	56	25	.327
Earl Smith	OF158	163	604	81	169	103	31	4	16	49	42	10	.280
Pat Duncan	OF54	60	204	32	70	27	11	0	2	17	10	3	.343
Hugh McMullen	C74	76	230	26	72		9	1	1			2	.313
Ernie Orsatti	1B67,OF52	123	449	96	171	84	32	15	15	39	54	10	.381
Sam Bohne	3B51	101	221	36	65		19	0	2			13	.294
Zack Wheat	OF49	82	194	17	60	30	7	1	5	14	12	1	.309
Frank Emmer	SS30	64	153	14	45		11	1	0			1	.294
John Brillheart	P58	63	72	6	16		3	0	3			0	.222
Cliff Brady	2B52	61	193	33	52		9	0	0			4	.269
F. Warwick	C37	49	123	13	28		1	2	1			1	.228
Gus Mancuso	C45	48	129	10	38		7	0	1			0	.295
William Black	2B38	47	131	19	37		9	1	1			4	.282
Ad Liska	P46	46	71	9	12		0	0	0			0	.168
John Benton	P41	42	89	10	17		1	0	1			0	.191
Ed Kenna	C38	41	132	25	39		5	0	4			4	.296
Guy Williams	P39	39	37	3	6		0	1	0			0	.162

MINNEAPOLIS (cont.)
Millers

BATTERS	POS-GAMES	GP	AB	R	H	BI	2B	3B	HR	BB	SO	SB	BA
Clay Van Alstyne	P25	29	48	4	10		3	0	0			0	.208
Charles Miller	OF28	28	103	19	32		10	5	4			0	.311
Bernard DeViveiros	SS27	27	82	16	25		8	1	3			2	.305
W. Hubbell	P27	27	21	3	3		0	0	1			0	.143
Hod Lisenbee	P26	26	37	4	5		1	0	0			0	.135
Carl East		15	32	5	13		2	2	1			1	.406
Joe Pate	P14	14	0	0	0		0	0	0			0	----
Leo Moon	P12	12	15	2	5		0	0	1			0	.333
Ezzell	3B	9	11	5	3	2	0	0	1	2	0	1	.273
Leo Skidmore	P9	9	9	1	4	1	0	0	0	0	1	0	.444
James Oglesby	1B	5	2	0	0	1	0	0	0	0	0	0	.000
Charles Robertson	P4	4	7	0	0	0	0	0	0	2	1	0	.000
Herb Brett	P4	4	3	0	0	0	0	0	0	0	2	0	.000
Ernie Krueger	C	3	3	0	0	0	0	0	0	0	1	0	.000
Adolph Stemig	P1	1	0	0	0	0	0	0	0	0	0	0	----

PITCHERS	W	L	PCT	G	GS	CG	SH	IP	H	BB	SO	ERA
Ad Liska	20	4	.833	46				225	246	61	82	3.68
John Brillheart	15	9	.625	58				221	248	84	126	4.11
John Benton	15	13	.536	41				250	274	75	76	3.46
Hod Lisenbee	8	6	.571	26				122	149	27	46	4.64
Clay Van Alstyne	7	7	.500	25				119	126	52	41	4.69
Guy Williams	6	7	.462	39				133	126	65	81	3.38
W. Hubbell	5	5	.500	27				85	118	24	14	5.40
Joe Pate	2	0	1.000	14				18	15	1	10	
Leo Skidmore	2	1	.667	9				30	28	18	10	4.20
Charles Robertson	2	1	.67	4				28	27	5	9	
Leo Moon	2	2	.500	12				40	60	10	9	6.30
Adolph Stemig	0	1	.000	1				1	4	1	0	54.00
Herb Brett	0	0	----	4				13	15	5	7	6.39

MILWAUKEE   3rd   90-78   .536   -9.5   Jack Lelivelt
Brewers

BATTERS	POS-GAMES	GP	AB	R	H	BI	2B	3B	HR	BB	SO	SB	BA
Ivy Griffin	1B109	115	428	72	139	55	22	7	6	43	24	13	.325
Spence Adams	2B102,SS29	133	453	53	123	44	19	3	4	39	28	5	.272
Otis Miller	SS107,2B19,OF17	149	583	93	183	65	35	3	5	31	22	11	.314
Harry Strohm	3B162	164	625	91	202	101	40	12	4	32	35	9	.323
Frank Luce	OF123	127	445	80	150	81	21	6	17	32	55	15	.337
Ed Pick	OF113,SS36,1B10	165	593	123	175	112	34	14	14	73	71	14	.295
Herschel Bennett	OF107	111	452	55	125	45	19	9	4	12	38	4	.277
Bob McMenemy	C124	136	411	55	140	58	26	5	12	68	37	4	.341
Bunny Brief	OF64,1B15	90	259	56	80	59	12	3	18	48	41	2	.309
Ernie Wingard	P41	80	157	23	52		8	3	4			0	.331
Russ Young	C50	70	183	20	50		8	1	3			1	.273
Bevo LeBourveau	OF64	64	266	55	106	36	12	4	7	16	22	7	.399
William Batch	2B48	53	195	35	57		5	5	1			7	.292
Charles Bates	OF38	44	148	23	43		7	3	3			2	.291
Win Ballou	P42	42	84	5	9		1	0	0			0	.107
Roy Sanders	P42	42	44	2	6		1	0	0			0	.136
Claude Jonnard	P41	41	107	5	12		2	1	0			0	.112
Joe Eddleman	P39	39	70	6	11		0	0	0			0	.157
Guy Sturdy	1B34	36	125	16	37		8	2	0			8	.296
Charles Willis	P32	33	43	1	7		2	0	0			0	.163
Dennis Gearin	P28	28	28	2	5		0	0	0			0	.179
Fred Baldy		21	23	1	4		1	1	0			0	.174
Al Reitz	P10	16	2	4	0		0	0	0			0	.000
Al Fons	P14	15	17	0	4		0	0	0			0	.235
Alvin Krueger	P11	12	9	0	0		0	0	0			0	.000
Ollie O'Mara		11	37	6	10		0	2	1			2	.270
Durham	C	4	9	0	1		0	0	0			0	.111
Ross	OF	2	2	1	1		1	0	0			0	.500

PITCHERS	W	L	PCT	G	GS	CG	SH	IP	H	BB	SO	ERA
Ernie Wingard	24	10	.706	41				292	309	91	63	3.27
Claude Jonnard	20	11	.645	41				299	301	85	150	3.29
Win Ballou	14	14	.500	42				244	247	103	116	4.02
Joe Eddleman	11	14	.440	39				191	236	45	46	4.85

MILWAUKEE (cont.)
Brewers

PITCHERS	W	L	PCT	G	GS	CG	SH	IP	H	BB	SO	ERA
Dennis Gearin	7	7	.500	28				91	124	39	28	6.13
Roy Sanders	7	12	.368	42				152	180	62	52	4.56
Charles Willis	4	5	.444	32				124	135	47	25	4.57
Al Fons	2	4	.333	14				53	62	23	22	5.27
Alvin Krueger	1	1	.500	11				29	35	16	7	
Al Reitz	0	0	----	10				16	16	8	4	
R. McIntire	0	0	----	3				9	5	1	2	

ST. PAUL   4th (T)   88-80   .524   -11.5   Nick Allen
Saints

BATTERS	POS-GAMES	GP	AB	R	H	BI	2B	3B	HR	BB	SO	SB	BA
Oscar Roettger	1B121,P1	134	483	59	145	86	25	7	7	29	28	13	.304
Ray Morehart	2B154	157	652	123	203	57	25	11	3	56	31	42	.311
Paul Wanninger	SS155	155	597	66	147	43	18	1	1	81	40	6	.246
Deeby Foss	3B120,SS10	147	513	78	162	75	27	8	6	48	42	16	.316
Bruno Haas	OF135,1B13	151	564	76	185	76	34	5	10	26	26	18	.328
Liz Funk	OF133	139	507	77	154	71	20	9	5	26	28	13	.304
Russ Scarritt	OF110	129	421	69	149	61	29	4	2	35	27	6	.354
Alex Gaston	C133	136	400	51	110	62	24	2	10	64	46	2	.275
Harold Anderson	1B44,OF44,3B28,P1	129	424	62	127	53	21	2	2	23	31	18	.300
George Davis	OF108	126	400	64	124	81	20	5	4	37	28	10	.310
Bernard Tesmer	C63	72	160	16	36		4	0	1			0	.225
Walter Betts	P35	49	106	11	26		3	2	0			0	.245
Lou Polli	P40	43	76	8	12		2	1	0			0	.158
Jack Hopkins	P37	37	72	2	3		0	0	0			0	.042
Fred Heimach	P29	33	87	12	18		4	0	2			0	.207
Paul Zahniser	P30	33	73	7	13		1	2	0			0	.179
Robert Murray	SS12,2B12	33	72	17	18		4	1	0			1	.250
George Kirsch	P29	29	25	0	3		0	0	0			0	.120
Julian Wera	3B27	27	104	19	35		7	3	3			1	.337
H. McQuaid	P24	24	32	1	4		0	0	0			0	.125
Al Shealy	P11	15	28	6	6		0	1	1			0	.214
Joe Giard	P15	15	23	2	3		0	0	0			0	.130
Archie Campbell	P13	14	13	0	0		0	0	0			0	.000
Robert Fenner	C	4	4	0	1		0	0	0			0	.250
Mangan	1B	1	0	0	0		0	0	0			0	----
Roy Chesterfield	P1	1	0	0	0		0	0	0			0	----

PITCHERS	W	L	PCT	G	GS	CG	SH	IP	H	BB	SO	ERA
Fred Heimach	18	10	.643	29				228	223	36	63	**2.76**
Walter Betts	16	12	.571	35				253	283	49	65	3.81
Paul Zahniser	13	10	.565	30				212	258	60	49	3.56
Lou Polli	13	15	.464	40				232	263	67	70	3.53
Jack Hopkins	9	11	.450	37				205	208	78	106	2.94
Al Shealy	5	5	.500	11				75	82	24	31	3.00
George Kirsch	4	5	.444	29				78	89	43	26	5.43
H. McQuaid	4	6	.400	24				100	124	27	24	4.86
Archie Campbell	3	2	.600	13				47	51	20	23	4.02
Joe Giard	3	3	.500	15				62	71	48	23	6.25
Oscar Roettger	0	1	.000	1				3	11			
Roy Chesterfield	0	0	----	1				1	3	1	0	
Bruno Haas	0	0	----	1								
Harold Anderson	0	0	----	1								

KANSAS CITY   4th (T)   88-80   .524   -11.5   Dutch Zwilling
Blues

BATTERS	POS-GAMES	GP	AB	R	H	BI	2B	3B	HR	BB	SO	SB	BA
Joe Kuhel	1B120	121	511	85	167	57	32	11	2	21	40	11	.327
Bill Wambsganss	2B162	163	637	88	190	62	18	8	0	46	34	15	.298
Charles Chatham	SS82	113	340	42	99	39	18	6	0	24	24	8	.291
Ralph Michaels	3B111,1B23	136	453	69	136	56	15	7	0	37	20	8	.300
Denver Grigsby	OF152	154	534	77	169	91	31	8	6	59	32	10	.316
Fred Nicholson	OF150	152	577	72	158	81	23	12	6	40	52	9	.274
James Moore	OF104	124	381	53	115	54	22	3	3	42	16	6	.302
John Peters	C130	133	431	52	136	64	31	7	1	25	21	2	.316

KANSAS CITY (cont.)
Blues

BATTERS	POS-GAMES	GP	AB	R	H	BI	2B	3B	HR	BB	SO	SB	BA
Emory Rigney	SS79,3B11	102	296	50	74	45	9	5	0	54	21	4	.250
James Zinn	P45	77	151	19	41		6	4	0			1	.272
Joe Cronin	3B59,SS14	74	241	34	59	32	10	6	2	31	28	1	.245
Frank McGowan	OF62,1B10	73	244	31	58	29	11	1	2	27	14	2	.236
Elwood Wirts	C67	71	180	24	44		4	0	1			1	.244
W. Warmoth	P38	53	79	14	11		3	0	0			0	.139
Frank Wilson	OF51	52	181	21	64		13	2	0			1	.354
Tom Sheehan	P43	46	98	16	28		4	1	0			0	.286
George Murray	P40	40	66	8	16		5	2	0			0	.242
Lynn Nelson	P35	38	46	7	9		1	2	0			0	.196
Frank Davis	P31	31	46	3	7		0	0	0			0	.152
John Morrison	P30	30	26	0	3		0	0	0			0	.115
Heinie Meinie	P15	24	50	8	15		2	0	1			0	.300
Matt Donohue	OF19	19	69	6	17		3	1	0			0	.247
Ed Schaack	P12	13	13	2	6		0	0	0			0	.462
Max Thomas	P5	6	2	0	1		0	0	0			0	.500
Mullen	3B	5	13	3	2		0	0	0			1	.154
Lou Fette	P2	2	4	2	4	1	1	1	0			0	1.000
Fitzberger	PH	2	2	0	0		0	0	0			0	.000
William Swift	P1	1	4	1	2		0	0	0			0	.500
Richard Landrum	P1	1	4	0	0		0	0	0			0	.000

PITCHERS		W	L	PCT	G	GS	CG	SH	IP	H	BB	SO	ERA
James Zinn		23	13	.639	45				323	334	84	90	3.58
Tom Sheehan		16	16	.500	43				240	279	73	66	4.09
George Murray		11	7	.611	40				200	224	63	59	3.96
W. Warmoth		10	16	.385	38				218	222	76	82	3.55
Frank Davis		8	6	.571	31				141	158	74	55	5.17
Heinie Meinie		7	4	.636	15				111	106	34	37	3.58
Lynn Nelson		7	8	.467	35				128	137	60	35	3.87
Ed Schaack		2	2	.500	12				31	39	14	7	4.11
Lou Fette		1	0	1.000	2				5	7	3	0	7.73
Richard Landrum		1	0	1.000	1				9	7	0	0	
William Swift		1	0	1.000	1				9	12	4	1	
Max Thomas		0	2	.000	5				8	9	8	3	

TOLEDO   6th   79-88   .473   -20   Casey Stengel
Mud Hens

BATTERS	POS-GAMES	GP	AB	R	H	BI	2B	3B	HR	BB	SO	SB	BA
Cliff Crawford	1B74,3B39	113	429	58	149	70	27	10	2	30	15	9	.347
John Rawlings	2B		(see multi-team players)										
Glen Messner	SS50	51	147	14	32		5	3	0			1	.218
William Marriott	3B45,SS29	77	315	50	84		12	5	3			7	.267
Bobby Veach	OF149	151	566	93	216	102	32	6	7	58	25	19	.382
Horace Koehler	OF99,SS32,3B22	154	588	83	167	57	23	10	1	34	17	10	.284
Clarence Mueller	OF89	99	339	60	113	60	14	8	4	49	34	3	.333
George O'Neil	C128	130	392	42	104	39	13	4	0	33	28	5	.265
Sanford Hamby	C58	66	153	16	39		6	1	0			1	.255
Otis Carter	OF43	60	164	18	33		7	2	1			4	.201
Chick Fullis	OF56	56	225	47	62		10	1	5			10	.275
John Scott	P31	51	78	9	21		5	0	1			0	.269
T. Gaffney	3B20	43	111	16	28		2	4	1			0	.252
Walt Huntzinger	P42	43	59	6	13		0	0	0			0	.220
Ed Moore	OF21,2B19	40	156	28	56		7	5	0			9	.359
Wilfred Ryan	P38	39	69	6	9		0	0	0			0	.130
James Sweeney	3B34	36	104	6	25		3	1	0			4	.240
Emilo Palmero	P28	35	51	9	14		2	0	0			0	.274
Baxter Jordan	3B19	29	98	10	37		4	2	1			5	.378
Jess Barnes	P29	29	76	6	15		0	1	0			0	.198
Tim McNamara	P28	28	28	3	2		0	0	0			0	.072
Casey Stengel		26	32	5	14		5	0	0			0	.438
Ed Pfeffer	P25	25	56	4	9		1	0	0			0	.161
Al DeVormer	C11	25	46	6	16		5	1	0			0	.348
Aaron Ward	2B23	24	79	8	18		4	1	3			1	.228
Ernie Maun	P19	24	23	2	6		0	0	1			0	.261
Garland Buckeye	P12	21	41	3	14		2	0	0			0	.341
George Milstead	P18	19	9	0	2		0	0	0			0	.222
John Cortazzo	SS16	16	50	4	12		2	0	0			1	.240
Rufus Smith	P14	16	21	2	2		1	0	0			0	.095
Dewey Stover	OF10	13	35	4	9		0	1	0			1	.257
Ed Taylor	SS	8	24	4	5		1	0	1	2		1	.208

TOLEDO (cont.)
Mud Hens

BATTERS	POS-GAMES	GP	AB	R	H	BI	2B	3B	HR	BB	SO	SB	BA
Jack Smith	1B	7	18	2	5		1	0	0			0	.278
William Walker	P7	7	17	2	3		0	0	0			0	.176
John Mundy	OF	7	10	2	4		0	0	0			0	.400
Lawrence Boerner	P4	4	4	0	0		0	0	0			0	.000
William Rabb	P2	2	3	0	0		0	0	0			0	.000
LeRoy Parmelee	PH	2	2	0	0		0	0	0			0	.000
F. Scott	SS	2	0	0	0		0	0	0			0	----
David Klinger	P1	1	3	0	0		0	0	0			0	.000
Guy Jones	P1	1	2	0	0		0	0	0			0	.000
Greg Mulleavy	SS1	1	1	0	0		0	0	0			0	.000

PITCHERS		W	L	PCT	G	GS	CG	SH	IP	H	BB	SO	ERA
John Scott		13	9	.591	31				180	217	44	78	4.35
Walt Huntzinger		12	12	.500	42				184	212	53	48	4.36
Wilfred Ryan		11	5	.688	38				171	184	59	74	3.05
Jesse Barnes		11	12	.478	29				220	258	45	50	3.81
Jeff Pfeffer		8	10	.444	25				170	186	39	59	3.18
Emilo Palmero		7	12	.368	28				153	170	60	43	4.47
Garland Buckeye		6	5	.545	12				88	100	20	24	3.78
Ernie Maun		4	2	.667	19				49	64	20	9	4.04
Rufus Smith		3	5	.375	14				43	53	13	15	
William Walker		2	5	.286	7				52	51	23	35	3.81
Tim McNamara		2	6	.250	28				101	124	36	18	5.26
William Rabb		0	1	.000	2				9	10	5	1	
David Klinger		0	1	.000	1				9	7	2	2	
George Milstead		0	2	.000	18				37	57	13	15	
Lawrence Boerner		0	0	----	4				12	14	10	1	
Guy Jones		0	0	----	1				3	0	1	0	

COLUMBUS   7th   68-100   .405   -31.5   Harry Leibold
Senators

BATTERS	POS-GAMES	GP	AB	R	H	BI	2B	3B	HR	BB	SO	SB	BA
Jim Geygan	1B74,2B28,3B25	145	502	71	133	73	25	6	4	27	41	9	.265
Emmett McCann	2B121,1B11	141	547	81	164	73	34	5	1	20	19	18	.300
Fred Nicolai	SS134,2B12	154	536	79	150	54	12	8	2	47	35	3	.280
Lute Boone	3B85	87	302	39	78	30	12	3	1	20	13	7	.258
Walt Christensen	OF141	143	550	91	161	54	19	3	0	54	14	18	.293
James Horn	OF102,1B22	133	426	62	128	41	29	5	2	37	25	9	.300
Pat McNulty	OF83	89	325	48	107	51	14	5	1	19	21	10	.329
Richard Ferrell	C100	126	339	51	113	65	31	5	2	44	4	4	.333
Harry Leibold	OF79	98	279	34	91		12	1	0			2	.326
Charles High	OF78	80	268	47	92	38	16	5	9	47	24	7	.343
Joe Stripp	3B62	64	227	49	95	51	19	7	7	42	14	8	.419
Pete Harris	P37	61	63	10	22		4	3	0			0	.349
John Tobin	1B27	53	137	15	39		4	2	0			3	.285
Walter Rehg	OF46	48	182	28	63		9	1	1			2	.346
Lawrence Winters	P36	44	78	13	28		4	1	1			1	.359
Richard Wyckoff	P38	40	72	6	21		3	0	1			0	.292
Harry Schwab	1B35	36	127	14	37		12	2	0			1	.291
Roy Meeker	P33	34	73	8	14		1	0	1			0	.191
Ken Ash	P26	34	61	12	11		2	0	1			0	.180
Elmer Myers	P32	33	72	5	23		2	0	0			0	.319
Emory Zumbro	P28	30	30	5	7		1	0	0			0	.233
George Lyons	P22	22	25	2	5		1	0	1			0	.200
Kenzie Kirkham		20	20	2	6		1	1	0			0	.300
Ray Wolf	1B15	16	54	5	15		4	1	0			1	.278
Harry Fishbaugh	P16	16	24	0	3		0	0	0			0	.125
Frank Miller	P15	15	17	3	7		2	0	0			0	.412
Tony Cuccinello	2B14	14	53	11	21		5	2	1			0	.396
John Doljack		14	22	0	5		0	0	0			0	.227
Hal Sullivan		12	25	3	5		0	0	1			0	.200
P. Jablonski	P8	8	18	3	4		1	1	0			1	.222
Henry Vick	C	5	18	2	5		1	0	0			0	.278
Harlan Wysong	P3	3	6	1	2		1	0	0			0	.333
Herb Tashijan	SS,3B	3	1	0	1		0	0	0			0	1.000
Lloyd	P1	1	3	0	1		0	0	0			0	.333

PITCHERS		W	L	PCT	G	GS	CG	SH	IP	H	BB	SO	ERA
Ken Ash		12	10	.545	26				172	168	40	47	2.77

COLUMBUS (cont.)
Senators

PITCHERS	W	L	PCT	G	GS	CG	SH	IP	H	BB	SO	ERA
Lawrence Winters	12	11	.522	36				187	257	54	40	5.10
Roy Meeker	11	13	.458	33				215	253	53	57	3.77
Elmer Myers	10	14	.417	32				188	225	43	37	4.46
Emory Zumbro	7	7	.500	28				107	145	21	11	4.55
Richard Wyckoff	7	13	.350	38				216	273	51	51	4.55
Pete Harris	3	12	.200	37				135	198	38	15	5.27
Frank Miller	2	1	.667	15				53	54	11	10	2.72
P. Jablonski	2	2	.500	7				39	50	6	14	5.54
Harry Fishbaugh	2	5	.286	16				72	101	14	14	6.50
Harlan Wysong	0	1	.000	3				17	17	2	2	
George Lyons	0	11	.000	22				82	114	48	27	7.25
Lloyd	0	0	----	2				5	10	1	1	

LOUISVILLE   8th   62-106   .369   -37.5   Bill Meyer
Colonels

BATTERS	POS-GAMES	GP	AB	R	H	BI	2B	3B	HR	BB	SO	SB	BA
Dud Branom	1B170	**170**	659	69	204	**128**	33	11	17	38	21	11	.310
Ed Sicking	2B166	168	658	114	**242**	72	38	4	1	55	25	14	.368
Joe Olivares	SS152	156	537	52	162	45	21	2	0	23	26	21	.302
Art Funk	3B133	146	523	59	125	34	11	11	1	23	31	17	.239
Richard Loftus	OF163	163	655	105	185	47	26	6	1	50	25	15	.282
Clarence Nachand	OF149	152	478	52	108	45	21	5	9	47	**106**	12	.226
Foster Ganzel	OF79	79	276	50	89	43	21	6	1	46	20	5	.322
Enoch Shinault	C			(see multi-team players)									
Maurice Shannon	3B49,OF10	101	242	24	70	31	11	1	1	23	21	0	.289
Dan Rutherford	OF50,SS31	93	244	22	53		7	1	0			1	.217
Ben Tincup	P38	60	100	7	17		4	2	0			0	.170
Malcolm Moss	P46	54	83	6	8		1	0	0			0	.096
Joe DeBerry	P41	52	96	8	21		0	0	0			0	.219
Roy Wilkinson	P37	40	72	4	12		2	1	0			0	.166
Ernie Koob	P39	39	59	2	5		1	0	0			0	.085
Larry Merville	OF29	30	103	9	22		5	1	1			0	.214
Bill Meyer	C30	35	84	4	23		5	2	0			1	.273
Rudy Sommers	P28	35	58	5	16		2	0	0			0	.276
Joe Guyon	OF20	25	79	9	19		3	3	0			1	.241
Norman Cullop	P25	25	35	2	7		1	0	0			0	.200
Larry Creson	P21	25	27	3	5		0	1	0			0	.185
Wayland Dean	P4	19	16	2	4		1	0	0			0	.250
John Kloza	OF15	16	40	4	4		1	0	0			1	.100
Baldomero Acosta	OF12	16	32	5	5		1	0	0			1	.156
John Riffe		11	26	4	8		1	2	0			1	.308
Seimer	C	9	23	1	3		1	0	0			0	.131
Billy Herman	2B	4	15	5	5	4	1	1	0			0	.333
Everett Henegar	P4	4	8	0	3	1	1	0	0		2	0	.375
Leon Austin	P4	4	1	0	0		0	0	0			0	.000
Earle Browne	P1,LF	3	11	0	1		1	0	0			0	.091
Ellis	OF	2	2	0	1	2	0	0	0			0	.500

PITCHERS	W	L	PCT	G	GS	CG	SH	IP	H	BB	SO	ERA
Ben Tincup	14	10	.583	38				208	229	55	87	3.42
Roy Wilkinson	12	16	.429	37				214	224	66	85	3.41
Joe DeBerry	11	19	.367	41				268	**334**	38	58	3.93
Malcolm Moss	10	**22**	.313	46				262	305	**117**	86	4.37
Ernie Koob	7	17	.292	39				187	249	67	54	5.49
Larry Creson	3	6	.333	21				74	93	40	22	5.11
Norman Cullop	2	6	.250	25				110	123	28	24	4.10
Rudy Sommers	2	8	.200	28				126	140	38	27	4.36
Everett Henegar	1	0	1.000	4				22	36	6	1	6.23
Wayland Dean	0	1	.000	4				15	22	8	2	6.60
Browne	0	1	.000	1				9	20	0	0	
Leon Austin	0	0	----	4				8	11	12	7	5.80

MULTI-TEAM PLAYERS

BATTERS	POS-GAMES	TEAMS	GP	AB	R	H	BI	2B	3B	HR	BB	SO	SB	BA
John Rawlings	2B123,SS14	MIN-TOL	141	508	64	149	63	31	6	6	46	36	8	.293

MULTI-TEAM PLAYERS (cont.)

BATTERS	POS-GAMES		GP	AB	R	H	BI	2B	3B	HR	BB	SO	SB	BA
Harvey Cotter	1B134	MIN-KC-MIN	140	457	68	136	65	23	7	10	50	45	9	.298
Roy Grimes	1B93	TOL-KC	114	359	51	119	71	21	8	5	28	39	9	.331
Enoch Shinault	C95	LOU-COL	114	307	36	72	36	11	2	2	45	34	2	.235
Ray Thompson	C88	MIL-LOU	103	302	24	83	41	13	6	2	23	22	0	.275
Joe Bird	C57	COL-LOU	64	166	10	48		4	2	0			1	.289
William Jacobsen	OF53	IND-TOL	55	199	26	68	27	7	3	1	18	16	2	.342
John White	SS44	TOL-COL	46	125	22	38		2	4	0			3	.304
Paul McCullough	P44	TOL-MIN	46	80	12	22		3	0	2			0	.275
Ray Jacobs	SS20,2B15	TOL-MIN	40	141	23	47		5	4	4			2	.333

PITCHERS		TEAMS	W	L	PCT	G	GS	CG	SH	IP	H	BB	SO	ERA
Paul McCullough		TOL-MIN	13	16	.448	44				221	244	91	95	4.32

TEAM BATTING

TEAMS	GP	AB	R	H	BI	2B	3B	HR	BB	SO	SB	BA
INDIANAPOLIS	167	5691	857	1717		274	103	69			132	.302
MINNEAPOLIS	169	5849	927	1765		313	63	120			125	.302
MILWAUKEE	170	5818	885	1733		287	83	98			105	.298
ST. PAUL	169	5838	835	1685		270	64	57			134	.289
KANSAS CITY	170	5785	803	1665		265	90	25			80	.288
TOLEDO	168	5755	775	1682		252	88	42			110	.292
COLUMBUS	169	5861	849	1757		292	76	39			111	.300
LOUISVILLE	170	5738	663	1566		238	68	34			104	.273
	676	46355	6594	13570		2191	635	484			901	.293

1929
Five of Nine

During the history of post-season baseball play, the standard length of each playoff series has usually been set at the best of seven games, with the winner having to win four. But there have been exceptions. For several years following World War I, the major leagues' World Series and the minor leagues' Little World Series were played using a best of nine format, with the winner having to win five.

The World Series went to best of nine in 1919, during the postwar boom. The change was ostensibly for financial reasons as more playing dates meant more paying customers. In 1920, the American Association and International League followed suit with the Little World Series.

During the first five years of the longer format, two Little World Series (1923 and 1924) went the full distance. In 1929, it happened again with probably the best Little World Series of the decade.

The 1929 American Association pennant was won by Kansas City in a spirited race over St. Paul with each team winning over 100 games. The rest of the teams (Minneapolis, Indianapolis, Louisville, Columbus, Milwaukee, and Toledo) finished far behind. Toledo's Art Ruble won the batting title (.376), while Allen Cooke of St. Paul finished with the most home runs (33) and runs batted in (148). Lou Polli of St. Paul won the most games (22), while teammate Archie Campbell had the lowest earned run average (2.79), and John Brillheart of Minneapolis struck out the most batters (134).

Kansas City's opponent in the 1929 Little World Series was the International League champion Rochester team. The series opened on October 2 in Kansas City with a 4–3 win by the hosts. Rochester took the next game, 11–2, before Kansas City won the next pair 1–0, and 6–2. When the series moved to Rochester, the home club quickly evened the series with a pair of wins (8–1, and 4–2). Kansas City then nosed into the lead with a win in game seven (9–1). With a 5–4 lead in the ninth inning, Kansas City looked to close out Rochester, but the home team tied the game in the ninth, and won in the eleventh, 6–5, to knot the series at four games apiece. In the deciding ninth game, Rochester established a four-run lead before a three-run Kansas City rally late in the game tied the score. Kansas City pushed home a run in the top of the eleventh to win the game 6–5, and the series five games to four.

The Little World Series would remain in the best of nine format until 1934, when it reverted to a best of seven contest. But the longer format had led to some thrilling playoff tilts, none better than the classic series of 1929.

KANSAS CITY 1st 111-56 .665 Dutch Zwilling
Blues

BATTERS	POS-GAMES	GP	AB	R	H	BI	2B	3B	HR	BB	SO	SB	BA
Joe Kuhel	1B161	161	649	135	211	83	27	**26**	6	50	58	19	.325
Fred Spurgeon	2B112,SS14	127	492	81	129	46	20	3	3	19	24	13	.262
George Knothe	SS141	142	544	78	137	48	12	5	2	46	46	14	.262
Ralph Michaels	3B91	101	327	40	89	37	10	3	1	36	29	6	.272
Denver Grigsby	OF137	140	499	91	172	94	29	10	4	61	34	11	.345
George Gerken	OF129	135	461	84	129	86	18	12	11	54	58	14	.280
Ollie Tucker	OF124	129	447	88	150	108	31	4	20	49	21	6	.336
John Peters	C126	129	375	44	120	63	20	7	2	51	23	4	.320
Bill Wambsganss	2B67,3B27	103	359	54	106	33	15	5	0	30	22	7	.295
Bob Seeds	OF90	100	322	53	110	57	21	3	4	29	23	10	.342
Fred Nicholson	OF68	98	241	48	83	46	9	7	4	19	21	5	.344
Harry Riconda	3B59,SS20	79	331	67	106	36	24	7	3	25	19	6	.320
Tom Angley	C64	76	208	31	81	43	15	6	6	20	2	1	.389
Marion Thomas	P50	53	84	7	16		2	1	1			0	.190
Lou Fette	P46	47	60	5	13		1	2	0			0	.216
Bob Murray	P41	42	85	13	24		6	1	3			0	.282
Tom Sheehan	P37	39	91	10	31		4	1	0			0	.341
Lynn Nelson	P38	39	69	7	11		5	1	1			0	.159
Clyde Day	P36	36	61	2	11		1	0	0			0	.180
W. Warmoth	P27	33	68	6	12		1	0	0			0	.176
Frank Davis	P21	21	29	2	4		0	0	0			0	.138
Keith Clarke	C	8	10	0	1	1	0	0	0	1	1	0	.100
Roy Grimes	1B	7	13	3	4		1	0	0		5	0	.308
Pember	2B	6	16	4	8	2	1	1	0	1	0	0	.500
Brozovitch	OF	6	10	1	2		1	0	0	2	2	0	.200
John Morrison	P6	6	10	1	2	1	0	0	0		2	0	.200
Frank Snyder	C	5	10	2	4		1	0	0		1	0	.400
John Hendee	1B	3	6	0	1		0	0	0		0	0	.167
Dennis Burns	P3	3	6	0	0		0	0	0		3	0	.000
Harvel	OF	3	5	1	2	2	1	0	0	0	0	0	.400

PITCHERS		W	L	PCT	G	GS	CG	SH	IP	H	BB	SO	ERA
Marion Thomas		18	11	.621	50				231	210	88	82	3.11
Bob Murray		17	8	.680	41				218	258	87	46	4.63
Tom Sheehan		16	11	.593	37				243	257	59	74	3.78
Lynn Nelson		15	6	.714	38				190	184	77	78	2.99
W. Warmoth		14	4	.778	27				176	164	79	61	3.38
Clyde Day		12	5	.706	36				178	162	33	76	2.98
Frank Davis		8	5	.615	21				84	84	35	30	4.07
Lou Fette		7	3	.700	46				154	171	71	43	4.33
John Morrison		3	2	.600	6				29	25	14	9	
Dennis Burns		1	1	.500	3				16	23	5	5	

ST. PAUL 2nd 102-64 .614 -8.5 Bubbles Hargrave
Saints

BATTERS	POS-GAMES	GP	AB	R	H	BI	2B	3B	HR	BB	SO	SB	BA
Oscar Roettger	1B163	164	629	84	205	132	45	3	13	41	34	1	.326
Ray Morehart	2B119	124	449	89	122	40	21	7	0	57	32	10	.272
Bill Rogell	SS90,2B58	162	657	134	221	90	34	18	9	66	68	7	.336
Bill Chapman	3B167	168	660	**162**	222	137	43	17	31	72	76	27	.336
Harold Anderson	OF153	158	600	107	181	73	30	2	7	72	54	16	.302
Allen Cooke	OF152	152	564	153	202	**148**	39	16	**33**	105	120	12	.358
Bruno Haas	OF133	135	510	56	151	60	31	4	3	24	21	6	.296
Bubbles Hargrave	C88	104	317	57	117	85	20	3	9	48	18	5	.369
George Davis	OF77	99	308	48	97	52	13	3	5	25	16	13	.315
Robert Fenner	C70	91	259	34	78	45	15	1	3	18	16	2	.301
Paul Wanninger	SS76	82	297	48	80	33	5	9	1	13	20	4	.269
Walter Betts	P39	52	121	12	27		4	0	1			0	.223
Lou Polli	P41	43	112	22	26		6	0	1			0	.232
Emory Zumbro	P40	43	30	6	6		0	1	0			0	.200
Bryan Harriss	P40	40	84	3	11		1	0	0			0	.131
Al Shealy	P32	40	71	11	24		5	1	2			0	.338
Russ Van Atta	P34	34	35	2	4		2	0	0			0	.114
Archie Campbell	P24	25	68	3	6		0	0	0			0	.088
Meredith Hopkins	SS13	16	45	8	14		3	1	1			0	.311
Jack Hopkins	P14	14	28	2	4		0	0	0			0	.143
Shefflot	C	9	19	2	1	2	0	0	0			0	.053
McCarter	P3	6	6	1	1		0	1	0		1	0	.167
John Connolly	P5	5	4	0	0		0	0	0	1	3	0	.000

ST. PAUL (cont.)
Saints

BATTERS	POS-GAMES	GP	AB	R	H	BI	2B	3B	HR	BB	SO	SB	BA
Mangan	1B1	1	0	0	0		0	0	0			0	----

PITCHERS		W	L	PCT	G	GS	CG	SH	IP	H	BB	SO	ERA
Lou Polli		**22**	9	.710	41				**288**	310	88	85	3.75
Walter Betts		21	13	.618	39				284	322	54	65	3.90
Bryan Harriss		18	10	.643	40				240	256	50	86	3.38
Archie Campbell		15	3	**.833**	24				174	152	53	82	**2.79**
Al Shealy		10	6	.625	32				165	197	68	68	4.64
Emory Zumbro		7	6	.538	40				128	148	37	26	4.01
Jack Hopkins		4	6	.400	14				70	85	30	41	5.66
Russ Van Atta		4	9	.308	34				115	127	46	65	4.93
McCarter		1	0	1.000	3				11	17	8	8	
John Connolly		0	0	----	5				12	20	9	3	

MINNEAPOLIS   3rd   89-78   .533   -22   Mike Kelley
Millers

BATTERS	POS-GAMES	GP	AB	R	H	BI	2B	3B	HR	BB	SO	SB	BA
Leo Cotter	1B157	158	547	105	160	120	22	5	27	84	63	18	.293
John Rawlings	2B121	125	470	80	126	39	28	3	4	40	43	2	.268
Frank Emmer	SS152	162	637	121	202	111	42	14	22	49	78	36	.317
Elmer Yoter	3B153,SS12	167	**687**	148	218	65	50	7	4	86	42	31	.317
Spence Harris	OF154	154	594	139	202	100	42	7	14	92	50	19	.340
Earl Smith	OF145	151	580	111	188	124	27	10	20	42	27	14	.324
Charles High	OF			(see multi-team players)									
Hugh McMullen	C97	100	334	43	96	51	15	4	4	17	31	9	.287
Ed Kenna	C85	95	252	36	60	36	18	2	3	51	26	8	.238
Wes Griffin	OF36,P7	75	154	28	54	42	7	3	6	26	15	0	.351
Stan Keyes	OF58	59	237	43	73	47	12	4	8	18	35	3	.308
Sam Bohne	2B18	57	83	18	20		3	0	1			9	.241
John Brillheart	P54	54	94	10	16		4	0	1			0	.170
Joe Pate	P52	52	50	4	9		1	0	1			0	.180
George Dumont	P49	49	77	7	12		2	0	0			1	.156
Bill Bagwell	OF29	48	119	22	42	36	14	2	7	10	9	1	.353
Ernest Shirley	OF20,1B13	47	133	32	44	35	10	1	7	13	9	2	.330
John Benton	P45	45	104	9	23		3	0	0			0	.221
Ed Delker	2B33	41	136	16	36		7	3	1			3	.265
Jim Middleton	P41	41	70	6	18		4	0	0			0	.257
Charles Rhem	P23	23	45	7	11		0	1	1			0	.244
John Butler	2B14	15	66	9	12		1	1	2			2	.182
Eulas Morgan	P12	12	28	2	4		1	0	1			0	.143
Fred Wingfield	P7	12	6	0	0		0	0	0			1	.000
Pat Duncan	OF,P1	7	14	3	3	2	1	0	0			0	.214
Hack Miller	OF	6	14	0	2	1	1	0	0			0	.143
Lester Ferguson	P6	6	4	1	1		1	0	0			0	.250
Dan Oberholzer	3B	5	11	4	4	2	0	1	1			0	.364
James Oglesby	1B	3	8	0	0		0	0	0			0	.000
Allen Benson	P3	3	4	1	2		0	0	0	1		0	.500

PITCHERS		W	L	PCT	G	GS	CG	SH	IP	H	BB	SO	ERA
John Benton		20	14	.588	45				284	303	78	78	3.69
John Brillheart		20	16	.556	**54**				267	**322**	115	**134**	5.02
George Dumont		13	7	.650	49				208	254	76	102	4.59
Joe Pate		11	5	.688	52				165	191	50	48	4.42
Jim Middleton		10	9	.526	41				197	249	77	38	5.12
Charles Rhem		5	11	.313	23				123	159	47	42	5.85
Eulas Morgan		3	5	.375	12				66	51	41	34	3.95
Fred Wingfield		1	0	1.000	7				14	16	4	1	
Lester Ferguson		1	1	.500	6				17	20	10	6	
Wes Griffin		0	1	.000	7				18	30	13	1	
Allen Benson		0	1	.000	3				16	29	6	11	8.44
Pat Duncan		0	0	----	1				1	0	0	0	0.00

INDIANAPOLIS 4th 78-89 .467 -33 Bruno Betzel
Indians

BATTERS	POS-GAMES	GP	AB	R	H	BI	2B	3B	HR	BB	SO	SB	BA
Pete Monahan	1B169	169	636	107	188	100	37	4	11	50	20	18	.296
M. Connolly	2B163	163	575	64	157	83	32	1	5	58	25	11	.273
Rabbit Warstler	SS152	153	574	86	164	70	35	7	6	56	41	11	.286
Leonard Metz	3B71,SS18,2B10	101	301	28	66	32	9	4	0	23	26	2	.219
Clyde Barnhart	OF146	155	552	91	167	109	31	12	16	64	25	5	.303
Herman Layne	OF146	151	570	107	175	60	41	6	4	45	35	23	.307
Wid Matthews	OF128	130	513	82	147	35	19	5	0	48	25	12	.287
Joe Sprinz	C131	138	463	63	142	68	17	6	4	48	32	7	.307
James Stroner	3B66	72	239	35	65	32	6	2	6	14	29	4	.272
John Riddle	C48	60	170	19	46	29	9	0	1	6	8	6	.271
Aloysius Bejma	OF52	56	171	23	49	26	5	2	1	15	11	3	.287
Bill Burwell	P38	51	116	9	22		3	0	1			0	.190
Byron Speece	P36	44	46	8	13		2	2	1			0	.283
Albert Russell	OF27	41	92	10	24		3	1	5			1	.261
Ken Penner	P24	38	82	7	22		3	0	1			0	.268
Art Teachout	P32	38	73	9	19		0	1	0			1	.260
Ferd Schupp	P33	33	85	4	8		0	0	0			0	.094
Len Koenecke	OF21	32	79	11	25		4	1	0			1	.316
Ruel Love	P25	26	51	4	12		5	0	0			0	.235
Ed Judd	3B22	22	88	6	22		0	0	0			2	.250
Carl Boone	P20	20	16	3	4		1	1	0			0	.250
Charles Gorman	3B13	18	39	7	9		0	0	1			0	.231
Claude Jonnard	P13	13	35	3	8		1	0	0			0	.229
Leo Skidmore	P13	13	7	1	2		0	0	0			0	.286
John Riffe	OF11	11	46	5	10		1	1	0			3	.217
Prentice Hall	P11	11	14	0	2		0	0	0			0	.143
Swanson	3B	9	22	4	5		0	0	0			0	.227
Meadows	P7	7	16	1	5	2	0	1	0			0	.313
Art Daney	P5	5	12	0	1		0	0	0			0	.083
Elmer Ambrose	P2	2	9	2	3		1	0	0			0	.333
Walter Wolf	P2	2	5	2	1		0	0	0			0	.200
Bruno Betzel	PH	2	2	0	0		0	0	0			0	.000
Reynolds	PH	1	1	0	0		0	0	0			0	.000
Osborn	P1	1	1	0	0		0	0	0			0	.000

PITCHERS	W	L	PCT	G	GS	CG	SH	IP	H	BB	SO	ERA
Bill Burwell	15	20	.429	38				271	284	48	68	3.69
Ken Penner	13	7	.650	24				191	170	51	71	3.25
Ferd Schupp	12	14	.462	33				235	233	117	123	3.64
Art Teachout	10	14	.417	32				194	213	68	63	4.46
Byron Speece	9	2	.818	36				109	109	35	44	3.80
Claude Jonnard	6	5	.545	13				108	96	43	58	2.92
Ruel Love	5	10	.333	25				133	168	32	32	5.27
Elmer Ambrose	2	0	1.000	2				18	12	6	1	0.50
Carl Boone	2	3	.400	20				54	69	28	9	5.50
Leo Skidmore	1	1	.500	13				27	39	12	8	7.67
Walter Wolf	1	1	.500	2				16	15	12	10	4.50
Prentice Hall	1	3	.250	11				46	53	9	16	4.70
Meadows	1	5	.167	7				45	67	13	13	5.00
Art Daney	0	4	.000	5				30	39	13	7	7.50
Osborn	0	0	----	1				1	1	0	0	0.00

LOUISVILLE 5th 75-90 .455 -35 Al Sothoron
Colonels

BATTERS	POS-GAMES	GP	AB	R	H	BI	2B	3B	HR	BB	SO	SB	BA
Dud Branom	1B147	151	597	92	198	129	35	8	17	32	17	8	.332
Ed Sicking	2B143	148	593	108	184	62	22	8	2	60	22	16	.310
Joe Olivares	SS149	150	566	65	161	58	22	6	2	26	32	11	.284
Maurice Shannon	3B70,SS11	95	323	47	95	36	15	3	0	18	27	2	.294
Elmer Smith	OF154	156	594	103	169	112	28	10	25	66	58	7	.285
Melbern Simons	OF145	150	630	121	214	71	27	13	7	40	33	13	.340
Foster Ganzel	OF109,3B40	157	568	85	183	80	31	15	2	62	25	7	.322
Ray Thompson	C133	143	464	51	129	56	19	9	5	27	20	3	.278
Richard Loftus	OF70	94	280	45	78	38	15	5	1	20	7	9	.278
Malcolm Moss	P43	44	78	7	14		3	1	0			0	.179
Ben Tincup	P33	50	77	11	25		2	0	1			0	.325
Larry Creson	P38	47	34	8	7		1	0	0			0	.205
Guy Williams	P43	44	78	7	14		3	1	0			0	.179
Joe DeBerry	P40	42	70	12	16		3	0	0			0	.228
Roy Wilkinson	P37	37	47	11	13		2	1	0			0	.277

LOUISVILLE (cont.)
Colonels

BATTERS	POS-GAMES	GP	AB	R	H	BI	2B	3B	HR	BB	SO	SB	BA
Art Funk	3B17,SS11	36	108	16	27		1	3	1			4	.250
Anthony Welzer	P33	34	65	6	7		0	0	0			0	.108
George O'Neil	C10	27	39	2	11		2	0	1			0	.282
Rolla Mapel	P25	25	20	1	1		0	0	0			0	.050
Billy Herman	2B24	24	93	17	30		3	4	1			5	.323
Larry Merville	OF21	21	76	8	24		2	2	0			3	.316
Joe Bird	C16	20	28	6	11		1	1	0			0	.390
Walter Beck	P8	9	7	1	2		0	1	0			0	.286
Earle Browne	P7	7	13	0	2		0	0	0			0	.154
Norman Cullop	P6	6	3	0	0		0	0	0			0	.000
Clarence Nachand	OF	4	4	1	2		0	0	0			0	.500
Carl Thomas	P4	4	1	0	1		0	0	0			0	1.000
Corey	OF	3	6	0	1		0	0	0			0	.167
Earl Ober	P2	2	0	0	0		0	0	0			0	----

PITCHERS		W	L	PCT	G	GS	CG	SH	IP	H	BB	SO	ERA
Guy Williams		16	9	.640	43				218	232	126	89	4.83
Joe DeBerry		13	10	.565	40				208	265	43	42	4.76
Roy Wilkinson		12	7	.632	37				144	177	50	36	4.00
Anthony Welzer		10	13	.435	33				211	246	50	52	4.73
Malcolm Moss		9	18	.333	43				274	320	110	87	4.80
Ben Tincup		7	16	.304	33				172	219	61	70	5.45
Larry Creson		3	5	.375	38				106	127	87	27	5.52
Earle Browne		2	2	.500	5				28	39	10	7	
Rolla Mapel		2	7	.222	25				78	98	27	17	4.84
Walter Beck		1	3	.250	8				18	27	14	14	
Cullop		0	0	----	6				14	15	4	3	
Carl Thomas		0	0	----	4				10	19	7	3	
Nachand		0	0	----	3				4	8	6	0	
Earl Ober		0	0	----	2				4	7	1	3	

COLUMBUS   6th   75-91   .452   -35.5   Harry Leibold
Senators

BATTERS	POS-GAMES	GP	AB	R	H	BI	2B	3B	HR	BB	SO	SB	BA
Emmett McCann	1B119,2B29	150	566	79	156	70	29	7	1	32	21	18	.276
Tony Cuccinello	2B136,3B26	162	635	136	227	111	56	10	20	57	79	2	.358
Grant Gillis	SS88	89	342	45	91	46	12	8	5	21	26	4	.266
Deeby Foss	3B72,1B14	86	327	59	92	37	13	10	4	25	19	21	.281
Marty Callaghan	OF149	152	595	105	212	75	46	6	4	51	22	14	.356
Estel Crabtree	OF142	152	583	112	179	129	28	10	21	36	52	9	.307
Bernie Neis	OF123	129	488	100	153	75	25	4	10	78	45	25	.314
Enoch Shinault	C110	117	320	43	93	52	24	4	5	40	28	2	.291
Lute Boone	3B54,SS36,1B10	107	351	60	112	75	18	5	4	39	17	8	.319
Harry Leibold	OF52	88	201	29	55		7	2	1			1	.274
Mike Devine	C76	78	223	20	47		9	2	0			0	.211
Pete Jablonowski	P41	57	114	13	31		8	6	1			1	.272
Lawrence Winters	P46	52	61	6	15		1	0	1			0	.246
Richard Wyckoff	P30	51	54	7	18		4	1	2			0	.333
Silas Johnson	P44	49	89	8	11		0	0	0			2	.124
Harlan Wysong	P41	44	84	4	14		3	1	0			0	.167
Fred Nicolai	SS38	40	140	29	41		6	0	1			2	.293
Herm Kemner	P28	32	58	9	15		2	1	0			0	.259
Frank Miller	P28	28	39	3	5		2	0	0			0	.128
Elmer Myers	P22	22	37	1	7		0	0	0			0	.189
C. Crossley	3B18	18	65	10	17		1	0	1			0	.262
John White	SS10	14	35	3	6		0	1	0			1	.171
Charles Maxton	P12	13	9	1	1		0	0	0			0	.111
Pete Harris	P9	10	7	0	2		0	0	0			0	.286
Pat McNulty	OF	9	35	10	11	4	2	0	0			2	.315
Pankratz	C	8	4	1	1		1	0	0			0	.250
E. Proffitt	P5	5	3	0	2		0	0	0			0	.600
Ryan	P4	4	4	0	0		0	0	0			0	.000
Harry Fishbaugh	P3	3	6	1	2	1	0	0	0			0	.333
Sears	OF1	1	2	0	0		0	0	0			0	.000
Durant	PH	1	1	0	0		0	0	0			0	.000
Spitaleri	P1	1	0	0	0		0	0	0			0	----

PITCHERS		W	L	PCT	G	GS	CG	SH	IP	H	BB	SO	ERA
Pete Jablonowski		18	12	.600	41				246	290	73	74	4.72

COLUMBUS (cont.)
Senators

PITCHERS	W	L	PCT	G	GS	CG	SH	IP	H	BB	SO	ERA
Silas Johnson	16	13	.552	44				251	267	82	123	4.52
Herm Kemner	11	11	.500	28				160	194	41	64	5.35
Harlan Wysong	9	12	.429	41				214	250	69	108	4.04
Lawrence Winters	7	14	.333	46				164	217	45	40	5.44
Frank Miller	5	9	.357	28				123	147	43	39	4.17
Charles Maxton	3	1	.750	12				36	48	13	5	6.00
Richard Wyckoff	3	4	.429	30				103	155	20	8	5.42
E. Proffitt	1	0	1.000	4				7	8	7	4	5.41
Ryan	1	1	.500	4				13	19	7	5	
Elmer Myers	1	12	.077	22				96	120	30	21	5.25
Pete Harris	0	1	.000	9				19	26	7	8	8.53
Harry Fishbaugh	0	1	.000	3				13	25	2	1	10.38
Spitaleri	0	0	----	1				2	4	4	0	18.00

MILWAUKEE   7th   69-98   .413   -42   Lelivelt - Berghammer
Brewers

BATTERS	POS-GAMES	GP	AB	R	H	BI	2B	3B	HR	BB	SO	SB	BA
Ivy Griffin	1B	(see multi-team players)											
Otis Miller	2B117	123	470	83	163	64	24	4	3	31	16	6	.347
Ed Grimes	SS158	160	645	99	184	92	28	13	9	54	64	15	.285
Harry Strohm	3B107	123	446	60	117	54	21	3	4	20	32	9	.262
Frank Luce	OF133	135	447	79	132	85	19	11	12	63	46	12	.296
Bevo LeBourveau	OF107	108	416	83	137	61	32	11	6	40	29	10	.329
Tom Jenkins	OF105	105	401	66	132	66	25	13	6	35	29	9	.329
Russ Young	C87	103	310	39	86	33	14	3	4	21	29	3	.278
Ed Pick	OF47,1B37,3B29,SS12	144	509	84	150	105	26	15	14	70	39	6	.295
Bob McMenemy	C87	97	295	42	79	37	13	9	9	41	39	0	.268
Red Badgro	OF41	43	158	26	45		11	3	5			1	.285
Wilfred Ryan	P43	43	95	5	19		0	1	0			1	.200
Dennis Gearin	P35	43	58	9	17		0	2	0			0	.293
Herb Cobb	P40	40	71	8	9		2	2	2			1	.127
R. Eldred	OF34	38	108	14	23		3	2	0			1	.213
John Buvid	P34	38	64	10	15		6	0	0			0	.235
Joe Eddleman	P37	37	68	5	9		0	0	0			0	.132
Oswald Orwoll	1B34,P1	35	138	25	41		5	0	3			4	.297
Joe Hauser	1B30	31	105	18	25		2	0	3			2	.238
Louis Temple	P31	31	28	3	3		0	0	0			0	.107
Charles Robertson	P30	30	65	4	9		0	0	0			0	.138
Ed Strelecki	P28	28	44	3	6		0	0	0			0	.136
Larry Bettencourt	OF20	24	74	12	19		5	1	1			0	.257
Frank Wilson		15	34	2	8		1	0	0			0	.235
Al Fons	P10	10	9	1	0		0	0	0			0	.000
R. McIntire	P8	8	6	0	1		0	0	0			0	.167
Charles Willis	P4	4	2	0	0		0	0	0			0	.000
Steele	P3	3	5	0	1		0	0	0			0	.200
Dunham	C	2	2	0	0		0	0	0			0	.000
William Thomas	P2	2	2	0	0		0	0	0			0	.000
Alvin Krueger	P2	2	0	0	0		0	0	0			0	----
Roman	C1	1	2	1	1		0	0	0			0	.500
Judd	PH	1	1	1	1		0	0	0			0	1.000
Leslie Cox	P1	1	1	1	0		0	0	0			0	.000

PITCHERS	W	L	PCT	G	GS	CG	SH	IP	H	BB	SO	ERA
Wilfred Ryan	15	14	.517	43				258	278	70	100	4.61
Herb Cobb	14	17	.452	40				215	258	74	82	5.73
John Buvid	9	6	.600	34				170	189	84	73	5.29
Dennis Gearin	8	15	.348	35				151	182	55	52	5.54
Ed Strelecki	7	11	.389	28				134	144	62	38	4.50
Charles Robertson	6	15	.286	30				190	235	51	60	4.36
Joe Eddleman	5	14	.263	37				172	241	44	38	6.38
Louis Temple	2	2	.500	31				106	125	52	21	5.52
Al Fons	1	0	1.000	10				33	38	16	12	6.55
Oswald Orwoll	1	0	1.000	1				9	5	3	6	
Charles Willis	1	2	.333	4				11	19	6	2	9.00
R. McIntire	0	1	.000	8				19	27	8	7	6.16
Steele	0	1	.000	4				12	18	8	4	10.50
William Thomas	0	0	----	2				5	5	2	0	1.93
Alvin Krueger	0	0	----	2				1	9	0	0	72.00
Leslie Cox	0	0	----	1				1	2	1	1	0.00

TOLEDO 8th 67-100 .401 -44 Casey Stengel
Mud Hens

BATTERS	POS-GAMES	GP	AB	R	H	BI	2B	3B	HR	BB	SO	SB	BA
Jack Smith	1B69,2B40	110	408	59	106	59	22	3	9	23	33	11	.260
Max Rosenfeld	2B45,OF56	101	372	60	131	64	14	6	2	20	13	12	.352
John Warner	SS106,3B37	145	578	90	191	88	34	9	3	27	31	16	.331
Howard Freigau	3B53	58	208	38	72	33	19	2	1	20	9	5	.346
Ed Brown	OF147	155	599	86	188	71	44	12	3	27	25	15	.314
Horace Koehler	OF123,3B32	156	640	98	198	70	30	12	3	25	22	17	.309
Art Ruble	OF88	89	367	63	138	53	24	7	7	34	17	6	**.376**
Harry McCurdy	C91	105	308	34	99	52	15	7	5	24	11	5	.321
Ernie Wingard	1B42,P35	100	275	42	82	45	13	5	7	11	24	0	.298
Bobby Veach	OF67	79	255	39	68	36	11	1	4	31	4	3	.267
Red Hayworth	C71	73	218	33	72	30	9	0	4	20	16	3	.330
George Redfern	2B32,SS28	60	242	35	58		10	2	0			9	.240
James Sweeney	3B49	57	200	28	62		3	2	0			1	.310
John Neun	1B53	53	221	32	63		12	2	0			14	.285
Herb Thomas	2B42	46	159	19	37		5	2	0			5	.233
Al DeVormer	C33	44	116	11	30		4	2	0			2	.259
LeRoy Parmelee	P36	40	93	15	23		2	3	4			0	.247
Ray Lucas	P28	28	42	2	7		1	0	0			0	.167
Ed Moore	OF10	27	110	15	29		8	1	1			4	.263
Hugh McQuillan	P25	25	47	0	6		1	1	0			0	.128
Ed Pfeffer	P23	23	32	2	6		1	0	0			0	.188
Jess Doyle	P21	23	26	4	7		1	0	0			0	.269
Ed Taylor	SS20	22	78	10	14		3	1	2			0	.179
Casey Stengel		20	31	2	7		1	1	0			1	.226
Alex Ferguson	P19	19	49	4	10		3	0	0			0	.205
Vern Parks	P19	19	35	6	6		0	1	0			0	.171
Floyd Patterson	OF13	17	42	8	15		2	0	0			1	.357
Paul Zahniser	P15	15	17	3	4		2	0	0			0	.235
Emilio Palmero	P13	13	22	2	7		1	1	0			0	.318
Robert Weiland	P10	11	21	5	6		1	1	1			0	.286
William Rabb	P11	11	8	0	0		0	0	0			0	.000
Greg Mulleavy	SS	7	21	2	6	5	1	1	0			1	.286
John Lindley	OF	7	17	1	4	1	1	1	0			0	.235
Wayne Wright	P6	6	7	0	1	1	0	0	0			0	.143
David Klinger	P4	4	7	1	2		0	0	0			0	.286
John Tate	P4	4	7	1	5	1	0	0	0			0	.714
Ted Blankenship	P4	4	5	0	0		0	0	0			0	.000
Jim Ring	P3	3	4	0	0		0	0	0			0	.000
Tim McNamara	P3	3	3	0	0		0	0	0			0	.000
Edward Baecht	P2	2	1	0	1		0	0	0			0	1.000
Alex Lindstrom	P2	2	0	0	0		0	0	0			0	----
Butcher	P1	1	0	0	0		0	0	0			0	----

PITCHERS	W	L	PCT	G	GS	CG	SH	IP	H	BB	SO	ERA
LeRoy Parmelee	12	14	.462	36				234	237	**154**	94	4.77
Ernie Wingard	10	15	.400	35				213	265	63	48	5.03
Alex Ferguson	8	8	.500	19				142	163	37	34	4.50
Hugh McMillan	7	7	.500	25				135	167	53	39	4.33
Ed Pfeffer	6	5	.545	23				97	136	23	18	5.10
Vern Parks	6	6	.500	19				101	120	21	33	5.17
Robert Weiland	3	4	.429	10				54	57	34	40	4.50
Emilio Palmero	3	5	.375	13				72	97	40	29	7.00
Ray Lucas	3	10	.231	28				126	134	59	44	4.28
Paul Zahniser	3	10	.231	15				78	110	29	18	7.04
Wayne Wright	2	3	.400	6				22	38	10	3	
David Klinger	1	0	1.000	4				14	25	5	2	9.00
Alex Lindstrom	1	0	1.000	2				4	4	3	2	7.38
Jess Doyle	1	3	.250	21				69	120	24	31	7.05
William Rabb	1	4	.200	11				39	41	24	21	3.46
Edward Baecht	0	1	.000	2				4	7	1	1	6.24
Jim Ring	0	2	.000	3				15	17	6	2	4.80
Ted Blankenship	0	0	----	4				12	26	7	4	12.75
Tim McNamara	0	0	----	3				4	7	4	1	4.50
Butcher	0	0	----	1				1	0	1	0	0.00

MULTI-TEAM PLAYERS

BATTERS	POS-GAMES	TEAMS	GP	AB	R	H	BI	2B	3B	HR	BB	SO	SB	BA
Jim Geygan	3B82,2B42,OF10	C-L-MIL	138	498	75	144	95	27	8	9	47	47	6	.289
Charles High	OF87	COL-MIN	113	323	75	98	87	15	0	28	43	23	2	.303
Ivy Griffin	1B83	MIL-LOU-MIL	97	351	63	115	49	22	4	5	20	20	9	.328

MULTI-TEAM PLAYERS (cont.)

BATTERS	POS-GAMES	TEAMS	GP	AB	R	H	BI	2B	3B	HR	BB	SO	SB	BA
Ernest Vache	OF51,1B19	MIL-COL	90	258	32	75	48	19	5	2	19	27	2	.291
Bernard Tesmer	C67	SP-LOU	76	192	27	49		9	1	2			2	.255
Garland Buckeye	P32	TOL-MIN	36	56	5	17		2	0	1			0	.304
Joe Giard	P9	SP-COL	9	6	0	0	0	0	0	0	0	2	1	.000

PITCHERS		TEAMS	W	L	PCT	G	GS	CG	SH	IP	H	BB	SO	ERA
Garland Buckeye		TOL-MIN	5	11	.313	32				145	192	36	54	5.40
Joe Giard		SP-COL	0	2	.000	9				23	36	16	8	

TEAM BATTING

TEAMS	GP	AB	R	H	BI	2B	3B	HR	BB	SO	SB	BA
KANSAS CITY	**170**	5888	958	1764		271	**103**	70	528	468	113	.300
ST. PAUL	169	**5958**	1054	**1822**		324	85	122	581	602	102	**.306**
MINNEAPOLIS	168	5876	**1076**	1738		**331**	68	**158**	**653**	626	**159**	.296
INDIANAPOLIS	168	5703	802	1583		264	58	63	500	450	107	.278
LOUISVILLE	167	5842	889	1723		253	94	66	465	373	94	.295
COLUMBUS	166	5691	923	1666		310	79	85	518	429	114	.293
MILWAUKEE	169	5782	896	1646		277	97	97	572	**628**	91	.285
TOLEDO	167	5917	853	1765		298	85	58	404	413	130	.298
	672	46657	7451	13707		2328	669	719	4221	3989	910	.294

1930
Rabbit Ball

Hitting in the American Association had been on the rise since the end of World War I. During the 1920s, batting averages gradually rose before reaching an unmatched crescendo at the end of the decade, a crescendo which would touch all the teams in the league, from top to bottom.

In 1921, after several years in the .270s, the league batting average jumped more than 20 points, finishing at a lofty .297 level. During the rest of the decade, the league average hovered between a low of .290 (1922) and a high of .298 (1927). In 1930, however, this high level would be raised a notch.

Before the 1930 season, to combat lagging Depression-era attendance, baseball moguls once again decided to tinker with baseball manufacturing. Thinking that high scoring games would result in more fan interest, baseballs were changed by featuring a more tightly wrapped core. This feature made the ball positively jump off the bat, causing some to declare that there must be a rabbit in the ball.

Batting levels all across baseball soared in 1930. When the results of the 1930 American Association season were tabulated, they echoed this trend, for they showed a record 43 batting championship qualifiers hitting over .300. This in turn led each team to the .300 level. From first place (.306), through fourth (.312), all the way to last (.300), each and every Association team batted at or over .300 for the season.

Louisville survived a battle with St. Paul to win the pennant by two and one-half games over the Saints. Toledo bounced back to third, while Minneapolis finished in fourth. The second division was comprised of Kansas City, Columbus, Milwaukee, and Indianapolis. Batting honors went to Bevo LeBourveau of Toledo (.380), while the home run mark was shattered in Minneapolis by Nick Cullop (54), who also had the most runs batted in (152). Pitching took it on the chin this year, as the earned run average winner, Hugh McQuillan of Toledo, finished with the highest winning mark to date (3.33). Other leaders included Wilcy Moore of St. Paul, who won 22 games, and Louisville's Phil Weinert, who struck out 132.

After the terrific pounding pitchers received in 1930, baseball manufacturing would return to its previous method, and batting averages would eventually slide down to a more manageble level. But for one glorious season the American Association achieved a hitting level previously unknown at the top level of the minor leagues. Although all teams in all leagues benefitted from the rabbit ball, only the Association managed to pull even its last place team to the .300 level.

LOUISVILLE Colonels

LOUISVILLE Colonels	1st	93-60	.608		Al Sothoron

BATTERS	POS-GAMES	GP	AB	R	H	BI	2B	3B	HR	BB	SO	SB	BA
Dud Branom	1B154	154	617	90	194	123	20	4	14	54	13	9	.314
Billy Herman	2B143	143	617	108	188	86	40	7	8	38	38	8	.305
Joe Olivares	SS154	154	567	100	168	72	34	9	5	44	23	24	.296
Foster Ganzel	3B126	128	464	83	157	77	33	6	9	56	35	10	.338
Melbern Simons	OF153	154	668	134	248	88	49	15	11	51	27	13	.371
Herman Layne	OF151	151	628	124	209	88	33	19	10	34	46	40	.333
Clarence Nachand	OF115,3B13	127	460	82	128	96	30	8	10	51	67	6	.278
Ray Thompson	C81	88	283	38	95	56	14	4	9	19	9	5	.336
Larry Merville	OF49	76	184	23	44		6	3	4			1	.239
Art Funk	3B26	62	106	22	28		4	0	1			3	.264
Ken Penner	P41	59	97	12	26		5	0	0			1	.268
John Barnes	C44,P1	58	146	19	32		3	3	1			2	.219
Ben Tincup	P43	46	45	8	10		1	0	0			1	.222
Martin Autry	C40	44	125	19	40	25	3	1	5	16	16	1	.320
Joe DeBerry	P41	43	94	13	22		4	0	1			0	.232
Lou Polli	P37	40	54	16	12		3	0	1			0	.222
Phil Weinert	P36	36	95	10	22		4	0	1			0	.232
Roy Wilkinson	P36	36	92	6	15		1	0	1			0	.163
Guy Williams	P32	32	31	2	6		0	0	0			0	.194
John Marcum	OF18,P5	25	76	11	30		3	1	0			0	.395
Bill Wambsganss		10	22	1	2		0	0	0			0	.090
Grover Hartley	C	6	15	2	3	0	0	0	0	0	0	0	.200
Vorhoff	3B	5	10	1	2	1	0	0	0	0	0	0	.200
Earle Browne	P4	4	4	0	2	1	0	1	0	0	0	0	.500

PITCHERS	W	L	PCT	G	GS	CG	SH	IP	H	BB	SO	ERA
Joe DeBerry	19	10	.655	41				252	311	35	68	3.79
Roy Wilkinson	17	11	.607	36				261	285	84	88	3.90
Phil Weinert	16	11	.593	36				243	252	82	132	3.63
Ben Tincup	14	3	.824	43				123	119	42	66	3.51
Ken Penner	10	8	.556	41				202	284	67	67	6.15
Lou Polli	8	13	.381	37				167	221	80	47	5.82
Guy Williams	5	3	.625	32				86	95	48	44	6.17
John Marcum	4	0	1.000	5				38	39	11	9	2.36
Earle Browne	0	1	.000	4				9	29	8	4	15.00
John Barnes	0	0	----	1				0	0	0	0	

ST. PAUL Saints

ST. PAUL Saints	2nd	91-63	.591	-2.5		Al Leifield

BATTERS	POS-GAMES	GP	AB	R	H	BI	2B	3B	HR	BB	SO	SB	BA
Oscar Roettger	1B145	148	605	110	213	128	38	4	16	34	28	3	.352
Jack Saltzgaver	2B154	154	654	122	202	100	43	11	19	55	67	13	.309
Paul Wanninger	SS143	143	496	69	143	50	24	8	1	19	14	7	.288
Meredith Hopkins	3B144	146	533	65	143	89	21	7	16	57	65	3	.268
Ben Paschal	OF135	144	583	116	204	98	33	8	10	30	63	13	.350
George Davis	OF134	143	522	119	191	95	45	13	16	21	45	16	.366
Harold Anderson	OF133,1B12	146	604	121	178	65	31	4	9	62	45	34	.295
John Grabowski	C94	102	348	48	99	63	9	8	9	19	30	0	.284
Robert Fenner	C78	98	279	54	109	61	21	10	5	31	18	2	.391
Bruno Haas	OF71	82	262	40	98	46	11	5	3	16	13	6	.374
Walter Betts	P44	56	103	19	32		5	1	1			0	.311
Walter Gerber	SS36	55	113	13	27		4	2	0			0	.239
Bryan Harriss	P46	46	95	1	15		3	0	1			1	.157
John Murphy	P39	45	74	11	21		4	0	4			0	.284
Wilcy Moore	P44	44	103	1	17		1	0	0			0	.165
Russ Van Atta	P29	37	40	8	10		4	0	1			0	.250
Francis Nekola	P26	26	22	1	3		1	0	0			0	.136
Don Hankins	P23	23	35	1	9		1	1	0			0	.257
Merwin Jacobson	OF12	18	43	9	12		1	0	1			1	.279
Lefty Gomez	P17	18	28	5	6		3	1	0			0	.214
John Winsett	OF	7	5	2	1	0	0	0	0		3	0	.200
Hjortaas	SS	6	0	1	0	0	0	0	0	0	0	0	----
Les Munns	P5	5	5	0	1	0	0	0	0		1	0	.200
Bernard Tesmer	C	3	3	0	1	0	0	0	0		1	0	.333

PITCHERS	W	L	PCT	G	GS	CG	SH	IP	H	BB	SO	ERA
Wilcy Moore	22	9	.710	44				272	325	58	101	4.07
Bryan Harriss	18	13	.581	46				252	301	83	102	4.50

ST. PAUL (cont.)
Saints

PITCHERS	W	L	PCT	G	GS	CG	SH	IP	H	BB	SO	ERA
Walter Betts	17	12	.586	44				265	278	64	80	4.14
John Murphy	11	10	.524	39				195	246	64	71	5.68
Don Hankins	8	4	.667	23				103	112	35	28	4.28
Lefty Gomez	8	4	.667	17				86	83	37	57	4.08
Francis Nekola	4	5	.444	26				79	104	33	20	5.24
Russ Van Atta	3	5	.375	29				113	137	50	47	5.34
Les Munns	0	1	.000	5				16	15	9	4	5.06

TOLEDO   3rd   88-66   .571   -5.5   Casey Stengel
Mud Hens

BATTERS	POS-GAMES	GP	AB	R	H	BI	2B	3B	HR	BB	SO	SB	BA
Ernie Wingard	1B92,P18	120	412	89	141	104	26	7	24	42	47	2	.342
John Butler	2B64,3B13	86	255	40	77	48	7	1	4	30	16	5	.302
Greg Mulleavy	SS71	71	283	47	100	50	18	6	2	18	14	6	.358
Horace Koehler	3B111,OF40	149	616	101	199	94	36	11	4	32	28	12	.323
Bevo LeBourveau	OF136	138	526	122	200	100	36	16	8	50	43	36	.380
Max Rosenfeld	OF89,2B10	107	400	63	132	49	27	6	0	32	17	13	.330
Johnny Mostil	OF88	91	287	61	96	35	16	4	2	43	39	11	.334
Walt Henline	C101	103	308	63	107	64	22	8	6	51	26	7	.347
Jack Smith	1B46,C36,2B21	100	333	63	85	48	10	4	3	42	25	9	.255
John Conlan	OF66	69	279	46	81		13	2	2			9	.290
Bill Hunnefield	SS25,2B24	60	237	44	68	29	9	2	1	12	15	10	.287
Karl Swanson	2B53	57	168	32	53		11	3	0			3	.315
Frank Wilson	OF33	48	128	30	44	28	11	2	3	10	11	0	.344
Irv Jeffries	SS45	45	185	27	61		13	3	5			5	.330
George Connally	P42	43	80	7	17		7	0	0			0	.213
Earl S. Smith	OF30	42	117	16	37	25	8	1	3	13	5	2	.316
John Tate	P36	39	41	8	14		1	1	0			0	.341
Al DeVormer	C32	36	100	12	24		3	2	2			3	.240
Fred Heimach	P27	32	61	12	18		5	1	1			0	.295
Alex Ferguson	P30	30	72	7	13		0	1	0			0	.181
Hugh McQuillan	P24	30	42	3	7		1	0	0			0	.167
John Warner	3B18	29	96	8	28		5	1	0			2	.291
William Rabb	P25	25	28	0	5		0	0	0			2	.179
Sam Leslie	1B19	23	79	10	26		5	4	0			1	.329
Warren Ogden	P19	19	24	4	6		1	0	1			0	.250
John Scott	P13	18	30	2	8		1	0	0			0	.267
Elam Vangilder	P13	15	25	3	11		0	0	0			0	.440
James Sweeney	3B12	12	35	6	7		2	0	0			0	.200
Leroy Jones	OF	8	24	6	9	7	3	1	1	0	0	1	.375
Clarence Fisher	P7	7	8	0	3	1	1	0	0	0	1	0	.375
Ed Ainsmith	C	6	12	2	1	1	1	0	0	3	1	0	.083
John Wright	1B	5	17	4	8	1	1	0	0	0	0	0	.471
Norm Kies	C	5	15	5	6	4	2	1	0	0	0	0	.400
LeRoy Bachman	P5	5	9	1	1	0	0	0	0	0	1	0	.111
Owen Carroll	P4	4	14	1	3	3	0	0	0	0	0	0	.214
Robert Weiland	P4	4	8	1	0	0	0	0	0	0	2	0	.000
John Hopkins	P3	3	0	0	0	0	0	0	0	0	0	0	----
Bill Knickerbocker	SS	2	7	0	0	0	0	0	0	0	0	0	.000
James Richardson	P2	2	7	0	0	0	0	0	0	0	0	0	.000
Emilio Palmero	P2	2	1	0	0	0	0	0	0	0	0	0	.000
Frank Cash	P2	2	1	0	0	0	0	0	0	0	0	0	.000
William Moore	P1	1	0	0	0	0	0	0	0	0	0	0	----

PITCHERS	W	L	PCT	G	GS	CG	SH	IP	H	BB	SO	ERA
George Connally	18	10	.643	42				235	266	102	116	4.60
Alex Ferguson	14	7	.667	30				185	250	61	55	4.87
Fred Heimach	11	7	.611	27				145	167	20	39	4.87
Ernie Wingard	8	7	.533	18				110	142	36	27	4.34
Hugh McQuillan	6	6	.500	24				116	137	39	30	3.33
John Scott	5	3	.625	13				64	63	25	40	3.65
William Rabb	4	1	.800	25				81	91	46	24	3.89
John Tate	4	4	.500	36				104	152	50	31	6.67
Elam Vangilder	4	4	.500	13				62	71	30	29	4.07
Carl Mays	3	1	.750	6				42	52	4	6	3.21
Owen Carroll	3	1	.750	4				33	27	11	8	2.73
Warren Ogden	3	6	.333	19				76	113	27	29	7.23
LeRoy Bachman	2	0	1.000	5				21	22	10	10	3.00
James Richardson	1	1	.500	2				14	19	1	6	4.50
Robert Weiland	0	1	.000	3				10	19	8	8	7.20

TOLEDO (cont.)
Mud Hens

PITCHERS	W	L	PCT	G	GS	CG	SH	IP	H	BB	SO	ERA
Emilio Palmero	0	1	.000	1				3	7	2	0	18.00
Clarence Fisher	0	2	.000	7				23	36	15	14	11.74
John Hopkins	0	2	.000	3				4	10	5	4	20.25
Frank Cash	0	0	----	2				4	9	2	0	9.00
William Moore	0	0	----	1				0	1	1	0	

MINNEAPOLIS   4th   77-76   .503   -16   Mike Kelley
Millers

BATTERS	POS-GAMES	GP	AB	R	H	BI	2B	3B	HR	BB	SO	SB	BA
George Kelly	1B34	34	147	25	53	38	9	1	6	13	11	3	.361
Ed Sicking	2B			(see multi-team players)									
Ernest Smith	SS76,3B35	111	442	90	141	77	28	7	9	37	29	17	.319
Dan Oberholzer	3B55	76	215	36	49		9	1	2			5	.228
Nick Cullop	OF127,P1	139	515	**150**	185	**152**	28	9	54	69	**110**	8	.359
Charles High	OF83	104	275	79	105	82	18	2	25	53	23	2	.382
Bernie Neis	OF			(see multi-team players)									
Mike Gonzalez	C90	92	266	30	70	38	11	2	5	34	17	1	.262
Frank Emmer	SS64,3B12	105	294	61	103	55	16	8	8	21	31	15	.350
Wes Griffin	C80	103	288	54	92	63	17	3	10	44	23	4	.319
Spence Harris	OF74,1B19	93	369	99	134	46	24	7	10	70	28	13	.362
Elmer Smith	OF60	84	241	60	80	67	13	3	16	38	19	3	.332
Paul McCullough	P62	62	75	5	11		2	0	1			0	.147
John Brillheart	P59	60	104	15	26		5	0	4			0	.250
Newell Morse	2B35	44	143	21	34		8	1	2			1	.238
George Dumont	P42	42	64	3	9		5	0	0			0	.141
Richard Morgan	P42	42	39	5	8		1	0	0			0	.205
John Benton	P41	41	65	4	11		2	0	0			0	.169
Carmen Hill	P36	36	42	1	7		1	0	0			0	.167
John Cortazzo	SS23,2B11	34	121	17	38		6	0	0			4	.314
Leo Cotter	1B33	34	107	14	29		3	0	1			2	.272
Charles Tolson	1B28	28	113	30	35	35	8	2	8	11	18	0	.310
Charles Miller	OF23	27	88	16	32		6	1	6			2	.364
Del Lundgren	P19	19	19	2	3		1	0	0			0	.158
Malcolm Moss	P12	12	26	1	6		1	0	0			0	.231
Bruce Caldwell		10	24	5	8		0	0	1			0	.333
Polvogt	C	7	19	2	2	4	1	0	0	0	1	1	.105
Ferd Schupp	P7	7	7	1	3	3	1	0	0	0		1	.429
Hugh McMullen	C	5	9	1	2	1	0	0	0	1		0	.222
Lyle Tinning	P4	4	11	2	3	4	0	0	1	0	0	1	.273
Holmes	P3	3	1	0	0		0	0	0			0	----
Bouza	OF	2	7	1	3	1	0	0	0	0		0	.429
Leo Norris	2B	2	1	0	0	0	0	0	0	0	1	0	.000

PITCHERS	W	L	PCT	G	GS	CG	SH	IP	H	BB	SO	ERA
John Brillheart	18	16	.529	59				270	**344**	111	106	5.57
George Dumont	13	3	.813	42				192	248	67	78	5.39
Paul McCullough	13	14	.481	62				224	291	89	78	5.43
Carmen Hill	8	9	.471	36				128	174	42	54	6.05
John Benton	8	12	.400	41				183	264	63	53	6.35
Richard Morgan	7	6	.538	42				126	168	65	48	6.50
Malcolm Moss	5	3	.625	12				63	82	23	26	6.86
Ferd Schupp	2	2	.500	7				19	33	12	12	6.63
Lyle Tinning	1	0	1.000	4				27	29	6	10	6.00
Del Lundgren	1	6	.143	19				61	93	30	7	7.67
Holmes	0	0	----	3				5	8	1	1	5.40
Nick Cullop	0	0	----	1				3	1	1	1	3.00

KANSAS CITY   5th   75-79   .487   -18.5   Dutch Zwilling
Blues

BATTERS	POS-GAMES	GP	AB	R	H	BI	2B	3B	HR	BB	SO	SB	BA
Joe Kuhel	1B93	93	374	77	139	65	28	12	8	29	12	13	.372
Norm McMillan	2B128,SS18,3B14	151	582	75	190	113	32	15	9	31	28	21	.326
George Knothe	SS117	118	472	62	139	36	22	3	0	22	37	12	.294
Harry Riconda	3B			(see multi-team players)									
Denver Grigsby	OF133	144	507	90	177	97	33	15	6	66	29	9	.349
Fred Nicholson	OF105	114	386	71	125	53	22	7	1	31	16	7	.324

KANSAS CITY (cont.)
Blues

BATTERS	POS-GAMES	GP	AB	R	H	BI	2B	3B	HR	BB	SO	SB	BA
Ed Pick	OF			(see multi-team players)									.304
George Susce	C42	45	125	13	38		5	1	1			4	.304
Fred Spurgeon	2B44,SS35	96	286	40	84	26	14	3	0	16	14	11	.294
Marion Thomas	P46	52	80	10	18		2	1	0			0	.225
John Peters	C38	51	121	4	35		6	1	0			0	.289
Charlie Gooch	3B45	48	194	30	42		13	2	0			4	.217
John Smith	OF35	47	127	24	33		8	2	1			3	.260
Harley Boss	1B40	46	157	20	53	31	7	1	2	9	6	1	.338
Pat Collins	C36	44	109	19	39		7	0	3			0	.358
Tom Sheehan	P40	42	77	14	20		6	0	1			0	.260
Joe Maley	P40	40	69	6	13		2	0	1			0	.189
Lou Fette	P40	40	58	4	14		3	0	1			0	.241
W. Warmoth	P39	39	39	8	9		2	0	0			2	.231
Clyde Day	P37	37	92	4	16		1	1	0			0	.174
Ed Holley	P32	32	58	3	8		0	0	0			0	.155
Vince Graber	OF13	25	61	5	14		1	1	0			3	.230
Morgan Snyder	C13	15	35	2	8		0	0	0			1	.229
Ralph Michaels	3B11	12	39	4	10		0	0	0			2	.256
Robert Murray	P9	11	13	3	3		1	1	0			0	.231
Roy Carlyle		10	27	7	11		2	0	0			0	.407
Frank Davis	P4	4	3	0	1	0	0	0	0	0	0	0	.333
Eldon Breese	SS	3	13	2	2	0	0	0	0	0	1	0	.154

PITCHERS		W	L	PCT	G	GS	CG	SH	IP	H	BB	SO	ERA
Marion Thomas		15	13	.536	46				216	242	72	89	4.50
Clyde Day		13	14	.481	37				243	252	45	107	4.20
Joe Maley		12	13	.480	40				203	260	50	56	4.19
Lou Fette		11	9	.550	40				177	185	66	64	4.12
Tom Sheehan		9	5	.643	40				194	240	56	54	4.78
W. Warmouth		6	7	.462	29				126	154	52	41	4.79
Ed Holley		6	12	.333	32				159	159	65	61	3.79
Robert Murray		2	2	.500	9				30	38	13	10	4.50
William Swift		1	2	.333	6				25	26	5	12	3.96
Frank Davis		0	2	.000	4				12	16	5	3	5.25

COLUMBUS   6th   67-86   .438   -26   Harry Leibold
Senators

BATTERS	POS-GAMES	GP	AB	R	H	BI	2B	3B	HR	BB	SO	SB	BA
Emmett McCann	1B151	151	617	92	207	105	37	9	4	30	21	28	.335
Ray Morehart	2B114	120	465	84	143	57	28	11	6	60	36	10	.308
Westcott Kingdon	SS106	108	392	60	105	58	23	9	3	42	45	15	.268
Elmer Yoter	3B			(see multi-team players)									
Everett Purdy	OF137	137	537	116	189	106	31	11	15	55	25	15	.352
Estel Crabtree	OF136	136	571	89	154	83	30	11	7	44	32	16	.301
Earl L. Smith	OF			(see multi-team players)									
Leo Dixon	C97	100	291	34	73	32	11	4	0	25	28	4	.251
Lute Boone	3B45,2B31,SS11	107	319	53	94	57	15	6	4	31	13	15	.295
Mike Devine	C83	85	256	35	58	34	6	3	0	12	10	6	.227
Lawrence Winters	P36,OF23	82	164	25	56	36	12	2	4	11	15	0	.341
Harry Leibold	OF42	73	159	31	43		6	4	2			3	.271
Herm Kemner	P45	56	105	17	35		3	1	0			3	.333
Russ Miller	P43	45	50	4	10		1	0	0			0	.200
Joe Benes	SS43	43	174	39	47		4	4	2			4	.270
Jess Doyle	P36	38	60	8	12		1	0	0			2	.200
Harlan Wysong	P30	37	65	12	19		2	0	4			1	.292
Charles Maxton	P30	31	25	3	3		1	0	0			0	.120
Percy Jones	P27	29	37	4	7		2	0	0			0	.189
Richard Wyckoff	P17	28	41	2	11		4	0	0			0	.268
Deeby Foss	3B15	21	49	7	18		4	1	1			2	.367
Harold King	2B14	14	52	8	22		5	1	0			2	.423
Walter Shaner		14	29	6	8		2	1	0			0	.276
Albert Eckert	P10	10	19	6	5		0	0	0			1	.263
Dumford	P5	5	6	0	3		0	0	0			0	.500
James Davis	P5	5	6	2	2	1	0	0	1	1	2	0	.333
James	C	5	6	0	2	0	0	0	0	0	0	1	.333
Ray Lucas	P4	4	3	0	0		0	0	0			0	.000
Shefflot	C	3	4	0	1		0	0	0			0	.250
Frank Coleman	P2	2	4	0	0		0	0	0			0	.000
Deeds	P2	2	3	0	0		0	0	0			0	.000

COLUMBUS (cont.)
Senators

PITCHERS	W	L	PCT	G	GS	CG	SH	IP	H	BB	SO	ERA
Lawrence Winters	13	11	.542	36				198	267	59	41	4.59
Harlan Wysong	10	10	.500	30				153	176	66	68	4.64
Herman Kemner	10	13	.435	45				226	312	61	74	5.37
Russ Miller	9	11	.450	43				147	192	59	23	5.81
Percy Jones	7	6	.538	27				107	140	27	50	4.12
Jess Doyle	6	6	.500	36				155	204	48	33	5.23
Albert Eckert	3	1	.750	10				51	78	14	21	6.17
Charles Maxton	3	5	.375	30				96	112	26	21	4.50
Campbell	2	4	.333	9				34	42	13	11	6.62
Richard Wyckoff	2	9	.182	17				81	106	22	22	5.22
James Davis	0	1	.000	5								
Dumford	0	1	.000	5				17	21	18	4	8.47
Frank Coleman	0	2	.000	2				12	16	10	8	8.25
Ray Lucas	0	0	----	4				9	18	7	2	18.00
Deeds	0	0	----	2				7	10	4	2	2.57

MILWAUKEE
Brewers
7th   63-91   .409   -30.5   Marty Berghammer

BATTERS	POS-GAMES	GP	AB	R	H	BI	2B	3B	HR	BB	SO	SB	BA
George Stanton	1B125	131	504	82	162	96	23	13	11	28	33	5	.321
E. Turgeon	2B100,P1	110	417	78	133	63	21	11	8	25	29	3	.319
Dan Bloxsom	SS47,3B57,OF30	134	551	88	177	116	25	2	29	30	68	6	.321
Ed Grimes	3B100,SS54	154	670	121	194	87	28	11	12	46	57	15	.291
Tom Jenkins	OF153	153	626	120	216	127	38	16	24	63	58	10	.345
Fred Bennett	OF87	92	301	47	91	52	23	7	4	41	33	4	.302
Walt Christensen	OF84	87	315	51	114	48	16	6	2	22	7	10	.362
Russ Young	C84,1B15	109	365	57	114	70	26	6	6	33	28	2	.312
Merv Shea	C76	81	256	26	64		15	0	4			2	.250
Wayne Windle	2B51,SS19	77	265	37	68	28	8	3	4	24	28	4	.257
Stan Benton	SS38	62	163	36	50		9	4	0			3	.307
John Buvid	P45	45	90	5	23		1	0	0			0	.257
Dennis Gearin	P35	45	69	10	17		3	0	0			0	.247
Wilfred Ryan	P44	44	60	9	14		1	1	1			0	.233
Ed Strelecki	P42	42	84	7	22		2	1	0			2	.262
Charles Robertson	P31	31	85	8	19		2	0	0			0	.224
Fred Stiely	P26	28	72	6	16		1	0	1			0	.222
Oscar Stark	P19	19	13	1	1		1	0	0			0	.077
Elmer Klumpp		13	22	9	7		1	2	0			1	.318
Paul Hopkins	P12	12	7	0	0		0	0	0			0	.000
Herb Cobb	P10	10	21	1	1		1	0	0			0	.047
Jim Geygan	2B	6	18	2	6	2	2	1	0	1	2	0	.333
Barrer	P4	4	2	0	0		0	0	0			0	.000
Blatz	P3	3	1	1	1		0	0	0			0	1.000
Enoch Shinault	C	2	5	0	2		1	0	0			0	.400
R. McIntire	P2	2	1	0	0		0	0	0			0	.000
Anton Kubek	OF1	1	5	1	1		0	0	0			0	.200
Hackbarth	PH	1	1	0	0		0	0	0			0	.000
Corbelli	PR	1	0	0	0		0	0	0			0	----
Block	P1	1	0	0	0		0	0	0			0	----
Zuvognick	P1	1	0	0	0		0	0	0			0	----

PITCHERS	W	L	PCT	G	GS	CG	SH	IP	H	BB	SO	ERA
Ed Strelecki	13	10	.565	42				215	266	71	54	5.23
Fred Stiely	11	12	.478	26				193	213	56	65	4.19
John Buvid	10	11	.476	45				224	279	122	89	5.79
Charles Robertson	10	19	.345	31				229	311	69	63	5.11
Wilfred Ryan	8	14	.364	44				188	255	37	70	5.60
Dennis Gearin	6	11	.353	35				152	212	73	37	6.98
Herb Cobb	4	4	.500	10				59	62	33	16	5.95
R. McIntire	1	1	.500	2				5	8	4	2	9.00
Paul Hopkins	0	1	.000	12				27	29	16	1	4.33
Blatz	0	1	.000	3				4	11	5	2	27.00
Oscar Stark	0	3	.000	19				44	67	17	9	8.39
Barrer	0	0	----	5				9	10	6	2	4.00
Block	0	0	----	1				1	2	3	0	18.00
Zuvognick	0	0	----	1				0	2	1	0	81.00
E. Turgeon	0	0	----	1				0	0	0	0	-----

INDIANAPOLIS   8th   60-93   .393   -33   John Corriden
Indians

BATTERS	POS-GAMES	GP	AB	R	H	BI	2B	3B	HR	BB	SO	SB	BA
Peter Monohan	1B141	141	531	82	157	62	25	5	6	42	46	6	.296
M. Connolly	2B95,SS19,1B10	133	479	85	162	75	33	7	7	37	19	8	.338
Rabbit Warstler	SS88	88	380	73	110	39	29	9	6	26	39	8	.289
Howard Freigau	3B98,1B16	120	434	59	141	59	24	5	2	30	33	4	.325
Clarence Hoffman	OF133	134	528	94	176	97	30	8	11	40	40	7	.333
Clyde Barnhart	OF123	123	473	84	145	71	19	5	13	50	28	3	.307
Charles Dorman	OF	(see multi-team players)											
Joe Sprinz	C48	54	167	17	46	27	7	4	0	30	8	0	.275
Bill Narlesky	3B52,SS37	85	337	73	105	38	18	6	3	25	26	11	.312
Len Koenecke	OF62	67	252	41	63	28	11	6	9	7	27	6	.250
Mike Cvengros	P35	53	103	15	26		2	0	3			1	.252
Ollie Tucker	OF50	52	184	40	65	44	11	2	9	27	15	1	.358
Bill Burwell	P51	51	108	14	28		2	0	2			0	.259
Paul Wolf	2B18	46	110	20	30		7	0	0			4	.273
John Riddle	C28,3B11	41	142	20	51	28	7	1	3	7	9	2	.359
Claude Jonnard	P34	34	89	5	10		1	0	0			0	.113
Foy Frazier	OF32	33	119	20	41		2	1	3			3	.345
Peter Mondino	C28	29	75	8	15		1	2	0			1	.200
Clyde Crouse	C23	28	84	7	32		2	1	1			0	.380
Elmer Ambrose	P25	28	51	2	12		2	1	0			0	.235
Oral Hildebrand	P25	25	38	1	6		1	0	0			0	.158
John Ryan	SS18	19	58	9	11		2	1	2			0	.190
Walter Wolf	P18	19	14	1	4		0	0	0			0	.286
Lee Daney	P18	18	16	1	3		1	0	0			0	.187
Joe Cicero	OF16	17	41	3	7		2	0	0			0	.171
Frank Mulrooney	P16	16	15	1	4		1	0	0			0	.267
Bill Parks	P13	13	15	2	5		1	0	0			0	.333
Aloysius Bejma	OF11	11	16	2	2		0	0	0			0	.125
Walter House	P11	11	12	1	0		0	0	0			0	.000
Carl Boone	P7	7	4	1	1	1	0	0	1	1	0	0	.250
George Payne	P5	5	5	0	0	0	0	0	0	0	2	0	.000
Patrick Simmons	P4	4	5	1	1	0	0	0	0	0	0	0	.200
Ted Blankenship	P4	4	3	0	1	2	0	0	0	0	1	0	.333
George Jones	P3	3	5	0	1	0	0	0	0	0	0	0	.200
Sidney Dyer	P2	2	4	0	0	0	0	0	0	0	0	0	.000
Floyd Olds	P2	2	3	1	1	0	0	0	0	0	0	0	.333
Prentice Hall	P1	1	1	0	0	0	0	0	0	0	1	0	.000

PITCHERS	W	L	PCT	G	GS	CG	SH	IP	H	BB	SO	ERA
Bill Burwell	17	12	.586	40				237	271	55	56	4.02
Mike Cvengros	15	9	.625	35				233	270	110	93	5.18
Claude Jonnard	11	17	.393	34				232	285	85	122	5.71
Elmer Ambrose	5	8	.385	25				123	151	45	45	5.27
Frank Mulrooney	3	4	.429	16				53	60	10	22	5.44
Oral Hildebrand	3	10	.231	25				110	108	47	65	4.34
Lee Daney	2	4	.333	18				54	87	33	25	8.33
Walter House	1	0	1.000	11				36	45	29	15	7.50
George Jones	1	1	.500	3				12	18	8	4	6.00
Walter Wolf	0	1	.000	18				44	45	47	17	6.75
Carl Boone	0	1	.000	7				19	21	11	3	5.68
Patrick Simmons	0	1	.000	4				13	25	9	5	5.54
Floyd Olds	0	1	.000	2				9	17	5	6	5.00
Sidney Dyer	0	1	.000	2				8	11	3	5	5.63
Ted Blankenship	0	2	.000	3				7	9	7	0	5.14
Bill Parks	0	3	.000	13				46	68	20	11	7.63
George Payne	0	3	.000	5				13	13	4	5	2.07
Prentice Hall	0	0	----	1				4	2	1	4	2.25

MULTI-TEAM PLAYERS

BATTERS	POS-GAMES	TEAMS	GP	AB	R	H	BI	2B	3B	HR	BB	SO	SB	BA
Earl L. Smith	OF145	MIN-COL	150	603	103	198	130	43	4	16	31	31	11	.328
Ed Pick	OF112,1B41	MIL-KC	150	538	114	167	97	30	14	8	**107**	48	19	.310
Ed Sicking	2B142	IND-MIN	148	609	129	190	69	36	5	4	77	34	17	.312
George Gerken	OF143	KC-MIL	145	596	111	196	65	28	15	10	52	64	19	.329
Elmer Yoter	3B136	MIN-COL	142	562	110	178	49	30	8	4	64	36	24	.317
Bernie Neis	OF123	COL-MIN	134	453	103	156	88	35	5	11	55	25	25	.344
Tom Angley	C104	KC-IND	116	332	47	111	54	21	4	6	48	12	3	.334
Harry Riconda	3B103	KC-MIN	106	440	76	146	50	39	7	5	27	35	4	.332
Charles Dorman	OF82	IND-KC	104	314	45	93	60	16	7	8	35	43	3	.296

MULTI-TEAM PLAYERS (cont.)

BATTERS	POS-GAMES	TEAMS	GP	AB	R	H	BI	2B	3B	HR	BB	SO	SB	BA
Bill Barrett	OF50,1B16	MIN-KC	76	252	39	67	34	10	6	4	30	19	7	.266
Clay Van Alstyne	P32	MIN-IND	37	53	6	12		1	1	1			0	.226
Frank Miller	P24	C-MIL-IND	24	26	4	3		0	1	0			0	.115
Alex Hooks	1B11	MIN-IND	16	39	8	11		3	1	0			2	.282
Harold Smith	P16	TOL-MIN	16	12	0	0		0	0	0			0	.000

PITCHERS		TEAMS	W	L	PCT	G	GS	CG	SH	IP	H	BB	SO	ERA
Clay Van Alstyne		MIN-IND	3	15	.167	32				124	154	67	53	5.95
Harold Smith		TOL-MIN	2	5	.286	16				45	65	12	13	7.00
Frank Miller		C-MIL-IND	2	10	.167	24				76	114	30	25	7.94

TEAM BATTING

TEAMS	GP	AB	R	H	BI	2B	3B	HR	BB	SO	SB	BA
LOUISVILLE	154	5499	925	1683		287	77	89	446	390	125	.306
ST. PAUL	155	5556	936	**1736**		304	81	126	415	543	100	.312
TOLEDO	154	5412	953	1705		302	89	72	517	454	137	**.315**
MINNEAPOLIS	154	5414	**1088**	1690		**316**	57	**183**	**618**	**598**	123	.312
KANSAS CITY	155	5449	842	1656		298	93	54	465	404	121	.304
COLUMBUS	155	5479	939	1654		294	90	75	479	406	**161**	.302
MILWAUKEE	154	**5591**	919	1701		275	**103**	119	480	574	89	.304
INDIANAPOLIS	**157**	5528	873	1656		274	72	90	492	502	72	.300
	619	43928	7475	13481		2350	662	808	3912	3871	928	.307

1931
Birds of a Feather

Most minor league team owners during the first part of the century were independent operators who relied on their own wiles and judgment to succeed. Most of their money was made from ticket sales and from selling their players farther up the minor league chain.

There were some exceptions to this trend. Several minor league teams had working relationships with major league teams. Some teams (including the American Association's Toledo franchise) were even owned outright by major league owners. This would give these major league teams a steady influx of minor league talent, an advantage that did not go unnoticed.

During the early 1920s, the St. Louis Cardinals of the National League began to purchase minor league teams with the intent of creating a stable of ballplayers that could be nurtured up to the big leagues. Led by Cardinal general manager Branch Rickey, St. Louis gobbled up more than a half-dozen teams by the end of the decade. Rickey desired another link in his growing chain of teams, and to accomplish this, he next turned his attention to the American Association.

The Columbus Senators were one of the eight charter members of the league. On the field, the team had suffered through a miserable decade of the 1920s, and thus were ripe for the picking. It was no surprise to anyone that in 1931, the St. Louis Cardinals purchased the Senators and added them to their collection of teams.

St. Paul returned to the top spot in 1931, featuring a hard hitting club which saw eight players crack more than ten homers apiece. Finishing a distant 14 games back was Kansas City, followed by Indianapolis, Columbus, Milwaukee, Minneapolis, Louisville, and Toledo. Art Shires of Milwaukee won the batting title (.385), while Cliff Crawford of Columbus hit the most home runs (28), and had the most runs batted in (154). On the pitching front, Frank Henry of Minneapolis won the most games (23), while Toledo's John Cooney had the best earned run average (2.49). Claude Jonnard from Milwaukee struck out the most batters, finishing with 130.

After its purchase by the Cardinals, the Columbus team saw an almost immediate turnaround. The Cardinals stocked their new farm team with many top players who would lead the team to pennant glory during the decades to come. They also built the team a new stadium to showcase its first division talents. One other significant change was also made. Not content to keep the Senators nickname, the parent Cardinals gave their Association franchise a moniker that would reflect their ownership. From then on, the Columbus team would be known as the Red Birds.

ST. PAUL Saints

1st	104-63	.623		Al Leifield

BATTERS	POS-GAMES	GP	AB	R	H	BI	2B	3B	HR	BB	SO	SB	BA
Oscar Roettger	1B141	145	608	97	217	123	38	7	15	31	25	7	.357
Jack Saltzgaver	2B166	167	679	150	231	91	37	13	19	77	55	26	.340
Joe Morrissey	SS160	167	673	123	223	114	34	3	22	34	19	14	.331
Meredith Hopkins	3B167	167	622	87	176	99	34	5	23	69	59	3	.283
George Davis	OF150	152	623	134	214	136	36	15	26	51	45	24	.343
Harold Anderson	OF136	140	611	126	192	95	36	6	23	37	53	24	.314
Cedric Durst	OF126,1B20	144	557	88	167	98	43	8	11	40	32	12	.300
Robert Fenner	C116	127	397	57	118	54	26	6	7	58	25	3	.297
Ben Paschal	OF105	121	441	86	148	85	29	0	14	36	51	13	.336
Frank Snyder	C68	73	219	25	51	30	10	1	5	27	16	0	.233
John Prudhomme	P42	56	114	13	33		5	0	1			1	.289
John Murphy	P38	50	111	17	25		5	1	0			0	.225
Bryan Harriss	P45	45	90	7	10		2	0	1			1	.111
Walter Betts	P41	44	102	18	25		4	1	0			0	.245
Russ Van Atta	P35	36	62	12	13		4	0	1			0	.210
Les Munns	P24	25	35	3	7		1	0	0			0	.200
Morris Bream	P24	24	34	7	7		1	0	0			0	.206
Paul Wanninger	SS16	18	43	9	14		0	1	0			0	.326
Leroy Jones		13	9	4	5		2	0	0			0	.556
Chet Nichols	P12	12	22	7	6		1	0	0			0	.273
Eugene Trow	P1	1	1	0	0	0	0	0	0	0	0	0	.000

PITCHERS	W	L	PCT	G	GS	CG	SH	IP	H	BB	SO	ERA
Walter Betts	22	13	.629	41				285	322	52	69	3.60
Bryan Harriss	20	11	.645	45				238	274	69	83	4.43
John Prudhomme	17	10	.630	42				256	311	99	88	4.73
John Murphy	16	13	.552	38				256	273	108	118	4.01
Russ Van Atta	13	5	.722	35				162	189	62	82	5.01
Morris Bream	7	5	.583	24				106	154	32	21	6.11
Chet Nichols	5	1	.833	12				61	74	17	10	4.87
Les Munns	4	4	.500	24				112	136	60	68	6.11
Eugene Trow	0	1	.000	1				3	3	2	0	

KANSAS CITY Blues

2nd	90-77	.539	-14	Dutch Zwilling

BATTERS	POS-GAMES	GP	AB	R	H	BI	2B	3B	HR	BB	SO	SB	BA
Peter Monohan	1B	(see multi-team players)											
Al Marquardt	2B92,SS12	103	449	80	134	49	16	10	1	24	32	6	.298
Bill Akers	SS109,2B10	119	456	105	151	97	34	7	20	58	42	2	.331
Ray Treadaway	3B91,2B14	111	436	73	140	52	26	11	5	41	17	9	.321
Ed Pick	OF164	165	672	125	214	128	58	14	9	91	39	19	.318
Denver Grigsby	OF159	162	606	129	192	99	33	7	4	83	38	13	.317
Gus Dugas	OF86	93	327	65	137	79	25	11	8	27	33	2	.419
John Peters	C102	126	363	37	118	53	14	9	2	27	13	4	.325
Robert Boken	3B61,2B30	106	365	66	104	46	19	9	8	17	40	5	.285
Tom Padden	C78	94	254	38	79	46	8	4	3	26	30	5	.311
Bill Dunlap	OF70	84	274	42	74	44	7	6	6	18	40	7	.270
Lou Fette	P45	55	77	12	21		3	3	0			0	.273
William Bayne	P49	51	67	6	10		2	1	0			0	.149
Lou Brower	SS50	50	208	32	63	25	10	3	3	17	13	7	.303
Joe Maley	P44	49	52	7	5		1	0	0			0	.096
Fred Nicholson	OF33	46	129	11	26		7	4	0			0	.202
William Swift	P43	45	89	11	16		2	1	0			0	.180
Marion Thomas	P41	41	55	6	15		1	0	0			1	.273
Herb Sanders	P35	41	50	7	9		0	0	0			0	.180
O. McDaniel	1B29	36	112	16	37	28	5	3	5	12	9	4	.330
Ed Holley	P34	34	90	5	21		7	1	0			0	.233
Norm McMillan	3B28	30	113	16	40		4	2	1			7	.354
Fred Spurgeon	2B22	30	87	19	23		4	1	0			5	.264
Pat Collins	C12	27	44	3	8		0	1	0			0	.182
Peter Donohue	P19	20	54	5	14		2	0	0			0	.259
George Knothe	2B16	16	58	9	10		2	1	0			0	.172
Don Hankins	P14	14	14	3	2		1	0	0			0	.143
Ed Rose		12	38	7	10		1	0	1			1	.263
Murl Prather	1B	8	25	4	6	6	0	0	1	3		0	.240
George Susce	C	8	17	1	5	1	1	0	0			0	.294
Vern Blenkiron	OF	8	9	2	3	2	0	0	0			0	.333
Bailey Clarke	OF6	6	15	0	2		0	0	0			0	.133
Glen Larson	P2	2	6	1	3	1	0	0	0			0	.500
House	P2	2	0	0	0		0	0	0			0	----

KANSAS CITY (cont.)
Blues

BATTERS	POS-GAMES	GP	AB	R	H	BI	2B	3B	HR	BB	SO	SB	BA
Schultz	P1	1	3	0	0		0	0	0			0	.000

PITCHERS		W	L	PCT	G	GS	CG	SH	IP	H	BB	SO	ERA
William Swift		16	7	.696	43				204	234	44	106	4.55
William Bayne		14	10	.583	49				199	232	82	64	4.66
Ed Holley		14	12	.538	34				233	227	63	91	4.01
Marion Thomas		11	10	.524	41				149	203	47	55	4.47
Peter Donohue		10	4	.714	19				138	183	30	34	4.44
Joe Maley		9	8	.529	44				157	220	41	49	6.08
Lou Fette		7	11	.389	45				183	235	88	59	6.00
Herb Sanders		6	8	.429	35				142	170	59	30	4.56
Glen Larson		1	0	1.000	2				16	19	9	3	
Schultz		0	1	.000	1				8	8	8	1	
House		0	0	----	2				1	2	0	1	

INDIANAPOLIS   3rd   86-80   .518   -17.5   Corriden - McCann
Indians

BATTERS	POS-GAMES	GP	AB	R	H	BI	2B	3B	HR	BB	SO	SB	BA
Emmett McCann	1B101,2B12	126	448	76	141	80	29	8	5	23	16	5	.315
Frank Sigafoos	2B101	107	420	59	137	70	30	4	6	21	39	7	.326
Jonah Goldman	SS81	82	315	57	84	26	24	2	2	39	24	4	.267
Elmer Yoter	3B	(see multi-team players)											
Len Koenecke	OF160	163	634	141	224	131	23	19	24	81	55	13	.353
Curtis Walker	OF130	143	494	103	159	85	23	7	8	88	31	1	.322
Ray Fitzgerald	OF	(see multi-team players)											
John Riddle	C103	116	346	42	101	46	18	3	5	23	11	1	.292
Tom Angley	C91	115	363	68	136	99	16	5	18	17	16	1	.375
Ed Montague	SS65	67	271	58	77	30	9	3	3	33	36	4	.284
Howard Fitzgerald	OF56	62	226	42	59	28	13	2	3	26	21	2	.261
George Smith	P41	43	39	7	10		1	0	1			1	.256
Bill Burwell	P36	41	100	16	27		5	0	1			0	.270
John Kroner	3B36	37	130	17	34		5	2	2			2	.262
Berly Horne	P30	36	49	7	9		2	0	0			0	.184
Carl Lind	2B32	35	127	18	35		7	0	1			2	.276
Harry Rosenberg	OF24	35	112	15	37		10	1	0			3	.330
Oral Hildebrand	P33	33	61	6	11		1	1	0			0	.180
Prentice Hall	P30	30	23	2	4		0	0	0			1	.174
Zeke Bonura	1B16	23	52	9	14		2	0	0			0	.269
Walt Miller	P17	17	44	3	11		0	1	0			0	.250
Ray White		15	52	9	13		4	2	0			1	.250
Leslie Barnhart	P13	16	11	2	3		1	0	0			0	.273
Lee Daney	P14	14	18	0	4		1	0	0			0	.222
Clyde Barnhart		14	21	3	6		1	0	0			0	.286
Willard Morrell	P13	13	18	1	1		0	0	0			0	.056
Martin Griffin	P12	12	13	1	1		0	0	0			0	.077
Edwin Lowell		10	34	8	11		2	0	0			0	.324
Pence	P8	8	10	0	0		0	0	0			0	.000
Herman Holzhauser	P8	8	9	0	1		0	0	0			0	.111
Paul Wolf	SS	7	1	1	0		0	0	0			0	.000
William Thomas	P6	6	5	0	1		0	0	0			0	.200
Frank Mulrooney	P6	6	0	0	0		0	0	0			0	----
Robert Logan	P5	5	10	3	2	2	0	0	0			0	.200
Prince	P5	5	8	0	0		0	0	0			0	.000
Charles Dorman	OF	5	4	0	0		0	0	0			0	.000
Eugene Jones	P5	5	3	0	0		0	0	0			0	.000
J. Jones	P3	3	5	0	0		0	0	0			0	.000

PITCHERS		W	L	PCT	G	GS	CG	SH	IP	H	BB	SO	ERA
Bill Burwell		17	10	.630	36				239	311	59	46	4.52
Oral Hildebrand		11	8	.579	33				165	184	64	99	5.18
Walt Miller		9	5	.643	17				115	135	26	40	4.70
Berly Horne		9	9	.500	30				136	149	61	66	4.50
George Smith		8	8	.500	41				109	136	58	41	4.63
Robert Logan		3	0	1.000	4				25	21	5	6	
Prentice Hall		3	3	.500	30				86	112	33	30	4.71
William Thomas		2	2	.500	4				20	26	4	6	
Willard Morrell		2	3	.400	13				59	72	21	14	4.88
Lee Daney		2	6	.250	14				54	59	28	20	4.50
Martin Griffin		2	6	.250	12				44	56	17	19	

INDIANAPOLIS (cont.)
Indians

PITCHERS	W	L	PCT	G	GS	CG	SH	IP	H	BB	SO	ERA
Leslie Barnhart	1	0	1.000	13				33	34	17	11	
Herman Holshauser	1	2	.333	8				15	29	11	4	
Prince	1	2	.333	5				22	22	11	4	
Pence	1	3	.250	8				26	40	14	8	
J. Jones	0	1	.000	3				15	18	4	7	
Frank Mulrooney	0	0	----	6				8	13	3	3	
Eugene Jones	0	0	----	5				10	16	8	2	

COLUMBUS   4th   84-82   .506   -19.5   Harry Leibold
Red Birds

BATTERS	POS-GAMES	GP	AB	R	H	BI	2B	3B	HR	BB	SO	SB	BA
Cliff Crawford	1B156	157	633	142	237	154	41	13	**28**	67	21	18	.374
Burgess Whitehead	2B68,SS62	135	515	85	169	68	19	7	1	14	32	20	.328
George Binder	SS51	63	227	28	53		10	3	0			8	.233
Bill Narlesky	3B		(see multi-team players)										
Ernest Swanson	OF135	146	528	117	175	83	38	14	8	52	34	21	.331
Everett Purdy	OF98	111	371	80	122	61	27	3	5	49	20	8	.329
Lew Riggs	OF83,3B38	138	510	83	149	82	18	10	18	29	42	11	.292
Gordon Hinkle	C91	100	271	25	60	27	13	2	3	23	48	4	.221
Marv Gudat	P30,OF22,1B12	102	213	37	73	34	10	1	4	21	12	6	.343
Gene DesAutels	C89	96	275	45	75	32	16	1	0	35	17	3	.273
Joel Hunt	OF66	77	281	52	78	49	6	9	4	29	33	10	.278
William Rollings	3B33	58	178	31	55		10	3	3			0	.309
Earl L. Smith	OF51	56	200	42	63	50	14	2	8	26	13	7	.315
Al Moore	OF46	50	173	34	48	33	10	6	1	22	11	5	.277
Harold King	2B48	50	157	34	50	40	7	0	13	23	13	3	.318
Ed Delker	SS37	47	187	34	56	39	18	4	4	22	19	2	.299
Ken Ash	P37	43	75	6	20		4	0	0			0	.267
LeRoy Parmelee	P30	36	67	7	25		4	0	0			0	.373
Al Grabowski	P28	31	60	6	12		1	0	1			0	.200
Ed Chapman	P30	31	47	3	6		2	0	0			0	.128
Al Eckert	P20	20	27	1	5		1	0	0			0	.185
Harold Bohl	3B13	16	47	9	13		1	2	0			1	.277
Floyd Rose	P16	16	11	5	2		0	0	0			0	.182
Al Baker	P15	15	13	1	3		0	0	0			0	.231
Carlisle Littlejohn	P14	14	11	0	3		0	0	0			0	.273
Burton Bruckman	C10	12	35	8	6		2	0	0			0	.171
Paul Dean	P12	12	9	0	2		1	0	0			0	.222
Bill Delancey	C	11	32	3	8		0	0	1			0	.250
John Brown	P5	5	6	1	1		0	0	0			0	.167
Tucker	OF	3	5	0	1		0	0	0			0	.200
Blair Kunes	P3	3	2	0	1		0	0	0			0	.500
Bill Lee	P2	2	6	0	1		1	0	0			0	.167
Harry Leibold	OF1	1	3	0	1		1	0	0			0	.333
Burns	P1	1	2	0	0		0	0	0			0	.000
Kaines	3B1	1	0	0	0		0	0	0			0	----
Bellman	C1	1	0	0	0		0	0	0			0	----

PITCHERS	W	L	PCT	G	GS	CG	SH	IP	H	BB	SO	ERA
Ken Ash	16	10	.615	37				201	255	60	57	5.28
Al Grabowski	10	6	.625	28				141	167	40	57	4.66
LeRoy Parmalee	8	6	.571	30				154	174	78	80	4.73
Ed Chapman	8	9	.471	30				129	108	103	73	4.54
Al Eckert	4	3	.571	20				75	101	28	28	5.16
Marv Gudat	4	4	.500	30				142	187	24	29	4.31
Al Baker	3	5	.375	15				43	43	18	13	5.44
Clarence Heise	2	0	1.000	4				26	26	7	7	
Percy Jones	2	0	1.000	3				18	18	9	9	
Bill Lee	2	0	1.000	2				17	6	4	17	
William Beckman	2	1	.667	5				23	41	12	10	
Floyd Rose	2	2	.500	16				42	43	31	21	
Carlisle Littlejohn	2	4	.333	14				40	62	12	11	
Lawrence Winters	1	0	1.000	4				5	11	1	0	
John Brown	0	1	.000	5				17	17	13	3	
Bill Kermode	0	1	.000	3				12	29	5	3	
James Winford	0	1	.000	3				11	18	6	6	
Ted Kleinhans	0	1	.000	3				8	11	8	2	
Paul Dean	0	2	.000	12				36	40	24	11	
Blair Kunes	0	0	----	3				17	13	5	1	
Burns	0	0	----	1				4	8	1	1	

MILWAUKEE   5th   83-85   .494   -21.5   Berghammer - O'Rourke
Brewers

BATTERS	POS-GAMES	GP	AB	R	H	BI	2B	3B	HR	BB	SO	SB	BA
Art Shires	1B157	157	623	120	**240**	131	45	8	11	71	30	8	**.385**
M. Connolly	2B113,3B42	161	670	118	211	85	35	5	15	46	28	22	.315
Jack Tavener	SS166	167	**703**	119	186	73	30	10	15	73	74	11	.265
Dan Bloxsom	3B56	72	260	35	67	47	12	0	10	21	31	9	.258
Alex Metzler	OF161	163	623	119	213	96	38	10	14	81	30	21	.342
John Kloza	OF129	133	492	107	157	89	24	9	22	53	59	12	.319
Anton Kubek	OF73	101	280	50	100	45	19	9	5	15	31	2	.357
Clyde Manion	C127	138	464	64	164	80	21	5	6	55	21	7	.353
George Gerken	OF53	64	211	32	57		13	2	1			9	.270
Walt Christensen	OF54	59	209	34	68	26	15	1	3	18	6	7	.325
Frank O'Rourke	3B47	50	214	40	65		12	1	1			4	.304
Ted Gullic	OF34,1B10	50	173	25	39		7	5	3			0	.225
Merton Nelson	P40	46	39	3	6		1	0	0			0	.154
Earl Caldwell	P45	45	91	6	19		3	2	0			1	.209
Claude Jonnard	P43	43	83	8	8		0	0	2			0	.096
Dennis Gearin	P35	43	62	5	16		3	0	0			0	.258
Lou Polli	P42	42	99	12	20		1	0	0			0	.202
Jack Knott	P37	37	75	8	11		1	0	1			0	.147
Jack Crouch	C31	36	110	17	32		5	1	3			2	.291
Fred Stiely	P27	32	67	12	20		0	0	5			0	.299
Benny Bengough	C20	21	61	6	15		1	0	2			0	.246
Walter Euller	3B17	17	54	3	12		0	0	1			0	.222
Marvin Ferrell	P16	16	15	1	3		2	0	0			0	.200
Garland Buckeye	P14	15	13	2	4		1	0	0			0	.308
Howard Taylor	P11	11	2	0	0		0	0	0			0	.000
Bernard Hungling		10	25	5	8		2	0	1			0	.320
John Buvid	P5	5	4	0	0		0	0	0			0	.000
Herb Cobb	P4	4	5	1	0		0	0	0	2	2	0	.000
Edward Linke	P3	3	0	0	0		0	0	0			0	----
John Dickshot	OF1	1	3	0	0		0	0	0			0	.000
Hurst	1B1	1	1	0	0		0	0	0			0	.000
Harold Wiltse	P1	1	0	0	0		0	0	0			0	----
Larry Kessenich	P1	1	0	0	0		0	0	0			0	----

PITCHERS	W	L	PCT	G	GS	CG	SH	IP	H	BB	SO	ERA
Lou Polli	21	15	.583	42				281	337	80	102	4.90
Earl Caldwell	15	15	.500	45				263	300	74	68	4.31
Jack Knott	11	9	.550	37				197	224	48	57	4.98
Claude Jonnard	11	15	.423	43				240	281	91	**130**	5.18
Fred Stiely	10	11	.476	27				152	182	45	54	4.68
Dennis Gearin	7	7	.500	35				139	194	50	35	5.82
Merton Nelson	6	8	.429	40				127	162	33	44	4.96
John Buvid	1	0	1.000	5				10	15	8	2	
Herb Cobb	1	1	.500	3				15	24	8	2	
Marvin Ferrell	0	1	.000	16				40	41	31	13	6.53
Garland Buckeye	0	2	.000	14				32	55	15	10	
Howard Taylor	0	0	----	11				15	28	5	5	
Edward Linke	0	0	----	3				3	5	3	2	
Larry Kessenich	0	0	----	1				0	1	2	0	
Harold Wiltse	0	0	----	1				0	0	2	0	

MINNEAPOLIS   6th   80-88   .476   -24.5   Mike Kelley
Millers

BATTERS	POS-GAMES	GP	AB	R	H	BI	2B	3B	HR	BB	SO	SB	BA
George Kelly	1B155	155	606	84	194	112	34	2	20	39	55	5	.320
Ed Sicking	2B125	142	523	118	169	59	28	2	5	71	24	14	.323
Ernest Smith	SS149	153	554	94	178	80	35	4	7	61	37	21	.321
Charles Dressen	3B99	101	397	65	102	34	17	2	4	42	28	3	.257
Spence Harris	OF150,1B16	163	642	**156**	223	108	40	12	15	**104**	40	18	.347
Bernie Neis	OF109	129	462	90	145	74	19	7	9	44	21	**26**	.314
Art Ruble	OF	(see multi-team players)											
Bubbles Hargrave	C100	117	361	67	110	63	19	2	12	32	24	5	.305
Leo Norris	3B49,2B45	112	384	68	112	89	20	9	17	35	43	8	.292
Wes Griffin	C78	96	302	55	100	58	19	2	9	38	27	3	.331
Frank McGowan	OF63	65	251	51	93	70	20	6	11	28	26	3	.371
Bob Meusel	OF45	59	187	30	53	59	8	2	8	15	14	5	.283
Frank Henry	P50	54	114	18	28		5	1	0			0	.246
Phil Hensick	P47	47	72	7	11		3	0	0			0	.153
John Brillheart	P41	43	61	7	12		2	0	0			0	.197

MINNEAPOLIS (cont.)
Millers

BATTERS	POS-GAMES	GP	AB	R	H	BI	2B	3B	HR	BB	SO	SB	BA
Al Wright	OF25	27	84	13	30		4	0	1			3	.357
John Benton	P36	36	77	9	15		1	0	0			0	.195
Bill Wilson	P22	23	38	4	6		0	0	1			0	.158
Frank Emmer	SS14	22	54	10	13		1	0	0			0	.241
Paul McCullough	P22	22	11	2	3		0	0	2			1	.273
Harry Riconda	3B17	20	78	10	25		5	0	0			2	.321
Hy Vandenberg	P16	18	14	4	4		2	0	0			0	.286
George Dumont	P16	16	8	0	0		0	0	0			0	.000
Richard Morgan	P13	13	19	0	2		0	0	0			0	.105
Hugh McMullen	C12	12	32	5	7		2	0	1			1	.219
Robert Schleicher	3B	9	20	4	3	4	0	3	0	1	0	0	.150
Stan Keyes	OF	9	19	5	5	5	1	0	1	7	4	0	.263
Gordon Nell	OF	9	13	2	3	3	1	0	1	0	2	0	.231
Vern Parks	P7	7	7	0	0		0	0	0			0	.000
Lyle Tinning	P5	5	8	0	1		0	0	0	1		0	.000
Elmer Smith	OF	4	14	2	3	1	1	0	0	2	1	0	.214
Wilbur Wehde	P3	3	2	0	0	1	0	0	0			0	.000
Joe Mowry	OF	3	2	1	0		0	0	0			0	.000
Gharrity	C	2	4	0	0		0	0	0			0	.000
Charles Tolson	1B1	1	1	0	0		0	0	0			0	.000

PITCHERS		W	L	PCT	G	GS	CG	SH	IP	H	BB	SO	ERA
Frank Henry		23	10	.697	50				292	352	78	109	4.41
John Benton		13	13	.500	36				209	264	49	47	4.61
Phil Hensick		8	13	.381	47				209	265	117	68	6.11
John Brillheart		8	15	.348	41				156	214	66	73	6.63
Bill Wilson		4	4	.500	22				84	110	19	28	6.86
George Dumont		3	0	1.000	16				40	59	21	16	
Hy Vandenberg		2	0	1.000	16				36	48	23	9	
Paul McCullough		2	4	.333	22				42	67	24	16	9.21
Lyle Tinning		1	2	.333	5				19	24	9	2	
Richard Morgan		1	7	.125	13				67	85	30	22	5.64
Vern Parks		0	1	.000	7				24	38	9	9	
Wilbur Wehde		0	0	----	3				8	14	6	1	

LOUISVILLE   7th   74-94   .440   -30.5   Al Sothoron
Colonels

BATTERS	POS-GAMES	GP	AB	R	H	BI	2B	3B	HR	BB	SO	SB	BA
Dud Branom	1B168	168	670	98	201	134	30	6	15	54	22	3	.300
Billy Herman	2B118	118	486	100	170	59	24	3	7	43	39	9	.350
Joe Olivares	SS144	154	545	62	137	44	27	7	2	29	26	7	.251
Foster Ganzel	3B130	133	481	64	147	57	35	4	4	57	30	1	.306
Liz Funk	OF147	150	561	101	158	73	24	15	5	72	40	19	.282
Herman Layne	OF138	150	564	102	195	44	22	7	3	30	33	25	.346
Clarence Nachand	OF111	124	350	50	92	73	21	6	6	31	52	3	.263
Ray Thompson	C96	110	344	31	87	39	14	5	2	11	17	1	.253
Art Funk	3B51,SS37,2B27	121	351	38	86	35	12	6	2	12	15	5	.245
John Marcum	OF42,P35	109	253	34	75	46	13	2	7	24	7	3	.296
Clarence Hoffman	OF73	92	298	36	90	50	14	4	3	15	24	1	.302
Ken Penner	P33	64	118	10	31		5	0	2			0	.263
Guy Williams	P49	51	50	7	10		2	0	0			1	.200
Joe DeBerry	P41	43	64	2	10		2	0	0			0	.156
Roy Wilkinson	P32	32	28	1	5		1	0	0			0	.179
Clyde Hatter	P31	31	56	2	8		0	0	0			0	.143
Robert Weiland	P28	29	65	5	16		2	0	0			0	.246
Phil Weinert	P25	25	37	3	12		1	0	0			0	.324
Billy Jurges	2B11	14	44	4	9		1	0	1			1	.205
Bill Berwanger	2B11	11	39	3	8		1	0	0			0	.205
Henry Erickson	C	8	28	1	5		0	1	0			0	.179
Larry Merville	OF	7	29	3	6		0	0	0			0	.205

PITCHERS		W	L	PCT	G	GS	CG	SH	IP	H	BB	SO	ERA
Ken Penner		17	8	.680	33				218	229	56	64	4.17
Robert Weiland		11	8	.579	28				171	191	82	95	3.90
Clyde Hatter		11	12	.478	31				164	204	70	81	4.66
Guy Williams		8	5	.615	49				167	207	75	61	5.01
Joe DeBerry		8	14	.364	41				215	265	28	53	4.31
John Marcum		8	14	.364	35				168	229	56	64	5.63
Roy Wilkinson		2	6	.250	32				95	120	36	23	4.55
Phil Weinert		1	11	.083	25				109	153	33	62	6.11

TOLEDO   8th   68-100   .405   -36.5   Casey Stengel
Mud Hens

BATTERS	POS-GAMES	GP	AB	R	H	BI	2B	3B	HR	BB	SO	SB	BA
Ernie Wingard	1B117,P15	141	507	90	155	98	29	13	18	50	62	1	.306
Greg Mulleavy	2B118,SS34	153	569	76	168	81	31	7	2	35	24	17	.295
Bill Knickerbocker	SS66,3B28	108	389	50	110	36	21	5	2	14	27	6	.283
Horace Koehler	3B		(see multi-team players)										
John Cooney	OF64,P25,1B24	117	342	46	99	29	19	2	3	21	12	2	.289
Fred Walker	OF52	58	228	33	69	31	10	2	4	22	14	8	.303
Bruno Haas	OF		(see multi-team players)										
Al DeVormer	C90	98	329	34	95	40	13	4	2	14	20	9	.289
Jack Smith	1B45,2B25,3B20	94	326	77	117	44	20	9	3	37	13	11	.359
Bill Werber	3B29,SS27	59	221	34	61		4	4	4			11	.276
Melbern Simons	OF52	52	225	36	80	34	10	0	4	6	15	7	.356
LeRoy Bachman	P31,OF14	50	94	10	19		2	1	0			0	.202
Alex Nigro	OF45	48	142	14	39		6	5	1			1	.275
Walt Henline	C42	44	159	22	43		8	3	0			3	.270
Norm Kies	C41	42	150	13	40		7	0	2			0	.267
James Sweeney	SS21,3B12	38	124	10	27		3	1	0			1	.218
Wilfred Ryan	P37	37	78	3	13		0	0	0			0	.167
William Rabb	P33	33	41	0	3		0	0	0			0	.073
Elam Vangilder	P29	31	56	9	13		1	0	0			0	.232
Clarke Pittenger	SS29	30	111	7	36		3	0	0			0	.324
George Connally	P21	22	60	6	15		4	0	0			0	.250
John Tate	P14	19	17	2	4		0	0	0			0	.235
Alex Ferguson	P16	16	14	2	6		2	1	0			0	.429
John Scott	P12	15	21	1	6		0	0	1			0	.286
William Eissler	P15	15	16	1	2		0	0	0			0	.125
Milt Shoffner	P11	13	19	3	4		0	0	2			1	.211
Richard Stahlman	C	6	19	2	3	1	3	0	0	0	0	0	.158
Casey Stengel	OF	3	11	0	4	2	2	0	0			0	.364
James Richardson	P2	2	0	0	0		0	0	0			0	----
John Ward	C1	1	1	1	0		0	0	0			0	.000

PITCHERS		W	L	PCT	G	GS	CG	SH	IP	H	BB	SO	ERA
George Connally		12	5	.706	21				159	165	50	66	3.29
John Cooney		10	7	.588	25				166	172	36	55	2.49
Wilfred Ryan		9	17	.346	37				211	250	35	68	4.14
Ernie Wingard		7	7	.500	15				118	153	39	25	5.34
Elam Vangilder		5	9	.357	29				135	157	87	99	4.87
LeRoy Bachman		4	15	.211	31				138	189	64	43	6.07
John Scott		3	2	.600	12				48	59	23	13	3.75
William Eissler		2	1	.667	15				45	54	31	14	5.60
Alex Ferguson		2	7	.222	16				45	72	14	11	6.60
William Rabb		2	10	.167	33				134	169	67	35	6.18
John Tate		1	3	.250	14				38	61	19	7	
Milt Shoffner		1	6	.143	11				56	70	24	13	6.43
James Richardson		0	0	----	1				3	6	5	3	

MULTI-TEAM PLAYERS

BATTERS	POS-GAMES	TEAMS	GP	AB	R	H	BI	2B	3B	HR	BB	SO	SB	BA
Bill Narlesky	3B104,SS31,2B29	IND-COL	164	660	110	195	114	38	6	12	48	49	15	.295
Horace Koehler	3B112,OF47	TOL-MIL	158	619	83	168	80	28	7	3	39	21	12	.271
Peter Monohan	1B137	IND-KC	143	541	90	163	83	26	8	6	60	44	8	.301
Ray Fitzgerald	OF132	KC-IND	140	493	105	161	100	24	9	11	45	39	14	.327
Bruno Haas	OF125	TOL-MIN	138	488	65	139	73	26	2	6	36	28	3	.285
Fred Bedore	1B48,2B43,3B38	COL-IND	134	478	74	142	59	30	8	2	35	33	9	.297
Bevo LeBourveau	OF112	TOL-COL	114	440	89	165	83	33	6	12	42	36	23	.375
Merv Shea	C88	MIL-LOU	97	267	39	71	32	21	1	2	31	38	0	.266
Art Ruble	OF88	TOL-MIN	93	343	65	112	79	21	6	17	24	23	7	.327
E. Turgeon	2B78	MIL-TOL	90	318	38	90	43	10	3	2	15	29	4	.283
Elmer Yoter	3B83	COL-IND	89	342	71	103	40	16	3	2	32	22	10	.301
Charles High	OF68	MIN-IND	84	249	44	73	58	13	2	14	36	13	0	.293
Eugene Moore	OF46	MIN-LOU	58	169	34	52	31	9	6	4	9	14	0	.308
Ed Walsh	P46	LOU-MIN	53	66	8	20		3	0	1			0	.303
Mike Cvengros	P37	IND-COL	48	86	10	22		3	1	1			1	.256
Archie Campbell	P41	COL-IND	41	67	6	11		1	0	0			0	.164
Tom Sheehan	P39	KC-MIN	41	35	6	8		0	1	1			0	.229
Carl Mays	P32	TOL-LOU	37	87	13	18		1	0	2			0	.207
Deland Wetherell	P37	COL-TOL	37	51	6	14		2	1	0			0	.275
Russ Miller	P29	COL-IND-COL	31	30	4	7		0	0	0			0	.233
Frank Miller	P21	MIL-MIN	21	20	2	2		0	0	0			2	.100

MULTI-TEAM PLAYERS (cont.)

BATTERS	POS-GAMES	TEAMS	GP	AB	R	H	BI	2B	3B	HR	BB	SO	SB	BA
Ben Tincup	P14	MIN-LOU	15	13	4	3		1	0	0			0	.231

PITCHERS	TEAMS	W	L	PCT	G	GS	CG	SH	IP	H	BB	SO	ERA
Archie Campbell	COL-IND	13	15	.464	41				195	221	110	63	4.90
Carl Mays	TOL-LOU	11	15	.423	32				204	248	54	54	4.32
Mike Cvengros	IND-COL	10	10	.500	37				191	222	72	58	5.23
Ed Walsh	LOU-MIN	8	15	.348	46				184	277	68	90	7.05
Deland Wetherell	COL-TOL	7	13	.350	37				158	210	57	57	5.53
Frank Miller	MIL-MIN	5	3	.625	21				66	98	29	8	6.54
Russ Miller	COP-IND-COL	4	2	.667	29				95	133	25	19	5.30
Tom Sheehan	KC-MIN	4	9	.308	39				116	161	44	52	5.98
Greenfield	LOU-IND	2	1	.667	5				16	23	6	2	
Ben Tincup	MIN-LOU	1	4	.200	14				28	33	18	6	

TEAM BATTING

TEAMS	GP	AB	R	H	BI	2B	3B	HR	BB	SO	SB	BA
ST. PAUL	167	6059	1072	**1885**		**345**	75	**167**	506	536	121	**.311**
KANSAS CITY	170	6147	1030	1852		314	**115**	80	556	531	107	.301
INDIANAPOLIS	167	6015	1045	1819		306	79	107	583	484	77	.303
COLUMBUS	168	6078	1080	1843		327	92	108	537	529	**150**	.303
MILWAUKEE	**171**	**6217**	1020	1852		307	73	126	575	**610**	118	.302
MINNEAPOLIS	168	6027	**1103**	1836		322	63	152	**627**	522	123	.305
LOUISVILLE	169	5929	829	1686		279	71	66	459	470	71	.285
TOLEDO	168	5980	841	1740		295	71	68	446	482	118	.291
	674	48452	8020	14513		2495	639	874	4289	4164	885	.300

1932
LeRoy Parmelee

Some American Association pitching records are set by players with long and storied careers. Others are set by one-season phenoms. The record set by one pitcher falls into neither category. Although he had a lengthy baseball career, he set his record in a short span of 18 games. This pitcher's name was LeRoy Parmelee.

LeRoy Parmelee's career started in 1927 in the lower minors, continuing to the Toledo Mud Hens in 1929. After a respectable 12–14 record for a last place team, he was called up to the New York Giants late in the season, where he would stay off and on for the next three years. Midway through the 1932 season, he rejoined the American Association, this time with the Columbus Red Birds. In the brief span of 18 games, Parmelee won 14 of 15 decisions to establish an Association single season winning percentage record of .933. (Note: some sources show the winning percentage leader to be Ben Tincup, who went 9–0 in 1921, but since all percentage leaders catalogued in league play have had at least 11 decisions, Tincup appears to be ineligible.)

Minneapolis, after a 17-year absence, returned to the top spot in 1932. Riding the crest of a 188–home run barrage, the Millers bested LeRoy Parmelee's Red Birds by 10 1/2 games, and Milwaukee by 11. Toledo rose from last to fourth, while Indianapolis, Kansas City, St. Paul and Louisville finished in the second division. The best batter, for the second time, was Minneapolis outfielder Art Ruble, who won with the exact same figure (.376) as his first title in 1929. His teammate Joe Hauser won the home run title (49), while a third Miller, Foster Ganzel, had the most runs batted in with 143. Miller pitcher Wilfred Ryan won the most games (22), while Paul Dean of Columbus had the most strikeouts (169). (Note: For all but a handful of pitchers, no official earned run averages were calculated for 1932 because no official box scores from Columbus were sent to the statisticians. With an unofficial mark of 2.38 [calculated by the author], LeRoy Parmelee would appear to have won the title.)

Parmelee returned to the New York Giants in 1933, staying for another three years before joining the Cardinals and later the Cubs. After another good year in the Association for Minneapolis, Parmelee had a last fling in the majors for the Athletics, before winding down his career with two years for Louisville.

Of all the records set in the early years of the American Association, LeRoy Parmelee's .933 winning percentage would be one of the few broken. Some 60 years after Parmelee won 14 of 15, another Association pitcher, Chris Hammond, would best him by winning 15 of 16, thus setting a new record of .938.

MINNEAPOLIS   1st   100-68   .595   Donie Bush
Millers

BATTERS	POS-GAMES	GP	AB	R	H	BI	2B	3B	HR	BB	SO	SB	BA
Joe Hauser	1B143	149	522	132	158	129	31	3	**49**			12	.303
Andy Cohen	2B93	93	420	66	122	41	16	3	1			0	.290
Ernest Smith	SS164	164	636	108	202	111	56	10	7			25	.318
Foster Ganzel	3B159	163	633	120	197	**143**	46	3	23			4	.311
Joe Mowry	OF167	**168**	**739**	**175**	**257**	98	48	11	19			5	.348
Art Ruble	OF133	141	561	126	211	141	25	11	29			7	**.376**
Harry Rice	OF98	117	391	82	135	55	15	3	11			6	.345
Wes Griffin	C74	96	276	32	78	43	19	1	6			0	.283
Spence Harris	OF96,1B21	129	469	125	165	113	33	7	17			5	.352
Richards	C74	78	269	45	97	69	14	3	16			1	.361
Ed Sicking	2B63	84	262	50	72	15	4	2	0			8	.275
Wilfred Ryan	P60	60	71	8	18	4	2	0	0			0	.254
Jesse Petty	P52	52	88	5	9	5	1	0	0			0	.102
Hy Vandenberg	P36	44	79	11	14	11	4	0	1			0	.177
Hugh McMullen	C41	42	114	16	27	14	5	2	1			0	.237
Hensiek	P40	42	42	7	7	3	1	0	0			0	.167
Clyde Day	P37	37	51	6	6	6	0	0	1			0	.118
John Benton	P35	35	90	5	10	7	0	0	0			0	.111
Flowers	2B14	23	76	9	16	14	4	0	1			1	.211
John Brillheart	P21	21	14	1	3	0	0	0	0			0	.214
Frank Henry	P10	12	24	2	5	3	1	0	1			0	.208
BillWilson	P10	11	10	2	2	2	0	0	0			0	.200
Rodda		10	26	2	7	2	0	0	0			0	.269
Ad Liska	P8	8	6	0	0		0	0	0				.000
Charles Dressen	3B	4	2	2	1		1	0	0				.500
Al Wright	OF	4	2	0	1		1	0	0				.500
Ray Phelps	P4	4	1	2	0		0	0	0				.000
John Poser		3	1	1	0		0	0	0				.000
Joe Genewich	P1	1	1	0	0		0	0	0				.000

PITCHERS		W	L	PCT	G	GS	CG	SH	IP	H	BB	SO	ERA
Wilfred Ryan		**22**	13	.629	**60**				196	215	71	54	
John Benton		18	7	.720	35				220	281	58	50	
Jesse Petty		16	10	.615	52				236	287	39	116	
Hy Vandenberg		11	6	.647	36				199	233	87	99	
Clyde Day		9	8	.529	37				145	230	44	54	
Hensiek		6	5	.545	40				118	151	67	49	
John Brillheart		3	1	.750	21				55	70	29	23	
Frank Henry		2	4	.333	10				56	87	15	23	
Frank Miller		1	0	1.000	5				19	26	6	2	3.32
Ad Liska		1	2	.333	9				28	46	8	5	6.11
Bill Wilson		0	1	.000	10				28	33	16	11	
Ray Phelps		0	2	.000	4				9	19	6	5	16.00
Joe Genewich		0	0	----	1				4	8	1	0	0.00

COLUMBUS   2nd   88-77   .533   -10.5   Leibold - Southworth
Red Birds

BATTERS	POS-GAMES	GP	AB	R	H	BI	2B	3B	HR	BB	SO	SB	BA
Cliff Crawford	1B160	160	640	116	236	140	34	5	30			14	.369
Burgess Whitehead	2B156	162	675	115	211	66	36	9	1			39	.313
Ossie Bluege	SS106	110	392	51	116	40	18	3	1			7	.296
Lew Riggs	3B154	162	588	89	172	102	32	10	20			13	.293
Ernest Swanson	OF150	151	619	128	232	131	50	18	9			**45**	.375
Nick Cullop	OF112	128	442	97	154	99	37	4	26			8	.348
Bevo LeBourveau	OF86	93	348	69	108	57	24	3	9			16	.310
Joe Sprinz	C74	84	257	33	67	24	10	2	2			3	.261
Harold Anderson	OF68	69	283	42	88	22	14	2	1			5	.311
Clarke	SS24,3B14	47	143	34	40	16	4	2	3			1	.280
George Rensa	C38	46	151	20	42	13	6	2	0			3	.278
Bill Lee	P42	45	101	12	29	15	6	0	1			0	.287
Fran Healy	C39	44	144	24	50	30	4	3	3			4	.347
George Selkirk	OF32	41	128	18	28	28	4	0	7			5	.219
Al Grabowski	P38	41	64	9	11	5	0	1	1			0	.172
Paul Dean	P40	40	78	7	24	4	1	0	0			0	.308
Ken Ash	P38	39	49	7	16	8	4	0	0			1	.327
Fred Blake	P34	37	64	7	10	3	0	0	0			1	.156
Joel Hunt	OF24	29	85	25	23	4	3	1	1			4	.271
Carey	SS20	20	68	9	13	8	0	2	1			0	.191
LeRoy Parmelee	P18	20	48	5	12	7	3	1	1			0	.250
Parker	OF18	19	65	10	18	10	2	2	0			1	.277

COLUMBUS (cont.)
Red Birds

BATTERS	POS-GAMES	GP	AB	R	H	BI	2B	3B	HR	BB	SO	SB	BA
Bilgere	SS13	18	45	4	11	9	2	1	0			0	.244
Ken O'Dea	C14	17	42	3	15	5	3	0	0			0	.357
Goodman	OF13	13	42	11	14	8	1	2	3			1	.333
Earl Webb		11	25	1	2	1	0	0	0			0	.080
W. Miller	P11	11	18	3	5	4	1	0	0			0	.278
Gordon Hinkle		10	26	6	8	6	0	1	1			0	.308
Harold King		10	19	5	8	6	0	1	1			1	.421
Harlan Wysong	P6	10	13	2	2	0	0	0	0			0	.154
Ray Mondron	OF	8	25	5	7	5	1	0	2				.280
Keane	SS	8	22	2	4		1	0	0				.182
Holm	SS	7	23	5	7		2	0	0				.304
Harry Leibold	OF	6	6	0	0		0	0	0				.000
Robert Klinger	P5	5	2	0	0		0	0	0				.000
William Beckman	P5	5	2	0	0		0	0	0				.000
Thomas West	C	3	9	2	2		0	0	0				.222
Moore	OF	3	7	1	0	1	0	0	0				.000
Clise Dudley	P3	3	6	2	2	1	1	0	0				.333
Billy Southworth	OF	3	6	0	1	0	0	0	0			0	.167
James Lyons	P3	3	5	0	1		0	0	0				.200
Ward Cross	P2	2	7	1	1	1	1	0	0				.143
Moxley	OF	2	4	0	1		0	0	0				.250
Harold Bohl	3B1	1	6	1	1		0	0	0				.167
Chapman	P1	1	3	0	1		0	0	0				.333
Seldon Bryant	P1	1	3	0	0		0	0	0				.000
Sparks	3B1	1	1	0	0		0	0	0				.000

PITCHERS	W	L	PCT	G	GS	CG	SH	IP	H	BB	SO	ERA
Bill Lee	20	9	.690	42				255	263	115	150	
LeRoy Parmelee	14	1	.933	18				119	92	50	102	
Ken Ash	10	9	.526	38				139	143	57	58	
Fred Blake	9	7	.563	34				161	184	92	56	
Al Grabowski	9	11	.450	38				173	205	69	90	
Paul Dean	7	16	.304	40				212	191	113	169	
Ward Cross	2	0	1.000	2				17	15	10	3	
Harlan Wysong	2	1	.667	6				23	37	13	5	7.83
Walter Miller	1	1	.500	11				46	48	17	11	
William Beckman	1	1	.500	5				9	10	5	3	
Robert Klinger	0	1	.000	5				9	12	3	8	
James Lyons	0	1	.000	3				17	23	2	5	
Seldon Bryant	0	1	.000	1				8	6	5	4	
Don Whittenburg	0	1	.000	1				2	4	3	0	
Clise Dudley	0	2	.000	3				11	19	8	2	12.27
Chapman	0	0	----	2				9	10	8	3	

MILWAUKEE   3rd   88-78   .530   -11   Frank O'Rourke
Brewers

BATTERS	POS-GAMES	GP	AB	R	H	BI	2B	3B	HR	BB	SO	SB	BA
George Stanton	1B161	164	667	131	194	89	36	16	6			16	.291
M. Connolly	2B165	165	657	111	190	84	26	4	14			18	.289
Jack Tavener	SS163	164	652	113	177	53	19	11	4			6	.271
Horace Koehler	3B142	152	571	79	167	91	27	4	8			5	.292
Alex Metzler	OF158	159	587	107	189	106	42	8	14			11	.322
Christensen	OF117	120	428	78	139	74	23	4	5			12	.325
Ted Gullic	OF113,1B10	141	491	117	174	123	25	6	27			9	.354
Russ Young	C90	105	336	39	98	51	16	5	4			2	.292
Jack Crouch	C78	94	258	38	82	33	11	7	3			4	.318
Clarence Hoffman	OF64	79	244	44	86	62	20	2	5			3	.352
Anton Kubek	OF48	66	175	27	56	27	7	4	3			4	.320
H. Hillin	P50	50	96	5	22	10	1	1	0			.0	.229
Caldwell	P44	48	113	16	27	25	2	1	5			1	.239
Garland Braxton	P48	48	45	2	2	0	0	0	0			1	.044
Frank O'Rourke	3B27	43	139	21	38	12	3	0	0			1	.273
Fred Stiely	P41	42	96	9	24	16	4	0	1			1	.250
Jack Knott	P39	39	80	4	4	4	0	0	0			0	.050
Fisher	OF34	36	122	28	44	21	8	3	2			4	.361
Larry Kessenich	P32	35	16	4	4	2	2	0	0			0	.250
Lou Polli	P27	28	60	8	10	3	0	0	0			0	.167
Al Bool	C16	19	56	5	11	7	1	0	0			0	.196
Rollie Stiles	P15	15	19	2	4	1	0	0	0			0	.211
Martin Nelson	P10	10	7	1	2	2	0	0	0			0	.286

MILWAUKEE (cont.)
Brewers

BATTERS	POS-GAMES	GP	AB	R	H	BI	2B	3B	HR	BB	SO	SB	BA
McNeely	OF	4	3	1	0		0	0	0				.000
George Gerken	OF	2	5	0	0		0	0	0				.000
Seitz	SS1	1	1	0	0		0	0	0				.000
Harold Wiltse	P1	1	0	0	0		0	0	0				----

PITCHERS		W	L	PCT	G	GS	CG	SH	IP	H	BB	SO	ERA
Fred Stiely		17	12	.586	41				243	294	122	78	
Jack Knott		17	12	.586	39				238	258	73	106	
H. Hillin		15	15	.500	50				254	332	99	59	
Lou Polli		14	6	.700	27				168	181	52	59	
Caldwell		14	17	.452	44				271	358	93	68	
Garland Braxton		8	11	.421	48				152	182	49	90	
Larry Kessenich		1	0	1.000	32				64	80	38	19	
Martin Nelson		1	0	1.000	10				28	38	8	15	
Rollie Stiles		1	5	.167	16				60	97	25	28	
Harold Wiltse		0	0	----	1				1	4	2	0	20.30

TOLEDO
Mud Hens

4th   87-80   .521   -12.5   Bibb Falk

BATTERS	POS-GAMES	GP	AB	R	H	BI	2B	3B	HR	BB	SO	SB	BA
Bill Sweeney	1B148	148	608	97	187	81	37	13	2			8	.308
E. Turgeon	2B144	152	582	69	151	46	23	8	1			8	.259
Bill Knickerbocker	SS160	160	697	116	234	70	69	8	5			7	.336
Odell Hale	3B158	158	618	110	206	110	36	22	7			15	.333
Max West	OF146	151	583	77	181	109	32	9	4			3	.310
Ellis Powers	OF118	121	482	104	179	72	34	11	10			4	.371
Ward	OF106	117	396	66	109	56	14	3	5			14	.275
Walt Henline	C76	89	294	35	74	48	14	4	2			2	.252
Bibb Falk	OF68	79	246	42	79	46	11	5	5			1	.321
White	2B30,3B15	63	174	26	39	17	8	0	0			2	.224
Ralph Winegarner	P35	63	119	27	41	33	4	1	11			0	.345
Pytlak	C53	54	179	33	58	32	9	4	2			3	.324
Milt Galatzer	OF44	48	165	30	59	30	5	6	1			7	.358
Steve O'Neill	C41	44	131	13	34	16	7	2	2			0	.260
Roxie Lawson	P39	43	87	8	16	4	0	1	0			1	.184
Howard Craghead	P41	41	85	5	11	3	0	0	0			0	.129
Belve Bean	P38	39	121	15	28	15	5	1	1			1	.231
Forrest Twogood	P26	31	60	6	17	9	1	0	0			1	.283
J. Moore	P31	31	45	5	9	2	0	0	0			0	.200
Monte Pearson	P21	26	45	3	9	2	0	1	0			0	.200
Hudson		18	22	3	5	1	0	0	0			0	.227
Al DeVormer	C10	11	35	3	10	7	1	1	0			1	.286
William Rabb	P11	11	4	0	1	1	0	0	0			0	.250
Lester Burke	2B	7	16	2	4	1	0	0	0	2			.250
Thornton Lee	P7	7	13	1	1	1	0	0	0				.077
Leo Moon	P7	7	12	0	3	1	1	0	0				.250
Hugh Wise	C	3	2	1	0		0	0	0	1			.000
LeRoy Bachman	P2	2	3	0	0		0	0	0		2		.000
Hal Trosky	OF	2	1	1	1		0	0	0				1.000
Leon Rhodes	P1	1	1	0	0		0	0	0				.000

PITCHERS		W	L	PCT	G	GS	CG	SH	IP	H	BB	SO	ERA
Belve Bean		20	14	.588	38				304	334	56	116	
Howard Craghead		18	15	.545	41				253	292	98	112	
Roxie Lawson		12	11	.522	39				233	272	100	67	
Ralph Winegarner		11	7	.611	35				116	113	58	73	
Forrest Twogood		10	6	.625	26				131	148	84	75	
J. Moore		6	8	.429	31				136	213	37	34	
Monte Pearson		3	9	.250	21				124	122	55	82	
William Rabb		1	0	1.000	11				28	38	12	9	
Thornton Lee		1	3	.250	8				38	49	19	14	
Leo Moon		0	3	.000	7				32	45	3	7	
LeRoy Bachman		0	0	----	2				7	10	4	2	6.14
Leon Rhodes		0	0	----	1				3	2	3	0	2.70

INDIANAPOLIS Indians

5th 86-80 .518 -13 Emmett McCann

BATTERS	POS-GAMES	GP	AB	R	H	BI	2B	3B	HR	BB	SO	SB	BA
Ernie Wingard	1B85,P18	116	391	76	134	75	21	15	13			2	.343
Frank Sigafoos	2B154,3B10	163	635	105	199	77	29	11	10			14	.313
Jonah Goldman	SS135	136	508	85	137	44	20	4	1			2	.270
S. Hale	3B100	104	421	56	128	63	28	1	1			4	.304
Harry Rosenberg	OF138	144	516	69	164	79	27	6	7			6	.318
Doug Taitt	OF135	137	526	70	158	89	29	11	9			9	.300
Ray Fitzgerald	OF	(see multi-team players)											
John Riddle	C104	109	346	34	98	41	26	0	3			5	.283
Tom Angley	C82	95	283	45	88	46	15	3	9			9	.311
Cooney	P37,1B20	78	175	29	51	21	9	0	0			2	.291
Emmett McCann	1B54	69	221	37	73	26	12	5	1			5	.330
Everett Purdy	OF49	61	172	22	47	30	8	5	1			1	.273
Joe Heving	P49	51	73	14	27	5	5	1	0			0	.370
Archie Campbell	P46	46	77	2	8	5	2	0	0			0	.104
Kroner	3B40	40	154	35	53	35	13	3	4			1	.344
Irwin Hufft	OF35	38	133	15	31	21	10	2	2			0	.233
Fred Bedore	3B20	37	121	19	29	16	7	2	1			2	.240
Chapman	OF27	33	99	15	31	12	2	1	3			1	.313
Bill Thomas	P25	27	57	5	11	0	2	0	0			0	.193
Stewart Bolen	P26	26	47	7	12	8	1	0	1			0	.255
Bill Burwell	P24	24	52	7	16	5	4	0	0			0	.308
Leslie Barnhart	P21	22	32	5	3	6	0	1	0			0	.094
Ray White	SS16	16	57	5	13	2	1	0	0			1	.228
Robert Logan	P15	15	19	2	5	0	0	0	0			0	.263
Edwin Lowell	1B13	13	44	6	16	7	1	3	0			1	.364
John Berly	P10	10	20	4	4	5	1	0	1			1	.200
James Crawford	OF	9	28	1	5	3	1	0	0				.179
Peter Daglia	P9	9	24	1	4	3	0	0	1				.167
George Smith	P7	7	5	0	0		0	0	0				.000
Berly Horne	P4	4	2	0	0		0	0	0		1		.000
Roy Carlyle	OF	2	8	0	2		0	0	0				.250
Gueisser	C1	1	2	0	1		0	0	0				.500
Al Butzberger	P1	1	2	0	0		0	0	0				.000
Robert Wolf	P1	1	1	0	1		0	0	0				1.000
McDonald	P1	1	0	0	0		0	0	0				----

PITCHERS	W	L	PCT	G	GS	CG	SH	IP	H	BB	SO	ERA
Joe Heving	15	9	.625	49				173	180	59	91	
Bill Thomas	12	6	.667	25				157	148	28	58	
Cooney	10	6	.625	37				174	205	40	71	
Archie Campbell	10	19	.345	46				234	233	103	146	
Wingard	7	7	.500	18				111	122	37	43	
Stewart Bolen	7	11	.389	26				129	159	62	74	
Leslie Barnhart	5	5	.500	21				94	111	39	48	
Bill Burwell	5	8	.385	24				141	170	39	31	
John Berly	4	1	.800	10				54	58	40	31	
Peter Daglia	4	3	.571	9				57	58	24	31	
Robert Logan	2	1	.667	15				52	61	21	29	
Berlyn Horne	1	0	1.000	4				10	12	4	4	5.40
Al Butzberger	1	0	1.000	1				6	5	3	2	
George Smith	0	1	.000	7				18	30	4	4	
Robert Wolf	0	0	----	1				4	2	0	2	0.00
Prentice Hall	0	0	----	1				2	2	1	2	
McDonald	0	0	----	1				1	4	0	2	27.00

KANSAS CITY Blues

6th 81-86 .485 -18.5 Dutch Zwilling

BATTERS	POS-GAMES	GP	AB	R	H	BI	2B	3B	HR	BB	SO	SB	BA
Peter Monohan	1B145	145	522	79	156	86	27	4	7			15	.299
Al Marquardt	2B141,3B13	155	681	107	197	51	31	10	1			17	.289
Robert Boken	SS120,3B39	161	642	95	180	113	26	9	5			19	.280
Ray Treadaway	3B96	114	406	74	130	51	21	12	3			11	.320
Ed Pick	OF163	163	616	111	212	121	39	15	7			8	.344
Denver Grigsby	OF147	152	556	105	173	75	31	9	1			19	.311
Herb Kelly	OF98	116	382	60	113	49	23	8	5			23	.296
Pat Collins	C93	105	291	47	78	48	14	3	4			4	.268
Jim Mosolf	OF95	96	362	61	108	50	17	8	4			9	.298
Hassler	3B29,2B13	74	239	31	62	29	8	3	0			4	.259
M. Snyder	C61	74	227	24	60	30	11	3	2			3	.264

KANSAS CITY (cont.)
Blues

BATTERS	POS-GAMES	GP	AB	R	H	BI	2B	3B	HR	BB	SO	SB	BA
Lou Fette	P46	47	113	13	34	15	5	3	0			0	.301
Ed Taylor	SS43	43	174	40	56	19	8	4	2			2	.322
Harold Smith	P37	37	74	1	13	8	1	0	0			0	.176
HaroldCarson	P34	37	60	7	13	12	0	2	2			0	.217
Dunlap	1B20,OF11	33	109	15	31	23	4	0	1			1	.284
John Tising	P30	30	58	8	20	11	2	2	0			0	.345
Joe Dawson	P27	27	70	8	26	9	6	0	0			1	.371
M. Thomas	P25	27	23	2	4	2	1	1	0			0	.174
Phillips	C23	26	79	15	21	13	2	2	4			1	.266
William Bayne	P18	18	24	3	7	1	0	0	0			0	.292
Pember	2B13	14	56	8	16	6	0	1	0			1	.286
Frank Gabler	P13	14	27	3	7	4	1	2	0			0	.259
Joe Blackwell	P7	7	17	2	2	2	0	0	0				.118
Ralph Birkofer	P3	3	11	3	5	3	3	0	0				.455
Glen Larson	P3	3	1	0	0		0	0	0				.000
Ray Davis	P3	3	0	0	0		0	0	0				----

PITCHERS		W	L	PCT	G	GS	CG	SH	IP	H	BB	SO	ERA
Hal Smith		17	8	.680	37				205	218	55	75	
Lou Fette		15	18	.455	46				282	348	72	81	
Harold Carson		11	8	.579	34				147	202	41	36	
Joe Dawson		11	10	.524	27				172	192	59	55	
John Tising		5	12	.294	30				153	168	64	68	
Joe Blackwell		3	2	.600	7				40	38	25	24	
Frank Gabler		3	6	.333	13				58	73	31	18	
Frank Birkofer		2	1	.667	3				24	14	6	11	
Bayne		2	3	.400	18				72	95	26	23	
M. Thomas		1	5	.167	25				77	101	25	29	
Glen Larson		0	0	----	3				4	8	6	3	14.55
Ray Davis		0	0	----	3				3	2	0	0	0.00

ST. PAUL
Saints

7th 70-97 .419 -29.5 Al Leifield

BATTERS	POS-GAMES	GP	AB	R	H	BI	2B	3B	HR	BB	SO	SB	BA
Phil Todt	1B168	168	697	95	194	115	38	20	14			4	.278
Irv Jeffries	2B152	166	690	106	213	82	52	8	20			7	.309
Clyde Beck	SS150	151	496	50	106	57	15	10	6			3	.214
Hopkins	3B167	167	608	91	158	83	20	4	17			2	.260
Fred Koster	OF147	152	621	112	197	52	32	11	5			6	.317
Ben Paschal	OF137	147	591	97	192	89	37	11	14			9	.325
Willis Norman	OF131	139	496	85	154	93	29	3	23			5	.310
Robert Fenner	C98	122	358	52	118	63	25	6	7			1	.330
Cedric Durst	OF100	117	408	53	128	49	16	11	6			4	.314
Guilliani	C50	80	196	20	54	22	3	2	2			1	.276
Frank Snyder	C49	59	158	14	41	18	10	0	1			0	.259
Russ Van Atta	P51	58	116	13	24	12	6	0	0			0	.207
Paul Wanninger	SS44	54	102	7	18	5	4	0	0			2	.176
Adkins	P53	53	52	1	9	2	0	1	0			0	.173
Ed Strelecki	P48	51	87	9	14	7	2	2	0			0	.161
Bryan Harriss	P50	50	119	4	17	10	5	0	0			0	.143
Les Munns	P45	49	104	10	23	16	4	3	1			0	.221
Reese	2B17	25	61	10	12	5	2	2	1			0	.197
Eugene Trow	P19	19	42	3	8	4	1	0	0			0	.190
Oswald Orwoll	P5	12	15	2	5	0	0	1	0			0	.333
Lou McEvoy	P8	8	10	1	2	0	0	0	0	0	1	0	.200
Harold Elliott	P6	6	2	0	0	0	0	0	0	0	1	0	.000
William McWilliams	3B1	1	1	0	0	0	0	0	0	0	0	0	.000

PITCHERS		W	L	PCT	G	GS	CG	SH	IP	H	BB	SO	ERA
Russ Van Atta		22	17	.564	51				303	318	123	129	
Bryan Harriss		13	22	.371	50				310	355	134	105	
Les Munns		11	16	.407	45				260	293	147	115	
Ed Strelecki		10	17	.370	48				243	289	99	48	
Adkins		9	9	.500	53				169	221	54	48	
EugeneTrow		3	5	.375	19				101	108	80	63	
Lou McEvoy		1	6	.143	7				30	41	12	3	
Harold Elliott		0	1	.000	6				15	16	9	3	
Oswald Orwoll		0	1	.000	5				18	41	7	5	

LOUISVILLE Colonels

	8th	67-101	.399	-33	Bruno Betzel

BATTERS	POS-GAMES	GP	AB	R	H	BI	2B	3B	HR	BB	SO	SB	BA
Dud Branom	1B168	168	652	71	177	110	27	6	17			3	.271
James Adair	2B126,SS11	149	553	83	177	72	25	12	7			27	.320
Joe Olivares	SS161	161	654	92	179	54	20	5	1			16	.274
Art Funk	3B140	145	552	78	172	67	23	14	6			6	.312
Herman Layne	OF145	150	557	91	168	56	23	9	2			41	.302
Melbern Simons	OF143	147	608	77	191	80	21	8	3			8	.314
Art Weis	OF130	137	470	77	120	74	26	5	11			0	.255
Merv Shea	C106	114	355	43	98	38	16	0	4			1	.276
Clarence Nachand	OF82	97	282	39	71	25	14	4	4			4	.252
John Marcum	P34,OF18	84	175	24	57	26	12	1	5			1	.325
Henry Erickson	C66	81	236	42	71	31	9	6	1			1	.301
Ken Penner	P40	47	108	5	26	12	1	0	1			0	.241
Archie McKain	P41	44	85	3	13	8	0	1	1			0	.153
Fred Maguire	2B40	40	145	20	33	9	7	4	0			3	.228
Claude Jonnard	P40	40	82	11	13	10	3	1	1			0	.159
Roy Wilkinson	P30	30	35	5	6	3	2	1	0			0	.171
Clyde Hatter	P29	29	38	2	4	4	0	0	0			0	.105
Lester Bell	3B24	24	88	5	23	10	2	1	1			1	.261
Joe DeBerry	P24	24	31	8	7	0	0	0	0			0	.226
Sharpe	P20	20	16	1	2	2	1	0	0			0	.125
Richard Bass	P17	17	25	3	5	1	0	0	1			0	.200
Kron		15	25	3	3	1	0	0	0			1	.120
Eldon McLean	P12	12	20	1	4	0	2	0	0			0	.200
Liz Funk	OF8	8	32	8	8	2	1	0	0	6	1	0	.250
Moore	C	8	3	0	0		0	0	0		1		.000
Louis Russell	OF	6	19	3	4	2	0	0	1				.211
Ray Thompson	C	4	12	1	4	2	1	1	0			0	.333
Guy Williams	P1	1	1	0	0		0	0	0		1		.000
Irving Cohen	P1	1	0	0	0		0	0	0				----

PITCHERS		W	L	PCT	G	GS	CG	SH	IP	H	BB	SO	ERA
Claude Jonnard		18	15	.545	40				249	294	91	135	
Ken Penner		11	17	.393	40				246	337	42	76	
Archie McKain		9	19	.321	41				247	318	88	80	
John Marcum		8	9	.471	34				130	154	46	85	
Eldon McLean		3	2	.600	12				53	53	30	23	
Joe DeBerry		3	3	.500	24				94	158	19	21	
Roy Wilkinson		3	7	.300	30				98	125	39	33	
Clyde Hatter		3	12	.200	29				116	153	67	65	
Richard Bass		2	6	.250	17				70	96	24	27	
Sharpe		0	5	.000	20				58	87	12	22	
Guy Williams		0	0	----	1				3	3	1	1	2.70
Irving Cohen		0	0	----	1				1	1	1	0	9.00

MULTI-TEAM PLAYERS

BATTERS	POS-GAMES	TEAMS	GP	AB	R	H	BI	2B	3B	HR	BB	SO	SB	BA
Ray Fitzgerald	OF110	IND-MIN	120	436	76	117	57	23	5	11			10	.268
Curtis Walker	OF62	IND-TOL	64	224	41	62	40	16	4	3			3	.277
Leo Norris	3B19,2B14	MIN-IND	46	129	22	34	13	5	2	0			3	.264
Elam Vangilder	P38	TOL-IND-MIN	46	72	5	22	10	1	1	2			0	.306
Fowler	P45	COL-KC	45	66	4	7	0	1	0	0			0	.106
Carmen Hill	P42	COL-MIN	42	63	2	11	4	3	0	0			0	.175
Phil Weinert	P34	LOU-COL	34	58	3	13	8	0	0	0			0	.224
Osborne	P33	KC-COL	34	54	3	14	6	1	1	0			0	.259
Peter Donohue	P9	COL-MIN	10	7	1	1	0	0	0	0			0	.143
Albert Harvin	P7	SP-TOL	7	9	1	2		0	0	0				.222

PITCHERS		TEAMS	W	L	PCT	G	GS	CG	SH	IP	H	BB	SO	ERA
Carmen Hill		COL-MIN	12	13	.480	42				183	252	66	45	
Elam Vangilder		TOL-IND-MIN	11	8	.579	38				160	219	83	88	
Phil Weinert		LOU-COL	11	9	.550	34				162	166	72	86	
Fowler		COL-KC	9	12	.429	45				188	232	52	93	
Osborn		KC-COL	6	8	.429	33				151	185	52	49	
Peter Donohue		COL-MIN	1	0	1.000	9				18	28	8	5	
Albert Harvin		SP-TOL	1	3	.250	7				32	49	17	2	7.31

TEAM BATTING

TEAMS	GP	AB	R	H	BI	2B	3B	HR	BB	SO	SB	BA
MINNEAPOLIS	168	**6054**	**1162**	**1856**		**332**	58	**188**			79	.307
COLUMBUS	166	5899	989	1813		307	74	125			**175**	**.308**
MILWAUKEE	169	5930	992	1745		273	76	101			97	.294
TOLEDO	168	5985	920	1791		318	101	60			80	.299
INDIANAPOLIS	167	5884	881	1721		310	87	77			64	.293
KANSAS CITY	168	5928	930	1745		282	**103**	48			138	.295
ST. PAUL	**169**	6053	839	1692		302	94	117			46	.280
LOUISVILLE	**169**	5908	801	1645		235	80	67			112	.279
	672	47641	7514	14008		2359	673	783			791	.294

1933
Joe Hauser

The cannonade started in April 1933, continuing unabated through the spring and summer, before tapering off in September. When it ended, a baseball-wide record lay shattered, crushed under the mighty onslaught. The man responsible for this carnage was Joe Hauser.

Joe Hauser started his baseball life in Providence with the Eastern League in 1918. After a brief stay with the Association's Milwaukee team, Hauser joined the Philadelphia Athletics for a six-year visit. In 1927, he made another stopover in the Association in Kansas City before an additional two years in the majors. In 1930, Joe Hauser joined the Baltimore Orioles of the International League and proceeded to electrify the baseball world. Previous to this, Hauser had shown moderate power, hitting twenty home runs in three separate seasons. This level was stepped up several notches, as Hauser broke the all-time home run record by clubbing 63.

After two years with the Orioles, Joe Hauser joined the Minneapolis Millers for the 1932 season. Finding tiny Nicollet Park to his liking, Hauser led the Association with 49 home runs. Good as this was, it was only a tune-up for the next year.

Joe Hauser hit four home runs in April 1933; May saw thirteen more; June's total was fifteen; twenty more were hit in July; only ten in August; and finally seven in September. All totalled, Joe Hauser swatted an incredible 69 homers during the 1933 season, the most ever in any league, anywhere.

The Minneapolis Millers, despite being the beneficiaries of Hauser's prowess, only finished a distant second as the Columbus Red Birds flew to their first pennant in more than 25 years. Behind Minneapolis, Indianapolis and St. Paul finished in the first division; while Toledo, Louisville, Milwaukee, and Kansas City occupied the last four rungs. The best hitter was Frank Sigafoos of Indianapolis (.370), while not too surprisingly Joe Hauser knocked in the most runs (182). All the pitching honors were garnered by one man as Paul Dean of the Red Birds won the triple crown by finishing with the most victories (22), lowest earned run average (3.15), and most strikeouts (222).

Joe Hauser went on to play another three, mostly injury filled, years with the Millers, before finishing up with a long stint for Sheboygan in the Wisconsin State League. Hauser's sixty-nine-homer record would stand until the 1950s, when a player in the Longhorn League managed to hit three more. But as an American Association record, Hauser's total has never been approached. For in all the years since 1933, no one has come within spitting distance of a 69–home run season.

COLUMBUS
Red Birds

1st   101-51   .664   Ray Blades

BATTERS	POS-GAMES	GP	AB	R	H	BI	2B	3B	HR	BB	SO	SB	BA
Minor Heath	1B92,P1	92	333	46	77	61	14	5	8	52	55	5	.231
Burgess Whitehead	2B80	89	347	51	120	49	20	6	1	15	11	6	.346
Bernhard Borgmann	SS88	90	377	69	128	29	11	1	2	36	19	28	.340
Lew Riggs	3B148	148	574	90	161	80	26	12	12	41	25	12	.280
Nick Cullop	OF147	150	587	110	184	143	37	22	28	65	131	5	.313
Harold Anderson	OF147	147	629	109	171	62	35	5	3	62	54	32	.272
John Rothrock	OF105,2B21	126	498	96	173	94	26	7	11	40	30	19	.347
Bill Delancey	C119	123	421	81	120	97	17	11	21	62	56	3	.285
Ray Blades	OF48	62	149	35	43	20	9	2	3	25	24	6	.289
Gordon Slade	SS45	45	187	32	66	20	18	7	1	11	20	4	.353
Art Shires	1B44	44	176	35	55	30	12	1	5	16	11	2	.313
Paul Dean	P43	43	94	7	17		3	0	0			0	.181
Charles Wilson	2B41	41	174	37	62	46	7	5	7	12	4	2	.356
Mike Gonzales	C32	39	111	11	36		3	1	1			0	.324
Art Teachout	P34	39	99	12	17	13	4	1	0	6	15	3	.172
Bill Lee	P34	37	92	12	26	12	4	1	0	6	17	0	.283
Clarence Heise	P33	34	82	9	19	13	3	3	1	8	9	0	.232
Ralph Judd	P20	28	49	4	12		0	0	0			0	.245
James Winford	P22	23	56	5	8		0	0	1			0	.143
Bevo LeBourveau	OF19	20	72	10	21		6	1	1			0	.292
Andy High	2B13	20	53	11	18		0	0	0			1	.340
Bill Narlesky	SS11	14	43	6	10		1	1	0			0	.233
Jim Lindsey	P13	13	25	1	5		1	0	0			0	.200
Neil Caldwell	1B10	11	36	2	10		4	0	0			1	.278
Ed Heusser	P9	9	12	1	1		1	0	0		9		.083
Hal Funk	C	5	17	2	2	2	0	0	0				.118
Len Hinchman	2B	5	16	0	4		0	0	0				.250
Fred Blake	P4	5	8	1	3	2	0	0	0	1	1		.375
Phillips Turner	2B	5	6	0	1		0	0	0				.167
Ken Ash	P4	4	6	0	0		0	0	0		1		.000
Ed Chapman	P4	4	4	1	1	2	1	0	0		1		.250
Gilbert	PH	4	3	0	0	0	0	0	0	1	2		.000
John Ward	C	3	7	0	0		0	0	0				.000
Ward Cross	P3	3	1	0	0		0	0	0				.000
Lew Whitehead	OF	2	2	0	0		0	0	0				.000
Thomas West	C	2	1	1	0		0	0	0	1			.000
Osborne	P2	2	0	0	0		0	0	0				----
Joe Sprinz	C1	1	4	0	0		0	0	0				.000

PITCHERS		W	L	PCT	G	GS	CG	SH	IP	H	BB	SO	ERA
Paul Dean		**22**	7	.759	43				254	228	117	**222**	3.15
Bill Lee		21	9	.700	34				252	227	114	141	3.79
Clarence Heise		17	5	**.773**	33				211	212	67	131	3.88
Art Teachout		15	10	.600	34				223	250	64	79	3.79
James Winford		10	6	.625	22				147	151	60	72	3.80
Jim Lindsey		7	2	.778	13				78	75	29	31	3.69
Ralph Judd		5	6	.455	20				97	111	26	39	4.82
Ed Heusser		1	1	.500	9				31	57	21	11	10.18
Ken Ash		1	1	.500	4				16	19	8	5	4.50
Ed Chapman		1	1	.500	4				13	10	10	12	6.23
Fred Blake		1	2	.333	4				25	30	18	18	7.12
Ward Cross		0	1	.000	3				9	8	8	6	7.00
Osborne		0	0	----	2				1	4	0	2	27.00
Minor Heath		0	0	----	1				0	0	0	0	0.00

MINNEAPOLIS
Millers

2nd   86-67   .562   -15.5   Dave Bancroft

BATTERS	POS-GAMES	GP	AB	R	H	BI	2B	3B	HR	BB	SO	SB	BA
Joe Hauser	1B153	153	570	153	189	182	35	4	**69**	138	88	1	.332
Andy Cohen	2B121	123	545	70	149	49	29	2	3	22	17	4	.273
Ernest Smith	SS112	124	431	84	125	52	30	2	3	55	22	16	.290
Foster Ganzel	3B117	124	437	76	137	74	30	5	11	67	26	6	.314
Spence Harris	OF152	152	631	141	224	106	47	10	22	85	36	13	.355
Art Ruble	OF151	153	623	113	187	87	33	9	15	52	30	15	.300
Robert Holland	OF110	111	470	91	167	99	37	3	17	37	37	8	.355
Joe Glenn	C125	137	439	65	146	91	36	5	17	49	62	1	.333
Leo Norris	SS48,2B35,3B	132	480	84	153	97	32	4	20	34	57	13	.319
Hy Vandenberg	P41	50	76	11	16		3	2	0			0	.211
Harry Holsclaw	P46	46	72	3	8		2	0	1			0	.111

MINNEAPOLIS (cont.)
Millers

BATTERS	POS-GAMES	GP	AB	R	H	BI	2B	3B	HR	BB	SO	SB	BA
Walt Tauscher	P44	46	54	5	15		2	0	1			0	.278
Walter Hilcher	P43	43	63	5	11		2	0	0			0	.175
Jesse Petty	P40	40	99	9	15	10	0	0	1	0	30	0	.152
John Benton	P31	31	78	4	10		0	0	0			0	.128
Bob Fothergill	OF26	30	96	19	33	14	6	1	2	10	3	0	.344
George Murray	P27	27	47	3	13		0	0	0			0	.277
Wes Griffin	C18	24	72	8	19		5	0	0			0	.264
Joe Mowry	OF20	20	89	20	32	15	7	1	4	6	7	2	.360
Frank Packard	OF10	15	50	9	14		2	0	1			0	.280
Westcott Kingdon		11	26	5	5		1	0	1			0	.192
Phil Hensick	P11	11	2	1	1		0	0	0			0	.500
Elam Vangilder	P10	10	9	2	1		0	0	1			0	.111
John Poser	P4,OF	7	6	1	0		0	0	0	1	1		.000
Dud Branom	1B	4	4	0	2	2	1	0	0				.500
Edward Baecht	P3	3	1	0	0		0	0	0				.000
Dave Beauchaine	SS	2	2	0	0		0	0	0				.000
Silas Williamson	P2	2	0	0	0		0	0	0				----
Al Wright	OF1	1	1	0	0		0	0	0	1			.000
James McCarter	PR	1	0	1	0		0	0	0				----

PITCHERS	W	L	PCT	G	GS	CG	SH	IP	H	BB	SO	ERA
Jesse Petty	18	8	.692	40				234	286	30	102	4.65
Walt Tauscher	15	8	.652	44				145	181	46	40	5.46
Harry Holsclaw	14	16	.467	46				227	277	60	102	5.19
Walter Hilcher	12	8	.600	43				176	223	79	79	6.29
John Benton	11	12	.478	31				206	247	62	39	4.67
George Murray	7	5	.583	27				126	180	47	38	6.29
Hy Vandenberg	7	6	.538	41				175	226	74	56	5.81
Phil Hensick	1	1	.500	11				15	22	9	10	8.40
Elam Vangilder	1	2	.333	10				27	32	15	11	5.67
Ed Baecht	0	1	.000	3				5	9	5	1	14.40
John Poser	0	0	----	4				9	18	2	1	12.00
Silas Williamson	0	0	----	2				0	1	3	0	inf.

INDIANAPOLIS   3rd   82-72   .532   -20   Wade Killefer
Indians

BATTERS	POS-GAMES	GP	AB	R	H	BI	2B	3B	HR	BB	SO	SB	BA
Ernie Wingard	1B142,P1	142	557	78	165	84	25	14	8	45	71	2	.296
Frank Sigafoos	2B152	152	635	108	235	126	53	11	6	26	49	24	.370
Dud Lee	SS129	130	514	81	143	37	14	4	2	69	52	11	.278
Fred Bedore	3B115,1B14	139	526	79	161	67	21	9	6	38	42	13	.306
John Cooney	OF125,P6	138	519	91	171	73	35	12	3	38	22	8	.329
Glenn Chapman	OF118	123	493	84	144	82	26	13	14	22	60	17	.292
Marty Callaghan	OF87	92	346	48	105	39	15	3	0	23	32	3	.303
John Riddle	C89	89	306	34	89	37	24	0	1	12	16	7	.291
Tom Angley	C76	92	307	35	93	47	12	3	7	9	10	3	.303
Ray White	3B44,SS32	78	270	27	65	29	6	5	0	20	22	1	.241
Jim Turner	P41	48	105	14	25		1	1	2			0	.238
Harry Rosenberg	OF39	44	146	20	41	20	8	2	2	11	13	2	.281
Robert Logan	P39	41	79	4	13	13	2	2	0	1	6	0	.165
Bill Thomas	P32	36	78	9	17		2	0	0			1	.218
Stewart Bolen	P34	35	81	8	24	16	2	1	2	5	17	0	.296
John Tising	P33	34	77	8	16		2	0	1			0	.208
Peter Daglia	P25	26	61	7	12		0	0	1			0	.197
Bill Burwell	P13	13	40	3	12		1	0	0			0	.300
Al Butzberger	P9	11	8	1	1		0	0	0			0	.125
Irwin Hufft		10	25	1	7		0	0	0			0	.280
Russ Scarritt	OF	8	30	2	9	3	1	0	0	3	1	0	.300
George Smith	P4	4	5	0	1	2	0	0	0	0	0	0	.200

PITCHERS	W	L	PCT	G	GS	CG	SH	IP	H	BB	SO	ERA
Jim Turner	17	9	.654	41				226	266	62	83	4.66
Stewart Bolen	14	9	.609	34				201	203	98	135	3.72
Robert Logan	12	13	.480	39				220	243	56	111	3.76
John Tising	11	13	.458	33				204	187	94	112	3.70
Bill Thomas	10	12	.455	32				215	265	41	76	4.35
Peter Daglia	9	9	.500	25				175	200	53	60	4.22
Bill Burwell	6	5	.545	13				102	107	23	18	3.26
John Cooney	2	1	.667	6				20	26	11	12	5.40

INDIANAPOLIS (cont.)
Indians

PITCHERS	W	L	PCT	G	GS	CG	SH	IP	H	BB	SO	ERA
Al Butzberger	1	1	.500	9				25	42	6	14	6.84
George Smith	0	0	----	4				14	13	4	3	3.21
Ernie Wingard	0	0	----	1				1	2	1	0	9.00

ST. PAUL   4th   78-75   .510   -23.5   McCann - Todt
Saints

BATTERS	POS-GAMES	GP	AB	R	H	BI	2B	3B	HR	BB	SO	SB	BA
Phil Todt	1B151	152	621	95	190	105	45	13	13	40	61	2	.306
Irv Jeffries	2B150	153	686	125	236	102	45	11	17	39	36	4	.344
Clyde Beck	SS147	147	524	61	144	69	20	5	5	50	49	4	.275
Meredith Hopkins	3B145,SS13	153	553	85	147	88	36	4	17	83	70	5	.266
Jesse Hill	OF129	129	555	101	166	54	42	8	11	62	42	15	.299
Ray Radcliff	OF124	128	511	77	186	99	36	10	6	29	19	9	.364
Ben Paschal	OF120	130	485	86	132	69	30	7	13	41	49	5	.272
Robert Fenner	C122	125	475	74	160	78	28	9	9	60	26	0	.337
Larry Rosenthal	OF55	74	231	53	68	33	14	4	4	74	35	3	.294
Les Munns	P44	50	120	22	34	11	3	3	2	2	3	1	.283
Emmett McCann	2B14	50	70	11	23		4	0	1			1	.329
Angelo Giulani	C41	48	144	17	47	19	7	2	0	6	7	0	.326
Bryan Harriss	P43	43	99	3	9		1	0	2			0	.091
Myles Thomas	P37	40	92	6	19		4	1	0			0	.207
Floyd Newkirk	P38	39	77	11	12		0	1	0			0	.156
Emil Yde	P17	30	43	4	11		1	0	0			0	.256
Fred Koster	OF28	29	118	15	32	12	6	1	0	19	9	2	.271
Eugene Trow	P25	25	29	1	4		0	0	0			0	.138
Hormidas Aube	P7	7	2	0	0		0	0	0				.000
George Quellich	OF	4	16	2	3	2	1	0	0				.188
James Minogue	P2	2	1	0	0		0	0	0				.000

PITCHERS	W	L	PCT	G	GS	CG	SH	IP	H	BB	SO	ERA
Les Munns	19	16	.543	44				284	301	119	111	4.66
Myles Thomas	15	14	.517	37				252	279	86	79	3.96
Bryan Harriss	15	15	.500	43				253	304	79	76	4.41
Floyd Newkirk	12	9	.571	38				219	232	76	67	4.15
Eugene Trow	6	7	.462	25				96	112	53	27	5.34
Emil Yde	3	4	.429	17				77	107	44	14	6.90
Hormidas Aube	0	0	----	7				12	16	10	7	7.50
James Minogue	0	0	----	2				3	6	4	0	12.00

TOLEDO   5th (T)   70-83   .458   -31.5   Steve O'Neill
Mud Hens

BATTERS	POS-GAMES	GP	AB	R	H	BI	2B	3B	HR	BB	SO	SB	BA
Bill Sweeney	1B84,2B13	95	380	44	115	52	21	7	1	22	19	15	.302
George Detore	2B81,3B27,C22,P1	137	508	103	179	82	37	7	11	54	41	16	.352
Ed Montague	SS145	145	588	82	137	46	19	8	3	65	100	14	.233
Robert Reis	3B123,2B10	132	551	96	178	20	31	14	10	10	8	15	.323
Max West	OF140	145	562	74	156	81	31	3	6	47	37	3	.278
Ellis Powers	OF84	84	352	60	113	60	20	9	6	27	26	5	.321
Frank Doljack	OF82	84	324	47	113	57	18	6	3	43	22	5	.349
Fran Healy	C	(see multi-team players)											
Hal Trosky	1B77,OF44	132	461	86	149	92	25	5	33	58	77	2	.323
Frank Reiber	C36,OF33	81	268	42	72	40	15	5	5	30	29	0	.269
Ralph Winegarner	P41	73	128	18	38	26	7	3	6	4	30	1	.297
Milt Galatzer	OF64	66	274	42	85	19	13	2	1	16	20	4	.310
E. Turgeon	2B57	66	202	15	38	15	6	1	0	9	10	1	.188
Roxie Lawson	P43	46	83	15	22		1	0	1			1	.265
LeRoy Bachman	P40	40	53	3	14	12	2	1	0	2	7	0	.264
Thornton Lee	P38	38	88	7	29	16	6	0	1	3	22	0	.330
Forrest Twogood	P30	31	45	6	11		1	0	0			0	.244
Bill Rhiel	OF19	30	97	10	20		5	1	0			1	.206
Francis Nekola	P28	28	35	3	6		1	0	0			0	.171
Monte Pearson	P23	23	56	4	15	11	3	0	2	1	6	0	.268
Howard Craghead	P21	21	38	2	7		0	0	0			0	.184
Steve O'Neill	C18	18	53	4	16		0	1	1			0	.302
Robert Asbjornson	C10	10	37	1	10		1	0	1			2	.270

TOLEDO (cont.)
Mud Hens

BATTERS	POS-GAMES	GP	AB	R	H	BI	2B	3B	HR	BB	SO	SB	BA
Marcel Bellande	3B	9	21	3	3	3	0	0	0	2	4	0	.143
Joe Doljack	P5	5	10	1	2		0	0	0		6		.200
Carl Schoof	P2	2	3	0	1		0	0	0		1		.333
Irvin Pawlicki	C1	1	1	0	1		0	0	0				1.000
Leo Reynolds	SS1	1	1	0	1		0	0	0				1.000
Sewell Glidden	OF1	1	1	0	1		1	0	0				1.000
Hobart Scott	P1	1	0	0	0		0	0	0				----
Dan DiLoreto	C1	1	0	0	0		0	0	0				----
William Rabb	P1	1	0	0	0		0	0	0				----

PITCHERS		W	L	PCT	G	GS	CG	SH	IP	H	BB	SO	ERA
Roxie Lawson		18	14	.563	43				248	284	106	56	4.57
Thornton Lee		13	11	.542	38				220	239	84	119	3.72
Monte Pearson		11	5	.688	23				148	139	49	96	3.41
Ralph Winegarner		11	15	.423	41				227	271	86	99	4.40
Howard Craghead		5	9	.357	21				119	154	44	45	5.90
Forrest Twogood		5	10	.333	30				130	169	65	43	6.44
Francis Nekola		4	11	.267	28				106	162	52	44	6.71
LeRoy Bachman		3	6	.333	40				146	177	51	61	5.12
Joe Doljack		0	1	.000	3				12	11	6	4	1.50
Carl Schoof		0	1	.000	2				8	5	2	4	4.50
Hobart Scott		0	0	----	1				5	3	1	0	9.00
George Detore		0	0	----	1				1	1	1	0	0.00
Willaim Rabb		0	0	----	1				0	3	1	0	inf.

LOUISVILLE   5th (T)   70-83   .458   -31.5   Bruno Betzel
Colonels

BATTERS	POS-GAMES	GP	AB	R	H	BI	2B	3B	HR	BB	SO	SB	BA
Al Van Camp	1B159	159	645	98	182	76	28	8	6	51	53	7	.282
James Adair	2B144	147	562	104	175	96	34	13	3	54	25	33	.311
Joe Olivares	SS137	139	503	47	141	46	16	4	0	23	19	6	.280
Art Funk	3B158	158	625	64	193	97	30	13	5	20	21	11	.309
Melbern Simons	OF151	152	621	94	201	82	44	7	1	37	31	18	.324
Goody Rosen	OF144	146	585	106	176	43	22	12	3	59	57	16	.301
Willis Norman	OF136	138	493	105	144	108	29	9	24	84	74	7	.292
Henry Erickson	C95	105	352	57	105	57	18	4	2	31	30	3	.298
Ray Thompson	C72	93	279	22	82	39	10	3	5	16	14	3	.294
John Marcum	P37	80	145	14	44	20	6	1	0	12	11	0	.303
Paul Wanninger	SS35,2B19	68	158	19	39	13	2	1	0	4	11	1	.247
Archie McKain	P46	51	78	11	11		0	0	1			0	.141
Richard Bass	P46	46	73	3	15		1	0	0			0	.205
Clyde Hatter	P44	44	35	3	7		1	0	0			0	.200
Ken Penner	P37	39	80	2	14		4	0	0			0	.175
Phil Weinert	P29	29	68	5	14		1	0	0			1	.206
Eldon McLean	P26	26	36	2	5		0	0	0			0	.139
Claude Jonnard	P20	20	17	1	2		0	0	0			0	.118
Gil Brack	OF	5	6	1	0	1	0	0	0	0	0	1	.000

PITCHERS		W	L	PCT	G	GS	CG	SH	IP	H	BB	SO	ERA
John Marcum		20	13	.606	37				272	278	78	153	3.74
Archie McKain		11	10	.524	46				238	256	67	88	3.93
Phil Weinert		11	12	.478	29				186	211	62	80	4.02
Richard Bass		10	12	.455	46				196	261	73	83	5.83
Ken Penner		10	13	.435	37				219	268	37	49	5.10
Eldon McLean		4	6	.400	26				111	140	62	53	5.68
Clyde Hatter		3	10	.231	44				115	117	84	74	5.24
Claude Jonnard		1	7	.125	20				48	72	29	25	8.06
Clarence Nachand		0	0	----	6				7	7	11	4	9.00

MILWAUKEE   7th   67-87   .435   -35   Frank O'Rourke
Brewers

BATTERS	POS-GAMES	GP	AB	R	H	BI	2B	3B	HR	BB	SO	SB	BA
George Stanton	1B155	156	633	94	184	87	33	7	9	48	57	15	.291
Al Marquardt	2B101	112	449	56	126	53	16	4	3	34	38	4	.281
Ed Grimes	SS86	88	325	33	80	34	12	5	2	88	42	5	.246

MILWAUKEE (cont.)
Brewers

BATTERS	POS-GAMES	GP	AB	R	H	BI	2B	3B	HR	BB	SO	SB	BA
Horace Koehler	3B124,OF29	155	644	96	205	85	30	6	6	42	16	8	.318
Walt Christensen	OF132	139	473	63	145	70	18	1	3	57	38	6	.307
Anton Kubek	OF112	123	453	80	140	45	17	10	5	46	55	8	.309
Alex Metzler	OF112	116	409	85	126	48	20	8	8	65	21	11	.308
Russ Young	C113	130	417	48	126	72	20	3	4	53	47	1	.302
Tom Connolly	2B64,SS58	148	550	100	166	79	33	3	18	84	31	11	.302
John Kloza	OF78	89	308	53	90	62	9	6	9	27	38	0	.292
Benny Bengough	C54	70	191	16	45	24	6	2	1	16	14	0	.236
H. Hillin	P50	52	74	4	10		0	1	0			0	.135
Lou Polli	P41	47	83	11	21		2	1	0			0	.253
Earl Caldwell	P42	45	89	7	17		2	1	0			0	.191
Forest Presnell	P44	44	64	8	14		1	0	0			0	.219
George Fisher	OF34	38	116	15	25		6	0	2			3	.216
Garland Braxton	P31	31	72	5	6		0	0	0			0	.083
Frank O'Rourke		22	38	6	5		0	1	0			0	.132
Fred Stiely	P21	21	35	6	6		1	0	0			0	.171
Dick Coffman	P17	17	30	0	8		1	0	0			0	.267
Paul Gregory	P16	16	27	2	5		0	0	0			0	.185
Harold Wiltse	P7	7	7	1	2		0	0	0				.286
Robert Lipschin	P7	7	3	0	1	1	0	0	0		1		.333
A. Kohler	3B	5	15	2	5	2	1	0	1	0	2	1	.333
Larry Bettencourt	OF	3	9	0	4	3	1	0	0	1	1		.444
Lester White	P3	3	0	0	0		0	0	0				----
Thomas Heath	C1	1	1	0	1		0	0	0				1.000

PITCHERS	W	L	PCT	G	GS	CG	SH	IP	H	BB	SO	ERA
Garland Braxton	16	7	.696	31				203	238	62	104	4.17
Lou Polli	15	14	.517	41				248	303	72	87	4.94
Forest Pressnell	10	13	.435	44				194	236	50	72	5.01
Earl Caldwell	10	18	.357	42				236	296	71	83	4.96
Paul Gregory	5	5	.500	16				86	139	19	27	7.22
Fred Stiely	4	4	.500	21				95	118	43	40	6.06
H. Hillin	4	15	.211	50				204	264	102	81	6.00
Harold Wiltse	0	1	.000	7				18	13	9	5	8.50
Robert Lipschin	0	0	----	7				13	18	16	3	10.39
Lester White	0	0	----	3				3	4	0	1	6.00

KANSAS CITY   8th   57-93   .360   -43   Speaker - Allen
Blues

BATTERS	POS-GAMES	GP	AB	R	H	BI	2B	3B	HR	BB	SO	SB	BA
James Keesey	1B64	65	257	31	87	39	10	5	1	14	10	0	.339
James Cronin	2B100,SS15	123	449	58	127	53	24	5	1	25	15	8	.283
Chet Wilburn	SS102	103	393	49	99	37	13	8	1	36	50	5	.252
Ed Taylor	3B92,SS39	137	545	72	165	51	41	4	3	49	39	12	.303
Denver Grigsby	OF145	147	563	86	170	74	32	6	6	71	41	10	.302
Stanley Schino	OF127	143	524	83	148	93	22	17	12	62	55	7	.282
Jim Mosolf	OF57	63	243	44	94	37	16	9	1	27	15	3	.387
Bill Brenzel	C98	106	325	32	85	28	16	4	0	11	16	1	.262
Bruce Connatser	1B50,OF34,2B26	112	457	68	144	63	29	12	3	37	44	9	.316
Ed Pick	OF56	65	230	34	67	31	13	2	3	31	19	1	.291
Alex Gaston	C51	58	170	14	34	14	4	2	0	30	23	0	.200
Peter Monohan	1B37	38	131	19	33	12	5	1	0	17	10	1	.252
Hugh Willingham	3B28	34	116	20	25	23	3	6	6	11	21	0	.216
Mace Brown	P33	33	58	6	8		2	0	0			0	.138
Joe Blackwell	P33	33	45	2	4		0	0	0			0	.089
Harold Carson	P23	31	72	8	13	13	1	1	1	2	22	0	.181
Fred Browning	P29	31	33	5	8		0	0	0			0	.242
Bill Shores	P25	26	60	5	17	11	4	1	0	6	16	1	.283
Walter Mails	P24	24	55	3	7		0	0	0			0	.127
Ray Treadaway	3B20	21	74	7	16	12	1	1	1	4	4	1	.216
Ed Connolly	C20	20	56	7	17		4	0	0			0	.304
John Niggeling	P17	19	41	7	12		2	0	0			0	.293
Aaron Ward		18	64	4	9		0	1	0			0	.141
Herb Kelly	OF15	18	57	2	15		4	0	0			0	.263
Fred Brickell	OF10	14	44	7	12		0	2	0			0	.273
Roy Hudson	OF12	14	38	6	6		3	0	0			0	.158
Al Marchand		10	29	3	8		1	0	0			0	.276
Frank Gabler	P9	9	9	0	1		0	0	0		1		.111
Charles Wood	P7	7	14	1	3		0	0	0		1		.214
Cliff Clay	P5	5	1	0	0		0	0	0				.000

KANSAS CITY (cont.)
Blues

BATTERS	POS-GAMES	GP	AB	R	H	BI	2B	3B	HR	BB	SO	SB	BA
Roberts	P3	3	10	0	3	1	1	0	0		3		.300
Leo Ogorek	OF	3	2	0	1		0	0	0		1		.333
Max Thomas	P2	2	4	0	1	1	0	0	0				.250
Frank Snyder	C1	1	1	0	0		0	0	0				.000

PITCHERS		W	L	PCT	G	GS	CG	SH	IP	H	BB	SO	ERA
Harold Carson		11	9	.550	23				153	176	36	25	4.59
Walter Mails		9	8	.529	24				140	148	58	79	3.79
Bill Shores		8	11	.421	25				168	171	63	88	4.13
Joe Blackwell		5	11	.313	33				137	163	73	66	5.12
John Niggeling		4	11	.267	17				113	154	23	31	5.10
Mace Brown		4	16	.200	33				194	200	84	68	4.41
Fred Browning		3	7	.300	29				108	136	29	35	4.75
Frank Gabler		1	2	.333	9				28	34	9	6	5.79
Wood		1	3	.250	7				39	45	19	16	4.38
Roberts		0	2	.000	3				25	30	3	2	3.04
Cliff Clay		0	0	----	5				5	11	3	2	10.80
Max Thomas		0	0	----	2				7	24	2	1	18.00

MULTI-TEAM PLAYERS

BATTERS	POS-GAMES	TEAMS	GP	AB	R	H	BI	2B	3B	HR	BB	SO	SB	BA
Herman Layne	OF131	LOU-IND	135	559	83	153	40	21	10	5	31	38	21	.274
Fran Healy	C67	COL-TOL	73	243	26	66	37	9	3	3	16	21	6	.272
Lou Fette	P36	KC-SP	60	130	23	44	20	8	2	5	0	16	3	.338
Walt Henline	C40	MIN-TOL	56	126	12	26		4	1	0			1	.206
Clarence Nachand	OF29	SP-LOU	48	115	17	30	19	5	3	2	2	6	1	.261
Louis Garland	P38	SP-KC	38	57	3	8		0	0	0			0	.140
Clarence Hoffman		MIL-IND	10	26	2	8		1	0	0			0	.308

PITCHERS		TEAMS	W	L	PCT	G	GS	CG	SH	IP	H	BB	SO	ERA
Lou Fette		KC-SP	10	13	.435	36				205	305	71	45	6.28
Louis Garland		SP-KC	9	10	.474	38				168	221	83	57	5.57

TEAM BATTING

TEAMS	GP	AB	R	H	BI	2B	3B	HR	BB	SO	SB	BA
COLUMBUS	153	5357	889	1573	734	263	92	106	386	536	131	.294
MINNEAPOLIS	153	5564	993	1688	925	340	49	190	604	579	82	.303
INDIANAPOLIS	158	5629	805	1665	774	267	89	58	405	553	105	.296
ST. PAUL	153	5556	861	1653	832	326	81	104	513	579	53	.298
TOLEDO	154	5494	796	1604	725	271	77	94	499	612	91	.292
LOUISVILLE	159	5597	792	1611	722	253	79	53	577	541	114	.288
MILWAUKEE	158	5532	792	1567	721	231	59	71	449	487	72	.283
KANSAS CITY	152	5287	698	1469	628	256	88	40	485	552	59	.278
	620	44016	6626	12830	6061	2207	614	716	3918	4439	707	.291

1934
East and West

Before the 1933 season started, the American Association unveiled a bold new plan. The eight teams of the league would be divided into two four-team groupings, with the winners squaring off to determine the league's participant in the Junior World Series. (The name of the Little World Series had been changed to Junior World Series in 1932.) Although still maintaining an eight-team grouping to determine overall standings, the clubs were divided into an east group and a west group. The east group consisted of Columbus, Toledo, Louisville, and Indianapolis. The west group included Minneapolis, St. Paul, Milwaukee, and Kansas City. League owners surmised that fan interest would be maintained longer if more than one team had a chance for the gold.

Conveniently enough, the best of the east (Columbus) and the best of the west (Minneapolis) finished first and second in the overall standings in 1933 and met in the best of seven championship series. After splitting the first four games, Columbus prevailed in the fifth and sixth games (7–5, and 14–11) to win the inaugural tilt.

When the 1934 season started, the same groupings were in place. When the season was over, the same two teams, Columbus and Minneapolis, finished first in the east and west, as well as first (Minneapolis) and second (Columbus) in the overall standings. Behind Columbus in the east was Louisville, Toledo and Indianapolis. In back of Minneapolis in the west finished Milwaukee, St. Paul, and Kansas City.

Milwaukee's Earl Webb won the batting title (.368), while Buzz Arlett of the Millers hit the most home runs (41). Milwaukee's John Kloza had the most runs batted in (148). Minneapolis pitcher Walt Tauscher posted the most wins (21), while James Elliott of Columbus had the best earned run average (3.27) and Stewart Bolen of Indianapolis had the most strikeouts (177).

In the post-season series, the Millers took only one of the first three games played in Minneapolis. When the series shifted to Columbus, the Millers took the next two, 5–2, and 10–8. Minneapolis was on the verge of taking the series the next day before Columbus rallied in a five run ninth inning to win 7–6. The Red Birds closed out the Millers in game seven 7–3 to emerge triumphant.

The divisional format without real divisions would end after two years, its inherent flaw recognized. The regular season pennant would mean little if the fifth place team could potentially win it all. However, the playoff idea itself would not dissappear. In a few years it would rise again, albeit in a slightly different form.

MINNEAPOLIS Millers

	1st	85-64	.570		Donie Bush

BATTERS	POS-GAMES	GP	AB	R	H	BI	2B	3B	HR	BB	SO	SB	BA
Joe Hauser	1B76	82	287	81	100	88	7	3	33	67	41	1	.348
Andy Cohen	2B144	145	**666**	106	207	62	33	4	0	24	26	0	.311
Leo Norris	SS135	143	564	105	175	116	35	7	23	46	76	7	.310
Foster Ganzel	3B134	141	498	81	150	83	43	4	8	77	33	0	.301
Al Wright	OF145	148	606	111	214	131	47	9	29	49	61	6	.353
Buzz Arlett	OF115	116	430	106	137	132	32	1	**41**	92	66	8	.319
Spence Harris	OF99,1B53	150	614	**138**	198	100	29	8	16	85	44	8	.322
Bubbles Hargrave	C144	147	547	118	195	108	29	7	16	69	29	4	.356
Ernest Smith	3B23,OF20,SS17	95	249	45	81	41	23	2	3	24	13	3	.325
Walt Tauscher	P50	55	92	13	21	11	5	0	1	9	19	0	.228
Wilfred Ryan	P50	50	57	2	11		1	0	0			0	.193
Ray Starr	P42	43	102	10	17		0	0	1			0	.167
Charles Marrow	P43	43	60	5	10		1	0	1			0	.167
A. Joyner	OF16,1B11	42	90	10	22	12	3	1	1	4	13	1	.244
Jesse Petty	P40	40	86	7	12		0	1	0			0	.140
Homer Peel	OF31	31	122	14	36	14	7	0	1	10	8	0	.295
David Barbee	OF24	25	88	12	25		7	1	0			2	.284
James Chaplin	P18	22	45	8	12		0	1	0			0	.267
Harry Holsclaw	P18	18	27	1	4		0	0	0			0	.148
Leo Ogerek		11	38	9	6		1	0	0			0	.158
Hy Vandenberg	P8	10	6	1	1		0	0	0			0	.167
John Gill	OF	8	22	2	6	4	2	1	1	3	2	1	.273
Schmidt	C	8	11	3	2		1	0	0		4		.182
Spurgeon Chandler	P8	8	8	2	4		1	0	0		1		.500
George Murray	P8	8	8	1	3	2	2	0	0		1		.375
Beryl Richmond	P7	7	7	0	1		0	0	0		4		.143
Sydney Cohen	P6	6	5	0	1	1	0	0	0				.200
Shatzer	C	5	9	0	2	2	0	0	0				.222
William Wyss	C	4	4	0	0		0	0	0				.000
Arthur Cuisinier	PR	3	0	3	0		0	0	0				----
Charles Johnson	P3	3	0	0	0		0	0	0				----
Joe Shaute	P2	2	3	0	0	1	0	0	0				.000
Rea	C	1	2	0	0		0	0	0				.000
Arnold	C1	1	1	0	0		0	0	0				.000

PITCHERS	W	L	PCT	G	GS	CG	SH	IP	H	BB	SO	ERA
Walt Tauscher	**21**	7	.750	50				222	226	80	90	3.89
Jesse Petty	19	7	.731	40				220	264	40	96	4.58
Ray Starr	16	17	.485	42				260	296	**123**	110	5.23
Charles Marrow	9	10	.474	43				170	212	54	78	5.61
James Chaplin	8	5	.615	18				107	132	15	35	3.70
Wilfred Ryan	8	8	.500	50				163	220	38	62	5.74
Sydney Cohen	2	0	1.000	6				12	19	6	5	8.76
Joe Shaute	1	0	1.000	2				10	10	1	8	2.70
Harry Holsclaw	1	5	.167	18				73	94	29	33	7.15
Hy Vandenberg	0	1	.000	8				16	34	9	14	14.88
George Murray	0	2	.000	8				26	38	11	9	7.62
Beryl Richmond	0	2	.000	7				23	31	13	14	9.39
Spurgeon Chandler	0	0	----	6				16	26	11	2	7.88
Charles Johnson	0	0	----	4				8	6	7	3	1.13

COLUMBUS Red Birds

	2nd	85-68	.556	-2	Ray Blades

BATTERS	POS-GAMES	GP	AB	R	H	BI	2B	3B	HR	BB	SO	SB	BA
Minor Heath	1B149	150	508	115	142	101	14	5	29	**123**	109	10	.280
Charles Wilson	2B143	145	600	85	195	86	36	11	14	37	45	16	.328
Bill Myers	SS155	**155**	604	112	189	67	37	13	10	70	**110**	9	.313
Lew Riggs	3B132	132	560	81	155	83	28	11	11	35	28	13	.277
Nick Cullop	OF140	147	587	97	178	130	34	13	27	56	98	8	.303
Terry Moore	OF130	130	558	99	183	84	36	11	14	37	45	16	.328
Gene Moore	OF82	85	308	56	105	47	23	9	8	35	39	8	.341
Ken O'Dea	C100	111	374	55	99	37	19	2	4	31	29	5	.265
Harold Anderson	OF67,2B14,3B13	98	340	44	88	41	12	2	2	33	27	7	.259
Ray Blades	OF36	63	140	18	37	20	6	1	0	22	13	3	.264
Art Teachout	P39	60	118	15	32	18	4	0	0	3	16	0	.271
Tom Angley	C34	57	136	21	46	31	7	0	5	11	8	1	.338
Ward Cross	P47	48	37	8	10		2	1	0			0	.270
Joe Sims	P46	46	26	5	4		0	0	0			0	.154
Robert Klinger	P40	42	68	5	15		2	0	0			0	.200
John Gooch	C33	39	96	9	17		3	0	1			0	.177

COLUMBUS (cont.)
Red Birds

BATTERS	POS-GAMES	GP	AB	R	H	BI	2B	3B	HR	BB	SO	SB	BA
Ed Greer	P39	39	83	4	9		2	0	0			0	.108
Clarence Heise	P32	34	72	6	14		0	1	0			0	.194
Tom Oliver	OF25	29	94	11	23		3	1	0			1	.245
Glenn Spencer	P24	25	26	3	4		0	0	0			0	.154
James Elliott	P17	17	35	0	7		2	0	0			0	.200
Urban Hodapp		10	32	7	11		0	0	0			0	.344
Martin	2B	9	14	3	4	1	0	0	0	1	2	0	.286
Ed Heusser	P9	9	11	2	3	3	0	1	0	1	2	0	.273
Bill Sweeney	1B	6	18	5	8	5	2	0	0	1	1	0	.444
William Beckman	P6	6	12	0	1		0	0	0				.083
Milton Bocek	OF	4	14	2	4	1	0	0	1		1		.286
Ken Ash	P4	4	4	0	0	0	0	0	0	2	0	0	.000
Ed Delker	3B3	3	11	0	3	1	1	0	0		1		.273
Mort Cooper	P3	3	2	0	0		0	0	0				.000
Keith Frazier	P1	1	1	0	0		0	0	0				.000

PITCHERS		W	L	PCT	G	GS	CG	SH	IP	H	BB	SO	ERA
Art Teachout		17	13	.567	39				240	294	62	83	4.39
Ed Greer		15	11	.577	39				251	249	70	88	3.51
Robert Klinger		15	13	.536	40				189	209	82	93	4.76
Clarence Heise		9	7	.563	32				175	189	80	85	4.78
James Elliott		8	4	.667	17				99	106	39	45	**3.27**
Joe Sims		7	4	.636	46				116	139	60	56	5.28
Ward Cross		6	5	.545	47				117	104	75	57	3.46
Glenn Spencer		4	4	.500	24				83	109	50	43	6.40
Ed Heusser		2	0	1.000	9				32	30	12	27	3.09
William Beckman		2	3	.400	6				34	48	15	9	6.08
Mort Cooper		0	1	.000	3				11	16	6	5	5.73
Keith Frazier		0	1	.000	1				3	4	5	1	15.00
Ken Ash		0	2	.000	4				17	19	8	1	5.82

MILWAUKEE   3rd   82-70   .539   -4.5   Al Sothoron
Brewers

BATTERS	POS-GAMES	GP	AB	R	H	BI	2B	3B	HR	BB	SO	SB	BA
Ernie Wingard	1B		(see multi-team players)										
Lin Storti	2B146	147	567	98	187	145	32	2	35	60	70	2	.330
Ed Marshall	SS129	129	548	95	157	55	23	4	4	63	29	1	.286
Bill Sullivan	3B137,1B13	151	648	124	222	93	30	11	17	61	39	5	.343
John Kloza	OF151	152	629	130	205	148	28	14	26	74	77	4	.326
Ted Gullic	OF135,1B10	142	593	112	198	97	53	6	14	32	86	11	.334
Earl Webb	OF104	106	424	72	156	84	27	4	11	42	29	1	**.368**
George Rensa	C86	100	308	54	92	54	21	5	7	33	16	2	.299
Anton Kubek	OF81	103	275	50	78	23	9	4	2	33	35	5	.284
Rudy Laskowski		51	97	9	26	10	3	2	0	7	10	1	.268
Forest Pressnell	P48	48	80	9	19		2	0	0			0	.238
Ed Hope	SS22,3B10	46	118	11	19	11	1	1	0	10	33	0	.161
George Susce	C41	43	154	23	57	30	6	4	1	11	22	4	.370
Lou Polli	P34	40	89	10	17		2	1	0			0	.191
Lee Stine	P33	36	94	18	32	14	2	1	3	5	19	1	.340
Garland Braxton	P34	34	86	8	18		2	0	0			1	.209
James Walkup	P34	34	63	6	10		2	1	0			0	.159
Dud Branom	1B18	18	75	7	20		2	0	1			2	.267
Irving Cohen	P6	6	7	2	1		0	0	0		4		.143
Ray Wallentoski	P5	5	1	0	0		0	0	0		1		.000
Paul Wanninger	SS	4	21	6	9	5	1	1	0		1		.429
Clarence Fieber	P3	3	5	2	3	3	1	0	1		1		.600
Joe Bartulis	P2	2	0	0	0		0	0	0		0		----
Ed Baecht	P2	2	0	0	0		0	0	0		0		----

PITCHERS		W	L	PCT	G	GS	CG	SH	IP	H	BB	SO	ERA
Garland Braxton		20	7	.741	34				238	303	56	121	4.05
Lee Stine		17	9	.654	33				221	247	83	97	4.19
Lou Polli		16	15	.516	34				241	279	87	108	4.63
Forest Pressnell		15	11	.577	48				223	268	72	68	4.28
James Walkup		7	10	.412	34				166	162	103	105	3.85
Clarence Fieber		2	0	1.000	3				13	19	6	5	9.00
Ernie Wingard		0	2	.000	4				16	19	8	11	3.38
Irving Cohen		0	0	----	6				15	25	13	3	9.00
Ray Wallentoski		0	0	----	5				9	8	3	3	3.00

MILWAUKEE (cont.)
Brewers

PITCHERS	W	L	PCT	G	GS	CG	SH	IP	H	BB	SO	ERA
Joe Bartulis	0	0	----	2				1	2	2	1	9.00
Ed Baecht	0	0	---	2				2	1	3	0	0.00

LOUISVILLE   4th   78-74   .513   -8.5   Betzel - Penner
Colonels

BATTERS	POS-GAMES	GP	AB	R	H	BI	2B	3B	HR	BB	SO	SB	BA
Ray Radcliff	1B86,OF65	142	565	90	189	102	27	19	5	46	25	7	.335
James Adair	2B130	131	469	83	141	68	16	15	3	53	37	15	.301
Joe Olivares	SS137	138	481	53	138	61	17	8	1	29	19	6	.287
Al Van Camp	3B66,1B56	134	534	73	154	67	24	10	4	38	30	3	.288
Melbern Simons	OF147	150	612	100	201	80	38	3	3	38	34	13	.328
Goody Rosen	OF137	140	563	106	174	50	20	10	2	73	41	25	.309
Gil Brack	OF111	126	417	70	128	66	25	13	6	48	85	11	.307
Ray Thompson	C102	113	393	42	113	66	17	2	2	16	18	2	.288
Henry Erickson	C56	69	216	27	57	30	10	5	2	14	22	0	.264
Art Funk	3B64	67	260	27	70	16	8	5	0	11	4	6	.269
Eldon McLean	P52	52	66	6	16		3	1	1			0	.242
Richard Bass	P46	48	76	10	22	10	2	1	0	1	7	0	.289
James Peterson	P41	43	90	12	18		1	0	1			0	.200
Walter Ringhoefer	C11	39	85	17	26	10	1	0	0	9	12	3	.306
Archie McKain	P33	39	62	8	9		1	0	1			0	.145
Clyde Hatter	P36	36	69	6	11		0	0	0			0	.159
Ken Penner	P22	23	36	4	8		0	0	0			0	.222
Charles Bloedorn		12	32	1	4		0	0	0			0	.125
Clarence Nachand	P9	10	2	1	0		0	0	0			0	.000
Klein	3B	3	7	2	2		0	0	0		1		.286
Al LeComte	P2	2	3	0	0		0	0	0		1		.000

PITCHERS	W	L	PCT	G	GS	CG	SH	IP	H	BB	SO	ERA
Richard Bass	17	8	.680	46				206	234	77	91	4.28
James Peterson	13	14	.481	41				263	318	75	88	4.76
Archie McKain	11	11	.500	33				171	194	76	84	5.11
Eldon McLean	9	11	.450	52				189	226	106	100	6.14
Clyde Hatter	8	12	.400	36				178	164	101	170	3.39
Ken Penner	7	4	.636	22				98	127	18	31	3.77
Clarence Nachand	0	0	----	9				13	13	3	0	9.69
Al LeComte	0	0	----	1				2	2	1	1	9.00

INDIANAPOLIS   5th   77-75   .507   -9.5   Wade Killefer
Indians

BATTERS	POS-GAMES	GP	AB	R	H	BI	2B	3B	HR	BB	SO	SB	BA
John Sherlock	1B115	115	452	57	108	50	17	8	3	32	37	10	.239
Vince Sherlock	2B145	145	546	92	163	67	21	7	1	51	65	7	.299
Dud Lee	SS132	132	505	69	126	42	19	4	1	76	31	22	.250
Fred Bedore	3B131,1B19	150	584	87	188	103	32	9	4	38	29	7	.322
Vern Washington	OF135	144	558	104	205	120	40	13	16	44	28	2	.367
Harry Rosenberg	OF112	126	450	74	148	65	18	11	2	31	37	2	.329
Como Cotelle	OF101	114	420	66	126	53	22	5	3	22	20	8	.300
Joe Sprinz	C84	87	300	32	83	36	10	2	0	39	29	2	.277
John Cooney	OF99	109	461	79	142	38	26	10	0	23	15	3	.308
Frank Sigafoos	OF30,3B26,2B14	109	394	52	111	36	19	1	1	15	15	10	.282
John Riddle	C77	87	282	38	83	54	23	2	5	15	21	2	.294
Robert Logan	P45	50	89	10	16		1	2	0			0	.180
Hal Chamberlain	P43	43	37	3	6		1	0	0			0	.162
Al Butzberger	P39	42	36	3	7		0	1	0			0	.194
Stewart Bolen	P35	36	110	9	25	11	6	0	2	5	12	1	.227
Jim Turner	P24	24	61	4	13		1	2	0			0	.213
Vance Page	P20	24	44	4	10		0	1	0			0	.227
Bill Burwell	P14	17	49	2	14		0	0	0			0	.286
Joe Lawrie		14	16	2	4		0	1	0			0	.250
John Miljus	P13	13	18	1	5		0	1	1			0	.278
Jim Shevlin	1B10	12	33	10	8		2	1	0			0	.242
Clifton Wright	P10	10	2	1	1		0	0	0			0	.500
Ray White	3B	7	8	0	1	1	0	0	0	2	1		.125
William Thomas	P3	3	1	1	0		0	0	0				.000

INDIANAPOLIS (cont.)
Indians

BATTERS	POS-GAMES	GP	AB	R	H	BI	2B	3B	HR	BB	SO	SB	BA
Al Baringer	P2	2	1	0	0		0	0	0				.000

PITCHERS		W	L	PCT	G	GS	CG	SH	IP	H	BB	SO	ERA
Robert Logan		20	14	.588	45				256	286	54	100	3.66
Stewart Bolen		14	11	.560	35				269	273	106	177	4.05
Bill Burwell		8	4	.667	14				107	132	15	35	3.70
Hal Chamberlain		8	7	.533	43				128	116	60	91	3.80
Jim Turner		7	8	.467	24				159	162	41	63	4.13
Vance Page		6	10	.375	20				126	148	32	47	4.57
Al Butzberger		3	5	.375	39				108	126	57	43	4.83
John Miljus		2	4	.333	13				46	63	15	22	6.46
Clifton Wright		1	0	1.000	10				17	22	4	1	2.12
William Thomas		0	1	.000	2				6	11	4	3	12.00
Al Baringer		0	0	----	2				3	4	1	2	3.00

TOLEDO   6th   68-84   .447   -18.5   Steve O'Neill
Mud Hens

BATTERS	POS-GAMES	GP	AB	R	H	BI	2B	3B	HR	BB	SO	SB	BA
Harry Davis	1B134	136	508	93	161	90	25	9	15	61	50	12	.317
Robert Allaire	2B114,3B11	128	479	87	140	57	16	7	1	52	22	5	.292
Ed Montague	SS131,2B14	149	529	100	159	73	26	7	3	78	72	23	.301
John Calvey	3B81,2B23	108	431	48	106	32	14	6	0	18	48	14	.247
Mike Powers	OF119	121	459	74	154	58	27	10	5	57	14	6	.336
Alta Cohen	OF101,P1	115	381	59	127	47	31	2	2	50	45	6	.333
Milt Galatzer	OF95,1B21	114	490	75	172	59	24	9	5	46	25	1	.351
Gene DesAutels	C83	88	280	33	75	38	13	3	0	36	17	1	.268
Robert Reis	3B58,OF47,SS29	138	516	90	153	89	28	16	12	40	51	13	.297
Joe Zapustas	OF67	82	275	52	84	38	21	5	3	21	50	6	.305
Bob Garbark	C54	59	179	23	61	36	7	1	2	19	15	2	.341
Rip Sewell	P38	50	98	16	28	13	5	1	0	5	15	1	.286
Bill Perrin	P49	49	69	7	12		0	0	0			0	.174
Roxie Lawson	P42	48	77	5	16	11	1	0	0	2	19	0	.208
Francis Nekola	P38	38	63	6	9		2	0	0			0	.143
George Uhle	P19,OF12	37	68	7	17	10	1	0	0	7	15	0	.250
Steve Sundra	P37	37	54	3	11		2	1	0			0	.204
Grant Bowler	P35	35	35	4	7		1	0	0			0	.200
Steve O'Neill	C19	30	67	9	21	16	5	0	0	9	7	0	.313
Joe Doljack	P23	26	23	3	8		2	1	0			0	.348
E. Turgeon		10	34	2	8		0	2	0			0	.235
Steve Larkin	P10	10	14	0	2		1	0	0			0	.143
Walter Laskowski	C	8	21	1	5	4	0	0	0	3	2	0	.238
LeRoy Bachman	P8	8	3	0	0		0	0	0				.000
Edward Marlow	P7	7	4	1	0		0	0	0		1		.000
Roy James	P6	6	8	0	0		0	0	0		4		.000
Bill Jackson	C	5	5	2	1	2	0	0	0		1		.200
Max West	OF	4	10	0	3	2	0	0	0		1		.300
Gilbert Kersey	P4	4	1	0	0		0	0	0	1	1		.000
Len Shires	2B	3	4	0	0		0	0	0	2			.000
Rheas	PR	1	0	1	0		0	0	0				----

PITCHERS		W	L	PCT	G	GS	CG	SH	IP	H	BB	SO	ERA
Rip Sewell		14	12	.538	38				218	289	71	86	6.07
Bill Perrin		14	18	.438	49				240	280	92	108	4.58
Francis Nekola		13	19	.406	38				202	243	77	71	5.52
Roxie Lawson		9	14	.391	42				202	256	83	65	5.66
Steve Sundra		7	7	.500	37				156	216	54	99	5.02
Grant Bowler		6	5	.545	35				102	120	47	28	5.82
Steve Larkin		2	3	.400	10				46	48	24	26	5.28
George Uhle		2	4	.333	19				70	77	16	30	3.73
Edward Marlow		1	0	1.000	7				12	18	8	5	9.75
Joe Doljack		0	1	.000	23				57	63	17	15	4.42
LeRoy Bachman		0	1	.000	9				14	21	7	2	7.71
Roy James		0	0	----	6				18	17	14	10	4.00
Gilbert Kersey		0	0	----	3				7	9	6	0	6.43
Alta Cohen		0	0	----	1				1	0	2	1	0.00

ST. PAUL   7th   67-84   .444   -19   Bob Coleman
Saints

BATTERS	POS-GAMES	GP	AB	R	H	BI	2B	3B	HR	BB	SO	SB	BA
Phil Todt	1B151	151	597	63	164	84	35	5	8	29	47	0	.275
John Warner	2B152	152	620	100	191	95	34	6	12	41	52	8	.308
Otto Bluege	SS119	124	416	50	86	22	17	4	1	45	20	4	.207
William McWilliams	3B120	130	468	41	115	65	14	5	12	26	82	3	.246
Fred Koster	OF134	137	552	89	172	52	33	9	4	58	47	11	.312
Larry Rosenthal	OF120	131	494	68	125	48	22	10	10	51	94	7	.253
Ivey Shiver	OF95	108	383	68	109	75	18	7	19	35	105	12	.285
Robert Fenner	C100	111	383	47	113	54	34	2	7	38	25	1	.295
Angelo Giulani	C64	76	220	20	57	23	5	3	4	9	19	1	.259
Lou Fette	P45	71	133	8	26	10	4	1	2	2	18	0	.195
Willis Norman	OF61	65	237	44	71	51	12	5	18	29	36	4	.300
Ed Leishman	SS43	60	129	23	29		5	0	0			5	.225
Meredith Hopkins	3B27,OF15	51	165	21	33	19	8	1	1	23	25	0	.200
Eugene Trow	P45	45	78	4	14		1	0	0			0	.179
Ray Phelps	P41	43	76	7	14		2	0	2			0	.184
Myles Thomas	P36	38	74	6	15		0	0	0			0	.203
Gowell Claset	P36	37	51	1	9		1	0	1			0	.176
Ralph Judd	P15	27	37	4	9		1	0	0			0	.243
George Gerken	OF16	19	51	5	8		3	0	0			0	.157
Ralph Erickson	P19	19	12	1	1		0	0	0			0	.083
Joe Hutcheson	OF15	15	58	9	12		2	0	4			0	.207
James Brown	P13	13	14	0	1		0	0	0			0	.071
Tony Freitas	P8	8	11	0	0	0	0	0	0	3	3	0	.000
Ted Norbert	OF	5	18	3	3		0	0	0				.167
Scharein	SS	2	10	3	1		0	0	0				.100
James	2B1	1	1	0	0	0	0	0	0	0	0	0	.000

PITCHERS		W	L	PCT	G	GS	CG	SH	IP	H	BB	SO	ERA
Ray Phelps		17	10	.630	41				244	249	87	81	3.76
Gene Trow		13	14	.481	45				214	228	113	92	5.68
Myles Thomas		12	14	.462	36				212	222	78	75	3.99
Lou Fette		12	19	.387	45				248	303	79	78	4.39
Gowell Claset		7	11	.389	36				165	236	65	58	6.38
Tony Freitas		2	3	.400	8				46	38	8	17	3.13
Ralph Judd		2	6	.250	15				63	98	19	21	8.00
Ralph Erickson		1	2	.333	19				51	65	19	25	5.65
James Brown		0	1	.000	13				48	67	15	8	6.56
Fred Heimach		0	1	.000	4				9	18	1	4	9.00

KANSAS CITY   8th   65-88   .425   -22   Roger Peckinpaugh
Blues

BATTERS	POS-GAMES	GP	AB	R	H	BI	2B	3B	HR	BB	SO	SB	BA
Glenn Wright	1B52,SS22	89	345	56	97	59	16	8	8	24	37	4	.281
Herman Schulte	2B45	46	151	19	34	11	5	2	0	11	11	0	.225
Al Niemiec	SS128	137	518	60	156	61	20	7	1	35	69	4	.301
Mike Kreevich	3B83,OF68	152	626	104	200	75	39	20	9	58	57	23	.319
Mel Almada	OF135	135	580	85	190	86	29	12	1	45	40	29	.328
Jim Mosolf	OF130	133	539	83	153	66	19	8	3	50	49	6	.284
George Stumpf	OF122	131	514	68	152	65	26	13	3	59	41	6	.296
Bill Brenzel	C103	113	395	53	112	50	7	6	0	19	17	1	.284
Fritz Knothe	3B51,2B37	95	336	43	83	35	19	3	2	46	41	6	.247
James Crandall	C52	66	197	17	53	16	7	1	0	16	8	0	.269
Bruce Connatser	1B48	48	193	21	54	37	10	2	1	16	12	5	.280
George Hockette	P39	48	102	19	33	13	1	0	0	5	8	0	.324
Curtis Fullerton	P44	46	72	5	17		1	0	0			0	.236
Harold Carson	P39	44	90	10	21		5	0	1			0	.233
Walt Gautreau	2B39	42	141	18	41	20	6	1	0	17	8	2	.291
William Rollings	1B20	37	89	14	29		3	0	1			0	.326
Al Shealy	P28	28	37	4	10		2	0	1			0	.270
Ed Taylor	3B20	27	95	14	27	10	3	1	0	13	5	0	.284
Phil Page	P27	27	60	4	15		0	0	0			0	.250
Wilcy Moore	P22	22	21	0	3		0	0	0			0	.143
J. Horn	1B11	20	60	3	13		1	0	0			2	.217
Fred West	1B19	19	71	10	15		0	0	0			0	.211
Joe Valenti	2B19	19	70	10	17		2	0	1			0	.243
Bill Shores	P10	10	11	1	3		2	0	0			0	.273
John Monroe	2B	6	16	2	6	3	1	0	0	5	1		.375
Alex Gaston	C6	6	10	3	4	3	0	0	1	2	0	0	.400
Mace Brown	P6	6	8	1	1		0	0	0	2		1	.125
Art Jones	P6	6	5	0	1		0	0	0		2		.200

KANSAS CITY (cont.)
Blues

BATTERS	POS-GAMES	GP	AB	R	H	BI	2B	3B	HR	BB	SO	SB	BA
Howard Taylor	P5	5	9	0	0		0	0	0	2	3		.000
Max Beard	P4	4	8	0	0		0	0	0		3		.000
Fred Browning	P4	4	1	0	0		0	0	0				.000
Al Marchand	OF	3	4	1	2		1	0	0		1		.500
Eldon Breese	OF,C	2	9	2	4	2	1	0	0				.444
Joe Blackwell	P2	2	2	0	0		0	0	0				.000
Rebman	C1	1	3	0	0	1	0	0	0		1		.000
John Niggeling	P1	1	1	0	0		0	0	0				.000

PITCHERS	W	L	PCT	G	GS	CG	SH	IP	H	BB	SO	ERA
George Hockette	16	15	.516	39				260	299	35	57	3.84
Phil Page	10	8	.556	27				164	203	54	77	4.34
Curtis Fullerton	10	17	.370	44				208	254	76	94	4.76
Harold Carson	9	15	.375	39				239	312	48	41	4.56
Al Shealy	4	5	.444	28				105	126	32	55	4.54
Bill Shores	2	3	.400	10				31	44	7	11	4.35
Max Beard	1	1	.500	4				20	22	7	8	5.85
Howard Taylor	1	2	.333	5				25	31	6	6	5.04
Art Jones	1	3	.250	6				23	29	12	10	5.48
Wilcy Moore	1	5	.167	22				66	106	16	16	5.59
John Niggeling	0	1	.000	1				3	3	3	2	6.00
Mace Brown	0	2	.000	6				26	33	8	8	7.27
Fred Browning	0	0	----	4				7	13	2	1	10.29
Joe Blackwell	0	0	----	2				5	8	5	2	7.20

MULTI-TEAM PLAYERS

BATTERS	POS-GAMES	TEAMS	GP	AB	R	H	BI	2B	3B	HR	BB	SO	SB	BA
George Detore	1B47,2B14,3B10	LOU-MIL	113	380	51	102	45	18	5	6	32	37	8	.268
Ernie Wingard	1B103	IND-MIL	105	416	65	121	67	21	7	8	24	61	2	.291
Russ Young	C58,1B15	MIL-MIN	82	221	32	49	23	1	0	3	29	23	1	.222
Rollie Stiles	P43	MIL-KC	43	72	8	18		1	0	0			0	.250
John Tising	P41	IND-LOU	42	70	4	10		4	0	0			0	.143
Phil Weinert	P34	LOU-TOL	34	66	5	15		1	0	0			0	.227
Bryan Harriss	P29	KC-MIL	29	42	2	9		2	0	0			0	.214
Ira Hutchinson	P25	MIL-SP	25	29	2	6		1	0	0			0	.207

PITCHERS	TEAMS	W	L	PCT	G	GS	CG	SH	IP	H	BB	SO	ERA
John Tising	IND-LOU	11	14	.440	41				186	191	110	171	4.45
Phil Weinert	LOU-TOL	10	11	.476	34				169	228	67	77	6.07
Rollie Stiles	MIL-KC	10	12	.455	43				209	238	82	76	4.52
Bryan Harriss	KC-MIL	3	8	.273	29				125	183	46	49	6.91
Ira Hutchinson	MIL-SP	3	10	.231	25				93	114	52	34	6.10

TEAM BATTING

TEAMS	GP	AB	R	H	BI	2B	3B	HR	BB	SO	SB	BA
MINNEAPOLIS	150	5448	1012	1676	939	309	50	176	603	600	42	.308
COLUMBUS	155	5487	870	1586	795	273	76	123	544	659	97	.289
MILWAUKEE	153	5598	949	1720	903	277	68	136	508	642	44	.307
LOUISVILLE	153	5373	771	1561	677	221	96	33	431	498	70	.291
INDIANAPOLIS	155	5552	812	1616	722	265	82	39	426	419	77	.291
TOLEDO	153	5347	830	1590	732	265	79	54	550	561	102	.297
ST. PAUL	152	5288	683	1379	621	250	58	105	441	719	56	.261
KANSAS CITY	153	5453	735	1557	657	220	83	33	478	530	89	.286
	612	43546	6662	12685	6046	2080	592	699	3981	4628	577	.291

1935
Marshall's Streak

Most holders of long batting streaks put up incredible numbers during their record setting seasons. Joe DiMaggio, when he hit in a record 61 games during the 1933 Pacific Coast League campaign, ended up batting .340 for the season. In the International League, Bill Sweeney's 36-game streak led to his .357 season average. However, in the American Association this was not the case. The record for the longest hitting streak was set by Milwaukee shortstop Ed Marshall, who finished with a solid but hardly spectacular season during his record setting year.

Ed Marshall, after several part-time seasons with the New York Giants, joined the Milwaukee Brewers as their shortstop for the 1934 season. During that campaign he batted a respectible .286. Certainly no one expected what would happen the next year.

In 1935, Marshall returned as the Brewer shortstop. In early May, Marshall hit safely in one game, and then continued getting hits in game after game. He hit safely in every game for the rest of the month, continuing into June. During the second week of the month, Marshall passed the existing record of 38, set by Frank Sigafoos in 1933. On June 15, Marshall failed to get a hit, and his streak was over. But his 43-game hitting streak still stands as the Association's best.

Overall, Marshall's season was average at best. With a monster streak like his, one would expect at least a .300 average. However, Marshall's average finished at .290, three points below the league average.

Minneapolis duplicated its pennant of 1934. Second place honors went to Indianapolis, while Kansas City and Columbus finished tied for third. St. Paul, Milwaukee, Toledo, and Louisville placed in the last four spots. John Cooney of Indianapolis won the batting title (.371), and Minneapolis' John Gill hit the most home runs (43) and knocked in the most runs (154). Dominic Ryba of Columbus won the most games (20), while Clyde Hatter of Milwaukee had the lowest earned run average (2.88) and John Tising of Louisville had the most strikeouts (230).

Ed Marshall went on to play several more years in the American Association before drifting out of the league. His hitting streak stands as a testament that a good, solid player can accomplish a spectacular achievement. Certainly, Ed Marshall's 43-game mastery of Association pitching qualifies as an example.

MINNEAPOLIS Millers

1st   91-63   .591   Donie Bush

BATTERS	POS-GAMES	GP	AB	R	H	BI	2B	3B	HR	BB	SO	SB	BA
Joe Hauser	1B118	131	409	74	107	101	18	1	23	94	75	3	.262
Andy Cohen	2B153	153	665	90	182	55	30	7	2	29	29	0	.274
Leo Norris	SS154	154	599	87	174	105	39	11	22	51	96	5	.290
Robert Holland	3B87,OF24	118	459	88	142	89	30	3	20	37	44	3	.309
John Gill	OF148	148	610	**148**	220	**154**	41	5	**43**	64	68	7	.361
Fabian Gaffke	OF118	135	447	87	135	76	29	4	19	25	64	2	.302
Buzz Arlett	OF113	122	425	90	153	101	26	2	25	60	36	6	.360
Bubbles Hargrave	C63	65	219	20	53	29	8	0	4	24	20	0	.242
Spence Harris	OF82,1B42	127	486	121	164	69	25	4	16	73	31	0	.337
Foster Ganzel	3B60	71	218	35	64	30	13	1	6	31	13	1	.294
Al Leitz	C54	69	173	15	43	21	8	1	3	12	12	0	.249
Bill Perrin	P47	47	84	5	13	0	0	0	0	1	33	1	.155
Wilfred Ryan	P46	46	37	4	6	1	0	1	1	5	13	0	.162
Walt Tauscher	P37	38	87	14	21	3	3	1	0	5	8	0	.241
Denny Galehouse	P35	37	71	10	16	5	2	1	1	4	20	0	.225
Francis Hogan	C35	36	102	12	30	21	6	1	2	26	6	0	.294
Ray Kolp	P34	34	71	7	11	3	1	0	0	3	7	0	.155
Steve Sundra	P28	30	43	8	8	1	0	0	1	1	12	0	.186
Belve Bean	P13	13	26	1	4	1	1	0	0	0	5	0	.154
Henry Fiarito	3B10	10	30	3	9	1	1	0	0	5	3	1	.300

PITCHERS	W	L	PCT	G	GS	CG	SH	IP	H	BB	SO	ERA
Walt Tauscher	18	9	.667	37				226	250	61	77	4.38
Denny Galehouse	15	8	.652	35				192	232	71	140	5.39
Bill Perrin	14	13	.519	47				231	288	106	119	4.83
Wilfred Ryan	11	4	.733	46				129	155	32	72	4.88
Ray Kolp	11	9	.550	34				196	242	32	63	4.27
Steve Sundra	4	6	.400	28				102	136	46	64	6.18
Ray Starr	2	1	.667	5				25	27	12	9	
Belve Bean	2	3	.400	13				61	85	17	19	5.02
Jesse Petty	1	0	1.000	2				8	11	1	4	
Herbert May	0	0	----	2				3				
Charles Johnson	0	0	----	1				1				

INDIANAPOLIS Indians

2nd   85-67   .559   -5   Wade Killefer

BATTERS	POS-GAMES	GP	AB	R	H	BI	2B	3B	HR	BB	SO	SB	BA
Minor Heath	1B153	153	551	115	166	98	32	7	20	**127**	73	20	.301
Vince Sherlock	2B128	128	484	66	144	57	25	2	2	37	56	23	.298
Otto Bluege	SS149	149	618	114	149	42	24	5	0	89	69	6	.241
Fred Bedore	3B129,2B20	146	575	80	180	96	33	8	2	49	49	10	.313
Riggs Stephenson	OF144	147	545	107	187	107	33	5	4	87	41	11	.343
John Cooney	OF140	142	603	111	**224**	92	37	7	3	37	21	9	**.371**
John Stoneham	OF97	113	389	62	111	67	22	10	12	48	28	4	.285
Joe Sprinz	C107	109	375	44	97	43	11	2	0	45	34	4	.259
Como Cotelle	OF88,P3	109	381	55	122	45	15	3	1	20	23	11	.320
John Riddle	C56,3B20	82	282	28	92	44	20	4	0	6	12	2	.326
Jim Turner	P33	48	106	13	25	14	5	1	0	1	2	0	.236
Phil Gallivan	P47	48	94	14	18	8	4	0	0	8	15	0	.191
Robert Logan	P35	38	80	6	13	4	2	0	0	2	11	0	.163
Vance Page	P33	34	75	9	20	8	4	1	0	1	11	1	.267
Clifton Wright	P30	31	26	4	5	7	0	0	1	2	11	0	.156
James Elliott	P25	25	32	4	5	7	0	0	1	2	11	0	.156
Stewart Bolen	P22	22	66	7	18	11	2	1	0	2	8	0	.273
Joe Lawrie		21	46	5	11	3	1	0	0	2	11	1	.239
James Sharp	P12	12	1	0	0	0	0	0	0	0	0	0	.000
Ralph Rhein		10	29	4	12	4	0	0	0	0	1	1	.414
Hal Chamberlain	P10	10	24	4	3	5	0	0	1	3	1	0	.125
Tom Gallivan	P10	10	12	1	2	0	0	0	0	1	1	0	.167

PITCHERS	W	L	PCT	G	GS	CG	SH	IP	H	BB	SO	ERA
Vance Page	17	7	.708	33				188	213	58	61	3.93
Phil Gallivan	15	17	.469	47				246	279	91	122	4.39
Stewart Bolen	13	6	.684	22				164	161	64	87	3.79
Jim Turner	13	11	.542	33				217	257	54	77	4.02
Robert Logan	12	11	.522	35				206	215	54	94	3.58
Hal Chamberlain	4	2	.667	10				55	72	26	19	6.38
James Elliott	4	5	.444	25				83	100	51	38	5.53

INDIANAPOLIS (cont.)

Indians

PITCHERS	W	L	PCT	G	GS	CG	SH	IP	H	BB	SO	ERA
Clifton Wright	3	3	.500	30				76	80	40	38	4.14
James Sharp	1	0	1.000	12				15	18	17	9	
Robert Walsh	1	0	1.000	5				20	18	15	6	
Paul Trout	0	1	.000	1				8	11	2	3	4.50
Tom Gallivan	0	3	.000	10				36	44	7	10	
Como Cotelle	0	0	----	3				5				
Paul Bouchet	0	0	----	2				7				
C. Bouchet	0	0	----	1				2				

COLUMBUS   3rd (T)   84-70   .545   -7   Ray Blades
Red Birds

BATTERS	POS-GAMES	GP	AB	R	H	BI	2B	3B	HR	BB	SO	SB	BA
Frank Hurst	1B83	91	317	47	88	63	8	3	11	27	26	2	.278
Earl Adams	2B85,3B26	110	420	57	120	59	20	6	0	30	13	7	.286
Fred Ankenman	SS157	157	702	123	219	87	26	11	4	44	32	21	.312
Don Gutteridge	3B98,2B22	121	492	77	143	63	34	5	6	23	62	12	.291
Nick Cullop	OF138	145	559	102	190	128	40	14	24	70	104	4	.340
John Winsett	OF101	108	368	91	128	90	29	5	20	45	60	3	.348
Chick Fullis	OF104,2B13	125	468	83	141	42	22	5	1	49	48	6	.301
Ambrose Ogrodowski	C129	130	490	66	146	76	31	7	5	32	34	8	.298
Harold Anderson	OF51,2B25,3B25	116	309	47	87	40	15	4	0	38	24	7	.282
Dominic Ryba	P48,C19,3B11	94	245	32	78	30	7	1	1	15	27	3	.318
John Hasset	1B73	78	288	52	97	45	14	2	5	31	12	11	.337
Robert Klinger	P49	51	93	6	18	4	1	0	0	3	5	1	.194
Don Padgett	OF43	46	176	21	48	30	5	2	3	9	21	3	.273
John Chambers	P45	45	42	2	6	3	0	0	0	6	15	0	.143
Hal Epps	OF42	43	162	33	52	19	7	2	2	20	12	3	.321
James Winford	P39	39	81	1	13	0	1	0	0	5	32	0	.160
James Moore	OF28	35	103	11	29	12	5	0	0	13	8	0	.282
Mort Cooper	P27	33	35	3	7	3	1	0	0	3	9	0	.200
James Mooney	P29	32	23	2	4	1	1	0	0	5	3	0	.174
Lyle Tinning	P27	28	50	6	13	9	2	1	0	2	7	0	.260
Ed Delker	2B10	16	44	13	14	7	2	3	1	8	7	3	.318
Mays Copeland	P14	14	18	2	6	2	1	0	0	3	4	0	.333
Stu Martin	2B11	13	37	3	14	5	1	2	0	4	1	1	.378
Robert Schelfing		10	26	3	6	4	1	0	0	2	6	0	.231
Joe Sims	P9	10	7	1	1	0	0	0	0	0	2	0	.143

PITCHERS	W	L	PCT	G	GS	CG	SH	IP	H	BB	SO	ERA
Dominic Ryba	20	8	.714	48				252	265	52	138	3.29
James Winford	14	11	.560	39				244	266	80	119	3.65
Robert Klinger	14	14	.500	49				255	322	85	113	4.27
Lyle Tinning	11	9	.550	27				143	161	50	65	4.22
Mort Cooper	6	7	.462	27				101	109	59	62	3.65
Mays Copeland	5	2	.714	14				52	49	13	20	2.77
John Chambers	5	6	.455	45				151	199	46	63	4.83
James Mooney	4	5	.444	29				86	115	35	31	6.17
Joe Sims	2	3	.400	9				26	34	15	8	
William Cox	1	0	1.000	2				7	8	2	3	
Oscar Judd	1	1	.500	5				7	8	10	2	
Nathan Andrews	1	2	.333	5				24	25	7	10	
Richard Elston	0	1	.000	5				10	9	7	1	
Deland Wetherell	0	1	.000	2				5	6	2	2	
Eddie Maximovich	0	0	----	5				12				
Ed Hurley	0	0	----	4				8				

KANSAS CITY   3rd (T)   84-70   .545   -7   Dutch Zwilling
Blues

BATTERS	POS-GAMES	GP	AB	R	H	BI	2B	3B	HR	BB	SO	SB	BA
Dale Alexander	1B111,P1	120	461	84	165	95	29	6	16	46	42	5	.358
Herman Schulte	2B145	147	524	52	138	54	21	7	2	33	42	6	.263
Ray French	SS151	151	621	115	161	38	22	8	1	69	63	9	.259
Wilbur Brubaker	3B87,1B45	133	484	85	142	73	41	15	7	55	94	11	.293
George Stumpf	OF150	150	580	84	187	105	32	13	3	66	57	16	.322
Mike Kreevich	OF131,3B29	156	643	130	222	115	36	14	13	44	45	20	.345
Ernest Sulik	OF112	124	443	93	129	43	23	11	6	44	28	5	.291

KANSAS CITY (cont.)
Blues

BATTERS	POS-GAMES	GP	AB	R	H	BI	2B	3B	HR	BB	SO	SB	BA
Ed Madjeski	C98	98	381	41	116	52	16	4	3	16	31	6	.304
Eldon Breese	OF28,C28,3B10	91	242	38	65	27	13	4	1	19	37	3	.269
Joe Valenti	3B36,2B21	75	193	34	73	42	5	6	0	28	19	5	.378
Walter Carson	OF64	72	246	43	76	35	10	5	4	34	31	5	.309
Clarence Struss	P41	52	92	10	24	11	8	1	0	1	10	0	.261
Wilcy Moore	P49	49	44	5	9	6	1	0	1	4	17	0	.205
Curtis Fullerton	P47	48	77	4	13	4	1	0	0	7	16	0	.169
Phil Page	P37	39	78	6	13	14	2	0	0	7	24	0	.167
Rollie Stiles	P35	35	86	7	15	5	1	0	0	2	27	0	.174
Harold Smith	P30	30	66	4	9	3	0	0	0	6	23	0	.136
Dallas Warren	C20	21	76	6	21	13	5	3	0	5	14	0	.276
Vance Cauble	P17	17	24	1	2	1	1	0	0	0	9	0	.138
Herman Bell	P14	14	9	2	0	0	0	0	0	3	2	0	.000
Cage Keaton		11	7	1	2	1	0	0	0	0	2	0	.286

PITCHERS	W	L	PCT	G	GS	CG	SH	IP	H	BB	SO	ERA
Wilcy Moore	15	5	.750	49				136	141	33	55	3.44
Phil Page	14	11	.560	37				210	283	47	74	5.10
Harold Smith	13	8	.619	30				191	201	59	63	3.53
Rollie Stiles	13	11	.542	35				218	228	71	77	3.39
Clarence Struss	12	12	.500	41				217	236	115	103	5.18
Curtis Fullerton	9	11	.450	47				206	274	58	83	5.33
Vance Cauble	4	3	.571	17				73	87	34	27	3.58
Bill Shores	2	1	.667	8				31	41	13	15	
Herman Bell	2	4	.333	14				42	72	9	19	
Gene Morris	0	1	.000	9				16	15	7	7	
John Niggeling	0	1	.000	3				12	16	3	6	
Fred Browning	0	2	.000	3				13	23	3	8	
James Parker	0	0	----	7				13				
Dale Alexander	0	0	----	1				3				

ST. PAUL
Saints

5th   75-78   .490   -15.5   Marty McManus

BATTERS	POS-GAMES	GP	AB	R	H	BI	2B	3B	HR	BB	SO	SB	BA
Phil Todt	1B139	141	600	80	177	93	29	9	9	22	39	0	.295
John Warner	2B154	154	667	113	208	74	38	5	12	45	56	8	.312
Robert Boken	SS114	129	477	68	142	75	25	5	10	28	56	6	.298
William McWilliams	3B107	117	414	58	116	75	24	5	13	32	77	5	.280
Larry Rosenthal	OF155	156	629	120	190	80	35	9	13	90	75	7	.302
Ivey Shiver	OF137	144	555	107	176	125	25	10	31	49	109	5	.317
Willis Norman	OF128	137	463	80	146	81	27	7	14	62	61	2	.315
Angelo Giulani	C109	109	311	39	86	37	18	5	2	18	14	0	.277
Robert Fenner	C85	101	288	30	84	44	14	3	5	36	22	0	.292
Marty McManus	3B52,1B21,P1	93	276	33	76	46	14	2	7	32	27	6	.275
Fred Koster	OF63	93	269	50	67	23	12	5	0	31	20	3	.249
Joe Rezotko	SS59	69	182	24	49	11	11	2	0	11	16	0	.269
Lou Fette	P43	54	85	19	16	7	3	1	0	2	8	2	.188
Lee Stine	P46	48	92	18	25	11	3	4	0	11	20	1	.272
Miles Hunter	P43	43	25	4	7	3	0	0	0	4	10	0	.280
Burleigh Grimes	P31	38	15	6	3	1	1	0	0	1	0	0	.200
Monty Stratton	P33	34	91	12	25	9	2	2	1	3	17	1	.275
Howard Mills	P34	34	45	6	8	4	2	1	0	2	20	0	.178
John Rigney	P32	32	35	5	11	3	1	1	0	2	9	0	.314
Eugene Trow	P28	28	38	2	3	1	1	0	0	1	8	0	.079
Gowell Claset	P13	13	20	1	2	0	0	0	0	1	8	0	.100
Glenn Spencer	P10	10	25	1	3	0	0	0	0	1	4	0	.120

PITCHERS	W	L	PCT	G	GS	CG	SH	IP	H	BB	SO	ERA
Lee Stine	18	11	.621	46				254	301	84	89	4.68
Monty Stratton	17	9	.654	33				226	261	63	120	4.02
Lou Fette	10	17	.370	43				239	263	81	67	4.71
J. Rigney	8	4	.667	32				107	136	48	26	5.64
Howard Mills	7	8	.467	34				146	170	84	70	5.36
Miles Hunter	5	5	.500	43				105	113	56	41	4.54
Glenn Spencer	3	7	.300	10				65	72	28	20	5.40
Eugene Trow	3	10	.231	28				106	125	79	38	6.03
Gowell Claset	2	2	.500	13				57	82	23	26	5.21

ST. PAUL (cont.)
Saints

PITCHERS	W	L	PCT	G	GS	CG	SH	IP	H	BB	SO	ERA
Burleigh Grimes	1	1	.500	31				54	73	29	19	6.83
Harry Kinzy	1	2	.333	7				18	21	20	13	
Charlie Barnabe	0	2	.000	3				7	9	4	2	
Marty McManus	0	0	----	1				1				

MILWAUKEE	6th	75-79	.487	-16	Al Sothoron

Brewers

BATTERS	POS-GAMES	GP	AB	R	H	BI	2B	3B	HR	BB	SO	SB	BA
Ernie Wingard	1B	(see multi-team players)											
Lin Storti	2B143,3B11	152	605	123	178	87	31	10	29	71	65	6	.294
Ed Marshall	SS155	155	677	110	196	71	29	6	8	59	42	1	.290
George Trapp	3B59	60	197	25	47	23	6	3	1	15	19	2	.239
Earl Webb	OF137	144	533	98	180	98	33	6	6	69	30	0	.338
Frank Doljack	OF115	123	467	75	145	63	30	10	9	42	37	7	.310
Ted Gullic	OF100,1B57	155	607	118	196	131	44	9	33	48	66	18	.323
George Rensa	C78	89	291	27	81	37	9	2	3	30	16	4	.278
George Detore	3B53,C52	120	375	65	107	68	23	5	7	56	51	11	.285
John Kloza	OF91	95	377	61	115	68	22	11	8	26	42	4	.305
Ed Hope	3B43,2B16	75	204	19	43	15	5	4	0	22	53	7	.211
Wayne LeMaster	P34	51	86	12	26	13	1	0	3	9	19	0	.302
Forest Pressnell	P38	38	50	2	9	4	0	0	0	1	8	0	.180
Lou Polli	P32	35	82	11	20	11	0	1	0	7	16	1	.244
Garland Braxton	P33	33	90	9	15	6	1	0	0	7	22	0	.167
Luke Hamlin	P30	33	66	9	12	2	2	0	0	3	19	0	.182
Anton Kubek	OF24	31	84	9	16	8	3	1	0	9	7	1	.190
Paul Florence	C26	28	101	11	26	13	1	3	0	6	8	0	.257
Steve Larkin	P27	27	49	3	8	1	1	1	0	0	15	0	.163
Gil Torres	P15,1B10	25	48	3	15	4	3	0	0	4	6	0	.313
Clyde Hatter	P14	14	36	1	5	3	0	0	0	2	7	0	.139

PITCHERS	W	L	PCT	G	GS	CG	SH	IP	H	BB	SO	ERA
Garland Braxton	17	10	.630	33				246	261	65	116	3.22
Lou Polli	13	12	.520	32				209	219	62	93	4.69
Wayne LeMaster	12	9	.571	34				184	213	103	105	4.65
Forest Pressnell	9	11	.450	38				161	207	47	64	5.25
Luke Hamlin	8	14	.364	30				178	202	46	90	4.04
Clyde Hatter	7	3	.700	14				100	93	38	74	**2.88**
Steve Larkin	6	10	.375	27				134	137	82	54	5.31
Gil Torres	2	6	.250	15				62	85	24	21	5.37
Ray Mackey	0	1	.000	7				30	37	13	9	
John Rowe	0	0	----	2				5				
Robert Duzich	0	0	----	2				5				
Jack Hallett	0	0	----	1				1	1	1	0	

TOLEDO	7th	64-86	.427	-25	Fred Haney

Mud Hens

BATTERS	POS-GAMES	GP	AB	R	H	BI	2B	3B	HR	BB	SO	SB	BA
Bob Garbark	1B48,C71	136	456	72	145	79	18	5	3	50	23	5	.318
Robert Allaire	2B141	144	550	79	148	59	19	7	1	44	30	9	.269
Frank Parker	SS148	149	555	82	159	59	34	7	1	33	58	7	.286
Fred Haney	3B134,P1	142	533	93	171	53	24	6	3	68	37	29	.321
Ellis Powers	OF125	131	489	81	166	90	19	5	14	55	37	3	.339
Alta Cohen	OF106,P11	128	452	67	126	47	16	2	1	74	43	14	.279
Chet Morgan	OF105	107	442	57	142	79	19	12	3	35	29	8	.321
George Susce	C68	72	275	41	83	57	18	2	4	20	13	4	.302
John Calvey	OF45,3B33,SS13,P1	115	393	54	115	43	16	6	3	29	44	15	.293
Harvey Walker	OF77,1B34	113	412	89	138	63	24	14	11	58	69	8	.335
Irvin Stein	P42	43	65	2	8	3	1	0	0	2	21	0	.123
Roxie Lawson	P29	40	92	14	26	10	3	0	0	6	15	0	.283
Joe Doljack	P27	39	37	5	7	4	1	0	0	2	10	0	.189
Walter Laskowski	C27	37	83	10	16	9	5	1	1	14	11	0	.193
Carl Boone	P37	37	80	5	15	9	0	0	0	4	11	0	.188
Oscar Roettger	1B32	35	115	15	25	13	8	0	0	16	9	0	.217
Carl Edmonds	1B24	35	92	13	23	10	1	2	0	5	18	0	.250

TOLEDO (cont.)
Mud Hens

BATTERS	POS-GAMES	GP	AB	R	H	BI	2B	3B	HR	BB	SO	SB	BA
Gus Walsh	P31	33	57	3	13	6	0	1	0	0	6	0	.228
Grant Bowler	P30	31	23	1	2	1	0	0	0	0	6	0	.087
Paul Sullivan	P28	29	55	4	14	4	0	0	0	4	9	0	.255
Joe Zapustas	OF20	24	54	7	11	3	1	1	0	3	20	0	.204
Thomas Leonard	OF10	14	42	4	15	4	3	0	0	1	2	1	.357
Kenneth Weafer	P10	10	10	1	2	1	0	0	0	0	1	0	.200

PITCHERS		W	L	PCT	G	GS	CG	SH	IP	H	BB	SO	ERA
Roxie Lawson		14	8	.636	29				211	243	81	87	3.92
Carl Boone		11	16	.407	37				232	276	54	104	4.66
Paul Sullivan		9	11	.450	28				151	149	78	55	4.89
Irvin Stein		6	12	.333	42				194	252	50	51	4.55
Alta Cohen		4	3	.571	11				55	75	15	24	4.58
Gus Walsh		4	9	.308	31				130	181	57	36	6.92
George Buchanan		3	1	.750	8				23	31	9	3	
Joe Doljack		2	6	.250	27				79	104	37	26	6.72
Grant Bowler		2	7	.222	30				83	97	47	27	6.07
Kenneth Weafer		1	1	.500	10				21	38	13	13	
Joe Bartulis		1	1	.500	3				10	18	1	4	
Al Curry		0	1	.000	6				27	35	10	18	
William Perry		0	0	----	3				5				
Oliver Thomas		0	0	----	2				3				
Ed Nichols		0	0	----	2				2				
Ed Myers		0	0	----	2				2				
Herbert Kiger		0	0	----	1				3				
Alfred Pederson		0	0	----	1				1				
Roy James		0	0	----	1				1				
John Calvey		0	0	----	1				1				
Sam Dailey		0	0	----	1				0				
Fred Haney		0	0	----	1				0				

LOUISVILLE 8th 52-97 .349 -36.5 Ken Penner
Colonels

BATTERS	POS-GAMES	GP	AB	R	H	BI	2B	3B	HR	BB	SO	SB	BA
William Rollings	1B		(see multi-team players)										
James Adair	2B106	118	443	52	124	57	22	10	3	35	32	13	.280
Joe Olivares	SS73,2B13	94	355	40	92	23	14	0	0	12	16	7	.259
Frank Sigafoos	3B96	98	398	51	125	52	18	5	3	26	15	6	.314
Goody Rosen	OF145	148	648	104	190	50	21	12	3	61	78	18	.293
Gil Brack	OF140	140	564	133	181	71	28	16	11	59	99	14	.321
Melbern Simons	OF125	134	525	80	185	74	31	5	1	44	25	10	.352
Ray Thompson	C97	115	378	38	111	55	15	7	6	22	13	0	.294
Art Funk	SS70,3B34	108	404	40	109	49	15	4	1	24	23	8	.270
Al Van Camp	1B41,OF30,3B19	96	362	39	106	50	13	4	4	26	22	3	.293
Walter Ringhoefer	C69	93	269	31	86	43	14	2	2	20	30	3	.320
Rip Sewell	P44	64	96	11	21	9	4	0	0	2	18	1	.219
Al LeComte	P34	49	91	15	26	11	5	1	2	15	28	0	.286
Richard Bass	P46	48	70	4	15	6	3	0	0	2	7	0	.214
James Peterson	P45	46	83	5	13	3	0	0	0	9	17	0	.157
John Tising	P43	43	100	11	25	8	3	3	0	2	14	0	.250
Vince Klein	2B28	31	106	11	28	13	2	2	0	8	9	1	.264
Francis Nekola	P27	27	26	1	1	1	0	0	0	3	15	0	.038

PITCHERS		W	L	PCT	G	GS	CG	SH	IP	H	BB	SO	ERA
John Tising		13	15	.464	43				269	246	142	230	4.88
James Peterson		12	18	.400	45				247	325	79	112	5.28
Richard Bass		8	18	.308	46				211	265	66	69	5.67
Rip Sewell		6	20	.231	44				194	278	102	84	8.12
Al LeComte		3	2	.600	34				96	130	77	49	7.88
Francis Nekola		2	7	.222	27				92	114	43	51	5.77
D. Southard		1	0	1.000	5				18	20	6	9	
Eldon McLean		0	2	.000	9				14	23	10	5	
Ken Penner		0	0	----	6				13				
Al Masek		0	0	----	2				3				

MULTI-TEAM PLAYERS

BATTERS	POS-GAMES	TEAMS	GP	AB	R	H	BI	2B	3B	HR	BB	SO	SB	BA
Ernie Wingard	1B107	MIL-TOL	122	447	53	129	71	27	7	7	36	41	1	.289
William Rollings	1B110	KC-LOU	120	459	60	151	72	18	5	6	33	30	9	.329
Charles Marrow	P46	MIN-LOU	47	67	7	14	6	0	0	3	2	14	0	.209
Archie McKain	P41	LOU-MIN	41	57	5	15	7	2	1	1	4	18	0	.263
Charles George	C35	KC-MIN	37	132	9	40	16	3	0	3	4	17	1	.303
Myles Thomas	P19	IND-TOL	25	48	5	8	5	1	0	0	1	4	0	.167
Rudy Laskowski		TOL-IND	13	30	6	5	1	0	0	0	7	7	0	.167

PITCHERS	TEAMS	W	L	PCT	G	GS	CG	SH	IP	H	BB	SO	ERA
Charles Marrow	MIN-LOU	12	14	.462	46				184	223	79	91	5.82
Myles Thomas	IND-TOL	8	8	.500	19				126	152	43	35	4.64
Archie McKain	LOU-MIN	8	11	.421	41				155	204	58	74	6.04
Orlin Collier	IND-MIL	1	1	.500	5				14				
Ernie Wingard	MIL-TOL	1	5	.167	16				68	83	33	14	5.56

TEAM BATTING

TEAMS	GP	AB	R	H	BI	2B	3B	HR	BB	SO	SB	BA
MINNEAPOLIS	154	5430	934	1601	881	284	44	191	573	639	29	.295
INDIANAPOLIS	154	5449	852	1617	773	276	56	47	579	513	104	.297
COLUMBUS	155	5614	890	1678	828	276	74	84	501	591	93	.299
KANSAS CITY	156	5525	854	1611	748	268	97	59	495	644	93	.292
ST. PAUL	156	5607	876	1620	803	285	76	117	486	678	46	.289
MILWAUKEE	155	5459	839	1557	788	266	80	111	522	602	63	.285
TOLEDO	154	5544	822	1616	731	237	71	48	544	562	103	.291
LOUISVILLE	150	5460	737	1605	658	229	75	47	408	517	93	.292
	617	44088	6804	12905	6210	2121	573	704	4108	4746	624	.293

1936
Shaughnessy's Plan

During the decade of the 1930s, all of minor league baseball suffered. The depression had hit the country hard, and people didn't have an abundance of money to spend on such frivolities as baseball. Baseball owners had to think hard to find ways of convincing the public they should come to the ballpark. One innovation was the onset of night baseball during the early thirties. Another was the development of the Shaughnessy playoff plan.

Frank Shaughnessy was a baseball executive in the International League, and in 1932 he developed a plan for a playoff system. The plan called for four teams in an eight-team circuit to participate in post-season play. Concurrently, the first and third and the second and fourth place clubs would conduct series, with the winners squaring off for the championship. The idea was to generate interest in an otherwise lackluster season by making even the race for fourth place mean something.

After the 1933 season, the International and Texas Leagues instituted the Shaughnessy playoff plan. In 1935, the Southern Association followed suit. After the 1936 season, two new participants joined the fray, the Pacific Coast League and the American Association.

Milwaukee came out of nowhere to win the pennant by five games over St. Paul, the Brewers' first since 1914. Kansas City and Indianapolis captured the last two playoff spots, with Minneapolis missing out by a single game. Columbus, Louisville and Toledo brought up the rear. Lead batting honors went to Vern Washington of St. Paul (.390), while John Winsett of Columbus swatted 50 home runs and knocked in 154 to lead the Association in both categories. Pitching leaders included St. Paul's Lou Fette who won 25 games, Columbus' Bill McGee who had an earned run average of 2.93, and Milwaukee's Clyde Hatter, who struck out 190.

In the inaugural series of playoffs, first place Milwaukee polished off third place Kansas City in four straight, while fourth place Indianapolis took second place St. Paul in five. In the final round, Milwaukee bumped off Indianapolis in five games to earn the right to participate in the Junior World Series.

Shaughnessy's plan would gain almost universal acceptance, as most minor leagues adopted some form of playoff system, despite complaints that the regular season was meaningless if the fourth place team could win it all. This led some leagues to adopt a dual championship trophy, one for the first place team and one for the playoff winners. Nonetheless, the playoffs would prove to be an enduring institution, surviving in much the same format to the present day.

MILWAUKEE Brewers

1st　　　90-64　　　.584　　　　　　　Al Sothoron

BATTERS	POS-GAMES	GP	AB	R	H	BI	2B	3B	HR	BB	SO	SB	BA
Rudy York	1B157	157	619	119	207	148	25	21	37	76	105	7	.334
Ed Hope	2B139	139	482	47	117	47	21	3	6	49	122	4	.243
Chet Wilburn	SS154	154	626	111	182	77	29	7	9	70	52	5	.291
Lin Storti	3B140,2B21	157	600	98	184	108	25	10	31	56	46	5	.307
Chet Laabs	OF157	157	627	119	203	151	27	16	42	48	136	6	.324
Bernard Uhault	OF111	116	456	104	147	55	32	4	7	52	27	36	.322
Chet Morgan	OF99	113	448	81	133	39	21	8	1	23	21	10	.297
George Detore	C77	89	264	46	87	38	10	5	6	38	38	10	.330
Ted Gullic	OF95	101	395	82	130	78	20	6	22	32	67	4	.329
Bill Brenzel	C73	77	274	24	79	42	17	3	1	15	23	1	.288
Luke Hamlin	P44	48	94	7	16	5	1	0	0	10	21	0	.170
Joe Heving	P41	44	98	9	27	4	4	1	0	3	13	0	.276
Salvador Ramos	3B22	41	120	11	31	15	3	4	0	7	13	0	.258
Garland Braxton	P39	39	59	4	12	3	0	0	0	1	14	0	.203
Clyde Hatter	P38	38	83	6	14	5	1	0	0	6	18	0	.169
Forest Pressnell	P36	36	79	8	20	7	3	0	0	6	8	0	.253
Allan Johnson	P21	21	22	0	0	0	0	0	0	1	15	0	.000
John Kloza		19	18	2	2	4	1	0	1	0	5	0	.111
Henry McDonald		13	13	2	4	0	0	0	0	0	4	0	.308
Richard Smith		12	24	1	10	3	0	0	0	1	1	0	.417
LeRoy Mahaffey	P11	11	22	2	4	3	1	0	1	0	11	0	.182
Herman Bell	P	11	10	0	0	2	0	0	0	1	1	0	.000
Gil Torres	OF,P2	7	19	1	3	0	0	0	0			0	.158
Al Mele	OF	4	17	1	2	2	1	0	0			0	.118
Harry Griswold	C	3	11	2	4	1	0	0	0			0	.364

PITCHERS		W	L	PCT	G	GS	CG	SH	IP	H	BB	SO	ERA
Forest Pressnell		19	9	.679	36		17		219	243	34	84	3.53
Joe Heving		19	12	.613	41		20		256	255	87	123	3.48
Luke Hamlin		19	14	.576	44		18		273	316	69	159	3.82
Clyde Hatter		16	6	.727	38		13		211	224	100	190	4.52
Garland Braxton		9	12	.429	39		5		179	232	81	95	5.43
LeRoy Mahaffey		5	4	.556	11		5		65	91	28	17	5.82
Allan Johnson		1	5	.167	21		2		68	105	32	18	8.47
Gil Torres		0	0	----	2		0		2	7	0	0	

ST. PAUL Saints

2nd　　　84-68　　　.553　　　-5　　　　　Gabby Street

BATTERS	POS-GAMES	GP	AB	R	H	BI	2B	3B	HR	BB	SO	SB	BA
Phil Todt	1B147	148	584	80	174	86	42	7	6	39	53	1	.298
John Warner	2B136	138	612	84	176	69	35	11	8	17	51	2	.288
Gordon Slade	SS98	107	421	82	130	51	38	3	9	44	44	3	.309
William McWilliams	3B105	120	412	71	126	73	22	6	14	38	62	0	.306
Henry Steinbacher	OF138	142	607	109	214	97	49	9	15	24	26	7	.353
Joe Mowry	OF93	97	380	71	105	54	19	4	3	48	23	2	.276
Willis Norman	OF80	108	317	83	95	62	19	3	17	63	37	4	.300
Robert Fenner	C118	122	438	60	124	85	32	6	8	51	24	1	.283
Robert Boken	SS59,3B47,2B16	127	462	72	136	78	19	5	15	30	45	6	.294
Vern Washington	OF72	73	305	55	119	53	25	4	7	12	6	3	.390
Larry Rosenthal	OF65	65	263	49	87	30	16	7	5	41	41	7	.331
John Pasek	C45	49	150	19	39	21	5	2	1	13	8	1	.260
Lou Fette	P38	43	118	17	37	19	8	0	3	3	15	0	.314
Art Herring	P37	41	86	11	21	9	0	4	1	1	8	0	.244
John Rigney	P41	41	78	4	13	5	2	1	0	1	26	0	.167
Ira Hutchinson	P39	39	62	1	13	7	3	0	0	0	17	0	.210
Glenn Spencer	P37	37	46	6	9	3	1	0	0	3	7	0	.196
Phil Weinert	P36	36	50	4	15	4	3	0	0	5	2	0	.300

PITCHERS		W	L	PCT	G	GS	CG	SH	IP	H	BB	SO	ERA
Lou Fette		25	8	.758	38		28		291	319	81	113	3.90
Ira Hutchinson		13	8	.619	39		9		184	236	62	86	4.89
John Rigney		12	11	.522	41		11		213	261	98	111	5.49
Art Herring		12	12	.500	37		14		227	246	85	123	4.64
Glenn Spencer		9	8	.529	37		8		140	177	73	54	5.46
Phil Weinert		6	6	.500	36		5		136	167	63	65	4.70

KANSAS CITY   3rd   84-69   .549   -5.5   Dutch Zwilling
Blues

BATTERS	POS-GAMES	GP	AB	R	H	BI	2B	3B	HR	BB	SO	SB	BA
Dale Alexander	1B153	154	612	81	193	100	30	9	5	57	45	4	.315
Herman Schulte	2B150	150	614	96	183	50	24	10	2	51	22	9	.298
Ed Marshall	SS134	139	507	56	140	55	24	5	2	48	47	3	.276
Meredith Hopkins	3B90	96	287	36	66	39	14	2	4	42	42	3	.230
Malin McCullough	OF134	139	521	77	156	63	17	24	6	47	50	9	.299
George Stumpf	OF128	130	489	69	141	62	22	8	5	48	52	15	.288
Al Marchand	OF98	107	358	59	105	39	15	7	3	31	40	10	.293
Ed Madjeski	C138	141	564	79	167	89	21	15	4	23	43	14	.296
Joe Valenti	3B82	114	318	31	95	39	15	2	0	42	34	2	.299
Milton Bocek	OF81	104	348	66	104	53	19	10	8	32	46	6	.299
Eldon Breese	OF46,C22	80	258	41	77	27	11	2	3	22	31	4	.298
Ray French	SS38,2B11	67	148	20	42	18	2	1	0	23	8	4	.284
Joe Vance	P39	61	88	19	22	10	1	1	0	2	11	1	.250
John Niggeling	P48	48	89	10	21	12	2	0	2	10	13	0	.236
Wilcy Moore	P43	43	28	1	5	2	1	0	0	3	13	0	.179
Phil Page	P34	36	89	12	27	9	1	1	0	3	16	0	.303
Whit Wyatt	P24	26	72	6	14	8	3	2	1	4	12	0	.194
Charles Moncrief	P25	25	29	0	4	0	3	1	0	1	1	1	.143
Harold Smith	P24	24	44	3	11	9	1	0	0	2	17	0	.250
Bill Shores	P23	23	54	5	10	3	0	0	0	2	20	0	.185
Russ Scarritt	OF16	17	72	11	21	9	3	2	1	5	2	2	.292
George Susce	C	8	25	1	6	3	1	0	0			0	.240

PITCHERS		W	L	PCT	G	GS	CG	SH	IP	H	BB	SO	ERA
John Niggeling		18	15	.545	48		16		267	271	87	147	3.64
Joe Vance		16	9	.640	39		13		211	238	67	89	3.97
Phil Page		15	12	.556	34		16		240	285	56	63	3.56
Whit Wyatt		12	7	.632	24		12		181	168	51	143	3.53
Wilcy Moore		8	7	.533	43		0		91	118	26	49	4.85
Harold Smith		6	2	.750	24		7		121	132	36	40	4.09
Bill Shores		6	5	.545	23		7		145	168	41	78	3.97
Charles Moncrief		2	4	.333	25		2		90	107	27	38	4.70

INDIANAPOLIS   4th   79-75   .513   -11   Wade Killefer
Indians

BATTERS	POS-GAMES	GP	AB	R	H	BI	2B	3B	HR	BB	SO	SB	BA
Dick Siebert	1B83,OF37	123	466	76	154	75	30	5	5	30	22	6	.330
Vince Sherlock	2B153	153	591	84	169	58	27	6	3	48	58	25	.286
Otto Bluege	SS134	137	526	76	144	45	19	4	1	63	37	1	.274
Robert Fausett	3B147,SS14	157	688	101	194	78	25	15	3	20	29	10	.282
Fred Berger	OF158	158	623	91	201	106	37	13	17	41	79	12	.323
Ox Eckhardt	OF127	128	541	95	191	69	26	11	4	26	39	3	.353
Hubert Bates	OF66	70	278	45	90	31	11	8	2	31	35	6	.324
John Riddle	C113	115	453	64	147	73	21	4	5	12	25	8	.325
Minor Heath	1B77	77	277	50	81	46	16	6	7	52	35	8	.292
James Crandall	C49	63	200	19	56	25	3	3	1	14	18	0	.280
Jim Turner	P34	51	117	14	33	21	6	2	1	5	14	0	.282
D'Arcy Flowers	3B16,SS15	48	133	21	44	24	7	2	8	9	11	0	.331
Robert Logan	P39	46	91	14	19	10	1	0	0	5	6	2	.209
Stewart Bolen	P36	38	76	7	23	13	4	0	2	5	19	0	.303
Paul Trout	P37	38	58	10	16	10	1	3	1	0	14	1	.276
Vance Page	P33	35	81	10	21	8	5	0	1	4	12	1	.259
Lyle Tinning	P33	33	82	10	21	15	3	0	0	3	8	1	.256
James Sharp	P28	28	13	0	0	1	0	0	0	3	11	0	.000
Como Cotelle	OF24	25	101	15	27	12	1	0	0	3	8	2	.267
Tom Gallivan	P23	23	15	0	1	0	0	0	0	0	4	0	.067
Dan Taylor	OF14	16	53	9	16	7	3	3	0	7	2	1	.302
George Payne	P	12	1	0	0	0	0	0	0	0	1	0	.000
Paul Dunlap		10	28	0	4	0	3	1	0	1	1	1	.143

PITCHERS		W	L	PCT	G	GS	CG	SH	IP	H	BB	SO	ERA
Jim Turner		18	13	.581	34		21		245	298	53	79	3.89
Robert Logan		16	9	.640	39		19		238	282	46	113	3.82
Vance Page		15	13	.536	33		13		217	263	41	79	4.31
Lyle Tinning		13	15	.464	33		14		213	254	50	83	4.18
Paul Trout		8	7	.533	37		9		144	180	84	70	5.13
Stewart Bolen		5	14	.263	36		10		198	234	91	114	4.95
Tom Gallivan		2	2	.500	23		0		56	66	26	14	4.34
James Sharp		1	2	.333	28		0		57	74	39	46	6.95

MINNEAPOLIS   5th   78-76   .509   -12   Donie Bush
Millers

BATTERS	POS-GAMES	GP	AB	R	H	BI	2B	3B	HR	BB	SO	SB	BA
Joe Hauser	1B114	125	437	95	117	87	20	2	34	83	101	1	.268
Andy Cohen	2B109	112	485	76	147	65	23	5	7	19	16	0	.303
John Ryan	SS125	129	510	83	146	62	24	3	11	37	80	4	.286
Robert Holland	3B71	81	314	51	82	38	20	1	7	28	30	4	.261
Fabian Gaffke	OF147	148	622	109	213	132	37	10	25	41	65	7	.342
Spence Harris	OF145	150	595	108	179	79	30	10	15	83	45	5	.301
Earl Browne	OF111,1B49	155	629	135	206	126	39	11	35	74	79	4	.328
Charles George	C101	107	381	68	114	56	25	4	11	26	49	1	.299
Roy Pfleger	2B58,SS40,3B26	121	465	76	139	104	22	5	25	19	31	2	.299
Buzz Arlett	OF50	74	193	55	61	52	10	4	15	41	24	1	.316
Bubbles Hargrave	C54	70	175	15	47	21	2	0	6	21	11	1	.269
Fresco Thompson	3B68	69	265	53	96	47	17	5	14	16	21	2	.362
Archie McKain	P45	50	105	18	22	11	3	0	1	8	36	0	.210
Reg Grabowski	P44	45	80	7	15	7	4	0	1	5	22	0	.188
Al Milnar	P31	42	76	16	19	8	5	0	5	5	19	0	.250
Belve Bean	P37	37	64	8	17	7	4	0	0	1	12	0	.266
James Baker	P36	36	33	3	7	2	0	0	0	2	8	0	.212
Walt Tauscher	P31	33	81	9	22	15	6	1	0	2	11	0	.272
Wilfred Ryan	P25	25	20	0	5	2	0	0	0	1	3	0	.250
Adam Comorosky	OF20	24	72	4	20	4	4	1	0	3	4	1	.278
Ray Kolp	P23	23	24	2	6	0	0	0	0	1	6	0	.250
Ted Olson	P21	21	18	0	3	2	0	0	0	1	7	0	.167
James Wasdell		12	13	3	3	0	0	0	0	0	2	0	.231
James Henry	P10	10	31	5	7	5	1	0	1	1	7	0	.226

PITCHERS		W	L	PCT	G	GS	CG	SH	IP	H	BB	SO	ERA
Archie McKain		19	12	.613	45		17		275	327	73	127	4.52
Walt Tauscher		13	9	.591	31		16		185	235	58	89	5.11
Reg Grabowski		12	13	.480	44		11		231	298	73	103	5.57
Belve Bean		9	9	.500	37		8		169	227	43	64	5.91
Al Milnar		8	15	.348	31		12		169	182	95	118	5.17
James Henry		6	3	.667	10		6		66	76	28	34	6.41
James Baker		5	2	.714	36		0		97	126	46	34	4.73
Wilfred Ryan		2	3	.400	25		0		59	79	17	22	6.25
Ted Olson		2	3	.400	21		3		64	75	28	21	5.34
Ray Kolp		2	7	.222	23		2		75	120	21	19	7.56

COLUMBUS   6th   76-78   .494   -14   Burt Shotton
Red Birds

BATTERS	POS-GAMES	GP	AB	R	H	BI	2B	3B	HR	BB	SO	SB	BA
Edwin Morgan	1B109	118	398	69	119	77	21	7	19	50	78	11	.299
Louis Bush	2B49,SS56	109	447	68	129	26	14	8	0	21	43	7	.289
Fred Ankenman	SS46,2B16	64	278	43	80	20	13	6	0	14	13	4	.288
Don Gutteridge	3B143	147	578	88	172	99	25	15	11	39	78	36	.298
Nick Cullop	OF142	145	560	108	181	114	30	11	24	61	95	4	.323
John Winsett	OF137	141	536	144	190	154	34	9	50	57	99	6	.354
Don Padgett	OF81	81	362	74	119	37	20	5	6	10	31	5	.329
Mickey Owen	C107	125	426	64	143	58	20	4	3	38	21	9	.336
Harold Anderson	OF55,2B23,1B22	103	344	64	99	42	17	4	2	31	31	10	.288
Paul Chervinko	C59	65	189	27	55	24	9	2	1	22	23	0	.291
Max Macon	P47	49	86	10	25	15	3	0	2	1	10	0	.291
Russ Peters	SS43	43	156	28	49	27	8	2	4	11	24	0	.314
Frank Doljack	OF38	40	151	20	41	20	9	4	0	12	17	1	.272
Dominic Ryba	P30	36	83	10	18	9	3	0	0	7	8	0	.217
Al Fisher	P28	36	47	5	11	10	1	1	3	2	7	0	.234
Bill McGee	P32	32	83	3	13	7	2	0	1	0	17	0	.157
Lyle Judy	2B30	31	102	10	26	14	1	2	1	7	9	2	.255
Allyn Stout	P30	30	40	3	4	1	1	0	0	1	16	0	.100
Tony Freitas	P25	25	46	2	9	2	2	0	0	5	10	0	.196
Phil Weintraub	1B22	22	83	14	30	13	5	2	1	14	11	1	.361
Tom Robello	2B13	22	70	11	20	15	1	2	5	4	17	0	.286
Chick Fullis	OF18	19	72	14	24	10	5	1	0	6	6	3	.333
Al Cuccinello	2B16	19	63	4	17	7	5	0	0	5	8	0	.270
Mort Cooper	P17	18	34	2	7	5	0	0	0	0	7	0	.206
Joe Hassler		17	45	4	10	8	1	1	0	4	12	1	.222
Francis Hawkins	2B13	16	49	5	15	4	3	0	0	4	4	1	.306
John Clark		12	18	3	8	3	3	0	0	1	0	0	.444
Ed Delker		11	34	5	9	4	1	1	0	2	4	1	.265
Robert Klinger	P11	11	19	1	4	0	0	0	1	0	0	0	.211

COLUMBUS (cont.)
Red Birds

BATTERS	POS-GAMES	GP	AB	R	H	BI	2B	3B	HR	BB	SO	SB	BA
George Nelson		10	11	0	2	0	1	0	0	0	3	0	.182

PITCHERS		W	L	PCT	G	GS	CG	SH	IP	H	BB	SO	ERA
Dominic Ryba		14	7	.667	30		16		199	220	39	107	4.03
Bill McGee		13	8	.619	32		12		203	213	51	101	2.93
Max Macon		12	12	.500	47		9		202	216	88	109	4.23
Tony Freitas		10	8	.556	25		8		126	170	30	49	5.86
Nelson Potter		8	4	.667	37		1		108	122	38	79	4.42
Mort Cooper		5	7	.417	17		4		85	90	33	68	4.76
Allyn Stout		5	8	.385	30		4		124	172	29	56	5.66
Al Fisher		4	7	.364	28		2		101	140	31	31	5.79
Robert Klinger		2	5	.286	11		3		59	70	19	25	4.42
Tom Seats		0	0	----	3		0		4	7	3	3	
Lee Sherrill		0	0	----	2		0		3	9	1	0	

LOUISVILLE   7th   63-91   .409   -27   Burleigh Grimes
Colonels

BATTERS	POS-GAMES	GP	AB	R	H	BI	2B	3B	HR	BB	SO	SB	BA
Julian Foster	1B134	137	537	66	179	94	36	15	5	38	58	15	.333
James Adair	2B77,SS14	107	322	47	88	50	22	3	10	36	26	15	.273
Anthony Malinosky	SS142	143	584	77	178	78	26	6	1	29	41	16	.305
Frank Sigafoos	3B100	114	434	79	148	61	24	7	5	17	29	10	.341
Melbern Simons	OF148	149	624	89	220	80	34	10	1	37	28	22	.353
Gil Brack	OF147	148	576	120	172	93	28	16	22	54	108	28	.299
Goody Rosen	OF130	135	526	104	165	41	25	11	5	75	66	15	.314
Ray Thompson	C105	111	363	31	110	60	18	6	4	27	19	2	.303
Walter Ringhoefer	C78	108	289	29	89	47	17	3	2	20	26	2	.308
Leo Ogorek	OF50,2B29	106	308	64	93	16	12	4	2	25	30	9	.302
Wilbur Buchanan	2B74	80	246	23	60	22	2	3	0	9	26	4	.244
William Rollings	3B46,1B17	68	257	32	69	37	17	4	6	14	22	4	.268
Wayne LaMaster	P30	65	111	14	30	14	3	0	1	4	23	1	.270
Yank Terry	P39	44	41	5	11	3	2	0	0	1	8	0	.268
Richard Bass	P40	42	49	3	10	1	1	1	0	0	10	2	.204
James Peterson	P37	37	84	5	16	6	0	0	0	6	25	0	.190
Charles Marrow	P37	37	77	11	22	8	3	0	0	3	14	0	.286
Fred Shaffer	P33	36	71	11	19	14	2	4	2	6	15	1	.268
John Tising	P32	32	61	6	17	5	2	0	0	1	12	0	.279
John DeMaisey	P14	14	15	1	2	1	0	0	0	0	5	0	.133
Ed Holley	P13	13	19	1	1	0	0	0	0	0	5	0	.053

PITCHERS		W	L	PCT	G	GS	CG	SH	IP	H	BB	SO	ERA
Wayne LaMaster		13	10	.565	30		10		183	196	66	135	4.52
Charles Marrow		11	14	.440	37		12		210	245	80	95	4.97
John Tising		10	9	.526	32		9		161	172	69	124	4.58
Fred Shaffer		9	13	.409	33		11		194	243	91	81	5.24
James Peterson		9	19	.321	37		16		241	269	71	86	4.15
Yank Terry		4	6	.400	39		2		115	121	50	59	5.63
Richard Bass		3	11	.214	40		4		135	180	47	53	6.00
Ed Holley		2	6	.250	13		4		55	62	20	34	5.56
John DeMaisey		1	2	.333	14		0		45	63	27	14	5.40

TOLEDO   8th   59-92   .391   -29.5   Fred Haney
Mud Hens

BATTERS	POS-GAMES	GP	AB	R	H	BI	2B	3B	HR	BB	SO	SB	BA
Harry Davis	1B146	147	563	93	168	90	29	6	12	61	33	22	.298
Al Vincent	2B146	149	566	82	141	60	23	4	3	61	65	14	.249
Frank Parker	SS106	106	405	48	120	44	21	6	2	32	29	6	.296
Gil English	3B94	102	412	74	138	78	21	15	5	39	32	4	.335
Walter Carson	OF137	140	554	107	166	71	32	13	10	73	108	15	.300
Ellis Powers	OF122	127	480	83	144	69	32	9	11	56	26	5	.300
Bob Garbark	OF82,C18	106	390	59	113	66	21	3	0	45	28	6	.290
Claude Linton	C97	105	332	43	96	52	15	1	13	40	40	0	.289
Mike Tresh	C55,OF27	93	282	37	78	49	11	5	2	27	39	1	.277
Alva Cohen	P41,PF17	79	128	19	40	21	5	4	0	14	17	1	.313

TOLEDO (cont.)
Mud Hens

BATTERS	POS-GAMES	GP	AB	R	H	BI	2B	3B	HR	BB	SO	SB	BA
Fred Haney	3B17,SS13	58	117	25	32	12	4	2	0	22	13	7	.274
Clyde Smoll	P49	49	45	2	5	2	0	0	0	1	8	2	.104
Joseph Hare	P45	48	75	7	12	4	1	1	1	7	31	0	.160
Don Ross	3B41	41	173	22	47	20	9	0	0	13	8	8	.272
Millard Howell	SS21,OF16	41	162	28	47	15	4	4	0	16	17	5	.290
Paul Sullivan	P36	38	74	3	16	9	3	0	1	4	14	0	.216
Charles Flowers	P29	31	61	8	8	4	1	0	0	7	18	2	.131
Art Weis	OF29	30	111	17	30	9	8	0	1	16	12	2	.270
Raymond Fritz	P18	29	55	11	17	12	4	0	1	1	6	2	.309
Thomas Leonard	OF16	27	65	7	15	8	2	0	0	3	4	1	.231
Louis Garland	P27	27	48	4	8	4	1	0	2	1	12	0	.167
Hubert Shelley	OF15	20	70	7	14	1	2	0	0	2	6	3	.200
Herman Clifton	SS18	19	64	8	18	7	2	1	0	7	7	0	.281
Carl Boone	P17	17	47	4	10	5	1	0	0	6	5	0	.213
John Calvey	OF12	16	48	2	5	2	0	0	0	1	8	2	.104
Oliver Thomas	OF10	14	6	0	0	0	0	0	0	0	3	0	.000
George Jansco		11	38	5	9	4	1	0	0	3	4	0	.237
John Clements	OF10	10	27	1	1	1	0	0	0	1	5	1	.037

PITCHERS		W	L	PCT	G	GS	CG	SH	IP	H	BB	SO	ERA
Alva Cohen		14	12	.538	41		9		197	265	57	61	5.21
Joseph Hare		12	17	.414	45		12		220	281	68	69	5.44
Charles Flowers		10	11	.476	29		14		181	224	52	65	4.97
Carl Boone		8	7	.533	17		10		132	158	27	40	4.16
Paul Sullivan		7	13	.350	36		8		192	211	**108**	89	4.69
Louis Garland		4	11	.267	27		4		133	205	63	28	7.58
Clyde Smoll		3	11	.214	**49**		3		152	205	45	67	6.16
Raymond Fritz		1	4	.200	18		1		60	97	30	16	7.35

MULTI-TEAM PLAYERS

BATTERS	POS-GAMES	TEAMS	GP	AB	R	H	BI	2B	3B	HR	BB	SO	SB	BA
Ivey Shiver	OF41	SP-IND	50	165	29	43	34	10	0	8	20	30	3	.261
William Cox	P37	COL-SP	37	50	2	4	2	0	0	0	3	10	0	.080
George Dickey	C28	MIL-MIN	28	96	11	20	6	2	0	0	12	20	0	.208
Fred Koster	OF18	SP-TOL	21	76	5	10	6	4	0	1	3	7	1	.132

PITCHERS		TEAMS	W	L	PCT	G	GS	CG	SH	IP	H	BB	SO	ERA
William Cox		COL-SP	7	12	.368	37		5		151	186	58	66	5.54

TEAM BATTING

TEAMS	GP	AB	R	H	BI	2B	3B	HR	BB	SO	SB	BA
MILWAUKEE	157	5526	891	1629	842	243	88	164	501	**787**	88	.295
ST. PAUL	152	5533	891	1656	812	**345**	73	113	448	527	39	.299
KANSAS CITY	157	5632	784	1617	693	228	**101**	46	500	578	86	.287
INDIANAPOLIS	**158**	5689	842	1701	767	260	86	70	403	526	101	.299
MINNEAPOLIS	**158**	**5758**	**1008**	**1703**	**924**	296	60	**212**	527	706	33	.296
COLUMBUS	154	5500	908	1649	822	259	90	134	436	721	103	.300
LOUISVILLE	155	5597	819	1702	732	275	93	66	403	597	**146**	**.304**
TOLEDO	153	5436	810	1502	721	254	72	64	**563**	635	108	.276
	622	44671	6953	13159	6313	2160	663	869	3781	5077	704	.295

1937
Three Up, Four Down

Most teams, when ahead three games to none in a best of seven game series, feel that they have matters well in hand. That is precisely how the 1937 American Association champions felt. Unfortunately for them, their grasp on the prize wasn't as tight as they thought.

The Columbus Red Birds, a preseason sixth place pick, scrambled to win the 1937 pennant by a single game over Toledo, and only three over Minneapolis. Defending champion Milwaukee dropped to fourth, while Kansas City, Indianapolis, St. Paul, and Louisville rounded out the standings. Enos Slaughter from Columbus won the batting title with a .382 mark, while Roy Pfleger of Minneapolis hit the most home runs (29). Pfleger's teammate, Red Kress had the most runs batted in with 157. Columbus pitcher Max Macon finished with the most victories (21), while his fellow moundsman Bill McGee had the lowest earned run average (2.97). Louisville's John Tising won his second strikeout crown finishing with 174.

After the season, Columbus dispatched Minneapolis in six games in the first round of the playoffs, duplicating the feat against Milwaukee in the final round. This gave the Red Birds the dubious honor of facing the powerful Newark Bears, the 1937 International League's best, in the Junior World Series

Some consider the 1937 Newark Bears the most powerful International League team in history. A top New York Yankee farm team, well stocked with future and former major league stars, the Bears won an impressive 109 games. Much to the Bears' surprise, the Red Birds marched right in and spanked them in their home stadium by a 5–4 score. Even more surprising, Columbus won the next game, and the game after (5–4, and 6–3) to send themselves homeward leading three games to none.

The Bears blitzed the Red Birds in game four by an 8–1 score and edged them in game five, 1–0, to climb back into the series. The following day, Newark crushed Columbus 10–1 to send the series to a deciding seventh game. The demoralized Red Birds were no match for the surging Bears, and they were mown down 10–4.

On paper, the Newark Bears should have won the Junior World Series as they were a far superior team. But Columbus' winning momentum could have carried it to victory, had not three key players sustained injuries during the latter stages of the series. Instead of achieving a dark horse victory, Columbus would be remembered as the only team to be three games up in the Little and Junior World Series, only to lose four games in a row, and the series with them.

COLUMBUS
Red Birds

	1st	90-64	.584		Burt Shotton

BATTERS	POS-GAMES	GP	AB	R	H	BI	2B	3B	HR	BB	SO	SB	BA
Dick Siebert	1B87	88	352	54	112	62	15	6	7	28	20	7	.318
James Jordan	2B132	135	522	77	149	63	29	2	1	20	31	6	.285
James Webb	SS137	139	525	70	152	70	26	7	4	28	60	10	.290
Justin Stein	3B103,2B29	131	511	62	141	80	31	7	4	43	48	4	.276
Enos Slaughter	OF153	154	642	**147**	**245**	122	42	13	26	64	50	18	**.382**
John Rizzo	OF150	150	584	117	209	123	38	**18**	21	78	57	15	.358
Lynn King	OF138	138	592	107	179	59	30	2	1	59	49	**28**	.302
Jack Crouch	C89	89	269	39	60	33	14	1	0	30	29	0	.223
Fred Ankenman	3B54,SS21	85	277	41	82	24	13	3	0	14	18	5	.296
Nelson Potter	P44	71	96	8	26	7	7	1	0	4	15	0	.271
William Prout	1B67	70	247	30	71	28	5	2	3	20	34	4	.287
Max Macon	P45	65	13	28	51	23	8	1	1	2	9	0	.357
Chick Fullis	OF30	44	97	13	26	8	3	0	1	1	4	0	.263
Mort Cooper	P39	43	69	10	17	7	2	0	1	1	10	0	.246
John Clark	C35	39	98	12	34	12	8	1	0	6	2	0	.347
Max Lanier	P38	38	52	7	16	7	0	0	0	3	9	0	.308
Paul Chervinko	C32	32	107	8	26	9	4	3	0	11	11	0	.243
Bill McGee	P31	31	78	7	18	16	1	0	0	2	15	0	.231
John Chambers	P31	31	64	4	14	6	1	0	0	3	13	0	.219
Ed Heusser	P25	25	36	1	6	5	0	0	0	0	12	0	.167
Wilmer Schroeder	P21	21	19	4	7	2	2	1	0	0	3	0	.368
Frank Grube	C17	17	47	4	10	2	0	0	0	3	6	0	.213
Robert Davis	3B11	13	38	3	10	8	3	0	1	1	4	0	.263
Louis Kahn	C10	11	18	2	3	2	0	0	0	1	3	0	.167
John Lynch	C	4	5	1	1	1	0	0	0			0	.200
Bob Scheffing	C	2	6	2	4	1	1	0	0			0	.667

PITCHERS		W	L	PCT	G	GS	CG	SH	IP	H	BB	SO	ERA
Max Macon		**21**	12	.636	45	34	16		265	273	114	163	3.46
Bill McGee		17	7	.708	31	27	13		206	193	56	165	**2.97**
Mort Cooper		13	13	.500	39	24	10		178	183	68	147	4.10
John Chambers		12	7	.632	31	25	10		181	210	43	60	3.78
Nelson Potter		11	11	.500	44	10	6		162	168	53	81	3.56
Max Lanier		10	4	**.714**	38	12	4		147	138	73	78	3.06
Ed Heusser		4	5	.444	25	14	4		103	132	38	39	5.50
H. Moore		1	0	1.000	5		0		17	18	11	2	5.29
Wilmer Schroeder		1	3	.250	21	0	0		63	75	19	17	4.29
Hank Gornicki		0	2	.000	9		0		26	28	17	13	5.54
Humphries		0	0	----	8		0		12				

TOLEDO
Mud Hens

	2nd	89-65	.578	-1	Fred Haney

BATTERS	POS-GAMES	GP	AB	R	H	BI	2B	3B	HR	BB	SO	SB	BA
Irving Burns	1B141	142	614	106	179	63	34	11	4	54	43	6	.292
James Adair	2B116	118	452	51	119	73	21	4	2	49	43	8	.263
Frank Croucher	SS152	152	604	73	167	80	22	8	2	26	65	9	.276
Roy Cullenbine	3B71,OF66,1B15	145	533	123	164	109	44	9	20	99	73	16	.308
Ed Coleman	OF134	138	517	95	159	123	29	5	25	72	61	1	.308
Chet Morgan	OF128	132	506	90	156	79	22	10	3	46	22	2	.308
Babe Herman	OF82	85	336	76	117	79	37	4	12	40	28	4	.348
Frank Reiber	C83	87	270	31	75	37	17	2	4	42	36	0	.278
Herman Clifton	3B67,2B38	107	443	86	112	33	18	3	4	39	60	17	.253
Claude Linton	C69	74	223	31	70	32	10	1	1	44	13	4	.314
Alva Cohen	P30,OF10	60	95	20	25	11	2	1	0	18	13	0	.263
Fred Haney	3B24	54	90	24	27	12	5	1	1	22	7	5	.300
Joe Sullivan	P37	49	75	11	13	4	2	0	0	10	18	1	.173
Paul Trout	P41	41	97	12	20	8	1	2	0	5	19	1	.206
Ben McCoy	OF21	31	69	17	19	12	2	3	1	8	6	0	.275
Fred Johnson	P31	31	60	4	10	7	1	0	0	1	9	0	.167
Vic Sorrell	P23	23	32	1	8	5	1	0	0	0	7	1	.250
Chet Laabs	OF21	21	83	27	34	17	8	5	3	12	22	1	.410
Hubert Bates	OF14	17	49	5	8	5	1	0	0	0	8	1	.163
Fred Marberry	P13	13	30	4	6	3	2	0	0	4	4	0	.200
Ralph Birkofer	P12	12	13	2	2	0	0	0	0	2	0	0	.154
Mitchell Frankovich	C10	11	27	1	7	4	0	0	0	3	5	0	.259
Joseph Hare	P11	11	6	0	1	0	0	0	0	1	2	0	.167
Mike Tresh	C	9	29	2	8	3	2	0	0			0	.276
John Brown	SS	4	10	1	2	0	0	0	0			0	.200
Don Ross	3B	3	12	0	1	0	0	0	0			0	.083

TOLEDO (cont.)
Mud Hens

PITCHERS	W	L	PCT	G	GS	CG	SH	IP	H	BB	SO	ERA
Alva Cohen	15	7	.682	30	24	15		187	211	52	52	4.14
Joe Sullivan	14	14	.500	37	29	14		228	255	87	126	4.66
Paul Trout	14	16	.467	41	31	14		259	294	118	109	4.42
Fred Johnson	9	7	.563	31	15	10		169	192	42	55	3.57
Fred Marberry	7	2	.778	13	9	5		80	88	21	40	3.26
Dick Coffman	6	1	.857	8	8	6		62	57	13	10	3.05
Vic Sorrell	6	5	.545	23	9	4		88	112	28	55	5.22
Ralph Birkofer	4	4	.500	12		1		42	55	20	21	7.50
Clyde Hatter	3	0	1.000	9		3		43	39	19	22	3.98
Joseph Hare	1	2	.333	11		1		28	34	8	5	5.14
Louis Garland	0	0	----	4		0		15				
Patchin	0	0	----	1		0		0				
Coleman	0	0	----	1		0		0				

MINNEAPOLIS   3rd   87-67   .565   -3   Donie Bush
Millers

BATTERS	POS-GAMES	GP	AB	R	H	BI	2B	3B	HR	BB	SO	SB	BA
Harry Taylor	1B153	155	612	97	173	83	24	5	12	50	43	6	.283
Andy Cohen	2B123	131	497	76	159	82	28	12	11	22	16	3	.320
Red Kress	SS158	158	649	136	217	157	43	9	27	71	66	12	.334
Roy Pfleger	3B87,2B39	126	485	83	158	121	21	4	29	35	23	2	.326
Allen Cooke	OF149	151	583	141	201	84	47	8	18	114	88	11	.345
Carl Reynolds	OF144	147	614	145	218	110	49	17	17	39	36	20	.355
Stan Spence	OF104	117	386	88	124	46	16	4	9	50	26	9	.321
John Peacock	C94	109	373	65	116	54	17	2	7	30	16	4	.311
George Dickey	C81	91	287	36	71	56	19	1	8	20	29	1	.247
Spence Harris	OF52,1B11	88	258	50	84	50	12	4	9	38	25	1	.326
Fresco Thompson	3B75	82	274	43	85	44	11	5	7	17	20	2	.310
Charles Wagner	P45	54	110	11	15	9	1	1	0	2	23	0	.136
Reg Grabowski	P49	49	53	2	8	1	0	0	0	4	17	0	.151
Walt Tauscher	P42	44	106	14	21	12	4	1	2	6	24	0	.198
Fabian Gaffke	OF40	41	163	32	53	29	12	1	7	9	17	0	.325
Belve Bean	P37	38	94	16	29	16	7	0	4	6	26	1	.309
James Henry	P36	36	82	6	16	6	1	2	1	1	28	0	.195
James Baker	P35	35	26	3	3	2	0	0	0	2	8	0	.115
Leon Pettit	P28	29	24	3	5	3	0	0	0	10	10	0	.208
Bill Burwell	P10	10	11	1	2	0	1	0	0	0	1	0	.182
John Newman	OF	7	12	1	4	2	0	0	1			0	.333
Lindsay Deal	OF	6	13	1	3	3	2	0	0			0	.231
Mike Christoff	PH	1	1	0	0	0	0	0	0			0	.000

PITCHERS	W	L	PCT	G	GS	CG	SH	IP	H	BB	SO	ERA
Charles Wagner	20	14	.588	45	34	20		278	295	76	132	3.53
Belve Bean	16	11	.593	37	35	18		237	316	54	68	4.86
Walt Tauscher	16	14	.533	42	35	18		260	320	85	75	4.88
James Henry	14	11	.560	36	32	9		205	243	115	100	5.84
Reg Grabowski	8	6	.571	49	8	2		157	168	48	59	4.70
James Baker	5	3	.625	35	4	2		94	113	35	36	4.31
Bill Burwell	4	0	1.000	10		0		30	36	5	4	3.00
Leon Pettit	4	6	.400	28	8	4		83	113	38	46	4.99
Phil Weinert	0	2	.000	6		0		18	25	14	7	13.50
Bill Butland	0	0	----	5		0		11	17	5	4	
Wilson Hayes	0	0	----	4		0		5	4	4	2	
Bowers	0	0	----	3		0		6				

MILWAUKEE   4th   80-73   .523   -9.5   Al Sothoron
Brewers

BATTERS	POS-GAMES	GP	AB	R	H	BI	2B	3B	HR	BB	SO	SB	BA
Minor Heath	1B156	156	537	107	159	113	31	11	25	132	66	11	.296
Lin Storti	2B79,3B76	155	603	107	186	125	45	6	25	77	63	7	.308
John Ryan	SS	(see multi-tean players)											
Ken Keltner	3B79,OF53	142	549	120	170	96	26	5	27	65	92	4	.310
Ted Gullic	OF150	151	601	109	193	138	35	8	26	56	87	9	.321
John Heath	OF100	100	447	79	164	64	34	9	14	22	47	7	.367
John Glynn	OF86	101	379	72	116	50	23	4	6	32	38	5	.306
Bill Brenzel	C91	91	339	40	86	44	12	3	3	19	23	1	.254

MILWAUKEE (cont.)
Brewers

BATTERS	POS-GAMES	GP	AB	R	H	BI	2B	3B	HR	BB	SO	SB	BA
Bernard Uhault	OF75	98	319	67	98	30	17	7	1	46	19	10	.307
Hank Helf	C68	85	259	29	71	42	11	5	7	11	29	1	.274
Ed Hope	2B64,SS12	77	220	24	52	18	10	2	1	25	40	0	.236
Ralph Winegarner	P34	53	103	17	27	13	8	1	1	9	9	1	.262
James Shilling	2B35	46	136	21	41	24	6	2	3	6	20	1	.301
Al Milnar	P41	42	103	13	23	14	3	1	3	7	31	1	.223
Forest Pressnell	P41	41	95	6	22	9	3	0	0	3	11	0	.232
George Blaeholder	P39	39	97	6	16	7	3	1	0	1	28	0	.165
Bill Zuber	P35	35	100	8	25	11	1	1	0	0	21	0	.250
Otto Bluege	SS34	34	128	24	32	8	3	1	1	33	18	1	.250
Newt Kimball	P26	26	32	4	6	3	0	0	1	1	10	0	.188
Harry Griswold	C	5	19	4	7	3	3	0	0			0	.368

PITCHERS	W	L	PCT	G	GS	CG	SH	IP	H	BB	SO	ERA
Forest Pressnell	18	12	.600	41	29	15		255	**327**	41	72	3.74
Al Milnar	16	13	.552	41	34	20		251	293	124	158	4.91
Bill Zuber	15	11	.577	35	29	19		250	275	**146**	101	4.79
George Blaeholder	15	16	.484	39	31	17		257	323	57	73	4.34
Ralph Winegarner	6	7	.462	34	6	6		138	143	43	62	3.59
Newt Kimball	4	8	.333	26	13	3		98	147	55	33	7.07
Allan Johnson	2	1	.667	5		1		31	43	9	7	7.55
Peter Sivess	0	0	----	2		0		8				

KANSAS CITY   5th   72-82   .468   -18   Dutch Zwilling
Blues

BATTERS	POS-GAMES	GP	AB	R	H	BI	2B	3B	HR	BB	SO	SB	BA
James Oglesby	1B150	150	595	97	182	106	38	11	9	57	28	8	.306
Herman Schulte	2B127	136	478	66	140	53	29	7	1	40	26	5	.293
Ed Marshall	SS	(see multi-team players)											
Charles English	3B138,2B19	154	624	80	204	98	44	15	1	23	38	2	.327
George Stumpf	OF134	137	523	81	140	58	27	10	6	59	39	1	.268
Al Marchand	OF108	129	453	85	132	44	21	7	8	56	42	5	.291
Ralph Boyle	OF75	82	279	54	88	25	11	5	3	38	20	9	.315
Christian Hartje	C86	100	305	56	89	40	17	2	4	29	35	8	.292
Eldon Breese	C83,OF18	109	360	31	109	52	18	5	0	21	17	6	.303
Fern Bell	OF65	75	262	43	77	22	11	6	3	16	26	2	.294
Milton Bocek	OF45	70	222	37	55	30	11	4	6	10	15	2	.248
Lee Stine	P43	51	67	4	13	8	1	1	1	3	12	0	.194
Earl Bolyard	OF49	50	203	26	53	27	8	0	0	9	18	6	.261
Wilcy Moore	P49	49	38	3	3	1	0	1	0	3	19	0	.079
Joe Vance	P38	41	71	9	16	10	2	0	1	0	15	1	.225
Mike Haslin	SS28	40	144	13	43	22	8	3	2	5	12	0	.299
Ted Kleinhans	P37	37	83	7	13	6	2	0	0	0	21	0	.157
Meredith Hopkins	3B17,SS13	33	80	8	14	8	3	0	0	10	16	0	.175
John Niggeling	P29	29	53	1	6	2	0	0	0	2	16	0	.113
Joe Gibbs	P29	29	37	1	6	5	0	0	0	1	3	0	.162
Beryl Richmond	P22	22	23	0	4	0	1	0	0	2	10	0	.174
Phil Page	P19	19	32	5	9	5	1	0	0	2	4	0	.281
Marv Breuer	P13	13	23	0	2	0	0	0	0	1	9	0	.087
Al Piechota	P11	11	18	1	8	1	1	0	0	3	5	0	.444
Norman Branch	P10	10	15	1	4	2	1	0	0	1	1	0	.267
John Dellasega	C	5	7	0	2	0	1	0	0			0	.286
David Goodman	PH	4	2	0	0	0	0	0	0			0	.000

PITCHERS	W	L	PCT	G	GS	CG	SH	IP	H	BB	SO	ERA
Joe Vance	17	9	.654	38	29	12		208	243	53	44	4.28
Ted Kleinhans	15	9	.625	37	29	14		230	255	90	122	4.03
John Niggeling	7	12	.368	29	19	3		149	175	66	71	5.38
Lee Stine	7	14	.333	43	18	6		154	211	72	72	6.02
Joe Gibbs	6	7	.462	29	15	4		114	145	49	34	6.00
Marv Breuer	4	5	.444	13	8	3		75	83	22	36	3.36
Norman Branch	3	2	.600	10	7	2		47	56	24	36	4.40
Beryl Richmond	3	4	.429	22	6	1		82	100	39	35	4.28
Wilcy Moore	3	6	.333	49	0	0		121	151	36	24	3.57
Phil Page	3	6	.333	19	14	4		100	153	31	30	5.22
Al Piechota	3	6	.333	11	8	3		52	63	18	44	5.19
Charles Moncrief	1	1	.500	4		0		13	13	1	5	2.77
Nusser	0	1	.000	3		0		9	20	5	3	12.00
LaFlamme	0	0	----	1		0		2				

INDIANAPOLIS   6th   67-85   .441   -22   Wade Killefer
Indians

BATTERS	POS-GAMES	GP	AB	R	H	BI	2B	3B	HR	BB	SO	SB	BA
George Archie	1B	(see multi-team players)											
Vince Sherlock	2B149	149	614	94	180	52	18	8	1	52	69	12	.293
Robert Fausett	SS79,3B38	133	508	66	141	53	14	7	3	21	15	18	.278
Robert Kahle	3B114	121	421	51	129	53	17	6	4	27	44	2	.306
Dan Taylor	OF144	146	556	87	182	98	28	7	10	73	43	7	.327
Ox Eckhardt	OF139	142	589	97	201	79	20	8	7	36	39	14	.341
Fred Berger	OF120	127	471	72	138	75	18	3	11	39	60	5	.293
John Riddle	C97	104	402	44	132	65	18	3	2	11	14	2	.328
Vic Mettler	OF63	78	249	37	67	16	13	4	0	12	30	3	.269
Bill Lewis	C58	78	232	27	67	25	8	3	0	24	15	1	.289
Frank Parker	SS61	61	188	23	46	21	14	2	1	26	21	2	.245
Robert Latshaw	1B46	60	173	13	40	19	6	1	1	17	36	1	.231
James Crandall	P38	45	67	8	13	11	2	0	0	4	10	0	.194
Clarence Phillips	P34	38	106	12	29	13	3	2	0	2	12	1	.274
Lloyd Johnson	P38	38	65	6	12	6	1	1	0	3	20	0	.185
Robert Logan	P27	37	69	4	18	6	1	0	0	0	7	1	.261
Vance Page	P33	34	83	4	21	11	5	0	0	5	17	0	.253
Robert Hoover	SS19	30	77	9	21	12	3	0	0	3	17	0	.273
Pat McLaughlin	P28	29	51	2	9	3	1	0	0	0	10	0	.176
James Sharp	P11	11	9	0	0	0	0	0	0	0	6	0	.000
Joe Lawrie		10	36	4	9	3	1	0	0	1	3	1	.250
Otto Meyers	OF	2	5	0	1	0	0	0	0			0	.200
Francis Hogan	C	7	22	1	4	0	1	0	0			0	.182

PITCHERS		W	L	PCT	G	GS	CG	SH	IP	H	BB	SO	ERA
Robert Logan		12	8	.600	27	25	14		181	199	26	51	4.23
Lloyd Johnson		11	10	.524	38	22	11		189	189	76	84	4.14
Clarence Phillips		11	11	.500	34	28	18		235	266	66	49	4.10
Vance Page		9	19	.321	33	30	17		223	278	53	83	4.60
Pat McLaughlin		8	11	.421	28	18	6		139	161	57	67	4.53
James Crandall		6	5	.545	38	0	0		139	164	34	26	4.21
Elmer Riddle		2	2	.500	5		1		26	26	16	12	5.88
Tom Gallivan		1	2	.333	6		0		14	15	5	5	5.14
James Sharp		0	6	.000	11		1		36	46	30	26	8.00

ST. PAUL   7th   67-87   .435   -23   Street - Todt
Saints

BATTERS	POS-GAMES	GP	AB	R	H	BI	2B	3B	HR	BB	SO	SB	BA
Phil Todt	1B131	131	499	61	154	66	28	6	2	25	31	5	.309
John Warner	2B88	91	380	59	97	43	17	5	1	28	38	2	.255
Robert Boken	SS73,1B25,3B14,2B13	134	504	67	151	75	28	7	18	29	55	7	.300
Joe Coscarart	3B109,SS18	129	482	56	134	52	17	2	4	29	33	2	.278
Malin McCullough	OF139	144	577	103	168	74	41	5	9	70	71	5	.291
Henry Steinbacher	OF114	116	490	76	152	79	28	6	26	29	4	.310	
Willis Norman	OF98	116	380	73	115	81	29	4	21	66	61	2	.303
John Pasek	C96	97	351	57	108	38	34	3	1	33	17	0	.308
Joe Morrissey	SS72,2B58	130	561	95	177	66	28	2	13	31	28	9	.316
Vern Washington	OF96	110	399	49	124	65	33	7	9	18	16	1	.311
Robert Fenner	C62	76	225	28	63	34	15	2	1	43	15	0	.280
William Cox	P44	48	98	9	19	6	4	0	0	2	11	0	.194
Jesse Landrum	3B37	40	138	15	48	17	7	0	5	11	25	0	.348
John Welch	P38	38	75	1	11	6	1	1	0	4	21	0	.147
Sal Gliatto	P37	37	30	3	7	2	0	0	0	3	8	0	.233
Ray Phelps	P35	36	95	9	17	5	3	0	1	3	29	0	.179
Art Herring	P27	29	75	14	23	13	4	2	1	1	12	0	.307
Joe Mowry	OF27	28	104	14	23	12	3	2	1	10	5	2	.221
Italo Chelini	P26	26	68	7	14	6	0	1	0	6	9	0	.206
Vern Wilshere	P23	23	21	2	3	0	0	0	0	0	9	0	.143
Ray Coombs	P12	12	29	4	8	0	0	0	0	2	2	0	.276
Mike Rocco	1B	6	20	2	3	3	2	0	0			0	.150
Ted Brissman	C	2	3	0	0	0	0	0	0			0	.000

PITCHERS		W	L	PCT	G	GS	CG	SH	IP	H	BB	SO	ERA
Art Herring		14	11	.560	27	24	17		184	213	56	72	4.45
Ray Phelps		13	11	.542	35	32	14		228	253	86	88	4.93
William Cox		13	16	.448	44	28	17		262	322	89	119	4.36
John Welch		12	19	.387	38	31	16		220	287	76	64	4.95
Italo Chelini		10	13	.435	26	21	13		175	235	44	46	4.83

ST. PAUL (cont.)
Saints

PITCHERS	W	L	PCT	G	GS	CG	SH	IP	H	BB	SO	ERA
Ray Coombs	3	8	.273	12	12	6		86	109	27	23	5.13
Sal Gliatto	1	3	.250	37	0	0		94	133	42	39	7.37
Vern Wilshere	1	3	.250	23	3	3		68	85	34	26	5.96
Needham	0	1	.000	3		0		11	15	14	6	10.63
Hugo Klaerner	0	1	.000	8		0		10	13	5	3	4.50
Johnson	0	0	----	5		0		9				
Pate	0	0	----	2		0		3				

LOUISVILLE   8th   62-91   .405   -27.5   Bert Niehoff
Colonels

BATTERS	POS-GAMES	GP	AB	R	H	BI	2B	3B	HR	BB	SO	SB	BA
Julian Foster	1B143	148	555	77	153	86	18	10	7	66	48	4	.276
Leo Ogorek	2B76	87	329	46	94	35	9	3	4	21	28	5	.286
Ray French	SS	(see multi-team players)											
Bill Matheson	3B	(see multi-team players)											
Goody Rosen	OF157	157	642	94	200	80	38	7	11	67	72	11	.312
Melbern Simons	OF156	157	630	98	199	73	35	8	1	36	25	4	.316
Nick Tremark	OF85	85	330	64	96	36	16	6	1	48	12	2	.291
Ray Berres	C126	127	425	57	103	39	12	5	4	29	54	1	.242
Walt Ringhoefer	C47,3B22	99	258	26	68	29	15	1	1	24	33	1	.264
Frank Sigafoos	3B20,2B18	76	182	19	46	23	9	4	0	7	17	2	.253
Edwin Morgan	OF51,1B10	60	220	26	57	24	9	2	3	22	28	2	.259
John Hudson	SS48,3B12	60	219	25	64	25	8	0	2	19	32	1	.292
John Tising	P45	48	82	8	23	9	3	1	0	4	19	0	.280
Richard Bass	P44	45	65	5	15	6	2	0	0	4	6	0	.231
Charles Marrow	P41	42	84	5	17	11	4	2	0	2	18	0	.202
Fred Shaffer	P39	40	33	4	5	2	1	0	0	5	12	0	.152
Yank Terry	P32	34	27	6	7	1	1	0	0	2	7	0	.259
Fred Koster	OF13	32	54	6	11	6	1	1	0	5	5	0	.204
James Peterson	P30	30	57	4	9	6	0	0	0	8	10	0	.158
Harry Eisenstat	P25	27	55	8	15	4	0	1	0	6	9	0	.273
William Rollings	3B23	26	92	6	22	10	2	2	0	8	1	0	.239
Walter Signer	P26	26	24	2	4	2	0	0	0	3	10	0	.167
Gerald Feille	3B22	24	65	10	18	6	3	1	0	11	6	0	.277
John DeMaisey	P20	20	23	2	6	7	0	0	0	0	5	0	.261
Leslie McNeece		14	17	3	2	1	0	1	0	3	7	0	.118
Woody Williams	SS	5	17	1	2	1	0	0	0			0	.118
Ed Williford	2B	3	12	2	4	3	0	0	0			0	.333

PITCHERS	W	L	PCT	G	GS	CG	SH	IP	H	BB	SO	ERA
Charles Marrow	14	14	.500	41	31	15		231	237	98	93	4.56
James Peterson	11	11	.500	30	24	10		176	204	55	86	4.19
Richard Bass	9	16	.360	44	26	9		200	248	67	64	5.49
John Tising	9	18	.333	45	28	15		218	257	97	174	4.91
Harry Eisenstat	8	9	.471	25	17	10		155	166	41	81	3.83
Fred Shaffer	4	8	.333	39	18	2		121	170	54	38	5.50
Yank Terry	3	5	.375	32	7	3		94	115	40	29	5.74
John DeMaisey	2	2	.500	20	4	2		65	99	18	18	7.20
Walter Signer	2	7	.222	26	8	2		86	110	38	20	5.02
D. Southard	0	1	.000	5		0		9	13	7	3	6.00
Cook	0	0	----	2		0		2				
Rutherford	0	0	---	1		0		0				

MULTI-TEAM PLAYERS

BATTERS	POS-GAMES	TEAMS	GP	AB	R	H	BI	2B	3B	HR	BB	SO	SB	BA
Ray French	SS81,2B65	KC-LOU	145	543	66	139	53	12	8	0	36	44	7	.256
Ed Marshall	SS144	KC-MIL	144	499	51	142	49	22	4	0	45	43	4	.285
George Archie	1B117	TOL-IND	130	521	106	164	68	24	8	11	53	44	17	.315
Bill Matheson	3B63,SS50,2B10	LOU-KC	130	500	63	154	85	27	10	11	15	73	12	.308
John Ryan	SS57,3B16	MIN-MIL	77	290	30	82	34	13	2	3	20	30	1	.283
Ellis Powers	OF46	LOU-TOL	76	196	28	60	40	10	4	3	21	10	2	.306
Don French	P35	TOL-IND	35	25	1	2	0	1	0	0	1	9	0	.080
Garland Braxton	P30	MIL-IND	30	37	6	6	3	0	0	0	4	5	0	.162
G. Nelson	P28	IND-TOL	28	42	4	4	5	1	0	1	2	17	0	.095
Carl Boone	P17	TOL-MIL	17	28	1	4	0	0	0	0	0	8	0	.143

MULTI-TEAM PLAYERS (cont.)

PITCHERS	TEAMS	W	L	PCT	G	GS	CG	SH	IP	H	BB	SO	ERA
G. Nelson	IND-TOL	8	3	.727	28	11	7		120	137	37	63	4.50
Garland Braxton	MIL-IND	7	11	.389	30	15	5		122	168	44	77	5.53
Don French	TOL-IND	3	3	.500	35	9	2		93	140	49	46	8.03
Carl Boone	TOL-MIL	3	6	.333	17	10	2		79	120	25	27	5.92

TEAM BATTING

TEAMS	GP	AB	R	H	BI	2B	3B	HR	BB	SO	SB	BA
COLUMBUS	154	5511	858	1671	781	285	68	70	439	529	97	.303
TOLEDO	154	5516	924	1567	833	292	72	86	621	615	79	.284
MINNEAPOLIS	158	5792	1058	1785	977	319	76	170	530	564	71	.308
MILWAUKEE	156	5522	904	1610	849	292	70	146	582	715	62	.292
KANSAS CITY	156	5446	755	1547	671	277	85	46	436	502	59	.284
INDIANAPOLIS	157	5577	774	1633	689	218	63	51	421	558	88	.293
ST. PAUL	156	5617	804	1621	747	322	61	93	440	532	39	.289
LOUISVILLE	157	5452	725	1507	655	219	69	44	450	571	52	.276
	624	44433	6802	12941	6202	2224	564	706	3919	4586	547	.291

1938
The Kid Comes of Age

As the 1938 season started, Minneapolis manager Donie Bush had a problem. His 19-year-old outfielder, fresh from the San Diego Padres of the Pacific Coast League, didn't appear to be a serious student of the game. Although an excellent hitter, he didn't take fielding seriously. Sometimes, as the game unfolded in front of him, he would practice his batting stance and swing while playing in the field. To him, batting was the important part of the game; fielding and other mundane chores were boring and incidental.

This attitude did not sit well with his manager. Donie Bush, a veteran of 30 years in the game, was not amused by the young outfielder's hijinks. Time after time, Bush would take the young man aside, explaining to him that all aspects of the game, even fielding, were important. Finally completely exasperated with the situation, Bush confronted management and insisted that one of them, the outfielder or him, would have to go. Since the kid was tearing the cover off the ball, management explained to Mr. Bush that he would definitely finish second in such a contest. With that, Bush managed to reach enough of an understanding with the youngster so that they could both complete the season on the same team.

In 1938, St. Paul returned to the top spot after a seven-year absence. Kansas City, Milwaukee, and Indianapolis finished in the playoff spots. Toledo and Minneapolis missed the playoffs by one game, while Columbus and Louisville finished well out of contention. Donie Bush's "one dimensional" outfielder won the triple crown with a .366 batting average, 43 home runs, and 142 runs batted in. Triple crown laurels also went to Milwaukee pitcher Whit Wyatt who finished with 23 wins, a 2.37 earned run average, and 208 strikeouts.

In 1939, Donie Bush's young protégé would go on to the Boston Red Sox, embarking on a 22-year career and enshrinement in the Hall of Fame. While always a superb hitter, this outfielder, though not the best, could certainly hold his own in Fenway Park's left field. This outfielder was affectionately called "the kid" for most of his career, but he was also known as Mr. Williams—Ted Williams.

ST. PAUL Saints

ST. PAUL   1st   90-61   .596   Foster Ganzel

BATTERS	POS-GAMES	GP	AB	R	H	BI	2B	3B	HR	BB	SO	SB	BA
Leroy Anton	1B138	138	493	83	143	64	27	4	14	39	38	14	.290
Aloysius Bejma	2B145	145	555	106	181	114	32	8	25	60	57	6	.326
Tony York	SS145	145	597	77	144	58	26	7	12	20	86	9	.241
Robert Boken	3B101,SS10	128	465	87	138	75	19	4	21	35	53	8	.297
George Stumpf	OF151	151	582	104	161	51	25	10	9	73	43	9	.277
Malin McCullough	OF141	144	499	90	150	83	41	14	5	77	65	9	.301
Fred Berger	OF89	102	319	49	93	57	14	2	10	31	47	8	.292
Ken Silvestri	C95,1B13	114	371	54	101	69	22	8	11	40	39	11	.272
John Pasek	C68	70	207	10	40	19	4	0	0	19	16	0	.193
Art Weis	OF50	56	160	16	34	21	4	1	5	28	19	0	.213
Jesse Landrum	3B29	41	131	22	39	17	11	2	5	7	24	2	.298
Lloyd Brown	P36	37	66	7	13	7	2	0	0	8	15	0	.197
Hugo Klaerner	P37	37	49	7	11	7	1	1	2	0	11	0	.224
Art Herring	P33	35	74	6	14	10	4	0	1	4	11	0	.189
Vern Washington	OF32	34	129	22	55	23	8	1	3	9	6	2	.426
Ray Phelps	P33	33	77	12	13	5	1	0	1	4	22	0	.169
Victor Frasier	P32	32	68	6	15	5	0	0	0	6	15	0	.221
Italo Chelini	P30	30	68	6	10	9	0	1	2	6	15	1	.147
Merritt Cain	P28	28	49	3	8	1	0	0	0	1	16	0	.163
Mervyn Connors	3B19	20	70	11	18	10	3	0	3	9	13	1	.257
Al Marchand	OF13	16	44	3	9	3	0	0	0	3	1	0	.205
Jack Peerson	3B,SS,OF	14	27	1	4	0	0	0	0	2	5	0	.148
Harry Taylor	P14	14	16	2	4	1	0	2	0	0	2	0	.250
Grey Clarke	OF	3	8	0	1	0	0	0	0	0		0	.125
James Adair	OF	3	2	0	1	0	0	0	0	0		0	.500
Russell Maxcy	SS	2	3	0	0	0	0	0	0	0		0	.000

PITCHERS		W	L	PCT	G	GS	CG	SH	IP	H	BB	SO	ERA
Victor Frasier		17	7	.708	32	22	13	1	187	194	54	91	3.27
Art Herring		16	6	.727	33	24	14	1	200	211	48	84	3.74
Lloyd Brown		12	8	.600	36	26	13	1	189	193	83	74	3.52
Ray Phelps		12	8	.600	33	28	16	3	219	233	46	66	2.96
Merritt Cain		12	11	.522	28	18	12	0	147	147	53	65	4.04
Italo Chelini		10	6	.625	30	20	10	0	169	199	50	48	4.90
Hugo Klaerner		8	8	.500	37	10	4	0	134	149	65	57	4.50
Harry Taylor		2	3	.400	14		0	0	42	55	25	15	4.93
Andrew Dobernic		1	1	.500	7		0	0	9	2	12	7	3.00
Ray Coombs		0	3	.000	8		0	0	22	27	12	9	6.13
Dwain Sloat		0	0	----	1		0	0	1				
George Schoenecker		0	0	----	1		0	0	0	1	1	0	

KANSAS CITY Blues

KANSAS CITY   2nd   84-67   .556   -6   Bill Meyer

BATTERS	POS-GAMES	GP	AB	R	H	BI	2B	3B	HR	BB	SO	SB	BA
Harry Davis	1B147	147	602	107	180	64	31	7	10	63	51	25	.299
Jack Saltzgaver	2B113,3B12	129	440	81	122	69	20	11	8	71	28	12	.277
Ed Miller	SS146	147	531	70	154	80	33	11	14	39	30	13	.290
Ed Joost	3B113,2B25,SS10	145	578	96	167	70	33	6	5	56	44	23	.289
Joe Gallagher	OF152	152	583	95	200	119	35	4	24	27	77	23	.343
Walt Judnich	OF148	150	557	94	152	104	34	10	22	61	47	8	.273
Ralph Boyle	OF104	120	353	43	99	47	11	6	5	46	19	7	.280
Eldon Breese	C47	53	151	21	36	13	5	0	1	17	9	7	.238
Bill Matheson	OF69,3B13	107	318	49	92	41	19	6	1	10	38	13	.289
Clyde McCullough	C43	46	132	20	33	12	2	2	3	13	17	5	.250
Christian Hartje	C41	44	128	23	37	17	5	2	2	10	10	0	.289
George Washburn	P35	42	61	14	19	6	3	0	0	2	9	0	.311
Fred Gay	P31	37	33	3	10	1	0	0	0	1	12	1	.303
Marv Breuer	P36	36	63	5	7	1	1	0	0	7	29	0	.111
Leo Norris	2B27	32	90	8	19	12	2	0	1	8	9	1	.211
Al Piechota	P29	30	60	4	11	1	1	0	0	6	11	0	.183
Robert Miller	P30	30	37	3	5	2	1	0	0	2	18	0	.135
Kemp Wicker	P27	27	59	4	9	4	4	0	0	1	15	0	.153
Frank Makosky	P24	24	22	2	3	3	0	0	0	1	5	0	.136
Gil English	3B18	20	58	5	9	7	2	0	0	6	6	0	.155
John Riddle	C19	20	52	9	13	4	3	0	0	7	2	1	.250
John LaRocca	P19	19	32	2	7	4	1	1	0	2	11	0	.219
Joe Vance	P13	18	31	5	9	4	1	1	1	2	7	3	.290
Norman Branch	P16	18	22	2	4	1	2	0	0	0	3	0	.182
Ambrose Ogrodowski	C15	16	44	2	11	3	1	0	0	0	3	0	.250

KANSAS CITY (cont.)
Blues

BATTERS	POS-GAMES	GP	AB	R	H	BI	2B	3B	HR	BB	SO	SB	BA
Ernie Bonham	P10	10	24	2	3	0	0	0	0	1	6	0	.125
Frank Kelleher	OF	8	15	2	2	0	1	0	0			0	.133
Homer Warren	C	7	16	2	4	0	0	0	0			0	.250
John Glynn	OF	7	16	0	1	0	0	0	0			0	.063
John Rosette	C	2	8	0	0	0	0	0	0			0	.000
William Holm	C	2	5	0	0	0	0	0	0			0	.000

PITCHERS	W	L	PCT	G	GS	CG	SH	IP	H	BB	SO	ERA
George Washburn	12	4	.750	35	15	6	0	131	115	96	76	3.98
Marv Breuer	12	12	.500	36	25	13	1	213	210	79	109	3.85
Al Piechota	10	10	.500	29	25	12	2	173	175	47	82	3.59
Kemp Wicker	9	9	.500	27	22	10	1	161	161	41	59	3.41
Joe Vance	8	1	.889	13	10	6	2	84	79	19	23	2.68
Robert Miller	7	5	.583	30	9	3	0	109	121	55	47	5.20
Frank Makosky	7	5	.583	24	1	0	0	69	64	19	35	2.61
John LaRocca	6	5	.545	19	19	5	0	95	98	64	59	4.17
Norman Branch	4	3	.571	16	6	2	0	56	58	25	14	3.21
Fred Gay	4	7	.364	31	8	4	0	92	91	70	36	5.09
Ernie Bonham	3	4	.429	10	9	5	0	71	81	22	34	3.42
Prendergast	1	0	1.000	2		0	0	6	10	4	2	4.50
Yocke	1	1	.500	8		0	0	22	18	9	9	4.09
George Jeffcoat	0	1	.000	2		0	0	3	4	2	0	6.00
Charles Stanceu	0	0	----	2		0	0	3				

MILWAUKEE		3rd	81-70		.536		-9			Al Sothoron		
Brewers

BATTERS	POS-GAMES	GP	AB	R	H	BI	2B	3B	HR	BB	SO	SB	BA
Minor Heath	1B139	141	514	117	151	81	21	4	32	109	56	13	.294
Lin Storti	2B93	112	362	59	96	79	9	2	21	57	54	5	.265
Thomas Irwin	SS125	125	476	72	141	68	23	4	8	35	22	12	.296
Oscar Grimes	3B125,2B17	143	503	107	154	81	28	9	12	81	72	17	.306
Ted Gullic	OF133	135	537	98	168	107	40	4	28	31	71	4	.313
Roy Johnson	OF128	128	491	86	148	86	29	6	7	69	41	14	.301
Fred Schulte	OF120	124	454	56	136	70	20	3	9	38	3	2	.300
Joe Becker	C75	79	265	37	81	25	15	1	4	28	12	2	.306
Bill Hankins	OF65,C22	92	338	40	88	37	11	3	5	12	22	1	.260
Ed Hope	2B45,SS29	83	268	35	58	27	7	3	7	35	35	0	.216
Joe Just	C60	74	199	35	52	38	10	0	12	39	44	2	.261
Ralph Winegarner	P29,3B17,1B14	62	173	38	55	29	8	2	12	7	29	3	.318
Whit Wyatt	P33	36	106	10	25	14	5	1	2	2	22	0	.236
George Blaeholder	P29	30	61	2	1	0	0	0	0	2	34	0	.016
Allan Johnson	P29	29	43	6	9	4	2	0	0	4	12	0	.209
Ken Jungels	P21	21	48	4	11	2	0	0	2	3	14	0	.229
Joe Heving	P19	19	47	8	10	8	2	0	1	2	8	0	.213
Tom Reis	P17	17	21	3	5	5	0	0	1	4	5	0	.238
Charles Marrow	P12	12	34	2	6	4	0	0	0	1	9	0	.176
Bill Zuber	P10	11	27	2	3	1	0	0	0	1	8	0	.111
Jose Gonzalez	P11	11	26	4	11	3	2	1	0	1	4	0	.423
Bert Haas	OF	9	33	3	11	3	2	0	0			1	.333
Ramos Hernandez	C	2	3	1	2	0	0	0	0			0	.667
Harry Griswold	C1	1	1	0	0	0	0	0	0			0	.000
Ernest Talos	PH	1	1	0	0	0	0	0	0			0	.000

PITCHERS	W	L	PCT	G	GS	CG	SH	IP	H	BB	SO	ERA
Whit Wyatt	23	7	.767	33	32	26	9	254	194	62	208	2.37
Allan Johnson	10	7	.588	29	18	6	1	114	154	40	33	6.32
George Blaeholder	9	12	.429	29	22	11	0	174	221	31	49	4.86
Joe Heving	8	8	.500	19	17	12	2	131	144	33	54	4.60
Charles Marrow	7	3	.700	12	12	8	0	91	95	27	46	3.66
Ken Jungels	7	7	.500	21	15	10	0	128	151	52	36	4.71
Ralph Winegarner	6	10	.375	29	9	4	0	113	143	33	42	5.73
Tom Reis	4	3	.571	17	4	3	0	66	71	15	30	3.95
Bill Zuber	3	4	.429	10	10	5	0	73	79	43	45	4.32
Jose Gonzalez	3	5	.375	11	6	4	0	65	95	19	21	6.23
Loafman	1	2	.333	8		0	0	37	42	43	17	7.54
Ahlf	0	1	.000	7		0	0	14	22	7	6	9.64
Jake Drake	0	1	.000	4		1	0	16	22	11	5	6.75
Sullivan	0	0	----	2		0	0	4				
Stephens	0	0	----	1		0	0	1				

INDIANAPOLIS   4th   80-74   .519   -11.5   Ray Schalk
Indians

BATTERS	POS-GAMES	GP	AB	R	H	BI	2B	3B	HR	BB	SO	SB	BA
Robert Latshaw	1B133	135	482	65	131	76	38	6	11	56	101	6	.271
Vince Sherlock	2B137	138	527	74	146	56	24	5	5	51	69	9	.277
Stephen Mesner	SS83,3B39	127	441	79	146	91	37	9	7	47	32	2	.331
Robert Fausett	3B121	139	502	89	170	40	27	11	3	45	19	28	.339
Glenn Chapman	OF148	149	568	93	175	103	20	8	8	42	52	13	.308
Myron McCormick	OF91	99	344	49	86	33	10	3	1	28	53	16	.250
Milt Galatzer	OF74,1B22	96	333	60	100	54	16	8	0	41	15	4	.300
Bill Lewis	C83	92	255	31	71	42	14	2	1	44	13	5	.278
Bill Baker	C79	90	280	40	86	38	18	3	7	33	24	2	.307
Jim Pofahl	SS64,2B22	88	299	45	73	31	12	3	5	41	58	5	.244
Andrew Pilney	OF68	81	265	35	69	21	8	3	0	22	29	5	.260
Carl Jorgenson	OF31	42	99	10	20	13	0	3	3	13	15	3	.202
Don French	P39	40	48	3	7	4	0	0	0	1	8	0	.146
Lloyd Johnson	P39	39	70	6	16	7	3	1	0	12	19	0	.229
James Wasdell	OF30	36	119	19	34	18	9	3	1	19	22	2	.286
Elmer Riddle	P32	35	26	4	4	3	1	0	0	6	9	0	.154
John Niggeling	P32	32	69	4	6	1	0	0	0	7	13	0	.087
Bobby Mattick	SS21	29	67	6	8	6	3	0	0	4	7	1	.119
Vance Page	P26	26	70	9	14	4	1	0	0	5	17	0	.200
Hod Lisenbee	P25	25	19	0	5	0	0	0	0	1	4	0	.263
Al Epperly	P18	18	30	1	4	1	1	0	0	1	14	0	.133
Robert Logan	P14	15	26	2	6	3	1	0	0	1	3	0	.231
Lauri Myllykangas	P12	12	13	0	0	0	0	0	0	0	4	0	.000
Clarence Phillips	P10	10	10	1	3	0	1	0	0	2	0	0	.300
Frank Doljack	OF	8	30	3	6	5	1	1	0			0	.200
Vic Mettler	OF	6	9	2	2	1	0	0	0			0	.222
LeGrant Scott	OF	3	12	0	2	1	1	0	0			0	.167
Louis Menendez	2B,SS	3	5	0	0	0	0	0	0			0	.000
Otto Meyers	PH	3	3	0	0	0	0	0	0			0	.000

PITCHERS	W	L	PCT	G	GS	CG	SH	IP	H	BB	SO	ERA
Vance Page	15	5	.750	26	23	15	3	192	178	26	68	2.53
John Niggeling	14	11	.560	32	28	15	2	211	200	86	113	4.31
Lloyd Johnson	13	13	.500	39	26	13	0	205	236	57	93	4.00
Don French	11	6	.647	39	17	4	0	146	138	61	66	4.38
Robert Logan	4	5	.444	14	9	4	0	77	97	22	41	4.91
Al Epperly	4	6	.400	18	13	5	0	86	92	36	29	4.92
Hod Lisenbee	4	8	.333	25	4	2	0	76	85	27	32	3.91
Elmer Riddle	3	4	.429	32	4	1	0	91	87	61	42	4.35
Clarence Phillips	2	3	.400	10		1	0	36	50	14	7	6.25
Lauri Myllykangas	0	3	.000	12		0	0	44	65	16	16	6.14
Smith	0	0	----	2		0	0	3				
Tom Gallivan	0	0	----	2		0	0	3				

TOLEDO   5th   79-74   .516   -12   Fred Haney
Mud Hens

BATTERS	POS-GAMES	GP	AB	R	H	BI	2B	3B	HR	BB	SO	SB	BA
George Archie	1B154	154	602	97	188	109	33	10	5	54	61	28	.312
Ben McCoy	2B151	154	615	105	190	98	27	16	17	53	52	15	.309
Chet Wilburn	SS154	154	658	110	196	63	31	6	2	71	46	6	.298
Charles Gelbert	3B137	143	490	99	139	91	30	11	8	87	43	7	.284
Roy Cullenbine	OF117,3B11	127	479	115	148	89	34	11	15	97	50	17	.309
Ed Coleman	OF111	119	437	77	145	89	27	8	15	54	43	3	.332
Chet Laabs	OF73	73	290	61	85	54	16	6	11	29	69	6	.293
Claude Linton	C94	97	287	29	90	37	7	2	3	56	24	1	.314
Chet Morgan	OF71	71	283	46	101	52	12	7	0	24	10	11	.357
Homer Peel	OF40	59	162	31	53	21	9	2	1	24	12	0	.327
Ox Eckhardt	OF48	55	201	29	46	29	9	3	2	15	18	3	.229
Robert Harris	P35	48	63	11	13	6	3	1	0	1	8	0	.206
Morris Hancken	C36	47	125	12	30	18	4	0	0	13	13	0	.240
John Johnson	P37	45	48	7	6	4	0	0	1	2	9	0	.125
Pat McLaughlin	P41	42	20	3	3	2	1	0	0	0	3	0	.150
Emmett Nelson	P34	34	51	4	8	6	2	0	0	0	16	0	.157
Charles Treadway	2B,3B	30	33	4	4	2	1	0	0	0	5	0	.121
Fred Johnson	P23	23	56	2	10	1	2	0	0	0	5	0	.179
Julio Bonetti	P18	18	38	4	6	4	1	1	0	1	10	0	.158
Joe Rogalski	P16	17	26	3	4	2	0	0	0	8	9	0	.154
Al Benton	P17	17	22	1	2	3	0	0	0	0	11	0	.091
Cletus Poffenberger	P14	15	33	7	10	3	1	1	0	0	3	1	.303

TOLEDO (cont.)
Mud Hens

BATTERS	POS-GAMES	GP	AB	R	H	BI	2B	3B	HR	BB	SO	SB	BA
Ed Selway	P11	15	29	1	7	6	5	0	0	1	7	0	.241
Fred Marberry	P14	14	25	1	5	1	0	0	0	0	3	0	.200
Stan Corbett	P14	14	4	1	1	0	0	0	0	1	0	0	.250
James Walkup	P13	13	30	2	6	4	2	0	0	0	7	0	.200
Truman Connell	3B,OF	13	20	2	2	1	0	0	0	1	7	0	.100
Joe Greenberg	3B	11	33	4	5	3	1	0	0	2	1	0	.152
Cecil Dunn	OF	10	22	4	4	4	0	0	1	1	5	0	.182
Fred Haney	PH	3	2	1	0	0	0	0	0			0	.000
John Zapor	PH	2	2	0	0	0	0	0	0			0	.000
Roy House	PH	1	1	0	0	0	0	0	0			0	.000

PITCHERS	W	L	PCT	G	GS	CG	SH	IP	H	BB	SO	ERA
Robert Harris	13	12	.520	35	22	8	1	175	185	83	81	4.11
Fred Johnson	12	4	.750	23	16	11	1	140	155	26	56	4.56
Cletus Poffenberger	8	3	.727	14	11	6	1	78	87	26	30	3.92
John Johnson	7	2	.778	37	11	3	0	138	141	75	80	4.24
James Walkup	7	5	.583	13	12	4	0	82	95	25	34	4.06
Emmett Nelson	7	9	.438	34	16	8	0	152	190	51	56	5.63
Julio Bonetti	5	8	.385	18	14	6	0	111	136	16	43	3.41
Pat McLaughlin	4	4	.500	41	5	0	0	82	117	39	41	6.70
Joe Rogalski	4	4	.500	16	12	5	0	91	110	20	39	4.35
Fred Marberry	4	7	.364	14	11	4	0	64	82	26	28	5.20
Al Benton	3	6	.333	17	8	3	0	67	88	26	33	5.24
Ed Selway	3	6	.333	11	10	5	0	59	68	25	22	5.64
Vic Sorrell	1	0	1.000	2		0	0	7	3	2	3	2.57
Paul Trout	1	2	.333	5		3	0	30	39	8	18	4.50
Stan Corbett	0	1	.000	14		0	0	24	36	18	9	7.88
Ralph Birkofer	0	1	.000	3		0	0	8	16	4	4	6.75
W. Miller	0	0	----	9		0	0	20				

MINNEAPOLIS   6th   84-68   .513   -12.5   Donie Bush
Millers

BATTERS	POS-GAMES	GP	AB	R	H	BI	2B	3B	HR	BB	SO	SB	BA
Harry Taylor	1B145	145	523	79	136	60	28	5	13	51	39	3	.260
Andy Cohen	2B144	145	597	66	150	55	24	4	4	11	37	4	.251
Roy Pfleger	SS95,3B38	135	484	66	120	89	13	2	20	43	44	5	.248
Jim Tabor	3B103	103	437	76	144	72	30	4	13	20	30	7	.330
Ted Williams	OF148	148	528	130	193	142	30	9	43	114	75	6	.366
Stan Spence	OF130	136	506	106	163	77	26	4	19	57	28	10	.322
Coaker Triplett	OF94	105	366	70	105	54	16	6	10	32	26	5	.287
Earl Grace	C	(see multi-team players)											
Otto Denning	C49,1B18	81	228	34	78	42	18	4	9	15	14	1	.342
John Mihalic	SS58,2B15	78	239	45	70	18	10	0	3	37	27	1	.293
Walt Tauscher	P47	48	65	4	17	6	3	0	0	3	20	0	.262
Fabian Gaffke	OF42	42	167	29	49	24	13	1	3	6	20	3	.293
LeRoy Parmelee	P35	42	101	14	22	12	3	0	1	5	25	0	.218
James Galvin	C38	41	129	16	35	11	10	0	2	15	13	2	.271
Belve Bean	P39	39	81	6	15	7	0	1	1	5	26	0	.185
Alva Cohen	P23	34	41	2	11	5	1	1	0	11	9	0	.268
James Henry	P32	32	51	9	14	7	3	1	0	2	12	0	.275
Jennings Poindexter	P22	23	42	1	7	3	1	0	0	0	8	0	.167
Wilfrid Lefebvre	P23	27	57	8	16	5	2	0	1	3	12	0	.281
Ken Richardson	3B19	22	61	3	12	8	2	0	1	5	7	1	.197
Dick Midkiff	P16	16	22	0	1	0	0	0	0	1	12	0	.045
Charles Wagner	P15	15	34	3	6	1	1	0	0	2	11	0	.176
Willie Duke	OF	15	28	6	7	2	1	1	1	2	2	0	.250
Henry Camelli	C10	10	26	6	6	3	1	2	0	6	4	0	.231
Calvin Chapman	SS,2B	9	28	4	8	8	1	0	1			1	.286
Cecil Trent	OF	5	18	3	5	1	1	1	0			1	.278

PITCHERS	W	L	PCT	G	GS	CG	SH	IP	H	BB	SO	ERA
LeRoy Parmelee	17	13	.567	35	32	18	0	240	219	167	128	4.20
Belve Bean	15	12	.556	39	30	17	2	223	260	59	64	4.44
Jennings Poindexter	9	7	.563	22	16	6	0	114	118	69	72	4.66
Walt Tauscher	9	11	.450	47	13	7	1	189	225	75	77	4.95
Charles Wagner	8	3	.727	15	12	8	1	83	90	30	44	3.90
Wilfrid Lefebvre	8	8	.500	23	14	8	0	127	156	35	45	4.25
James Henry	7	9	.438	32	19	5	1	142	144	66	62	5.39
Alva Cohen	2	5	.286	23	6	2	0	67	111	18	24	6.99

MINNEAPOLIS (cont.)
Millers

PITCHERS	W	L	PCT	G	GS	CG	SH	IP	H	BB	SO	ERA
Dick Midkiff	2	5	.286	16	9	2	0	69	94	32	25	6.52
W. Clarke	0	1	.000	3		0	0	12	7	4	0	1.50
Reg Grabowski	0	0	----	5		0	0	9				
Fletcher	0	0	----	1		0	0	5				
Pat Malone	0	0	----	1		0	0	0	4	2	0	

COLUMBUS	7th	64-89	.418	-27	Burt Shotton

Red Birds

BATTERS	POS-GAMES	GP	AB	R	H	BI	2B	3B	HR	BB	SO	SB	BA
Charles Hassan	1B112	123	414	71	114	97	23	4	19	60	57	0	.275
James Bucher	2B101,3B12	121	501	86	159	64	37	5	6	29	26	11	.317
Fred Ankenman	SS112,2B16	137	452	67	122	49	15	5	2	52	29	12	.270
Art Garibaldi	3B117,2B29	149	549	75	145	72	27	4	3	59	50	20	.264
Lynn King	OF153	153	620	106	196	54	25	11	3	79	45	30	.316
Edwin Morgan	OF126	131	438	75	138	69	29	10	10	44	48	20	.315
Earle Browne	OF104,1B23	125	469	79	143	98	23	6	17	49	46	7	.305
Dominic Ryba	C54,P18	72	207	15	51	25	7	0	0	17	14	1	.246
Joe Schultz	C50	57	176	15	49	19	8	0	1	18	7	2	.278
James Grilk	C22,1B14	50	137	14	32	16	4	5	2	6	20	0	.234
Al Fisher	P33	50	87	11	18	13	3	2	1	3	7	0	.207
James Lynn	P50	50	59	4	7	1	1	0	0	1	11	0	.119
Mike Martynik	P39	41	59	13	12	5	1	3	0	8	11	0	.203
Nathan Andrews	P37	37	71	8	4	1	0	0	0	11	37	0	.056
Ken Miller	OF24	34	80	6	19	12	3	1	3	7	12	3	.238
John Morrow	3B22	27	83	8	15	3	2	1	0	2	12	0	.181
Harold Kelleher	P22	26	46	10	13	6	6	0	0	3	9	0	.283
George Hader	P20	21	21	2	4	4	1	0	1	0	3	0	.190
Justin Stein	2B11	20	73	2	18	6	3	1	0	5	7	0	.247
Anthony Malinosky	SS20	20	63	3	14	6	1	0	0	3	5	0	.222
Jim Thompkins	P19	19	12	1	1	0	0	0	0	1	7	0	.083
George Turbeville	P15	17	21	3	6	1	0	0	0	0	2	1	.286
Sammy Baugh	SS16	16	59	3	13	3	2	0	0	1	13	0	.220
Milt Bocek	OF13	14	45	4	7	4	0	0	1	4	5	0	.156
Herschel Lyons	P13	13	23	2	4	0	1	0	0	1	4	0	.174
Phil Clark	OF11	12	37	4	8	4	2	0	0	0	4	1	.216
Bill Seinsoth	P4	11	10	0	1	0	0	0	0	1	2	0	.100
Dick Siebert	1B	9	36	5	12	7	1	0	0			3	.333
Dennis Gleason	C,OF	9	16	2	3	1	1	1	0			0	.188
Bob Blattner	SS,3B	8	13	1	2	0	0	0	0			0	.154
Jim Dillingham	3B	2	7	0	0	0	0	0	0			0	.000
Paul Easterling	OF1	1	3	0	0	1	0	0	0			1	.000
Charles Martin	C1	1	1	0	0	0	0	0	0			0	.000

PITCHERS	W	L	PCT	G	GS	CG	SH	IP	H	BB	SO	ERA
Al Fisher	14	6	.700	33	23	12	1	162	166	44	82	3.94
Nathan Andrews	11	19	.367	37	29	14	0	222	238	95	134	4.91
James Lynn	8	11	.421	50	12	4	0	175	173	78	104	4.42
Mike Martynik	8	14	.364	39	26	8	1	182	188	97	87	5.29
Harold Kelleher	7	6	.538	22	16	4	0	110	123	59	42	5.32
Max Lanier	3	1	.750	8		4	0	44	45	26	26	2.25
George Hader	3	3	.500	20	4	2	0	62	66	26	23	4.06
Dominic Ryba	3	9	.250	18	7	4	0	86	90	17	52	3.24
Herschel Lyons	2	7	.222	13	10	4	0	70	72	41	47	4.24
George Turbeville	1	1	.500	15	2	0	0	50	62	24	29	4.86
Toten	1	1	.500	5		1	0	19	27	12	15	6.63
Jim Thompkins	1	3	.250	19		0	0	42	58	49	10	9.64
Bill Seinsoth	0	2	.000	4		0	0	9	13	7	3	10.00
Quante	0	1	.000	3		0	0	12	15	5	3	7.50
Berg	0	0	----	1		0	0	2				
Clem Dreisewerd	0	0	----	1		0	0	1				
Humphries	0	0	----	1		0	0	0				

LOUISVILLE	8th	53-100	.346	-38	Bert Niehoff

Colonels

BATTERS	POS-GAMES	GP	AB	R	H	BI	2B	3B	HR	BB	SO	SB	BA
Johnny Sturm	1B155	155	600	69	180	70	31	4	0	26	34	10	.300

LOUISVILLE (cont.)
Colonels

BATTERS	POS-GAMES	GP	AB	R	H	BI	2B	3B	HR	BB	SO	SB	BA
Leo Ogorek	2B139	146	566	79	170	55	18	8	6	47	34	14	.300
Pee Wee Reese	SS132	138	483	68	134	54	21	8	3	36	57	23	.277
Frank Madura	3B138,2B19	153	557	83	155	46	18	2	1	110	18	12	.278
Fred Koster	OF145	149	529	84	139	60	30	9	3	43	50	7	.263
Melbern Simons	OF137	144	511	54	139	49	17	4	0	30	14	2	.272
Fern Bell	OF129	129	511	73	167	90	30	13	9	29	62	6	.327
Walter Ringhoefer	C83	112	277	29	72	24	14	4	0	33	18	1	.260
Ed Madjeski	C73	92	270	27	71	45	8	2	3	8	12	5	.263
Ray French	SS33,3B22	74	197	18	44	20	4	1	0	18	12	3	.223
Nick Tremark	OF21	55	101	11	23	16	3	0	0	9	9	2	.228
Fred Shaffer	P48	49	50	4	7	8	3	0	0	5	13	0	.140
Lester Willis	P42	43	85	10	16	7	3	1	0	8	21	1	.188
Rufus Meadows	P39	41	77	8	18	5	2	2	1	1	17	0	.234
Yank Terry	P35	38	61	4	10	4	0	0	0	2	18	0	.164
Cooper Hampton	OF26	37	81	6	16	5	3	0	0	4	24	1	.198
Lewis Carpenter	P37	37	34	0	2	0	0	0	0	2	10	0	.059
Carl Boone	P25	26	22	3	3	5	1	0	1	2	2	0	.136
Anthony Governor	OF15	25	77	7	23	4	1	2	0	2	6	2	.299
John Owens	P22	23	12	1	2	0	1	0	0	0	6	0	.167
James Holbrook	C13	18	46	4	13	3	1	1	0	3	4	0	.283
Ernest Thomasson	P10	10	2	0	0	0	0	0	0	0	2	0	.000
Richard Hampton	C	3	5	0	0	0	0	0	0			0	.000

PITCHERS	W	L	PCT	G	GS	CG	SH	IP	H	BB	SO	ERA
Rufus Meadows	11	11	.500	39	29	10	1	206	240	81	59	4.67
Yank Terry	9	12	.429	35	24	10	1	179	176	83	91	4.32
Lester Willis	9	21	.300	42	31	13	0	239	261	80	90	4.33
Fred Shaffer	8	16	.333	48	16	7	0	163	205	66	54	5.47
Lewis Carpenter	2	9	.182	37	14	3	0	129	144	78	32	5.65
John Owens	1	4	.200	22	2	1	0	50	73	25	17	5.94
Carl Boone	1	8	.111	25	11	2	0	80	117	27	28	7.20
Ernest Thomasson	0	2	.000	10		0	0	14	14	9	5	5.14
Ray Kolp	0	0	----	9		0	0	18				
John DeMaisey	0	0	----	4		0	0	5				
Rutherford	0	0	----	1		0	0	1				
Brittsan	0	0	----	1		0	0	0				

MULTI-TEAM PLAYERS

BATTERS	POS-GAMES	TEAMS	GP	AB	R	H	BI	2B	3B	HR	BB	SO	SB	BA
Dan Taylor	OF111	MIN-COL-IND	125	412	65	137	58	25	7	2	52	33	9	.333
Earl Grace	C115	MIN-COL	117	356	38	83	50	13	1	11	46	37	1	.233
Gordon Hinkle	C56	IND-TOL	62	157	18	32	19	7	0	0	18	33	0	.204
John Tising	P37	LOU-IND	37	71	4	7	4	1	0	0	4	19	0	.099
Charles Flowers	P35	IND-LOU	35	60	2	15	5	3	0	0	1	19	0	.250
John Chambers	P17	COL-MIN	17	24	2	4	1	0	0	0	3	4	0	.167

PITCHERS	TEAMS	W	L	PCT	G	GS	CG	SH	IP	H	BB	SO	ERA
Charles Flowers	IND-LOU	11	11	.500	35	20	11	0	172	206	75	63	5.08
John Tising	LOU-IND	11	16	.407	37	29	13	1	206	228	66	128	4.28
John Chambers	COL-MIN	3	5	.375	17	11	3	0	74	93	40	14	6.81

TEAM BATTING

TEAMS	GP	AB	R	H	BI	2B	3B	HR	BB	SO	SB	BA
ST. PAUL	152	5138	784	1401	708	244	65	129	487	628	80	.273
KANSAS CITY	153	5139	776	1421	689	251	68	97	469	545	145	.277
MILWAUKEE	151	5054	830	1426	773	234	44	163	571	629	76	.282
INDIANAPOLIS	157	5212	757	1433	673	256	71	52	550	633	102	.275
TOLEDO	154	5352	893	1544	824	264	85	82	612	588	97	.288
MINNEAPOLIS	152	5239	830	1491	769	258	50	154	488	561	52	.285
COLUMBUS	154	5218	738	1421	680	239	63	73	526	537	119	.272
LOUISVILLE	155	5233	647	1419	574	211	61	27	423	473	90	.271
	614	41585	6255	11556	5690	1957	507	777	4126	4594	761	.278

1939
Kansas City Blues

The most powerful American Association club in almost 20 years emerged from the westernmost reaches of the league in the late 1930s. This team would dominate the circuit in the years leading up to World War II, with the help of friends in the east.

The Kansas City Blues had known modest success, winning three pennants (1918, 1923, and 1929) during the Association's first thirty years. Although sparsely spaced, the latter two teams (1923 and 1929) finished their seasons with 112 and 111 victories respectively, the second and third most victories by any Association team. The team's fortunes took a sudden upswing during the 1930s because of one event. In 1937, the Kansas City Blues had become one of the top farm teams of the mighty New York Yankees, to be blessed with the largess inherent in such a relationship.

This relationship soon paid off, as the 1938 Blues jumped from the second division to second place. The team went on to win both playoff rounds in the Association, continuing with a victory over Newark in the Junior World Series.

In 1939, the Kansas City team stepped up their performance a notch. After battling with Minneapolis in the first half, the Blues ran away in the second to finish with 107 victories, eight more than the second place Millers. The Blues were led by a host of fine players including home run and runs batted in leader Vince DiMaggio (46 and 136), Jerry Priddy (.333, 24 HR, 107 RBI), Phil Rizzuto (.316), and Johnny Sturm (.309). None of their pitchers won twenty games, but three of them won seventeen: Tom Reis (17-4), John Babich (17-6), and Marv Breuer (17-6). In addition, these three pitchers finished in the first three spots in the earned run average race: Breuer (2.28), Reis (2.30) and Babich (2.55). All in all, this was one of the most dominant teams to ever grace the circuit. Second place Minneapolis did not go down without a fight as they set a record of 217 home runs hit in one season (six of their players had over twenty each). The rest of the pack consisted of Indianapolis, Louisville, St. Paul, Milwaukee, Columbus, and Toledo. Among the few honors not garnered by Blues players was the batting title, won by Gil English of St. Paul (.343), and the mark for most strikeouts, made by Minneapolis pitcher Herb Hash (143).

The Kansas City Blues would continue to dominate the American Association for the next few years, winning two more firsts and a third. This 1939 club was something special. Although four other Association clubs finished with more wins than the 1939 Blues, all of them had the benefit of a 168-game season. This Kansas City team played only a 154-game schedule, so the 107 wins resulted in a .695 winning percentage, the second best in all of the years of the American Association.

KANSAS CITY Blues

1st   107-47   .695   Bill Meyer

BATTERS	POS-GAMES	GP	AB	R	H	BI	2B	3B	HR	BB	SO	SB	BA
Johnny Sturm	1B130	131	528	76	163	59	31	6	7	29	25	9	.309
Jerry Priddy	2B154	155	580	110	193	107	44	15	24	45	61	12	.333
Phil Rizzuto	SS129	135	503	99	159	64	21	6	5	36	27	33	.316
Jack Saltzgaver	3B88,OF20,1B19	129	436	74	126	58	18	8	4	73	38	14	.289
Vince DiMaggio	OF154	154	544	122	158	136	32	9	46	89	123	21	.290
Bill Matheson	OF105	115	379	64	114	57	20	9	9	16	51	21	.301
Art Metheny	OF86	95	298	55	94	57	24	4	10	42	37	4	.315
John Riddle	C97	100	265	25	62	25	12	1	3	27	16	3	.234
Billy Hitchcock	3B76,SS29	116	369	52	97	40	17	11	4	23	51	15	.263
Clyde McCullough	C90	108	282	55	78	42	18	9	11	35	55	9	.277
Ralph Boyle	OF68	83	212	32	67	39	12	8	5	42	21	6	.316
Rupert Thompson	OF42	44	125	18	28	17	3	1	2	26	16	3	.224
John Lindell	P23	40	81	8	15	8	1	1	0	3	6	0	.185
Joe Vance	P32	38	58	9	19	10	0	2	1	0	6	1	.328
John Babich	P36	37	79	11	22	10	3	1	1	0	18	1	.278
Frank Makosky	P36	36	18	2	3	2	1	0	0	0	2	0	.167
Tom Reis	P34	34	52	4	7	3	1	0	0	4	16	0	.135
Al Piechota	P33	33	66	6	15	7	3	0	0	3	10	0	.227
Ernie Bonham	P32	32	67	6	12	4	1	0	0	5	13	0	.179
Marv Breuer	P26	26	56	5	4	2	0	0	0	4	17	0	.071
Tommy Holmes	OF	7	20	2	3	1	0	0	0			0	.150
Herman Schulte	3B,2B	7	16	1	4	1	1	0	0			0	.250
John Stonebraker	OF	5	9	1	3	0	0	0	0			1	.333
Ed Kearse	PH	1	1	0	0	0	0	0	0			0	.000

PITCHERS	W	L	PCT	G	GS	CG	SH	IP	H	BB	SO	ERA
Tom Reis	17	4	.810	34	17	11	3	164	140	61	77	2.30
John Babich	17	6	.739	36	27	15	4	208	196	78	117	2.55
Marv Breuer	17	6	.739	26	25	15	4	178	154	56	93	2.28
Al Piechota	16	7	.696	33	22	15	2	181	162	56	93	2.88
Joe Vance	10	4	.714	32	19	9	0	152	148	61	49	4.32
Ernie Bonham	10	9	.526	32	26	12	3	198	172	62	143	3.18
Frank Makosky	9	3	.750	36	0	0	0	74	76	30	50	4.74
John Lindell	8	5	.615	23	16	7	0	131	143	45	53	4.40
Don Hendrickson	0	0	----	5			0	11	8	5	3	

MINNEAPOLIS Millers

2nd   99-55   .643   -8   Tom Sheehan

BATTERS	POS-GAMES	GP	AB	R	H	BI	2B	3B	HR	BB	SO	SB	BA
Phil Weintraub	1B149	149	507	127	168	126	36	9	33	110	67	3	.331
Lin Storti	2B145	147	502	88	141	105	28	5	30	87	78	5	.281
Jim Pofahl	SS143	146	582	128	176	74	35	9	19	60	75	7	.302
Robert Fausett	3B110,OF19	131	463	66	141	53	18	6	3	22	10	23	.305
Al Wright	OF152	152	582	113	196	134	36	6	21	53	78	6	.337
Harvey Walker	OF148	148	570	145	173	63	26	7	24	106	78	23	.304
James Wasdell	OF97	102	387	79	125	90	23	4	29	39	37	18	.323
George Lacy	C101	108	340	45	98	66	15	2	20	25	24	5	.288
Roy Pfleger	3B53,SS16,2B10	90	284	44	78	49	14	2	13	24	26	1	.275
Otto Denning	C33,OF22	71	195	31	59	47	10	2	13	17	17	1	.303
Walt Tauscher	P41	45	62	9	13	4	1	0	1	7	11	0	.210
Harry Smythe	P41	44	87	10	26	8	3	0	1	4	7	0	.299
Elon Hogsett	P37	42	84	4	18	4	1	1	1	2	17	0	.214
Earl Grace	C36	41	112	9	28	13	4	0	4	12	19	0	.250
Marvin Ulrich	P38	38	45	4	10	2	4	0	0	2	12	0	.222
Herb Hash	P37	37	99	8	19	8	3	0	1	2	16	1	.192
Bill Butland	P37	37	82	9	21	8	2	0	2	4	27	0	.256
Cecil Trent	OF26	28	98	9	21	9	6	1	0	4	5	0	.214
Russ Rolandson	OF16	21	46	4	8	7	2	0	0	5	5	2	.174
Belve Bean	P13	13	41	3	10	5	1	1	1	0	6	0	.244
Andy Cohen	PH	2	1	0	0	1	0	0	0	0	0	0	.000

PITCHERS	W	L	PCT	G	GS	CG	SH	IP	H	BB	SO	ERA
Herb Hash	22	6	.786	37	30	20	2	256	222	94	144	3.27
Bill Butland	19	10	.655	37	29	18	1	218	227	71	117	3.96
Elon Hogsett	16	9	.640	37	25	14	1	199	217	64	100	4.03
Walt Tauscher	13	6	.684	41	12	5	1	160	181	68	62	5.23
Harry Smythe	12	12	.500	41	25	11	1	208	261	58	102	4.89
Belve Bean	8	3	.727	13	12	9	0	96	101	17	23	3.75

MINNEAPOLIS (cont.)
Millers

PITCHERS	W	L	PCT	G	GS	CG	SH	IP	H	BB	SO	ERA
Marvin Ulrich	6	6	.500	38	15	6	0	130	166	72	50	6.16
Al Baker	0	0	----	1			0	1	1	1	0	

INDIANAPOLIS   3rd   82-72   .532   -25   Schalk - Griffin
Indians

BATTERS	POS-GAMES	GP	AB	R	H	BI	2B	3B	HR	BB	SO	SB	BA
Robert Latshaw	1B106	112	360	49	91	43	14	7	9	53	57	4	.253
James Adair	2B60	60	240	32	58	16	9	7	1	27	35	1	.242
Nolen Richardson	SS98	98	359	35	99	38	8	3	1	17	14	4	.276
Don Lang	3B149	149	536	83	143	66	20	12	13	67	75	14	.267
Myron McCormick	OF148	149	547	100	174	61	33	9	2	60	42	15	.318
Milt Galatzer	OF129	135	501	79	163	42	22	9	0	46	20	4	.325
Allen Hunt	OF85	87	321	53	98	54	12	9	2	29	38	3	.305
Bill Baker	C84	98	302	35	102	58	31	1	3	32	14	1	.338
Jesse Newman	1B49,2B44,OF17	126	426	61	128	87	19	8	9	45	67	2	.300
Dee Moore	C65	77	230	28	54	26	14	1	3	16	39	1	.235
Glenn Chapman	OF41	52	142	16	34	24	7	0	1	18	18	3	.239
Fred Vaughn	2B40	45	149	25	48	21	8	3	2	20	25	2	.322
Kermit Lewis	OF32	40	108	16	24	9	4	2	2	14	28	4	.222
Charles Barrett	P38	38	83	3	19	5	2	0	0	0	13	0	.299
Don French	P35	36	89	11	24	12	5	1	1	3	22	0	.270
Mitchell Balas	P29	31	38	6	10	4	0	1	1	2	13	0	.263
John Wilson	P31	31	16	1	1	1	0	0	0	0	5	1	.063
Robert Logan	P29	30	63	4	16	5	0	0	0	2	9	0	.254
Lloyd Johnson	P29	29	54	3	7	1	1	0	0	4	22	0	.130
James Sharp	P26	26	31	0	3	0	0	0	0	3	19	0	.097
Hod Lisenbee	P26	26	8	0	0	0	0	0	0	0	3	0	.000
Einar Sorensen	2B18	25	69	6	17	5	2	0	0	6	5	3	.246
John Niggeling	P22	22	57	7	10	4	2	1	0	6	8	0	.175
LeGrant Scott	OF12	21	54	14	17	13	2	1	3	3	5	2	.315
Roy Easterwood	C	7	18	1	3	3	0	1	0			0	.167
Nino Bongiovanni	OF	5	18	2	2	2	1	0	0			0	.111
Paul Dunlap	OF	4	14	1	4	4	0	0	1			0	.286

PITCHERS	W	L	PCT	G	GS	CG	SH	IP	H	BB	SO	ERA
Charles Barrett	16	12	.571	38	30	17	1	227	229	51	79	3.41
John Niggeling	15	7	.682	22	22	18	2	164	142	54	108	3.13
Don French	15	11	.577	35	29	14	2	227	239	72	124	3.69
Robert Logan	13	8	.619	29	23	13	1	167	171	47	90	3.66
Lloyd Johnson	8	11	.421	29	18	9	0	154	155	47	54	3.74
John Wilson	6	2	.750	31	4	2	1	74	72	25	44	3.41
Mitchell Balas	5	7	.417	29	13	9	0	116	139	40	50	5.20
James Sharp	4	8	.333	26	13	3	1	103	102	62	59	4.89
Hod Lisenbee	0	5	.000	26			0	50	63	9	16	4.86
Art Jacobs	0	0	----	1			0	3	4	0	2	

LOUISVILLE   4th   75-78   .490   -31.5   Bush - Burwell
Colonels

BATTERS	POS-GAMES	GP	AB	R	H	BI	2B	3B	HR	BB	SO	SB	BA
Paul Campbell	1B148	149	597	77	168	51	20	9	2	16	61	26	.281
Vince Sherlock	2B151	152	542	75	147	66	26	6	1	62	35	9	.271
Pee Wee Reese	SS149	149	506	78	141	57	22	18	4	69	47	35	.279
Ernest Andres	3B71	73	265	36	79	32	14	2	4	12	17	0	.298
Chet Morgan	OF147	152	597	79	174	38	22	11	1	46	19	8	.291
Stan Spence	OF132	136	485	82	140	70	25	12	12	47	30	5	.289
Fabian Gaffke	OF94	105	337	48	81	44	16	8	4	32	56	4	.240
Ed Madjeski	C78	83	268	28	84	52	15	3	3	11	13	2	.313
Fred Sington	OF79	83	264	48	67	55	17	3	13	58	48	1	.254
Thomas Irwin	3B44	53	168	21	46	20	11	0	1	21	12	1	.274
Wes Flowers	P37	37	58	2	8	2	1	0	0	0	11	0	.138
Fred Shaffer	P35	35	38	3	9	5	1	1	1	5	10	0	.237
James Weaver	P31	31	68	4	4	0	0	0	0	4	31	0	.059
Ted Olson	P31	31	60	3	11	4	0	0	0	5	13	0	.183
Wilfrid Lefebvre	P30	31	38	2	8	1	2	0	0	2	7	0	.211
Charles Wagner	P28	30	58	5	6	1	0	0	0	1	16	0	.103

LOUISVILLE (cont.)
Colonels

BATTERS	POS-GAMES	GP	AB	R	H	BI	2B	3B	HR	BB	SO	SB	BA
LeRoy Parmelee	P22	22	48	1	9	4	1	0	0	0	10	0	.188
Eldon Breese		19	37	5	9	8	0	1	0	2	4	0	.243
Yank Terry	P17	17	22	0	5	4	1	1	0	0	5	0	.227
Bob Elliott	OF14	14	53	5	14	4	0	2	0	4	5	0	.264
Monte Weaver	P13	14	32	1	8	2	1	0	0	4	4	0	.250
Wayman Kerksieck		14	10	0	0	0	0	0	0	0	5	0	.000
John Barrett	OF	9	18	0	3	2	1	0	0			0	.167
Pat Colgan	C	7	9	1	1	0	0	0	0			0	.111
Walter Ringhofer	C	5	12	1	1	1	0	0	0			0	.083

PITCHERS		W	L	PCT	G	GS	CG	SH	IP	H	BB	SO	ERA
James Weaver		14	8	.636	31	22	16	0	196	169	70	122	2.98
Ted Olsen		12	10	.545	31	25	10	0	168	167	80	62	4.23
Charles Wagner		10	11	.476	28	22	13	3	177	151	52	87	2.90
Fred Shaffer		9	4	.692	35	7	2	0	119	110	38	37	3.86
LeRoy Parmelee		7	7	.500	22	16	8	2	123	111	82	81	3.88
Wes Flowers		7	11	.389	37	19	9	0	163	170	65	63	4.14
Wilfrid Lefebvre		6	10	.375	30	18	7	2	116	142	43	42	5.51
Monte Weaver		4	7	.364	13	11	7	0	89	92	37	43	4.35
Yank Terry		3	4	.429	17	10	3	1	74	75	35	40	3.16
Rufus Meadows		0	0	----	4			0	6	11	2	0	
Lyle Tinning		0	0	----	1			0	2	6	2	0	

ST. PAUL   5th   73-81   .474   -34   Foster Ganzel
Saints

BATTERS	POS-GAMES	GP	AB	R	H	BI	2B	3B	HR	BB	SO	SB	BA
LeRoy Anton	1B136	136	469	82	124	53	23	3	22	62	42	15	.264
Frank Madura	2B		(see multi-team players)										
Tony York	SS140	141	515	63	127	54	18	5	9	25	89	7	.247
Gil English	3B139	139	501	96	172	92	35	7	19	53	35	4	**.343**
George Fleming	OF146	151	536	94	162	107	25	12	19	52	51	10	.302
George Stumpf	OF146	147	536	82	148	55	33	7	6	76	47	9	.276
Malin McCullough	OF137	139	501	73	124	53	21	8	3	51	51	5	.248
John Pasek	C66	68	219	15	60	21	10	1	0	24	8	0	.274
Robert Reis	OF37,1B18,3B15,2B13	107	306	32	83	44	8	4	10	16	38	0	.271
Leo Wells	SS28,2B25	67	180	22	37	12	7	2	3	18	41	1	.206
Ken Silvestri	C44	60	177	32	48	31	6	4	3	31	33	5	.271
Avitus Himsl	P42	53	73	13	24	8	0	2	2	0	13	0	.329
Rufus Jackson	C30	52	105	12	26	8	3	1	0	13	13	0	.248
Norm Schlueter	C36	36	94	15	26	13	3	1	1	11	11	1	.277
Ray Phelps	P34	34	57	9	19	8	4	0	2	1	10	0	.333
Merritt Cain	P32	32	77	4	11	1	1	0	0	2	23	0	.143
Lloyd Brown	P31	32	68	6	11	7	0	0	0	4	14	0	.162
James Taylor	P31	32	35	1	8	1	2	0	0	1	4	1	.229
Victor Frasier	P21	21	32	1	4	1	0	0	0	2	6	0	.125
Italo Chelini	P17	20	31	2	4	2	0	1	0	3	5	0	.129
Art Herring	P18	18	47	4	9	4	1	1	1	4	8	0	.191
Harry Boyles	P15	15	22	1	3	2	0	0	0	0	6	0	.136
Maurice Jacobs	2B13	14	55	8	12	3	2	0	1	2	4	0	.218
Frank Gabler		13	7	0	0	0	0	0	0	0	3	0	.000
Wilbur Cearley	OF	9	25	2	6	1	1	0	0			0	.240
Eddie Feinberg	2B	5	5	0	1	0	0	0	0			0	.200

PITCHERS		W	L	PCT	G	GS	CG	SH	IP	H	BB	SO	ERA
Ray Phelps		13	9	.591	34	19	8	1	156	173	57	49	5.14
Lloyd Brown		13	12	.520	31	24	16	1	190	214	64	78	4.74
Merritt Cain		11	13	.458	32	28	14	1	206	**243**	82	86	4.11
Avitus Himsl		10	9	.526	42	17	8	0	172	201	44	74	4.55
Art Herring		9	9	.500	18	18	14	1	137	128	34	56	3.55
Harry Boyles		4	5	.444	15	10	5	1	69	66	40	26	5.48
Victor Frasier		4	6	.400	21	17	7	0	98	108	34	32	5.33
Italo Chelini		3	3	.500	17	9	2	1	71	85	27	32	4.18
James Taylor		2	9	.182	31	7	1	0	102	131	39	33	4.59
Mearl Strachan		0	0	----	4			0	7	10	3	5	
Frank Laminski		0	0	----	2			0	4	6	1	1	

MILWAUKEE Brewers

6th   **70-83**   **.458**   **-36.5**   Minor Heath

BATTERS	POS-GAMES	GP	AB	R	H	BI	2B	3B	HR	BB	SO	SB	BA
Minor Heath	1B100	117	336	65	87	53	15	7	16	71	68	6	.259
Justin Stein	2B94	98	337	35	84	44	13	2	8	31	32	2	.249
Stephen Mesner	SS71,2B13	85	309	47	100	54	21	4	5	23	25	4	.324
John Hill	3B140	140	552	82	183	76	21	9	9	18	9	2	.332
Ted Gullic	OF146	146	54	89	167	97	29	5	26	37	52	6	.301
Roy Johnson	OF121	127	433	64	128	60	23	5	11	58	40	5	.296
Oris Hockett	OF87	94	299	36	84	36	17	3	5	24	35	7	.281
Ramos Hernandez	C95	101	303	31	90	35	20	3	5	44	32	3	.297
Ralph Winegarner	1B66,OF10	93	263	42	79	43	15	1	11	37	36	1	.300
Fred Schulte	OF69	76	235	36	70	39	16	3	2	20	19	0	.298
Bobby Mattick	SS68	68	273	47	78	16	13	3	5	27	18	3	.286
Joe Just	C63	66	179	15	30	18	7	0	4	20	46	0	.168
Edwin Carnett	P26	53	106	11	29	11	3	2	1	6	16	1	.274
Barney Walls	2B51	52	191	24	56	21	9	6	2	13	32	2	.293
Newt Kimball	P41	41	54	5	12	4	0	0	0	13	7	1	.222
Ken Jungels	P35	46	78	12	24	12	3	1	0	1	11	1	.308
Charles Marrow	P35	36	70	6	17	8	2	0	1	1	11	0	.243
George Blaeholder	P35	35	43	2	3	1	0	0	0	7	10	0	.070
Lester Willis	P33	33	37	5	6	0	0	1	0	1	9	0	.162
James Carleton	P30	31	74	9	13	5	2	0	0	9	18	0	.176
Al Epperly		15	10	0	1	0	0	0	0	2	4	0	.100
Gordon Foth		14	30	5	10	4	2	0	0	1	4	0	.333
Stanley Galle	SS11	11	42	6	11	8	1	0	2	2	5	0	.262
Lou Novikoff	OF11	11	42	6	9	3	4	0	1	3	0	1	.214
Joe Skurski		11	39	6	17	7	4	0	1	1	5	1	.436
Eddie Zydowski	3B	9	34	1	9	3	1	0	0			0	.265
Ed Hope	2B	3	10	0	0	0	0	0	0			0	.000
Joe Becker	C	2	7	1	1	0	0	0	0			0	.143
Red Smith	C	2	5	1	2	1	1	0	0			0	.400

PITCHERS				W	L	PCT	G	GS	CG	SH	IP	H	BB	SO	ERA
Charles Marrow				15	9	.625	35	25	13	1	196	196	66	106	4.36
James Carleton				11	9	.550	30	25	12	1	202	218	89	107	4.23
Ken Jungels				10	16	.385	35	29	14	0	196	215	100	86	4.73
Newt Kimball				9	18	.333	41	25	11	1	185	191	74	122	4.52
George Blaeholder				7	6	.538	35	13	5	0	132	158	41	41	3.75
Lester Willis				6	8	.429	33	12	5	0	108	117	52	43	4.33
Edwin Carnett				4	11	.267	26	15	8	0	138	158	58	76	4.37

COLUMBUS Red Birds

7th   **62-92**   **.403**   **-45**   Burt Shotton

BATTERS	POS-GAMES	GP	AB	R	H	BI	2B	3B	HR	BB	SO	SB	BA
Joe Mack	1B93	93	326	46	91	56	22	5	6	49	38	5	.279
Danny Murtaugh	2B83,3B24	111	415	53	106	29	16	2	2	26	42	6	.255
Bobby Sturgeon	SS151	151	559	53	166	52	24	2	0	14	25	4	.297
James Bucher	3B111	116	437	62	126	33	25	2	2	30	20	14	.288
Earle Browne	OF112	116	369	49	99	62	13	3	12	36	38	3	.268
Coaker Triplett	OF108	116	395	66	127	55	27	2	15	41	30	12	.322
Edwin Morgan	OF		(see multi-team players)										
Herb Bremer	C57	61	167	14	35	28	5	2	6	14	28	1	.210
Al Fisher	1B51,P24	96	264	31	80	39	19	5	4	11	33	1	.303
Elvin Adams	OF80	84	273	47	70	38	10	5	4	32	44	10	.256
John Winsett	OF64	67	221	37	58	50	11	3	14	22	40	2	.262
Herm Franks	C55	58	175	22	52	18	5	0	4	17	13	2	.297
George Hader	P53	57	47	2	10	4	2	0	0	3	12	1	.213
Max Macon	P30	52	71	2	13	2	2	0	0	1	2	1	.183
Creepy Crespi	2B47	49	152	22	37	14	9	4	1	15	13	3	.243
William Curlee	P47	47	37	6	8	2	1	0	0	1	17	0	.216
Richard Tichacek	C37	42	120	10	26	12	3	0	0	8	12	0	.217
Max Lanier	P33	34	69	5	16	2	1	0	0	4	9	0	.232
Ernie Orsatti	OF15,1B12	31	80	6	24	10	3	0	0	12	11	1	.300
Norbert Kleinke	P30	30	48	2	8	2	0	0	0	1	12	0	.167
Nathan Andrews	P29	29	69	5	7	1	0	0	0	1	22	0	.101
Joe Schultz	C21	28	55	7	18	9	0	0	0	12	4	0	.327
Whitey Kurowski	2B18	18	60	5	19	8	1	0	2	2	4	2	.317
Lee Sherrill	P13	13	21	1	4	1	0	0	0	0	7	0	.190
Walt Schuerbaum	OF,2B	10	26	1	4	0	2	0	0	0	1	1	.154
John Echols	2B,3B	9	10	1	5	1	0	0	0			0	.500
Gerry Burmeister	C	7	6	0	0	0	0	0	0			0	.000

COLUMBUS (cont.)
Red Birds

BATTERS	POS-GAMES	GP	AB	R	H	BI	2B	3B	HR	BB	SO	SB	BA
Hal Epps	OF	6	24	3	4	1	0	0	0			0	.167
Vernon Horn	2B	6	16	3	4	2	0	1	0			0	.250
Ray Smith	C	6	5	1	2	2	0	0	0			0	.400
Dave Danaher	PH	1	0	0	0	0	0	0	0			0	----

PITCHERS		W	L	PCT	G	GS	CG	SH	IP	H	BB	SO	ERA
Nathan Andrews		17	9	.654	29	25	17	2	200	177	48	92	2.70
Max Lanier		10	16	.385	33	28	12	4	200	202	105	148	4.14
Al Fisher		7	9	.438	24	18	8	0	127	155	33	46	4.61
Max Macon		6	9	.400	30	16	4	0	133	162	65	52	4.74
Norbert Kleinke		6	14	.300	30	23	8	2	152	160	43	78	4.44
Lee Sherrill		5	1	.833	13	5	1	0	56	42	29	21	3.86
William Curlee		3	7	.300	47	7	2	0	116	137	58	62	4.81
George Hader		3	16	.158	53	15	3	0	165	187	80	67	5.24
Jake Drake		0	0	----	6			0	16	15	11	4	
Lew Krausse		0	0	----	3			0	4	9	0	1	
John Dagenhard		0	0	----	1			0	1	1	1	0	

TOLEDO   8th   47-107   .305   -60   Myles Thomas
Mud Hens

BATTERS	POS-GAMES	GP	AB	R	H	BI	2B	3B	HR	BB	SO	SB	BA
Harry Taylor	1B	(see multi-team players)											
Ben McCoy	2B81	81	300	55	97	57	13	7	14	32	26	2	.323
Boyd Perry	SS75,2B12	101	342	53	79	28	15	5	5	33	42	3	.231
Fred Muller	3B122	126	454	51	112	78	18	3	20	26	61	1	.247
Frank Secory	OF142	143	517	84	149	79	19	12	18	51	99	7	.288
Leslie Fleming	OF116,1B11	126	446	71	120	92	15	6	27	59	83	4	.269
Joe Dwyer	OF67	79	260	27	82	24	13	3	2	15	9	0	.315
Vern Mackie	C93	99	306	29	94	36	17	1	2	26	15	3	.307
Conrad Flippen	SS27,3B20,2B18	73	259	28	62	19	8	2	0	15	30	5	.239
Ed Parsons	C61	67	207	16	41	19	7	3	5	15	37	1	.198
Ken Huff	3B28,SS10	57	151	19	28	7	2	2	2	8	28	1	.185
Joe Grace	OF51	52	181	26	54	34	8	3	3	19	23	1	.298
Fred Petoskey	OF39	51	138	14	32	3	7	0	0	4	7	2	.232
Andrew Sabota	SS46	48	154	13	39	10	8	1	2	11	35	1	.253
Milt Lenhardt	OF37	44	144	32	32	15	5	1	2	26	21	0	.222
Lloyd Dietz	P41	42	40	2	5	3	0	0	0	2	6	0	.125
Junie Barnes	P38	39	71	8	18	6	2	2	0	0	12	1	.254
Pat McLaughlin	P38	38	51	4	8	0	0	1	0	3	8	0	.157
Joe Rogalski	P36	36	50	4	5	3	2	0	0	4	14	0	.100
Albert Smith	2B33	33	118	14	31	6	8	1	0	8	16	1	.263
Clarence Phillips	P21	29	49	2	9	4	4	0	1	1	7	0	.184
Fred Hutchinson	P21	23	57	8	16	5	3	0	0	9	5	0	.281
Cecil Dunn	1B14	20	75	5	20	8	5	1	1	4	12	0	.267
Fred Johnson	P19	19	16	1	2	0	0	0	0	0	3	0	.125
Ralph Younker	OF11	18	53	10	15	9	4	2	0	2	11	2	.283
Jackie Reid	P13	13	18	3	4	1	0	0	0	1	5	0	.222
Ewald Pyle	P13	13	17	2	3	0	0	0	0	1	3	0	.176
Floyd Gieball	P12	12	32	1	5	2	2	0	1	2	2	0	.156
John Johnson		12	14	0	1	0	0	0	0	0	4	0	.071
Tom Tighe		10	28	3	6	0	0	0	0	2	5	0	.214
James Morris		10	9	0	3	1	0	0	0	0	2	0	.333
James Brown	OF	7	13	2	3	1	0	0	0			0	.231
Carl Foldenauer	C	4	11	0	3	2	0	0	0			0	.273

PITCHERS		W	L	PCT	G	GS	CG	SH	IP	H	BB	SO	ERA
Fred Hutchinson		9	9	.500	21	18	14	0	137	128	34	56	3.55
Joe Rogalski		8	9	.471	36	22	6	0	155	187	36	68	4.99
Junie Barnes		7	18	.292	38	29	9	0	182	251	62	59	5.79
Clarence Phillips		6	10	.375	21	18	8	0	104	142	25	25	5.19
Pat McLaughlin		6	12	.333	38	17	7	0	175	239	51	58	5.14
Lloyd Dietz		3	17	.150	41	19	5	0	147	181	41	67	5.69
Jackie Reid		2	4	.333	13	2	1	0	55	69	9	32	4.75
Ewald Pyle		2	5	.286	13	7	1	1	52	68	24	23	7.44
Fred Johnson		1	6	.143	19	3	1	0	59	59	14	25	4.27
Floyd Gieball		1	10	.091	12	11	9	0	93	102	21	37	3.58
Eli Birmingham		0	0	----	1			0	6	9	2	0	

MULTI-TEAM PLAYERS

BATTERS	POS-GAMES	TEAMS	GP	AB	R	H	BI	2B	3B	HR	BB	SO	SB	BA
Edwin Morgan	OF127	COL-MIL	138	493	76	161	54	29	9	7	34	46	16	.327
Harry Taylor	1B130	MIN-TOL	131	484	48	123	32	15	2	3	43	31	7	.254
Frank Madura	2B96	LOU-SP	117	367	51	108	26	18	2	1	58	14	8	.294
Lindsay Brown	SS62,3B25,2B15	IND-COL	105	312	35	59	27	7	3	1	22	48	5	.189
Robert Boken	3B48,2B21,1B11	SP-LOU	101	289	43	79	56	12	4	9	20	42	5	.273
Bill Lewis	C76	IND-LOU	83	246	30	72	24	7	2	0	34	12	2	.293
Emmett Nelson	P26	TOL-MIL	26	21	0	2	1	0	0	0	0	5	0	.095

PITCHERS	TEAMS	W	L	PCT	G	GS	CG	SH	IP	H	BB	SO	ERA
Emmett Nelson	TOL-MIL	5	2	.714	26	4	4	0	72	79	26	37	4.00

TEAM BATTING

TEAMS	GP	AB	R	H	BI	2B	3B	HR	BB	SO	SB	BA
KANSAS CITY	155	5054	835	1447		264	91	132			154	.286
MINNEAPOLIS	154	5190	937	1534		268	53	217			95	.296
INDIANAPOLIS	155	5030	691	1383		219	78	55			66	.275
LOUISVILLE	153	5049	668	1357		213	83	52			96	.269
ST. PAUL	156	5113	728	1374		223	61	105			69	.269
MILWAUKEE	154	5076	706	1436		249	58	117			48	.283
COLUMBUS	155	5104	640	1384		228	44	77			86	.271
TOLEDO	154	5077	635	1304		200	58	108			41	.257
	618	40693	5840	11219		1864	526	863			655	.276

1940
Unlikely Champions

The 1939 Kansas City Blues were overwhelming favorites going into the playoffs. The team had just throttled the rest of the league with one of the finest team performances in regular season history. However, much to their chagrin, a team with more than 30 fewer wins went on to represent the Association in the Junior World Series. If this wasn't enough, the same team would duplicate the feat in 1940.

The fourth place Louisville Colonels staggered into the 1939 playoffs with the worst record of any playoff team to date (75–78). They then proceeded to stun the baseball world by knocking off their first round playoff opponent Minneapolis, in five games, to reach the Association finals. The favored Kansas City, meanwhile, had lost to Indianapolis in five games as well. Much to everyone's surprise, Louisville went on to rout Indianapolis and reach the Junior World Series.

The Rochester Red Wings were the favorites entering the series but the Colonels whipped out two quick wins to draw first blood. Rochester won the next two to even the series. Games five and six were split to knot the series at three apiece. The deciding game went into extra innings before Louisville put up a four spot in the eleventh inning to win the series. The stunning upset was complete.

In 1940, Louisville once again lurched into fourth place with a 75-victory season. Kansas City, Columbus, and Minneapolis finished ahead of the Colonels, while St. Paul, Indianapolis, Toledo, and Milwaukee finished behind them. Top batting honors fell to Al Wright of Minneapolis, who won the triple crown with a .369 average, 39 home runs, and 159 runs batted in. The top pitchers included Robert Logan of Indianapolis and John Lindell of Kansas City, who each won 18; Ernie White of Columbus who had a 2.25 earned run average; and Frank Melton of Columbus, who struck out 142.

In the playoffs, lightning struck twice as Louisville polished off Columbus in six games, while Kansas City did the same to Minneapolis. In the finals, Louisville quashed any hope of Kansas City's advancement by beating the Blues four games to two to reach the Junior World Series for the second straight year. Only a defeat by Newark in the final series prevented a duplicate of 1939 for the Louisville Colonels.

The Kansas City Association entry had finished first two years in a row in convincing fashion. But thanks to the playoff wizardry of Louisville, the Blues stayed home while the upstart Colonels represented the league in the Junior World Series. They were an unlikely champion for sure, and a clear example of the fact that a team didn't need to win even half of its games to count its season a success.

KANSAS CITY Blues

1st	95-57	.625	Bill Meyer

BATTERS	POS-GAMES	GP	AB	R	H	BI	2B	3B	HR	BB	SO	SB	BA
Johnny Sturm	1B144	144	580	86	181	73	27	5	4	42	43	15	.312
Jerry Priddy	2B154	154	566	92	173	112	38	10	16	71	73	23	.306
Phil Rizzuto	SS146	148	579	124	201	73	28	10	10	48	33	35	.347
Bill Hitchcock	3B117,SS15	131	447	64	120	61	18	6	6	30	52	15	.268
Frenchy Bordagaray	OF154	154	598	113	214	83	39	8	4	44	18	31	.358
Nino Bongiovanni	OF136	142	564	82	152	55	29	6	6	38	22	14	.270
Russ Derry	OF66	67	228	45	53	47	11	4	9	47	43	8	.232
John Riddle	C109	111	314	39	88	35	15	1	4	24	23	3	.280
Jack Saltzgaver	3B49,1B13	103	262	38	64	31	12	3	1	35	19	6	.244
Anthony DePhillips	C80	85	201	19	51	26	8	2	1	26	24	3	.254
Bill Matheson	OF61	68	222	27	57	39	13	6	1	17	24	6	.257
Ralph Boyle	OF11	51	64	10	16	9	0	0	0	6	6	1	.250
John Lindell	P31	41	88	12	24	11	2	1	1	3	13	1	.273
Charles Stanceu	P37	37	69	3	5	1	1	0	0	1	30	0	.072
Al Gerheauser	P34	37	29	3	7	5	2	0	0	2	12	0	.241
Colonel Mills	OF36	36	132	18	46	25	7	1	1	11	13	3	.348
Charles Wensloff	P35	35	63	5	12	4	2	0	1	3	18	0	.190
Don Hendrickson	P35	35	56	2	7	2	1	0	0	1	10	0	.125
John Haley	P33	33	33	3	9	3	3	0	0	1	9	0	.273
Al Moran	P32	32	31	2	3	1	2	0	0	1	13	0	.097
Ernie Bonham	P16	16	44	5	12	6	1	0	0	4	5	0	.273
Herm Caldwell	OF11	14	31	3	7	3	1	0	1	4	2	1	.226
Joe Callahan	P11	11	13	1	0	0	0	0	0	0	7	0	.000
Tom Reis	P10	10	11	1	1	0	0	0	0	0	6	0	.091
William Gill	P8	8	12		1								.083
Edwin Carnett	P8	8	11		5								.455
James Nicholson	3B	6	8	1	3	0	0	0	0			1	.375
I. Andrews	P3	3	3		1								.333
Aaron Robinson	C	3	3	1	1	2	0	0	0			1	.333

PITCHERS	W	L	PCT	G	GS	CG	SH	IP	H	BB	SO	ERA
John Lindell	18	7	.720	31	27	16	3	203	179	69	82	2.70
Don Hendrickson	16	7	.696	35	21	10	2	167	164	40	48	3.02
Charles Stanceu	15	8	.652	37	24	16	6	214	170	109	126	2.69
Charles Wensloff	13	8	.619	35	27	11	0	178	169	55	70	3.19
Ernie Bonham	10	4	.714	16	15	9	4	124	107	29	50	2.32
Al Moran	6	4	.600	32	11	3	0	99	108	58	29	4.91
Al Gerheauser	5	5	.500	34	4	1	0	95	89	39	58	3.22
John Haley	5	5	.500	33	9	2	0	108	94	59	37	3.17
William Gill	2	0	1.000	8			0	31				
Joe Callahan	2	2	.500	11			0	36				
Edwin Carnett	2	2	.500	8			0	28				
Tom Reis	1	4	.200	10			0	44				
I. Andrews	0	1	.000	3			0	13				

COLUMBUS Red Birds

2nd	90-60	.600	-4	Burt Shotton

BATTERS	POS-GAMES	GP	AB	R	H	BI	2B	3B	HR	BB	SO	SB	BA
Maurice Sturdy	1B80,3B38,2B20	128	478	56	141	66	27	3	3	39	23	6	.295
James Bucher	2B108,3B19	127	523	75	149	48	27	8	6	40	22	9	.285
Jim Hitchcock	SS91,3B14	106	354	40	92	38	12	4	0	35	24	3	.260
Robert Repass	3B90,SS31,2B18	135	464	68	138	59	22	9	0	36	45	6	.297
Morris Jones	OF128	129	484	81	156	100	30	12	9	75	47	7	.322
Harry Walker	OF122,SS20	140	537	94	168	74	39	7	17	66	43	17	.313
Coaker Triplett	OF116	120	466	112	158	78	27	12	11	52	42	12	.339
Walker Cooper	C130	131	477	61	144	53	29	12	3	24	22	12	.302
George Fleming	OF57	83	239	29	67	37	13	4	1	19	22	0	.280
Larry Barton	1B53	57	167	25	42	35	12	2	8	22	16	3	.251
Harry Brecheen	P34	48	100	10	26	16	0	1	2	5	17	0	.260
Frank Barrett	P47	47	33	4	5	3	0	0	0	4	8	0	.152
John Bolling	1B34	45	128	16	27	12	8	0	0	9	12	3	.211
Frank Melton	P43	43	66	4	11	4	3	0	1	3	27	0	.167
Richard Tichacek	C38	41	101	13	24	11	8	1	1	13	11	0	.238
Murry Dickson	P36	41	94	10	24	12	2	1	1	0	5	0	.255
William Rabe	OF25	36	105	15	29	17	6	1	2	8	19	3	.276
Lee Sherrill	P35	35	42	5	10	9	2	0	0	2	12	0	.238
Tom Sunkel	P31	31	69	7	11	3	0	0	0	3	19	0	.159
Lynn Meyers	SS25	29	103	17	20	7	4	2	0	11	14	2	.194
Ernie White	P26	27	50	4	7	3	2	0	0	1	9	0	.140
Averett Thompson	OF10	18	47	4	13	6	3	0	0	1	1	0	.277

COLUMBUS (cont.)
Red Birds

BATTERS	POS-GAMES	GP	AB	R	H	BI	2B	3B	HR	BB	SO	SB	BA
William Curlee	P17	17	7	1	1	0	0	0	0	0	2	0	.143
Robert Moers		11	40	8	9	4	1	1	0	5	3	0	.225
Vernon Horn	P11	11	11	0	0	0	0	0	0	0	3	0	.000
Goody Rosen		10	33	6	7	6	1	0	2	4	2	1	.212
George Hader	P7	7	7		2								.286
Al Unser	3B	7	3	0	1	0	0	0	0			0	.333
James Winford	P4	4	4		0								.000
Milt Lowrey	P4	4	1		0								.000
Fred Martin	P3	3	1		1								1.000
Joe Niedson	PH	3	1	0	0	0	0	0	0	0	0	0	.000

PITCHERS		W	L	PCT	G	GS	CG	SH	IP	H	BB	SO	ERA
Murry Dickson		17	8	.680	36	28	15	3	219	212	86	105	3.33
Harry Brecheen		16	9	.640	34	24	15	1	216	207	52	124	2.75
Ernie White		13	4	**.765**	26	16	10	3	136	102	59	92	**2.25**
Tom Sunkel		13	7	.650	31	27	9	2	181	155	117	113	3.53
Lee Sherrill		10	7	.588	35	13	5	1	126	109	62	63	3.64
Frank Melton		10	10	.500	43	28	4	1	207	195	**139**	**142**	3.48
Frank Barrett		8	8	.500	47	10	5	2	126	123	84	62	3.07
William Curlee		1	1	.500	17			0	32				
Vernon Horn		1	2	.333	11			0	37				
George Hader		1	3	.250	7			0	23				
James Winford		0	1	.000	4			0	12				
Milt Lowrey		0	0	----	4			0	5	8	8	2	
Fred Martin		0	0	----	3			0	5	9	6	1	9.00

MINNEAPOLIS   3rd   86-59   .593   -5.5   Tom Sheehan
Millers

BATTERS	POS-GAMES	GP	AB	R	H	BI	2B	3B	HR	BB	SO	SB	BA
Phil Weintraub	1B135	137	487	106	169	109	34	4	27	107	48	8	.347
Frank Trechock	2B90,SS14	110	319	45	79	33	10	1	0	31	31	5	.248
Eugene Geary	SS129	131	529	110	163	58	31	3	10	51	48	8	.308
Robert Fausett	3B108,SS12	129	456	59	129	52	10	4	2	29	7	27	.283
Al Wright	OF146	146	578	137	213	**159**	35	9	**39**	61	64	4	**.369**
Bobby Estella	OF137,3B11	147	531	**147**	181	121	36	5	32	**132**	91	14	.341
Harvey Walker	OF88	103	352	88	112	58	28	3	25	72	47	10	.318
Otto Denning	C103,1B10	130	410	59	135	74	22	8	11	53	46	6	.329
Lin Storti	2B78,3B33	120	384	50	120	80	10	1	20	54	66	2	.313
Fabian Gaffke	OF81	104	327	60	96	52	21	2	12	31	45	3	.294
Russ Rolandson	C58	65	200	15	49	14	7	1	1	9	34	2	.245
Walt Tauscher	P53	53	56	6	11	7	5	0	0	2	8	0	.196
Harry Smythe	P38	48	71	11	22	16	2	1	2	5	9	0	.310
Elon Hogsett	P41	43	81	9	16	7	2	1	0	6	14	0	.198
Harry Kelley	P42	42	94	10	18	8	4	0	0	8	6	0	.191
Milt Haefner	P40	40	62	5	13	7	1	0	0	15	18	0	.210
Russ Evans	P39	39	79	6	15	8	0	0	0	3	17	0	.190
Bill Barnacle	OF	7	9	2	1	1	0	0	1			0	.111
Jose Gonzalez	P4	4	5		4								.800
Belve Bean	P4	4	1		0								.000
Kash	P2	2	3		0								.000
Sowada	P2	2	2		1								.500
Lee Rogers	P2	2	1		0								.000
Earl Grace	PH	1	1	0	0	0	0	0	0			0	.000

PITCHERS		W	L	PCT	G	GS	CG	SH	IP	H	BB	SO	ERA
Harry Kelley		16	9	.640	42	29	12	2	249	**295**	69	90	4.30
Elon Hogsett		16	11	.593	41	26	11	1	210	249	70	104	4.03
Walt Tauscher		15	9	.625	53	10	7	2	167	183	59	48	4.04
Milt Haefner		14	8	.636	40	29	14	2	205	236	83	104	4.74
Harry Smythe		13	9	.591	38	23	12	0	173	196	43	76	3.80
Russ Evans		10	11	.476	39	29	11	0	215	250	80	105	4.40
Belve Bean		1	0	1.000	2			0	5				
Kash		1	0	1.000	2			0	6				
Sowada		0	2	.000	2			0	6				
Jose Gonzales		0	0	----	4			0	15	12	4	3	
Lee Rogers		0	0	----	2			0	6	11	4	2	

LOUISVILLE   4th   75-75   .500   -19   Bill Burwell
Colonels

BATTERS	POS-GAMES	GP	AB	R	H	BI	2B	3B	HR	BB	SO	SB	BA
Paul Campbell	1B149	150	627	101	178	50	23	17	4	42	64	30	.284
Vince Sherlock	2B103	108	380	43	90	34	9	2	1	46	44	5	.237
Woody Williams	SS143	143	521	57	130	56	20	5	1	47	21	7	.250
Ernest Andres	3B91,2B13	111	369	36	102	35	17	2	1	32	33	1	.276
Chet Morgan	OF150	150	602	87	191	69	23	7	0	44	9	3	.317
Art Parks	OF136	139	487	68	145	62	30	7	5	79	23	0	.298
Fred Sington	OF115	123	425	55	115	76	19	7	10	56	56	1	.271
George Lacy	C77	83	275	30	64	49	13	1	8	29	29	0	.233
Baxter Jordan	3B65	94	250	23	72	18	8	2	2	21	7	5	.288
Bill Lewis	C55	69	179	28	49	28	5	5	0	38	8	1	.274
James Shilling	2B37	57	185	15	42	16	10	2	0	10	13	1	.227
Ed Madjeski	C19,OF11	50	139	17	42	20	9	0	0	4	13	1	.302
Cecil Hughson	P44	44	66	2	13	3	1	0	0	3	12	0	.197
Thomas Gavin	OF31	41	96	19	26	8	2	0	0	12	4	2	.271
James Weaver	P32	32	68	2	5	2	0	0	0	4	33	0	.074
LeRoy Parmelee	P27	31	50	7	8	7	2	2	1	3	18	0	.160
Yank Terry	P25	26	55	6	8	2	0	0	0	1	10	0	.145
Wes Flowers	P24	24	53	1	11	6	2	0	0	2	11	0	.208
Al Hollingsworth	P17	17	29	4	9	1	2	0	0	1	3	0	.310
Sam Nahem	P17	17	21	2	5	0	0	1	0	0	2	0	.238
Fred Shaffer	P16	16	12	1	3	0	0	0	0	0	2	0	.250
Monte Weaver	P15	15	12	0	3	0	1	1	0	1	1	0	.250
Dale Gentil	P15	15	8	0	2	2	1	0	0	0	0	0	.250
Woody Rich	P12	12	9	1	1	0	0	0	0	0	2	0	.111
Stan Spence	OF11	11	39	4	10	7	2	0	2	6	2	0	.256
Charles Wagner	P11	11	28	2	4	3	0	0	0	3	5	0	.143
Forest Pressnell	P11	11	20	2	5	0	1	0	0	3	1	0	.250
Leo Nonnenkamp	OF	6	17	2	5	3	1	0	0			0	.294
Davis	P5	5	4		0								.000
Art Mahan	PH	4	4	2	2	0	0	0	0			0	.500
Fred Walters	C	3	9	1	2	2	0	0	0			0	.222
Francis Walsh	3B	3	8	0	2	0	0	0	0			0	.250
Aloysius Hodkey	P1	1	4		2								.500

PITCHERS	W	L	PCT	G	GS	CG	SH	IP	H	BB	SO	ERA
Wes Flowers	13	6	.684	24	16	9	2	154	149	57	45	2.86
James Weaver	13	9	.591	32	27	9	1	198	219	72	75	3.95
Charles Wagner	9	1	.900	11	10	9	1	83	65	22	37	1.84
Yank Terry	7	9	.438	25	17	10	3	151	140	52	88	3.70
LeRoy Parmelee	7	10	.412	27	17	8	1	132	145	80	70	4.09
Cecil Hughson	7	11	.389	44	21	10	2	209	240	40	84	3.92
Forest Pressnell	4	5	.444	11	8	5	2	68	70	14	29	3.04
Fred Shaffer	3	3	.500	16	6	2	0	52	75	26	7	6.23
Sam Nahem	3	5	.375	17	6	2	0	63	75	25	30	4.43
Al Hollingsworth	3	7	.300	17	11	5	0	78	86	39	35	4.85
Davis	2	2	.500	5			0	13				
Aloysius Hodkey	1	0	1.000	1	1	1	0	9				
Dale Gentil	1	1	.500	15			0	30				
Woody Rich	1	2	.333	12			0	26				
Monte Weaver	1	4	.200	15			0	35				

ST. PAUL   5th   69-79   .466   -24   Foster Ganzel
Saints

BATTERS	POS-GAMES	GP	AB	R	H	BI	2B	3B	HR	BB	SO	SB	BA
Jesse Newman	1B		(see multi-team players)										
Aloysius Bejma	2B146	149	549	92	163	69	33	2	14	68	37	9	.297
John Gerlach	SS81,3B12	99	316	30	78	31	3	0	1	23	25	8	.247
Gil English	3B124	127	480	65	152	89	15	9	19	45	39	6	.317
George Stumpf	OF148	149	532	69	145	53	26	5	1	81	64	9	.273
Ralph McLeod	OF101	103	386	73	104	23	11	5	1	61	40	11	.269
Edwin Morgan	OF		(see multi-team players)										
Norm Schlueter	C86	96	294	30	60	37	13	6	4	29	61	0	.204
Robert Reis	OF46,3B19,1B16	110	315	34	86	66	11	2	16	35	39	6	.273
Lou Roggino	SS67	67	203	32	49	21	7	1	3	39	45	5	.241
Avitus Himsl	P37	45	87	8	17	9	6	0	0	3	21	0	.195
Neil Clifford	C38	44	126	6	27	12	5	1	0	8	21	0	.214
LeRoy Anton	1B40	43	153	30	35	21	7	1	8	17	13	2	.229
Harry Taylor	P39	42	51	5	8	0	1	0	0	3	15	0	.157
Art Herring	P32	34	95	10	25	19	3	1	2	5	15	0	.263

ST. PAUL (cont.)
Saints

BATTERS	POS-GAMES	GP	AB	R	H	BI	2B	3B	HR	BB	SO	SB	BA
Tom Earley	P32	32	45	3	7	5	0	1	0	2	6	0	.156
William Swift	P30	30	66	4	14	5	0	0	0	0	11	0	.212
Frank Madura		18	24	9	6	3	1	0	1	8	1	0	.250
Victor Frasier	P18	18	24	0	4	1	0	0	0	4	6	0	.167
Rufus Jackson	C15	15	49	4	12	6	2	1	1	6	3	0	.245
Al Fisher	P8	11	19	0	0	0	0	0	0	3	4	0	.000
Edwin Weiland	P7	7	6		1								.167
M. Beddingfield	P7	7	6		0								.000
Howard Belknap	P7	7	4		1								.250
Ed Hoffman	OF	6	17	7	8	4	1	0	1			0	.471
Keith Bissonette	1B	5	20	0	3	3	0	0	0			0	.150
Nathan Andrews	P5	5	12		4								.333
Dwain Sloat	P5	5	2		0								.000
Dubernic	P5	5	0		0								----
Ray Phelps	P4	4	0		0								----
Wilcy Moore	P1	1	1		0								.000

PITCHERS		W	L	PCT	G	GS	CG	SH	IP	H	BB	SO	ERA
Art Herring		17	10	.630	32	32	23	0	239	275	76	100	3.80
William Swift		13	10	.565	30	24	16	5	186	163	51	97	3.29
Avitus Himsl		13	15	.464	37	26	17	1	222	257	53	58	4.05
Tom Earley		12	12	.500	32	17	5	0	139	166	51	42	4.47
Harry Taylor		5	15	.250	39	22	8	2	150	178	68	54	5.88
Victor Frasier		3	4	.429	18	7	3	0	65	94	30	19	5.40
Al Fisher		1	3	.250	8			0	44				
Nathan Andrews		1	3	.250	5			1	24				
Howard Belknap		0	1	.000	7			0	15				
Dubernic		0	1	.000	5			0	6				
Wilcy Moore		0	1	.000	1			0	5				
Edwin Weiland		0	0	----	7			0	21	33	14	8	
M. Beddingfield		0	0	----	7			0	20	33	4	8	
Dwain Sloat		0	0	----	5			0	8	11	5	4	
Ray Phelps		0	0	----	4			0	6	6	3	1	
Jack Gerlach		0	0	----	1			0	1	4	6	0	

INDIANAPOLIS   6th   62-84   .425   -30   Griffith - Ens
Indians

BATTERS	POS-GAMES	GP	AB	R	H	BI	2B	3B	HR	BB	SO	SB	BA
Robert Prichard	1B56	56	183	26	51	31	7	4	5	31	28	1	.279
Ben Zientara	2B142	142	559	76	147	63	28	3	3	50	49	9	.263
Roland Harrington	SS85	85	359	46	88	37	11	7	3	17	24	3	.245
Wayne Blackburn	3B62	75	247	38	77	37	15	5	0	20	16	9	.312
Milt Galatzer	OF130,1B18	147	568	98	191	53	24	9	2	81	30	6	.336
LeGrant Scott	OF87	92	320	51	97	37	17	4	5	41	28	4	.303
Allen Hunt	OF82	95	307	42	79	43	17	5	4	40	30	13	.257
Dick West	C99	113	401	56	114	50	23	4	7	30	53	7	.284
Don Lang	3B49	60	182	20	40	33	5	3	7	26	29	1	.220
Joe Mack	OF31,1B18	59	181	16	40	17	8	1	3	14	26	2	.221
John Pasek	C48	55	149	15	47	26	11	1	0	22	11	1	.315
Nolen Richardson	SS54	54	187	10	41	15	3	1	0	16	5	1	.219
John Hill	3B40	46	146	26	38	14	2	4	1	14	9	1	.260
Walter Berger	OF41	41	155	27	38	19	8	1	5	15	34	0	.245
Don French	P37	38	39	3	2	2	0	0	0	4	9	0	.051
Robert Logan	P36	36	99	4	12	5	0	0	0	1	23	0	.121
John Wilson	P33	33	19	1	2	1	0	0	0	4	10	0	.105
Peter Sivess	P26	26	56	1	8	4	1	0	0	0	14	0	.143
Earl Caldwell	P26	26	39	3	6	1	1	0	0	1	10	0	.154
Charles Barrett	P25	25	52	4	12	4	1	0	0	0	7	0	.231
James Sharp	P25	25	23	0	2	0	0	0	0	1	14	0	.087
Johnny VanderMeer	P14	15	36	4	8	9	2	2	0	0	9	0	.222
Art Jacobs	P13	13	0	1	0	0	0	0	0	2	0	0	----
Robert Latshaw		10	28	3	8	3	2	0	0	3	2	0	.286
Mitchell Balas	P9	9	8		0								.000
Dee Moore	C	6	16	2	5	4	1	0	0			1	.313
Glenn Fletcher	P6	6	11		1								.091
Bauers	P6	6	4		2								.500
Art Doll	P5	5	7	0	2	1	0	0	0			0	.286
Tony Archinski	P4	4	1		0								.000
Harry Wolfe	P2	2	3		0								.000

INDIANAPOLIS (cont.)
Indians

PITCHERS	W	L	PCT	G	GS	CG	SH	IP	H	BB	SO	ERA
Robert Logan	18	14	.563	36	34	24	3	267	267	77	104	3.10
Peter Sivess	7	12	.368	26	24	8	1	149	174	51	46	4.89
Johnny VanderMeer	6	4	.600	14	14	10	2	105	76	65	109	2.40
Don French	6	8	.429	37	9	4	0	113	154	49	32	5.18
Earl Caldwell	5	12	.294	26	15	6	2	129	141	57	44	3.56
Charles Barrett	5	13	.278	25	22	10	1	150	172	51	40	4.74
Glenn Fletcher	4	0	1.000	6			0	32				
John Wilson	3	3	.500	33	1	0	0	70	66	27	35	3.86
Balas	2	3	.400	9			0	25				
Art Jacobs	1	2	.333	13			0	13				
James Sharp	1	5	.167	25	5	1	0	76	79	56	38	3.91
Bauers	0	1	.000	6			0	14				
Art Doll	0	0	----	5			0	18	24	13	4	
Tony Archinski	0	0	----	4			0	10	13	5	1	
Harry Wolfe	0	0	----	2			0	7	6	3	1	

TOLEDO
Mud Hens

7th 59-90 .396 -34.5 James Taylor

BATTERS	POS-GAMES	GP	AB	R	H	BI	2B	3B	HR	BB	SO	SB	BA
Harry Taylor	1B139	140	464	57	124	41	22	0	3	44	32	8	.267
John Lucadello	2B141	141	518	81	173	102	35	11	9	87	15	4	.334
Mark Christman	SS133,3B21	151	577	73	152	45	19	7	0	42	32	13	.263
Art Whitney	3B46	49	187	15	50	32	15	1	2	7	13	3	.267
Henry Steinbacher	OF131	140	502	74	143	62	17	8	7	52	28	3	.285
Tony Criscola	OF111	125	443	64	125	44	22	3	7	31	40	5	.282
Milt Byrnes	OF84	109	321	58	82	37	16	3	3	43	43	3	.255
Harold Spindel	C97	101	350	41	101	46	13	1	3	17	34	5	.289
Ralph Winegarner	3B26,1B24,OF16	77	214	24	57	31	18	3	1	26	16	1	.266
Joe Dwyer	OF58	74	239	31	74	28	8	4	1	14	9	3	.310
John Marcum	P36	73	127	15	41	30	10	0	1	13	10	0	.323
Robert Neighbors	3B36,SS22	71	204	20	57	14	10	2	0	14	36	2	.279
Jesse Landrum	3B37	64	161	19	37	20	4	2	3	8	25	3	.230
Glenn McQuillen	OF60	61	234	38	78	23	10	12	3	18	21	4	.333
George Gill	P40	48	64	11	18	7	3	1	0	1	16	0	.281
Armand Payton	C38	47	122	13	29	15	4	1	0	9	9	0	.238
Harry Kimberlin	P41	41	88	4	13	8	0	0	0	6	19	0	.148
Lester Wirkkala	P39	40	65	3	10	6	2	0	0	4	11	0	.154
Charles Wagener	P37	37	17	2	1	0	0	0	0	1	1	0	.059
Art McDougall	P31	31	10	0	0	0	0	0	0	2	3	0	.000
Jacob Wade	P22	26	8	1	3	2	0	0	0	2	2	0	.375
Ed Silber	OF15	17	57	12	11	2	3	0	0	10	8	0	.193
John Whitehead	P16	16	21	2	8	1	0	0	0	3	4	0	.381
Frank Grube	C15	15	43	1	10	3	0	0	0	7	5	0	.233
John Kramer	P13	13	11	1	1	0	1	0	0	1	4	0	.091
Edward Cole	P12	12	18	0	2	1	0	0	0	0	3	0	.111
John Johnson	P9	9	11		2								.182
William Cox	P7	7	11		1								.091
Harry Bailey	P6	6	0		0								----
Zach Taylor	C	4	8	0	1	1	0	0	0			0	.125
Ben SoRelle	P3	3	0		0								----
Junie Barnes	P2	2	0		0								----
Robert Jones	PH	1	1	0	0	0	0	0	0			0	.000
Dan Scudder	C1	1	1	0	0	0	0	0	0			0	.000

PITCHERS	W	L	PCT	G	GS	CG	SH	IP	H	BB	SO	ERA
Harry Kimberlin	16	16	.500	41	33	17	2	246	275	107	131	4.39
Johnny Marcum	13	12	.520	36	29	14	0	228	285	32	93	5.21
Lester Wirkkala	9	13	.409	39	24	9	0	196	223	91	54	4.82
George Gill	8	12	.400	40	21	7	1	169	212	57	41	4.79
John Whitehead	6	7	.462	16	11	7	0	80	86	12	22	2.70
Jacob Wade	2	2	.500	22			0	34				
John Johnson	1	1	.500	9			0	18				
William Cox	1	4	.200	7			0	42				
John Kramer	1	6	.143	13			0	37				
Charles Wagener	1	7	.125	37	6	0	0	78	104	35	26	5.65
Edward Cole	1	7	.125	12	8	3	0	61	70	15	25	4.28
SoRelle	0	1	.000	3			0	2				
Art McDougall	0	2	.000	31	1	0	0	50	52	28	9	5.04
Harry Bailey	0	0	----	6			0	9	10	6	6	
Junie Barnes	0	0	----	2			0	3	4	2	0	

MILWAUKEE   8th   58-90   .392   -35   Heath - Schalk
Brewers

BATTERS	POS-GAMES	GP	AB	R	H	BI	2B	3B	HR	BB	SO	SB	BA
Leslie Powers	1B134	135	514	74	119	58	15	2	12	43	45	4	.232
Barney Walls	2B144	145	522	52	146	56	26	8	1	35	72	7	.280
Claude Corbitt	SS134	136	526	92	171	42	23	10	2	64	40	17	.325
Charles English	3B148	148	568	80	171	93	29	4	17	41	37	7	.301
Ted Gullic	OF144,P1	146	554	106	179	100	40	5	31	41	58	5	.323
Harold Peck	OF127	136	527	76	155	66	19	14	9	30	51	11	.294
Ted Abernathy	OF		(see multi-team players)										
Bob Garbark	C96	101	295	31	64	29	11	0	0	46	16	1	.217
Paul Dunlap	OF61	93	226	29	56	41	5	2	7	30	13	0	.248
Bill Hankins	C66	77	213	20	57	18	9	0	2	17	19	1	.268
Chet Wilburn	SS18,1B15,2B11,P1	75	188	16	42	19	5	0	4	15	25	1	.223
Frank Makosky	P41	42	55	4	9	4	2	0	0	4	7	0	.164
Joe Dickinson	P41	41	25	4	6	2	2	0	0	1	4	0	.240
George Blaeholder	P39	39	54	2	5	2	1	0	0	5	22	0	.093
Robert Kline	P39	39	32	3	5	1	0	0	0	0	5	0	.156
Jimmy DeShong	P35	36	64	11	13	7	2	1	0	7	11	0	.203
Charles Marrow	P35	35	68	7	17	7	1	0	0	7	14	0	.250
Ken Jungels	P28	30	56	12	16	8	1	0	1	1	8	1	.286
Paul Sullivan	P27	27	42	2	6	3	0	0	0	1	15	0	.143
Art Herring	P11	12	11	1	2	0	1	0	0	1	3	0	.182
Joe Skurski	OF	7	15	2	4	2	1	0	0			1	.267
Minor Heath	1B	4	3	0	1	0	0	0	0	0		0	.333
Justin Stein	PH	2	1	0	0	0	0	0	0	0		0	.000
Stanley Galle	PH	1	1	0	0	0	0	0	0			0	.000
John Schmitz	P1	1	0		0								----

PITCHERS	W	L	PCT	G	GS	CG	SH	IP	H	BB	SO	ERA
George Blaeholder	10	10	.500	39	17	9	1	175	209	44	45	3.39
Jimmy DeShong	10	15	.400	35	30	8	0	193	271	97	50	6.16
Robert Kline	8	5	.615	39	9	4	1	112	120	42	32	3.78
Frank Makosky	8	13	.381	41	20	8	2	182	216	57	59	4.15
Charles Marrow	8	19	.296	35	27	14	2	205	254	76	71	5.58
Ken Jungels	6	11	.353	28	19	5	1	132	157	55	40	5.11
Paul Sullivan	4	9	.308	27	22	6	1	130	153	86	60	5.54
Joe Dickinson	2	4	.333	41	2	0	0	97	118	45	32	5.29
Art Herring	2	4	.333	11			0	30				
Tedd Gullic	0	0	----	1			0	4	5	3	2	
John Schmitz	0	0	----	1			0	3	6	1	3	
Chet Wilburn	0	0	----	1			0	2	6	0	1	

MULTI-TEAM PLAYERS

BATTERS	POS-GAMES	TEAMS	GP	AB	R	H	BI	2B	3B	HR	BB	SO	SB	BA
Jesse Newman	1B133	IND-SP	139	464	68	140	88	34	3	7	87	65	9	.302
Ted Abernathy	OF128	SP-MIL	135	506	60	142	87	35	4	10	36	48	5	.281
Gil Brack	OF121	SP-IND	134	475	78	131	99	26	7	18	65	89	7	.276
Edwin Morgan	OF114	MIL-SP	128	435	85	127	48	30	7	7	53	38	14	.292
Vern Mackie	C40	TOL-SP	52	125	7	28	10	3	0	1	10	9	0	.224
Lloyd Johnson	P39	IND-SP	39	64	4	11	3	2	0	0	1	15	0	.172
Damon Phillips	SS12	SP-IND	16	49	3	9	2	1	1	0	4	7	0	.184

PITCHERS		TEAMS	W	L	PCT	G	GS	CG	SH	IP	H	BB	SO	ERA
Lloyd Johnson		IND-SP	8	11	.421	39	23	7	0	183	213	69	59	4.67

TEAM BATTING

TEAMS	GP	AB	R	H	BI	2B	3B	HR	BB	SO	SB	BA
KANSAS CITY	156	5261	803	1514	714	261	64	66	462	527	167	.288
COLUMBUS	152	5230	765	1483	702	278	80	67	483	482	84	.284
MINNEAPOLIS	147	5038	928	1547	863	260	43	183	672	583	89	.307
LOUISVILLE	150	5052	619	1346	560	201	60	35	483	437	58	.266

TEAM BATTING (cont.)

TEAMS	GP	AB	R	H	BI	2B	3B	HR	BB	SO	SB	BA
ST. PAUL	149	4963	703	1331	654	217	48	95	586	**625**	78	.268
INDIANAPOLIS	147	4893	642	1281	589	213	60	56	522	583	65	.262
TOLEDO	152	5137	661	1413	600	233	59	43	474	452	60	.275
MILWAUKEE	151	5044	683	1379	631	225	50	95	433	520	63	.273
	602	40618	5804	11294	5313	1888	464	640	4115	4209	664	.278

1941
Three Crowns for Columbus

During the decade of the 1930s, the Columbus Red Birds had finished in the playoffs three times. This was about average, considering that fully half of the teams made the playoffs starting in 1936. What is not average is the Red Birds' performance in those playoffs.

The first two Columbus playoff appearances came in 1933 and 1934. In those years, before the Shaughnessy playoff system, Columbus dumped their Association opponent Minneapolis (the winner of the west grouping) in both years to reach the Junior World Series. Once there, the Red Birds whipped their International League opponent each time to win the championship. Again in 1937, Columbus waltzed through the Association playoffs, only to lose in heartbreaking fashion to Newark in the Junior World Series. Impressive as their 1930s feats were, the Red Birds' most convincing playoff run came during the next decade.

The Columbus Red Birds won the 1941 pennant going away, beating second place Louisville by eight games. Kansas City and Minneapolis rounded out the first division, while Toledo, Indianapolis, St. Paul, and Milwaukee filled positions five through eight. The league's leading batter came from Milwaukee, as Lou Novikoff (.370) won the title. Al Wright of Minneapolis won his second consecutive home run championship (26), while Bert Haas of Columbus finished with the most runs batted in (131). On the pitching front, Columbus' Murray Dickson finished with the most wins (21) and strikeouts (153), while his teammate, John Grodzicki had the lowest earned run average (2.58).

In the playoffs, Columbus returned to its winning ways. In the first round, the Red Birds polished off the Kansas City Blues in six games. In the second round, they finished off Louisville in five to reach the Junior World Series, where their opponent would be the Montreal Royals. After spotting the Royals a two games to one lead in Montreal, the Red Birds returned home to dust off Montreal with three straight wins (5–4, 13–3, and 9–8).

In the next two years, Columbus would duplicate its 1941 efforts with two more crowns, both coming from third place Association finishes. As the decade of the forties turned the corner, the team won another Junior World Series championship. In all, between 1934 and 1950, Columbus finished in the playoffs nine times. Of those nine, seven times the team reached the Junior World Series. Of these, the Red Birds won six, making them the undisputed ruler of the American Association's post-season kingdom.

COLUMBUS 1st 95-58 .621 Burt Shotton
Red Birds

BATTERS	POS-GAMES	GP	AB	R	H	BI	2B	3B	HR	BB	SO	SB	BA
Ray Sanders	1B151	152	587	**119**	181	120	**40**	9	14	76	63	6	.308
George Myatt	2B101	110	402	84	119	33	17	2	1	44	55	24	.296
Lou Klein	SS101	112	362	67	133	54	22	11	5	53	23	10	.367
Bert Haas	3B153	**156**	594	102	187	**131**	37	12	15	64	41	10	.315
Milo Marshall	OF133	138	493	79	149	101	19	11	17	41	68	6	.302
Harry Walker	OF120	121	445	79	124	58	25	1	4	54	23	13	.279
Morris Jones	OF78	87	279	53	75	43	17	4	4	29	41	1	.269
Thomas Heath	C97	99	263	35	67	43	12	1	3	57	28	1	.255
Robert Repass	SS63,2B38	117	391	68	124	56	18	6	0	45	32	11	.317
Hugh Poland	C83	85	242	20	59	25	7	1	2	15	21	0	.244
Carden Gillenwater	OF63	66	215	33	57	28	12	1	1	29	25	2	.265
Murry Dickson	P44	63	132	18	45	27	3	1	1	1	7	0	.341
James Bucher	2B28	52	116	23	30	11	8	0	3	13	10	2	.259
Augie Bergamo	OF57	57	214	31	57	23	9	4	1	25	14	0	.266
Harry Brecheen	P35	45	79	11	17	5	2	1	1	7	18	0	.215
Frank Barrett	P42	42	42	5	9	5	0	0	0	5	11	0	.214
John Grodzicki	P32	34	74	10	16	6	6	0	0	7	17	0	.216
George Hader	P30	31	36	3	9	3	1	1	0	2	9	0	.250
Preacher Roe	P30	30	46	3	7	1	0	0	0	4	11	0	.152
Hooper Triplett	OF21	21	76	15	19	9	6	2	1	12	4	1	.250
Ed Wissman	P20	21	23	2	6	5	0	1	0	1	6	0	.261
Frank Gabler	P20	20	37	3	6	3	0	0	0	5	8	0	.162
Bill Brumbeloe	P13	13	12	1	3	4	0	0	1	0	4	0	.250
William Rabe	OF11	11	29	9	12	4	1	0	0	9	6	1	.414
Jack Creel	P11	11	6	0	0	1	0	0	0	0	0	0	.000
Sam Nahem	P5	5	8		1								.125
Averette Thompson	OF	4	5	1	1	3	0	0	0			0	.200
John Griffore	P4	4	4		2								.500
James Winford	P2	2	1		0								.000
Joe Neidson	C1	1	3	0	1	2	0	0	0			0	.333
Richard Tichacek	C1	1	3	0	1	0	1	0	0			0	.333
Vernon Horn	P1	1	1		0								.000
Al Thomas	P1	1	1		0								.000
Bill Ramsey	PH	1	1	0	0	0	0	0	0			0	.000
Carl Boyer	PH	1	1	0	0	0	0	0	0			0	.000

PITCHERS	W	L	PCT	G	GS	CG	SH	IP	H	BB	SO	ERA
Murry Dickson	**21**	11	.656	44	31	22	4	259	244	**124**	153	3.30
John Grodzicki	19	5	**.792**	32	24	17	4	199	169	83	136	**2.58**
Harry Brecheen	16	6	.727	35	25	11	2	188	175	66	112	3.64
Preacher Roe	11	9	.550	30	20	9	2	159	156	41	82	3.57
George Hader	8	5	.615	30	13	5	1	106	122	51	49	5.01
Francis Barrett	7	5	.583	42	13	8	2	145	161	76	73	4.47
Frank Gabler	6	6	.500	20	8	3	0	104	103	25	38	3.20
Ed Wissman	3	4	.429	20	11	1	0	63	77	34	29	5.43
Jack Creel	2	2	.500	11		0	0	20	22	10	6	3.15
John Griffore	1	0	1.000	4	1	1	0	14	12	15	6	5.79
Bill Brumbeloe	1	3	.250	13	4	2	0	35	46	25	17	6.43
Sam Nahem	0	2	.000	5		0	0	22	45	7	6	9.41
James Winford	0	0	----	2		0	0	3	2	5	1	
Al Thomas	0	0	----	1		0	0	4	4	2	1	
Vernon Horn	0	0	----	1		0	0	2	7	1	0	

LOUISVILLE 2nd 87-66 .569 -8 Bill Burwell
Colonels

BATTERS	POS-GAMES	GP	AB	R	H	BI	2B	3B	HR	BB	SO	SB	BA
Tony Lupien	1B154	154	564	74	163	59	22	8	6	45	29	16	.289
Alphonse Mazer	2B151	151	499	69	136	59	20	7	1	91	68	13	.273
Johnny Pesky	SS146	146	600	93	195	48	25	5	1	45	37	16	.325
Ernest Andres	3B153	154	577	85	167	100	33	2	15	46	41	3	.289
Walter Cazen	OF147	149	536	92	159	82	28	12	10	75	65	17	.297
Chet Morgan	OF140	142	528	64	148	78	17	9	3	40	11	4	.280
Art Parks	OF121	128	443	77	120	58	23	4	8	76	31	7	.271
Joe Glenn	C93	96	296	35	72	43	15	5	2	34	29	8	.243
George Lacy	C70	74	213	17	51	22	9	0	6	17	22	0	.239
Thomas Gwin	OF20	49	67	15	15	2	2	1	0	6	5	5	.224
Oscar Judd	P24	45	71	8	15	9	2	0	0	9	12	0	.211
Joe Vosmik	OF37	42	144	15	42	20	9	2	1	15	14	1	.292
Charles Gelbert	SS10,P1	40	74	8	20	10	3	1	0	14	8	1	.270

LOUISVILLE (cont.)
Colonels

BATTERS	POS-GAMES	GP	AB	R	H	BI	2B	3B	HR	BB	SO	SB	BA
Bill Butland	P35	35	65	2	11	2	1	0	0	11	22	0	.169
Wilfrid Lefebvre	P33	34	57	7	11	1	0	0	0	6	5	0	.193
Bill Sayles	P30	32	67	5	19	8	3	1	0	2	11	0	.284
Owen Scheetz	P29	29	36	1	7	3	1	0	0	1	7	0	.194
Fred Shaffer	P24	25	14	2	3	1	0	0	0	1	3	0	.214
Les Fleming	P20	20	31	1	6	3	0	0	0	1	4	0	.194
Emerson Dickman	P15	15	38	1	6	0	1	0	0	0	4	0	.158
Cecil Hughson	P13	13	29	1	2	3	0	0	0	7	13	0	.069
Herb Hash	P9	9	20		5								.250
Woody Rich	P9	9	8		2								.250
Henry Fiarito	2B,3B,SS,OF	8	9	1	3	1	1	0	1			0	.333
Lawrence Powell	P7	7	9		1								.111
Francis Walsh	C	6	11	1	3	1	0	0	0			0	.273
Charles Harris	P6	6	5		1								.200
Aloysius Hodkey	P6	6	2		0								.000
Andy Gilbert	OF	5	16	3	3	1	0	0	0			1	.188
John Lazor	PH	3	3	0	0	0	0	0	0			0	.000

PITCHERS	W	L	PCT	G	GS	CG	SH	IP	H	BB	SO	ERA
Oscar Judd	13	5	.722	24	18	11	2	148	143	57	72	3.16
Bill Sayles	13	12	.520	30	23	11	3	169	188	61	107	4.37
Wilfrid Lefebvre	12	7	.632	33	21	11	1	169	192	52	51	3.51
Wilburn Butland	12	11	.522	35	26	13	1	201	187	83	126	3.76
Owen Scheetz	8	7	.533	29	9	5	2	115	94	39	40	3.05
Cecil Hughson	7	1	.875	13	11	7	3	91	86	23	40	2.97
Emerson Dickman	7	5	.583	15	13	8	1	102	90	32	31	1.94
Les Fleming	6	6	.500	20	13	4	1	89	85	40	62	4.15
Herb Hash	3	4	.429	9	9	4	1	59	68	15	23	4.73
Woody Rich	2	2	.500	9		0	0	27	35	15	28	3.33
Lawrence Powell	2	2	.500	7	4	2	0	28	25	26	16	7.85
Charles Harris	1	1	.500	6	2	1	0	24	27	16	9	6.38
Fred Shaffer	1	2	.333	24	1	1	0	54	57	20	13	3.83
Aloysius Hodkey	0	1	.000	6		0	0	16	15	6	10	4.50
Charles Gelbert	0	0	----	1		0	0	3	7	0	1	

KANSAS CITY   3rd   85-69   .552   -10.5   Bill Meyer
Blues

BATTERS	POS-GAMES	GP	AB	R	H	BI	2B	3B	HR	BB	SO	SB	BA
Mike Chartak	1B84,OF64	150	533	87	156	82	28	13	16	100	106	24	.293
Al Glossop	2B141	144	551	97	166	96	28	10	16	50	64	14	.301
Billy Hitchcock	SS149	150	554	77	164	59	28	8	3	43	43	21	.296
Russ Bergmann	3B62,2B10	77	290	45	86	35	9	3	1	37	12	10	.297
Colonel Mills	OF137	141	495	85	152	63	34	7	6	54	34	7	.307
Art Metheny	OF128	136	466	50	112	59	18	2	3	42	68	6	.240
Lloyd Christopher	OF69	72	241	36	54	39	9	1	7	31	47	4	.224
Aaron Robinson	C96	105	319	46	86	52	13	3	7	32	27	3	.270
Russ Derry	OF61	69	217	27	44	30	8	5	3	32	43	1	.203
Ed Kearse	C62	69	184	22	44	20	7	1	2	25	26	0	.239
Ed Whitner	1B64	64	233	32	72	30	10	3	4	8	21	11	.309
Jack Saltzgaver		59	98	8	25	13	3	1	0	21	7	1	.255
Louis Blair	3B54	57	189	17	43	16	4	1	1	10	16	6	.228
Edwin Carnett	P26	49	48	15	16	11	4	0	0	2	10	0	.333
Charles Wensloff	P36	36	62	7	11	7	1	0	0	9	19	0	.177
Don Hendrickson	P36	36	50	6	9	1	1	0	0	7	9	0	.180
Milo Candini	P35	35	44	5	9	5	1	0	0	2	11	0	.205
Al Gerheauser	P32	33	49	5	6	0	2	0	0	0	21	0	.122
George Barley	P30	33	46	7	10	4	2	0	0	8	15	1	.217
Tom Reis	P30	30	50	7	8	8	1	2	0	5	17	0	.160
Rinaldo Ardizoia	P27	27	50	9	9	8	2	0	0	9	14	0	.180
James Nicholson	3B14	15	46	6	13	1	3	1	0	3	6	0	.283
Lou Bartola	C12	13	31	7	10	5	1	0	0	6	4	0	.323
Randall Gumpert	P3	4	2		0								.000
John Haley	P4	4	0		0								----
Thomas Ananicz	P3	3	0		0								----
Walter Stewart	P2	2	2		0								.000
Mel Queen	P1	1	3		1								.333
William Gill	P1	1	1		0								.000

KANSAS CITY (cont.)
Blues

PITCHERS	W	L	PCT	G	GS	CG	SH	IP	H	BB	SO	ERA
Charles Wensloff	15	8	.652	36	22	11	0	197	224	62	77	3.93
Don Hendrickson	13	10	.565	30	19	8	1	167	200	51	59	4.15
Rinaldo Ardizoia	12	9	.571	27	24	12	2	169	154	84	67	3.46
George Barley	11	13	.458	30	24	13	4	167	174	68	77	3.50
Tom Reis	9	6	.600	30	21	9	2	161	164	75	64	3.91
Milo Candini	9	7	.563	35	15	6	3	141	112	64	84	3.26
Al Gerheauser	8	11	.421	32	21	9	2	153	153	61	74	3.76
Edwin Carnett	4	2	.667	26		0	0	77	88	32	26	4.91
Mel Queen	1	0	1.000	1	1	1	1	7	1	3	9	0.00
Walter Stewart	0	1	.000	2		0	0	7	6	7	2	6.43
William Gill	0	1	.000	1		0	0	3	3	7	0	15.00
John Haley	0	0	----	4		0	0	5	12	7	1	
Randall Gumpert	0	0	----	3		0	0	7	10	3	1	6.43
Thomas Ananicz	0	0	----	3		0	0	3	2	2	0	

MINNEAPOLIS	4th	83-70	.542	-12	Tom Sheehan

Millers

BATTERS	POS-GAMES	GP	AB	R	H	BI	2B	3B	HR	BB	SO	SB	BA
Frank Houska	1B59	68	194	18	55	19	8	2	1	22	24	2	.284
Frank Trechock	2B126,SS20	145	449	47	103	45	20	1	7	44	41	2	.229
Eugene Geary	SS139	142	528	85	148	56	33	3	12	47	48	15	.280
Bill Barnacle	3B71,OF17	92	331	63	100	32	30	4	4	31	26	4	.302
Babe Barna	OF137	142	521	102	175	105	22	3	24	66	74	29	.336
Al Wright	OF126	138	461	90	131	103	29	5	26	64	86	5	.284
Fabian Gaffke	OF126	133	499	100	152	97	39	7	21	43	60	11	.305
Otto Denning	C86,1B56	144	510	85	168	105	34	4	17	64	40	4	.329
Harvey Walker	OF91	111	319	70	81	42	18	2	10	58	52	12	.254
Robert Fausett	3B63,P14	93	294	37	67	22	12	1	1	15	18	15	.228
Frank Danneker	2B54,3B24	88	232	39	64	45	10	3	11	26	38	4	.276
Robert Kline	P52	52	18	0	2	0	0	0	0	0	5	0	.111
Zeke Bonura	1B46	46	172	47	63	38	9	1	7	28	4	2	.366
Harry Kelley	P44	44	88	1	18	4	1	0	0	5	4	0	.205
Mike Kash	P43	43	49	2	3	3	1	0	0	7	18	0	.061
Walt Tauscher	P41	41	59	7	17	4	2	0	0	3	6	0	.288
Elon Hogsett	P38	39	88	8	12	3	1	0	0	3	24	0	.136
Milt Haefner	P35	38	83	7	22	6	4	0	1	10	14	1	.265
Angelo Giulani	C37	37	143	15	42	21	6	0	1	11	1	0	.294
George Rensa	C34	35	92	6	12	5	1	0	0	12	9	1	.130
Joe Hatten	P26	26	34	4	4	9	2	1	0	1	17	0	.118
Frank Nessoth	P13	13	16	1	1	2	0	0	0	0	13	0	.063
Russ Rolandson	C	6	9	1	3	0	0	0	0	0		0	.333
Harry Smythe	P2	2	4		2								.500
Wes Westrum	PH	1	1	0	0	0	0	0	0	0		0	.000
Phil Coggswell	C1	1	0	0	0	0	0	0	0	0		0	----

PITCHERS	W	L	PCT	G	GS	CG	SH	IP	H	BB	SO	ERA
Elon Hogsett	18	9	.667	38	30	15	3	233	264	76	105	4.17
Harry Kelley	16	13	.552	44	33	15	3	248	288	88	113	4.10
Walt Tauscher	13	6	.684	41	14	5	1	155	192	53	36	4.82
Milt Haefner	12	16	.429	35	33	20	2	241	251	92	136	3.96
Mike Kash	10	7	.588	43	15	7	2	164	157	69	69	4.28
Joe Hatten	5	6	.455	26	16	2	0	97	105	53	58	4.64
Robert Kline	3	3	.500	52		0	0	85	98	30	19	2.96
Robert Fausett	3	4	.429	14	7	6	0	61	64	34	20	5.75
Frank Nessoth	3	5	.375	13	6	1	0	40	52	27	7	5.85
Harry Smythe	0	1	.000	2		0	0	4	7	2	0	9.00

TOLEDO	5th	82-72	.532	-13.5	Taylor - Haney

Mud Hens

BATTERS	POS-GAMES	GP	AB	R	H	BI	2B	3B	HR	BB	SO	SB	BA
Charles Stevens	1B144	145	558	74	162	72	19	6	6	29	41	4	.290
Mark Christman	2B53,3B53	141	470	65	132	52	27	5	2	53	27	8	.281
Vern Stephens	SS152	153	616	95	173	74	33	11	14	43	72	10	.281
Sigmund Gryska	3B	(see multi-team players)											
Glenn McQuillen	OF152	155	583	88	192	93	25	11	11	51	28	14	.329
Milt Byrnes	OF126	132	447	89	126	50	22	5	9	89	40	17	.282

TOLEDO (cont.)
Mud Hens

BATTERS	POS-GAMES	GP	AB	R	H	BI	2B	3B	HR	BB	SO	SB	BA
Henry Steinbacher	OF83	88	301	28	81	52	18	3	2	37	16	8	.269
Harold Spindel	C106	111	393	43	108	53	13	3	4	29	37	2	.275
Jack Bradsher	OF65	83	196	33	44	25	11	2	2	20	28	3	.224
John Marcum	P30	77	134	18	48	19	7	1	0	17	11	0	.358
Sam Harshany	C55	71	181	34	45	19	4	0	0	42	13	0	.249
Ralph Winegarner	P30	47	68	8	15	10	4	0	0	7	10	0	.221
Ben SoRelle	P38	43	60	6	6	4	0	0	0	3	14	0	.100
Lester Wirkkala	P37	38	54	5	9	4	0	0	0	6	13	0	.167
Harry Kimberlin	P37	37	58	1	5	2	0	0	0	2	15	0	.086
Bobby Estalella	OF31	31	114	16	33	23	6	0	4	19	12	2	.289
Tony Criscola	OF26	31	76	11	17	7	0	3	0	11	13	0	.224
Emil Bildilli	P20	26	33	7	12	7	0	0	0	0	1	0	.364
Herb Nordquist	P26	26	20	0	3	0	0	0	0	0	4	0	.150
LeRoy Parmelee	P23	24	35	1	3	2	0	0	0	0	10	1	.086
Frank Biscan	P23	23	44	0	5	4	0	0	0	0	15	0	.114
John Whitehead	P18	18	24	0	3	0	0	0	0	3	3	0	.125
Bob Dillinger	2B	7	23	3	4	3	0	1	0			1	.174
Harry Bailey	P3	3	2		0								.000

PITCHERS		W	L	PCT	G	GS	CG	SH	IP	H	BB	SO	ERA
John Marcum		17	7	.708	30	25	19	2	215	214	40	61	2.97
Ben SoRelle		12	7	.632	38	20	10	0	176	195	61	93	3.73
Lester Wirkkala		12	10	.545	37	20	10	0	164	165	71	41	4.06
Frank Biscan		9	7	.563	23	18	11	2	133	127	43	55	3.38
Harry Kimberlin		9	10	.474	37	24	9	2	183	185	61	107	3.59
Ralph Winegarner		6	3	.667	30	2	1	1	90	90	28	34	2.50
Herb Nordquist		5	3	.625	26	9	3	0	76	73	53	38	4.74
LeRoy Parmelee		5	7	.417	23	12	4	1	103	96	51	58	3.50
Emil Bildilli		5	9	.357	20	13	5	1	86	101	54	26	5.44
John Whitehead		2	9	.182	18	13	5	1	82	95	20	11	5.27
Harry Bailey		0	0	----	3		0	0	6	4	5	1	

INDIANAPOLIS   6th   65-88   .425   -30   Wade Killefer
Indians

BATTERS	POS-GAMES	GP	AB	R	H	BI	2B	3B	HR	BB	SO	SB	BA
Ed Shokes	1B78	81	283	27	67	28	13	2	2	18	31	2	.237
Ben Zientara	2B151	151	588	77	160	64	34	10	2	41	30	8	.272
Wayne Ambler	SS139	139	515	59	126	43	10	3	2	63	31	3	.245
Joe Bestudik	3B96,SS13	117	388	55	117	49	10	10	3	53	32	5	.302
Allen Hunt	OF133	133	457	75	134	61	15	7	4	63	41	12	.293
Kermit Lewis	OF111	120	425	57	119	59	15	7	4	28	50	15	.280
Wayne Blackburn	OF106	113	428	79	134	32	21	4	2	71	38	16	.313
John Pasek	C92	97	288	20	78	31	8	1	0	26	10	0	.271
Milt Galatzer	1B38,OF37	98	262	33	63	36	7	4	0	42	13	1	.240
Al Lakeman	C58	70	199	16	57	24	12	3	1	16	33	1	.286
Wilbur Brubaker	3B38	54	166	14	40	26	6	1	0	26	25	0	.241
Stan Mazgay	OF52	53	197	22	56	20	4	2	1	12	19	2	.284
Ray Starr	P42	42	97	2	8	4	0	0	0	4	42	0	.082
Joe Mack	1B32	35	113	9	22	12	5	0	0	11	11	3	.195
Ben Wade	P32	32	44	2	7	3	1	0	0	0	10	0	.159
Robert Logan	P26	31	55	5	11	3	0	0	0	1	5	0	.200
William Cox	P29	30	61	2	16	3	0	0	0	2	10	0	.262
George Gill	P30	30	60	5	14	8	2	0	1	7	15	0	.233
Glenn Fletcher	P27	29	41	4	6	4	0	2	0	3	8	0	.146
LeGrant Scott	OF17	22	72	5	19	9	3	0	0	2	4	0	.264
Charles Aleno	3B19	19	69	11	24	9	4	1	1	7	3	3	.348
Charles Moncrief	P19	19	14	2	2	0	0	0	0	1	2	0	.143
Carmel Castle	OF	14	26	3	5	2	0	1	0	1	5	0	.192
Italo Chelini	P14	14	21	0	1	1	0	0	0	2	5	0	.048
Joe Becker	C	10	28	1	7	2	1	0	0	5	4	0	.250
Art Graham	OF	9	18	0	5	0	0	0	0			0	.278
Peter Sivess	P6	7	3		0								.000
Jacob Wade	P7	7	2		1								.500
Orville Bolton	C	6	22	0	3	0	0	0	0			0	.136
Mike Naymick	P4	4	3		1								.333
Gil Brack	OF	3	11	1	3	3	0	0	0			0	.273
Jack Bastian	P2	2	5		0								.000
Ray Phebus	P2	2	2		1								.500

INDIANAPOLIS (cont.)
Indians

PITCHERS	W	L	PCT	G	GS	CG	SH	IP	H	BB	SO	ERA
Ray Starr	20	15	.571	42	35	22	6	273	245	112	145	3.43
George Gill	11	9	.550	30	20	12	2	163	194	63	44	3.75
Robert Logan	8	14	.364	26	25	14	1	166	192	48	61	4.72
William Cox	8	16	.333	29	24	14	4	185	185	73	68	3.75
Ben Wade	4	5	.444	32	9	5	0	127	104	84	40	2.83
Charles Moncrief	3	0	1.000	19		0	0	45	45	21	2	4.00
Glenn Fletcher	3	12	.200	27	15	6	1	114	116	65	41	4.66
Italo Chelini	2	8	.200	14	9	3	1	66	84	27	18	6.14
Jacob Wade	0	1	.000	7		0	0	9	19	6	3	9.00
Jack Bastien	0	1	.000	2	2	1	0	13	17	13	6	6.23
Peter Sivess	0	2	.000	6		0	0	16	24	7	5	8.44
Mike Naymick	0	0	----	4		0	0	9	11	11	7	
Ray Phebus	0	0	----	2		0	0	5	9	2	1	

ST. PAUL   7th   61-92   .399   -34   Red Kress
Saints

BATTERS	POS-GAMES	GP	AB	R	H	BI	2B	3B	HR	BB	SO	SB	BA
Red Kress	1B68,SS33,P2	118	382	36	112	57	11	2	10	34	36	6	.293
Aloysius Bejma	2B110	123	417	49	125	53	8	1	3	44	21	5	.300
Leo Wells	SS122,2B30	152	602	81	167	26	16	7	5	52	64	22	.277
Gil English	3B107,OF46,P1	152	551	84	174	93	32	5	13	70	37	9	.316
Fern Bell	OF151	151	567	96	161	80	31	1	18	59	51	10	.284
George Stumpf	OF135	144	472	43	120	51	18	6	1	59	33	6	.254
Frank Kalin	OF86	94	329	33	97	36	17	2	5	16	33	6	.295
Edward Fernandes	C82	102	257	33	69	48	16	1	4	89	41	2	.268
Avitus Himsl	P33	51	82	11	22	7	1	0	0	9	8	0	.268
Norm Schlueter	C46	47	157	10	38	10	5	2	0	11	30	2	.242
Art Herring	P31	36	61	5	9	3	1	0	1	6	9	0	.148
Ken Raffensberger	P32	32	51	3	3	2	0	0	0	2	24	0	.059
Clay Smith	P30	31	48	1	8	2	0	0	0	4	17	0	.167
Dwain Sloat	P30	31	29	1	5	0	0	0	0	3	11	0	.172
Richard Lanahan	P28	28	46	3	9	3	0	0	0	2	15	0	.196
Herman Bauer	C24	27	78	5	21	9	1	0	1	2	3	0	.269
William Swift	P16	16	45	3	7	3	0	0	0	3	6	0	.156
Oral Hildebrand	P16	16	25	1	4	3	0	0	0	2	4	0	.160
Mearl Strahan	P15	15	8	4	1	2	1	0	0	1	0	0	.125
Armond Payton	C	11	27	1	5	1	3	0	0	1	3	0	.185
Bill Clemensen	P11	11	9	1	1	1	0	0	0	1	4	0	.111
Dick Coffman	P11	11	5	1	2	0	0	0	0	0	0	0	.400
Frank Knox	2B	10	22	2	4	0	0	0	0	3	1	0	.182
Clarence Struss	P7	7	1		0								.000

PITCHERS	W	L	PCT	G	GS	CG	SH	IP	H	BB	SO	ERA
Avitus Himsl	12	15	.444	33	24	16	1	229	260	47	66	4.28
Art Herring	11	17	.393	31	26	13	1	190	200	82	76	4.59
Ken Raffensberger	10	9	.526	32	20	10	3	156	183	49	89	4.85
Clay Smith	8	10	.444	30	20	8	0	148	180	59	75	5.41
William Swift	7	8	.467	16	16	11	3	124	104	34	72	3.19
Oral Hildebrand	5	3	.625	16	12	4	1	78	98	28	38	4.27
Richard Lanahan	5	14	.263	28	18	8	2	134	156	66	49	6.37
Mearl Strahan	2	4	.333	15	5	1	0	35	52	27	12	7.46
Dwain Sloat	1	6	.143	30	5	3	0	105	126	93	50	7.03
Red Kress	0	1	.000	2		0	0	7	7	5	3	2.57
Bill Clemensen	0	2	.000	11	3	1	0	32	52	15	7	5.07
Dick Coffman	0	2	.000	11		0	0	23	32	4	2	5.48
Clarence Struss	0	0	----	7		0	0	11	11	8	4	
Gil English	0	0	----	1		0	0	2	7	1	0	

MILWAUKEE   8th   55-98   .359   -40   Wm. Killefer - Grimm
Brewers

BATTERS	POS-GAMES	GP	AB	R	H	BI	2B	3B	HR	BB	SO	SB	BA
Ted Gullic	1B91,OF46	139	523	80	148	89	31	4	22	42	54	5	.283
Barney Walls	2B85	85	322	28	80	29	10	2	0	20	34	3	.248
William Myers	SS51,2B21	72	260	43	62	32	5	1	5	35	63	0	.238
Stanley Galle	3B82,SS66	148	586	82	169	68	29	3	6	39	35	4	.288
Harold Peck	OF140	144	561	79	150	64	23	6	8	43	44	8	.267

MILWAUKEE (cont.)
Brewers

BATTERS	POS-GAMES	GP	AB	R	H	BI	2B	3B	HR	BB	SO	SB	BA
Lou Novikoff	OF90	90	365	53	135	66	23	6	8	25	24	0	.370
Arnold Moser	OF61	71	226	26	67	24	2	0	1	18	14	0	.296
Alfred Todd	C72	79	293	33	82	33	14	0	2	9	18	3	.280
Joe Abreu	2B47,3B40	100	345	53	98	46	12	2	11	43	46	0	.284
Aubrey Epps	OF49	54	171	25	41	25	7	2	5	35	32	0	.240
Stan Stencel	OF42	50	151	11	37	15	5	2	2	9	13	1	.245
Joe Just	C32	49	118	18	26	19	3	0	4	13	21	0	.220
John Schmitz	P33	46	72	12	19	9	1	1	0	1	15	0	.264
Lyn Lary	SS39	42	143	12	35	15	3	0	0	12	17	1	.245
Ray Hayworth	C34	40	116	15	29	8	3	0	0	11	15	1	.250
George Koslo	P35	40	76	8	12	8	0	2	2	6	23	0	.158
Frank Makosky	P37	38	34	1	1	0	0	0	0	0	6	0	.029
Bob Garbark	C25	31	77	6	21	10	3	0	1	9	6	0	.273
George Blaeholder	P31	31	37	4	3	1	0	0	0	5	16	0	.081
Heber Stroud	3B22	30	91	10	20	7	5	0	0	10	13	0	.220
Bernard Olsen	OF17	28	59	7	17	13	3	0	2	3	11	0	.288
Gus Suhr	1B25	27	77	11	18	9	3	0	2	16	5	1	.234
Andrew Dobernic	P24	26	26	4	7	0	0	0	0	3	9	0	.269
Leon Balser	P24	25	21	0	2	0	0	0	0	1	7	0	.095
Charles Workman	OF14	17	49	5	6	4	0	0	1	4	6	0	.122
Robert Latshaw	1B16	16	61	8	14	9	0	0	3	8	14	0	.230
Charles English	3B	14	36	4	11	1	0	0	0	1	1	0	.306
Hugh Gustafson	1B10	14	34	1	4	1	0	0	0	5	6	0	.118
Al Moran	P13	14	20	2	6	0	1	0	0	1	7	0	.300
Eugene Lambert	P13	13	9	1	1	0	0	0	0	2	5	0	.111
Nick Strincevich	P12	12	22	3	4	2	0	1	0	3	7	0	.182
Vallie Eaves	P11	11	20	1	4	0	1	0	0	0	5	0	.200
George Coffman	P10	10	21	4	6	2	1	0	1	0	5	0	.286
Nathan Andrews	P10	10	17	0	5	2	0	0	0	1	5	0	.294
Joe Dickinson	P10	10	13	1	1	0	0	0	0	1	3	0	.077
Raymond Campbell	P9	9	16		6								.375
Robert Weiland	P7	7	2		1								.500
Vance Page	P6	6	12		5								.417
George Binks	1B	5	18	5	8	5	1	0	1			0	.444
Roxie Lawson	P5	5	8		1								.125
James Walkup	P5	5	4		1								.250
Edwin Weiland	P3	3	2		0								.000
John Tising	P2	2	4		2								.500
Charles Grimm	1B1	1	1	0	1	0	0	0	0			0	1.000
Charles Marrow	P1	1	0		0								----

PITCHERS	W	L	PCT	G	GS	CG	SH	IP	H	BB	SO	ERA
George Koslo	13	13	.500	35	29	15	2	203	211	83	96	4.43
George Blaeholder	9	7	.563	31	13	3	1	125	147	31	41	3.96
John Schmitz	7	14	.333	33	22	8	0	157	169	91	87	4.87
Nick Strincevich	4	2	.667	12	7	4	0	63	72	21	31	4.57
Vallie Eaves	4	6	.400	11	8	5	0	58	46	28	35	2.95
Andrew Dobernic	4	8	.333	24	13	3	0	89	94	80	51	5.56
Ray Campbell	3	0	1.000	9	5	3	0	48	46	23	18	3.19
Vance Page	2	0	1.000	6	4	2	0	31	38	11	9	4.06
Eugene Lambert	2	2	.500	13	4	1	0	43	48	21	18	4.40
Al Moran	2	6	.250	13	7	1	0	53	54	37	10	4.58
Nathan Andrews	2	7	.222	10	10	2	1	58	80	30	20	7.91
Roxie Lawson	1	2	.333	5	5	1	0	21	27	8	3	5.57
Joe Dickinson	1	4	.200	10		0	0	33	24	18	14	5.18
George Coffman	1	8	.111	10	8	4	0	55	81	21	17	5.07
James Walkup	0	1	.000	5		0	0	15	20	13	5	7.80
Edwin Weiland	0	1	.000	3		0	0	7	11	3	0	5.14
Orville Jorgens	0	1	.000	1		0	0	4	9	4	1	9.00
Robert Weiland	0	2	.000	7		0	0	14	23	8	6	7.07
Frank Makosky	0	6	.000	37		0	0	109	136	39	41	4.38
Leon Balser	0	8	.000	24	7	3	0	85	98	48	31	5.19
John Tising	0	0	----	2		0	0	5	7	5	1	
Charles Marrow	0	0	----	1		0	0	1	2	1	0	

MULTI-TEAM PLAYERS

BATTERS	POS-GAMES	TEAMS	GP	AB	R	H	BI	2B	3B	HR	BB	SO	SB	BA
Sigmund Gryska	2B61,3B52,1B23	TOL-SP	136	450	58	98	49	19	1	14	45	78	9	.218
Jesse Newman	1B67,3B32	SP-TOL	111	354	62	100	30	13	7	3	55	50	4	.282

MULTI-TEAM PLAYERS (cont.)

BATTERS	POS-GAMES	TEAMS	GP	AB	R	H	BI	2B	3B	HR	BB	SO	SB	BA
Frank Silvanic	OF61,1B16	SP-KC	98	289	43	65	44	11	1	10	33	49	4	.225
Lin Storti	3B64,2B20	MIN-TOL	86	299	40	78	48	17	2	5	36	31	0	.261
Louis Berger	3B24	KC-TOL	25	91	14	19	14	2	0	2	6	10	2	.209
Lloyd Johnson	P22	SP-IND	22	35	1	3	1	0	0	0	0	18	1	.086
Paul Sullivan	P11	MIL-KC	11	16	1	6	4	1	0	0	1	3	0	.375

PITCHERS	TEAMS	W	L	PCT	G	GS	CG	SH	IP	H	BB	SO	ERA
Lloyd Johnson	SP-IND	5	6	.455	22	10	6	1	106	108	28	38	3.99
Paul Sullivan	MIL-KC	3	0	1.000	11	4	1	0	43	36	30	21	4.19

TEAM BATTING

TEAMS	GP	AB	R	H	BI	2B	3B	HR	BB	SO	SB	BA
COLUMBUS	156	5222	876	1517	803	262	69	74	602	551	87	.291
LOUISVILLE	154	5035	682	1386	614	215	57	54	548	459	92	.275
KANSAS CITY	155	4997	725	1339	665	220	61	71	550	667	113	.268
MINNEAPOLIS	155	5238	842	1453	777	285	37	143	569	651	107	.277
TOLEDO	156	5113	718	1384	649	216	55	63	547	512	76	.271
INDIANAPOLIS	154	4995	597	1310	536	172	58	23	512	508	71	.262
ST. PAUL	153	4960	610	1330	571	191	34	84	558	571	76	.268
MILWAUKEE	153	5124	665	1367	616	190	32	87	440	625	28	.267
	618	40684	5715	11086	5231	1751	403	599	4326	4544	650	.272

1942
Parity

Usually, the difference between a first place American Association team and a seventh is large. In some cases it is a whopping difference. In 1939, the Kansas City Blues finished 45 games ahead of seventh place Columbus. In 1920, the difference was even greater, as St. Paul finished 49 1/2 ahead of the seventh place Columbus Senators. But, if a seventh place team was particularly good (or the first place team bad) the advantage might be fewer than 15 games. In 1942, the race would be closer still.

Before the 1942 season started, the top teams were predicted to be Kansas City, Columbus, Milwaukee, and Minneapolis. Much to everyone's surprise, Toledo, Louisville, and Indianapolis joined the quartet as contenders as well, and this septet of teams remained in a tight cluster as the pennant race unfolded through the summer. The season entered its final month with these seven teams jostling one another for the pennant, separated by seven games or fewer. When the curtain fell, Kansas City, thanks to a 10 out of 14 game win spurt, ended up on top, with Milwaukee a close one and one-half games behind. Third place Columbus finished two and one-half behind the leader, while Toledo captured the last playoff spot only five games off the pace. Fifth place Louisville finished six and one-half back, while Indianapolis and Minneapolis finished tied, eight and one-half games behind. Only last place St. Paul was truly out of contention.

Batting honors went to Eddie Stanky of Milwaukee who hit .342. His teammate Willis Norman hit the most home runs (24), while Indianapolis Indian John McCarthy knocked in 113 runs. Pitcher Charles Wensloff of Kansas City won the most games (21), while Red Bird hurler Harry Brecheen had the lowest earned run average (2.09) and most strikeouts (156).

There was a simple corollary to the seven-team clump at the top of the American Association standings in 1942. The rules of mathematics state that for every Association win, there has to be an accompanying loss. For seven teams to finish high in the standings, none of them can win very many games. During the first fifty years of Association play, Kansas City's 84-win, .549 winning percentage season stands as the lowest ever to win the pennant.

KANSAS CITY
Blues

1st   84-69   .549   John Neun

BATTERS	POS-GAMES	GP	AB	R	H	BI	2B	3B	HR	BB	SO	SB	BA
Edward Levy	1B136	139	503	63	154	70	37	7	8	44	55	21	.306
Mike Milosevich	2B144,SS16	153	511	71	146	52	27	3	2	67	52	2	.286
George Scharein	SS121	123	451	43	114	29	21	2	0	32	28	7	.253
Don Lang	3B138	138	470	51	136	75	20	4	6	46	43	1	.289
Leo Nonnenkamp	OF152	153	546	86	124	35	22	7	1	87	53	17	.227
Larry Rosenthal	OF127	130	416	43	94	45	17	5	6	72	58	4	.226
Eric Tipton	OF90	91	318	50	97	44	17	9	5	40	25	12	.305
Ken Sears	C115	127	439	62	123	56	27	6	13	36	48	1	.280
Jack Saltzgaver	2B17,3B11,OF11	84	167	18	34	30	8	1	0	10	21	0	.204
Harry Craft	OF58	58	215	37	62	32	10	1	4	12	18	5	.288
Mike Garbark	C45	58	152	12	42	18	5	1	2	10	7	0	.276
Herb Karpel	P38	45	40	4	10	4	3	0	1	7	7	0	.250
Fred Collins	OF20,1B15	44	122	18	37	20	3	2	2	9	22	3	.303
Allen Gettel	P36	40	61	4	13	5	0	1	0	0	2	0	.213
Charles Wensloff	P33	33	80	4	12	4	1	0	0	10	18	0	.150
Rinaldo Ardizoia	P30	30	40	1	5	1	0	0	0	2	18	0	.125
John Johnson	P29	29	65	1	13	5	1	0	0	3	18	0	.200
Raymond Volpi	P29	29	65	1	13	5	1	0	0	3	18	0	.200
Boyd Perry	SS27	27	87	11	13	7	2	0	1	9	21	1	.149
Francis Shea	P27	27	32	2	3	0	1	0	0	2	9	0	.094
Tom Reis	P25	25	55	4	6	5	1	0	0	3	24	0	.109
Urban Pfeffer	OF14	16	37	1	6	1	0	1	0	1	5	1	.162
Emerson Roser	P11	11	9	1	2	0	0	0	0	0	1	0	.222
Steve Souchock	1B	8	28	4	6	5	1	0	2			0	.214
Fred Frankhouse	P8	8	2		1								.500
John Welaj	OF	5	6	1	1	1	1	0	0			0	.167
Don Hendrickson	P5	5	0		0								----
Frank Silvanic	OF	3	5	0	1	0	0	0	0	0		0	.200
Ed Kearse	C	1	3	0	0	0	0	0	0	0		0	.000
Mel Queen	P1	1	1		1								.000
Roman Pfeffer	P1	1	0		0								----
Paul Sullivan	P1	1	0		0								----

PITCHERS				W	L	PCT	G	GS	CG	SH	IP	H	BB	SO	ERA
Charles Wensloff				21	10	.677	33	31	25	4	244	209	64	104	2.47
Tom Reis				13	5	.722	25	24	9	2	159	134	83	41	2.83
Allen Gettel				12	11	.522	36	26	14	4	179	182	80	74	3.62
Herb Karpel				11	1	.917	38	4	4	0	116	93	51	50	2.48
John Johnson				8	11	.421	29	21	11	2	178	165	71	109	3.29
Raymond Volpi				7	6	.538	29	11	2	1	115	101	69	57	3.68
Rinaldo Ardizoa				6	12	.333	30	18	7	2	137	129	70	49	3.42
Francis Shea				5	8	.385	27	14	4	0	100	76	75	89	3.15
Emerson Roser				1	2	.333	11		0	0	34	39	17	18	2.38
Fred Frankhouse				0	1	.000	8		0	0	14	15	4	4	5.14
Don Hendrickson				0	2	.000	5		0	0	6	10	6	2	6.00
Roman Pfeffer				0	0	----	1		0	0	3	5	4	3	12.00
Mel Queen				0	0	----	1		0	0	2	1	3	3	13.50
Fred Collins				0	0	----	1		0	0	2	2	0	0	
Paul Sullivan				0	0	----	1		0	0	0	0	1	0	

MILWAUKEE
Brewers

2nd   81-69   .540   -1.5   Charles Grimm

BATTERS	POS-GAMES	GP	AB	R	H	BI	2B	3B	HR	BB	SO	SB	BA
Heinz Becker	1B136	143	500	76	170	94	30	12	6	71	41	8	.340
John Hudson	2B124,SS11	144	537	76	121	55	25	5	6	50	65	5	.225
Eddie Stanky	SS143	145	527	124	180	57	56	6	8	108	35	6	.342
Stan Rogers	3B		(see multi-team players)										
Harold Peck	OF141	141	568	90	189	94	24	10	10	40	45	9	.333
Willis Norman	OF122	129	418	80	126	85	22	3	24	88	53	2	.301
Ted Gullic	OF86,1B17,3B15	128	436	61	125	71	22	1	15	36	45	2	.287
Charles George	C83,OF12	109	359	31	100	36	16	6	3	19	52	2	.279
Harry Griswold	C76	86	262	27	74	35	1	2	4	16	23	0	.282
Frank Secory	OF70	78	257	31	64	47	14	2	9	24	63	1	.249
Grey Clarke	3B50	66	231	32	63	31	11	3	2	15	8	0	.273
Odell Hale	2B28	60	140	16	35	14	2	3	3	10	13	0	.250
Walt Lanfranconi	P42	48	85	14	19	5	2	1	1	2	25	0	.224
Hy Vandenberg	P42	46	90	7	21	7	2	0	0	2	10	0	.233
Emil Kush	P45	45	54	5	9	3	2	0	0	0	11	0	.167
Peter Naktenis	P36	36	39	9	11	7	2	1	0	2	9	0	.282

MILWAUKEE (cont.)
Brewers

BATTERS	POS-GAMES	GP	AB	R	H	BI	2B	3B	HR	BB	SO	SB	BA
George Blaeholder	P33	33	8	0	0	0	0	0	0	1	5	0	.000
Vance Page	P30	30	30	2	4	0	0	1	0	2	10	0	.133
Roxie Lawson	P27	27	45	2	6	3	1	0	0	2	10	0	.133
Ed Hanyzewski	P18	18	42	3	10	1	1	0	0	0	12	0	.238
Vallie Eaves	P12	12	21	1	2	2	0	0	0	2	6	0	.095
Ray Campbell	P7	12	2	0	0	0	0	0	0	0	2	0	.000
Gordon Goodell		11	24	3	7	3	0	0	0	2	0	0	.292
Harvey Storey		10	21	3	5	3	0	0	1	2	6	0	.238
Russ Mears	P10	10	14	3	4	2	0	0	0	1	2	0	.286
Harry Lowrey	OF	9	32	5	9	0	0	0	0			1	.281
John Christensen	P7	7	1	0									.000
Herschel Martin	OF	5	20	3	7	5	0	0	0			0	.350
John Berly	P5	5	3	0									.000
John Meketti	P2	2	2	0									.000
Murray Howell	OF1	1	2	1	0	0	0	0	0			0	.000

PITCHERS			W	L	PCT	G	GS	CG	SH	IP	H	BB	SO	ERA
Hy Vandenberg			17	10	.630	42	31	10	1	235	249	74	100	4.14
Walt Lanfranconi			15	13	.536	42	28	13	3	226	230	90	76	4.34
Emil Kush			9	12	.429	45	20	8	1	163	169	70	76	4.31
Peter Naktenis			8	8	.500	36	19	6	0	121	124	83	64	5.13
Ed Hanyzewski			7	2	.778	18	15	4	0	111	94	83	72	3.89
Vance Page			7	7	.500	30	8	1	0	95	123	26	41	4.83
Roxie Lawson			6	6	.500	27	17	6	0	125	142	56	32	5.54
Russ Mears			4	2	.667	10	6	2	0	41	36	39	23	4.17
Vallie Eaves			4	5	.444	12	9	1	0	61	69	34	26	5.46
Ray Campbell			2	0	1.000	12		0	0	15	24	8	4	8.40
George Blaeholder			2	3	.400	33	0	0	0	60	73	20	18	4.50
John Berly			0	1	.000	5		0	0	9	6	4	13	2.00
John Christensen			0	0	----	7		0	0	6	14	5	1	
John Meketti			0	0	----	2		0	0	7	8	8	1	

COLUMBUS   3rd   82-72   .532   -2.5   Ed Dyer
Red Birds

BATTERS	POS-GAMES	GP	AB	R	H	BI	2B	3B	HR	BB	SO	SB	BA
Dib Williams	1B72	85	263	26	72	43	10	1	2	24	20	2	.274
Floyd Young	2B99,SS42	143	541	64	125	49	16	4	3	34	90	2	.231
Lou Klein	SS119,3B16	138	465	68	116	63	24	0	14	43	48	18	.249
John Antonelli	3B103,2B29	131	468	57	121	48	20	1	0	53	34	3	.259
Jim Gleeson	OF134	134	451	74	119	55	16	6	8	91	56	15	.264
Ed Lukon	OF132	134	487	71	126	65	20	7	23	51	63	5	.259
Howie Moss	OF83	95	310	28	82	34	10	5	3	24	28	0	.265
Thomas Heath	C109	117	318	35	82	42	12	2	3	73	41	2	.258
George Myatt	2B40,OF38	116	322	60	90	35	11	10	0	54	39	32	.280
Augie Bergamo	OF63	90	244	32	74	30	12	2	1	32	25	3	.303
Rae Blaemire	C63	69	174	10	38	11	9	3	1	7	20	0	.218
Charles Aleno	1B33,3B30	66	197	22	43	22	2	2	0	21	27	0	.218
George Munger	P39	41	93	11	28	15	4	1	0	1	16	0	.301
Harry Brecheen	P33	40	95	10	21	9	5	2	0	4	15	1	.221
Frank Barrett	P39	39	25	3	7	1	1	0	0	3	8	0	.280
Frank Gabler	P36	36	39	1	9	1	1	0	0	2	6	0	.231
Ted Wilks	P32	34	49	4	4	1	1	0	0	1	15	0	.082
Preacher Roe	P33	33	51	4	9	3	0	0	0	3	12	0	.176
Bill Crouch	P32	32	59	6	17	7	1	0	0	5	10	0	.288
Harry Davis	1B29	29	102	9	23	8	5	0	1	15	14	0	.225
Ken Burkhart	P21	21	23	1	6	2	1	0	1	3	4	0	.261
Milo Marshall	OF16	17	60	16	21	6	4	3	0	12	6	1	.350
Jack Angle	1B17	17	60	3	11	7	0	0	0	3	5	0	.183
Hooper Triplett	OF13	15	41	5	8	7	3	0	0	6	2	1	.195
Cliff Hopkins	OF,P1	6	0	1	0	0	0	0	0			0	----
Floyd Beal	PH	4	4	0	1	2	0	0	0			0	.250
Ken Blackman	C	3	1	0	0	0	0	0	0			0	.000
Frank Kerr	PH	2	2	0	0	0	0	0	0			0	.000
Wilbur Buerckholtz	PH	1	1	0	0	0	0	0	0			0	.000
Gilbert Dobbs	P1	1	1	0									.000

PITCHERS			W	L	PCT	G	GS	CG	SH	IP	H	BB	SO	ERA
Harry Brecheen			19	10	.655	33	29	23	6	246	211	53	156	2.09
George Munger			16	13	.552	39	32	19	4	243	237	90	140	3.52

COLUMBUS (cont.)
Red Birds

PITCHERS	W	L	PCT	G	GS	CG	SH	IP	H	BB	SO	ERA
Ted Wilks	12	9	.571	32	20	12	3	164	136	40	78	2.41
Bill Crouch	11	12	.478	32	28	13	0	179	195	49	55	4.07
Frank Barrett	8	3	.727	39	6	2	0	106	84	46	57	2.72
Frank Gabler	7	9	.438	36	13	6	0	132	128	38	42	3.07
Preacher Roe	6	11	.353	33	17	7	2	158	146	61	92	3.02
Ken Burkhart	3	5	.375	21	9	3	1	80	90	35	39	3.60
Gilbert Dobbs	0	0	----	1		0	0	1	3	3	0	
Cliff Hopkins	0	0	----	1		0	0	1	1	1	0	

TOLEDO   4th   78-73   .517   -5   Fred Haney
Mud Hens

BATTERS	POS-GAMES	GP	AB	R	H	BI	2B	3B	HR	BB	SO	SB	BA
Charles Stevens	1B146	147	532	69	133	84	16	11	8	62	59	10	.250
Jim Bucher	2B62	62	245	32	83	32	13	2	0	16	10	2	.339
Mark Christman	SS145	147	533	75	147	43	28	4	6	34	25	8	.276
Bob Dillinger	3B64,2B53	132	491	81	150	45	21	7	4	20	30	23	.305
Milt Byrnes	OF146	147	503	88	128	75	30	9	10	110	59	8	.254
Roy Bell	OF117	127	444	42	121	67	28	2	6	43	33	0	.273
Ray Parrott	OF114	123	432	48	113	56	17	3	2	17	21	3	.262
Harold Spindel	C99	104	320	40	71	33	11	1	1	25	30	1	.222
Jack Bradsher	OF89	101	253	33	55	19	9	2	0	22	37	2	.217
Lin Storti	3B48,2B18	83	239	21	48	23	7	1	3	32	30	0	.201
Ardys Keller	C63	64	193	15	52	17	6	0	0	20	19	0	.269
John Marcum	P34	62	117	8	35	23	6	0	0	11	8	0	.299
Carl Schultz	2B35	56	107	18	22	4	4	1	0	17	20	1	.206
Stanley Galle	3B45	45	163	16	42	13	5	1	2	10	11	0	.258
Archie McKain	P40	41	70	10	18	8	1	0	1	7	19	0	.257
William Cox	P29	39	36	3	8	4	4	0	0	1	3	0	.222
Harry Kimberlin	P36	36	52	5	8	1	0	0	0	2	13	0	.154
Fred Sanford	P35	35	35	3	2	0	0	0	0	8	14	0	.057
LeRoy Parmelee	P26	27	28	7	9	8	4	1	2	1	7	0	.321
Ewald Pyle	P24	25	48	5	11	2	2	0	0	4	5	0	.229
Fred Ostermueller	P22	23	52	7	10	6	2	0	0	3	6	0	.192
Henry Steinbacher	OF10	16	40	6	10	4	1	0	0	6	1	0	.250
Loy Hanning	P7	7	13		1								.077
Arnold Funderburk	C	7	10	1	1	0	0	0	0			0	.100
Jack Hulsen	P3	3	1		0								.000

PITCHERS	W	L	PCT	G	GS	CG	SH	IP	H	BB	SO	ERA
Archie McKain	17	11	.607	40	30	16	3	215	218	65	75	3.81
John Marcum	14	16	.467	34	29	21	3	237	254	26	63	2.96
Fred Ostermueller	11	9	.550	22	18	12	1	145	139	45	77	3.23
Fred Sanford	9	9	.500	35	16	6	0	155	148	61	70	3.19
Ewald Pyle	8	6	.571	24	18	11	1	136	128	50	59	2.71
Harry Kimberlin	8	9	.471	36	23	10	4	181	200	58	83	3.18
William Cox	6	7	.462	29	7	1	0	97	108	61	38	5.20
LeRoy Parmelee	3	3	.500	26	5	2	1	80	77	41	41	4.28
Loy Hanning	2	3	.400	7	6	3	0	40	40	10	9	3.15
Jack Hulsen	0	0	----	3		0	0	3	6	5	2	

LOUISVILLE   5th   78-76   .506   -6.5   Bill Burwell
Colonels

BATTERS	POS-GAMES	GP	AB	R	H	BI	2B	3B	HR	BB	SO	SB	BA
Red Kress	1B69,2B24,P6	119	373	40	93	46	20	5	1	28	25	1	.249
Henry Fiarito	2B63	96	248	34	55	27	10	2	3	47	28	13	.222
Bill Wietelmann	SS133	133	527	69	137	35	21	3	0	55	42	7	.260
John Tobin	3B72,2B18	92	332	41	83	22	13	2	3	34	30	3	.250
Chet Morgan	OF155	155	564	67	156	61	22	3	1	59	20	12	.277
John Lazor	OF124	128	434	56	134	51	22	6	6	30	32	4	.309
Andy Gilbert	OF102,1B36,2B18	153	577	90	171	87	30	19	4	38	77	8	.296
George Lacy	C91	102	314	29	79	40	13	3	2	33	14	2	.252
Fred Walters	C74	86	241	22	60	43	6	5	2	25	27	6	.249
Al Lingua	OF56	83	166	30	34	15	7	1	0	14	25	9	.205
Nelson Potter	P38	58	93	7	28	14	6	0	2	6	9	0	.301

LOUISVILLE (cont.)
Colonels

BATTERS	POS-GAMES	GP	AB	R	H	BI	2B	3B	HR	BB	SO	SB	BA
Walter Cazen	OF49	52	167	16	35	14	3	3	1	23	27	3	.210
Stan Sperry	3B32	39	105	14	29	13	2	1	1	10	9	1	.276
Anton Karl	P39	39	46	5	12	4	2	0	1	1	8	0	.261
Stan Benjamin	3B38	38	145	19	44	13	3	3	3	12	20	8	.303
Bob Lotshaw	1B36	38	116	12	31	11	4	0	0	18	12	2	.267
Peter Blumette	P36	36	32	1	7	6	1	0	0	2	12	0	.219
Emery Rudd	P35	35	50	3	12	5	2	0	0	0	5	0	.240
Mel Deutsch	P34	34	33	0	5	3	0	0	0	0	7	0	.152
Lou Lucier	P33	33	64	5	11	5	2	1	0	3	4	0	.172
Bill Sayles	P29	32	68	4	14	8	3	0	1	2	8	0	.206
Joe Wood	P27	27	43	0	3	3	2	0	0	4	12	0	.070
William Johnson	3B11	24	66	5	13	4	3	0	0	5	9	0	.197
Eddie Pellagrini	SS18	19	68	8	14	1	4	0	0	8	9	0	.206
Emmett O'Neill	P11	18	14	0	1	1	1	0	0	2	1	0	.286
Richard Kalal	3B17	17	65	4	11	1	3	0	0	4	9	1	.169
George Byam		12	40	5	9	5	0	0	0	3	6	0	.225
James Browne		11	28	1	6	3	0	0	0	1	4	0	.214
Mars Lewis		10	24	1	3	1	0	0	0	0	6	1	.125
Cecil Dunn		10	23	4	6	3	1	1	0	2	5	0	.261
Art Parks		10	20	2	4	4	0	0	1	2	2	0	.200
Chet Covington	P10	10	12	2	4	2	0	0	0	0	0	0	.333
Lloyd Richards	C	3	6	1	1	0	0	0	0			0	.167
Emerson Dickman	P2	2	4		1								.250
Fred Shaffer	P2	2	2		0								.000

PITCHERS	W	L	PCT	G	GS	CG	SH	IP	H	BB	SO	ERA
Nelson Potter	18	8	.692	38	26	17	2	211	190	59	147	2.60
Lou Lucier	13	9	.591	33	25	11	1	206	160	76	94	2.45
Bill Sayles	11	12	.478	29	26	12	2	183	176	79	90	3.44
Peter Blumette	8	4	.667	36	10	3	1	103	97	58	51	3.84
Emery Rudd	7	11	.389	35	12	3	0	132	117	90	78	3.48
Anton Karl	6	13	.316	39	16	5	2	152	145	33	38	2.90
Emmett O'Neill	4	3	.571	11	7	2	1	47	39	42	34	3.26
Joe Wood	4	10	.286	27	19	7	0	137	141	69	81	3.74
Mel Deutsch	3	2	.600	34	7	1	0	103	97	56	41	2.88
Chet Covington	3	2	.600	10	6	2	1	32	43	11	19	5.91
Emerson Dickman	1	1	.500	2		0	0	13	10	2	3	4.15
Fred Shaffer	0	1	.000	2		0	0	5	6	1	1	9.00
Red Kress	0	0	----	6		0	0	13	14	6	3	

INDIANAPOLIS   6th (T)   76-78   .494   -8.5   Gabby Hartnett
Indians

BATTERS	POS-GAMES	GP	AB	R	H	BI	2B	3B	HR	BB	SO	SB	BA
John McCarthy	1B154	154	597	103	176	113	34	13	17	54	39	2	.295
Clyde McDowell	2B139	139	542	62	127	49	9	6	0	35	31	9	.231
William Skelley	SS144	152	520	44	127	69	10	6	2	55	62	5	.244
Joe Bestudik	3B154	154	568	91	185	94	37	11	6	62	53	11	.326
Wayne Blackburn	OF145	152	569	91	171	38	22	7	4	102	56	14	.301
Joe Moore	OF124	128	434	71	122	43	16	6	3	59	28	3	.281
Gil English	OF		(see multi-team players)										
Gabby Hartnett	C58	72	186	17	41	24	12	2	4	20	19	1	.220
Bob Seeds	OF49	66	186	19	50	17	15	1	0	20	23	1	.269
Milt Galatzer	OF34	47	118	7	29	11	4	0	0	17	7	1	.246
Woody Rich	P40	40	69	4	13	3	5	0	0	6	16	0	.188
Robert Logan	P35	35	76	1	9	5	1	0	0	2	10	0	.118
George Gill	P32	32	70	5	12	3	2	0	0	1	10	0	.171
Earl Reid	P30	31	43	9	11	4	2	1	0	0	9	0	.256
Raymond Poat	P29	29	55	1	4	1	0	0	0	5	30	0	.073
Elon Hogsett	P27	27	61	5	13	1	3	1	0	0	14	0	.213
Walt Tauscher	P24	25	21	2	3	1	0	0	0	3	5	0	.143
Steve Rachunok	P21	21	33	3	5	3	0	0	1	3	14	0	.143
Frank Staucet		12	16	1	2	1	0	0	0	0	2	0	.125
James Steiner	C	9	31	5	5	3	1	0	1			0	.161
John Hutchings	P4	4	11		4								.364
Oral Hildebrand	P4	4	6		2								.333
Al Falzone	P4	4	2		0								.000
Glenn Fletcher	P4	4	0		0								----
Otto Huber	2B	2	3	0	0	0	0	0	0			0	.000

INDIANAPOLIS (cont.)
Indians

PITCHERS	W	L	PCT	G	GS	CG	SH	IP	H	BB	SO	ERA
Raymond Poat	15	8	.652	29	22	11	2	176	150	96	112	2.86
Robert Logan	12	10	.545	35	27	17	3	225	222	59	68	2.72
Elon Hogsett	11	10	.524	27	22	14	2	162	174	59	56	3.50
Earl Reid	10	7	.588	30	13	5	1	116	123	51	45	4.11
Woody Rich	10	10	.500	40	20	12	1	201	198	102	114	3.54
George Gill	8	15	.348	32	22	12	2	193	186	52	60	2.98
John Hutchings	4	0	1.000	4	4	4	2	32	26	12	16	0.84
Walt Tauscher	3	3	.500	24	0	0	0	65	84	23	22	5.12
Steve Rachunok	3	10	.231	21	16	7	2	114	124	55	36	4.26
Al Falzone	0	2	.000	4	3	1	0	9	11	18	2	14.00
Oral Hildebrand	0	3	.000	4		0	0	21	28	13	9	6.86
Glenn Fletcher	0	0	----	4		0	0	7	10	5	0	

MINNEAPOLIS   6th (T)   76-78   .494   -8.5   Tom Sheehan
Millers

BATTERS	POS-GAMES	GP	AB	R	H	BI	2B	3B	HR	BB	SO	SB	BA
Frank Danneker	1B66	96	300	32	73	44	11	3	8	21	47	1	.243
Frank Trechock	2B88	111	328	29	65	14	17	3	1	33	48	5	.198
Eugene Geary	SS89	89	337	46	99	39	15	3	5	34	28	7	.294
Bill Barnacle	3B141	148	529	91	145	67	34	4	12	77	65	11	.274
Harvey Walker	OF144	149	547	97	151	63	34	4	18	83	74	13	.276
Al Wright	OF143	143	516	91	150	110	28	6	23	69	94	4	.291
Joe Vosmik	OF139	147	513	64	156	78	34	2	8	50	38	2	.304
Angelo Giulani	C103,1B12	120	370	32	81	43	14	1	1	20	17	0	.219
Claude Linton	C69	81	229	22	70	43	8	0	12	36	17	0	.306
Alf Anderson	SS63	63	235	44	64	22	13	0	1	18	22	4	.272
Stu Martin	2B59	59	217	42	59	28	5	1	6	22	17	10	.272
Frank Stasey	OF34	52	120	18	37	17	7	4	1	13	14	0	.308
Milt Haefner	P48	49	83	10	13	8	1	0	0	12	22	0	.157
Wilfrid Lefebvre	P47	48	52	6	8	5	1	1	0	4	12	2	.154
Owen Scheetz	P45	45	88	8	15	3	1	0	0	6	17	0	.170
Don Schoenborn	P41	44	32	3	5	1	1	0	0	2	13	0	.156
Joe Lafata	1B40	42	134	13	30	13	4	0	2	11	25	0	.224
Van Lingle Mungo	P24	40	65	11	19	7	3	0	1	2	12	0	.292
Norm Jaeger	1B38	39	139	11	37	18	7	0	2	10	16	1	.266
Harry Kelley	P39	39	73	4	14	4	1	0	0	0	2	0	.192
Don Wheeler	OF16	24	46	3	9	7	4	0	0	6	10	0	.196
Herbert Bain	P17	17	20	1	0	0	0	0	0	2	17	0	.000
Rabbit Warstler	2B10	10	31	3	6	0	1	0	0	2	10	0	.194
Reuben Fischer	P9	9	17		1								.059
Herb Hash	P9	9	11		2								.182
Clint Hartung	P3	6	15		0								.000
Russ Evans	P3	3	7		2								.286
Wes Westrum	C	3	1	1	0	0	0	0	0			0	.000
Robert Kline	P3	3	0		0								----
Frank Nessoth	P2	2	1		0								.000
Howard Steffens	PH	1	1	0	1	0	0	0	0			0	1.000
Werner Strunk	P1	1	0		0								----

PITCHERS	W	L	PCT	G	GS	CG	SH	IP	H	BB	SO	ERA
Milt Haefner	18	17	.514	48	33	17	2	260	283	90	113	4.22
Owen Scheetz	15	16	.484	45	27	16	2	251	255	84	69	3.73
Harry Kelley	13	13	.500	39	29	16	1	198	237	56	64	4.50
Van Lingle Mungo	11	3	.786	24	20	3	1	124	118	61	72	4.57
Wilfrid Lefebvre	9	11	.450	47	15	6	1	162	186	63	64	4.11
Herbert Bain	4	2	.667	17	7	3	0	76	68	37	37	3.20
Reuben Fischer	3	5	.375	9	9	4	0	57	58	25	20	4.74
Don Schoenborn	2	7	.222	41	9	2	0	116	131	42	34	4.73
Herb Hash	1	3	.250	9		0	0	33	34	19	9	6.27
Russ Evans	0	1	.000	3	1	1	0	16	9	6	8	2.81
Clint Hartung	0	0	----	3		0	0	9	12	5	4	3.86
Robert Kline	0	0	----	3		0	0	4	9	4	1	
Frank Nessoth	0	0	----	2		0	0	4	6	3	1	
Werner Strunk	0	0	----	1		0	0	8	7	4	1	

ST. PAUL   8th   57-97   .370   -27.5   Virgil Hannah
Saints

BATTERS	POS-GAMES	GP	AB	R	H	BI	2B	3B	HR	BB	SO	SB	BA
Phil Weintraub	1B		(see multi-team players)										
Frank Drews	2B148	148	519	65	133	58	21	6	11	77	50	2	.256
Dick Culler	SS143	143	570	64	148	43	15	4	4	47	35	8	.260
James Grant	3B135	141	512	52	160	70	36	11	6	49	68	1	.313
Guy Cartwright	OF99	103	347	54	101	45	14	4	13	43	39	4	.291
Allen Hunt	OF		(see multi-team players)										
Alvin Powell	OF,P		(see multi-team players)										
Stan Andrews	C119	124	375	35	90	41	20	3	2	30	22	0	.240
William Schalow	1B25,OF15,3B12	68	192	17	34	15	3	1	1	20	49	1	.177
Joe Bowman	P28	63	73	4	17	7	0	1	1	5	7	1	.233
Dave Philley	OF41	56	173	28	41	13	12	2	0	15	20	6	.237
Avitus Himsl	P37	43	100	7	23	5	3	0	0	3	28	0	.230
Keith Bissonette	OF27	42	135	6	32	19	4	0	0	8	16	0	.237
Art Graham	OF38	40	128	13	21	5	4	0	1	25	18	1	.164
George Stumpf	OF35	38	124	11	22	6	4	2	0	18	15	1	.177
Art Herring	P29	35	77	5	14	5	3	0	0	2	9	0	.182
Clay Smith	P31	32	50	4	6	3	0	0	0	2	20	0	.120
William Swift	P30	30	79	3	16	6	3	0	0	6	14	0	.203
Richard Lanahan	P25	25	43	5	9	3	3	0	0	0	8	0	.209
Morris Martin	P25	25	24	3	5	0	0	0	0	1	12	0	.208
George Coffman	P23	23	47	3	5	4	0	1	0	2	10	0	.106
Howard Belknap	P13	15	15	0	3	2	0	0	0	6	2	0	.189
Howard Schultz	1B12	12	52	5	15	8	4	2	1	0	5	0	.288
Sigmund Gryska	2B,OF	12	37	4	7	4	0	0	0	6	2	0	.189
Harold Younghans		1	0	0	0	0	0	0	0			0	----

PITCHERS		W	L	PCT	G	GS	CG	SH	IP	H	BB	SO	ERA
Avitus Himsl		16	13	.552	37	28	24	1	253	283	39	74	3.56
Art Herring		13	11	.542	29	25	18	1	207	187	89	93	3.30
William Swift		12	15	.444	30	28	19	1	220	197	56	103	3.15
Clay Smith		5	11	.313	31	17	9	0	139	182	53	72	5.44
Rich Lanahan		4	14	.222	25	17	8	1	124	142	61	31	4.72
Joe Bowman		3	12	.200	28	13	4	1	96	120	44	42	6.28
George Coffman		3	12	.200	23	19	8	1	145	142	61	43	3.48
Morris Martin		1	4	.200	25	0	0	0	71	80	37	19	4.69
Howard Belknap		0	5	.000	13	4	1	0	45	56	42	11	7.00
Alvin Powell		0	0	----	1		0	0	5	3	1	1	

MULTI-TEAM PLAYERS

BATTERS	POS-GAMES	TEAMS	GP	AB	R	H	BI	2B	3B	HR	BB	SO	SB	BA
Gil English	OF118,3B10	SP-IND	134	475	48	120	57	27	6	4	48	44	0	.253
Phil Weintraub	1B119,OF12	SP-TOL	134	429	70	115	67	34	1	13	94	58	2	.268
Alvin Powell	OF124	IND-SP	133	488	60	158	74	38	0	11	28	43	6	.324
Allen Hunt	OF97	IND-SP	105	372	53	92	27	21	6	5	30	24	8	.247
Stan Rogers	3B86	IND-MIL	103	353	39	82	36	13	3	3	32	37	2	.232
Norm Schlueter	C83	SP-IND	90	278	17	54	28	·13	2	0	22	58	0	.194
John Pasek	C65	IND-SP	66	184	9	35	11	4	0	0	23	11	1	.190

TEAM BATTING

TEAMS	GP	AB	R	H	BI	2B	3B	HR	BB	SO	SB	BA
KANSAS CITY	154	4901	597	1264	548	225	51	53	507	583	75	.258
MILWAUKEE	152	5083	**742**	**1437**	**695**	**246**	59	95	531	594	38	**.283**
COLUMBUS	154	4942	621	1253	565	188	49	60	**567**	611	**85**	.254
TOLEDO	152	5002	641	1295	579	223	45	46	481	473	58	.259
LOUISVILLE	**156**	**5109**	597	1309	555	207	57	32	474	507	81	.256
INDIANAPOLIS	154	5050	614	1305	570	223	**62**	39	529	540	50	.258
MINNEAPOLIS	154	5057	685	1311	633	245	32	**101**	538	**659**	60	.259
ST. PAUL	154	5054	568	1269	533	232	43	71	518	586	41	.251
	615	40198	5065	10443	4678	1619	398	497	4145	4553	488	.260

1943
Home Field Advantage

One of the most eccentric yet innovative owners to grace the American Association was Milwaukee Brewers owner Bill Veeck. During his tenure as the Brewers' owner, there wasn't anything he wouldn't try to lure fans to his ballpark or to give his team some kind of advantage.

Playing in ancient Borchert Park, the Brewers needed every advantage they could get, and Bill Veeck saw that they got plenty. When playing a nimble opponent, Veeck flooded the infield, turning it into a quagmire. Sometimes he would have the ground crew stall for several hours in order to receive better lighting conditions. But the stunt Bill Veeck played in 1943 outshone all the rest.

Earlier, Veeck had a 60-foot fence erected on the short right fence at Borchert Park to cut down on opposing home runs. Not content with this solution, he thought of an outrageous wrinkle in the plan. Veeck stated: "I designed a system for sliding the wire fence back and forth along the top of the wall by means of a hydraulic motor. When the visiting team had more left-handed power than we did, the fence would stay up. Otherwise, we would reel it back to the foul line." Originally designed for a series-to-series change, Veeck's device was carried to its extreme, yet logical, conclusion. Veeck continues: "In the best of all possible parks, the fence would be up for the opposition and down for us. We could do this without any trouble at all—and we did do it—by reeling the fence in and out between innings." Veeck had created for himself the ultimate edge.

Riding the antics of their colorful owner, the Milwaukee Brewers finished atop the American Association in 1943. Indianapolis, Columbus, and Toledo filled in the last three playoff spots, while Louisville, Minneapolis, Kansas City and St. Paul finished out of the running. Grey Clarke of Milwaukee finished with the top batting average (.346) while his Brewer teammate, Ted Norbert, had the most home runs (25) and runs batted in (117). Jim Trexler of Indianapolis won the most games (19) and had the best earned run average (2.14), while Preacher Roe of Columbus struck out the most hitters (136).

Bill Veeck's fence sliding plan worked for exactly for one game. The very next day the league passed a rule outlawing such home field tailoring. With this rule change a degree of integrity returned to games played in Milwaukee. But for the space of one day, Bill Veeck had built for his Brewers an undisputed, best ever, home field advantage.

MILWAUKEE   1st   90-61   .596   Charles Grimm
Brewers

BATTERS	POS-GAMES	GP	AB	R	H	BI	2B	3B	HR	BB	SO	SB	BA
Heinz Becker	1B101	101	353	59	115	61	22	8	4	60	34	1	.326
Don Johnson	2B139	139	509	71	144	71	28	5	6	29	38	5	.283
Tony York	SS150	150	651	109	187	55	28	8	10	40	78	2	.287
Grey Clarke	3B142	142	534	77	185	96	29	9	10	57	22	2	.346
Ted Norbert	OF144	146	512	94	150	117	22	3	25	78	39	2	.293
Herschel Martin	OF123,1B12	134	492	104	151	66	28	2	13	90	38	7	.307
Willis Norman	OF121	132	396	72	109	83	18	0	18	90	63	1	.275
Henry Helf	C126	127	427	49	111	55	16	5	9	40	63	0	.260
Tom Nelson	2B17,3B15,1B10	66	168	23	43	16	5	2	2	15	26	2	.256
Hugh Todd	OF34	57	132	20	33	14	7	2	4	17	18	1	.250
James Pruett	C38	52	122	19	35	17	5	3	3	14	12	0	.287
Frank Secory	OF37	50	128	14	28	12	4	1	2	12	24	0	.219
Joe Berry	P37	41	88	8	20	8	1	0	0	6	8	0	.227
Wes Livengood	P36	37	85	7	14	8	4	1	1	3	35	0	.165
Charles Sproull	P37	37	20	2	3	2	0	0	0	3	5	0	.150
Robert Bowman	P33	33	23	4	4	3	2	0	0	0	13	0	.174
Mervyn Connors	1B31	32	118	18	29	18	5	3	4	11	23	0	.246
Earl Caldwell	P32	32	59	4	10	8	1	0	1	5	10	0	.169
Charles Gassaway	P27	27	35	1	3	1	0	0	0	5	12	0	.086
Harold Peck	OF15	23	45	11	20	15	2	1	1	6	5	0	.444
Le Fleming	P21	21	46	2	6	5	0	0	1	3	8	0	.130
Prince Oana	P14	20	34	8	14	4	1	1	0	4	6	0	.412
Paul Erickson	P12	12	21	1	5	4	1	1	0	2	5	0	.238
Julio Acosta	P9	9	16		6								.375
Ed Hanyzewski	P8	8	24		8								.333
John Hudson	1B	4	3	1	1	0	0	0	0			0	.000
Harold Hoffman	C	2	1	0	0	0	0	0	0			0	.000
Bill Sahlin	P2	2	0		0								----
Ralph Pate	P1	1	1		0								.000
Vern Godfredson	P1	1	0		0								----

PITCHERS		W	L	PCT	G	GS	CG	SH	IP	H	BB	SO	ERA
Joe Berry		18	10	.643	37	28	18	2	236	224	63	98	2.78
Wes Livengood		18	10	.643	36	29	15	3	220	223	69	84	3.04
Earl Caldwell		10	11	.476	32	24	11	1	171	181	59	65	3.68
Les Fleming		8	6	.571	21	15	8	1	123	134	61	67	3.51
Charles Gassaway		7	6	.538	27	13	4	2	111	102	45	57	2.76
Robert Bowman		6	2	.750	33	4	2	0	80	84	25	37	3.04
Paul Erickson		6	4	.600	12	10	5	1	62	58	34	42	3.19
Ed Hanyzewski		5	1	.833	8	8	5	1	58	50	30	43	2.95
Charles Sproull		5	5	.500	37		0	0	92	79	55	51	4.01
Julio Acosta		3	1	.750	9	6	3	0	44	50	10	29	3.89
Prince Oana		3	5	.375	14	8	2	1	64	59	29	32	4.08
Bill Sahlin		0	0	----	2		0	0	2	0	4	0	
Ralph Pate		0	0	----	1		0	0	2	7	0	0	
Vern Godfredson		0	0	----	1		0	0	0	0	1	0	

INDIANAPOLIS   2nd   85-67   .559   -5.5   Donie Bush
Indians

BATTERS	POS-GAMES	GP	AB	R	H	BI	2B	3B	HR	BB	SO	SB	BA
Edwin Morgan	1B146	147	525	81	141	74	23	12	9	84	51	6	.269
Fred Vaughn	2B	(see multi-team players)											
Carl Fairly	SS148	148	487	56	109	46	12	4	2	40	46	3	.224
Mike Haslin	3B99,2B12	117	372	32	89	50	13	3	1	37	21	4	.239
Wayne Blackburn	OF153	153	583	114	169	50	22	7	1	95	46	10	.290
Joe Moore	OF134	136	514	85	157	53	23	9	4	51	16	5	.305
Jess Pike	OF104	107	355	62	113	64	13	6	7	61	40	4	.318
Stewart Hofferth	C130	134	495	63	149	83	31	10	3	24	23	1	.301
Gil English	OF69,3B64	141	543	80	175	83	26	3	3	49	28	0	.322
James Trexler	P29	56	114	15	32	20	5	4	2	12	18	0	.281
Eric McNair	2B27,SS15	53	137	6	23	8	4	0	0	7	16	2	.168
John Hutchings	P36	39	89	9	27	11	4	0	0	6	10	0	.303
Charles Glock	2B37	37	137	17	36	26	6	2	1	13	6	1	.263
Norm Schlueter	C29	32	90	5	23	9	5	1	0	5	19	0	.256
Woody Rich	P26	29	51	6	18	4	3	0	0	5	7	0	.353
Robert Logan	P25	29	47	3	10	4	1	2	0	2	5	0	.213
Glenn Fletcher	P27	27	51	6	10	5	1	0	0	7	5	0	.196
George Jeffcoat	P23	24	30	7	6	0	1	1	0	4	9	0	.200
George Diehl	P22	23	48	3	6	4	2	0	1	9	16	0	.125

INDIANAPOLIS (cont.)
Indians

BATTERS	POS-GAMES	GP	AB	R	H	BI	2B	3B	HR	BB	SO	SB	BA
Walt Tauscher	P20	20	11	1	3	1	1	0	0	1	2	0	.273
Al Bronkhurst	P17	17	7	0	1	0	0	0	0	0	2	0	.143
Earl Reid	P15	15	31	3	4	3	0	0	0	3	1	0	.129
William Barnes	2B11	12	32	3	5	2	0	0	0	2	5	1	.156

PITCHERS		W	L	PCT	G	GS	CG	SH	IP	H	BB	SO	ERA
James Trexler		19	7	.731	29	26	19	4	219	207	84	103	2.14
John Hutchings		17	12	.586	36	28	23	2	226	216	83	105	3.07
George Diehl		12	7	.632	22	19	10	2	140	159	28	59	3.92
Glen Fletcher		10	6	.625	27	20	6	2	150	143	66	66	3.00
Robert Logan		9	6	.600	25	14	4	1	124	139	42	46	3.85
Woody Rich		6	10	.375	26	16	11	2	138	142	74	83	3.98
George Jeffcoat		6	10	.375	23	11	4	0	91	102	39	50	4.25
Earl Reid		5	6	.455	15	15	7	2	98	107	34	24	3.31
Al Bronkhurst		1	1	.500	17		0	0	36	49	12	8	4.00
Walt Tauscher		0	0	----	20		0	0	41	51	16	8	

COLUMBUS		3rd	84-67		.556		-6			Nick Cullop			

Red Birds

BATTERS	POS-GAMES	GP	AB	R	H	BI	2B	3B	HR	BB	SO	SB	BA
Maurice Sturdy	1B97,3B10	109	383	57	92	45	7	1	2	51	31	5	.240
Emil Verban	2B121,SS30	151	588	72	151	48	16	9	0	31	18	11	.257
Floyd Young	SS112	112	388	34	90	57	17	1	2	36	55	3	.232
John Antonelli	3B116,2B29	149	565	65	149	74	25	9	4	50	32	3	.264
Augie Bergamo	OF144	144	500	85	162	51	35	9	0	109	41	6	.324
Chet Wieczorek	OF128,3B18	146	530	89	174	97	31	3	9	63	40	3	.328
George Stumpf	OF104	112	402	59	104	24	10	4	5	61	38	1	.259
Thomas Heath	C102	108	340	37	104	59	8	1	5	55	28	0	.306
Joe Garagiola	C62	81	205	27	60	27	7	3	4	18	20	2	.293
Lou Scoffic	OF63	79	239	24	65	31	6	2	1	12	28	0	.272
Frank Barrett	P51	51	46	5	6	0	1	0	0	2	9	1	.130
Jack McLain	OF22,1B11	47	79	14	18	12	2	1	0	10	10	2	.228
Nick Cullop	OF	42	45	5	10	8	2	0	1	13	14	0	.222
Joe Mack	1B38	38	132	34	44	21	13	2	1	31	13	1	.333
Ted Wilks	P38	38	84	3	17	7	3	1	1	2	20	0	.202
Jack Creel	P33	37	64	2	10	1	1	0	0	1	21	0	.156
Andrew Timko	SS16	35	93	14	25	12	5	2	0	6	14	1	.269
George Dockins	P27	34	60	12	19	5	0	0	0	13	9	0	.317
Ken Burkhart	P31	31	68	6	17	8	2	0	0	6	18	0	.250
William Beckmann	P30	30	26	3	6	6	1	1	0	4	7	0	.231
Preacher Roe	P24	24	59	2	5	3	1	0	0	2	17	0	.085
Bill Brumbeloe	P6	6	2		0								.000
John Boehringer	P4	5	2		0								.000
John Lohrey	P2	3	4		0								.000
Larry Whalen	SS	2	3	2	0	0	0	0	0			0	.000

PITCHERS		W	L	PCT	G	GS	CG	SH	IP	H	BB	SO	ERA
Ted Wilks		16	8	.667	38	26	13	0	240	236	46	132	2.66
George Dockins		16	8	.667	27	27	20	5	196	188	38	85	2.25
Preacher Roe		15	7	.682	24	22	16	6	167	123	60	136	2.37
Ken Burkhart		12	11	.522	31	28	10	1	198	208	79	68	3.14
Frank Barrett		11	10	.524	51	9	5	0	160	151	53	83	3.21
Jack Creel		8	13	.381	33	27	12	4	185	185	81	72	3.99
William Beckmann		5	9	.357	30	11	3	0	102	140	29	45	4.50
John Lohrey		1	0	1.000	2	1	1	0	10	8	7	0	2.70
Bill Brumbeloe		0	1	.000	6		0	0	11	23	13	3	15.54
John Boehringer		0	0	----	4		0	0	11	11	3	4	1.66

TOLEDO		4th	76-76		.500		-14.5			Jacques Fournier			

Mud Hens

BATTERS	POS-GAMES	GP	AB	R	H	BI	2B	3B	HR	BB	SO	SB	BA
Phil Weintraub	1B131	138	467	79	156	96	27	3	16	90	50	2	.334
James Bucher	2B143	144	570	82	160	63	35	7	6	44	24	6	.281
Dick Kimble	SS61,3B14	78	255	29	58	27	6	3	1	25	22	3	.227

TOLEDO (cont.)
Mud Hens

BATTERS	POS-GAMES	GP	AB	R	H	BI	2B	3B	HR	BB	SO	SB	BA
Lin Storti	3B92	99	301	26	72	40	16	0	3	51	32	3	.239
Nick Gregory	OF149	149	543	70	142	69	33	3	6	31	38	1	.262
Hal Epps	OF146	146	552	84	166	52	22	13	6	50	22	4	.301
Tony Criscola	OF86	86	315	46	100	45	13	3	6	31	23	8	.317
Myron Hayworth	C92	102	295	30	82	30	13	2	0	28	14	1	.278
Len Schulte	SS58,3B45	126	429	53	115	56	22	6	2	26	30	1	.268
Ardys Keller	C74	79	231	19	53	18	10	1	0	24	27	0	.229
Al Zarilla	OF57	57	209	36	78	32	10	2	5	16	13	3	.373
Robert Boken	OF10	54	93	5	31	10	7	0	0	13	8	2	.333
Bill Seinsoth	P31	51	94	10	20	12	1	1	5	14	32	0	.213
Robert Wren	1B18	45	62	16	16	5	0	2	1	3	10	0	.258
William Cox	P29	42	52	12	11	4	1	0	0	1	7	0	.212
Loy Hanning	P34	42	30	2	2	1	0	0	0	1	2	0	.067
Floyd Baker	SS37	37	149	21	38	14	3	1	1	18	12	1	.255
Harry Kimberlin	P33	33	56	4	7	1	0	0	0	1	8	0	.125
John Whitehead	P28	28	64	2	11	5	0	0	0	6	10	0	.172
Fred Sanford	P28	28	62	7	10	4	2	0	0	9	13	1	.161
Sidney Peterson	P28	28	43	3	10	8	1	0	0	1	11	0	.233
John Kramer	P10	11	26	4	6	5	0	0	0	7	8	0	.231
Earl Jones	P9	9	3		0								.000
Cliff Fannin	P8	8	5		1								.200
Robert Raney	P5	5	1		0								.000
George Corona	OF	4	9	0	1	0	0	0	0			0	.111
Ken Wood	OF	2	1	0	0	0	0	0	0			0	.000
Sylvester Goedde	P1	1	0		0								----

PITCHERS		W	L	PCT	G	GS	CG	SH	IP	H	BB	SO	ERA
Fred Sanford		13	9	.591	28	24	17	1	190	181	78	106	3.27
John Whitehead		13	12	.520	28	28	17	1	200	240	24	62	3.20
Harry Kimberlin		10	9	.526	33	21	9	1	173	150	72	90	3.23
William Cox		9	11	.450	29	23	10	1	149	159	77	59	4.53
Bill Seinsoth		9	15	.375	31	24	20	4	196	210	65	73	3.40
John Kramer		8	2	.800	10	10	8	3	84	55	26	59	2.46
Sydney Peterson		8	9	.471	28	15	5	0	128	138	39	39	3.73
Loy Hanning		6	7	.462	34		0	0	97	125	64	36	5.75
Earl Jones		0	1	.000	9		0	0	20	17	20	11	4.50
Cliff Fannin		0	1	.000	8	2	1	0	21	15	22	8	1.71
Robert Raney		0	0	----	5		0	0	8	11	7	2	
Sylvester Goedde		0	0	----	1		0	0	2	1	3	2	

LOUISVILLE   5th   70-81   .464   -20   Bill Burwell
Colonels

BATTERS	POS-GAMES	GP	AB	R	H	BI	2B	3B	HR	BB	SO	SB	BA
Earle Browne	1B142	144	543	62	147	46	26	9	4	49	35	3	.271
Ed Popowski	2B120	120	378	40	85	24	6	0	1	48	35	6	.225
Henry Coriggio	SS82	90	272	26	65	26	11	1	2	26	26	2	.239
Stephen Barath	3B119	121	393	59	103	37	20	11	8	40	61	2	.262
Tom McBride	OF125	128	465	42	143	59	19	6	0	27	22	15	.308
Ford Garrison	OF97	99	358	53	116	62	20	5	8	28	34	5	.324
Stan Benjamin	OF75,3B37,1B12	123	439	49	104	47	15	5	0	28	74	14	.237
Howard Doyle	C68	76	249	37	70	36	13	4	9	23	17	1	.281
Sam Lamitina	2B39,OF13,SS10	74	209	17	45	25	6	1	1	17	33	1	.215
Walter Millies	C54	65	203	16	54	17	7	1	0	13	10	1	.266
Chet Morgan	OF49	56	183	21	43	14	5	1	0	23	10	3	.235
Jack Albright	SS53	53	192	37	54	21	6	5	2	36	18	2	.281
Babe Barna	OF49	49	163	23	38	13	2	3	6	29	36	3	.233
Bill Campbell	C36	49	117	12	25	5	7	0	0	23	8	1	.214
Norm Brown	P39	44	88	7	17	4	4	0	1	2	15	0	.193
Charles Schupp	P39	39	45	3	9	0	0	1	0	3	10	0	.200
Mel Deutsch	P33	34	71	3	16	4	3	1	0	1	17	0	.225
James Wilson	P28	33	32	3	8	2	0	0	0	1	4	0	.250
Victor Johnson	P25	25	47	1	13	9	2	0	0	3	9	0	.277
George Toolson	P24	24	24	0	5	2	0	0	0	1	10	1	.208
Emmett O'Neill	P18	21	47	4	8	5	1	1	0	2	15	0	.170
Hugh Holliday	OF10	18	44	3	12	5	1	0	0	3	3	1	.273
Stan Sperry	2B11	16	38	3	5	3	1	0	0	4	0	0	.132
Lou Lucier	P14	16	27	2	4	1	1	0	0	0	7	0	.148
Darwin Cobb	P15	15	4	1	1	0	0	0	0	2	2	0	.250
George Woods	P11	12	28	1	7	2	0	0	0	0	1	0	.250

LOUISVILLE (cont.)
Colonels

BATTERS	POS-GAMES	GP	AB	R	H	BI	2B	3B	HR	BB	SO	SB	BA
Leon Culberson	OF10	10	41	3	7	2	0	0	0	5	4	0	.171
Bill D'Alessandro	SS,OF	10	23	2	2	0	1	0	0	2	6	0	.087
Orace Powers	C	3	3	1	1	0	0	0	0			0	.333
Fred Schulte	PH	3	3	1	0	0	0	0	0			0	.000
Ray Patton	P2	2	0		0								----
Robert Perina	2B1	1	4	0	1	1	0	0	0			0	.250
Chet Covington	P1	1	2		1								.500
Sam Scheivley	P1	1	0		0								----

PITCHERS		W	L	PCT	G	GS	CG	SH	IP	H	BB	SO	ERA
Norm Brown		16	11	.593	39	29	18	4	255	233	85	98	2.33
Mel Deutsch		12	11	.522	33	25	14	2	187	176	61	53	2.74
Charles Schupp		9	5	.643	39	17	7	1	153	140	38	55	3.06
Lou Lucier		6	5	.545	14	11	6	1	81	81	25	43	3.22
Emmett O'Neill		6	7	.462	18	16	9	3	127	108	74	80	2.48
Victor Johnson		6	12	.333	25	17	8	2	134	129	46	50	3.02
George Toolson		3	5	.375	24	5	1	1	76	80	55	34	5.33
George Woods		3	5	.375	11	9	4	1	68	78	26	24	3.31
Darwin Cobb		1	4	.200	15		0	0	20	19	17	8	5.40
Chet Covington		0	1	.000	1	1	1	0	5	9	3	2	9.00
James Wilson		0	5	.000	28		0	0	57	49	43	31	5.68
Ray Patton		0	0	----	2		0	0	2	1	4	0	
Sam Scheivley		0	0	----	1		0	0	2	1	0	1	0.00

MINNEAPOLIS   6th   67-84   .444   -23   Tom Sheehan
Millers

BATTERS	POS-GAMES	GP	AB	R	H	BI	2B	3B	HR	BB	SO	SB	BA
Frank Danneker	1B82,OF31	123	403	61	90	53	14	0	15	51	66	13	.223
Jim Pofahl	2B122,SS21	143	487	80	122	44	27	6	4	99	74	11	.251
Frank Trechock	SS97,1B13	113	367	44	100	40	15	5	1	34	43	10	.272
Herman Clifton	3B147	150	554	68	156	56	11	3	1	82	45	16	.282
Joe Vosmik	OF143	146	498	66	126	62	25	2	5	62	31	6	.253
Robert Dill	OF110	117	387	47	102	56	21	11	11	36	86	4	.264
Al Wright	OF98	101	364	49	102	69	15	2	16	28	66	4	.280
Mike Blazo	C96	100	310	26	69	30	4	0	0	30	24	1	.223
Russ Rolandson	OF72,C56	136	473	73	131	45	23	2	4	27	43	15	.277
Ed Skladany	SS42,1B14	66	187	22	42	6	5	1	0	18	21	5	.225
Cliff Johnson	OF30,P1	51	69	12	8	6	1	2	1	13	31	1	.116
Bill DeCarlo	1B19	42	79	4	19	12	6	0	0	4	13	0	.241
Wilfrid Lefebvre	P24	39	73	5	18	5	4	0	0	9	7	1	.247
William Clark	P36	37	69	6	12	6	0	0	0	8	13	1	.174
Herbert Bain	P35	35	48	1	6	0	0	0	0	1	22	0	.125
James Walsh	1B24	24	87	15	22	18	3	1	4	15	10	0	.253
Claude Horton	P22	22	40	4	11	9	2	0	1	1	9	0	.275
Lewis Carpenter	P21	21	38	6	6	0	1	0	0	2	13	0	.158
Roy Mosley	P20	20	12	0	2	0	0	0	0	1	4	0	.167
Ewald Pyle	P17	17	36	2	5	4	0	0	0	3	7	0	.139
Harold Wonson	P16	17	14	2	0	0	0	0	0	0	2	0	.000
Frank Papish	P5	5	8		1								.125
Vallie Eaves	P4	4	7		2								.286
Ray Roth	C	3	6	0	1	0	1	0	0			0	.167
Roy Fontaine	OF	2	2	0	0	0	0	0	0			0	.000

PITCHERS		W	L	PCT	G	GS	CG	SH	IP	H	BB	SO	ERA
Wilfrid Lefebvre		12	8	.600	24	18	15	1	162	145	38	53	2.22
William Clark		12	11	.522	36	28	11	2	213	236	98	59	4.44
Claude Horton		9	9	.500	22	17	7	0	110	139	48	33	4.91
Lewis Carpenter		8	8	.500	21	15	6	0	106	132	63	50	4.16
Herbert Bain		8	13	.381	35	22	9	0	161	194	80	55	4.70
Ewald Pyle		5	9	.357	17	13	9	0	104	108	46	41	4.50
Roy Mosley		2	3	.400	20		0	0	44	40	21	14	4.09
Frank Papish		0	3	.000	5	2	1	0	18	32	7	11	6.00
Vallie Eaves		0	3	.000	4	3	1	0	21	21	13	16	4.71
Harold Wonson		0	0	----	16		0	0	49	61	23	13	5.88
Cliff Johnson		0	0	----	1		0	0	2	7	1	1	

KANSAS CITY   7th (T)   67-85   .441   -23.5   John Neun
Blues

BATTERS	POS-GAMES	GP	AB	R	H	BI	2B	3B	HR	BB	SO	SB	BA
Roy Zimmerman	1B149	151	553	61	154	63	26	9	2	28	36	6	.278
Mike Milosevich	2B138	139	523	46	127	42	19	5	1	30	42	3	.243
George Scharein	SS105	105	419	53	121	29	12	5	2	23	34	8	.289
Jack Saltzgaver	3B52,OF14,2B12	103	259	44	68	22	12	5	1	58	18	2	.263
Hubert Shelley	OF130	130	495	43	128	38	20	2	0	33	45	8	.259
Jesse Landrum	OF110	117	406	32	117	43	14	7	3	16	38	4	.288
Albert Lyons	OF78	108	314	37	74	48	13	1	6	36	49	3	.236
Joe Glenn	C108	120	390	41	102	53	20	1	4	36	35	3	.262
Oliver Blakeney	3B52,SS40	98	272	31	71	31	9	2	4	42	32	1	.261
Lynn King	OF70	71	260	38	72	18	11	3	0	25	16	5	.277
Larry Smith	C38	41	133	14	40	20	9	0	2	5	18	0	.301
Clem Hausmann	P36	37	57	8	9	6	2	0	0	10	12	1	.158
Don Hendrickson	P37	37	42	2	2	3	0	0	0	5	14	0	.048
James McLeod	3B35	36	127	19	27	6	3	1	0	9	11	1	.213
Floyd Bevens	P34	34	43	1	5	2	2	0	0	2	18	0	.116
Frank Tincup	P20	33	35	0	11	2	1	0	0	1	2	0	.314
Lloyd Christopher	C30	32	87	13	21	12	1	1	6	12	15	0	.241
Tom Reis	P29	29	64	3	8	4	1	0	0	5	21	0	.125
Mel Queen	P25	25	53	2	7	0	1	0	0	0	22	0	.132
John Johnson	P22	24	45	3	7	3	1	0	0	5	20	0	.156
Russ Messerly	P24	24	20	1	2	0	0	0	0	0	6	0	.100
William Rabe	OF21	23	64	0	11	4	1	1	2	10	17	1	.172
Jerry Crosby	3B17	22	62	6	17	6	0	0	0	7	3	1	.274
Bill Cronin	C13	14	31	2	3	0	1	0	0	6	3	0	.097
Albert Smith	3B,SS	9	21	2	3	0	1	0	0	0			.143
Richard Korte	SS	9	10	1	3	0	0	0	0			0	.300
Jack Fallon	P9	9	14		0								.000
Harry Craft	OF	8	30	5	9	6	0	0	3			0	.300
Garrett McBryde	OF	8	27	5	5	0	1	0	0			1	.185
John Babich	P7	7	10		2								.200
Robert Dews	C	2	2	0	1	0	0	0	0	0		0	.000
George Feikert	P2	2	0		0								----
Svend Jessen	PH	1	0	0	0	0	0	0	0	0		0	----

PITCHERS		W	L	PCT	G	GS	CG	SH	IP	H	BB	SO	ERA
Clem Hausmann		14	14	.500	36	24	11	2	179	170	77	58	4.02
Tom Reis		12	14	.462	29	27	14	2	195	206	69	77	4.11
Don Hendrickson		9	12	.429	37	15	7	0	144	136	59	54	3.69
John Johnson		8	5	.615	22	20	7	1	143	145	46	58	3.27
Floyd Bevens		7	8	.467	34	19	7	2	149	145	82	87	3.08
Mel Queen		7	12	.368	25	22	8	3	160	133	100	90	3.43
Albert Lyons		4	6	.400	19		0	0	80	68	46	51	3.49
Frank Tincup		3	6	.333	20		0	0	53	61	40	19	5.09
Russ Messerly		2	2	.500	24	4	1	0	76	65	51	29	2.72
Jack Fallon		1	1	.500	9	2	2	0	44	43	21	12	3.68
John Babich		0	5	.000	7	7	2	0	34	44	23	10	9.00
George Feikert		0	0	----	2		0	0	3	2	3	1	
Jack McClure		0	0	----	1		0	0	1	0	2	0	0.00

ST. PAUL   7th (T)   67-85   .441   -23.5   Francis Parker
Saints

BATTERS	POS-GAMES	GP	AB	R	H	BI	2B	3B	HR	BB	SO	SB	BA
Howard Schultz	1B97	99	372	39	106	53	24	3	5	8	45	3	.285
Frank Drews	2B142	142	445	55	115	43	22	8	7	82	48	2	.258
Don Blanchard	SS91,2B11	104	350	36	70	27	8	0	0	20	33	7	.200
Francis Parker	3B127	132	434	57	107	51	25	3	2	47	44	3	.247
Allen Hunt	OF136	142	495	62	132	49	29	8	7	58	39	9	.267
Alvin Powell	OF94,P1	97	364	46	103	57	19	2	11	26	36	9	.283
Charles Baron	OF79,1B26	118	334	41	96	28	18	2	2	31	24	8	.287
Stan Andrews	C83	91	277	32	67	47	9	2	6	26	14	1	.242
Glenn Chapman	OF77	86	269	22	69	19	14	5	1	17	21	4	.265
Joe Vitter	3B32,SS14	75	237	26	65	15	5	5	2	27	22	10	.274
Rae Blaemire	C64	72	219	28	66	30	7	3	2	13	16	0	.301
Floyd Speer	P44	44	70	9	13	4	0	0	0	10	24	0	.186
John Marion	OF35	42	125	23	42	18	4	1	4	13	16	2	.336
Joe Orengo	SS35	37	119	21	34	25	4	1	5	17	17	1	.286
Otho Nitcholas	P36	36	78	3	13	5	1	0	0	1	9	0	.167
John Bolling	1B32	34	118	16	33	14	7	1	0	5	6	3	.280
Edwin Weiland	P34	34	61	7	13	2	1	1	0	2	26	0	.213

ST. PAUL (cont.)
Saints

BATTERS	POS-GAMES	GP	AB	R	H	BI	2B	3B	HR	BB	SO	SB	BA
Ed Patrew	SS22	28	70	9	13	1	2	0	0	21	17	0	.186
Art Herring	P25	27	71	6	15	7	1	0	0	3	7	0	.211
Vince Castino	C16	25	48	6	12	4	0	0	0	8	8	1	.250
Howard Belknap	P22	22	21	2	6	0	0	0	0	0	5	0	.286
Clay Smith	P21	21	33	0	0	0	0	0	0	1	9	0	.000
Robert Reis	P6	18	30	1	4	3	0	0	0	1	6	1	.133
Joe Strincevich	P13	13	9	2	0	0	0	0	0	1	4	0	.000
LeRoy Hewite	P10	10	6	0	0	0	0	0	0	0	3	0	.000
Frank Melton	P9	9	18		3								.167
Robert Mistele	P7	7	9		1								.111
Norm Dillard	P2	2	0		0								----
Julian Morgan	P2	2	0		0								----
Don Yohe	SS1	1	2	0	1	0	0	0	0			0	.500
Lou Cardinal	C1	1	2	0	0	0	0	0	0			0	.000

PITCHERS	W	L	PCT	G	GS	CG	SH	IP	H	BB	SO	ERA
Floyd Speer	15	12	.556	44	30	15	3	234	254	65	94	4.19
Art Herring	13	10	.565	25	25	22	2	195	189	77	83	3.37
Otho Nitcholas	13	14	.481	36	27	20	3	226	218	47	59	2.99
Edwin Weiland	11	16	.407	34	23	13	0	187	195	100	51	3.80
Clay Smith	5	12	.294	21	17	5	1	116	129	36	46	3.96
Howard Belknap	3	5	.375	22		0	0	73	68	59	30	5.79
Frank Melton	2	6	.250	9	8	6	0	60	54	34	40	3.30
Joe Strincevich	1	3	.250	13		0	0	28	39	22	7	7.71
LeRoy Hewite	0	1	.000	10		0	0	24	25	23	12	3.75
Robert Mistele	0	1	.000	7		0	0	26	26	21	8	5.54
Robert Reis	0	0	----	6		0	0	13	17	21	4	
Julian Morgan	0	0	----	2		0	0	4	13	3	2	
Norm Dillard	0	0	----	2		0	0	2	5	1	0	9.00
Alvin Powell	0	0	----	1		0	0	3	6	5	0	

MULTI-TEAM PLAYERS

BATTERS	POS-GAMES	TEAMS	GP	AB	R	H	BI	2B	3B	HR	BB	SO	SB	BA
Fred Vaughn	2B96,1B14	IND-MIN	119	376	47	90	53	11	12	9	46	64	6	.239
Arthur Rebel	OF84	LOU-SP	102	317	41	83	37	19	3	1	22	15	5	.262
Joe Bowman	P28	SP-LOU	53	97	7	27	11	4	3	0	7	7	1	.278
Owen Scheetz	P43	MIN-MIL	43	69	1	18	5	1	0	0	2	13	0	.261
Ernest Rudolph	P27	MIN-SP	27	26	1	5	1	1	0	0	3	9	0	.192
Elon Hogsett	P25	IND-MIN	26	16	1	4	0	0	0	0	0	5	0	.250

PITCHERS	TEAMS	W	L	PCT	G	GS	CG	SH	IP	H	BB	SO	ERA
Owen Scheetz	MIN-MIL	11	15	.423	43	29	15	1	203	218	60	53	3.50
Joe Bowman	SP-LOU	9	12	.429	28	21	10	0	159	180	54	64	4.02
Ernest Rudolph	MIN-SP	3	3	.500	27	7	3	0	93	123	46	39	6.58
Elon Hogsett	IND-MIN	1	4	.200	25	5	1	0	58	92	28	20	6.98

TEAM BATTING

TEAMS	GP	AB	R	H	BI	2B	3B	HR	BB	SO	SB	BA
MILWAUKEE	152	5049	785	1434	744	230	57	115	606	595	23	.284
INDIANAPOLIS	153	4989	688	1356	617	201	72	37	550	446	39	.272
COLUMBUS	151	4916	653	1328	596	193	49	35	580	512	39	.270
TOLEDO	152	4912	640	1344	586	222	47	58	491	438	37	.274
LOUISVILLE	152	4945	555	1268	504	191	59	43	458	559	66	.256
MINNEAPOLIS	151	4848	613	1219	558	185	39	69	548	680	92	.251
KANSAS CITY	152	4868	523	1228	464	183	43	36	419	553	49	.252
ST. PAUL	153	4896	570	1252	523	213	46	54	456	530	49	.256
	608	39423	5027	10429	4592	1618	412	447	3698	4313	394	.265

1944
Milwaukee Brewers

The World War II era was the golden era for one American Association franchise. Although this city had won back-to-back pennants 30 years previously, the mid–1940s would see its most impressive teams to date. This franchise was the Milwaukee Brewers.

The Brewers had won only three pennants during their first 40 years in the Association. The first two had come in the years immediately preceding World War I, as the Brewers won two in a row in 1913 and 1914. More than 20 years later, Milwaukee won their next flag in 1936. Another several years passed before the Brewers became competitive again.

Bill Veeck bought the Milwaukee franchise in 1941 and immediately pumped energy into the last place team. Veeck brought in several quality players and sank several thousand dollars into refurbishing the team's ballpark. The Brewers' fortunes quickly rose as they finished a close second in 1942 and won the pennant in 1943. In 1944, however, the Brewers were to step it up a notch more.

The 1944 Milwaukee Brewers ground up their American Association competition as they raced to their second consecutive pennant. This Brewer powerhouse of a team hit the ball hard and often as they became the first Association team in many years to bat over .300. Their best players included Heinz Becker (.346, 115 RBI), Harold Beck (.345), James Pruett (.312), Dick Culler (.308), Bill Nagel (.308, 23 HR, 117 RBI), and Tom Nelson (.303, 20 HR). Their pitching staff featured the work of Earl Caldwell, who won a league best 19 of 24 decisions.

Toledo climbed to an impressive second place finish with the best winning percentage in franchise history. Louisville and St. Paul finished third and fourth, while Columbus missed the playoffs by a scant percentage point. Indianapolis, Minneapolis, and Kansas City brought up the rear. John Wyrostek of Columbus led all Association batters with a mark of .358, while Minneapolis slugger Babe Barna hit the most home runs (24), and Nick Polly of Louisville brought home the most runs (120). James Wilson of Louisville shared the victory title with Earl Caldwell (19) as well as posting the most strikeouts (147). Another Louisville pitcher, Mel Deutsch, had the best earned run average (2.47).

Milwaukee would go on to win its third straight flag in 1945, ensuring its place in Association lore as a genuine dynasty. They were only the third team ever to win three pennants in a row, the first in more than thirty years.

MILWAUKEE Brewers

1st   102-51   .667   Grimm - Stengel

BATTERS	POS-GAMES	GP	AB	R	H	BI	2B	3B	HR	BB	SO	SB	BA
Heinz Becker	1B145	146	526	115	182	115	26	9	10	93	43	6	.346
Tom Nelson	2B146	146	518	78	157	97	25	7	20	61	48	10	.303
Dick Culler	SS148	148	629	131	194	54	30	4	5	46	33	19	.308
Bill Nagel	3B103	109	425	66	131	117	10	7	23	28	55	3	.308
Harold Beck	OF146	148	579	140	200	83	25	9	13	71	42	18	.345
Willis Norman	OF129	138	443	84	131	90	21	1	17	86	63	7	.296
Frank Secory	OF67	88	248	51	72	47	19	2	9	44	41	9	.290
James Pruett	C109	114	356	55	111	49	20	4	9	51	36	2	.312
George Binks	OF58,1B13	100	281	59	105	66	17	2	10	25	25	8	.374
Herschel Martin	OF58	58	218	49	78	56	8	2	8	30	9	3	.358
Edward Levy	OF17,3B15	46	126	17	36	15	5	2	1	12	12	3	.286
Charles Gassaway	P42	43	77	9	15	11	2	2	2	3	28	0	.195
Julio Acosta	P36	39	87	13	21	7	4	0	2	3	11	1	.241
Ray Easterwood	C37	37	106	13	30	20	4	1	4	12	16	2	.283
Charles Sproull	P35	35	69	6	14	5	2	0	0	2	14	0	.203
Jack Farmer	P34	34	21	2	1	2	0	0	0	1	5	0	.048
Earl Caldwell	P29	29	96	14	25	10	4	0	1	5	17	1	.260
Ken Raddant	C27	27	58	5	14	6	0	0	0	6	7	0	.241
Owen Scheetz	P25	25	53	10	9	6	0	1	1	3	6	0	.170
Floyd Speer	P24	24	20	2	2	4	0	1	0	2	12	0	.100
Dale Long	OF1	1	4	0	0	0	0	0	0			0	.000

PITCHERS		W	L	PCT	G	GS	CG	SH	IP	H	BB	SO	ERA
Earl Caldwell		19	5	.792	29	29	15	3	212	226	58	115	2.97
Charles Gassaway		17	8	.680	42	27	16	0	219	200	87	108	2.75
Charles Sproull		16	7	.696	35	26	11	3	187	179	71	87	2.50
Julio Acosta		13	10	.565	36	25	18	2	208	217	73	114	3.89
Owen Scheetz		11	7	.611	25	21	11	1	146	156	39	55	4.13
Jack Farmer		8	6	.571	34	2	1	0	79	73	39	30	2.96
Floyd Speer		7	2	.778	24	12	3	1	108	115	33	39	4.08
Louis Grasmick		0	1	.000	1		0	0	9	4	15	2	6.00

TOLEDO Mud Hens

2nd   95-58   .621   -7   Ollie Marquardt

BATTERS	POS-GAMES	GP	AB	R	H	BI	2B	3B	HR	BB	SO	SB	BA
Ed Ignasiak	1B136	136	463	76	125	69	18	3	7	89	81	5	.270
Len Schulte	2B84,1B54,SS13	153	607	112	175	98	30	9	11	42	31	6	.288
Dick Kimble	SS143	152	510	91	135	67	20	10	4	92	38	17	.265
Robert Wren	3B49,2B55	110	369	44	98	54	14	7	3	26	38	15	.266
George Corona	OF110,P1	122	442	67	136	68	29	4	3	41	47	6	.308
Bill Burgo	OF99	101	370	72	120	70	26	5	11	27	12	4	.324
Don Smith	OF87	101	324	71	98	34	14	6	4	31	27	17	.302
Joe Schultz	C87	93	298	39	94	38	23	0	1	52	18	4	.315
Boris Martin	OF64,C37	114	386	82	135	72	27	10	14	40	33	7	.350
Fred Reinhart	OF84	111	346	58	113	62	22	6	1	39	20	3	.327
Robert Boken	3B46,1B15,OF11	76	245	38	70	53	10	1	8	17	22	4	.286
Bill Seinsoth	P33	43	91	19	26	21	6	0	3	10	17	0	.286
Cliff Fannin	P40	41	36	5	7	4	2	0	0	4	10	0	.194
Harry Kimberlin	P37	37	45	4	6	5	1	0	0	2	5	0	.133
George Sebesak	OF29	31	94	14	26	11	6	0	0	10	6	1	.277
Earl Jones	P26	26	48	5	11	5	2	1	1	3	11	0	.229
James Bucher	2B25	25	96	12	25	13	6	0	1	11	2	1	.260
Sylvester Goedde	P24	25	56	4	10	5	0	0	0	3	25	0	.179
John Whitehead	P25	25	55	8	14	6	2	0	0	13	5	0	.255
Al LaMacchia	P23	25	37	8	5	1	0	0	0	7	13	0	.135
John Miller	P23	24	36	2	6	1	1	0	0	4	11	0	.167
Walt Missler	C17	17	41	3	5	1	2	0	0	2	15	0	.122
Mike Sertich	C16	16	55	7	11	3	2	0	0	6	6	0	.200
Walter Brown	P14	14	33	3	9	3	0	0	0	0	5	0	.273
Ernest Bickhaus	P6	11	8	1	2	0	0	0	0	1	3	0	.250
Herman Fink	P7	7	8		1								.125
Lew Flick	OF	5	17	2	1	1	0	0	0			0	.059
Lin Storti	3B	5	9	0	0	1	0	0	0			0	.000
Roy Smith	P5	5	2		1								.500
Don Spencer	P4	4	1		0								.000
Ken Gregory	SS,3B	3	8	0	1	1	0	0	0			0	.125
Paul Prpsh	C	3	2	0	0	0	0	0	0			0	.000
Robert Comyn	PH	2	1	0	1	0	0	0	0			0	1.000
Bill Sullivan	P2	2	0		0								----

TOLEDO (cont.)
Mud Hens

PITCHERS	W	L	PCT	G	GS	CG	SH	IP	H	BB	SO	ERA
Bill Seinsoth	16	11	.593	33	26	16	2	205	232	50	91	4.08
John Whitehead	13	8	.619	25	24	11	3	173	185	17	47	3.38
Al LaMacchia	12	3	.800	23	18	9	2	118	132	57	51	4.35
Cliff Fannin	11	7	.611	40	10	6	2	126	111	41	91	3.50
Harry Kimberlin	10	6	.625	37	13	4	0	134	153	44	49	4.43
Earl Jones	10	6	.625	26	19	6	1	144	127	76	122	3.69
Sylvester Goedde	9	4	.692	24	19	11	1	133	132	104	67	4.67
Walter Brown	7	5	.583	14	10	5	1	90	92	28	56	3.40
John Miller	6	4	.600	23	9	2	0	100	129	40	46	5.76
Herman Fink	0	2	.000	7		0	0	30	44	17	14	9.90
Ernest Bickhaus	0	3	.000	6	2	2	0	24	28	15	7	4.50
Roy Smith	0	0	----	5		0	0	9	5	9	4	
Don Spencer	0	0	----	4		0	0	5	4	6	3	
Bill Sullivan	0	0	----	2		0	0	2	3	4	0	
George Corona	0	0	----	1		0	0	4	9	3	0	

LOUISVILLE　　　　3rd　　　85-63　　　.574　　　-14.5　　　Harry Leibold
Colonels

BATTERS	POS-GAMES	GP	AB	R	H	BI	2B	3B	HR	BB	SO	SB	BA
Earle Browne	1B143	143	564	90	176	99	30	6	7	58	30	9	.312
Ben Steiner	2B147	149	617	122	195	68	25	10	3	64	60	17	.316
Frank Shofner	SS129	133	464	73	147	76	15	9	5	28	44	12	.317
Nick Polly	3B142	149	486	110	141	120	24	9	20	147	72	9	.290
Frank Genovese	OF147	148	527	130	147	55	22	11	7	115	43	33	.279
Bill Howerton	OF122	133	401	62	101	52	18	9	3	36	75	9	.252
Stephen Barath	OF94	111	347	71	114	77	25	9	15	63	64	10	.329
Fred Walters	C125	129	446	48	124	72	22	4	5	39	34	9	.278
James Wilson	P38	62	119	14	31	18	5	2	1	6	13	0	.261
Henry Marshall	OF36	39	92	14	20	3	3	0	0	2	5	3	.217
Mel Deutsch	P34	36	83	4	21	9	1	3	0	1	13	0	.253
Al Widmar	P31	31	61	3	10	3	0	0	0	4	22	0	.164
Sam Lamitina	SS20	27	82	13	26	6	4	3	1	7	9	5	.317
Ben Lady	C24	27	63	4	10	7	0	1	0	11	11	0	.159
Jimmy Ripple	OF20	24	68	7	14	6	1	1	0	13	5	2	.206
Lou Lucier	P20	22	26	5	7	3	0	0	0	3	2	0	.269
Victor Johnson	P19	19	36	5	10	4	0	1	0	1	4	0	.278
James McDonnell	C12	14	41	5	12	6	1	0	0	6	0	1	.293
Joe Wood	P12	13	17	2	2	2	0	0	0	2	5	0	.118
Dale Matthewson	P9	12	7	3	2	0	0	0	0	1	1	0	.286
Vance Dinges	OF,1B	11	21	2	4	2	0	0	0	0	3	1	.190
Dwight Simonds	P10	10	14	1	2	1	0	0	0	0	2	0	.143
George Savino	C	9	17	1	3	2	1	0	0			0	.176
Dick Callahan	P9	9	15		2								.133
Robert Ennis	P8	8	8		1								.125
Ray Patton	P5	5	6		1								.167
Andrew Latchic	OF	4	1	3	1	0	0	0	0			0	1.000
Victor Males	OF,2B	2	6	0	1	1	0	0	0			0	.167
Robert Kobrin	C	2	2	0	0	0	0	0	0			0	.000
Richard Kern	C	2	2	0	1	0	0	0	0			0	.500
Lewis Brock	P2	2	0		0								----
Charles Koney	PH	1	1	0	0	0	0	0	0			0	.000

PITCHERS	W	L	PCT	G	GS	CG	SH	IP	H	BB	SO	ERA
James Wilson	19	8	.704	38	27	22	1	237	189	98	147	2.77
Mel Deutsch	14	11	.560	34	26	14	1	211	215	60	73	2.47
Al Widmar	12	11	.522	31	22	9	0	174	181	78	59	4.66
Lou Lucier	7	3	.700	20	10	4	0	82	103	33	33	4.83
Victor Johnson	5	3	.625	19	11	4	0	90	86	30	24	3.60
Dwight Simonds	4	2	.667	10	2	1	0	41	41	19	12	3.29
Joe Wood	3	3	.500	12	8	3	1	61	85	32	36	5.16
Ray Patton	1	0	1.000	5	3	1	0	20	20	17	7	4.50
Lewis Brock	1	0	1.000	2		0	0	1	1	4	0	36.00
Dale Matthewson	1	1	.500	9		0	0	18	22	13	11	6.00
Robert Ennis	1	1	.500	8		0	0	24	34	12	8	6.38
Dick Callahan	1	6	.143	9	6	4	0	43	46	34	16	5.86

ST. PAUL Saints

ST. PAUL   4th   85-66   .563   -16   Ray Blades

BATTERS	POS-GAMES	GP	AB	R	H	BI	2B	3B	HR	BB	SO	SB	BA
Charles Baron	1B148	148	541	100	164	73	29	11	5	45	31	15	.303
Frank Drews	2B94	95	298	35	74	46	11	1	3	57	17	10	.248
Frank Piet	SS		(see multi-team players)										
Leighton Kimball	3B134	143	511	73	124	60	20	5	16	57	76	10	.243
Carden Gillenwater	OF149	152	550	111	163	70	25	9	19	83	63	15	.296
Glenn Chapman	OF146	146	528	85	172	93	28	4	4	54	48	13	.326
John Marion	OF111	114	394	67	136	80	21	3	10	45	37	8	.345
Dominic Castro	C127	128	389	35	80	42	9	3	3	23	55	1	.206
Joe Vitter	2B53,SS45,OF20,3B15	140	447	70	122	57	15	6	4	50	50	19	.273
Walt Tauscher	P36	39	48	3	10	1	2	0	0	1	10	0	.208
Cyril Buker	P25	37	65	3	13	1	2	0	0	2	6	0	.200
William Webb	P32	36	56	5	9	6	0	0	0	2	8	0	.161
Mike Sandlock	P35	35	120	17	37	15	5	0	1	15	16	0	.308
Ernest Rudolph	P34	35	63	5	9	3	1	0	0	6	14	0	.143
Loy Camp	P34	34	62	6	8	4	1	0	0	2	16	0	.129
Joe Strincevich	P17	33	34	6	7	3	1	0	0	1	11	0	.206
Otho Nitcholas	P29	30	70	7	16	10	1	0	0	2	9	0	.229
Frank Pugsley	P30	30	12	1	1	1	0	0	0	3	2	0	.083
Ed Badke	OF27	28	97	14	23	7	0	0	0	11	14	3	.237
Art Herring	P15	27	45	6	17	4	5	0	0	1	3	0	.378
Ken Mauer		16	26	3	6	4	1	0	0	3	2	0	.231
Walter King	SS	9	9	3	1	1	0	0	0			0	.111
Claude Weaver	P8	8	18		3								.167
Richard Furey	P5	7	4		1								.250
Gene Werth	P6	6	2		1								.500
James Riskosky	OF	5	18	0	5	1	0	0	0			0	.278
Lou Rochelli	2B	5	16	1	2	0	1	0	0			0	.125
Roy Eder	PH	2	0	1	0	0	0	0	0			0	----
Don Froehle	PH	1	1	0	0	0	0	0	0			0	.000
Don Ernst	P1	1	0		0								----

PITCHERS	W	L	PCT	G	GS	CG	SH	IP	H	BB	SO	ERA
Otho Nitcholas	14	11	.560	29	28	19	6	218	231	40	75	2.89
Ernest Rudolph	14	14	.500	34	27	12	3	200	161	81	123	2.88
Loy Camp	14	14	.500	34	31	9	4	167	195	88	70	4.69
Cyril Buker	11	3	.786	25	23	8	1	128	125	49	62	3.23
William Webb	10	7	.588	32	17	11	1	144	158	48	50	3.56
Art Herring	8	5	.615	15	12	11	1	103	89	23	41	2.18
Walt Tauscher	6	7	.462	36	13	6	1	139	152	43	53	3.88
Claude Weaver	4	1	.800	8	6	4	0	48	50	15	14	3.94
Frank Pugsley	2	2	.500	30		0	0	62	71	55	20	5.81
Joe Strincevich	2	2	.500	17	4	2	0	58	58	32	14	4.03
Gene Werth	0	0	----	6		0	0	8	11	5	6	
Richard Furey	0	0	----	5		0	0	8	9	4	5	
Don Ernst	0	0	----	1		0	0	0	0	2	0	

COLUMBUS Red Birds

COLUMBUS   5th   86-67   .562   -16   Nick Cullop

BATTERS	POS-GAMES	GP	AB	R	H	BI	2B	3B	HR	BB	SO	SB	BA
Joe Mack	1B155	155	543	95	156	102	36	5	7	115	61	5	.287
John Antonelli	2B83,3B56	139	526	77	164	88	31	6	6	39	14	4	.312
Glenn Crawford	SS82,3B44	130	495	87	144	71	21	8	8	61	43	11	.291
John Price	3B57,SS18	82	283	38	76	24	14	2	0	27	11	0	.269
James Mallory	OF153	153	637	91	189	82	34	10	1	36	33	15	.297
George Stumpf	OF144	144	554	118	156	68	36	4	19	72	57	3	.282
John Wyrostek	OF109	110	416	87	149	69	50	5	10	60	36	11	.358
Gerry Burmeister	C72	74	221	28	49	32	3	2	7	30	21	0	.226
Floyd Young	SS67,2B55	121	419	44	103	59	17	3	6	37	57	4	.246
Thomas Heath	C65	68	216	20	58	33	11	3	1	26	19	0	.269
Lou Scoffic	OF25	46	97	9	22	20	8	0	1	10	10	1	.227
Wes Cunningham	P40	40	29	4	5	0	0	1	0	5	7	0	.172
Eugene Crumling	C37	39	125	16	32	19	4	0	0	7	16	0	.256
Jack McLain	OF26	39	102	20	24	11	2	3	1	11	16	7	.235
Arthur Lopatka	P27	39	73	6	26	4	3	2	0	3	17	0	.356
Jack Creel	P32	36	75	6	7	2	2	0	1	2	20	1	.093
Ken Burkhart	P33	33	91	10	22	9	2	1	1	4	11	0	.243
John Herr	P30	30	38	2	5	0	0	0	0	2	8	0	.132
John Burman	2B23	29	91	8	17	4	1	0	0	9	3	2	.187
Arthur Rebel	OF22	22	88	16	32	19	10	2	0	11	3	2	.364

COLUMBUS (cont.)
Red Birds

BATTERS	POS-GAMES	GP	AB	R	H	BI	2B	3B	HR	BB	SO	SB	BA
LeRoy Pfund	P19	19	25	3	4	0	3	1	0	1	11	0	.160
John Podgajny	P13	18	30	1	4	4	2	0	0	2	5	0	.133
Frank Barrett	P16	16	21	3	2	2	0	0	0	4	8	0	.095
Thomas Ananicz	P12	12	15	3	3	4	0	0	1	1	4	0	.200
Arthur Frantz	P8	12	11	2	4	0	0	0	0	3	0	0	.364
Nick Cullop	PH	10	6	0	3	1	0	0	0	4	0	0	.500
Vaughn Hazen	OF	9	5	3	3	2	1	0	0			0	.600
Edward Blake	P8	9	10		2								.200
Elmer Burkart	P8	8	18		4								.222
John Bucha	C	2	2	0	0	0	0	0	0			0	.000
Joe Garagiola	C1	1	3	1	0	0	0	0	0			0	.000
Larry Drake	PH	1	1	0	0	1	0	0	0			0	.000

PITCHERS	W	L	PCT	G	GS	CG	SH	IP	H	BB	SO	ERA
Ken Burkhart	15	9	.625	33	31	17	1	231	**259**	69	86	4.05
Arthur Lopatka	11	9	.550	27	21	16	5	170	154	97	88	3.49
Jack Creel	11	15	.423	32	28	13	1	199	221	86	99	4.25
John Herr	9	5	.643	30	13	4	0	122	116	73	63	3.98
John Podgajny	6	2	.750	13	11	5	0	80	114	22	22	4.61
Wes Cunningham	5	5	.500	40		0	0	113	105	40	41	2.95
Frank Barrett	4	3	.571	16		0	0	67	53	24	44	2.28
Elmer Burkart	4	3	.571	8	8	4	0	48	52	19	13	3.56
LeRoy Pfund	4	4	.500	19	9	1	0	70	96	36	25	5.91
Thomas Ananicz	3	3	.500	12	7	4	1	46	62	18	18	5.87
Arthur Frantz	1	2	.333	8		0	0	28	38	11	14	3.86
Edward Blake	1	3	.250	8	4	1	0	26	23	6	5	6.58

INDIANAPOLIS   6th   57-93   .380   -43.5   Bush - Kelly
Indians

BATTERS	POS-GAMES	GP	AB	R	H	BI	2B	3B	HR	BB	SO	SB	BA
Kirby Farrell	1B123,P6	123	458	53	134	44	9	5	2	34	24	7	.293
Ed Borom	2B55,3B19	79	311	50	84	16	9	2	0	20	26	9	.270
Joe Aliperto	SS87	94	288	20	62	25	7	3	1	23	57	4	.215
Gil English	3B48,OF32,1B15	91	332	59	107	47	18	6	4	34	14	2	.322
Wayne Blackburn	OF134,3B17	149	535	104	180	65	23	7	1	99	29	25	.336
Chet Clemens	OF101	101	405	82	119	43	10	10	3	31	30	21	.294
Ed Morgan	OF43,1B20	65	213	27	67	33	10	3	1	31	12	4	.315
Hugh Poland	C113	123	413	37	115	64	20	4	2	19	23	6	.278
Bill Heltzel	SS58,3B15	70	235	16	50	18	7	1	0	20	20	1	.213
Robert Logan	P33,OF31	66	168	13	38	16	4	1	0	7	18	2	.226
Russ Lyon	C45	64	167	17	59	15	14	1	2	16	13	1	.353
Mike Sabena	3B25,2B17,OF16	61	205	22	65	12	8	0	0	11	13	3	.317
Joe Burns	2B48	59	232	29	70	34	12	3	1	16	22	4	.302
Harry Kelley	P43	43	57	4	12	8	1	0	0	2	3	0	.211
Woody Rich	P26	41	76	2	19	8	2	0	0	3	5	0	.250
George Mitrus	3B29	39	113	15	21	5	6	0	1	7	15	0	.186
Nick Rhabe	OF30	38	115	12	27	12	0	0	0	7	8	1	.235
John Hutchings	P22	34	55	2	11	6	2	0	0	9	9	0	.200
Carl Lindquist	P28	32	41	3	6	3	1	1	0	2	19	0	.146
Roy Herndon	OF11	25	54	6	12	10	1	0	1	7	5	3	.222
David Odom	P21	21	29	4	6	2	1	0	0	2	11	0	.207
Charles Anderson	2B12	18	54	2	12	3	3	0	0	5	10	0	.222
Frank Wilkie		16	30	6	6	2	1	0	0	6	9	1	.200
Wes Flowers	P14	15	31	5	7	4	1	0	0	2	8	0	.226
Paul Bowman	OF11	13	29	4	5	2	0	0	0	3	8	0	.172
Norm Schlueter	C12	12	33	4	9	2	2	0	0	4	2	0	.273
John Lehman	OF,1B	11	22	0	4	0	0	0	0	1	3	2	.182
Stan Klopp	P10	10	11	0	2	0	1	0	0	3	4	0	.182
John Donahue	P9	9	14	3	5	1	0	0	0			0	.357
Nick Kanavas	P6	6	5		0								.000
Al Bronkhurst	P4	4	3		0								.000
Allyn Stout	P3	3	3		0								.000
Preston Wint	OF	3	1	1	0	0	0	0	0			0	.000
Robert Martin	P3	3	0		0								----

PITCHERS	W	L	PCT	G	GS	CG	SH	IP	H	BB	SO	ERA
Robert Logan	12	11	.522	33	24	18	1	225	224	57	98	3.08
Harry Kelley	9	9	.500	43	14	7	0	163	201	49	58	3.81
Wes Flowers	6	4	.600	14	10	0	0	80	83	41	36	3.94

INDIANAPOLIS (cont.)
Indians

PITCHERS	W	L	PCT	G	GS	CG	SH	IP	H	BB	SO	ERA
Carl Lindquist	6	13	.316	28	18	8	0	124	145	73	45	5.81
John Hutchings	6	13	.316	22	18	11	1	132	147	46	81	4.70
Woody Rich	4	14	.222	26	20	11	1	168	204	94	103	4.50
Stan Klopp	3	4	.429	10	7	2	2	46	53	33	24	4.70
John Donahue	2	3	.400	9	6	1	0	33	46	25	16	9.55
David Odom	2	4	.333	21	11	2	0	81	84	61	43	6.33
Al Bronkhurst	1	1	.500	4	2	1	0	12	11	3	5	2.25
Allyn Stout	0	1	.000	3		0	0	7	7	6	3	7.71
Nick Kanavas	0	2	.000	6	3	1	0	17	17	11	5	4.24
Kerby Farrell	0	0	----	6		0	0	22	33	8	5	6.95
Robert Martin	0	0	----	3		0	0	3	6	4	2	

MINNEAPOLIS   7th   54-97   .358   -47   Wilfred Ryan
Millers

BATTERS	POS-GAMES	GP	AB	R	H	BI	2B	3B	HR	BB	SO	SB	BA
Bill Ebranyi	1B116,P7	134	390	37	100	39	12	0	4	75	43	2	.256
Fred Vaughn	2B123	125	445	73	143	62	24	9	17	39	70	16	.321
Frank Danneker	SS108,3B34	142	497	91	133	51	24	7	14	85	45	32	.268
Mike Blazo	3B97,C47	142	495	64	132	63	21	4	2	51	34	10	.267
Jim Cookson	OF138	141	564	87	172	42	19	2	0	44	41	47	.305
Babe Barna	OF98	106	325	67	97	85	20	2	24	61	44	12	.298
Robert Dill	OF91	112	320	39	88	46	22	7	3	44	59	9	.275
Jack Aragon	C117	127	372	35	74	43	16	2	7	52	76	7	.199
Hugh Todd	OF74	96	280	42	81	43	13	6	4	37	21	5	.289
Vern Curtis	P44	46	82	6	12	1	0	0	0	6	24	1	.146
Harold Wonson	P38	42	42	3	6	0	1	0	0	2	10	0	.143
Bill Sahlin	P41	41	32	6	5	1	3	0	0	6	14	0	.156
Joe Vosmik	OF29,P1	39	111	17	31	16	3	0	1	14	5	0	.279
Bill Schaedler	1B21	36	89	11	24	14	7	0	4	14	17	1	.270
Herbert Bain	P35	35	72	2	6	3	0	0	0	3	21	0	.083
Al Wright	OF28	32	101	15	27	15	4	0	4	16	14	2	.267
Elon Hogsett	P31	31	33	9	9	6	1	0	0	0	7	0	.273
Larry Bettencourt	OF16	29	69	10	17	7	4	0	0	7	7	4	.246
Harley Boss	1B25	27	87	3	21	9	0	0	0	3	6	1	.241
Arnold Lehrman	SS24	24	78	13	15	9	3	0	1	6	10	2	.192
Harold Swanson	P20	21	40	5	12	0	1	0	0	1	10	0	.300
Greg Lippold	P20	20	22	1	2	1	0	0	0	1	15	0	.091
Ray Mosley	P16	16	13	0	2	0	0	0	0	0	5	0	.154
Claude Horton	P13	13	13	2	2	2	0	0	0	1	4	1	.154
Ed Lichenstein	SS,3B	12	20	2	2	1	0	1	0	4	3	0	.100
Henry Nicklasson	SS11	11	42	6	17	1	3	0	0	5	2	2	.405
Wayne Johnson	P10	10	3	0	1	0	0	0	0	0	2	0	.333
Sam Rooney	3B	9	25	3	6	2	1	1	0			0	.240
Joe Frantz	2B	7	26	2	6	4	0	0	0			0	.231
Clarence Dowling	OF	7	6	1	1	0	0	0	0			0	.167
Richard Meyers	3B	6	11	0	0	0	0	0	0			0	.000
Pedro Gomez	SS	5	14	0	0	0	0	0	0			1	.000
Jesse Pinkston	OF	5	8	0	2	0	0	0	0			0	.250
John Dowling	OF	4	8	1	1	1	0	0	0			0	.125
Mike Kash	P2	2	2		1								.500
Joe Hanzlik	P2	2	1		0								.000
Charles Johnson	P1	1	2		0								.000

PITCHERS	W	L	PCT	G	GS	CG	SH	IP	H	BB	SO	ERA
Vern Curtis	15	17	.469	44	30	16	2	249	256	114	135	4.01
Herbert Bain	11	17	.393	35	30	9	2	197	249	81	82	5.44
Harold Swanson	8	10	.444	20	16	6	0	110	143	28	37	5.07
Elon Hogsett	5	7	.417	31		0	0	87	118	33	38	6.83
Greg Lippold	4	10	.286	20	18	2	0	73	107	42	32	8.38
Roy Mosley	2	2	.500	16		0	0	40	59	19	4	6.08
Wayne Johnson	1	0	1.000	10		0	0	18	25	15	4	6.50
Claude Horton	1	3	.250	13	5	1	0	32	48	18	14	6.75
Bill Ebranyi	0	1	.000	7		0	0	17	22	9	6	6.35
Harold Wonson	0	6	.000	38	5	2	0	122	163	46	39	6.20
Bill Sahlin	0	14	.000	40	20	2	0	118	126	122	57	6.71
Joe Hanzlik	0	0	----	2		0	0	5	4	1	0	
Mike Kash	0	0	----	2		0	0	4	4	3	0	
Charles Johnson	0	0	----	1		0	0	6	9	3	2	
Joe Vosmik	0	0	----	1		0	0	4	9	6	0	

KANSAS CITY   8th   41-110   .272   -60   Jack Saltzgaver
Blues

BATTERS	POS-GAMES	GP	AB	R	H	BI	2B	3B	HR	BB	SO	SB	BA
Gene Corbett	1B103	103	364	39	98	42	22	4	3	42	39	4	.269
Charles Glunt	2B91,3B63	152	610	79	187	55	30	4	3	23	34	5	.307
Mike Portner	SS46	49	194	27	51	19	6	2	1	17	30	7	.263
Gene Roberts	3B35	39	118	6	15	9	2	0	0	10	31	2	.127
Jesse Landrum	OF144	148	562	78	175	82	22	10	10	36	33	5	.311
Stan Platek	OF129	137	455	46	116	63	15	4	3	58	44	5	.255
William Kats	OF69	73	271	47	85	10	8	2	0	36	32	5	.314
Q. Taylor	C43	51	149	9	33	9	3	1	0	16	22	1	.221
Jack Saltzgaver	2B47,3B20	85	210	42	73	22	12	4	1	53	13	1	.348
Golden Holt	OF55,3B10,P1	80	239	26	59	22	6	1	1	28	22	3	.247
Roy Musser	OF50	50	184	24	48	19	4	1	1	13	30	1	.261
Roy Zimmerman	1B46	47	174	19	51	22	14	2	0	12	5	3	.293
Herb Upton	SS43	43	149	2	18	3	0	0	0	3	53	0	.121
Fred Pepper	P36	42	78	8	19	6	5	0	0	3	21	0	.244
Richard Morgan	C28	41	87	10	16	5	1	1	0	6	26	0	.184
Elmer Singleton	P26	32	53	12	11	2	1	0	0	4	14	0	.208
Vince DiBiasi	P29	31	67	6	12	6	1	0	0	4	14	1	.179
William Davis	P31	31	57	5	12	4	0	0	0	4	21	0	.211
Ed Patrow	3B27	29	87	10	21	2	1	1	0	14	19	0	.241
Joe Bodner	SS28	28	93	9	22	7	4	1	0	6	11	2	.237
Marvin McNulty	C19	28	65	5	13	5	1	0	0	8	8	0	.200
Walt Sierotko	C16	25	59	4	11	4	0	0	0	3	15	0	.186
Chris McKenna	OF11	21	45	1	9	8	3	0	1	3	13	0	.200
Don Johnson	P18	18	46	1	7	2	0	0	0	2	13	0	.152
Charles Shanklin	P18	18	28	0	0	1	0	0	0	1	14	0	.000
James Goff	P14	15	7	0	0	0	0	0	0	1	3	0	.000
Bill Wiley	P14	14	13	0	1	1	0	0	0	0	12	0	.077
Carl Hower	C13	13	27	2	9	7	2	0	0	2	2	0	.333
Ken Gables	P9	9	4		0								.000
John Phillips	P7	8	11		2								.182
John Rager	P5	5	3		1								.333
Ray Uniak	P5	5	2		0								.000
Jerry Crosby	3B	4	11	0	0	0	0	0	0			0	.000
Roger Gruenewald	P2	3	3		0								.000
Eldon Clark	P3	3	2		0								.000
Charles Carter	P2	2	5		0								.000
Alex Zych	OF	2	2	0	0	0	0	0	0			0	.000
Maurice Belshe	P2	2	0		0								----
Robert Musulas	2B1	1	3	1	1	0	0	0	0			0	.333
James Propst	P1	1	3		0								.000
Al Wittmer	P1	1	1		0								.000
Gene McCready	C	1	1	0	0	0	0	0	0			0	.000
Don King	P1	1	0		0								----

PITCHERS	W	L	PCT	G	GS	CG	SH	IP	H	BB	SO	ERA
Elmer Singleton	7	11	.389	26	21	12	0	150	163	71	63	4.38
Vince DiBiasi	7	18	.280	29	25	15	1	194	201	107	98	4.59
William Davis	6	17	.261	31	25	12	1	175	217	84	53	5.55
Fred Pepper	5	18	.217	36	26	11	2	176	215	100	47	5.83
Don Johnson	3	11	.214	18	18	9	0	131	147	53	67	4.40
Charles Shanklin	2	10	.167	18	11	7	0	96	130	52	19	5.72
James Propst	1	0	1.000	1	1	1	0	7	4	3	4	1.29
Charles Carter	1	1	.500	2		0	0	10	12	11	2	7.20
John Phillips	1	5	.167	7	5	1	0	28	44	30	10	11.57
John Rager	0	1	.000	5		0	0	13	23	6	5	8.31
Bill Wiley	0	2	.000	14	2	1	0	39	50	43	20	8.54
James Goff	0	2	.000	14		0	0	33	47	10	13	5.73
Ray Uniak	0	2	.000	5		0	0	13	13	10	7	4.85
Ken Gables	0	3	.000	9		0	0	19	31	15	11	10.42
Eldon Clark	0	0	----	3		0	0	5	8	3	1	
Roger Gruenewald	0	0	----	2		0	0	4	6	11	0	
Maurice Belshe	0	0	----	2		0	0	1	5	11	0	
Golden Holt	0	0	----	1		0	0	5	12	1	1	
Al Wittmer	0	0	----	1		0	0	4	3	3	2	
Don King	0	0	----	1		0	0	1	6	2	1	

MULTI-TEAM PLAYERS

BATTERS	POS-GAMES	TEAMS	GP	AB	R	H	BI	2B	3B	HR	BB	SO	SB	BA
Como Cotelle	OF110	IND-LOU	115	385	53	132	68	18	9	1	28	16	5	.343

MULTI-TEAM PLAYERS (cont.)

BATTERS	POS-GAMES	TEAMS	GP	AB	R	H	BI	2B	3B	HR	BB	SO	SB	BA
Frank Piet	SS76,OF13	SP-LOU	103	335	41	92	44	19	0	6	20	21	6	.275
Alton Biggs	3B38,SS38,2B33	KC-MIL	98	387	48	132	59	21	5	0	24	26	11	.341
Tom Padden	C55	MIN-SP	69	145	11	33	13	7	0	1	20	21	0	.228
Thomas Jordan	C57	MIL-KC	66	219	27	78	43	15	3	4	6	10	0	.356
Arnie Berge	2B23,SS18	LOU-MIN	57	137	16	28	13	3	0	0	11	14	4	.204
Richard Hearn	P39	MIL-KC	39	31	3	1	0	0	0	0	2	11	0	.032
Fred Schulte	OF25	SP-IND	37	99	9	19	5	5	0	0	7	6	0	.192
Don Hendrickson	P35	KC-MIL	35	50	4	11	2	2	0	0	4	11	0	.220
Otis Clark	P32	MIN-LOU	32	75	4	9	4	0	0	0	3	14	0	.120
Ed Schweiwe	SS14	MIL-KC	30	70	6	17	8	3	2	0	5	9	0	.243
Ollie Byers	P30	LOU-IND	30	68	9	6	1	0	0	0	10	13	0	.088
Stan Partenheimer	P27	LOU-COL	28	76	8	14	4	3	0	0	6	16	0	.184
George Diehl	P23	IND-LOU	23	46	2	7	2	0	0	0	3	15	0	.152
Pat Capri	2B16	COL-IND	20	66	12	21	9	2	0	0	9	5	0	.318
Charles Bates	C10	KC-SP	13	26	1	6	3	1	1	0	3	6	0	.231
Robert Bowman	P13	MIL-MIN	13	1	1	1	0	0	0	0	0	0	0	1.000
Phil Coggswell	C	TOL-COL	9	16	5	2	1	0	0	0			0	.125
Ray Campbell	P7	TOL-LOU	7	8		2								.250
H. McCormick	P5	MIN-KC	5	1		0								.000

PITCHERS	TEAMS	W	L	PCT	G	GS	CG	SH	IP	H	BB	SO	ERA
Stan Partenheimer	LOU-COL	16	7	.696	27	25	17	1	204	231	90	127	3.26
Don Hendrickson	KC-MIL	12	7	.632	35	11	6	2	161	160	40	77	2.57
Otis Clark	MIN-LOU	12	14	.462	32	30	17	0	211	235	57	58	4.01
Ollie Byers	LOU-IND	10	11	.476	30	21	11	1	184	216	61	74	4.84
Richard Hearn	MIL-KC	6	7	.462	39	10	5	0	103	123	75	47	7.34
George Diehl	IND-LOU	5	11	.313	23	20	8	1	136	185	48	48	5.96
Robert Bowman	MIL-MIN	1	0	1.000	13		0	0	12	22	13	3	12.00
Ray Campbell	TOL-LOU	1	0	1.000	7		0	0	16	24	16	6	11.25
H. McCormick	MIN-KC	0	0	----	5		0	0	8	5	10	2	

TEAM BATTING

TEAMS	GP	AB	R	H	BI	2B	3B	HR	BB	SO	SB	BA
MILWAUKEE	154	5226	954	1604	889	234	54	135	597	555	97	.307
TOLEDO	154	5161	854	1470	765	266	61	72	589	514	90	.285
LOUISVILLE	150	5039	852	1436	757	214	85	68	655	584	128	.285
ST. PAUL	153	4852	706	1311	630	200	43	72	504	544	100	.270
COLUMBUS	155	5340	814	1478	744	294	59	71	594	546	64	.277
INDIANAPOLIS	152	5084	640	1407	568	188	49	49	453	456	96	.277
MINNEAPOLIS	151	4939	661	1287	586	205	41	85	600	663	158	.261
KANSAS CITY	153	5056	573	1346	524	194	46	28	442	660	51	.266
	611	40697	6054	11339	5463	1795	438	580	4434	4522	784	.279

1945
Green Light

During World War I, baseball was treated as an enemy of the war effort. The United States issued a "work or fight" order designed to curtail frivolous activities such as baseball. The work order succeeded in that all minor leagues save one shut down their operations for the duration of the conflict. When World War II reared its ugly head, the United States was once again in a position of cutting nonessential activities. This time, however, the top level of baseball was largely spared.

The war years brought lean times to most of minor league baseball. Travel restrictions and lack of personnel caused many circuits to suspend operations. However some of the top leagues, including the American Association, kept going. This was largely due to intervention from the highest level. During the early part of the war, the major league commissioner sent inquiries to President Roosevelt about the status of baseball during the war, offering to shut it down. Roosevelt replied with what is known as the "green light" letter. Rightly perceiving the tremendous boost in morale that baseball provided a war-weary country, the President gave his thumbs up to its continuance, thus ensuring that baseball would not be shut down by the war.

Grateful for continued operation, the American Association responded by helping with the war effort. Some games were staged in the morning to offer night shift workers the pleasure of attending a game. Other activities included exhibition games staged with service teams to help raise money for the war effort.

In 1945, Milwaukee won its third straight pennant by a slim margin over Indianapolis. Louisville and St. Paul finished third and fourth, while Minneapolis, Toledo, Kansas City, and Columbus ended fifth through eighth. Lewis Flick of Milwaukee was the top batter (.374), and Babe Barna won his second straight home run title (25). Eugene Nance of Milwaukee had the most runs batted in (106). Pitching honors went to Owen Scheetz of the Brewers who won 19; James Wallace of Indianapolis, who had an earned run average of 1.83; and Cliff Fannin of Toledo, who struck out 126.

As the 1945 season entered its latter stages, World War II came to an end. Although not contributing directly to the Allies' victory, baseball gave its share by providing countless hours of enjoyment to the American people. This "green light" given baseball certainly proved to be a far better idea than the "red light" flashed a quarter century before.

MILWAUKEE Brewers

| | 1st | 93-61 | .604 | | | | Nick Cullop |

BATTERS	POS-GAMES	GP	AB	R	H	BI	2B	3B	HR	BB	SO	SB	BA
Otto Denning	1B141	143	483	79	148	92	21	5	9	82	30	15	.306
Joe Rullo	2B116	123	475	79	133	47	24	2	4	42	43	7	.277
Alton Biggs	SS89,2B41	135	513	93	164	70	26	5	6	64	42	7	.320
Eugene Nance	3B151	152	564	94	179	106	27	7	17	57	54	5	.317
Bill Burgo	OF144	147	530	60	147	86	27	3	6	42	43	7	.280
Lew Flick	OF139	142	575	90	215	92	32	10	11	25	23	12	.374
John Rosenthal	OF74	74	254	47	77	40	12	3	4	51	32	4	.303
Joe Stephenson	C120	123	405	54	111	50	15	6	4	35	62	0	.274
Ed Kobesky	OF46	57	175	18	33	16	4	0	2	25	17	2	.189
Willis Norman	OF49	53	148	20	35	12	7	1	0	51	24	6	.236
Julio Acosta	P29	34	70	12	16	8	1	0	1	6	13	0	.229
Floyd Speer	P33	33	60	3	11	3	1	0	0	5	12	0	.183
Elmer Weingartner	SS27	28	104	18	30	6	8	0	0	14	7	1	.288
Owen Scheetz	P27	28	83	3	19	17	3	0	0	5	12	1	.229
Wendell Davis	P26	28	50	10	19	12	6	0	1	1	1	0	.380
Tom Padden	C24	24	82	10	22	7	2	0	2	7	14	3	.268
Carl Lindquist	P24	24	50	5	10	8	3	1	1	2	22	0	.200
Michael Ulisney	C13	21	56	6	9	4	2	0	0	4	9	0	.161
Don Hendrickson	P18	18	33	4	8	4	2	0	0	6	3	0	.242
Ewald Pyle	P15	15	39	5	11	1	0	0	0	2	10	0	.282
John McGillen	P12	13	11	3	5	0	0	0	0	1	0	0	.455
Clarence Etchison	1B10	12	32	8	9	4	0	0	1	12	4	0	.281
Tony Mazurek	OF,1B	12	31	4	8	1	1	1	0	1	7	0	.258
Ray Davis	P12	12	9	1	3	1	0	0	0	2	2	0	.333
Felix Martignetti	1B	7	17	3	2	1	0	0	0			0	.118
Jack Farmer	P7	7	6		0								.000
Aldo Caravello	SS	6	4	2	2	0	0	0	0			0	.500
Charles Carroll	OF	5	11	1	2	0	1	0	0			0	.182
Florian Zielinski	SS	2	6	2	2	0	0	0	0			1	.333
Joe Sosnowski	PH	2	2	0	1	0	0	0	0			0	.500
Joe Roxbury	P2	2	0		0								----
Eugene Edwards	C1	1	2	0	1	0	0	0	0			0	.500

PITCHERS	W	L	PCT	G	GS	CG	SH	IP	H	BB	SO	ERA
Owen Scheetz	19	8	.704	27	25	20	4	226	206	40	90	1.95
Wendell Davis	15	4	.789	26	9	5	2	110	117	41	42	3.85
Julio Acosta	15	10	.600	29	22	17	2	186	178	83	84	3.44
Floyd Speer	12	8	.600	33	22	13	1	182	202	35	104	3.71
Don Hendrickson	8	2	.800	18	12	10	0	106	117	32	52	2.72
Carl Lindquist	8	5	.615	24	19	11	1	136	173	63	51	5.56
Ewald Pyle	7	5	.583	15	13	8	0	104	104	46	61	4.41
John McGillen	1	1	.500	12	3	1	0	32	32	18	7	3.66
Jack Farmer	0	2	.000	7		0	0	17	23	5	5	6.35
Ray Davis	0	3	.000	12	4	2	0	35	51	10	13	4.11
Joe Roxbury	0	0	----	2		0	0	1	8	5	0	
John Price	0	0	----	1		0	0	1	1	0	2	0.00

INDIANAPOLIS Indians

| | 2nd | 90-63 | .592 | -2.5 | | | Bill Burwell |

BATTERS	POS-GAMES	GP	AB	R	H	BI	2B	3B	HR	BB	SO	SB	BA
Joe Mack	1B80	80	279	56	93	46	15	1	5	55	37	0	.333
Ben Geraghty	2B116	117	411	63	111	25	11	5	0	69	41	5	.270
Bill Heltzel	SS141	142	496	64	125	48	24	1	5	59	56	2	.252
Gil English	3B114,OF26	137	504	81	144	97	26	6	9	48	37	2	.286
Stan Wentzel	OF154	154	574	102	184	103	35	11	14	48	75	30	.321
Art Parks	OF133	138	513	104	160	68	27	4	8	76	29	0	.312
Robert Dill	OF	(see multi-team players)											
Bob Brady	C107	116	387	40	109	63	17	8	1	35	35	2	.282
George Detore	C52	78	186	19	44	22	5	0	1	25	17	2	.237
Vince Shupe	1B73	73	295	47	93	47	15	10	3	18	15	2	.315
Norm Wallen	3B51	58	157	12	38	16	3	0	2	11	21	1	.242
Pedro Jimenez	P39	47	75	7	24	8	7	0	0	1	7	0	.320
Wes Flowers	P41	41	73	9	14	6	6	0	0	3	10	0	.192
Stephen Shemo	2B23	35	105	20	31	10	7	1	0	15	9	3	.295
Frank Wilkie	SS14,P3	31	56	10	12	6	3	0	0	7	25	1	.214
James Wallace	P25	30	68	11	12	2	3	1	0	7	21	0	.176
George Jeffcoat	P29	29	38	0	4	3	1	0	0	0	10	0	.105
Tom Davis	OF22	24	65	6	14	6	3	0	0	12	12	1	.215
Jess Pike	OF20	22	72	10	24	15	1	1	1	9	8	1	.333

INDIANAPOLIS (cont.)
Indians

BATTERS	POS-GAMES	GP	AB	R	H	BI	2B	3B	HR	BB	SO	SB	BA
Ed Wright	P20	21	62	12	19	8	3	0	0	2	2	0	.306
Harry Durheim	P21	21	20	3	6	2	0	0	0	2	1	0	.300
Glenn Fletcher	P20	20	40	3	9	2	2	0	0	1	4	0	.225
Woody Rich	P18	18	24	2	6	0	1	0	0	4	2	0	.250
Robert Fletcher	2B14	14	44	5	10	9	1	2	0	8	5	1	.227
Ira Hutchinson	P11	11	23	2	4	0	0	0	0	2	4	0	.174
Tom Earley	P10	10	15	1	3	1	0	0	0	0	3	0	.200
Mike Roscoe	P5	5	6		0								.000
Harold Schacker	P5	5	1		0								.000
Robert Logan	P4	4	9		2								.222
David Odom	P4	4	1		0								.000
Al Hazel	P1	1	1		0								.000
Al Haines	P1	1	0		0								----
Walt Dickerson	P1	1	0		0								----

PITCHERS		W	L	PCT	G	GS	CG	SH	IP	H	BB	SO	ERA
James Wallace		17	4	.810	25	22	15	7	177	153	59	124	1.83
Ed Wright		13	5	.722	20	18	12	2	146	118	54	51	3.08
Wes Flowers		13	12	.520	41	26	12	4	201	212	89	84	4.34
Pedro Jiminez		11	6	.647	39	16	9	0	160	175	58	59	3.77
Harry Durheim		8	3	.727	21	9	3	1	79	85	42	30	3.76
Glenn Fletcher		8	6	.571	20	13	6	2	104	97	59	55	3.38
George Jeffcoat		7	6	.538	29	12	5	3	104	108	52	43	3.63
Woody Rich		6	4	.600	18	11	3	0	73	82	38	47	4.56
Tom Earley		2	2	.500	10		0	0	35	51	11	10	6.94
Ira Hutchinson		2	6	.250	11	10	3	0	70	76	29	24	4.76
Robert Logan		1	1	.500	4	3	1	0	21	19	14	0	2.57
Mike Roscoe		0	2	.000	5	2	1	0	14	26	13	2	15.42
Harold Schacker		0	2	.000	5		0	0	11	13	5	5	5.73
David Odom		0	0	----	4		0	0	7	3	6	2	
Frank Wilkie		0	0	----	3		0	0	9	6	9	2	
Al Hazel		0	0	----	1		0	0	2	2	0	3	
Walt Dickerson		0	0	----	1		0	0	1	2	1	1	
Al Haines		0	0	----	1		0	0	1	3	0	0	

LOUISVILLE   3rd   84-70   .545   -10   Harry Leibold
Colonels

BATTERS	POS-GAMES	GP	AB	R	H	BI	2B	3B	HR	BB	SO	SB	BA
Earle Browne	1B145,P1	146	539	72	147	83	16	7	5	57	20	7	.273
Charles Koney	2B138	139	513	69	141	72	24	3	4	37	37	12	.275
Frank Shofner	SS128,3B17	144	524	75	156	68	18	13	1	39	47	13	.298
Nick Polly	3B		(see multi-team players)										
Frank Genovese	OF154	154	541	93	151	49	27	10	4	121	37	25	.279
Stephen Barath	OF108	121	381	65	111	66	27	4	15	63	65	6	.291
Bill Howerton	OF72,SS2	81	208	43	56	33	12	5	5	22	25	6	.269
Jack Aragon	C		(see multi-team players)										
Byron LaForest	OF42,3B21,SS14	91	306	57	108	43	15	5	2	35	41	14	.353
Como Cotelle	OF52	58	188	29	51	23	9	2	1	19	5	6	.271
Walter Millies	C42	50	120	12	26	12	5	0	0	16	3	0	.217
Dwight Simonds	P39	45	35	8	9	4	0	1	0	0	7	0	.257
Ben Steiner	3B42	44	167	17	36	16	9	2	1	16	11	7	.216
Gerard Lipscomb	3B10	40	92	13	24	11	5	0	1	14	7	0	.261
Lindsey Deal	OF23	39	90	15	33	15	5	1	0	11	2	3	.367
Dick Callahan	P29	35	64	7	16	9	2	0	0	2	21	0	.250
Don Thompson	P22,OF	34	46	9	12	6	2	3	0	7	5	0	.261
Al Widmer	P33	33	54	4	8	2	2	0	0	2	10	0	.148
Elwood Lawson	P33	33	39	4	8	5	2	0	0	7	10	0	.205
Fred Walters	C29	31	94	17	32	19	6	1	2	16	4	0	.340
Rex Cecil	P28	31	62	6	16	2	2	1	0	9	8	2	.258
George Diehl	P21	24	39	1	5	3	0	0	1	4	17	0	.128
Otis Clark	P23	23	45	3	9	5	1	0	0	1	8	0	.200
Joe Koney	SS17	17	53	7	13	8	2	2	0	3	7	0	.245
Ray Patton	P14	15	21	0	2	1	0	0	0	0	7	0	.095
Fred Chumley	P13	15	16	2	2	1	0	0	0	0	2	0	.125
Randolph Heflin	P8	9	22		4								.182
Yank Terry	P7	7	14		2								.143
Ed Zipay	1B	6	9	0	2	0	0	0	0			0	.222
Herschel Held	3B,OF	5	15	1	1	1	0	0	0			0	.067
Charles Roberts	C	5	12	1	1	0	0	0	0			0	.083
John Lund	P4	4	1		0								.000

LOUISVILLE (cont.)
Colonels

BATTERS	POS-GAMES	GP	AB	R	H	BI	2B	3B	HR	BB	SO	SB	BA
Frank Piet	3B,OF	3	7	1	1	0	0	0	0			0	.143
Vic Austin	3B	2	4	0	1	0	0	0	0			0	.250
Joe Langworthy	C1	1	2	1	0	0	0	0	0			0	.000
Bill Molyneaux	C1	1	1	0	0	0	0	0	0			0	.000

PITCHERS		W	L	PCT	G	GS	CG	SH	IP	H	BB	SO	ERA
Dwight Simonds		13	5	.722	39	7	5	1	116	137	46	40	3.80
Otis Clark		11	6	.647	23	19	11	1	126	123	51	46	4.07
Dick Callahan		10	5	.667	29	17	10	1	147	133	90	87	3.92
Al Widmar		10	8	.556	33	20	2	0	153	160	94	64	4.76
Rex Cecil		10	9	.526	28	20	12	2	161	149	70	98	2.96
Don Thompson		6	8	.429	22	16	7	3	113	91	101	94	3.66
George Diehl		6	9	.400	21	15	7	0	122	122	36	42	3.47
Elwood Lawson		5	6	.455	33	14	2	1	117	108	98	75	4.00
Yank Terry		4	2	.667	7	7	4	2	41	45	12	20	3.29
Randolph Heflin		3	2	.600	8	7	4	0	55	56	23	37	3.76
Ray Patton		3	4	.429	14	7	1	0	50	53	40	42	5.76
Fred Chumley		1	2	.333	13	1	1	0	43	43	37	10	5.02
John Lund		0	1	.000	4	0	0	0	9	15	3	4	7.00
Earle Browne		0	0	----	1		0	0	2	3	0	0	0.00

ST. PAUL   4th   75-76   .497   -16.5   Ray Blades
Saints

BATTERS	POS-GAMES	GP	AB	R	H	BI	2B	3B	HR	BB	SO	SB	BA
Paul Schoendienst	1B114	127	432	61	136	48	30	6	2	26	32	8	.315
Joe Vitter	2B95,OF31	127	468	80	117	45	25	5	5	67	48	9	.250
Tom Brown	SS80	85	301	54	86	48	13	3	10	33	38	5	.286
Leighton Kimball	3B147	148	505	101	159	95	39	1	22	83	60	5	.315
Glenn Chapman	OF117	124	439	55	135	80	26	4	3	27	42	2	.308
Ed Yaeger	OF91	93	330	49	75	23	5	3	0	49	49	10	.227
Don Lund	OF72	72	247	25	65	30	12	7	0	16	31	6	.263
Sam Narron	C78	90	292	29	74	53	23	3	5	15	22	1	.253
Bill Lewis	C74	90	195	24	57	30	7	3	1	47	8	0	.292
Ed Schweiwe	OF36,2B15	64	156	30	49	27	9	0	5	21	23	4	.314
Walt Tauscher	P61	61	21	2	1	0	0	0	0	3	5	0	.048
Stan Platek	OF51	60	192	23	46	23	8	2	0	22	19	2	.240
Claude Weaver	P45	45	53	5	8	1	1	0	0	9	6	0	.151
William Boaz	2B38	43	105	5	16	6	3	1	0	5	7	0	.152
Bill Hart	SS38	38	136	36	50	46	9	0	17	18	16	2	.368
Richard Lanahan	P37	37	53	2	9	6	2	0	0	1	9	0	.170
Tom Sunkel	P28	29	56	8	10	4	3	0	0	8	16	0	.179
Robert Tart	P25	29	26	2	2	1	0	0	0	1	13	0	.077
Eugene Kelly	P16	25	39	5	8	1	0	0	0	2	12	0	.205
Carl Tucker	2B10	24	38	5	6	1	1	0	0	5	9	0	.158
Otho Nitcholas	P22	23	52	4	11	6	2	0	0	0	9	0	.212
Howard Schultz	1B19	19	82	19	30	13	4	0	1	3	4	3	.366
Frank Powaski	OF10	16	30	3	4	3	1	0	0	2	8	1	.133
Ken Mauer		16	26	3	3	3	2	0	0	6	2	0	.115
Ralph Branca	P15	15	31	3	4	2	0	0	0	2	10	0	.129
Ernest Rudolph	P15	15	23	0	3	0	0	0	0	2	9	0	.130
George Coffman	P11	12	5	0	0	1	0	0	0	1	2	0	.000
Loy Camp	P11	11	17	1	1	0	1	0	0	1	2	0	.059
Cecil Dunn	1B10	10	19	2	3	2	0	0	0	1	9	0	.158
Gene Corbett	1B,2B	10	16	1	5	3	1	0	1	0	6	0	.313
Jack Miller	P10	10	7	0	1	0	0	0	0	0	2	0	.143
John Dantonio	C	9	27	4	11	3	2	0	0			0	.407
Henry Welch	OF	6	5	3	1	1	1	0	0			0	.200
Pat Riley	OF	3	10	1	2	0	0	0	0			0	.200
Jack Capelle	2B	3	5	0	1	0	0	0	0			0	.200
Gene Werth	P3	3	0		0								----
George Dannels	P2	2	3	0	1	0	0	0	0			0	.333
J. Ford	C	2	1	0	0	0	0	0	0			0	.000
Martin Radmer	C	1	2	0	0	0	0	0	0			0	.000
LeRoy Hewite	P1	1	0		0								----

PITCHERS		W	L	PCT	G	GS	CG	SH	IP	H	BB	SO	ERA
Claude Weaver		15	10	.600	45	20	10	2	186	185	46	54	3.19
Tom Sunkel		13	8	.619	28	28	8	1	170	177	85	134	4.02
Otho Nitcholas		11	6	.647	22	19	12	4	143	139	36	49	2.90

ST. PAUL (cont.)
Saints

PITCHERS	W	L	PCT	G	GS	CG	SH	IP	H	BB	SO	ERA
Richard Lanahan	11	9	.550	37	22	7	4	152	155	97	68	3.73
Walt Tauscher	8	7	.533	61		0	0	104	105	41	35	3.98
Ralph Branca	6	5	.545	15	14	6	2	100	87	64	94	3.33
Ernest Rudolph	3	7	.300	15	12	4	0	77	82	48	37	4.56
Robert Tart	3	11	.214	25	13	1	0	83	80	73	35	4.55
Eugene Kelly	2	3	.400	16		0	0	74	64	40	38	3.04
Jack Miller	1	1	.500	10		0	0	20	20	23	11	7.65
Loy Camp	1	3	.250	11	9	2	1	56	70	27	23	4.98
George Dannels	0	1	.000	2	1	1	0	8	8	5	3	4.50
George Coffman	0	0	----	11		0	0	21	25	13	6	
Gene Werth	0	0	----	3		0	0	3	4	3	3	
LeRoy Hewite	0	0	----	1		0	0	1	1	0	0	0.00

MINNEAPOLIS		5th		72-81		.471		-20.5		Wilfred Ryan			
Millers													

BATTERS	POS-GAMES	GP	AB	R	H	BI	2B	3B	HR	BB	SO	SB	BA
Joe Lafata	1B146	146	495	83	135	69	25	3	5	69	83	9	.273
Frank Danneker	2B141	142	536	94	165	76	21	4	12	64	44	50	.308
Victor Males	SS		(see multi-team players)										
Nick Picciuto	3B98	99	336	60	88	40	17	1	8	55	59	10	.262
Henry Nowak	OF148	150	586	110	193	72	33	1	9	53	47	8	.329
Babe Barna	OF129	132	421	106	130	96	21	4	25	126	70	14	.309
Joe Cicero	OF56	65	198	27	56	28	13	0	2	27	31	4	.283
Mike Blazo	C69,3B10	86	242	27	65	38	9	1	1	40	28	3	.269
Robert Albertson	P47	61	61	6	16	8	2	0	0	12	20	0	.262
Elwood Kresal	OF49	60	183	33	41	32	4	3	7	19	34	2	.224
Mike Kash	P51	51	86	10	23	6	2	0	0	5	15	0	.267
Arnold Lehrman	SS43	44	133	15	29	12	3	1	0	21	19	1	.218
Woody Abernathy	P32	35	67	1	6	5	0	0	0	5	20	0	.090
Lou Lucier	P22	33	48	8	11	5	2	0	0	2	9	0	.229
Harold Swanson	P29	32	64	3	12	4	0	0	0	0	15	0	.188
Tomas Maulini	OF22	24	72	6	14	6	2	0	0	14	22	1	.194
Juan Ruiz	3B18	24	69	11	20	4	8	1	0	5	18	3	.290
Nick Jackimchuk	SS22	22	78	11	14	3	1	0	0	7	11	1	.179
Richard Hearn	P21	21	20	3	2	0	0	0	0	2	11	0	.100
Isidoro Leon	P16	19	36	3	9	4	0	0	0	3	6	0	.250
Bruce Sloan	OF	17	32	4	7	7	0	0	0	8	4	4	.219
Greg Lippold	P15	15	15	3	2	0	0	1	0	2	8	0	.133
Virginio Arteaga	1B	11	22	2	4	1	0	0	0	1	3	0	.182
Bernard Morel	P9	9	6		1								.167
John Chambers	P7	7	1		0								.000
Leo Lillienthal	P4	4	7	1	3	0	0	0	0			0	.429
Onisio Gonzalez	SS	3	5	0	0	0	0	0	0			0	.000
Harold Wonson	P3	3	0		0								----
Jose Carabello	P2	2	1		0								.000
Bill Sisler	P2	2	1		0								.000
Reynolds Erickson	PH	2	1	0	0	0	0	0	0			0	.000

PITCHERS	W	L	PCT	G	GS	CG	SH	IP	H	BB	SO	ERA
Harold Swanson	13	11	.542	29	20	12	1	165	205	58	49	4.75
Mike Kash	13	16	.448	51	23	12	1	223	282	86	91	4.96
Lou Lucier	9	5	.643	22	17	8	1	109	147	40	15	5.04
Woody Abernathy	9	13	.409	32	25	11	0	190	230	70	80	4.59
Isidoro Leon	6	5	.545	16	14	7	2	94	100	22	43	4.40
Greg Lippold	4	4	.500	15		0	0	50	78	29	12	8.82
Robert Albertson	4	5	.444	47		0	0	128	179	106	44	7.52
Bernard Morel	2	1	.667	9		0	0	17	24	6	2	5.82
Leo Lillienthal	1	0	1.000	4		0	0	16	16	7	4	2.25
Richard Hearn	1	4	.200	21	5	1	0	63	74	45	13	6.71
Bill Sisler	0	2	.000	2		0	0	2	7	5	0	31.50
John Chambers	0	0	----	7		0	0	8	7	8	3	
Harold Wonson	0	0	----	3		0	0	3	11	4	4	
Jose Carabello	0	0	----	2		0	0	3	7	1	1	

TOLEDO Mud Hens

TOLEDO Mud Hens	6th	69-84	.451	-23.5	Ollie Marquardt

BATTERS	POS-GAMES	GP	AB	R	H	BI	2B	3B	HR	BB	SO	SB	BA
Ed Ignesiak	1B147	147	525	75	143	102	18	11	12	79	75	4	.272
Robert Wren	2B124	128	468	80	149	49	15	7	6	60	26	14	.318
Dick Kimble	SS107	113	392	51	104	49	20	7	2	64	30	6	.265
Stephen Collins	3B84,2B28	114	447	53	129	55	11	4	2	27	13	4	.289
Fred Reinhart	OF138	138	507	70	160	52	28	6	0	60	28	4	.316
George Corona	OF90	95	336	59	105	48	16	1	3	36	22	4	.313
Don Smith	OF88	92	323	56	76	20	8	4	2	44	27	22	.235
James Crandall	C57	66	202	12	40	24	8	0	2	20	17	1	.198
Blackstone Thompson	SS52,OF23,3B20	105	329	39	74	28	17	3	0	46	38	5	.225
Robert Okrie	OF77	100	250	35	70	26	9	3	1	9	31	1	.280
Ed Lanfersieck	3B32	40	115	16	25	17	6	2	2	24	7	4	.217
Elwood Knierim	P37	40	37	3	7	2	0	0	0	5	10	0	.189
Walter Missler	C31	38	85	10	23	8	4	1	0	4	20	0	.271
Robert Comyn	C37	37	105	7	23	17	0	0	0	8	7	0	.219
Jim Mains	P36	37	37	1	5	0	0	1	0	2	14	0	.136
Cliff Fannin	P25	31	55	8	12	3	0	0	0	6	9	0	.218
Ned Garver	P31	31	45	3	10	6	1	0	0	9	5	0	.222
John Whitehead	P23	28	60	3	15	5	1	0	0	8	7	0	.250
John Miller	P17	25	43	12	13	14	1	0	4	9	11	0	.302
Earl Smalling	P24	25	25	0	1	1	0	0	0	0	3	0	.040
Al LaMacchia	P18	24	36	4	7	3	0	0	0	5	14	0	.194
Robert Boken	OF14	22	50	3	16	12	4	0	1	7	5	0	.320
Frank Jeric		22	44	7	6	4	1	0	0	3	10	0	.135
Sidney Peterson	P13	13	11	3	0	1	0	0	0	2	3	0	.000
Bill Staker		12	25	2	3	0	0	0	0	4	13	0	.120
John Pavlick	P10	12	23	0	5	3	0	0	0	2	2	0	.217
George Kaufman	P10	10	4	0	1	0	0	0	0	2	2	0	.250
Boris Martin	OF	9	30	6	9	3	2	0	1			0	.300
Al Kaiser	OF	9	20	4	9	2	2	1	0			0	.450
John Fayad	OF	9	13	1	1	0	0	0	0			0	.077
Sylvester Goedde	P7	7	16		2								.125
Bill Massalsky	OF	4	13	1	3	1	0	0	0			0	.231
Frank Pack	OF	4	8	0	1	0	0	1	0			0	.125
Clyde Humphrey	P4	4	4		0								.000
Don Crist	P3	3	3	0	1	1	0	0	0			0	.333
Roger Powell	P1	1	0		0								----

PITCHERS	W	L	PCT	G	GS	CG	SH	IP	H	BB	SO	ERA
Cliff Fannin	11	9	.550	25	22	13	2	161	165	79	126	3.41
Elwood Knierim	8	8	.500	37	12	7	0	127	147	49	61	4.25
John Miller	8	8	.500	17	16	11	2	115	122	36	71	3.99
John Whitehead	8	12	.400	23	23	11	1	157	196	14	45	4.01
Al LaMacchia	6	8	.429	18	16	9	2	114	106	31	62	3.71
Earl Smalling	5	5	.500	24	9	3	1	85	99	57	27	4.55
Jim Mains	5	8	.385	36	8	2	0	118	107	64	62	3.28
Ned Garver	5	8	.385	31	15	7	1	132	150	76	68	4.64
John Pavlick	4	4	.500	10	9	5	0	63	67	38	20	4.57
Sylvester Goedde	2	1	.667	7	6	1	0	39	44	25	16	5.31
Sidney Peterson	2	5	.286	13	4	2	0	40	65	26	17	10.35
Clyde Humphrey	1	1	.500	4		0	0	7	9	9	3	5.14
George Kaufman	0	1	.000	10		0	0	22	28	23	11	5.73
Don Crist	0	1	.000	3	2	1	0	10	10	4	7	2.70
Roger Powell	0	0	----	1		0	0	1	0	0	0	0.00

KANSAS CITY Blues

KANSAS CITY Blues	7th	65-86	.430	-26.5	Casey Stengel

BATTERS	POS-GAMES	GP	AB	R	H	BI	2B	3B	HR	BB	SO	SB	BA
Walt Nowak	1B98,OF20	116	428	62	143	80	23	9	6	45	57	15	.334
Melvin Serafini	2B57,3B22,P1	95	260	36	87	43	25	2	3	47	51	5	.335
Frank Zak	SS104	104	376	87	108	30	13	3	0	78	51	19	.287
John Ostrowski	3B134,SS14	144	558	102	166	99	28	4	13	48	70	14	.297
Lynn King	OF132	135	477	76	123	40	16	2	0	72	34	9	.258
John Devincenzi	OF101	112	345	42	90	59	18	2	7	57	52	3	.261
John Kreevich	OF71	71	242	34	71	31	13	2	3	24	23	9	.293
Bill Steinecke	C53	60	181	21	51	28	7	2	0	20	8	0	.282
Anthony Sabol	2B35,OF33	72	232	38	76	41	12	1	1	26	18	15	.328
John Bogard	2B42,OF12	67	190	24	54	29	10	2	0	20	24	1	.284
Wayne Tucker	SS31,1B16,2B14	64	236	30	65	28	4	2	1	19	26	7	.275
Herb Crompton	C49	53	160	19	40	20	5	0	0	18	11	0	.250

KANSAS CITY (cont.)
Blues

BATTERS	POS-GAMES	GP	AB	R	H	BI	2B	3B	HR	BB	SO	SB	BA
Joe Passero	OF42	49	141	25	40	20	3	3	6	31	15	4	.284
Clarence Marshall	P39	42	68	4	18	4	2	0	0	4	17	1	.265
Charles Suytar	1B33	39	118	15	31	13	9	0	1	14	16	1	.263
Harold Danielson	C38	39	93	9	21	4	2	1	0	8	23	0	.226
Gale Pringle	P38	39	47	4	11	9	3	2	0	4	17	0	.234
Dominic Castro	C31	35	95	5	16	11	2	0	0	7	10	0	.168
Edson Bahr	P29	34	71	4	11	2	3	0	0	2	17	0	.155
Roy Musser	OF29	30	95	9	15	8	0	1	0	5	14	0	.158
Ed Marleau	P30	30	10	0	0	0	0	0	0	1	4	0	.000
John Moore	P27	28	47	4	6	2	0	1	0	5	16	0	.128
John Cooney	OF21	27	108	20	37	9	2	1	0	7	3	0	.343
William Davis	P24	24	13	1	2	0	0	0	0	2	3	0	.154
Otto Meyers	OF14	19	45	8	16	7	2	0	0	13	5	0	.356
Alex Martin	P14	18	29	1	6	1	1	0	0	0	9	0	.207
Elmer Singleton	P17	17	41	3	9	4	2	0	0	5	13	0	.220
John Orphal	P14	14	33	4	12	4	1	0	0	2	4	0	.364
Fred Pepper	P13	14	30	3	3	1	0	0	0	2	9	0	.100
Jack Saltzgaver	2B,1B	11	31	6	8	5	3	1	0	10	4	2	.258
Daniel Doy	SS,2B	9	29	2	4	2	0	0	0			1	.138
Alva Emmertson	P9	9	5		0								.000
Joe Valenzuela	P7	8	16		3								.188
Jerry Crosby	OF	8	8	1	1	1	0	0	0			0	.125
Ted Pfennig	P6	6	4		0								.000
Ray Uniak	P6	6	0		0								----
Charles Cozart	P4	5	14		4								.286
Loren Babe	2B	5	8	2	3		0	0	0			1	.375
Chris McKenna	OF	4	7	1	3	4	0	0	0			0	.429
Giles Knowles	P4	4	1		0								.000
Ray Stelmack	P1	1	4		0								.000
John Mahnen	P1	1	2		0								.000
Robert Koraleski	PH	1	0	1	0	0	0	0	0			0	----
Irl Henderson	P1	1	0		0								----
Andy Yurchak	C1	1	0	0	0		0	0	0			0	----

PITCHERS	W	L	PCT	G	GS	CG	SH	IP	H	BB	SO	ERA
Clarence Marshall	12	9	.571	39	20	15	1	173	176	**107**	121	4.27
Edson Bahr	12	9	.571	29	24	14	1	185	177	**107**	112	4.09
John Orphal	8	5	.615	14	12	8	1	87	80	46	45	4.14
Elmer Singleton	7	6	.538	17	15	8	1	115	99	56	66	2.43
John Moore	7	12	.368	27	21	5	0	147	173	59	74	4.86
Gale Pringle	6	13	.316	38	17	8	0	152	174	55	42	3.73
Joe Valanzuela	4	3	.571	7	7	5	0	48	53	19	14	3.38
Fred Pepper	3	7	.300	13	11	4	0	81	83	43	34	4.11
Charles Cozart	2	0	1.000	4	3	1	0	25	24	19	7	4.32
Alex Martin	2	6	.250	14	8	3	1	64	77	20	18	3.94
William Davis	1	2	.333	24	8	1	0	55	74	23	11	5.56
Ed Marleau	1	7	.125	30		0	0	51	59	19	11	3.53
Ted Pfennig	0	1	.000	6		0	0	13	17	4	1	6.23
Ray Uniak	0	1	.000	6		0	0	3	7	10	5	30.00
Giles Knowles	0	1	.000	4		0	0	5	8	4	0	3.60
Alva Emmertson	0	4	.000	9		0	0	23	35	14	10	7.83
Ray Stelmack	0	0	----	1		0	0	6	4	4	1	
John Mahnen	0	0	----	1		0	0	3	2	5	0	
Melvin Serafini	0	0	----	1		0	0	2	8	2	0	
Irl Henderson	0	0	----	1		0	0	1	5	2	0	

COLUMBUS   8th   63-90   .412   -29.5   Charlie Root
Red Birds

BATTERS	POS-GAMES	GP	AB	R	H	BI	2B	3B	HR	BB	SO	SB	BA
Maurice Sturdy	1B93	99	349	45	95	37	9	2	1	50	18	12	.272
George Davis	2B80	91	347	45	97	35	7	3	1	39	30	5	.280
Floyd Young	SS65,2B18	88	287	35	72	36	9	3	2	31	51	0	.251
Warren Huston	3B62,2B21	84	305	37	74	31	11	2	0	23	21	0	.243
Jack McLain	OF122,1B15	137	485	61	132	55	26	4	2	35	57	22	.272
Vaughn Hazen	OF100	113	408	59	11	36	14	6	3	28	58	10	.272
Arthur Rebel	OF93	94	340	69	110	70	16	4	10	55	24	6	.324
John Bucha	C107	119	396	54	130	47	17	5	3	40	38	4	.328
Richard Gracey	C25,2B23,1B11	73	238	35	70	42	10	2	0	45	20	4	.294
James Towns	SS60	62	234	28	65	18	8	3	0	15	9	2	.278
Steve Filipowicz	OF48	53	187	28	49	34	7	4	2	16	18	1	.262

COLUMBUS (cont.)
Red Birds

BATTERS	POS-GAMES	GP	AB	R	H	BI	2B	3B	HR	BB	SO	SB	BA
David Bartosch	OF50	50	184	18	41	24	6	2	0	13	26	0	.223
George Sumey	P41	41	63	8	17	6	2	3	0	4	4	0	.270
Vern Rider	OF30	39	114	9	21	7	3	1	0	16	14	1	.184
Charles Baron	1B38	38	146	22	46	32	9	3	1	9	9	2	.315
Roman Brunswick	P36	37	77	9	19	12	1	1	1	1	19	0	.247
Peter Mazar	P35	37	61	8	20	5	1	0	0	3	1	0	.328
Arthur Lopatka	P30	33	64	12	16	8	3	1	0	5	9	0	.250
Robert Rhawn	3B19,SS10	32	104	12	25	12	4	3	2	7	5	1	.240
Luco Lancelotti	3B28	29	113	17	37	22	7	0	1	12	15	0	.327
George Pratt	C16	28	63	3	12	10	0	0	2	7	7	0	.190
Paul Brock	P26	26	29	2	6	3	1	0	1	1	1	0	.207
Charlie Root	P22	22	39	0	6	1	1	0	0	3	10	0	.154
Clarence Strommen	P22	22	28	0	4	3	1	0	0	1	5	0	.143
Ed Storenski	SS16	21	58	6	11	7	0	1	1	6	10	0	.190
Milt Lowrey	P13	18	18	3	6	2	1	0	1	1	4	0	.333
James Mallory	OF16	16	61	10	17	1	3	1	1	6	8	0	.279
Conklyn Merriwether	P6	15	14	0	6	4	1	1	0	1	1	0	.429
Eugene Crumling	C12	13	35	7	8	1	3	0	0	1	4	0	.229
Nicholas Vucovich	P13	13	11	0	0	0	0	0	0	1	6	0	.000
Wes Cunningham	P12	12	15	2	2	1	0	0	0	2	0	0	.133
Peter Pronczik	OF	10	23	6	7	2	1	0	0	5	3	0	.304
Robert Archer	SS	7	17	1	3	2	0	0	0			0	.176
Chauncey Peffer	P7	7	7		0								.000
Stan Partenheimer	P6	6	9		2								.222
Joe Sugrue	SS	5	9	0	3	2	0	0	0			0	.333
Henry Koch	P5	5	2		0								.000
Joe Urso	2B	4	13	1	1	0	0	1	0			0	.077
Robert Matthews	P4	4	2		0								.000
Louis Zaden	2B,SS	3	5	0	1	0	0	0	0			0	.200
Charles Gooding	P3	3	0		0								----
George Stumpf	OF	2	7	2	1	0	1	0	0			0	.143
Ray Baughn	PH	2	2	0	0	0	0	0	0			0	.000
Frank Cronin	P2	2	2		0								.000
Robert Eisiminger	P2	2	0		0								----

PITCHERS	W	L	PCT	G	GS	CG	SH	IP	H	BB	SO	ERA
Peter Mazar	12	10	.545	35	18	10	2	166	170	55	60	3.85
Roman Brunswick	11	14	.440	36	26	13	1	210	227	83	85	3.47
Arthur Lopatka	10	13	.435	30	24	11	2	168	180	99	88	4.82
Charlie Root	9	8	.529	22	15	12	3	121	112	20	64	2.53
George Sumey	7	15	.318	41	24	10	1	190	215	95	94	4.26
Clarence Stommen	5	5	.500	22	11	4	0	93	105	64	44	4.55
Wes Cunningham	3	4	.429	12	5	3	0	48	51	7	12	3.94
Paul Brock	3	6	.333	26	10	3	0	94	99	54	53	4.40
Milt Lowrey	1	1	.500	14		0	0	39	52	34	16	5.77
Stan Partenheimer	1	3	.250	6	5	1	0	32	39	22	14	6.19
Conklyn Merriwether	0	1	.000	6		0	0	16	16	14	5	3.94
Henry Koch	0	1	.000	5		0	0	12	16	7	1	6.75
Frank Cronin	0	2	.000	2		0	0	4	7	9	1	15.75
Nicholas Vucovich	0	3	.000	13		0	0	34	36	28	26	6.09
Chauncey Peffer	0	3	.000	7		0	0	22	36	11	3	9.00
Robert Mathews	0	0	----	4		0	0	8	4	4	2	
Charles Gooding	0	0	----	3		0	0	5	3	7	3	
Robert Eisiminger	0	0	----	2		0	0	2	0	5	2	

MULTI-TEAM PLAYERS

BATTERS	POS-GAMES	TEAMS	GP	AB	R	H	BI	2B	3B	HR	BB	SO	SB	BA
Victor Males	SS98,3B18,2B14,OF10	L-MIN	137	461	58	103	48	22	4	3	57	84	2	.223
Robert Dill	OF127	MIN-IND	135	428	73	115	69	24	6	7	72	72	10	.269
Nick Polly	3B79,OF33	LOU-TOL	118	379	65	119	65	23	0	9	80	37	5	.314
John Marion	OF103	SP-LOU	116	348	57	89	44	16	1	1	82	50	4	.256
George Savino	C91	LOU-MIN	106	292	42	87	61	23	0	4	40	11	2	.298
Russ Lyon	C73	IND-TOL	92	244	20	63	37	15	0	3	23	12	0	.258
Arnie Berge	SS38,3B26,2B12,1B10	MIN-S	89	273	31	71	34	17	1	1	23	20	3	.260
Jack Aragon	C79	MIN-LOU	88	243	32	60	32	15	0	1	38	41	2	.247
Edwin Morgan	OF57,1B10	IND-MIN	77	196	34	52	25	8	2	0	32	22	3	.265
John Price	SS40,3B26	COL-MIL	70	263	46	77	19	9	1	2	12	5	1	.293
William Webb	P31	SP-MIN	35	59	7	13	4	5	0	1	1	10	0	.220
Harry Kimberlin	P34	TOL-LOU	34	28	2	6	3	0	0	0	1	4	0	.214
Robert Mistele	P25	MIL-MIN	25	52	4	11	3	2	0	0	1	12	0	.212

MULTI-TEAM PLAYERS (cont.)

BATTERS	POS-GAMES	TEAMS	GP	AB	R	H	BI	2B	3B	HR	BB	SO	SB	BA
Armond Cardoni	P22	IND-MIL	24	52	5	9	4	1	0	0	0	12	0	.173
Lou Cardinal	C21	MIN-SP	21	60	6	13	3	2	0	0	3	12	0	.217
Elmer Burkart	P17	COL-MIL	17	19	3	6	0	1	0	0	0	10	0	.316
Frank Martin	C,3B	COL-MIL	5	10	1	2	0	1	1	0			0	.200

PITCHERS		TEAMS	W	L	PCT	G	GS	CG	SH	IP	H	BB	SO	ERA
William Webb		SP-MIN	8	11	.421	31	17	7	0	148	176	43	46	5.72
Armand Cardoni		IND-MIL	7	10	.412	22	20	10	1	133	154	45	65	4.20
Harry Kimberlin		TOL-LOU	6	8	.429	34	10	4	0	107	131	37	48	4.54
Robert Mistele		MIL-MIN	5	12	.294	25	23	4	0	138	176	90	74	6.20
Elmer Burkart		COL-MIL	2	5	.286	17	8	2	0	59	89	25	15	7.02

TEAM BATTING

TEAMS	GP	AB	R	H	BI	2B	3B	HR	BB	SO	SB	BA
MILWAUKEE	154	5098	771	1487	699	233	45	71	560	483	71	.292
INDIANAPOLIS	154	5009	756	1407	667	234	56	53	578	553	61	.281
LOUISVILLE	154	4990	716	1358	652	229	61	46	610	518	105	.272
ST. PAUL	151	4879	713	1302	652	260	37	73	552	598	62	.267
MINNEAPOLIS	153	5023	790	1351	682	232	28	81	697	753	122	.269
TOLEDO	153	5050	680	1352	619	192	52	47	604	554	71	.268
KANSAS CITY	152	4898	710	1354	637	211	42	35	611	650	107	.276
COLUMBUS	153	5087	672	1380	622	187	57	35	495	574	71	.271
	612	40034	5808	10991	4578	1778	378	441	4707	4109	670	.275

1946
Most Valuable Player

In all sports, one strives to measure individual excellence. One way is through statistical domination. Another comes through recognition by your peers and associates. To some, this method is the best way to determine the year's best.

Off and on through the decades of the thirties and forties, American Association sportswriters voted informally for the best player of the league. In 1932, they selected Cliff Crawford of Columbus, and in 1936 the sportswriters voted for Rudy York of Milwaukee. In the years after World War II, this award was formalized and given a title: the Most Valuable Player Award.

In 1946, Louisville jumped to the head of the pack, winning its first pennant in 16 years. Indianapolis, St. Paul, and Minneapolis finished in the other playoff spots, while Milwaukee, Toledo, Kansas City, and Columbus trailed at the back. Sibbi Sisti of the Indianapolis Indians won the batting title (.343), while Jerome Witte of Toledo hit the most homers (46), and Minneapolis Miller John McCarthy had the most runs batted in (120). Three pitchers shared the lead in victories with the modest total of fifteen: Fred Sanford from Toledo, Harry Taylor from St. Paul, and Milwaukee's Ewald Pyle. Louisville's Al Widmar had the best earned run average (2.43), while the aforementioned Fred Sanford struck out the most batters (154). (Note: some sources give the earned run average title to Emerson Roser of Indianapolis with a mark of 1.73. However, Roser pitched in only 83 innings, too few to qualify.)

After the season, American Association sportswriters voted for the newly christened Most Valuable Player award. They selected the player who dominated a glamour statistic, Toledo firstbaseman Jerome Witte, who poled a league leading 46 home runs. Jerome Witte, a veteran of six minor league seasons, was enjoying his first taste of the American Association in 1946. His homer hitting binge earned him a brief trip to the major league St. Louis Browns in 1946 and 1947. Witte would play two more seasons in the Association before ending his career in the early 1950s after two home run titles in the Texas League.

The Most Valuable Player Award has remained a part of the American Association to the present day, its recipients ranging from sluggers to relief pitchers. All of the award winners have put up gaudy numbers during their big years, numbers which attest to their ability. But these numbers, individually achieved, take on greater significance when recognized by a player's sportswriting associates with the bestowal of the Most Valuable Player Award.

LOUISVILLE Colonels

1st   92-61   .601   Leibold - Walters

BATTERS	POS-GAMES	GP	AB	R	H	BI	2B	3B	HR	BB	SO	SB	BA
Albert Flair	1B131	132	466	56	125	64	20	10	7	49	35	7	.268
Charles Koney	2B142	143	518	70	148	56	24	6	5	27	50	6	.286
Jack Albright	SS109	110	363	47	82	41	10	7	5	63	35	1	.226
Frank Shofner	3B83,SS49	138	522	80	159	84	22	6	4	39	37	12	.305
John Welaj	OF142	142	573	108	172	74	21	10	6	60	51	37	.300
Frank Genovese	OF120	126	420	80	128	54	25	5	5	86	49	12	.305
George Bennington	OF62	83	245	47	62	18	7	1	0	30	32	8	.253
Fred Walters	C122	132	431	53	114	64	17	1	2	47	34	5	.265
Byron LaForest	3B32	52	155	17	37	17	3	1	0	19	27	8	.239
Harry Kimberlin	P41	42	26	1	1	2	0	0	0	2	6	0	.038
Mars Lewis	OF37	41	150	24	42	26	11	1	4	13	29	2	.280
Al Brancato	3B27	39	119	14	31	20	4	1	0	16	10	2	.261
Howard Doyle	C26	30	93	4	16	8	2	0	1	11	5	2	.172
Al Widmar	P30	30	62	2	6	3	0	0	0	4	22	0	.097
Harry Dorish	P28	28	49	3	7	6	1	1	0	3	23	1	.143
Joe Ostrowski	P24	28	39	8	7	4	2	0	0	6	13	0	.179
James Wilson	P22	26	68	4	11	5	1	0	0	0	8	0	.162
Emery Rudd	P21	24	50	7	13	5	0	0	0	2	6	0	.260
Bill Clark	P20	21	46	5	7	4	2	0	0	4	10	0	.152
Mel Deutsch	P21	21	41	3	8	3	1	0	0	4	9	0	.195
George Diehl	P20	21	39	4	5	3	2	0	0	9	12	0	.128
George Toolson	P16	17	24	5	5	5	0	0	0	2	8	0	.208
Fred Gerken	1B16	16	63	9	13	7	2	0	0	6	9	1	.206
Sam Mele	OF14	15	53	8	12	8	2	2	0	8	7	0	.226
Dwight Simonds	P12	12	4	0	1	0	0	0	0	0	0	0	.250
Jack Aragon	C11	11	23	1	5	3	0	0	0	5	3	0	.217
Al Mazur	2B	6	15	0	2	2	0	0	0			0	.133
Bill Butland	P5	5	12		1								.083
Randolph Heflin	P3	4	9		1								.111
Joe Langworthy	C	3	6	0	1	0	1	0	0			0	.167
Elwood Lawson	P3	3	5	2	2	0	0	0	0			0	.400
Vic Austin	2B,SS	3	4	0	1	1	1	0	0			0	.250
Herschel Held	PH	3	1	2	1	1	1	0	0			0	1.000
Dick Callahan	P2	2	3		0								.000
Ray Patton	P2	2	1		0								.000
Robert Sperry	PH	1	1	0	0	0	0	0	0			0	.000
Don Thompson	P1	1	1	0	0	0	0	0	0			0	.000

PITCHERS	W	L	PCT	G	GS	CG	SH	IP	H	BB	SO	ERA
Al Widmar	12	9	.571	30	23	9	2	185	156	94	73	**2.43**
Harry Dorish	11	4	.733	28	14	7	0	146	128	47	76	3.14
Bill Clark	11	7	.611	20	18	10	3	137	143	41	45	2.89
Joe Ostrowski	10	4	.714	24	11	6	1	116	123	35	54	2.87
James Wilson	10	6	.625	22	20	12	1	158	142	72	126	3.02
Emery Rudd	9	6	.600	24	19	8	0	133	109	117	81	3.72
Harry Kimberlin	8	3	.727	41	0	0	0	89	89	32	47	3.44
George Diehl	7	5	.583	20	14	7	1	114	126	29	49	4.03
George Toolson	5	3	.625	16	5	2	0	58	56	37	30	3.88
Mel Deutsch	5	8	.385	21	17	9	0	121	133	34	42	3.42
Elwood Lawson	1	0	1.000	3	1	1	0	11	7	5	6	3.27
Randolph Heflin	1	1	.500	3	3	1	1	18	20	10	6	2.00
Dwight Simonds	1	2	.333	12	0	0	0	25	29	3	6	3.96
Wilburn Butland	1	2	.333	5	4	1	0	31	37	18	23	2.90
Ray Patton	0	1	.000	2	0	0	0	5	7	4	1	7.20
Dick Callahan	0	0	----	2		0	0	10	16	2	9	
Don Thompson	0	0	----	1		0	0	4	6	3	2	9.00

INDIANAPOLIS Indians

2nd   88-65   .575   -4   Bill Burwell

BATTERS	POS-GAMES	GP	AB	R	H	BI	2B	3B	HR	BB	SO	SB	BA
Vince Shupe	1B153	153	585	77	174	73	**44**	6	4	50	85	4	.297
Al Roberge	2B90	93	374	63	116	48	26	4	4	27	28	1	.310
Sibbi Sisti	SS148	149	**592**	99	**203**	86	33	**14**	6	47	80	14	**.343**
Edward Turchin	3B53,SS13,2B10	83	255	39	63	20	7	3	0	36	48	8	.247
Stan Wentzel	OF153	154	565	94	169	79	30	3	12	62	71	20	.299
Joe Bestwick	OF123	139	484	76	135	109	25	2	15	73	57	7	.279
Chet Wieczorek	OF88	96	334	48	102	47	18	4	5	33	27	4	.305
John Riddle	C76	78	233	24	65	42	16	0	3	26	19	2	.279
Frank Drews	2B57,3B49	114	363	52	87	27	12	4	1	52	34	4	.240

INDIANAPOLIS (cont.)
Indians

BATTERS	POS-GAMES	GP	AB	R	H	BI	2B	3B	HR	BB	SO	SB	BA
Wayne Blackburn	OF50,3B12	100	225	45	60	15	5	5	1	31	25	3	.267
Bob Brady	C64	67	193	29	45	31	8	5	5	27	25	1	.233
Gil English	3B29	58	135	16	41	17	7	0	3	21	9	2	.304
Roy Weatherly	OF36	46	130	15	37	17	7	2	1	4	9	2	.285
Glenn Fletcher	P39	39	37	4	10	6	1	1	0	7	6	0	.270
George Woods	P38	38	44	4	9	3	1	0	1	1	8	0	.205
Rex Cecil	P33	33	59	3	11	4	1	0	0	3	9	1	.186
Paul Derringer	P32	32	68	7	13	4	0	0	0	0	20	0	.191
Hugh Poland	C29	30	90	12	30	14	3	1	1	7	5	0	.333
Earl Reid	P28	29	42	2	10	3	2	0	0	1	11	0	.238
John Hutchings	P26	26	58	4	10	3	1	0	0	1	11	0	.172
Elmer Nieman	OF22	25	86	14	14	6	4	0	1	13	13	0	.163
Frank Barrett	P25	25	20	0	0	0	0	0	0	0	8	0	.000
Art Parks		22	36	5	5	2	0	0	0	9	1	0	.139
Ed Klieman	P18	19	37	8	9	9	4	0	0	2	10	0	.243
Wes Flowers	P17	17	4	0	0	0	0	0	0	0	1	0	.000
Robert Logan	P15	15	4	0	0	0	0	0	0	0	1	0	.000
Al Treichel	P13	13	29	5	8	5	5	0	0	0	4	1	.276
Emerson Roser	P13	13	25	2	5	5	1	0	0	4	7	0	.200
Robert Detweiler		11	33	1	6	0	0	0	0	3	4	1	.182
Thaddeus Cieslak	3B	8	33	2	11	9	4	1	0			0	.333
George Lacy	C	6	16	2	5	4	1	0	1			0	.313
Elmer Singleton	P6	6	9		2								.222
Al Hazel	P6	6	7		1								.143
Chet Ross	OF	5	12	2	2	0	0	0	0			0	.167
Charles Schupp	P4	4	2	1	1	0	0	0	0			0	.250
Stephen Shemo	2B	2	2	0	0	0	0	0	0			0	.000
Morris Aderholt	PH,PR	2	1	0	0	0	0	0	0			0	.000
Frank Staucet	PH,PR	2	0	1	0	0	0	0	0			0	----
Woody Rich	P2	2	0		0								----
James Wallace	P1	1	5	1	2	0	1	0	0			0	.400

PITCHERS	W	L	PCT	G	GS	CG	SH	IP	H	BB	SO	ERA
John Hutchings	11	6	.647	26	20	9	1	155	141	62	59	3.54
Rex Cecil	11	13	.458	33	25	10	2	178	180	93	114	3.74
Earl Reid	10	2	.833	28	16	5	2	120	111	44	40	3.30
Paul Derringer	9	11	.450	32	24	12	4	180	185	55	84	2.65
Ed Klieman	8	5	.615	18	15	8	0	109	114	45	49	4.13
Glenn Fletcher	8	7	.533	39	12	4	0	124	130	74	73	3.77
Emerson Roser	7	3	.700	13	11	4	0	83	62	41	37	1.73
George Woods	7	6	.538	38	11	2	1	129	110	73	65	3.14
Frank Barrett	6	4	.600	25		0	0	65	45	32	40	2.77
Al Treichel	5	3	.625	13	11	3	0	77	68	52	55	3.74
Robert Logan	3	1	.750	15		0	0	24	33	8	13	6.38
James Wallace	1	0	1.000	1	1	1	0	9	7	6	6	2.00
Al Hazel	1	1	.500	6	4	1	0	25	28	6	6	3.60
Elmer Singleton	1	2	.333	6	4	1	0	23	25	18	10	6.26
Charles Schupp	0	1	.000	4		0	0	7	7	6	2	5.14
Wes Flowers	0	0	----	17		0	0	29	26	13	15	
Woody Rich	0	0	----	2		0	0	3	5	0	1	3.33

ST. PAUL   3rd   80-71   .530   -11   Ray Blades
Saints

BATTERS	POS-GAMES	GP	AB	R	H	BI	2B	3B	HR	BB	SO	SB	BA
John Douglas	1B144	144	579	87	178	41	14	3	0	62	59	9	.307
Ed Basinski	2B134	136	515	66	130	46	17	5	5	44	85	9	.252
Gene Mauch	SS149	149	536	74	133	55	19	3	6	91	68	9	.248
Leighton Kimball	3B113	124	391	51	100	63	15	2	13	68	75	2	.256
Eric Tipton	OF144	147	526	113	145	100	33	8	19	113	61	21	.276
Larry Rosenthal	OF133	135	457	85	127	57	26	3	8	101	53	7	.278
John Rizzo	OF95	110	369	60	110	88	16	4	12	51	31	3	.298
John Dantonio	C82	101	294	36	90	47	18	0	3	28	43	1	.306
Joe Vitter	OF65,1B12,3B11	110	281	44	64	26	12	4	2	59	50	9	.228
Lou Rochelli	3B35,2B22	58	156	21	37	27	6	2	5	12	22	2	.237
Homer Matney	OF46	57	153	17	41	22	8	2	0	13	12	1	.268
George Coffman	P50	50	25	1	6	3	1	0	0	1	2	0	.240
Lloyd Dietz	P39	49	48	3	7	7	1	0	1	2	10	0	.146
Al Sherer	P45	45	29	4	5	1	0	0	1	1	5	0	.172
Harry Taylor	P29	41	67	9	17	4	0	1	0	4	9	1	.254
Cliff Dapper	C29	37	100	8	21	17	4	0	1	15	13	0	.210

ST. PAUL (cont.)
Saints

BATTERS	POS-GAMES	GP	AB	R	H	BI	2B	3B	HR	BB	SO	SB	BA
Mike Sandlock	C12,3B10	37	79	12	14	11	2	1	1	5	10	0	.177
Edwin Weiland	P36	36	54	3	5	0	0	0	0	3	19	0	.093
Avitus Himsl	P27	34	12	2	2	2	1	0	0	0	2	0	.167
Walter Nothe	P33	33	47	4	9	4	2	0	1	1	15	0	.191
Otho Nitcholas	P32	32	67	6	17	11	3	0	1	0	14	0	.254
Tom Sunkel	P16	17	30	2	6	1	1	0	0	1	9	0	.200
Richard Lanahan	P16	16	21	1	5	1	2	0	0	1	5	0	.238
Don Lund	OF	14	15	3	3	0	0	0	0	2	3	0	.200
John Banta	P8	12	20	2	6	1	0	0	0	2	0	0	.300
Dwain Sloat	P11	11	2	0	0	0	0	0	0	1	0	0	.000
Eugene Kelly	P4	6	3		0								.000
Al Simonic	PR	4	0	2		0	0	0	0	0		0	----
Sam Narron	C	2	2	0	0	0	0	0	0	0		0	.000
Ernest Davis	OF1	1	5	1	2	2	0	0	0			0	.400
Ken Staples	OF1	1	0	0	0	0	0	0	0			0	----

PITCHERS		W	L	PCT	G	GS	CG	SH	IP	H	BB	SO	ERA
Harry Taylor		15	7	.682	29	25	13	5	181	149	98	91	3.33
Otho Nitcholas		12	10	.545	32	24	12	4	181	190	38	77	3.58
Edwin Weiland		10	12	.455	36	21	5	2	170	181	75	75	4.45
Lloyd Dietz		9	8	.529	39	17	3	0	155	154	55	53	3.83
George Coffman		8	5	.615	50		0	0	94	99	51	44	4.12
Tom Sunkel		6	6	.500	16	16	3	0	91	79	55	71	4.05
Al Sherer		6	7	.462	45	8	3	1	116	128	31	38	3.96
Richard Lanahan		5	1	.833	16	9	4	0	59	63	28	24	3.66
Al Banta		3	2	.600	8	7	3	0	56	49	28	49	2.89
Walter Nothe		3	11	.214	33	24	3	0	154	149	94	134	4.44
Dwain Sloat		2	2	.500	11		0	0	19	13	16	16	4.26
Avitus Himsl		1	0	1.000	27		0	0	51	63	15	9	5.29
Eugene Kelly		0	0	----	4		0	0	7	7	3	5	

MINNEAPOLIS   4th   76-75   .503   -15   Bonura - Ryan -
Millers   Sheehan

BATTERS	POS-GAMES	GP	AB	R	H	BI	2B	3B	HR	BB	SO	SB	BA
John McCarthy	1B126	126	484	84	161	122	30	4	16	58	23	4	.333
Frank Danneker	2B92	111	334	65	91	52	15	3	8	61	24	8	.272
Frank Trechock	SS91,2B41	135	435	49	126	34	11	3	0	43	42	16	.290
Ernest Andres	3B76,1B14	90	342	37	98	59	20	0	4	27	24	2	.287
Babe Barna	OF150	152	517	122	154	112	21	4	28	141	77	6	.298
James Maynard	OF104	104	390	72	103	45	9	1	9	57	34	14	.264
Cleston Ray	OF95	102	330	54	88	42	12	3	9	48	39	2	.267
James Pruett	C56	63	189	22	53	32	7	0	0	27	21	0	.280
Bill Barnacle	OF64,3B26	102	312	58	84	28	14	2	4	58	41	9	.269
Mel Harpuder	3B39,SS38	90	253	46	64	32	5	2	10	50	52	3	.253
Bill Lilliard	SS60,2B19	82	283	49	76	25	12	0	1	37	23	0	.269
Russ Rolandson	C50	52	161	12	36	15	9	2	0	17	22	1	.224
Don Wheeler	C38	52	159	15	42	18	6	0	0	15	14	2	.264
Wilfrid Lefebvre	P35	41	58	5	7	3	2	0	2	11	24	0	.121
William Webb	P38	38	41	4	14	8	3	0	0	4	9	0	.341
Don Schoenborn	P38	38	30	1	5	0	1	0	0	0	11	0	.167
Henry Nowak	OF28	34	110	15	27	7	3	0	0	8	6	0	.245
Bruce Campbell	OF22	31	71	16	19	13	4	0	3	11	12	0	.268
Werner Strunk	P26	29	26	4	5	1	1	0	1	1	10	0	.192
John Brewer	P27	27	62	2	10	2	1	0	0	2	11	0	.161
Ken Jungels	P24	24	48	3	7	4	3	0	0	1	11	0	.146
Phil Oates	P24	24	41	3	6	2	0	0	0	2	7	0	.146
Woody Abernathy	P22	22	47	7	9	4	0	0	0	6	10	0	.191
David Garcia	3B17	20	65	8	17	9	6	0	1	3	8	0	.262
Fabian Gaffke	OF18	18	64	9	16	15	4	2	1	10	10	0	.250
Robert Joyce	P12	13	24	2	5	4	0	0	0	2	1	0	.208
Robert Barthelson	P12	12	16	1	2	2	0	0	0	1	4	0	.125
Reuben Fischer	P10	10	22	0	4	0	1	0	0	1	7	1	.182
Zeke Bonura	1B	9	25	1	5	5	1	0	0			0	.250
Fred Reinhart	OF	9	19	2	4	2	2	0	0			0	.211
Harold Swanson	P9	9	10		1								.100
Joe Lafata	1B	8	22	1	3	1	1	0	0			1	.136
Anthony Jaros	1B	5	5	0	0	0	0	0	0			0	.000
Francis Hardy	P5	5	1		0								.000
Mike Kash	P5	5	1		0								.000
Lou Lucier	P2	4	3	0	1	0	0	0	0			0	.333

MINNEAPOLIS (cont.)
Millers

BATTERS	POS-GAMES	GP	AB	R	H	BI	2B	3B	HR	BB	SO	SB	BA
Robert Bowman	P3	3	6		1								.167
Alfred Dean	P2,1B	3	4	0	0	0	0	0	0	0		0	.000
Mike Mellis	P3	3	1		0								.000
Ed Skladany	2B,SS	2	1	0	0	0	0	0	0	0		0	.000

PITCHERS		W	L	PCT	G	GS	CG	SH	IP	H	BB	SO	ERA
John Brewer		14	9	.609	27	26	16	3	190	185	74	106	3.46
Wilfrid Lefebvre		11	12	.478	35	24	10	1	167	221	49	58	6.41
Ken Jungels		9	5	.643	24	12	6	0	126	128	70	41	5.07
Woody Abernathy		9	9	.500	22	19	11	4	149	127	34	73	3.44
William Webb		8	6	.571	38	9	4	0	122	135	41	42	3.84
Robert Joyce		5	3	.625	10	7	4	1	59	60	27	22	4.73
Reuben Fischer		5	3	.625	12	8	3	0	65	88	20	21	4.98
Phil Oates		5	6	.455	24	16	7	3	119	128	70	41	5.07
Don Schoenborn		4	8	.333	38	13	1	0	104	117	73	64	5.97
Harold Swanson		3	3	.500	9	5	2	2	34	40	13	9	6.09
Werner Strunk		2	3	.400	26		0	0	76	78	59	34	4.62
Robert Barthelson		1	4	.200	12	4	1	0	43	51	19	19	7.53
Alfred Dean		0	1	.000	2		0	0	6	11	3	0	13.50
Robert Bowman		0	3	.000	3	3	1	0	19	29	7	10	6.63
Mike Kash		0	0	----	5		0	0	10	13	4	2	
Francis Hardy		0	0	----	5		0	0	9	9	7	6	
Mike Mellis		0	0	----	3		0	0	8	11	6	2	
Lou Lucier		0	0	----	2		0	0	7	10	4	0	

MILWAUKEE   5th   70-78   .473   -19.5   Nick Cullop
Brewers

BATTERS	POS-GAMES	GP	AB	R	H	BI	2B	3B	HR	BB	SO	SB	BA
Joe Mack	1B114	116	383	55	109	63	26	4	4	83	57	4	.285
Floyd Baker	2B79,SS25,3B21	120	464	81	133	35	23	4	0	73	37	7	.287
Charles Brewster	SS104	104	427	65	128	50	17	5	4	24	49	9	.300
Eugene Nance	3B120	121	432	67	109	81	20	4	9	64	33	3	.252
Dave Philley	OF128	130	507	85	167	93	33	10	13	44	42	19	.329
John Dickshot	OF88	95	322	57	105	50	20	5	3	65	28	9	.326
Robert Johnson	OF83	94	307	53	83	53	14	2	13	57	46	7	.270
Manny Fernandez	C73	78	237	21	44	22	10	0	2	32	39	1	.186
Marv Felderman	C71	77	239	39	70	49	13	2	5	26	42	3	.293
Francis Walls	2B54	64	174	20	34	17	3	0	1	27	27	2	.195
James Delsing	OF40	40	157	21	50	20	5	2	0	10	22	2	.318
Russ Leach	1B13	40	72	9	23	16	0	0	3	7	12	1	.319
Alton Biggs	2B29	35	126	20	25	9	6	1	0	18	15	2	.198
Ira Hutchinson	P33	33	23	0	2	0	0	0	0	0	8	0	.087
Wendell Davis	P31	31	16	3	6	1	0	0	0	4	3	0	.375
Walt Lanfranconi	P30	30	57	4	9	2	2	0	0	4	26	0	.158
Frank Marino	P28	30	25	5	7	5	3	1	0	0	6	0	.280
Ed Mierkowicz	1B22	29	105	15	34	11	6	1	1	10	10	4	.324
Ewald Pyle	P26	26	72	7	23	7	3	1	0	6	19	0	.319
Carl Lindquist	P26	26	26	3	3	1	0	0	0	1	14	0	.115
Thomas Heath	C19	24	61	5	14	12	2	1	2	8	10	0	.230
Al Epperly	P22	23	54	3	12	4	1	0	0	0	11	0	.222
Owen Scheetz	P22	23	47	0	7	1	0	0	0	1	9	0	.149
Lee Ross	P21	21	36	1	7	2	0	0	0	3	13	0	.194
Lew Flick	OF19	21	81	7	21	10	4	2	2	4	2	1	.259
Milt Galatzer	OF10	17	26	3	3	1	0	0	0	5	2	1	.115
Bill Nagel	3B,SS,OF	15	47	7	12	7	2	0	2	3	5	0	.255
Wes Livengood	P14	14	30	1	3	1	1	0	0	0	11	0	.100
Pershing Thomassic	OF12	13	41	4	6	4	1	0	0	7	2	1	.146
John Russian	SS	9	28	3	7	6	0	0	2			0	.250
Dan Reynolds	SS	8	20	2	0	0	0	0	0	0		0	.000
Val Heim	OF	8	13	0	1	1	0	0	0	0		0	.077
Don Black	P7	8	13		1								.077
Hy Vandenberg	P7	7	6		1								.167
Len Perme	P6	6	8		1								.125
James Grant	OF	6	6	1	0	0	0	0	0	0		0	.000
Jack Christensen	P5	5	1	1	1	0	0	0	0	0		0	1.000
Homer Chapman	SS	3	3	0	1	1	1	0	0	0		0	.333
Leonard Gilmore	P2	2	6	0	0	0	0	0	0	0		0	.000
Claude Weaver	P2	2	2		0								.000
Ed Karas	P1	1	1		0								.000
Art Kundle	PH	1	1	0	0	0	0	0	0	0		0	.000

MILWAUKEE (cont.)
Brewers

BATTERS	POS-GAMES	GP	AB	R	H	BI	2B	3B	HR	BB	SO	SB	BA
Bill Trotter	P1	1	0		0								----

PITCHERS	W	L	PCT	G	GS	CG	SH	IP	H	BB	SO	ERA
Ewald Pyle	15	6	.714	26	26	15	4	203	191	91	148	3.01
Lee Ross	9	6	.600	21	14	8	1	110	121	31	43	3.27
Owen Scheetz	8	9	.471	22	20	9	2	131	146	35	35	3.78
Walt Lanfranconi	8	10	.444	30	19	8	1	158	165	68	75	3.70
Wes Livengood	7	3	.700	14	11	5	0	80	110	37	32	5.51
Al Epperly	7	10	.412	22	19	10	1	140	144	40	61	2.83
Frank Marino	5	8	.385	28	9	2	0	74	78	52	47	5.59
Carl Lindquist	4	7	.364	26	9	5	1	91	88	41	48	3.86
Len Perme	2	0	1.000	6	4	1	0	21	21	21	12	7.71
Wendell Davis	2	4	.333	31		0	0	68	81	47	24	5.56
Leonard Gilmore	1	1	.500	2	2	1	0	16	18	3	8	5.63
Hy Vandenberg	1	2	.333	7	2	1	0	25	27	11	12	3.96
Claude Weaver	0	1	.000	2		0	0	8	14	5	4	9.00
Don Black	0	5	.000	7	7	1	0	40	38	20	16	5.18
Ira Hutchinson	0	6	.000	33		0	0	87	86	22	28	3.62
Jack Christensen	0	0	----	5		0	0	10	10	9	8	
Ed Karas	0	0	----	1		0	0	3	3	0	1	
Bill Trotter	0	0	----	1		0	0	1	3	1	0	

TOLEDO   6th   69-84   .451   -23   Gutteridge - Detore
Mud Hens

BATTERS	POS-GAMES	GP	AB	R	H	BI	2B	3B	HR	BB	SO	SB	BA
Jerome Witte	1B151	152	589	99	184	120	26	3	46	58	75	2	.312
Robert Wren	2B91	108	389	53	109	41	16	6	6	24	28	8	.280
Dick Kimble	SS122	122	394	39	98	50	16	6	2	65	51	4	.249
Ellis Clary	3B76,2B30	112	406	64	114	30	24	2	3	42	30	7	.281
Paul Lehner	OF140	144	580	71	184	75	30	8	10	23	32	6	.317
Albert White	OF107	122	465	81	154	35	17	3	1	40	22	33	.331
Bernard Lutz	OF59	73	237	18	54	29	6	1	4	27	22	5	.228
Les Moss	C105	121	390	44	116	54	21	1	13	32	49	2	.297
Don Gutteridge	3B62	70	252	25	70	28	12	3	4	11	19	5	.278
Boris Martin	C22,OF11	50	136	24	36	17	7	0	3	17	17	2	.265
Len Schulte	3B25	48	166	19	40	18	2	1	1	16	13	1	.241
Pete Gray	OF30	48	96	14	24	7	3	0	0	5	0	2	.250
Maurice Newlin	P45	45	42	3	10	0	0	0	0	3	12	0	.238
Earl Jones	P37	37	47	3	6	6	2	0	0	1	10	0	.128
Chet Johnson	P36	36	65	5	9	1	2	0	0	6	24	0	.138
Walter Brown	P34	34	42	2	3	2	0	0	0	3	10	0	.071
John Pavlick	P32	32	38	1	3	1	0	0	0	1	10	0	.079
William Scott	P30	30	27	1	5	3	0	0	0	3	8	1	.185
Vince Castino	C27	29	86	3	14	3	2	0	1	9	12	1	.163
Fred Sanford	P29	29	81	8	9	5	1	0	0	7	30	0	.111
Stanley Galle	2B15,SS10	28	92	7	22	5	5	0	0	2	10	1	.239
Ken Wood	OF24	27	96	16	22	9	7	0	3	8	22	2	.229
Norbert Litzsinger	OF20	27	76	4	18	7	5	0	1	5	11	0	.237
George Corona	OF14	20	53	3	14	6	1	1	0	5	6	0	.264
Frank Croucher	SS13	16	51	3	10	1	1	0	0	4	7	0	.196
John Miller	P13	14	27	2	5	0	1	0	0	3	8	0	.185
Robert Doyle	P12	14	16	2	4	2	0	0	0	0	6	0	.250
John Gibson	P12	12	12	0	2	1	2	0	0	0	6	0	.167
Robert Raney	P12	12	7	0	0	0	0	0	0	0	2	0	.000
James Lucas	SS	11	24	2	4	3	0	0	0	5	4	0	.167
George Bradley	OF	9	31	4	5	1	0	0	1			0	.161
Sam Harshany	C	9	22	3	9	2	0	0	0			0	.409
Clarence Iott	P8	8	5		1								.200
Ray Parrott	PH	5	5		1								.200
Blackstone Thompson	SS	2	3	0	0	1	0	0	0			0	.000
Elwood Knierim	P2	2	1		0								.000
John Marcum	P1	1	0	0	0	0	0	0	0			0	----
Ed Redys	P1	1	0		0								----
James Robinson	PH	1	0	0	0	0	0	0	0			0	----
Earl Smalling	P1	1	0		0								----

PITCHERS	W	L	PCT	G	GS	CG	SH	IP	H	BB	SO	ERA
Fred Sanford	15	10	.600	29	28	21	2	230	199	77	154	2.74
Chet Johnson	12	12	.500	36	28	13	3	199	224	104	151	3.66

TOLEDO (cont.)
Mud Hens

PITCHERS	W	L	PCT	G	GS	CG	SH	IP	H	BB	SO	ERA
Earl Jones	9	7	.563	37	16	5	0	137	135	97	84	5.52
Walter Brown	9	8	.529	34	15	6	1	129	133	63	78	3.70
JohnMiller	5	5	.500	13	11	4	1	76	97	24	43	3.67
Maurice Newlin	5	9	.357	45	13	5	0	147	170	74	47	4.96
John Pavlick	5	13	.278	32	16	3	1	129	138	72	81	4.60
William Scott	3	6	.333	30	8	3	0	94	107	45	35	3.93
Robert Raney	2	0	1.000	12		0	0	28	16	30	15	2.57
John Gibson	2	2	.500	12	4	2	0	36	41	15	24	5.25
Robert Doyle	1	3	.250	12		0	0	47	43	48	31	4.60
John Marcum	0	1	.000	1		0	0	1	1	2	0	9.00
Clarence Iott	0	2	.000	8		0	0	24	17	23	36	3.00
Elwood Knierim	0	0	----	2		0	0	4	4	2	1	
Ed Redys	0	0	----	1		0	0	2	3	2	1	
Earl Smalling	0	0	----	1		0	0	1	2	1	0	

KANSAS CITY   7th   67-82   .450   -23   Meyer - Grimes
Blues

BATTERS	POS-GAMES	GP	AB	R	H	BI	2B	3B	HR	BB	SO	SB	BA
Wayne Tucker	1B57,2B14	82	285	30	64	30	9	2	3	17	27	8	.225
George Scharein	2B45,SS11	72	198	21	60	15	11	1	0	11	17	4	.303
Otis Strain	SS104,2B14	116	390	48	79	35	8	3	5	33	83	24	.203
Joe Beckman	3B144	144	528	73	160	95	27	4	12	78	59	29	.303
Art Metheny	OF100	101	367	48	92	42	14	5	6	49	37	5	.251
Don Smith	OF86	96	310	56	93	16	9	5	0	38	23	18	.300
Harry Croft	OF70	94	260	34	75	35	17	0	7	36	51	3	.288
Charlie Silvera	C87	91	284	22	71	45	13	2	3	34	42	5	.250
Russ Burns	OF67	78	263	40	62	44	10	5	8	24	54	1	.236
Milt Byrnes	OF62	77	211	33	58	24	10	5	1	65	18	4	.275
Frank Zak	SS53,2B16	68	217	26	48	11	6	2	0	33	32	9	.221
Bill Drescher	C53	60	162	15	35	14	4	3	0	29	20	1	.216
Ben Drake	1B50	53	178	18	53	15	4	2	1	11	21	5	.298
Al Lyons	P24	53	85	11	20	9	2	3	3	12	26	1	.235
David Douglas	OF45	46	169	28	48	11	8	2	0	18	12	6	.284
Johnny Sturm	1B44	45	161	14	43	22	11	0	3	13	19	1	.267
Irvin Hall	2B39	45	153	12	39	12	5	0	0	6	18	2	.255
Don Hendrickson	P42	42	13	0	4	1	0	0	0	1	4	0	.308
Mike Milosevich	2B37	38	121	17	27	6	5	0	0	22	15	1	.223
John Maldovan	P33	37	43	2	6	2	0	1	0	3	18	0	.140
Fred Bradley	P30	31	41	4	9	4	1	0	0	0	6	0	.220
Frank Secory	OF27	28	99	13	25	17	4	2	4	10	17	2	.253
Karl Drews	P24	28	66	9	10	5	0	0	0	7	16	0	.152
Carl DeRose	P25	25	56	1	5	0	1	1	0	4	16	0	.089
Tom Reis	P21	21	38	1	7	1	0	0	0	2	13	0	.184
Joe Valenzuela	P19	20	34	0	10	3	0	0	0	1	4	0	.294
Fred Collins	OF14	19	49	5	10	6	1	0	1	6	9	1	.204
Frank Makosky	P18	18	5	0	0	0	0	0	0	0	3	0	.000
Gus Niarhos	C17	17	51	8	12	3	2	0	0	4	5	2	.235
Charles Aleno	3B,1B,OF	12	29	3	5	1	0	0	0	4	1	0	.172
Porter Vaughan	P12	12	26	3	4	0	2	0	0	1	6	0	.154
Ken Holcombe	P10	10	4	0	0	0	0	0	0	2	0	0	.000
Mike Portner	OF,3B	9	10	3	2	1	0	1	0			0	.200
Ralph Houk	C	8	23	5	8	1	2	0	1			0	.348
Urban Pfeffer	OF	6	11	2	3	2	0	0	0			1	.273
Joe Murray	P6	6	7		0								.000
John Bianco	P6	6	6		1								.167
Ray Louthen	P6	6	1		0								.000
Golden Holt	3B,OF	5	10	0	2	0	0	0	0			0	.200
Herb White	C	5	8	2	4	3	0	0	0			0	.500
Robert Revels	P5	5	8		0								.000
Jerry Coleman	2B	5	3	0	1	0	0	0	0			0	.333
Willis Baker	P4	4	4		0								.000
Mario Russo	P3	3	2		0								.000
Gale Pringle	P3	3	1	0	1	0	0	0	0			0	1.000
Carl Ray	P2	2	0		0								----
Walt Carlson	P1	1	0		0								----

PITCHERS	W	L	PCT	G	GS	CG	SH	IP	H	BB	SO	ERA
Karl Drews	14	9	.609	24	24	13	0	182	174	75	89	3.36
Carl DeRose	12	6	.667	25	23	11	2	165	156	72	97	3.16
Tom Reis	7	5	.583	21	17	7	1	121	124	42	45	3.57

KANSAS CITY (cont.)
Blues

PITCHERS	W	L	PCT	G	GS	CG	SH	IP	H	BB	SO	ERA
Fred Bradley	7	9	.438	30	13	4	1	123	117	49	54	3.59
Al Lyons	7	12	.368	24	22	11	2	169	168	73	99	3.67
Joe Valenzuela	6	7	.462	19	12	7	0	100	100	46	33	3.60
John Maldovan	5	15	.250	33	18	6	1	156	128	122	105	4.38
Porter Vaughan	4	2	.667	12	9	2	0	69	65	29	24	2.22
Don Hendrickson	4	4	.500	42		0	0	82	80	35	30	4.06
Frank Makosky	1	1	.500	18		0	0	31	38	12	22	4.65
John Bianco	0	1	.000	6	3	1	0	19	24	10	10	7.11
Wissis Baker	0	1	.000	4		0	0	12	12	6	7	3.75
Mario Russo	0	1	.000	3		0	0	8	13	2	4	3.38
Gale Pringle	0	1	.000	3		0	0	6	13	2	5	15.00
Joe Murray	0	2	.000	6		0	0	18	20	16	9	6.00
Robert Revels	0	2	.000	5		0	0	21	27	10	13	6.43
Ken Holcombe	0	4	.000	10		0	0	21	29	13	9	6.00
Ray Louthen	0	0	----	6		0	0	12	16	7	7	
Carl Ray	0	0	----	2		0	0	1	0	3	0	18.00
Walt Carlson	0	0	----	1		0	0	1	3	2	0	

COLUMBUS   8th   64-90   .416   -28.5   Charlie Root
Red Birds

BATTERS	POS-GAMES	GP	AB	R	H	BI	2B	3B	HR	BB	SO	SB	BA
Michael Natisin	1B119	120	445	64	122	72	21	3	13	65	25	4	.274
Tom Nelson	2B104,SS21	133	502	62	154	74	22	1	7	40	55	5	.307
Robert Rhawn	SS60,3B76,OF12	145	545	62	153	65	24	3	11	37	54	3	.281
Lemuel Young	3B34,2B25	61	172	10	32	16	5	0	0	19	43	2	.186
Augie Bergamo	OF138	144	526	77	162	64	21	7	3	87	43	9	.308
Jack McLain	OF106	109	441	59	100	28	13	8	1	43	73	8	.227
Bill Howarton	OF68	73	268	44	81	40	16	4	10	36	54	3	.302
Delbert Wilber	C78	101	297	35	78	33	9	9	7	35	54	0	.263
Edward Malone	C74	101	266	30	63	27	17	2	2	45	41	1	.237
Vaughn Hazen	OF47	60	203	29	45	13	10	5	3	19	43	7	.222
Claude Wright	SS12	43	33	4	5	3	0	1	0	3	8	0	.152
Peter Mazar	P38	42	59	8	19	4	1	0	0	3	5	2	.322
John Herr	P38	38	34	3	4	1	0	0	0	6	15	0	.129
Richard Cole	3B23,2B11	37	108	8	26	12	2	0	1	15	15	0	.241
Jack Creel	P29	35	48	3	7	4	1	0	0	1	17	0	.146
John Griffore	P31	34	65	6	10	4	3	0	1	2	22	0	.154
Wayne McLeland	P34	34	57	2	3	2	1	0	0	1	22	0	.053
Bill Clemensen	P34	34	44	5	3	2	1	0	0	6	21	0	.068
Harry Marnie	2B14,SS11	27	79	8	10	4	0	0	0	12	8	1	.127
James Hearn	P24	24	35	4	12	6	2	0	0	1	7	0	.343
Don Fisher	P21	23	19	1	4	2	0	0	0	0	7	0	.211
Norman Richards	1B21	22	76	2	13	5	2	0	0	9	9	1	.171
Bill Burich		20	44	2	6	1	1	0	0	3	7	0	.136
George Stumpf	OF16	18	64	7	18	9	0	0	2	6	10	0	.281
Charles Sproull	P16	16	21	0	1	1	0	0	0	2	8	0	.048
Bill Wachtler		13	21	3	3	0	1	0	0	4	4	0	.143
Frank Karr		12	23	1	4	3	0	0	0	1	1	0	.174
Walt Goodall	P12	12	7	0	1	0	0	0	0	1	1	0	.143
Peter Kramer		11	30	1	3	3	0	1	0	3	5	0	.100
Richard Gracey	2B,SS	11	21	0	1	1	0	0	0	2	2	0	.048
Bill Brandt	P10	10	6	0	1	0	0	0	0	0	0	0	.167
Robert Collett	3B,SS	7	29	6	8	3	1	0	0			0	.276
Joe Shroba	P7	7	3		0								.000
Joe Demoran	P7	7	1		0								.000
John Bucha	C	6	10	2	2	0	0	0	0			1	.200
Clarence Beers	P6	6	0		0								----
Charlie Root	P5	5	10		0								.000
Joe King	3B,OF	4	16	2	1	1	0	0	0			0	.063
James Hopper	P4	4	5		0								.000
George Kleine	P4	4	0		0								----
Don Schuchmann		4	0		0								----
Adrian Thompson	2B	3	7	0	1	0	1	0	0			0	.143
Wilbur Buerckholtz	PH	2	1	0	0	0	0	0	0			0	.000
Art Nelson	P2	2	0		0								----
Hooper Triplett	PH	1	1	0	0	0	0	0	0			0	.000
Andreas Mohrlock	P1	1	0		0								----
Charles Gooding	P1	1	0		0								----

COLUMBUS (cont.)
Red Birds

PITCHERS	W	L	PCT	G	GS	CG	SH	IP	H	BB	SO	ERA
Wayne McLeland	11	9	.550	34	20	9	0	171	193	51	81	3.42
John Griffore	11	10	.524	31	25	13	1	184	186	55	84	3.62
Peter Mazar	9	13	.409	38	20	9	3	175	201	57	82	3.14
Bill Clemensen	8	11	.421	34	18	7	0	155	151	70	64	4.53
Jack Creel	8	11	.421	29	20	6	0	144	140	73	71	4.19
James Hearn	4	5	.444	24	8	3	0	98	103	46	48	4.13
Charlie Root	3	0	1.000	5		0	0	23	27	5	10	1.57
John Herr	3	6	.333	38	13	2	0	113	107	82	63	3.98
Ed Malone	2	0	1.000	4	2	2	0	21	20	13	7	1.71
Walt Goodall	2	1	.667	12		0	0	31	29	17	17	3.77
Charles Sproull	2	8	.200	16	9	1	0	72	75	45	30	5.25
Don Fisher	1	5	.167	21	5	1	0	52	54	33	16	5.02
Clarence Beers	0	1	.000	6		0	0	8	17	10	6	12.38
Don Schuchmann	0	1	.000	4		0	0	6	8	7	5	12.00
Joe Shroba	0	2	.000	7		0	0	16	19	13	9	5.06
Bill Brandt	0	3	.000	10		0	0	26	39	5	9	4.85
James Hopper	0	4	.000	4	4	1	0	15	25	10	5	8.40
Joe Demoran	0	0	----	7		0	0	14	20	5	5	
George Kleine	0	0	----	4		0	0	4	4	5	2	
Art Nelson	0	0	----	2		0	0	2	1	2	0	0.00
Andreas Mohrlock	0	0	----	1		0	0	2	0	1	0	0.00
Charles Gooding	0	0	----	1		0	0	1	0	1	0	0.00

MULTI-TEAM PLAYERS

BATTERS	POS-GAMES	TEAMS	GP	AB	R	H	BI	2B	3B	HR	BB	SO	SB	BA
Jim Gleeson	OF148	COL-LOU	148	559	80	171	94	22	8	7	78	66	8	.306
Don Lang	3B95	LOU-COL	110	339	45	82	38	6	5	1	59	38	2	.242
George Savino	C70	MIN-SP	85	235	16	52	30	9	2	0	29	30	0	.221
Andy Gilbert	OF61	LOU-TOL	76	245	36	67	30	8	5	3	21	42	3	.273
Jim Cookson	OF50	MIN-MIL	68	230	39	64	15	5	2	0	33	24	15	.278
Paul O'Dea	OF44	TOL-MIL	52	172	15	50	19	13	0	0	14	22	0	.291
Otto Denning	1B10,C10	MIL-LOU	40	60	8	19	9	3	0	0	8	9	1	.317
Robert Harris	P16	TOL-MIL	16	16	1	2	0	0	0	0	1	3	0	.125

PITCHERS		TEAMS	W	L	PCT	G	GS	CG	SH	IP	H	BB	SO	ERA
Robert Harris		TOL-MIL	2	6	.250	16	7	2	0	64	73	27	18	4.50

TEAM BATTING

TEAMS	GP	AB	R	H	BI	2B	3B	HR	BB	SO	SB	BA
LOUISVILLE	**155**	5194	732	1374	661	201	**58**	43	594	570	111	.265
INDIANAPOLIS	**155**	5227	749	**1461**	688	**269**	55	64	546	660	75	**.280**
ST. PAUL	152	5057	724	1321	653	207	39	79	717	668	74	.261
MINNEAPOLIS	152	5089	**784**	1360	**707**	208	27	97	**725**	620	70	.267
MILWAUKEE	149	4991	712	1342	666	229	47	66	636	580	90	.269
TOLEDO	154	**5300**	654	1424	575	219	38	**101**	459	612	84	.269
KANSAS CITY	151	4991	606	1256	530	187	49	58	578	710	**133**	.252
COLUMBUS	154	5196	632	1309	572	191	53	66	604	**779**	53	.252
	611	41045	5593	10847	5052	1711	366	574	4859	5199	690	.264

1947
Perfect

Once in a great while, an athlete sets aside personal adversity to perform a totally unexpected, stunning feat. Such an event happened during the 1947 American Association season. The player involved was a Kansas City Blues pitcher named Carl DeRose.

Carl DeRose first pitched in the American Association during the 1946 season for the Kansas City Blues. Compiling a decent 12–6 record, DeRose was penciled in as a starter for the Blues for 1947. Unfortunately, he was plagued with a sore arm, which sidelined him for nearly a month in June. With his arm still not well, and surgery imminent, DeRose asked and received permission for one final start. On June 26 he took the mound against the defending champion Louisville Colonels. After a tidy 5–0 whitewashing of the Colonels, DeRose's season ended with a four win and two loss record and a 5.48 earned run average. This record in and of itself was not memorable, but his last victory was. For Carl DeRose had not allowed one Louisville batter to reach base during his final game, thus tossing the first perfect game in Association history.

DeRose's team soared ahead without him. Following a seventh place finish in 1946, Kansas City leapfrogged to the top rung in 1947. Louisville finished second, while Milwaukee and Minneapolis came in third and fourth. Columbus, Indianapolis, St. Paul and Toledo brought up the rear. Milwaukee's Heinz Becker won the batting title (.363), his teammate Carden Gillenwater hit the most home runs (23), and Cliff Mapes from Kansas City had the most runs batted in (117). Clem Dreisewerd of Louisville won two legs of the triple crown by finishing with the most wins (18) and lowest earned run average (2.15), while the third leg was won by Phil Haugstad of St. Paul with 145 strikeouts.

DeRose went on to pitch only five more games in the American Association before drifting out of the league for good. Despite his perfect game, he never once pitched in the major leagues.

Carl DeRose did not hold the distinction of pitching the Association's only perfect game for long; within five years another performed the same feat. But certainly his performance, the best of his career, stands as a testament that adversity can be set aside to achieve a stunning victory, a perfect masterpiece.

KANSAS CITY
Blues

1st 93-60 .608 Bill Meyer

BATTERS	POS-GAMES	GP	AB	R	H	BI	2B	3B	HR	BB	SO	SB	BA
Steve Souchock	1B136	136	528	86	155	99	25	11	17	39	67	19	.294
Joe Muffoletto	2B96	99	343	44	87	59	9	9	5	33	31	3	.254
Otis Strain	SS125	125	395	55	84	37	7	4	1	63	73	17	.213
Jerry Coleman	3B97,SS43	131	446	60	124	57	15	6	6	47	86	12	.278
Cliff Mapes	OF152	155	542	107	167	117	27	11	21	119	104	17	.308
Hank Bauer	OF120	131	457	90	143	79	32	5	16	49	58	13	.313
Ed Stewart	OF116,3B22	145	528	107	189	102	33	17	7	52	33	16	.358
Gus Niarhos	C87	93	237	44	76	26	11	0	1	62	22	2	.321
Blas Monaco	2B40,3B36,1B20	112	284	74	73	48	16	3	7	92	47	4	.257
Harry Craft	OF79	88	267	42	84	32	16	6	4	33	31	5	.315
Ken Silvestri	C76	83	242	44	58	41	12	2	9	58	46	2	.240
David Douglas	OF23	53	90	21	24	10	4	0	0	21	5	0	.267
Forrest Main	P44	44	18	1	2	0	0	0	0	1	6	0	.111
John Lucadello	2B25	34	88	11	15	11	3	1	0	23	7	1	.170
Tommy Byrne	P19	33	74	13	19	10	6	2	0	8	10	0	.257
Clarence Marshall	P30	30	58	5	10	5	1	0	0	2	12	0	.172
William Wight	P29	29	65	5	8	5	0	0	1	6	21	1	.123
Fred Bradley	P28	28	55	8	20	6	2	0	0	4	9	0	.364
Frank Hiller	P22	22	61	10	19	12	3	0	0	4	6	1	.311
Don Hendrickson	P22	22	3	0	0	0	0	0	0	1	0	0	.000
Cal McLish	P16	16	30	3	5	3	0	0	0	2	10	0	.167
Fred Wolff	P16	16	15	0	1	0	0	0	0	0	7	0	.067
Ford Mullen	SS,2B,3B	14	45	2	8	9	2	0	0	2	3	0	.178
Charles Haag	P12	14	3	1	0	0	0	0	0	0	2	0	.000
James Dyck	3B	11	26	5	5	3	1	0	0	1	5	1	.192
Frank Secory	OF	11	10	0	1	3	0	0	0	2	1	0	.100
Kent Sterling	P10	10	5	1	0	0	0	0	0	2	3	0	.000
Vern Hoscheit	C	7	15	0	2	2	0	0	0			1	.133
John Moore	P7	7	9	2	5	2	1	0	0			0	.556
Dick Kryhoski	PH	2	2	0	0	0	0	0	0			0	.000

PITCHERS		W	L	PCT	G	GS	CG	SH	IP	H	BB	SO	ERA
William Wight		16	9	.640	29	28	17	5	199	202	71	75	2.85
Frank Hiller		15	5	.750	22	22	12	5	175	193	39	70	3.45
Fred Bradley		13	4	.765	28	21	11	1	157	163	51	74	2.98
Tommy Byrne		12	6	.667	19	18	13	0	149	109	106	138	3.26
Henry Marshall		11	6	.647	30	25	10	1	166	163	123	92	4.28
Forrest Main		7	6	.538	44	2	1	0	95	108	41	65	4.45
Cal McLish		6	7	.462	16	12	6	0	92	104	42	40	4.40
Mario Russo		4	1	.800	7	5	3	1	39	54	20	14	6.00
Carl DeRose		4	2	.667	8	8	1	1	46	49	25	19	5.48
Fred Wolff		2	2	.500	16	6	2	0	49	57	29	21	4.96
Charles Haag		1	1	.500	12		0	0	25	25	12	13	4.32
Roland Hoyle		1	1	.500	2		0	0	7	7	6	3	2.57
Don Hendrickson		1	4	.200	22		0	0	38	46	19	10	6.16
Kent Sterling		0	3	.000	10		0	0	26	36	28	13	10.03
John Moore		0	3	.000	7	3	1	0	26	33	9	10	3.81
Carmine Melignano		0	0	----	4		0	0	4	9	0	2	8.31
John Mackinson		0	0	----	2		0	0	7	7	6	3	13.50

LOUISVILLE
Colonels

2nd 85-68 .556 -8 Harry Leibold

BATTERS	POS-GAMES	GP	AB	R	H	BI	2B	3B	HR	BB	SO	SB	BA
Paul Campbell	1B152	152	601	93	183	71	24	14	6	56	58	8	.304
Charles Koney	2B150	154	607	88	177	78	28	4	4	42	52	8	.292
Frank Shofner	SS57,3B26	86	265	36	70	39	10	6	0	34	20	5	.264
Sam Dente	3B52,SS27	76	267	35	83	31	5	5	0	29	22	4	.311
John Welaj	OF142	151	516	82	137	74	17	9	5	60	30	26	.266
Jim Gleeson	OF131	139	437	65	116	78	29	5	8	101	54	10	.265
Peter Layden	OF70	71	257	29	68	36	9	3	3	21	35	8	.265
Ed McGah	C54	59	142	29	31	16	1	0	6	39	33	8	.218
Billy Goodman	SS56,OF32	94	329	55	112	49	18	8	2	52	27	8	.340
Ed Lavigne	OF36	50	133	16	42	32	5	1	4	7	15	1	.316
James Pruett	C35	38	113	11	36	10	5	1	0	8	13	2	.319
Ken Chapman	3B26	34	71	11	9	4	1	0	1	13	15	2	.127
George Toolson	P33	34	39	5	8	1	1	0	0	3	10	1	.205
Joe Ostrowski	P29	32	51	9	10	7	1	0	0	17	18	0	.196
Clem Dreisewerd	P31	31	71	5	6	0	0	0	0	5	39	0	.085
Bill Elbert	P27	31	40	4	6	0	0	0	0	1	10	1	.150

LOUISVILLE (cont.)
Colonels

BATTERS	POS-GAMES	GP	AB	R	H	BI	2B	3B	HR	BB	SO	SB	BA
Wes Bailey	P30	30	35	4	7	3	1	0	0	3	10	0	.200
Al Widmar	P29	29	39	3	4	0	0	0	0	4	13	0	.103
James Wilson	P12	13	33	1	12	5	0	1	0	1	4	0	.364
Hal Albright	SS	9	32	4	6	6	0	0	1			0	.188
Mickey McDermott	P5	5	10	2	5	2	0	0	0			0	.500
Mike Ovaduke	PH	3	1	1	0	0	0	0	0			0	.000
Don Thompson	P1	1	0	0	0	0	0	0	0			0	----
Leslie Aulds	C	1	0	0	0	0	0	0	0			0	----

PITCHERS		W	L	PCT	G	GS	CG	SH	IP	H	BB	SO	ERA
Clem Dreisewerd		**18**	7	.720	31	24	**17**	2	201	202	33	101	**2.15**
Joe Ostrowski		13	11	.542	29	22	13	4	184	160	43	66	2.98
George Toolson		11	6	.647	33	13	4	0	127	125	67	59	3.19
Al Widmar		8	8	.500	29	13	6	0	126	130	63	44	4.93
Bill Elbert		6	3	.667	27	11	4	0	117	117	65	58	3.85
Wes Bailey		6	8	.429	30	12	6	1	113	115	51	55	4.30
James Wilson		4	4	.500	12	10	3	2	68	45	38	47	2.65
Maurice McDermott		1	0	1.000	5	4	1	0	27	17	32	25	4.67
Mel Parnell		0	2	.000	4	3	1	0	18	24	11	11	7.50
Walker Cress		0	0	----	1		0	0	2	6	6	3	31.50
Don Thompson		0	0	----	1		0	0	1	1	3	1	9.00

MILWAUKEE   3rd   79-75   .513   -14.5   Nick Cullop
Brewers

BATTERS	POS-GAMES	GP	AB	R	H	BI	2B	3B	HR	BB	SO	SB	BA
Heinz Becker	1B131	131	457	90	166	90	23	8	11	92	53	1	**.363**
Danny Murtaugh	2B119	119	444	96	134	49	15	5	7	76	48	2	.302
Alvin Dark	SS149	149	**614**	121	186	66	49	7	10	60	39	14	.303
Damon Phillips	3B104	118	409	44	124	63	11	1	8	29	41	1	.303
Carden Gillenwater	OF145	146	500	84	156	92	28	5	**23**	86	63	4	.312
Thomas Neill	OF134	134	529	79	151	91	29	4	13	39	46	3	.285
Al Roberge	OF85,2B41,3B13	139	515	77	162	86	27	7	9	47	37	3	.315
Bob Brady	C46	46	150	16	31	21	6	3	3	21	17	0	.207
Max Macon	OF23,1B14,P2	62	150	17	46	21	3	2	0	9	12	0	.307
Eugene Nance	3B39	40	134	19	36	20	7	1	2	19	8	0	.269
Walter Linden	C34	39	109	8	25	7	3	0	0	8	10	0	.229
James Davis	P39	39	31	3	2	0	0	0	0	4	14	0	.059
John Dickshot	OF25	37	95	13	24	11	1	0	0	14	9	0	.253
Al Epperly	P30	33	60	9	12	3	3	0	0	5	10	0	.200
Lee Ross	P30	30	54	6	13	5	3	0	0	4	21	0	.241
Ewald Pyle	P28	29	65	6	10	1	1	1	0	2	22	0	.154
Vern Bickford	P29	29	45	2	11	5	1	0	0	4	9	0	.244
James Wallace	P29	29	36	6	6	2	1	0	0	6	12	0	.167
Earl Reid	P26	26	44	3	11	4	4	0	0	0	11	0	.250
Glenn Elliott	P24	24	39	3	6	3	0	0	0	9	13	0	.154
F. Younger	C20	22	59	6	14	7	2	0	0	5	8	0	.237
Joe Mack	1B16	16	52	4	12	12	1	0	2	7	5	0	.231
Chet Ross	OF13	16	40	5	9	1	1	0	0	4	9	0	.225
Emerson Roser	P15	15	15	2	1	1	0	0	0	1	7	0	.067
Ken Raddant	C14	14	37	4	7	4	1	0	0	3	4	0	.189
Wes Livengood	P12	12	10	2	1	3	0	0	0	0	5	0	.100
James Hill	C	6	15	2	3	2	0	0	0			0	.200
Ray Fletcher	OF	4	12	1	3	1	0	0	0			0	.250
Tom Whisenant	OF	2	4	2	1	1	0	0	1			0	.250
John Hennerich	PH	2	2	0	0	0	0	0	0			0	.000
Richard Manville	P2	2	1	1	1	0	0	0	0			0	1.000
James Paules	PH	1	1	0	0	0	0	0	0			0	.000
Bill Sanders	PH	1	0	0	0	0	0	0	0			0	----

PITCHERS		W	L	PCT	G	GS	CG	SH	IP	H	BB	SO	ERA
Glenn Elliott		14	5	.737	24	18	10	2	138	149	45	75	3.78
Al Epperly		14	7	.667	30	23	11	1	176	179	51	75	3.58
Ewald Pyle		10	12	.455	28	26	14	0	177	170	77	119	4.32
Lee Ross		10	13	.435	30	23	11	2	159	200	69	64	5.09
Vern Bickford		9	5	.643	29	14	10	3	143	131	72	69	3.78
Earl Reid		7	9	.438	26	17	9	1	116	154	52	34	5.35
James Wallace		6	10	.375	29	16	5	1	110	144	62	62	6.87
James Davis		3	5	.375	39	5	2	0	113	114	70	80	4.94
Emerson Roser		2	3	.400	15	6	3	0	51	62	27	31	4.76

MILWAUKEE (cont.)
Brewers

PITCHERS	W	L	PCT	G	GS	CG	SH	IP	H	BB	SO	ERA
Wes Livengood	1	1	.500	12	3	1	0	35	41	20	8	5.40
Ray Janikowski	0	1	.000	6		0	0	15	17	14	8	4.20
Richard Manville	0	1	.000	2		0	0	3	8	5	2	30.00
Max Macon	0	0	----	2		0	0	10	10	5	4	
Dave Sheehan	0	0	----	1		0	0	5	7	4	2	
Ed Karas	0	0	----	1		0	0	1	0	1	0	0.00
Aaron Kaye	0	0	----	1		0	0	0	1	3	0	0.00

MINNEAPOLIS	4th	77-77	.500	-16.5	Tom Sheehan

Millers

BATTERS	POS-GAMES	GP	AB	R	H	BI	2B	3B	HR	BB	SO	SB	BA
John McCarthy	1B131	142	504	81	174	102	23	2	22	37	31	2	.345
Len Schulte	2B73,SS17,3B16	104	348	51	98	41	12	1	1	43	35	1	.282
Frank Trechock	SS115	127	372	51	108	41	13	2	1	46	44	6	.290
Robert Rhawn	3B117,SS27	140	503	75	152	90	34	8	14	33	48	8	.302
Cleston Ray	OF142	143	525	90	148	77	21	7	15	68	56	14	.282
Babe Barna	OF134	143	472	97	153	79	23	5	21	105	66	5	.324
Andy Gilbert	OF	(see multi-team players)											
Wes Westrum	C119	134	398	85	117	87	24	3	22	74	90	10	.294
Jack Maguire	2B60,SS11	93	253	34	71	32	16	3	4	33	34	2	.281
Stephen Gerkin	P83	83	44	4	6	6	1	0	0	1	14	0	.136
Larry Miggins	OF47	60	202	28	47	31	7	0	6	17	46	1	.233
Earl McGowan	P44	47	86	13	17	8	3	1	0	2	19	0	.198
Dick Lajestic	2B40	42	145	16	35	13	8	0	1	24	23	0	.241
Francis Hardy	P33	41	68	8	10	3	0	0	0	7	20	0	.147
Norm Jaeger	1B19	38	73	16	19	9	3	1	1	13	5	0	.260
Marv Grissom	P37	37	53	4	9	7	1	0	0	2	22	0	.170
Reuben Fischer	P31	32	68	4	10	5	1	0	0	5	17	0	.147
Woody Abernathy	P27	27	40	2	7	7	0	0	0	2	12	0	.175
Bill Emmerich	P24	24	15	3	4	2	0	0	0	0	5	0	.267
Richard Hoover	P21	21	17	0	1	0	1	0	0	1	6	0	.059
Harold Gilbert	1B11	16	31	3	3	4	0	0	1	1	8	0	.097
Mel Harpruder	SS,2B,3B	13	34	3	10	4	1	1	1	6	7	1	.294
Fred Bell	OF12	12	44	7	9	3	1	0	0	1	0	1	.205
Eugene Geary	SS10	10	41	6	5	1	0	0	0	4	2	1	.122

PITCHERS	W	L	PCT	G	GS	CG	SH	IP	H	BB	SO	ERA
Earl McGowan	17	11	.607	44	29	10	2	221	242	70	130	3.95
Reuben Fischer	14	10	.583	31	30	17	2	197	197	104	85	4.43
Stephen Gerkin	10	2	.833	83		0	0	175	193	51	51	4.27
Francis Hardy	9	9	.500	33	24	12	2	202	169	103	136	3.97
Woody Abernathy	9	10	.474	27	17	3	0	118	136	45	52	5.19
Marv Grissom	9	16	.360	37	25	7	1	151	162	89	92	6.26
Bill Emmerich	3	3	.500	24		0	0	56	73	22	11	6.75
Richard Hoover	2	5	.286	21	6	1	0	52	70	28	17	5.54
Neil Saulia	0	0	----	3		0	0	4	6	7	2	
Art Fowler	0	0	----	2		0	0	3	5	3	1	12.00
Ed Wagner	0	0	----	1		0	0	4	5	6	0	

COLUMBUS	5th	76-78	.494	-17.5	Harold Anderson

Red Birds

BATTERS	POS-GAMES	GP	AB	R	H	BI	2B	3B	HR	BB	SO	SB	BA
Michael Natisin	1B146	146	540	93	168	108	35	5	22	59	36	11	.311
Charles Harrington	2B114	123	487	67	121	30	20	2	0	45	50	27	.248
Merrill Combs	SS	(see multi-team players)											
Don Lang	3B140	142	483	94	167	87	28	12	11	71	44	6	.346
Bill Howerton	OF149	150	532	76	131	86	29	4	17	85	97	4	.246
Bernard Olsen	OF133	142	507	82	139	62	25	6	8	66	65	7	.274
Roy Broome	OF79	99	301	43	83	32	11	4	2	20	35	4	.276
Bill Baker	C95	108	340	34	94	52	18	0	4	39	16	5	.276
Bill Conroy	C66	91	237	25	53	35	14	1	5	34	32	0	.224
Julius Schoendienst	SS35,3B19,2B18	86	264	31	63	31	10	1	3	15	35	2	.239
Ira Hutchinson	P62	62	17	1	1	0	0	0	0	2	3	0	.059
Rogers McKee		38	77	10	18	6	5	0	2	10	14	0	.234
Les Studener	P31	32	55	2	8	3	0	0	0	2	18	0	.145

COLUMBUS (cont.)
Red Birds

BATTERS	POS-GAMES	GP	AB	R	H	BI	2B	3B	HR	BB	SO	SB	BA
Charles Stanceu	P31	31	68	5	12	10	7	0	0	7	29	0	.176
Alex Patterson	P31	31	44	5	9	3	1	0	1	2	12	0	.205
John Caulfield	SS27	28	95	4	19	12	0	1	0	5	17	1	.200
Wayne McLeland	P27	27	40	1	5	3	0	0	0	2	12	0	.125
George Copeland	P24	24	12	0	3	0	0	0	0	2	5	0	.250
Art Herring	P20	20	23	4	6	3	1	0	0	2	2	0	.261
Ken Johnson	P18	19	23	4	5	3	1	0	0	1	5	0	.217
Edward Blake	P18	18	12	1	2	0	0	0	0	0	2	0	.167
Richard Cole	2B15	15	50	8	11	4	0	1	0	5	8	1	.220
A. Phillips	2B,SS,3B	13	29	1	4	1	0	1	0	2	4	0	.138
Peter Mazar	P12	13	12	1	1	1	0	0	0	1	2	0	.067
Gerald Staley	P12	12	24	2	7	3	1	0	0	0	5	0	.292
Andy Phillip	PH	2	2	0	1	1	0	1	0			0	.500

PITCHERS		W	L	PCT	G	GS	CG	SH	IP	H	BB	SO	ERA
Alex Patterson		14	8	.636	31	20	4	0	135	194	68	38	5.93
Charles Stanceu		12	12	.500	31	27	15	1	221	214	90	109	3.05
Ira Hutchinson		10	3	.769	62		0	0	102	98	29	44	2.91
Les Studener		10	8	.556	31	24	9	1	156	154	104	83	4.67
Wayne McLeland		7	10	.412	27	20	4	0	129	142	70	53	4.47
Gerald Staley		6	1	.857	12	9	4	0	66	74	21	17	3.95
Art Herring		6	2	.750	20	7	2	0	70	84	16	33	3.99
George Copeland		1	3	.250	24		0	0	53	44	44	36	4.42
Ken Johnson		1	3	.250	18	7	1	0	59	73	53	30	7.47
Rudy Rundus		0	1	.000	7		0	0	22	23	12	7	2.86
Ray Lee		0	1	.000	2		0	0	5	1	3	2	1.80
Wilber McCullough		0	2	.000	4		0	0	9	10	10	4	4.00
Peter Mazar		0	4	.000	12		0	0	34	58	18	10	7.94
Edward Blake		0	5	.000	18		0	0	50	52	29	19	5.22
John Klippstein		0	0	----	2		0	0	3	3	6	1	9.00

INDIANAPOLIS   6th   74-79   .484   -19   James Brown
Indians

BATTERS	POS-GAMES	GP	AB	R	H	BI	2B	3B	HR	BB	SO	SB	BA
Cyril Moran	1B146	148	556	80	157	71	29	5	8	47	59	5	.282
Gene Mauch	2B58	58	217	37	65	16	13	4	0	39	14	1	.300
Pete Castiglione	SS140	146	567	74	153	40	26	9	2	30	35	3	.270
Ernest Andres	3B150	150	537	69	143	84	24	2	13	44	26	2	.266
Roy Weatherly	OF136	140	503	79	153	81	27	7	14	52	34	3	.304
Ben Guintini	OF115	126	430	66	130	70	21	5	16	36	66	4	.302
Stan Wentzel	OF110	118	377	59	94	37	18	5	2	39	43	4	.249
John Riddle	C65	79	210	17	71	24	9	0	4	18	10	0	.338
Frank Kalin	OF64	85	241	32	75	48	9	5	9	25	28	2	.311
James Brown	2B47	66	194	25	46	14	5	1	0	25	8	6	.237
Frank Barrett	P65	65	22	1	2	0	0	0	0	2	6	0	.091
LeRoy Jarvis	C56	59	195	23	45	24	6	0	7	22	28	2	.231
James Bloodworth	2B43	50	187	23	56	22	11	2	4	15	18	1	.299
Woody Williams	2B11	36	70	5	15	7	4	0	0	6	5	1	.214
Bill Salkeld	C31	34	112	16	27	10	6	0	2	16	13	0	.241
Robert Malloy	P28	32	65	6	14	8	1	0	0	1	15	1	.215
Jack Hallett	P32	32	48	2	12	8	0	0	1	3	12	0	.250
Stanley Ferek	P28	29	16	1	3	2	1	0	0	3	5	0	.188
Stephen Nagy	P23	27	45	4	9	9	2	0	2	4	13	0	.200
Lou Tost	P25	26	67	7	11	4	1	0	0	7	19	1	.164
Manny Perez	P25	25	35	2	8	0	2	0	0	0	13	0	.229
Glenn Fletcher	P24	24	45	3	4	1	1	0	0	3	12	0	.089
Ken Gables	P21	21	21	0	4	2	1	0	0	3	5	0	.188
Royce Lint	P11	20	41	6	12	3	0	1	0	2	4	0	.293
Victor Barnhart	SS13	13	45	5	8	4	1	0	0	7	19	1	.164
Hugh Poland	C	10	26	1	7	2	0	0	0	2	3	0	.269
Charles Workman	OF,3B	9	31	3	7	6	2	0	1			0	.226
Bill Deininger	C	7	10	2	7	3	0	1	0			0	.700
Lee Howard	P2,PR	5	3	1	1	0	0	0	0			0	.333
William McKee	SS	4	12	0	3	1	0	0	0			0	.250
Ted Beard	PH,PR	2	1	0	0	0	0	0	0			0	.000

PITCHERS		W	L	PCT	G	GS	CG	SH	IP	H	BB	SO	ERA
Robert Malloy		14	9	.609	28	25	15	1	179	190	73	66	3.92

INDIANAPOLIS (cont.)
Indians

PITCHERS	W	L	PCT	G	GS	CG	SH	IP	H	BB	SO	ERA
Lou Tost	11	12	.478	25	24	12	1	178	208	54	98	4.35
Jack Hallett	10	11	.476	32	18	7	1	152	153	60	136	3.79
Charles Nagy	8	5	.615	23	20	9	2	132	147	50	90	4.43
Glenn Fletcher	7	7	.500	24	17	7	0	132	122	67	66	3.68
Frank Barrett	6	3	.667	65		0	0	115	114	43	66	3.83
Manny Perez	5	9	.357	25	17	8	1	118	113	73	56	3.74
Stanley Ferek	4	5	.444	28		0	0	76	78	38	43	4.26
Royce Lint	4	6	.400	11	11	4	0	74	72	46	47	4.74
Dewey Soriano	2	0	1.000	4	4	1	0	27	25	19	17	4.67
Ken Gables	2	8	.200	21	9	4	1	76	78	34	44	4.50
George Woods	1	2	.333	4		0	0	10	10	11	6	8.10
Aldon Wilkie	0	1	.000	5		0	0	11	9	6	6	2.45
Hank Gornicki	0	1	.000	1		0	0	3	6	3	0	15.00
Ed Albosta	0	0	----	2		0	0	3	10	5	0	
Lee Howard	0	0	----	2		0	0	7	5	3	0	
James Walsh	0	0	----	1		0	0	4	3	1	3	0.00

ST. PAUL   7th   69-85   .454   -24.5   Franks - Davis
Saints

BATTERS	POS-GAMES	GP	AB	R	H	BI	2B	3B	HR	BB	SO	SB	BA
John Douglas	1B155	155	594	80	195	88	25	11	1	65	55	8	.328
George Fallon	2B140	144	551	91	142	64	25	6	11	52	55	5	.258
Bob Ramazzotti	SS82	86	344	67	105	47	13	2	13	30	26	18	.305
Lew Riggs	3B101	115	378	85	119	62	17	9	11	64	24	2	.315
Eric Tipton	OF134	138	452	96	139	106	18	5	19	130	47	15	.308
Don Lund	OF84	90	325	68	91	49	18	4	16	21	51	8	.280
John Dantonio	C90	99	293	32	79	39	13	3	2	48	16	0	.270
Jack Paepke	C50,OF31,P5	96	292	29	76	45	13	2	4	50	42	2	.260
Marv Rackley	OF58	60	234	33	74	22	10	4	2	25	23	7	.316
George Coffman	P52	52	10	2	1	1	0	0	0	1	4	0	.100
Herm Franks	C38	49	102	3	21	16	3	2	2	29	10	0	.206
Lloyd Dietz	P35	46	67	10	11	2	3	1	0	2	13	0	.164
George Spears	SS22	38	88	8	19	8	1	0	0	7	9	0	.216
Phil Haugstad	P37	37	88	3	8	4	0	0	0			0	.091
John Gabbard	P35	35	71	4	8	7	1	1	0	4	23	0	.113
Harold Younghans	SS33	33	118	6	20	14	2	1	0	8	12	0	.169
Curt Davis	P26	30	28	2	7	3	2	1	1	1	10	0	.250
Joe Tepsic	OF18	21	63	10	19	12	2	2	1	8	13	0	.302
Otho Nitcholas	P19	19	32	3	6	1	1	0	0	2	4	0	.188
Morris Martin	P19	19	19	0	1	0	0	0	0	1	6	0	.053
LeRoy Pfund	P18	18	39	5	8	3	1	2	0	5	21	0	.205
Ed Head	P12	12	17	4	3	3	1	0	0	3	2	0	.176
Robert Tart	P11	12	13	1	2	0	0	0	0	0	4	0	.154
Ken Mauer	SS	6	21	1	4	3	1	1	0			0	.190
Ernest Davis	PH,PR	5	3	0	0	1	0	0	0			0	.000
Joe Vitter	OF,1B	5	3	3	1	0	0	0	0			0	.333
Wayne Blackburn	OF	4	7	1	2	1	0	0	0			0	.286
Ed Nulty	OF	3	12	0	3	2	0	0	0			0	.250

PITCHERS	W	L	PCT	G	GS	CG	SH	IP	H	BB	SO	ERA
Phil Haugstad	16	6	.727	37	28	16	0	230	199	114	145	3.80
John Gabbard	11	15	.423	35	27	8	0	191	228	78	56	5.26
Lloyd Dietz	9	17	.346	35	25	11	1	184	203	73	59	4.60
George Coffman	6	4	.600	52		0	0	71	84	44	20	3.93
Otho Nitcholas	6	5	.545	19	9	4	0	87	111	20	29	5.28
LeRoy Pfund	5	7	.417	18	16	6	1	123	132	42	28	4.32
Curt Davis	4	5	.444	26	5	2	0	77	90	16	26	3.97
Ed Head	3	3	.500	12		0	0	61	74	28	19	5.16
Morris Martin	2	3	.400	19	3	1	0	59	47	34	30	4.12
Melvin Himes	1	1	.500	3	2	2	1	23	20	8	10	1.96
Robert Tart	1	2	.333	11		0	0	37	40	35	22	5.59
Bill Eggert	0	1	.000	3		0	0	13	20	9	3	11.77
Al Sherer	0	3	.000	4	3	2	0	20	23	10	6	6.75
Edwin Weiland	0	4	.000	8		0	0	24	37	13	14	6.75
Jack Paepke	0	4	.000	5		0	0	24	32	21	13	7.88

TOLEDO   8th   61-92   .399   -32   Frank Snyder
Mud Hens

BATTERS	POS-GAMES	GP	AB	R	H	BI	2B	3B	HR	BB	SO	SB	BA
Charles Stevens	1B134	141	484	78	135	55	21	5	7	78	49	7	.279
Irvin Hall	2B69,SS23	97	337	34	96	32	7	1	1	25	21	0	.285
Dick Kimble	SS131	131	516	88	142	62	29	5	12	65	52	1	.275
Ellis Clary	3B108,2B46	153	542	85	154	72	26	5	9	71	21	8	.284
Glenn McQuillen	OF146	148	546	95	169	70	28	6	9	67	45	2	.310
Mizell Platt	OF138	141	531	76	162	98	30	8	16	35	61	1	.305
Albert White	OF121	125	454	60	147	50	16	4	5	45	21	13	.324
Boris Martin	C89	110	310	44	99	64	20	4	15	32	28	0	.319
Hank Helf	C79	91	261	27	53	38	10	0	8	16	59	1	.203
George Elder	OF64	90	247	34	77	25	5	4	1	18	40	5	.312
Jerome Witte	3B47	55	215	35	60	46	14	3	13	20	36	0	.279
Robert Wren	2B44	48	156	25	35	18	3	0	1	23	11	1	.224
William Scott	P40	41	41	3	5	1	0	0	0	2	8	0	.122
Al Milnar	P25	36	43	6	12	2	2	0	0	1	10	0	.279
Chet Johnson	P35	35	61	3	7	3	0	0	0	7	24	0	.115
Ray Shore	P35	35	49	7	9	6	0	0	0	0	11	0	.184
James Bilbrey	P35	35	25	5	6	5	2	0	1	4	5	0	.240
John Pavlick	P34	34	59	4	9	3	1	0	0	3	9	0	.153
Earl Jones	P23	23	40	5	14	9	2	0	0	3	6	0	.350
Newman Shirley	P18	23	30	7	6	3	1	0	0	0	6	1	.200
Robert Raney	P22	22	46	5	7	2	0	0	0	3	18	0	.152
Robert Payne	1B14	14	45	4	8	1	0	0	0	4	5	0	.178
Stan Ferens	P12	12	11	2	2	0	0	0	0	1	5	0	.182
Stan Benjamin	OF,1B	5	4	0	2	3	0	0	0			0	.000
Vince Castino	C	2	3	0	0	0	0	0	0			0	.000
George Corona	PH	1	1	0	0	0	0	0	0			0	.000
Carl Schultz	PH	1	1	0	0	0	0	0	0			0	.000
Glen Willard	PR	1	0	0	0	0	0	0	0			0	----

PITCHERS		W	L	PCT	G	GS	CG	SH	IP	H	BB	SO	ERA
Robert Raney		8	8	.500	22	19	10	3	130	134	87	103	5.12
Chet Johnson		8	20	.286	35	32	11	1	211	241	108	133	5.08
Ray Shore		7	11	.389	35	15	8	0	124	125	82	84	4.79
Earl Jones		6	5	.545	23	11	5	1	105	118	49	65	4.37
Newman Shirley		6	6	.500	18	13	3	0	82	80	62	44	5.71
William Scott		6	8	.429	40	12	4	0	135	158	72	55	4.33
John Pavlick		5	13	.278	34	22	6	0	180	187	101	90	4.35
James Bilbrey		4	8	.333	35	8	3	0	98	116	68	48	5.33
Stan Ferens		3	1	.750	12	4	2	0	40	59	10	13	6.98
Al Milnar		1	5	.167	25		0	0	70	82	45	27	4.63
Jim Mains		0	1	.000	1		0	0	2	2	2	1	0.00
Frank Biscan		0	0	----	5		0	0	10	18	14	5	10.45

MULTI-TEAM PLAYERS

BATTERS	POS-GAMES	TEAMS	GP	AB	R	H	BI	2B	3B	HR	BB	SO	SB	BA
Augie Bergamo	OF107	COL-MIN-LOU	123	379	58	92	42	13	4	5	60	35	0	.243
Joe Bestudik	OF60,3B38	MIL-SP	115	366	59	103	59	21	0	7	58	41	1	.281
Maurice Mozzali	OF99	MIN-COL	114	340	71	102	35	15	3	6	74	31	6	.300
Andy Gilbert	OF79,3B17,1B12	TOL-MIN	112	364	58	106	65	23	1	15	24	57	4	.291
Leighton Kimball	3B62,OF33	SP-LOU	104	301	45	71	46	8	2	11	54	52	1	.236
Merrill Combs	SS103	LOU-COL	103	346	46	82	19	10	4	4	55	35	4	.237
John Rosenthal	OF83	SP-IND	93	297	51	95	49	11	4	7	50	36	2	.320
Frank Genovese	OF63	LOU-MIN	92	217	48	52	29	9	1	3	63	27	7	.240
Russ Rolandson	C55	MIN-LOU	81	219	33	71	31	8	4	4	23	22	3	.324
Jack Aragon	C70	LOU-MIN	78	193	20	42	16	14	1	0	32	37	3	.218
Al Brancato	3B26,SS18,2B16	LOU-SP	76	232	33	66	23	10	3	4	35	37	1	.284
Norm Schlueter	C50	LOU-MIL	54	157	8	32	16	2	1	0	25	28	0	.204
Cyril Buker	P34	SP-MIL	34	42	3	11	7	1	0	0	4	10	0	.262
Otto Denning		LOU-MIN	34	41	8	12	3	3	0	0	7	7	0	.293
Ken Jungels	P32	MIN-LOU	32	27	2	6	1	0	0	0	3	6	0	.222
John Griffore	P31	COL-LOU	31	67	7	10	3	1	0	0	5	16	0	.149
Otis Clark	P29	LOU-COL	29	66	3	7	2	0	1	0	4	18	0	.106
Emery Rudd	P29	LOU-TOL	29	48	4	8	1	0	0	0	2	15	0	.167
Lum Harris	P24	LOU-MIN	24	37	3	4	0	0	0	0	3	12	0	.103

PITCHERS		TEAMS	W	L	PCT	G	GS	CG	SH	IP	H	BB	SO	ERA
Otis Clark		LOU-COL	12	13	.480	29	27	10	1	207	222	75	79	3.87
Cyril Buker		SP-MIL	8	8	.500	34	16	5	0	139	178	71	52	5.31

MULTI-TEAM PLAYERS (cont.)

PITCHERS	TEAMS	W	L	PCT	G	GS	CG	SH	IP	H	BB	SO	ERA
Emery Rudd	LOU-TOL	8	9	.471	29	20	7	0	132	145	121	73	5.93
John Griffore	COL-LOU	8	11	.421	31	27	8	0	189	194	52	111	3.76
Lum Harris	LOU-MIN	7	7	.500	24	14	6	0	115	130	50	35	4.46
Ken Jungels	MIN-LOU	2	10	.167	32	16	2	1	102	136	53	46	5.74
Owen Scheetz	MIL-LOU	0	0	----	8		0	0	14	23	4	5	

TEAM BATTING

TEAMS	GP	AB	R	H	BI	2B	3B	HR	BB	SO	SB	BA
KANSAS CITY	156	4981	852	1392	784	226	78	96	729	713	115	.279
LOUISVILLE	154	4956	695	1324	638	183	65	49	640	637	113	.267
MILWAUKEE	156	5097	775	1460	721	235	45	92	619	591	28	.286
MINNEAPOLIS	157	5320	839	1469	781	234	39	135	649	731	62	.276
COLUMBUS	155	5044	704	1315	633	235	47	85	619	655	75	.261
INDIANAPOLIS	154	5113	682	1398	629	224	49	90	498	533	39	.273
ST. PAUL	156	5206	806	1428	737	222	69	110	692	674	70	.274
TOLEDO	154	5125	742	1426	670	217	45	98	536	582	40	.278
	621	40842	6095	11212	5593	1776	437	755	4892	5116	542	.275

1948
Indianapolis Indians

In the first fifty years of the American Association, two teams failed to win two pennants in a row. One of the two was the Toledo Mud Hens, who had but a single title to their credit. The other was the Indianapolis Indians.

The Indianapolis Indians won the inaugural Association pennant in 1902, but their efforts since had earned them only a smattering of titles. Their second title followed in 1908, with another in 1917 and a fourth in 1928. Since then, the Indians had entered a long dry spell. However, after finishing sixth in 1947, the Indians put together a powerful team which would club the American Association into submission.

In 1948, Indianapolis rolled to the pennant by eleven games over second place Milwaukee. Finishing with exactly 100 victories, the Indians were paced by first baseman Les Fleming (.323, 26 HR, 143 RBI), catcher Earl Turner (.313), shortstop Pete Castiglione (.308), second baseman Jack Cassini (.305), and outfielders Ted Beard (.301) and Culley Rikard (107 RBI). (Fleming's RBI total led the league.) Indians pitchers were led by Robert Malloy's circuit leading twenty-one victories.

Behind second place Milwaukee finished St. Paul, Columbus, Minneapolis, Kansas City, Toledo, and Louisville. (Note: the American Association's first African-American player, Roy Campanella, made his debut in 1948 with the third place St. Paul Saints.) The batting leader was Glenn McQuillen of Toledo (.329), and the home run leader was Michael Natisin of Columbus (30). Glenn Elliott of Milwaukee won the earned run average title with an all-time high mark of 3.76, while Louisville's John McCall struck out a league leading 149. (Note: some sources indicate the earned run average titlist to be Ira Hutchinson of Columbus with a mark of 2.54. Hutchinson, however, pitched in only 85 innings, too few to qualify.)

The Indianapolis 100-victory season in 1948 would prove to be the high water mark of the club's first 50 years. But this team would also be remembered for something else—its popularity. This Indianapolis team drew nearly 500,000 fans to see them play. No other American Association team, to this point, had ever drawn more.

INDIANAPOLIS Indians

1st   100-54   .649   Al Lopez

BATTERS	POS-GAMES	GP	AB	R	H	BI	2B	3B	HR	BB	SO	SB	BA
Les Fleming	1B151	151	527	112	170	143	28	6	26	103	52	1	.323
Jack Cassini	2B129	131	518	101	158	63	27	6	0	54	53	33	.305
Pete Castiglione	SS148	148	578	87	178	88	33	16	5	41	37	3	.308
Don Gutteridge	3B89,2B11	107	366	58	94	51	17	2	5	31	50	6	.257
Tom Saffell	OF145	149	586	119	175	56	24	10	6	66	76	22	.299
Ted Beard	OF142	142	571	131	154	85	31	17	7	128	97	13	.301
Culley Rikard	OF141	142	491	99	140	107	29	6	11	85	58	2	.285
Earl Turner	C83	85	307	48	96	56	17	8	2	26	28	5	.313
Roy Weatherly	OF32,3B,2B	68	132	17	40	30	3	1	4	13	15	1	.303
Charlie Letchas	3B30,2B19	52	164	30	41	15	17	2	5	31	50	6	.257
Cal McLish	P29	51	77	22	22	2	0	1	0	6	17	3	.286
Robert Ganss	C43	49	131	19	35	20	5	1	2	18	23	0	.267
Frank Kalin	OF20,1B14	46	126	26	41	39	6	2	7	16	17	1	.325
Frank Barrett	P44	44	15	1	5	3	1	0	0	1	5	0	.333
Al Lopez	C42	43	127	13	34	21	4	1	2	12	13	1	.268
John Hutchings	P38	38	21	2	4	2	0	0	0	1	4	0	.190
Jim Bagby	P31	34	94	9	20	15	3	0	3	2	13	0	.213
Edson Bahr	P28	34	56	4	9	3	1	0	0	0	23	0	.161
Robert Malloy	P32	32	103	12	22	10	1	0	0	5	17	1	.214
Jack Hallett	P23	23	51	3	12	7	2	0	0	1	10	0	.235
Royce Lint	P16	23	19	3	5	2	1	0	0	2	6	0	.263
James Walsh	P13	13	15	2	1	1	0	0	0	1	7	0	.067
Glenn Crawford	3B,2B	12	17	3	6	1	0	0	0	6	2	0	.353
Stanley Ferek	P6	6	4		1								.250
Stephen Nagy	P3	3	4		1								.250
Charles Rushe	P3	3	0		0								----
Jim Kleckley	P2	2	0		0								----
Bill Sweiger	P2	2	0		0								----

PITCHERS		W	L	PCT	G	GS	CG	SH	IP	H	BB	SO	ERA
Robert Malloy		21	7	.750	32		18	0	242	270	99	105	4.17
Jim Bagby		16	9	.640	34		16	1	227	272	80	54	4.64
Cal McLish		12	9	.571	29		12	4	172	199	57	71	4.13
Jack Hallett		11	5	.688	23		9	1	132	126	62	91	4.91
John Hutchings		10	2	.833	38		1	0	92	88	37	59	3.52
Edson Bahr		10	6	.625	28		7	1	148	164	57	78	4.20
Frank Barrett		7	5	.583	44		0	0	73	64	42	25	3.21
James Walsh		4	2	.667	13		2	1	47	51	23	26	4.79
Royce Lint		4	4	.500	16		0	0	45	51	29	28	4.80
Stephen Nagy		1	0	1.000	3			0	14	12	8	8	2.57
Stanley Ferek		0	2	.000	6			0	14	31	9	8	18.00
Charles Rushe		0	0	----	3			0	3	9	4	1	
Jim Kleckley		0	0	----	3			0	5	4	1	0	
Bill Sweiger		0	0	----	2			0	1	2	1	0	0.00

MILWAUKEE Brewers

2nd   89-65   .578   -11   Nick Cullop

BATTERS	POS-GAMES	GP	AB	R	H	BI	2B	3B	HR	BB	SO	SB	BA
Heinz Becker	1B135	136	483	91	155	71	28	5	10	93	55	3	.321
Al Roberge	2B121	141	515	76	131	68	19	5	16	46	39	1	.254
Damon Phillips	SS110,3B36	145	560	87	150	78	22	3	16	42	48	5	.268
Gene Markland	3B115,2B31	147	560	120	157	82	25	3	20	96	86	12	.280
Froilan Fernandez	OF151	152	575	96	183	124	29	6	23	76	53	18	.318
Marv Rickert	OF120,1B10	128	510	99	154	117	22	13	27	50	65	5	.302
Jim Gleeson	OF			(see multi-team players)									
Paul Burris	C100	111	368	47	91	53	15	2	3	47	28	2	.247
Frank Kerr	C46	68	166	26	45	24	7	4	4	24	33	2	.271
Tom Triner	P46	50	30	5	8	0	0	0	0	0	7	0	.267
Norwood Ozark	1B18	43	91	12	26	20	5	1	0	8	12	2	.286
Johnny Logan	SS38	40	151	27	38	20	8	3	1	25	23	1	.252
Larry Rosenthal	OF15	34	56	9	10	2	0	0	0	11	12	2	.179
Glenn Elliott	P33	33	56	6	12	15	0	0	0	2	13	0	.213
Al Epperly	P29	32	69	14	22	7	1	2	0	10	16	1	.319
Raymond Martin	P30	31	49	8	10	7	2	0	1	6	23	0	.204
Ed Wright	P30	30	45	3	13	8	2	0	0	3	7	0	.289
Norman Roy	P27	27	43	4	8	3	1	0	0	0	8	0	.186
Carden Gillenwater	OF24	24	84	16	30	19	5	1	2	20	15	2	.357
Al Lyons	P11,OF	18	31	5	6	2	2	1	1	5	9	0	.194
Jim Prendergast	P17	17	25	4	3	1	0	0	0	4	2	0	.120

MILWAUKEE (cont.)
Brewers

BATTERS	POS-GAMES	GP	AB	R	H	BI	2B	3B	HR	BB	SO	SB	BA
Les Studener	P16	16	21	2	3	2	0	0	1	1	7	0	.143
Frank Bernardi	P9	9	2		0								.000
Norm Schlueter	C	7	23	0	1	1	0	0	0			0	.043
Del Crandall	C	5	12	1	1	0	0	0	0			0	.083
Walter Linden	C	5	9	0	2	1	0	0	0			0	.222
Harry MacPherson	P5	5	1		0								.000
Dave Sheehan	P4	4	5		1								.200
Dick Mulligan	P2	2	4		0								.000
Joe Bauman	PH	1	1	0	0	0	0	0	0			0	.000

PITCHERS		W	L	PCT	G	GS	CG	SH	IP	H	BB	SO	ERA
Glenn Elliott		14	7	.667	33		13	3	189	181	73	125	3.76
Al Epperly		14	8	.636	29		14	2	197	223	60	67	4.34
Norman Roy		10	6	.625	27		7	0	120	99	78	79	3.98
Raymond Martin		10	7	.588	30		7	0	144	157	79	85	4.75
Ed Wright		9	12	.429	30		9	0	139	183	50	37	5.37
Jim Prendergast		8	2	.800	17		7	0	87	110	13	41	3.10
Tom Triner		7	5	.583	46		1	0	105	108	66	58	4.71
Al Lyons		3	2	.600	11			0	38	49	27	35	4.50
Les Studener		3	4	.429	16		3	0	60	63	60	39	5.25
Frank Bernardi		1	1	.500	9			0	20	28	18	7	6.30
Dave Sheehan		1	1	.500	4			0	15	17	12	8	5.40
Dick Mulligan		0	1	.000	2			0	8	8	10	2	4.50
Harry MacPherson		0	0	----	5			0	7	12	4	5	

ST. PAUL   3rd   86-68   .558   -14   Walt Alston
Saints

BATTERS	POS-GAMES	GP	AB	R	H	BI	2B	3B	HR	BB	SO	SB	BA
John Douglas	1B138	143	578	75	175	73	22	11	2	68	54	5	.303
George Fallon	2B93	96	347	49	90	67	25	2	10	32	38	3	.259
Clarence Hicks	SS126	137	534	91	158	61	26	5	5	71	51	10	.296
Al Brancato	3B85,2B48	139	505	66	150	76	21	7	9	53	43	1	.297
Eric Tipton	OF146	148	540	111	169	126	35	10	28	115	64	14	.313
Earl Naylor	OF121	127	454	71	126	62	26	5	8	56	59	7	.278
Robert Addis	OF118	126	456	88	143	67	20	11	8	36	36	6	.314
Ferrell Anderson	C108	117	415	72	122	63	29	3	12	39	34	0	.294
David Pluss	OF53	73	203	41	55	33	8	4	7	42	28	1	.271
John Jorgensen	3B63	70	245	33	64	28	11	5	8	32	16	6	.261
Maurice Atwell	OF33,C21	60	203	37	70	39	16	3	3	32	11	3	.345
Bob Ramazzotti	SS31,2B,3B,OF	47	175	39	50	30	8	2	5	13	15	4	.286
Charles Samaklis	P39	39	38	5	5	3	1	0	0	5	16	0	.132
George Coffman	P38	38	11	1	1	0	0	0	0	0	3	0	.091
Roy Campanella	C29,OF	35	123	31	40	39	5	2	13	23	23	0	.325
Morris Martin	P35	35	66	5	11	11	1	1	0	3	11	0	.167
Jack Paepke	P27	35	65	13	17	5	3	2	0	5	13	0	.262
Ezra McGlothin	P32	33	62	8	10	7	2	0	0	4	10	0	.161
Phil Haugstad	P31	31	65	5	6	4	1	0	0	8	35	0	.092
Melvin Himes	P30	30	61	9	7	4	3	0	1	8	16	0	.115
James Romano	P28	28	32	0	2	0	2	0	0	2	12	0	.063
Danny Ozark	1B16	23	62	13	14	12	1	0	5	11	11	0	.226
Floyd Ross	P14	20	12	3	1	1	0	0	0	0	3	0	.083
Harry Taylor	P9	12	32	4	8	6	2	0	1	0	2	0	.250
Stewart Hofferth	C	7	9	0	0	2	0	0	0			0	.000
Dan Bankhead	P6	6	18	4	9	2	0	0	0			0	.500
James Phillips	OF	6	8	1	0	1	0	0	0			0	.000
LeRoy Pfund	P6	6	7		1								.143
Dmitrios Baxes	2B,1B	5	11	1	2	0	0	0	0			0	.182
John Gabbard	P4	4	3		0								.000
Charles Thompson	C	3	6	1	2	0	0	1	0			0	.333
Joe Bielmeier	P3	3	4		0								.000
Bill Eggert	P1	1	1		0								.000
Leon Griffeth	P1	1	0		0								----

PITCHERS		W	L	PCT	G	GS	CG	SH	IP	H	BB	SO	ERA
Ezra McGlothin		14	7	.667	32		10	4	172	158	85	125	4.81
Morris Martin		13	11	.542	35		15	3	186	171	71	129	4.16
Phil Haugstad		12	8	.600	31		9	2	182	154	106	95	4.25
Melvin Himes		11	6	.647	30		7	2	167	171	70	114	4.85

ST. PAUL (cont.)
Saints

PITCHERS	W	L	PCT	G	GS	CG	SH	IP	H	BB	SO	ERA
Charles Samaklis	10	10	.500	39		2	1	125	134	53	56	4.90
Jack Paepke	7	8	.467	27		7	2	149	146	98	70	3.93
James Romano	5	5	.500	28		3	0	109	100	63	59	3.06
George Coffman	5	6	.455	38		0	0	62	74	31	26	4.50
Dan Bankhead	4	0	1.000	6			0	35	34	18	22	3.60
Harry Taylor	3	4	.429	9		4	1	57	54	30	39	3.95
Floyd Ross	2	1	.667	14			0	40	46	31	16	7.20
LeRoy Pfund	0	1	.000	6			0	24	25	16	7	6.38
Joe Bielemeier	0	1	.000	3			0	12	19	3	2	8.25
John Gabbard	0	0	----	4			0	13	13	8	3	2.77
Bill Eggert	0	0	----	1			0	3	2	2	3	0.00
Leon Griffeth	0	0	----	1			0	1	2	0	1	0.00

COLUMBUS   4th   81-73   .526   -19   Harold Anderson
Red Birds

BATTERS	POS-GAMES	GP	AB	R	H	BI	2B	3B	HR	BB	SO	SB	BA
Michael Natisin	1B139	141	521	107	159	132	33	5	30	71	45	1	.305
Ben Steiner	2B86	89	336	60	95	36	13	7	2	47	23	5	.283
Bill Costa	SS151	151	532	55	145	70	23	6	5	64	50	2	.273
Tom Glaviano	3B98,2B2	106	349	82	100	77	17	7	18	72	51	10	.287
Bill Howerton	OF150	150	569	104	170	114	33	6	25	66	83	4	.299
Roy Broome	OF121	126	468	75	137	69	18	6	5	28	55	4	.293
Don Thompson	OF107	121	446	79	127	51	24	3	4	48	49	9	.285
Bill Baker	C59	64	190	25	58	28	10	1	3	48	6	2	.305
Bernard Olsen	OF55,3B38	109	332	47	93	59	16	11	4	40	40	4	.280
Maurice Mozzali	OF49,1B18	98	274	63	80	27	18	1	2	41	24	2	.292
Charles Harrington	2B71	97	341	70	103	22	24	4	1	22	29	7	.302
Joe Garagiola	C58	65	202	38	72	45	11	3	7	34	14	0	.356
Ira Hutchinson	P65	65	15	1	1	1	0	0	0	0	5	0	.067
Bill Conroy	C43	50	128	17	30	26	3	2	8	17	23	0	.234
Harvey Haddix	P32	45	92	12	31	12	5	0	0	4	18	0	.337
John Crimian	P40	43	50	5	5	0	0	0	0	4	10	0	.100
Kurt Krieger	P38	38	67	4	9	2	1	0	0	2	21	0	.134
Wayne McLeland	P34	34	50	4	9	7	0	1	0	1	21	0	.180
Charles Stanceu	P30	30	70	3	10	5	0	0	0	4	33	0	.143
Clarence Beers	P30	30	64	5	7	2	1	0	0	3	22	0	.109
Ray Yochim	P20	21	27	4	6	7	2	0	2	0	5	0	.222
Stephen Gerkin	P20	20	8	0	1	0	0	0	0	0	3	0	.125
Alex Patterson	P13	13	17	1	2	3	1	0	0	0	2	0	.118
Claude Wright	3B12	12	48	5	11	5	1	1	1	3	9	0	.229
Roy Huff	3B	10	17	2	4	0	0	0	0	0	7	0	.235
Vern Rapp	C	7	19	6	7	3	0	0	0	1		0	.368
George Copeland	P5	5	0		0								----
Gregory Masson	C	2	1	0	0	0	0	0	0	0		0	.000
Jack Frisinger	P2	2	1		0								.000
Tom Kelley	P2	2	0		0								----
Ken Siefert	P2	2	0		0								----
Bill Burda	PH	1	1	0	0	0	0	0	0	0		0	.000
John Klippstein	P1	1	0		0								----
Joe Ford	P1	1	0		0								----

PITCHERS	W	L	PCT	G	GS	CG	SH	IP	H	BB	SO	ERA
Kurt Krieger	12	11	.522	38		9	1	189	178	92	87	4.14
Charles Stanceu	12	12	.500	30		11	0	193	215	83	89	4.24
Harvey Haddix	11	9	.550	32		11	1	186	199	67	144	4.79
Clarence Beers	10	12	.455	30		7	0	158	188	68	80	5.35
Ira Hutchinson	9	3	.750	65		0	0	85	81	25	15	2.54
John Crimian	9	4	.692	40		4	0	149	181	64	65	4.65
Wayne McLeland	7	14	.333	34		5	2	164	167	72	65	3.79
Ray Yochim	5	1	.833	20		4	2	72	65	42	39	3.13
Alex Patterson	3	2	.600	13		3	0	54	67	26	9	5.83
Stephen Gerkin	3	3	.500	20			0	36	46	14	14	4.75
Ken Siefert	0	1	.000	2			0	2	7	2	1	18.00
Joe Ford	0	1	.000	1			0	1	4	0	1	36.00
George Copeland	0	0	----	5			0	7	10	5	6	
Jack Frisinger	0	0	----	2			0	7	8	3	2	7.71
Tom Kelley	0	0	----	2			0	2	6	3	1	27.00
John Klippstein	0	0	----	1			0	1	3	3	1	

MINNEAPOLIS   5th   77-77   .500   -23   Shellanback - Herman
Millers

BATTERS	POS-GAMES	GP	AB	R	H	BI	2B	3B	HR	BB	SO	SB	BA
Elbie Fletcher	1B107	110	347	73	106	79	26	5	19	96	29	2	.305
Linus Frey	2B69	70	265	51	70	31	15	3	7	54	25	3	.264
Dick Kimble	SS		(see multi-team players)										
Len Schulte	3B76,2B43	129	510	72	141	53	23	1	2	34	40	2	.276
Cleston Ray	OF126	136	453	111	138	61	25	7	18	84	56	1	.305
Babe Barna	OF98	104	344	79	99	83	17	2	23	93	56	0	.288
Joe Lafata	OF86,1B42	130	474	78	137	76	30	3	14	45	71	12	.289
Bennie Warren	C69	79	223	39	53	48	13	0	14	61	44	1	.238
Andy Gilbert	OF68,3B13	100	326	62	100	82	22	3	22	33	49	2	.307
Frank Genovese	OF82	97	243	74	71	36	13	1	14	105	28	4	.292
Jack Maguire	3B35,SS21	75	235	35	62	42	15	2	6	29	29	5	.264
Robert Rhawn	3B29,SS32	59	233	41	72	38	13	1	9	15	24	4	.309
Bill Emmerich	P55	55	18	2	2	2	0	0	0	0	8	0	.111
Francis Hardy	P42	50	56	4	8	4	2	0	0	3	17	0	.143
Mario Picone	P43	49	80	13	21	12	4	0	0	7	25	0	.263
Bill Ayers	P38	38	76	3	11	2	0	1	0	2	21	0	.145
Jack Conway	2B32	37	146	28	46	27	10	3	5	17	38	0	.315
Dick Culler	SS35	35	128	11	35	9	6	0	0	11	9	1	.273
Otis Clark	P35	35	68	2	11	4	0	0	0	5	19	0	.162
Reuben Fischer	P25	27	40	6	11	6	3	1	2	3	13	0	.275
Robert Cain	P22	27	37	4	10	6	2	0	1	3	6	1	.270
Werner Strunk	P13	14	10	1	1	1	0	0	0	1	3	0	.100
Harold Bamberger	OF	13	32	7	7	4	1	0	0	5	3	1	.219
Monte Kennedy	P13	13	28	2	3	1	0	0	0	1	12	0	.107
Hubert Andrews	P10	11	16	1	1	0	0	0	0	0	9	0	.059
Billy Herman	2B,3B,1B	10	31	9	14	9	4	0	2	4	3	0	.452
Clem Dreisewerd	P9	9	13		1								.077
Lum Harris	P9	9	6		1								.167
Ray Carlson	SS	8	5	0	0	0	0	0	0			0	.000
Harold Swanson	P4	4	2		0								.000
Earl McGowan	P4	4	0		0								----
John Uber	P3	3	1		0								----
Woody Abernathy	P2	2	0		0								----
Ed Wallner	C	1	3	0	2	0	1	0	0			0	.667
Sam Brewer	P1	1	1		0								.000

PITCHERS		W	L	PCT	G	GS	CG	SH	IP	H	BB	SO	ERA
Otis Clark		12	13	.480	35		11	2	186	238	96	64	5.66
Bill Emmerich		11	6	.647	55		0	0	94	111	34	38	4.60
Mario Picone		11	9	.550	43		9	1	202	216	150	104	5.93
Bill Ayers		11	12	.478	38		12	2	205	223	96	118	4.61
Francis Hardy		10	10	.500	42		4	0	169	205	102	97	6.66
Reuben Fischer		5	4	.556	25		6	1	116	157	47	43	5.74
Robert Cain		5	5	.500	22		3	0	78	88	51	48	6.58
Clem Dreisewerd		4	3	.571	9		4	0	49	70	10	15	5.69
Monte Kennedy		3	6	.333	13		5	2	78	62	51	77	3.81
Werner Strunk		1	0	1.000	13			0	35	46	16	21	4.89
John Uber		1	0	1.000	3			0	6	10	3	2	9.00
Lum Harris		1	1	.500	9			0	18	17	8	12	5.50
Earl McGowan		1	1	.500	4			0	5	9	0	4	10.80
Hubert Andrews		1	5	.167	10		2	0	49	82	19	20	8.45
Harold Swanson		0	2	.000	4			0	12	16	13	7	8.25
Woody Abernathy		0	0	----	2			0	1	5	2	1	
Sam Brewer		0	0	----	1			0	3	9	1	0	

KANSAS CITY   6th   64-88   .421   -35   Dick Bartell
Blues

BATTERS	POS-GAMES	GP	AB	R	H	BI	2B	3B	HR	BB	SO	SB	BA
Dick Kryhoski	1B145	145	545	78	160	87	30	7	13	50	58	7	.294
Nicholas Witek	2B		(see multi-team players)										
Al Stringer	SS65	68	196	25	49	10	9	1	1	31	29	1	.250
Al Rosen	3B102,SS31	127	462	102	151	110	29	8	25	73	36	10	.327
Hank Bauer	OF132	132	541	103	165	100	32	11	23	52	67	26	.305
James Dyck	OF91,3B15	106	407	71	115	61	25	4	2	52	41	8	.283
Leon Culberson	OF79	83	313	47	81	39	17	1	5	40	46	4	.259
Ralph Houk	C92,3B1	103	364	54	110	49	24	5	1	31	14	9	.302
Blas Monaco	3B50,OF15	114	260	56	75	50	17	6	5	84	32	7	.288
Bill Drescher	C57	88	213	35	68	52	13	2	7	28	20	1	.319
John Phillips	SS63,1B,OF	67	240	39	67	28	11	0	1	24	19	7	.279

KANSAS CITY (cont.)
Blues

BATTERS	POS-GAMES	GP	AB	R	H	BI	2B	3B	HR	BB	SO	SB	BA
Ford Garrison	OF48	53	171	28	55	34	11	1	3	22	12	0	.322
Joe Muffoletto	2B44	44	166	30	62	34	10	2	1	23	10	3	.373
David Madison	P35	38	68	3	10	4	1	0	0	7	13	0	.147
William Woop	P38	38	63	6	5	3	1	0	0	7	23	0	.079
Joe Beggs	P38	38	6	0	0	0	0	0	0	0	2	0	.000
Lee Dodson	P31	32	37	1	4	2	1	0	0	2	13	0	.108
John Mackinson	P27	30	19	3	4	1	0	0	0	2	9	0	.211
Charley Schanz	P28	28	40	5	4	5	1	1	0	1	16	0	.100
James Arnold	P24	26	17	0	1	0	0	0	0	0	9	0	.059
Malcolm Malette	P23	23	40	3	6	2	0	1	0	1	9	0	.150
Carmine Melignano	P22	22	14	0	1	0	0	0	0	2	8	0	.071
Malcolm Mick	OF11	21	33	5	5	2	2	0	0	10	3	4	.151
Don Johnson	P14	14	22	2	2	0	0	0	0	0	4	0	.091
Henry Ballinger	C10	13	33	3	12	6	2	0	1	1	2	0	.364
Robert Keegan	P9	13	23	1	8	4	1	0	0	0	3	0	.348
Harry Craft	OF	13	18	0	3	1	0	0	0	1	4	0	.167
Clarence Marshall	P10	11	12	1	3	1	0	0	0	2	1	0	.250
Henry Anderson	P7	8	6		1								.167
Leslie Mueller	P8	8	2		0								.000
Frank Verdi	SS	7	29	7	6	4	1	0	1			2	.207
Victor Fucci	OF	7	26	5	6	6	3	1	1			0	.231
Carl DeRose	P5	5	8		1								.125
Bill Houtz	P4	5	2		0								.000
Ray Louthen	P2	4	6		1								.167
James Tote	P3	3	2		0								.000
William Burgess	PH,PR	2	1	0	0	0	0	0	0	0			.000
Edwin Ehlers	2B1	1	1	0	0	0	0	0	0	0		0	.000
Frank Simanovsky	P1	1	0		0								----

PITCHERS		W	L	PCT	G	GS	CG	SH	IP	H	BB	SO	ERA
David Madison		14	9	.609	35		14	1	197	239	63	83	4.27
William Woop		9	14	.391	38		8	0	198	208	120	111	5.00
Malcolm Malette		7	5	.583	22		3	0	105	127	70	67	4.97
John Mackinson		5	4	.556	27		0	0	61	64	43	37	5.02
Charley Schanz		5	7	.417	28		3	2	119	152	54	62	5.45
Robert Keegan		4	1	.800	9		5	0	57	45	19	48	2.21
James Arnold		4	4	.500	24		1	0	60	82	35	22	6.00
Carmine Melignano		4	6	.400	22		1	0	57	71	39	32	6.16
Joe Beggs		3	6	.333	38		0	0	48	73	19	21	6.75
Don Johnson		3	7	.300	14		0	0	66	69	36	40	5.18
Henry Anderson		2	0	1.000	7			0	18	15	22	12	6.50
Clarence Marshall		1	2	.333	10			0	35	44	30	17	6.69
Carl DeRose		1	2	.333	5			0	21	31	13	7	8.57
Lee Dodson		1	8	.111	31		3	0	124	119	113	87	5.15
Leslie Mueller		0	1	.000	8			0	12	12	6	3	6.75
James Tote		0	1	.000	3			0	4	6	7	1	9.00
Ray Louthen		0	2	.000	2			0	12	20	8	2	12.75
Bill Houtz		0	0	----	4			0	4	1	4	2	0.00
Frank Simanovsky		0	0	----	1			0	1	5	0	0	

TOLEDO
Mud Hens

7th   61-91   .401   -38   George Detore

BATTERS	POS-GAMES	GP	AB	R	H	BI	2B	3B	HR	BB	SO	SB	BA
Henry Arft	1B98	99	366	57	106	67	18	5	15	47	48	6	.290
Ellis Clary	2B134	140	542	88	163	38	29	6	1	73	41	15	.301
Wesley Hamner	SS60	69	246	29	67	26	11	1	3	13	36	7	.272
Donald Richmond	3B136	146	496	80	150	75	28	3	13	42	44	8	.302
Glenn McQuillen	OF	147	538	76	177	90	37	3	14	58	21	10	.329
Boris Woyt	OF141	145	599	78	168	49	23	4	2	31	48	17	.280
Dick Kokos	OF82	84	314	70	99	44	14	3	13	51	39	9	.315
Frank Mancuso	C97	111	337	41	92	61	14	4	13	38	40	0	.273
Donald Palmer	C69	74	210	19	52	23	9	0	0	17	32	2	.248
George Corona	OF43	63	179	23	37	16	12	0	6	15	27	1	.207
George Binks	1B46,OF13	59	237	34	67	36	16	3	4	13	39	1	.283
Leighton Kimball	OF	53	104	14	23	13	5	1	2	10	15	0	.221
Salvador Madrid	SS49	49	174	13	38	26	5	1	3	8	30	0	.218
George Elder	OF36	49	145	20	41	22	9	2	0	8	28	1	.283
Walter Brown	P42	42	19	2	4	0	1	0	0	1	7	0	.211
Ernest Bickhaus	P28	40	44	8	5	3	1	0	1	1	12	0	.114
Robert Raney	P31	31	57	3	8	0	0	0	0	0	21	1	.140

TOLEDO (cont.)
Mud Hens

BATTERS	POS-GAMES	GP	AB	R	H	BI	2B	3B	HR	BB	SO	SB	BA
Charles Grant	2B12,3B,SS,OF	27	71	12	19	9	4	1	1	8	15	1	.268
James Wilson	P26	27	63	2	17	6	5	0	1	2	4	0	.270
Emery Rudd	P25	25	27	0	4	0	0	0	0	1	3	0	.148
Ralph Schwamb	P25	25	24	1	3	2	1	0	0	0	9	0	.125
Joe Ostrowski	P19	19	35	1	7	5	0	1	0	6	6	0	.200
Al Gerheauser	P16	16	24	1	1	0	0	0	0	0	9	0	.042
Ray Minor	P4	4	9		3								.333
Marlin Stuart	P4	4	3		2								.667
James Bilbney	P3	3	1		0								.000
Loy Hanning	P3	3	1		0								.000

PITCHERS		W	L	PCT	G	GS	CG	SH	IP	H	BB	SO	ERA
Robert Raney		9	13	.409	31		10	1	163	172	144	128	5.91
James Wilson		7	13	.350	26		11	2	175	177	75	108	4.01
Walter Brown		6	3	.667	42		1	0	93	119	44	59	5.13
Ernest Bickhaus		6	4	.600	28		5	0	125	129	61	57	4.90
Joe Ostrowski		6	9	.400	19		8	0	115	129	22	51	4.54
Al Gerheauser		4	7	.364	16		5	1	74	69	29	34	3.28
Ray Minor		1	1	.500	4			0	22	27	19	9	8.59
Ralph Schwamb		1	9	.100	25		5	0	77	79	52	45	5.14
Marlin Stuart		0	2	.000	4			0	11	15	12	10	11.45
Emery Rudd		0	6	.000	38		0	0	48	73	19	21	6.75
James Bilbrey		0	0	----	3			0	7	12	6	1	
Loy Hanning		0	0	----	3			0	6	8	7	2	

LOUISVILLE   8th   56-98   .364   -44   Leibold - Scheetz
Colonels

BATTERS	POS-GAMES	GP	AB	R	H	BI	2B	3B	HR	BB	SO	SB	BA
Jerome Witte	1B113,OF21,3B11	147	518	72	132	98	28	3	29	58	**122**	8	.255
Lambert Meyer	2B	(see multi-team players)											
George Strickland	SS95,2B,3B,1B	105	367	53	87	39	8	9	1	54	51	5	.237
Ken Chapman	3B101,2B33,SS11	143	521	73	130	45	31	9	7	75	68	12	.250
Tom Wright	OF148	151	563	89	173	85	31	10	13	79	85	12	.307
Augie Bergamo	OF104,1B13	129	422	61	116	44	22	8	2	65	36	8	.275
Ed Lavigne	OF90	97	329	45	92	49	9	6	5	35	41	7	.280
Leslie Aulds	C94	104	293	34	69	38	5	3	4	47	52	4	.235
Ellis Deal	OF15,P14	67	115	13	30	16	4	1	1	18	25	1	.261
Russ Rolandson	C59	64	181	13	37	10	2	2	1	12	16	0	.204
John McCall	P31	57	90	9	19	8	3	0	1	7	24	0	.211
Fred Hatfield	3B38	39	155	12	39	12	8	2	0	9	24	2	.252
George Toolson	P33	33	47	2	9	4	0	1	0	2	18	0	.191
John Griffore	P29	29	62	1	7	3	1	0	0	0	10	0	.113
Bill Zuber	P29	29	31	3	3	1	0	0	0	0	11	0	.097
Walt Dropo	1B28	28	109	9	22	12	1	2	3	8	18	2	.202
Maurice Craft	OF19	25	44	11	10	2	1	1	0	10	5	0	.227
Bill Elbert	P20	25	36	5	3	0	0	0	0	0	15	0	.083
James Shea	P22	22	10	0	2	0	1	0	0	2	4	0	.200
Hampton Coleman	P16	17	23	2	1	2	1	0	0	2	9	0	.043
Ed Rall	C13	13	36	1	8	6	1	0	0	1	5	0	.222
Peter Modica	P13	13	19	1	2	0	0	0	0	5	7	0	.105
James Pruett	C10	12	30	5	10	3	1	0	1	4	3	1	.333
Rollin Schuster	P10	10	5	0	0	0	0	0	0	1	1	0	.000
Charles Koney	2B	8	24	2	4	1	0	0	0			0	.167
Wes Bailey	P7	7	13		2								.154
Ken Jungels	P4	4	0		0								----
Nicholas Milan	P1	1	1		0								.000
Joe Jones	P1	1	0		0								----

PITCHERS		W	L	PCT	G	GS	CG	SH	IP	H	BB	SO	ERA
John Griffore		10	13	.435	29		9	1	176	193	60	80	3.84
John McCall		9	12	.429	31		14	0	183	182	99	**149**	4.67
Ellis Deal		5	7	.417	14		7	1	75	80	34	34	4.80
Hampton Coleman		4	7	.364	16		3	1	75	80	45	49	5.40
George Zuber		4	8	.333	29		3	1	105	119	74	55	6.09
George Toolson		4	10	.286	33		4	0	140	160	64	44	5.21
Wes Bailey		2	3	.400	7			0	40	48	17	14	4.28
Bill Elbert		2	7	.222	20		2	0	98	118	56	34	5.97
Peter Modica		2	7	.222	13		3	0	71	66	53	28	6.72
James Shea		1	4	.200	22		1	0	60	88	35	26	6.00

LOUISVILLE (cont.)
Colonels

PITCHERS	W	L	PCT	G	GS	CG	SH	IP	H	BB	SO	ERA
Rollin Schuster	0	1	.000	10			0	22	28	30	10	6.95
Ken Jungels	0	1	.000	4			0	6	7	5	1	6.00
Joe Jones	0	0	----	1			0	1	1	1	0	
Nicholas Milan	0	0	----	1			0	0	2	0	0	

MULTI-TEAM PLAYERS

BATTERS	POS-GAMES	TEAMS	GP	AB	R	H	BI	2B	3B	HR	BB	SO	SB	BA
James Gleeson	OF121	LOU-MIL	135	408	78	125	78	29	6	12	106	69	9	.306
Lambert Meyer	2B72,OF34	MIN-LOU	128	438	81	131	97	21	3	20	54	37	4	.299
Milt Byrnes	OF105	KC-LOU	121	409	59	123	63	21	3	3	74	51	9	.301
Nicholas Witek	2B115	LOU-KC	117	464	80	145	47	17	6	0	41	20	4	.313
Russ Peters	SS49,3B41	TOL-IND	114	344	48	96	48	13	3	7	38	60	2	.279
Bill Sinton	OF84	MIL-KC-LOU	108	292	56	77	29	17	5	3	58	65	4	.264
Dick Kimble	SS99	MIN-LOU	99	341	58	110	47	18	3	6	68	26	5	.323
Frank Trechock	2B30,SS27	MIN-LOU-MIL	74	205	27	44	19	13	0	0	25	25	5	.215
Don Grate	P39	LOU-MIL	40	30	4	7	3	0	0	0	5	6	0	.233
Earl Reid	P29	MIL-TOL	38	67	15	18	8	2	2	0	3	9	0	.269
John Robinson	P32	KC-LOU	35	52	8	12	4	2	0	0	7	12	0	.231
Chet Johnson	P34	TOL-IND	34	76	5	9	2	0	0	0	6	28	0	.118
Cyril Buker	P32	MIL-KC	32	19	2	4	3	0	1	0	0	2	0	.211
Lee Ross	P29	MIL-TOL	30	22	1	6	1	1	0	1	1	4	0	.273
Ewald Pyle	P27	MIL-LOU	28	59	5	8	3	1	0	0	4	16	0	.136

PITCHERS		TEAMS	W	L	PCT	G	GS	CG	SH	IP	H	BB	SO	ERA
Chet Johnson		TOL-IND	16	12	.571	34		13	1	215	218	134	148	4.06
Earl Reid		MIL-TOL	9	13	.409	29		7	1	153	185	53	51	5.18
Ewald Pyle		MIL-LOU	8	13	.381	27		12	1	162	192	79	104	5.33
John Robinson		KC-LOU	7	14	.333	32		7	1	163	191	79	70	4.36
Don Grate		LOU-MIL	4	4	.500	39		1	0	116	119	55	49	4.19
Cyril Buker		MIL-KC	4	4	.500	32		1	0	73	99	45	35	8.51
Lee Ross		MIL-TOL	3	6	.333	29		2	1	76	97	33	34	6.28

TEAM BATTING

TEAMS	GP	AB	R	H	BI	2B	3B	HR	BB	SO	SB	BA
INDIANAPOLIS	**154**	5244	**948**	**1514**	848	244	**81**	82	668	693	93	**.289**
MILWAUKEE	**154**	5108	862	1428	803	229	58	139	724	648	65	.280
ST. PAUL	**154**	**5351**	878	1508	826	269	75	126	670	625	60	.282
COLUMBUS	**154**	5233	874	1472	805	253	64	118	630	658	50	.281
MINNEAPOLIS	**154**	5175	932	1450	**876**	**280**	39	**185**	**827**	723	45	.280
KANSAS CITY	152	5159	851	1471	775	274	60	91	660	601	**102**	.285
TOLEDO	152	5170	715	1430	645	254	39	99	478	648	79	.277
LOUISVILLE	**154**	5057	666	1283	616	207	64	81	646	**781**	74	.254
	614	41497	6726	11556	6194	2010	480	821	5303	5377	568	.278

1949
Squeaker

Tight pennant races in any baseball league are a challenge to the participating players, nervewracking to their managers, but great for the fans. When the difference between first and second is only a single game, the situation becomes particularly exciting. In the history of the American Association, a single game had separated first and second place only one time, in 1937 when Columbus edged Toledo by a single digit. In 1949, the difference between the top two teams would prove even smaller.

As the 1949 season started, the Indianapolis Indians were the defending champions. Returning with much of their lineup from the previous year, the Indians were favored to repeat. Another team picked to be in contention was the St. Paul Saints. A third place finisher in 1948, this team was a top farm team of the powerful Brooklyn Dodgers. As a result, the Saints were well stocked with quality talent.

The Indians and the Saints entered the latter stages of the 1949 season in a dogfight for the top spot. As the last game approached, the Saints needed a doubleheader sweep on the final day of the season to clinch the flag. St. Paul responded to the challenge, winning the twin bill. Indianapolis finished with the same number of wins, but with one more loss. The Indians ended a buck short, one-half game behind the Saints.

Trailing well behind the leaders, Milwaukee and Minneapolis finished in the last two playoff spots, while Kansas City, Louisville, Columbus, and Toledo finished out of contention. Hitting honors went to Tom Wright of Louisville who hit for the highest average (.368); Minneapolis' Chuck Workman, who hit 41 home runs; and Froilan Fernandez of Indianapolis and St. Paul, who plated 128 runners. Pitching was dominated by one man, Mel Queen. Queen (of Indianapolis) won the most games (22), had the lowest earned run average (2.57), and finished with the most strikeouts (178), winning the pitching triple crown. Phil Haugstad of the Saints managed to tie Queen in one of the categories as he won 22 games as well.

The 1949 season will be remembered for the closest pennant race in American Association history. The second place Indianapolis Indians finished with the same number of victories as the first place Saints, but due to St. Paul rainouts, the Indians played one more game. Unfortunately, this extra game resulted in a loss, ensuring a final deficit of only half a game, the closest possible second place finish.

ST. PAUL Saints

ST. PAUL Saints   1st   93-60   .608   Walt Alston

BATTERS	POS-GAMES	GP	AB	R	H	BI	2B	3B	HR	BB	SO	SB	BA
Danny Ozark	1B75,OF1	92	277	53	85	48	14	2	13	35	36	4	.307
Henry Schenz	2B108,OF11,3B,SS	123	516	104	178	77	26	8	17	39	22	30	.345
Clarence Hicks	SS149	151	530	84	142	62	23	1	4	112	57	5	.268
Dan O'Connell	3B136	138	493	89	155	102	29	1	17	61	68	7	.314
Eric Tipton	OF145	146	516	105	165	106	35	12	13	106	60	11	.320
Robert Addis	OF126	127	492	90	170	74	36	10	6	68	38	12	.346
Earl Naylor	OF101	104	290	52	82	58	14	2	13	32	43	2	.283
Ferrell Anderson	C128	140	478	83	145	91	21	3	16	52	33	1	.303
James Pendleton	OF96	105	347	83	95	39	9	5	6	44	54	27	.274
Clem Labine	P64	64	34	3	5	7	2	0	1	3	15	0	.147
Al Brancato	2B49,3B,SS	63	201	19	46	25	19	1	1	21	23	0	.229
Sam Calderone	C35	60	136	20	43	29	5	0	4	13	20	1	.316
Leon Griffeth	P45	45	22	1	2	2	0	0	0	1	4	0	.091
James Romano	P36	36	57	8	11	9	1	0	1	3	12	0	.193
Phil Haugstad	P35	35	91	5	9	5	0	0	0	2	37	0	.099
George Brown	P31	31	41	6	7	5	0	0	1	5	16	0	.171
Wayne Belardi	1B26	28	99	14	24	18	4	0	4	13	15	1	.242
Harry Taylor	P24	25	50	7	12	8	0	2	1	0	12	0	.240
Louis Welaj	2B,3B	23	17	4	3	2	0	0	0	5	0	0	.176
Karl Morrison	P14	20	22	4	6	2	1	0	0	4	4	1	.273
Melvin Himes	P18	19	40	3	8	5	1	0	1	3	14	0	.200
Morris Martin	P16	16	24	2	2	0	1	0	0	2	4	0	.083
Bill Eggert	P12	13	13	0	1	0	0	0	0	2	8	0	.077
Donald Nicholas	PR	8	0	2	0	0	0	0	0			2	----
Oscar Grimes	3B	7	6	0	1	0	0	0	0			0	.167
Ray Dabek	C	1	2	0	0	0	0	0	0			0	.000

PITCHERS	W	L	PCT	G	GS	CG	SH	IP	H	BB	SO	ERA
Phil Haugstad	22	7	.759	35		17	2	243	216	150	140	2.85
Clem Labine	12	6	.667	64		0	0	139	124	88	70	3.50
Harry Taylor	11	6	.647	24		7	1	118	112	58	43	3.89
James Romano	10	12	.455	36		5	0	161	170	89	71	4.64
Melvin Himes	8	7	.533	18		6	1	112	110	69	36	4.90
George Brown	7	4	.636	31		3	0	123	130	101	61	5.34
Leon Griffeth	4	1	.800	45		0	0	83	75	42	49	3.47
Karl Morrison	4	2	.667	14		4	0	70	69	66	21	5.01
Bill Eggert	3	2	.667	12		2	0	44	47	34	18	5.73
Morris Martin	3	6	.333	16		4	1	79	83	31	51	3.87
Frank Laga	1	0	1.000	4			0	7	12	4	3	2.57
Nick Andromidas	0	1	.000	7			0	17	24	24	14	5.29
Floyd Ross	0	0	----	4			0	10	14	6	1	6.30

INDIANAPOLIS Indians

INDIANAPOLIS Indians   2nd   93-61   .604   -0.5   Al Lopez

BATTERS	POS-GAMES	GP	AB	R	H	BI	2B	3B	HR	BB	SO	SB	BA
Les Fleming	1B94	95	338	71	115	69	27	2	14	67	34	3	.340
Jack Cassini	2B129	131	524	86	157	67	22	4	3	49	45	14	.300
Jack Conway	SS139	140	505	72	129	68	17	6	13	58	94	4	.255
Froilan Fernandez	3B,SS		(see multi-team players)										
Ted Beard	OF120	127	426	108	118	40	17	16	5	132	86	23	.277
Frank Kalin	OF103,1B	113	378	51	116	80	18	4	13	43	46	2	.307
Gerard Scala	OF79	80	302	47	103	40	12	7	3	34	26	4	.341
Earl Turner	C85	99	308	46	81	53	11	7	12	36	53	0	.263
Russ Peters	3B42,SS24,2B1	85	177	22	47	30	8	4	3	26	21	0	.266
Royce Lint	P48	75	59	17	10	6	1	0	0	0	17	0	.169
Tom Saffell	OF67	69	236	39	65	38	6	4	9	35	38	13	.275
Dale Coogan	1B61	64	238	36	63	36	8	2	4	36	32	2	.265
Robert Ganss	C48	58	149	18	44	20	7	1	4	17	13	1	.295
Don Gutteridge	2B28,3B4	56	112	27	28	15	6	3	3	11	21	6	.250
Forrest Main	P54	54	23	7	9	2	0	0	0	4	2	0	.391
Clyde Kluttz	C34	46	129	11	32	14	8	1	0	11	5	0	.248
Dom Dallessandro	OF35	44	114	13	39	19	8	0	2	22	13	1	.342
Culley Rikard	OF42	43	137	23	45	21	11	0	0	41	3	4	.328
Mel Queen	P39	39	82	4	7	5	2	0	0	5	16	0	.085
Chet Johnson	P37	37	68	7	11	3	0	1	0	9	22	0	.162
Joe Muir	P33	36	43	2	7	1	2	0	0	0	3	0	.163
Robert Klinger	P32	32	5	0	0	0	0	0	0	0	1	0	.000
John Hutchings	P28	28	6	0	1	0	0	0	0	0	1	0	.167
James Walsh	P24	27	55	8	8	6	0	2	0	10	24	0	.145

INDIANAPOLIS (cont.)
Indians

BATTERS	POS-GAMES	GP	AB	R	H	BI	2B	3B	HR	BB	SO	SB	BA
Robert Malloy	P23	24	42	3	8	3	0	0	0	1	11	0	.190
Roy Weatherly	OF10	16	43	8	12	10	2	1	1	5	1	0	.279
William Plate	OF11	14	31	5	8	5	2	1	0	7	1	1	.258
Robert Kellogg	OF	12	9	2	1	2	0	1	0	2	1	1	.111
Dick Sinovic	PH	2	1	0	0	0	0	0	0			0	.000
Carlos Bernier	OF	2	0	0	0	0	0	0	0			0	----

PITCHERS		W	L	PCT	G	GS	CG	SH	IP	H	BB	SO	ERA
Mel Queen		**22**	9	.710	39		**24**	6	**266**	221	109	**178**	**2.57**
James Walsh		15	4	.789	24		12	1	181	181	93	94	3.83
Royce Lint		14	3	**.824**	48		5	1	174	182	74	77	3.41
Chet Johnson		11	9	.550	37		8	1	193	207	99	112	4.57
Forrest Main		9	7	.563	54		1	0	109	122	55	61	5.09
Joe Muir		9	8	.529	33		5	2	139	152	58	77	4.92
John Hutchings		4	2	.667	28			0	36	40	15	8	4.50
Robert Malloy		4	9	.308	23		2	0	125	165	51	44	5.77
Robert Klinger		3	4	.429	32			0	38	60	23	13	9.71
Clyde Shoun		1	1	.500	8			0	20	19	10	6	3.15
Elmer Riddle		1	2	.333	5		1	0	28	34	18	11	2.89
John Hahn		0	0	----	3			0	3	2	5	0	
Paul Erickson		0	0	----	1			0	1	3	0	1	
Jack Hallett		0	0	----	1			0	1	0	0	1	0.00

MILWAUKEE   3rd   76-76   .500   -16.5   Nick Cullop
Brewers

BATTERS	POS-GAMES	GP	AB	R	H	BI	2B	3B	HR	BB	SO	SB	BA
Nick Etten	1B147	148	518	82	145	82	22	4	20	108	26	4	.280
Roy Hartsfield	2B153	**154**	**640**	120	**203**	86	27	8	12	73	108	13	.317
Johnny Logan	SS154	**154**	548	84	157	69	21	5	7	81	67	7	.286
Damon Phillips	3B137	139	539	91	154	83	25	2	14	47	53	1	.286
Howie Moss	OF147	147	575	106	169	117	27	5	29	66	85	3	.294
Alvin Aucoin	OF95	103	361	48	109	42	13	1	6	36	41	3	.302
Milt Byrnes	OF		(see multi-team players)										
Paul Burris	C115	120	384	50	101	44	11	3	3	55	30	1	.263
Jim Gleeson	OF88	105	293	42	79	37	13	2	5	75	38	6	.270
Len Schulte	3B19,2B,1B	63	118	19	27	15	4	0	2	9	8	0	.229
Lewis Fox	P50	53	38	4	10	5	1	0	0	0	10	0	.263
Clint Conatser	OF48	49	170	23	47	25	10	1	5	27	28	2	.276
Tom Triner	P42	43	10	2	2	0	0	0	0	0	3	0	.200
Al Lakeman	C25,1B13	40	126	16	38	28	9	2	8	13	32	0	.302
Henry Perry	P34	34	70	6	12	10	1	0	1	7	18	0	.171
Richard Manville	P33	33	46	2	6	4	0	0	0	0	13	0	.130
Norman Roy	P31	31	56	2	12	6	1	0	0	2	8	0	.214
Don Grate	P28	31	6	3	3	0	0	0	0	0	0	0	.500
Al Epperly	P25	30	60	6	18	14	2	1	0	11	10	0	.300
Joe Just	C22	28	73	10	16	10	2	0	2	9	14	0	.219
Raymond Martin	P26	28	41	6	4	2	0	1	0	7	10	0	.098
Les Studener	P26	26	41	1	4	5	1	1	1	0	10	0	.098
Jim Prendergast	P14	14	32	3	5	2	0	0	0	1	8	1	.156
Homer Moore	OF11	12	40	9	11	9	1	2	0	7	10	0	.275
Jesse Levan	OF	12	29	5	3	2	0	0	0	4	1	0	.103
Paul Rambone	PH	8	8	2	2	3	0	0	1			0	.250
William Edwards	C	5	6	1	0	0	0	0	0			0	.000
Richard Donovan	P2	2	2	0	1	0	0	0	0			0	.500
Jack Weisenburger	PH	2	2	0	0	0	0	0	0			0	.000

PITCHERS		W	L	PCT	G	GS	CG	SH	IP	H	BB	SO	ERA
Henry Perry		15	15	.500	34		12	1	191	188	111	85	4.29
Al Epperly		12	10	.545	25		15	2	184	197	34	56	3.38
Norman Roy		11	6	.647	31		10	0	175	171	87	109	3.81
Richard Manville		9	7	.563	33		6	1	123	137	70	76	4.17
Les Studener		8	8	.500	26		7	0	143	145	99	76	4.85
Lewis Fox		6	7	.462	50		4	0	137	150	73	62	4.27
Raymond Martin		6	11	.353	26		8	1	142	167	51	47	4.37
Jim Prendergast		5	8	.385	14		6	1	91	117	25	25	4.25
Tom Triner		3	2	.600	42		0	0	69	66	36	38	3.65
Don Grate		1	1	.500	28		0	0	49	72	26	17	4.96
Richard Donovan		0	1	.000	2		0	0	7	8	2	4	7.71

MILWAUKEE (cont.)
Brewers

PITCHERS	W	L	PCT	G	GS	CG	SH	IP	H	BB	SO	ERA
Ernest Johnson	0	0	----	7			0	11	11	5	5	4.09

MINNEAPOLIS   4th   74-78   .487   -18.5   Thomas Heath
Millers

BATTERS	POS-GAMES	GP	AB	R	H	BI	2B	3B	HR	BB	SO	SB	BA
John Harshman	1B149	150	519	121	140	111	22	7	40	122	110	3	.270
Robert Hofman	2B92	92	395	66	111	38	15	4	9	38	24	2	.281
William Jennings	SS117	123	404	72	115	66	14	6	10	67	87	6	.285
Ray Dandridge	3B83,2B16	99	398	60	144	64	22	5	6	17	17	4	.362
Charles Workman	OF139	146	502	117	146	122	18	4	41	102	62	4	.291
Carvel Rowell	OF85,2B15,3B1	117	418	60	110	71	17	2	11	25	24	3	.263
Andy Gilbert	OF75,1B6	92	221	29	53	38	13	0	6	36	46	1	.240
Sal Yvars	C82	84	290	49	89	57	15	4	8	38	24	1	.307
Jack Maguire	OF64,3B25,SS22	122	428	88	149	71	26	7	12	97	42	5	.348
Roy Hughes	3B43,2B34,SS20,OF10	115	436	75	136	57	26	6	9	37	22	7	.312
Bob Brady	C77	97	256	49	72	59	10	1	21	30	45	1	.281
Gail Henley	OF45	62	170	38	47	39	4	1	13	16	30	2	.276
Lester Layton	OF58	59	208	37	56	36	9	1	9	31	31	4	.269
Alex Konikowski	P38	39	49	6	13	2	2	1	0	5	14	0	.265
Bill Ayers	P38	38	88	6	11	8	2	0	1	0	23	0	.125
Don Mueller	OF27	28	119	21	37	12	7	2	2	3	7	1	.311
David Barnhill	P28	28	47	5	10	12	3	0	0	5	12	0	.213
Don Robertson	P23	24	36	6	6	6	2	0	1	1	17	0	.167
Wes Bailey	P21	22	37	2	7	1	0	0	0	0	14	0	.189
Vern Kennedy	P20	22	25	3	4	1	0	0	0	0	2	0	.160
Robert Callan	P22	22	10	0	1	0	0	0	0	1	5	0	.100
Albert Sima	P20	20	10	1	1	1	0	0	0	1	6	0	.100
Bill Gardner	3B	17	28	7	5	6	0	0	2	3	7	0	.179
Harrel Toenes	P16	16	10	0	2	0	1	0	0	0	2	0	.200
Francis Hardy	P13	15	16	2	1	0	0	0	0	5	10	0	.063
Mario Picone	P14	14	24	5	9	2	4	0	1	1	7	0	.375
Robert Cain	P12	12	7	0	1	0	0	0	0	1	3	0	.143
Phil Tomkinson	C	7	24	4	6	2	0	0	0			0	.250
Ernest Yelen	C	4	10	1	1	0	0	0	0			0	.100
Harold Swanson	P4	4	5	1	2	3	0	1	0			0	.400
Stan Jok	PH	2	2	0	0	0	0	0	0			0	.000
Mike Colombo	PH	2	1	0	0	0	0	0	0			0	.000
Ed Wallner	C1	1	2	0	1	1	0	0	0			0	.500
Angelo Giulani	C	1	2	1	0	0	0	0	0			0	.000

PITCHERS	W	L	PCT	G	GS	CG	SH	IP	H	BB	SO	ERA
Bill Ayers	12	16	.429	38		14	0	233	242	98	118	5.02
Alex Konikowski	11	7	.611	38		5	0	154	181	103	65	5.90
Don Robertson	8	5	.615	23		3	0	105	150	52	52	6.09
David Barnhill	7	10	.412	28		8	3	144	154	82	91	5.75
Wes Bailey	6	6	.500	21		4	1	106	133	41	51	5.60
Francis Hardy	4	4	.500	13		3	1	54	61	14	23	5.50
Mario Picone	3	2	.600	14		2	0	53	72	43	21	7.47
Vern Kennedy	3	3	.500	20		2	1	68	86	46	29	7.15
Robert Callan	2	1	.667	22		0	0	46	57	29	13	4.11
Albert Sima	2	2	.500	20		1	0	40	37	21	27	4.50
Verne Williamson	1	0	1.000	9			0	17	20	17	7	6.88
Sam Brewer	1	1	.500	9			0	26	32	20	13	6.57
Harold Swanson	1	1	.500	4			0	12	17	9	9	8.25
Al LaMacchia	1	2	.333	8		1	0	30	47	19	8	8.70
Jack Kraus	1	2	.333	4			0	16	27	13	4	12.38
Robert Cain	0	1	.000	12			0	21	16	27	8	6.00
Harrel Toenes	0	4	.000	16		1	0	42	54	27	16	7.93
Earl McGowan	0	0	----	8			0	10	16	10	4	

KANSAS CITY   5th   71-80   .470   -21   Bill Skiff
Blues

BATTERS	POS-GAMES	GP	AB	R	H	BI	2B	3B	HR	BB	SO	SB	BA
Joe Collins	1B146	146	530	104	169	83	25	18	20	82	82	6	.319
Joe Muffoletto	2B75,3B47	124	435	68	116	62	24	9	4	44	35	6	.267
John Wallaesa	SS1112,3B1	117	414	75	128	71	19	3	18	63	68	4	.309

KANSAS CITY (cont.)
Blues

BATTERS	POS-GAMES	GP	AB	R	H	BI	2B	3B	HR	BB	SO	SB	BA
Nicholas Witek	3B32,2B,SS	41	157	19	44	14	8	1	1	15	9	2	.280
James Delsing	OF149	151	545	89	173	77	24	5	7	91	64	11	.317
Archie Wilson	OF120	122	451	64	129	47	13	10	6	21	56	16	.286
Henry Workman	OF67,1B2	70	249	44	62	30	9	4	12	30	36	3	.249
Ralph Houk	C88	95	313	47	86	36	18	1	0	40	8	3	.275
John Lucadello	SS43,2B29,3B27	111	350	55	100	42	16	4	2	58	30	3	.286
Bill Drescher	C68,1B1	101	232	27	64	47	14	2	2	49	22	1	.276
Ted Sepkowski	OF58,2B18,3B1	80	272	28	66	48	10	1	10	17	34	1	.243
Gene Valla	2B27,3B22	57	181	27	49	12	3	1	0	16	9	3	.271
Ford Garrison	OF40	54	155	20	37	19	6	0	2	13	19	1	.239
James Dyck	OF30,3B26	53	174	24	50	26	8	2	3	18	25	3	.287
Lew Burdette	P36	40	32	1	2	2	0	0	0	4	10	0	.063
Robert Keegan	P32	37	58	8	18	6	2	0	1	13	11	1	.310
David Madison	P33	33	61	5	13	5	1	0	0	5	9	0	.213
Bill Elbert	P22	29	55	6	6	0	0	1	0	1	16	0	.109
Ernest Groth	P28	28	56	1	10	5	0	0	0	1	12	0	.179
Paul Hinrichs	P26	28	30	4	6	3	2	0	0	4	9	0	.200
Frank Hiller	P23	27	61	3	12	9	6	0	0	6	11	0	.197
Aldon Wilkie	P23	23	10	1	2	1	0	0	0	0	2	0	.200
Pat Seerey	OF16	18	52	4	10	10	5	0	0	9	16	2	.192
Wallace Hood	P11	11	20	1	4	0	0	0	0	4	6	0	.200
Art Bohman	P10	10	7	0	1	0	0	0	0	0	0	0	.143
Mal Mallette	P10	10	3	0	1	0	0	0	0	0	0	0	.333
Ed Ehlers	3B	9	30	0	5	4	1	1	0			0	.167
Vic Mastro	C	9	12	2	2	0	1	0	0			0	.167
William Holm	C	7	5	2	1	0	0	0	0			0	.200
Keith Thomas	1B,OF	6	25	3	7	6	0	0	1			0	.280
Henry Foiles	C	5	3	0	1	0	0	0	0			0	.333
Emil Tellinger	OF	4	11	2	5	1	0	1	0			0	.455
Al Stringer	SS	3	9	1	4	1	1	0	0			0	.444
Gerald Snyder	SS	3	3	0	2	1	0	0	0			0	.667

PITCHERS	W	L	PCT	G	GS	CG	SH	IP	H	BB	SO	ERA
John Groth	12	9	.571	28		14	0	162	163	63	72	4.28
Frank Hiller	11	8	.579	23		14	1	169	180	44	101	3.57
David Madison	11	10	.524	33		13	2	186	202	82	94	4.02
Bill Elbert	9	8	.529	22		14	1	145	141	62	47	3.85
Robert Keegan	9	15	.375	32		7	0	172	180	88	92	4.81
Lew Burdette	6	7	.462	36		2	0	118	147	47	51	5.26
Wallace Hood	3	2	.600	11		3	1	66	69	37	38	3.27
Aldon Wilkie	3	3	.500	23			0	44	52	20	17	4.30
Paul Hinrichs	3	10	.231	26		5	1	107	117	73	47	4.79
Mal Mallette	2	1	.667	10			0	16	17	19	1	7.88
Art Bohman	1	0	1.000	10			0	24	31	20	4	9.00
Earl Harrist	1	2	.333	9			0	22	31	9	16	6.95
Lee Dodson	0	2	.000	9			0	18	12	27	12	6.00
James Tote	0	3	.000	7			0	22	25	26	6	9.41
James Arnold	0	0	----	5			0	7	6	7	2	
Carmine Melignano	0	0	----	2			0	2	4	1	2	
Delmar Owens	0	0	----	1			0	5	8	3	3	
George Vandrashek	0	0	----	1			0	2	4	2	1	
Henry Anderson	0	0	----	1			0	4	8	10	0	

COLUMBUS   6th (T)   70-83   .458   -23   Harold Anderson
Red Birds

BATTERS	POS-GAMES	GP	AB	R	H	BI	2B	3B	HR	BB	SO	SB	BA
Michael Natisin	1B127	130	457	89	121	89	15	2	24	91	49	1	.265
Ben Steiner	2B142	145	564	92	150	44	19	11	5	88	64	7	.266
Bill Costa	SS147	147	478	53	111	46	20	3	1	72	37	3	.232
Don Lang	3B126	128	435	81	129	76	22	7	13	89	51	3	.297
Bill Howerton	OF148	148	547	101	180	111	43	4	21	91	55	3	.329
Roy Broome	OF137	145	551	69	163	76	30	8	2	30	41	8	.296
Ernest Logan	OF94	115	352	55	98	75	12	7	15	43	26	0	.278
Les Fusselman	C89	97	332	34	93	57	13	6	7	32	40	2	.280
Mel McGaha	OF75,1B30,3B1	114	407	70	118	37	13	5	1	19	47	5	.290
Vern Rapp	C69,OF1	77	249	30	64	29	14	5	6	22	33	2	.257
Claude Wright	3B25,2B15,SS15	62	163	22	35	12	4	1	0	26	21	3	.215
John Crimian	P51	51	62	5	14	3	0	0	0	4	7	0	.226
Harvey Haddix	P35	44	82	6	21	9	2	0	1	9	14	0	.256

COLUMBUS (cont.)
Red Birds

BATTERS	POS-GAMES	GP	AB	R	H	BI	2B	3B	HR	BB	SO	SB	BA
Robert Habenicht	P37	38	45	3	8	2	0	0	0	4	6	0	.178
Charles Stanceu	P35	35	54	4	5	3	0	0	1	4	22	0	.093
Bernard Olsen	OF23	29	70	5	15	7	1	0	0	13	11	0	.214
Kurt Krieger	P28	28	43	4	10	0	0	0	0	1	14	0	.233
John Remke	P22	22	33	2	3	1	0	1	0	3	18	0	.091
Ira Hutchinson	P18	18	2	0	0	0	0	0	0	0	1	0	.000
Ray Yochim	P12	13	11	2	3	1	0	0	0	0	2	0	.273
James Bryant	P12	12	15	0	1	2	0	0	0	2	3	0	.067
John Mikan	P10	10	4	0	1	0	0	0	0	0	0	0	.250
Bill Hardin	3B	6	18	1	4	0	0	0	0			0	.222
Harvey Zernia	PH	1	1	0	0	0	0	0	0			0	.000

PITCHERS	W	L	PCT	G	GS	CG	SH	IP	H	BB	SO	ERA
Harvey Haddix	13	13	.500	35		14	4	219	206	94	177	3.49
John Crimian	11	9	.550	51		7	0	187	209	74	52	3.47
Robert Habenicht	7	9	.438	37		6	0	151	171	69	75	5.54
Charles Stanceu	7	13	.350	35		7	1	166	201	64	75	4.83
Kurt Krieger	6	7	.462	28		6	1	127	136	91	58	5.17
John Remke	5	9	.357	22		4	1	102	105	84	67	5.21
Ray Yochim	2	1	.667	12			0	39	36	24	16	3.46
James Bryant	2	5	.286	12		3	0	52	44	36	21	4.67
John Mikan	1	2	.333	10			0	20	34	11	6	9.90
Ira Hutchinson	1	4	.200	18			0	15	21	14	5	5.50
Wayne McLeland	0	1	.000	7			0	16	24	10	6	6.75
Robert Eisiminger	0	1	.000	3			0	9	12	9	4	11.00
Merlin Williams	0	1	.000	2			0	7	7	5	1	0.00
Jack Frisinger	0	0	----	1			0	1	3	2	1	67.16

LOUISVILLE   6th (T)   70-83   .458   -23   Walters - Ryba
Colonels

BATTERS	POS-GAMES	GP	AB	R	H	BI	2B	3B	HR	BB	SO	SB	BA
Murrell Jones	1B91	91	316	34	75	44	13	0	10	44	40	3	.237
Charles Harrington	2B	(see multi-team players)											
Mel Hoderlein	SS97,2B18,3B	127	444	71	119	44	22	1	2	80	35	7	.268
Ken Chapman	3B108,2B13	125	399	55	98	61	21	6	8	80	51	4	.246
Tom Wright	OF151	151	549	91	202	89	38	8	9	103	59	7	**.368**
George Wilson	OF134	141	528	90	141	67	28	1	17	74	38	7	.267
Jim Piersall	OF116	125	446	58	121	58	21	4	3	30	59	6	.271
Robert Scherbarth	C76,1B,2B	83	239	29	69	30	12	4	2	32	24	1	.289
Dick Kimble	SS54,1B,2B,3B	85	232	33	64	28	8	5	1	42	12	1	.276
Warren Robinson	C70	70	207	20	53	19	7	0	2	34	27	1	.256
Ed Lavigne	OF35	60	152	18	48	19	15	2	2	15	14	1	.316
John Barrett	OF22,1B	48	127	19	36	20	3	2	1	24	15	3	.283
Gordon Mueller	P47	47	28	0	2	0	0	0	0	1	7	0	.071
Milt Rutner	3B36	41	136	14	36	16	7	1	3	22	7	0	.265
Hector Brown	P33	35	70	3	18	6	1	1	1	5	5	0	.257
John Griffore	P33	33	71	5	9	6	1	0	0	6	11	0	.127
Richard Palm	P27	27	52	6	11	7	1	0	0	6	26	0	.212
John Robinson	P27	27	44	5	6	3	2	0	0	4	16	1	.136
Ewald Pyle	P27	27	26	0	0	1	0	0	0	0	6	0	.000
Robert Alexander	P25	25	48	3	4	4	0	0	0	3	14	0	.083
Tom Tatum	OF,3B,1B	17	53	4	18	7	4	0	0	6	0	0	.340
Allen Richter	SS14	15	40	3	9	1	0	0	0	5	0	0	.225
Harry Dorish	P15	15	31	5	6	2	0	0	0	4	10	0	.194
Hampton Coleman	P14	14	8	1	1	0	0	0	0	1	3	0	.125
Mickey McDermott	P11	13	30	5	10	4	2	0	1	4	5	1	.333
Leslie Aulds	C	9	27	1	5	4	0	0	1			0	.185
Sam White	C	8	21	3	3	3	0	1	0			0	.143
Russ Rolandson	C	7	17	0	1	2	0	0	0			0	.059
Willard Nixon	P4	4	8	0	3	0	0	0	0			0	.375
Norbert Zauchin	C	2	7	1	2	0	0	0	0			0	.286
Fred Walters	C	1	4	1	1	1	1	0	0			0	.250

PITCHERS	W	L	PCT	G	GS	CG	SH	IP	H	BB	SO	ERA
John Griffore	12	12	.500	33		13	1	212	207	57	99	3.31
Gordon Mueller	10	4	.714	47		0	0	104	95	62	68	3.81
Richard Palm	9	8	.529	27		8	2	147	173	74	65	4.47
Robert Alexander	8	8	.500	25		8	0	144	148	65	54	4.25

LOUISVILLE (cont.)
Colonels

PITCHERS	W	L	PCT	G	GS	CG	SH	IP	H	BB	SO	ERA
Hector Brown	8	13	.381	33		15	1	193	217	51	70	3.31
Mickey McDermott	6	4	.600	11		7	1	77	53	54	116	3.27
John Robinson	6	13	.316	27		6	1	145	163	52	52	5.03
John McCall	5	2	.714	8		1	0	46	39	42	15	5.09
Harry Dorish	3	3	.500	15		3	0	90	103	35	45	5.10
Hampton Coleman	1	3	.250	14			0	35	36	34	24	6.43
Ewald Pyle	1	8	.111	27		1	0	78	90	50	43	6.23
Harley Hisner	0	1	.000	2			0	4	9	2	4	13.50
Willard Nixon	0	3	.000	4		1	0	23	19	18	15	5.09
John Hoffman	0	0	----	4			0	5	6	4	4	1.80
Harry Payne	0	0	----	3			0	7	10	11	4	

TOLEDO   8th   64-90   .416   -29.5   Eddie Mayo
Mud Hens

BATTERS	POS-GAMES	GP	AB	R	H	BI	2B	3B	HR	BB	SO	SB	BA
Tony Lupien	1B124	125	460	58	136	60	14	4	6	66	13	6	.296
Robert Mavis	2B154	154	584	106	176	79	35	4	12	99	21	2	.301
John Bero	SS148	149	488	77	120	81	22	6	17	91	62	5	.246
Bruce Blanchard	3B126	128	466	63	131	45	9	2	0	63	53	4	.281
Austin Knickerbocker	OF123	135	483	76	138	104	26	8	23	49	66	2	.286
Bill Barnacle	OF109,3B10,SS1	124	447	87	128	48	21	3	6	90	48	4	.286
Don Lund	OF101,1B3	117	416	74	124	81	24	4	17	45	55	4	.298
Myron Ginsberg	C91	102	336	48	95	43	17	1	5	31	19	2	.283
George Lerchen	OF78	90	309	56	92	29	9	4	4	45	56	4	.298
Ed Mordaski	C74	78	232	31	63	30	9	3	6	40	23	1	.272
George Corona	OF47,P1,1B,3B	76	217	27	55	31	8	2	2	20	37	1	.253
Eddie Mayo	3B19,1B,2B,SS	41	108	9	28	13	2	2	3	8	6	0	.259
Bill Butland	P40	40	28	2	4	3	0	0	0	2	6	0	.143
Raymond Herbert	P35	35	57	3	12	5	4	0	0	3	12	0	.211
Bill Connelly	P34	34	61	6	13	4	3	0	1	4	18	0	.213
Walter Nothe	P33	33	41	2	5	2	0	0	0	4	10	0	.122
Ed March	P31	31	44	3	12	7	3	0	0	3	10	0	.273
Dwain Sloat	P30	31	41	5	14	6	0	0	0	2	8	0	.341
Anthony Foti	P31	31	41	0	6	3	2	0	0	0	15	0	.146
William Scott	P26	26	9	0	1	1	0	0	0	1	2	0	.111
Glen Russell	1B19	23	76	10	20	20	3	1	3	14	8	0	.263
Harold White	P22	23	46	5	4	5	0	0	1	4	14	0	.087
John Creel	OF14	18	52	10	12	11	1	2	0	8	2	2	.231
Art Moher	SS	6	11	2	2	0	0	0	0			0	.182
Keith Little	PH	1	0	1	0	0	0	0	0			0	.000

PITCHERS	W	L	PCT	G	GS	CG	SH	IP	H	BB	SO	ERA
Harold White	10	8	.556	22		11	0	139	130	52	59	3.24
William Butland	9	3	.750	40		0	0	100	127	31	65	4.86
Walter Nothe	8	8	.500	33		5	1	129	137	88	57	6.07
William Connelly	8	11	.421	34		10	2	172	172	142	134	6.17
Anthony Foti	7	6	.538	31		3	0	128	132	115	74	5.70
Raymond Herbert	6	17	.261	35		6	1	163	184	120	76	5.80
Marlin Stuart	4	2	.667	7		4	0	53	41	21	26	2.72
Ed March	3	9	.250	31		6	0	124	153	38	46	5.01
Dwain Sloat	3	11	.214	30		3	0	118	137	82	55	6.86
Rufus Gentry	1	0	1.000	6			0	24	40	27	10	11.63
William Scott	1	2	.333	26			0	40	46	32	5	4.50
Ed Albosta	1	2	.333	6		1	0	18	34	15	3	12.00
Len Perme	0	3	.000	6		1	0	18	31	25	9	10.00
George Coffman	0	0	---	3			0	9	18	4	2	
George Corona	0	0	----	1			0	0	1	4	0	

MULTI-TEAM PLAYERS

BATTERS	POS-GAMES	TEAMS	GP	AB	R	H	BI	2B	3B	HR	BB	SO	SB	BA
Froilan Fernandez	3B113,OF49	SP-IND	153	599	107	187	**128**	35	6	21	72	45	13	.312
Charles Harrington	2B124,3B4	COL-LOU	134	508	74	126	45	19	4	2	55	52	10	.248
Milt Byrnes	OF112	LOU-MIL	130	346	55	90	34	15	1	8	69	44	4	.260
John Douglas	1B108	SP-LOU	115	404	48	108	32	18	0	1	59	33	5	.267
Ellis Deal	P33,OF2	LOU-COL	73	116	12	26	16	0	0	4	17	25	0	.224

MULTI-TEAM PLAYERS (cont.)

BATTERS	POS-GAMES	TEAMS	GP	AB	R	H	BI	2B	3B	HR	BB	SO	SB	BA
Ike Pearson	P52	COL-MIN	52	13	2	2	0	0	0	0	1	2	0	.154
Grady Wilson	3B27	IND-SP	40	113	20	38	21	8	0	3	10	18	0	.336
Edson Bahr	P30,OF	IND-SP	33	48	7	6	1	0	0	0	1	7	0	.125
William Clark	P27	MIN-TOL	27	35	1	1	3	0	0	0	2	9	0	.029
Louis Lombardo	P10	MIN-TOL	10	7	0	2	1	1	0	0	0	2	0	.286

PITCHERS	TEAMS	W	L	PCT	G	GS	CG	SH	IP	H	BB	SO	ERA
Ellis Deal	LOU-COL	15	9	.625	35		19	2	221	216	88	119	2.97
Edson Bahr	IND-SP	8	9	.471	30		7	0	138	128	65	47	3.52
Ike Pearson	COL-MIN	7	5	.583	52		0	0	85	102	42	39	4.66
William Clark	MIN-TOL	6	14	.300	27		4	0	117	153	41	30	5.62
Louis Lombardo	MIN-TOL	2	0	1.000	10			0	16	22	17	10	9.56

TEAM BATTING

TEAMS	GP	AB	R	H	BI	2B	3B	HR	BB	SO	SB	BA
ST. PAUL	154	5199	898	**1500**	810	**262**	47	121	690	650	**112**	**.289**
INDIANAPOLIS	154	5122	838	1452	770	227	**73**	111	**738**	687	89	.283
MILWAUKEE	154	5142	792	1416	725	206	39	120	702	677	45	.275
MINNEAPOLIS	154	**5259**	**936**	1490	**890**	232	52	**202**	695	**719**	45	.283
KANSAS CITY	153	5018	735	1386	660	216	64	89	617	633	66	.276
COLUMBUS	154	5109	740	1378	692	209	59	101	662	600	37	.274
LOUISVILLE	**155**	5103	680	1362	620	238	40	70	724	576	55	.267
TOLEDO	154	5127	771	1403	711	215	47	106	704	595	37	.270
	616	41079	6390	11387	5878	1805	421	920	5532	5137	486	.277

1950
Staying Home

After World War II, the minor leagues experienced a phenomenal spurt of growth. From a total of 12 minor leagues in 1945, the number jumped to 43 in 1946, 52 in 1947, 58 in 1948, and 59 in 1949. In all, these 59 leagues included over 400 teams scattered all across the United States, Canada, and Mexico. By the start of the 1950 season, the number of leagues had dipped to 58. This drop in and of itself was not alarming, but an accompanying trend was. Although the count of teams and leagues remained virtually the same, the number of people attending the games did not.

The American Association had enjoyed the postwar boom along with the rest of baseball. In 1947, attendance for the league was 2,156,161. In 1948, the figure bumped up to 2,235,843, while in 1949 attendance dipped but still remained high at 1,999,270.

In 1950, Minneapolis ended a long pennant drought by chalking up their first flag in 15 years. The rest of the playoff teams, (Indianapolis, Columbus and St. Paul) finished close to the Millers, with the trailing quartet (Louisville, Milwaukee, Toledo and Kansas City) farther behind. Batting honors went to Milwaukee's Robert Addis who had the highest batting average (.323), and to Lou Limmer of St. Paul who hit the most home runs (29) and runs batted in (111). Pitching honors for the second year in a row went to one man as Harvey Haddix of Columbus won the triple crown. He finished with 18 wins, a 2.70 earned run average, and 160 strikeouts.

The 1950 attendance figures for the American Association showed a precipitous drop over the previous year. Only 1,210,688 fans saw Association games in 1950, nearly a 40 percent drop over the previous year. The culprit was television.

In the late 1940s, baseball started broadcasting on television major league games to most parts of the country. Now a fan had his choice: stay at home and root for your favorite major league team, or go to the ballpark and root for the same old minor league team. If that wasn't enough, television was offering many diverse entertainment choices to an eager American public. If there was no ballgame to view, chances are there was something else interesting to watch on television.

Through the decade of the 1950s, the number of minor leagues would drop to less than half their previous number, as people stayed away in droves. It wasn't a question of America losing interest in baseball, but a question of entertainment options. For the first time, people had lots of ways to spend their free time. Baseball was merely one of the choices.

MINNEAPOLIS Millers

1st   90-64   .584   Thomas Heath

BATTERS	POS-GAMES	GP	AB	R	H	BI	2B	3B	HR	BB	SO	SB	BA
Bert Haas	1B78,OF64	141	515	101	164	106	**36**	2	24	80	46	1	.318
Dave Williams	2B135	138	536	46	150	65	28	6	17	76	50	6	.280
William Jennings	SS145	145	467	80	133	85	13	7	23	83	84	3	.285
Ray Dandridge	3B136,2B17,SS	150	**627**	106	**195**	80	24	1	11	41	26	1	.311
John Kropf	OF155	155	516	86	131	97	15	3	21	99	85	4	.254
Carvel Rowell	OF70,2B5	95	316	43	82	47	14	3	8	23	13	4	.259
William Milne	OF54	54	215	44	67	27	11	8	3	29	44	6	.312
Bob Brady	C66	69	186	27	44	28	6	2	12	17	43	2	.237
Joe Lafata	OF53,1B1	78	202	48	55	38	12	2	9	36	24	3	.272
John Harshman	1B70	76	244	46	56	46	9	1	17	48	51	0	.230
John Jorgensen	OF29,3B22,SS10	64	215	32	71	47	6	4	8	38	10	1	.330
Jake Early	C62	63	182	21	45	35	9	2	6	28	29	0	.247
Phil Tomkinson	C54	55	159	17	41	24	5	1	1	16	26	0	.258
Mylon Vukmire	SS14,3B,OF,2B	54	81	20	20	13	5	1	3	15	17	1	.247
Millard Howell	P24	51	91	16	28	20	7	0	5	2	23	0	.308
Ike Pearson	P48	48	11	0	2	0	0	0	0	1	1	0	.182
Charles Workman	OF34	41	131	23	28	21	7	1	6	24	21	1	.214
Hoyt Wilhelm	P35	35	61	4	14	2	1	0	0	2	16	0	.230
Adrian Zabala	P33	33	50	11	10	7	1	0	1	2	9	0	.200
Dave Barnhill	P27	32	53	9	12	8	1	0	1	6	12	1	.226
Bill Ayers	P30	30	57	2	9	6	1	0	0	0	14	0	.158
Wes Bailey	P28	30	25	3	5	2	0	0	0	2	9	0	.200
Alex Konikowski	P25	25	21	3	2	0	0	0	0	4	13	0	.095
George McDonald	OF10,1B7	21	60	6	15	4	4	0	0	2	3	0	.250
Frank Fanovich	P21	21	38	3	10	5	1	0	0	3	3	0	.263
Kirby Higbe	P21	21	37	1	4	2	2	0	0	2	13	0	.108
Bob Lennon	OF3	16	22	4	8	6	2	1	0	1	4	0	.364
Ed Wright	P14	14	10	0	1	0	0	0	0	0	2	0	.100
Don Robertson	P8	10	8	1	1	0	0	0	0	2	6	0	.125
Joe Konitzki	C	7	11	1	1	0	0	0	0			0	.091
Harold Gilbert	1B	6	18	6	5	2	1	1	0			0	.278
Leslie Klesitz	P6	6	5	0	1	0	0	0	0			0	.200
William Lutes	OF	4	4	0	1	0	1	0	0			0	.250

PITCHERS		W	L	PCT	G	GS	CG	SH	IP	H	BB	SO	ERA
Hoyt Wilhelm		15	11	.577	35	25	10	1	180	190	64	99	4.95
Millard Howell		14	2	**.875**	24	23	10	2	145	162	67	91	4.78
Dave Barnhill		11	3	.786	27	16	9	1	140	124	48	128	3.60
Adrian Zabala		11	4	.733	33	14	5	2	130	151	54	52	4.92
Bill Ayers		11	10	.524	30	23	7	0	177	176	61	73	4.37
Frank Fanovich		8	5	.615	21	19	5	0	104	95	64	98	4.50
Wes Bailey		6	5	.545	28	6	3	0	95	117	34	40	5.49
Alex Konikowski		5	6	.455	25	10	2	0	92	98	45	62	4.99
Kirby Higbe		5	8	.385	21	12	6	1	105	109	49	60	4.71
Ike Pearson		3	6	.333	48	0	0	0	62	70	23	13	2.61
Don Robertson		1	2	.333	8			0	31	35	17	12	5.23
Ed Wright		0	1	.000	14			0	41	61	13	11	6.59
Leslie Klesitz		0	1	.000	6			0	13	16	9	4	8.31

INDIANAPOLIS Indians

2nd   85-67   .559   -4   Al Lopez

BATTERS	POS-GAMES	GP	AB	R	H	BI	2B	3B	HR	BB	SO	SB	BA
Dale Coogan	1B65	65	255	29	61	28	9	6	5	15	44	3	.239
Monty Basgall	2B133,SS1	133	462	63	130	58	29	4	13	52	58	5	.281
Dan O'Connell	SS84	84	322	65	113	50	20	4	8	33	23	5	.351
Joe Bockman	3B101	107	363	55	89	46	11	6	11	45	57	3	.245
Mizell Platt	OF116	126	418	47	115	71	21	1	12	19	57	1	.275
Tom Saffell	OF83	85	298	49	97	23	15	3	5	37	33	11	.326
Frank Kalin	OF60	85	238	38	70	51	13	5	14	22	43	1	.294
Ed Fitz Gerald	C94	103	310	43	97	42	14	6	0	34	38	3	.313
Dom Dallessandro	OF53,1B9	101	223	45	78	52	13	2	12	53	28	0	.350
Russ Peters	3B43,SS,2B	69	183	27	46	17	11	5	2	27	31	0	.251
Royce Lint	P46	67	49	14	5	4	1	0	0	6	15	2	.102
Froilan Fernandez	3B36,SS25,OF2	61	230	29	69	47	14	2	11	20	20	3	.300
Ed Stevens	1B56	61	198	26	52	27	3	2	5	34	24	0	.263
Delmont Ballinger	C47	52	137	15	33	16	11	0	0	20	2	0	.241
Don Gutteridge	2B28,3B7	52	98	19	19	9	5	2	0	4	13	0	.194
Forrest Main	P43	43	16	1	1	1	1	0	0	0	3	0	.063
David Bell	OF38	38	165	33	66	21	10	6	5	19	13	1	.400

INDIANAPOLIS (cont.)
Indians

BATTERS	POS-GAMES	GP	AB	R	H	BI	2B	3B	HR	BB	SO	SB	BA
Joe Muir	P38	38	72	9	15	4	0	0	0	0	9	0	.208
Elmer Riddle	P26	36	54	6	7	6	1	0	1	1	20	0	.130
Al Grunwald	1B28	35	117	22	39	29	9	1	3	8	13	0	.333
Paul LaPalme	P31	31	10	2	4	1	1	0	0	0	0	0	.400
Fred Strobel	P30	30	29	1	2	2	1	0	0	2	11	0	.069
Ted Beard	OF29	29	107	15	25	2	7	1	0	14	22	1	.234
William Pierro	P25	25	28	2	1	0	0	0	0	2	14	0	.036
Leo Wells	SS21	22	69	13	21	9	5	0	1	5	8	0	.304
Robert Kellogg	OF13	22	48	9	13	2	2	1	0	5	9	0	.271
Dino Restelli	OF21	21	81	10	13	6	3	1	1	10	14	1	.160
John McCall	P20	21	35	8	10	7	5	0	1	4	7	0	.286
Earl Turner	C14	19	55	3	17	8	2	1	0	1	9	0	.309
Frank Papish	P19	19	35	4	7	4	1	0	0	2	7	0	.200
Harold Gregg	P18	19	29	2	3	3	0	0	0	1	8	0	.103
John Hutchings	P19	19	1	0	0	0	0	0	0	0	1	0	.000
Bob Friend	P11	11	18	1	2	0	0	0	0	0	9	0	.111
Rolland Leveille	C10	10	25	3	6	6	3	0	1	3	1	0	.240
Robert Ganss	C	4	9	1	5	5	0	0	0			0	.556
Lloyd Gearhart	OF	4	5	2	1	0	0	0	0			0	.200

PITCHERS	W	L	PCT	G	GS	CG	SH	IP	H	BB	SO	ERA
Royce Lint	12	6	.667	46	18	7	2	177	196	76	100	3.97
Frank Papish	11	3	.786	19	15	8	1	109	84	47	47	2.81
Elmer Riddle	11	9	.550	26	25	10	1	165	168	85	70	4.04
Joe Muir	10	10	.500	38	25	9	2	205	**225**	52	97	3.91
William Pierro	8	3	.727	25	11	4	2	104	56	59	75	2.60
John McCall	7	7	.500	20	18	6	2	104	111	60	82	5.28
Paul LaPalme	6	5	.545	31	0	0	0	49	42	23	27	3.67
Forrest Main	5	4	.556	43	0	0	0	71	48	24	42	1.90
Fred Strobel	5	5	.500	30	14	4	1	108	122	56	49	4.17
John Hutchings	3	1	.750	19			0	29	23	13	15	1.55
Harold Gregg	3	9	.250	18	17	4	0	93	98	49	71	5.03
Bob Friend	2	4	.333	11	9	0	0	56	75	16	34	5.46
James Mims	1	0	1.000	7			0	11	10	4	3	2.45
Peter Modica	1	1	.500	3			0	10	11	11	7	5.40
William Kennedy	0	0	----	1			0	1	2	1	0	

COLUMBUS   3rd   84-69   .549   -5.5   Rollie Hemsley
Red Birds

BATTERS	POS-GAMES	GP	AB	R	H	BI	2B	3B	HR	BB	SO	SB	BA
Maurice Mozzali	1B87,OF11	115	375	74	115	47	20	4	4	46	37	3	.307
Solly Hemus	2B84,SS	84	296	51	88	49	23	4	6	48	26	11	.297
Bill Costa	SS150	150	510	60	134	55	22	3	1	51	28	7	.263
Frank Shofner	3B126	126	439	56	106	54	27	6	10	44	58	0	.241
Larry Miggins	OF146	146	532	73	149	92	26	9	18	46	69	4	.280
Roy Broome	OF112	112	407	49	113	55	15	4	3	37	42	6	.278
Vern Benson	OF102,2B10	119	363	75	92	55	18	7	8	71	55	4	.253
Bill Sarni	C130	132	429	52	120	47	21	8	3	42	37	2	.280
Michael Natisin	1B54	73	195	21	45	28	10	1	3	40	20	0	.231
Ben Steiner	2B52,SS2	70	197	26	48	17	3	3	0	27	20	2	.244
Roy Hughes	3B33,2B14,SS4,1B1	63	172	23	43	11	9	1	1	26	13	2	.250
Glenn Nelson	OF34,1B15	48	184	25	77	40	16	2	7	13	4	2	.418
John Crimian	P43	43	36	3	6	2	0	1	0	3	8	0	.167
Robert Habenicht	P40	42	48	2	5	5	0	1	0	1	17	0	.104
Harry Walker	OF41	41	144	26	40	14	11	2	3	31	16	2	.278
Ellis Deal	P29,OF1	38	68	1	12	5	0	0	0	9	15	0	.176
Harvey Haddix	P30	35	86	11	20	13	2	2	1	9	16	0	.233
Luis Arroyo	P33	33	39	7	9	2	0	1	0	3	6	0	.231
Mike Clark	P29	29	44	3	6	0	1	0	0	1	12	0	.136
Kurt Krieger	P27	27	72	5	12	8	2	2	1	0	22	0	.167
Les Fusselman	C16	20	50	4	9	2	0	2	0	4	5	0	.180
Eugene Major	P18	18	37	0	6	1	0	1	0	0	14	0	.162
Mel McGaha	OF16	17	50	3	11	5	3	2	0	1	5	1	.220
Vince Moreci	OF11	14	43	6	8	5	1	0	1	9	8	0	.186
Russ Kerns	C13	14	26	0	4	5	1	0	0	6	3	0	.154
Rollie Hemsley	C	12	17	1	2	2	0	0	0	0	3	0	.118
David Thomas	P9	9	2	0	1	0	0	0	0			0	.500
John Lindell	OF	5	10	1	2	2	0	0	0			0	.200
Fred Marolewski	1B	4	15	2	3	3	1	1	0			0	.200
Charles Frey	PH	2	2	1	1	0	1	0	0			0	.500

COLUMBUS (cont.)
Red Birds

PITCHERS	W	L	PCT	G	GS	CG	SH	IP	H	BB	SO	ERA
Harvey Haddix	**18**	6	.750	30	27	**17**	4	217	192	59	**160**	2.70
Kurt Krieger	17	5	.773	27	26	14	3	193	166	101	85	3.50
Robert Habenicht	10	10	.500	40	20	9	4	157	140	59	73	3.73
Ellis Deal	10	14	.417	29	24	13	2	166	174	97	65	4.61
Mike Clark	9	10	.474	29	19	5	1	135	146	55	75	5.07
John Crimian	6	8	.429	43	9	3	0	122	127	47	52	4.65
Glen Moulder	5	2	.714	8	7	4	1	49	49	11	17	3.12
Luis Arroyo	4	4	.500	33	8	3	0	116	107	77	64	4.11
Eugene Major	4	8	.333	18	13	5	1	101	109	54	36	4.81
David Thomas	1	1	.500	9			0	17	14	12	9	3.71
John Fasholz	0	1	.000	2			0	0	4	2	0	190.91
George Eyrich	0	0	----	1			0	2	1	0	0	
Joe Chuka	0	0	----	1			0	1	5	1	2	9.00

ST. PAUL   4th   83-69   .546   -6   Clay Hopper
Saints

BATTERS	POS-GAMES	GP	AB	R	H	BI	2B	3B	HR	BB	SO	SB	BA
Lou Limmer	1B142	144	501	98	139	111	23	6	29	96	70	7	.277
Jack Cassini	2B122,3B17	142	532	107	147	52	14	7	6	71	46	36	.276
James Pendleton	SS144	145	571	105	171	98	25	19	10	43	89	25	.299
Al Brancato	3B125,SS,2B,1B	134	468	51	110	62	16	4	4	51	40	1	.235
Eric Tipton	OF136	144	462	80	133	97	35	1	10	108	61	12	.288
Earl Naylor	OF76,P4,1B1	106	286	41	81	65	7	2	13	32	32	4	.283
Cliff Aberson	OF59	75	168	39	43	24	10	3	6	51	43	2	.256
Ferrell Anderson	C133	135	430	46	119	66	16	4	14	54	42	1	.277
Donald Nicholas	OF55,SS,3B	71	204	46	61	10	6	4	0	43	21	35	.299
Cal Abrams	OF57,1B1	58	192	56	64	16	8	1	3	64	33	5	.333
Harry Taylor	P34	46	80	13	19	7	3	0	2	4	18	0	.238
Guy Wellman	C40	43	59	4	9	6	1	0	0	13	3	0	.153
John Van Cuyk	P38	40	41	6	3	0	1	0	0	9	30	1	.073
Robert Bundy	3B17,2B10	39	119	12	29	11	7	0	1	8	10	6	.244
Clem Labine	P37	39	41	4	5	0	2	0	0	1	20	0	.122
William Antonello	OF37	38	136	17	33	15	6	2	6	10	18	0	.243
Ed Chandler	P37	37	50	4	6	2	0	0	0	5	10	0	.120
George Shuba	OF33	36	117	17	30	19	3	1	4	12	21	1	.256
Phil Haugstad	P36	36	76	2	7	2	0	0	0	5	31	0	.092
Edson Bahr	P25	34	35	4	3	3	0	0	0	2	16	0	.086
Morris Martin	P31	32	76	3	19	5	0	0	0	2	14	0	.250
John Simmons	OF24	31	85	12	21	17	4	1	2	10	10	2	.247
Leon Griffeth	P29	30	10	1	0	0	0	0	0	3	4	0	.000
Danny Ozark	1B13,3B,OF	24	54	9	10	6	0	0	1	4	3	0	.185
Dimitrios Baxes	2B13	13	53	4	7	8	2	1	1	4	13	1	.132
Ted Bartz	OF	12	29	3	5	1	2	0	0	2	3	0	.172
Stephen Lembo	C10	11	29	2	7	5	2	0	0	2	0	0	.241
James Hughes	P6	6	2	0	1	0	0	0	0			0	.500
Clint Conatser	OF	4	16	3	4	2	2	0	1			0	.250
James Romano	P2	2	5	2	2	3	0	0	1			0	.400

PITCHERS	W	L	PCT	G	GS	CG	SH	IP	H	BB	SO	ERA
Phil Haugstad	16	11	.593	36	32	12	0	229	216	125	137	3.89
Morris Martin	14	9	.609	31	28	13	1	197	216	62	114	3.65
Harry Taylor	13	9	.591	34	31	15	0	206	216	88	102	4.02
Clem Labine	11	7	.611	37	13	6	0	128	139	64	64	4.99
Ed Chandler	9	7	.563	37	19	4	0	154	178	56	53	4.44
Edson Bahr	7	7	.500	25	9	4	1	100	113	37	41	3.69
John Van Cuyk	7	9	.438	38	13	7	0	152	151	57	102	4.44
James Romano	2	0	1.000	2			0	16	6	4	14	0.00
Leon Griffeth	2	5	.286	29	3	0	0	53	74	33	18	5.94
James Hughes	1	0	1.000	6			0	7	19	9	7	23.14
Fred Waters	1	1	.500	5			0	12	17	7	6	6.75
Chester Kehn	0	1	.000	6			0	8	13	7	4	10.78
George Brown	0	1	.000	3			0	3	1	6	1	3.00
Nick Andromidas	0	2	.000	9			0	24	27	19	9	5.63
Earl Naylor	0	0	----	4			0	9	17	6	3	

LOUISVILLE   5th   82-71   .536   -7.5   Dominic Ryba
Colonels

BATTERS	POS-GAMES	GP	AB	R	H	BI	2B	3B	HR	BB	SO	SB	BA
John Douglas	1B124	131	468	64	125	36	12	6	1	39	55	5	.267
Edward Lyons	2B83	98	322	50	93	47	15	2	3	48	34	3	.289
Allen Richter	SS152	152	477	66	120	57	22	2	1	100	36	4	.252
Ken Chapman	3B149	150	561	69	150	82	27	9	8	63	49	5	.267
Taft Wright	OF129	134	481	72	153	92	31	4	15	67	22	2	.318
Jim Piersall	OF125	131	487	97	124	60	25	11	3	72	59	14	.255
George Wilson	OF101	126	380	68	104	82	19	2	17	56	36	2	.274
Robert Scherbarth	C74,1B1	80	250	28	61	28	17	2	0	29	34	1	.244
Mel Hoderlein	2B73,OF15,3B,SS,1B	107	377	66	110	50	21	2	5	41	35	1	.292
Tom O'Brien	OF81	93	274	39	72	49	7	3	15	33	37	0	.263
Peter Daley	C59	62	209	30	55	31	7	5	4	5	18	0	.263
Gordon Mueller	P39	39	14	1	1	1	0	0	0	0	5	0	.071
Bennett Flowers	P33	33	13	2	0	1	0	0	0	1	7	0	.000
Robert Alexander	P30	30	63	3	8	2	2	0	0	3	24	0	.127
Hampton Coleman	P26	27	19	0	2	0	0	0	0	4	8	0	.105
Dick Gernert	1B18	26	73	6	16	3	1	0	0	5	11	0	.219
Willard Nixon	P13	26	55	9	19	7	2	1	0	4	14	0	.345
John Robinson	P24	24	47	6	11	2	0	0	0	5	20	0	.234
John Griffore	P22	22	37	4	3	2	1	0	0	3	9	0	.081
Harley Hisner	P21	21	28	3	6	1	0	0	0	0	9	0	.214
William Boyce	OF20	20	76	12	25	7	5	2	0	9	10	2	.329
James McDonald	P18	19	47	5	12	7	0	0	0	8	11	0	.255
Earl Johnson	P15	15	31	2	2	2	0	0	0	4	13	0	.065
Richard Palm	P14	14	26	2	2	0	0	0	0	0	16	0	.077
Walt Dropo	1B11	11	47	5	12	11	1	1	2	5	5	0	.255
Jim Suchecki	P10	10	19	1	3	2	0	0	0	1	8	0	.158
Jack Parks	C	8	14	0	1	0	0	0	0			0	.057
Richard Burgett	OF	4	10	1	0	0	0	0	0			0	.000
Sal Federico	P3	3	3	0	1	0	0	0	0			0	.333

PITCHERS		W	L	PCT	G	GS	CG	SH	IP	H	BB	SO	ERA
Robert Alexander		12	10	.545	30	26	13	4	186	167	90	73	3.44
Willard Nixon		11	2	.846	13	13	11	2	117	95	59	97	2.69
James McDonald		11	4	.733	18	17	10	3	137	117	50	47	3.35
John Robinson		8	8	.500	24	22	6	0	137	163	44	62	4.93
Gordon Mueller		7	4	.636	39	0	0	0	63	54	35	42	3.71
Earl Johnson		6	6	.500	15	13	7	1	92	70	27	45	2.54
John Griffore		6	7	.462	22	16	7	2	121	134	34	57	4.09
Harley Hisner		5	6	.455	21	12	4	1	91	101	31	42	4.65
Jim Suchecki		4	4	.500	10	9	5	1	66	57	32	39	3.41
Bennett Flowers		3	4	.429	33	1	1	0	77	68	46	49	3.39
Richard Palm		3	7	.300	14	12	4	0	74	85	48	42	6.57
Ira Godin		2	3	.400	7			0	44	46	26	15	3.89
Hampton Coleman		2	6	.250	26	3	0	0	83	77	46	45	4.55
Sal Federico		1	0	1.000	3			0	12	9	10	5	7.50

MILWAUKEE   6th   68-85   .444   -21.5   Bob Coleman
Brewers

BATTERS	POS-GAMES	GP	AB	R	H	BI	2B	3B	HR	BB	SO	SB	BA
Len Pearson	1B63	63	223	29	68	24	10	2	4	13	18	0	.305
William Reed	2B123	131	473	65	148	39	19	3	3	40	27	9	.313
Johnny Logan	SS154	154	558	73	165	57	28	2	6	42	46	10	.296
Jack Weisenburger	3B76,OF24,2B15	121	386	52	93	43	20	2	13	43	87	1	.241
robert Addis	OF136	136	529	80	171	76	32	10	9	54	58	6	.323
Howie Moss	OF117,3B1	123	435	60	124	87	15	2	26	35	71	0	.285
Robert Montag	OF115,1B18	142	490	87	131	53	24	6	20	79	82	2	.267
Al Lakeman	C87,1B11	107	363	52	86	73	21	4	19	35	115	0	.237
Robert Jaderlund	OF83	103	249	40	68	30	9	3	2	42	17	3	.273
Walter Linden	C71	81	260	27	64	29	14	0	4	21	25	0	.246
Mark Christman	1B20,2B20,3B5	68	172	24	38	16	4	0	5	17	16	0	.221
James Clarkson	3B58	59	205	34	62	33	11	1	7	26	30	0	.302
Paul Rambone	3B21,OF10	59	90	15	20	11	2	0	0	14	22	3	.222
Raymond Sanders	1B43	55	159	15	31	16	4	2	1	26	15	0	.195
David Cole	P30	38	37	8	6	5	2	0	1	2	13	0	.162
George Estock	P36	36	69	3	9	3	1	0	0	4	30	0	.130
Raymond Martin	P32	34	57	6	8	6	2	0	1	5	18	0	.140
Glenn Elliott	P31	31	50	3	10	5	0	0	0	9	20	0	.200
Ben Johnson	P30	30	24	2	0	1	0	0	0	8	12	0	.000
Chet Nichols	P29	29	41	2	2	0	0	0	0	2	19	0	.049

MILWAUKEE (cont.)
Brewers

BATTERS	POS-GAMES	GP	AB	R	H	BI	2B	3B	HR	BB	SO	SB	BA
Les Studener	P16,1B1	24	22	1	0	0	0	0	0	0	9	0	.000
John Podgajny	P22	22	5	1	2	1	1	1	0	0	1	0	.400
Richard Donovan	P19	20	30	1	5	2	2	0	1	1	11	0	.167
John Smith	P19	19	4	0	0	0	0	0	0	0	2	0	.000
Tom Whisenant	OF17	17	48	8	15	10	4	2	1	2	15	0	.313
Murray Wall	P13	13	19	1	4	1	0	0	0	2	8	0	.211
Charles Gorin	P13	13	6	2	2	0	0	0	0	0	2	0	.333
Joe Della Monica	2B,PR	9	1	0	0	0	0	0	0			0	.000
Joe Just	C	3	10	1	0	0	0	0	0			0	.000
Harold Daniels	OF	3	5	0	0	0	0	0	0			0	.000
Chester Hajduk	1B	3	3	0	0	0	0	0	0			0	.000
Glenn Thompson	P2	2	5	0	2	1	0	1	0			0	.400
Frank Baldwin	PH	1	1	0	0	0	0	0	0			0	.000

PITCHERS		W	L	PCT	G	GS	CG	SH	IP	H	BB	SO	ERA
George Estock		16	8	.667	36	24	16	1	196	194	91	76	3.35
Glenn Elliott		11	12	.478	31	24	13	1	176	189	61	87	4.50
Raymond Martin		11	13	.458	32	22	11	1	180	168	86	75	4.00
Chet Nichols		7	14	.333	29	19	9	3	128	121	74	76	3.73
David Cole		6	5	.545	30	11	4	0	112	101	60	107	4.18
Ben Johnson		3	5	.375	30	14	4	0	100	109	52	48	5.40
Les Studener		3	5	.375	16	9	3	0	72	76	34	40	5.38
Richard Donovan		3	6	.333	19	10	1	0	75	102	33	44	6.24
John Smith		2	2	.500	19			0	27	28	14	11	4.33
Murray Wall		2	5	.286	13	9	3	1	69	68	20	25	3.91
Richard Manville		1	1	.500	8			0	31	42	24	12	7.55
Henry Perry		1	1	.500	5			0	17	18	8	6	4.24
Charles Gorin		1	2	.333	13			0	28	28	10	15	2.89
John Podgajny		1	3	.250	22			0	34	49	19	9	4.50
Glenn Thompson		0	1	.000	2			0	14	9	11	13	6.43
Charles Bicknell		0	2	.000	7			0	15	17	11	9	9.60
Sam Webb		0	0	----	1			0	5	6	3	1	7.20
Don Liddle		0	0	----	1			0	1	2	0	0	13.43
Robert Malloy		0	0	----	1			0	0	5	0	0	54.54

TOLEDO   7th   65-87   .428   -24   Eddie Mayo
Mud Hens

BATTERS	POS-GAMES	GP	AB	R	H	BI	2B	3B	HR	BB	SO	SB	BA
Paul Campbell	1B96,OF22	119	440	56	132	51	36	4	4	33	50	5	.300
Al Federoff	2B133	136	520	64	145	36	16	3	0	43	37	14	.279
John Bero	SS113,3B13	127	440	76	111	57	14	4	18	78	66	3	.252
Bill Barnacle	3B112,OF31	146	522	81	14	82	23	3	10	78	65	4	.276
Don Lund	OF149,1B1	150	555	88	136	66	22	2	23	62	87	1	.245
George Lerchen	OF148	148	522	80	141	97	36	3	26	72	97	3	.270
Emil Restaino	OF66	86	226	24	48	27	5	0	3	19	27	5	.212
Ed Mordarski	C66	77	198	20	41	16	5	0	6	33	39	0	.207
Austin Knickerbocker	OF52	69	197	15	40	19	3	0	5	18	40	1	.203
Robert Mavis	3B26,2B18	67	170	20	45	14	7	1	2	22	11	1	.265
Myron Ginsberg	C60	63	214	32	72	39	13	2	7	25	15	0	.336
Alex DeLaGarza	SS46,2B,3B	63	178	21	34	10	5	1	3	7	23	0	.191
Dwain Sloat	P38	46	26	3	6	0	3	0	0	1	6	0	.231
Ken Fremming	P34	35	61	4	14	7	4	0	0	2	12	0	.230
Ed Neville	P35	35	50	6	12	7	0	2	0	10	9	0	.240
Richard Marlowe	P33	33	55	2	4	0	0	0	0	1	22	0	.073
Harvey Riebe	C28	30	93	6	22	5	4	0	1	4	12	0	.237
Raymond Herbert	P30	30	62	9	10	6	3	0	0	7	16	0	.161
Dick Kryhoski	1B29	29	120	18	40	22	11	1	6	3	16	1	.333
Marv Grissom	P28	28	46	2	4	2	0	0	0	0	16	0	.087
George Vico	1B26	26	92	12	21	16	4	0	2	15	6	0	.228
Bill Connelly	P20	21	25	1	1	0	1	0	0	0	10	0	.040
Bill Butland	P16	16	6	2	2	0	0	0	0	0	1	0	.333
Marlin Stuart	P13	13	30	5	5	2	0	0	0	6	3	0	.167
Halbert Simpson	OF	8	14	1	3	7	1	1	1			0	.214
Floyd Fogg	3B	7	16	0	2	1	0	0	0			0	.125
Art McConnell	P5	5	3	0	2	0	0	0	0			0	.600
Saul Rogovin	PH	1	1	0	0	0	0	0	0			0	.000

PITCHERS		W	L	PCT	G	GS	CG	SH	IP	H	BB	SO	ERA
Raymond Herbert		11	12	.478	30	24	12	2	188	174	106	90	3.69

TOLEDO (cont.)
Mud Hens

PITCHERS	W	L	PCT	G	GS	CG	SH	IP	H	BB	SO	ERA
Marlin Stuart	9	3	.750	13	12	10	3	97	84	22	48	2.23
Marv Grissom	9	10	.474	28	20	8	1	156	157	54	99	3.46
Richard Marlowe	7	10	.412	33	24	8	1	181	181	83	81	4.57
Ken Fremming	7	15	.318	34	25	8	3	169	173	74	99	4.95
Ed Neville	6	15	.286	35	20	11	1	174	181	94	72	4.14
Kapuscinski	4	3	.571	9	7	3	2	51	46	17	18	2.82
Dwain Sloat	3	4	.429	38	6	0	0	90	73	65	54	4.50
Bill Connelly	3	5	.375	20	7	4	1	64	58	48	49	4.78
Wilbur Butland	2	1	.667	16			0	26	32	10	12	7.27
Walter Beck	2	2	.500	7			0	18	16	10	10	4.00
Frank Laga	1	1	.500	4			0	14	18	11	4	6.43
Ed March	1	2	.333	6			0	18	23	7	6	6.00
Al Piechota	0	1	.000	7			0	18	27	10	10	7.50
Art McConnell	0	1	.000	5			0	14	22	10	10	9.64
William Clark	0	1	.000	5			0	8	15	3	6	10.13
James Parton	0	0	----	3			0	4	8	2	1	
Milo Johnson	0	0	----	2			0	3	2	2	1	3.00

KANSAS CITY   8th   54-99   .353   -35.5   Joe Kuhel
Blues

BATTERS	POS-GAMES	GP	AB	R	H	BI	2B	3B	HR	BB	SO	SB	BA
Fenton Mole	1B59,OF18	86	273	38	71	51	10	0	15	44	40	1	.260
Joe Muffeletto	2B64	98	239	25	51	19	7	2	2	34	19	0	.213
Gerald Snyder	SS96,2B41,3B8	145	526	68	149	48	28	2	1	30	50	9	.283
Gene Valla	3B77,SS39,2B21	136	517	73	150	46	12	3	1	39	34	9	.290
Archie Wilson	OF138	144	518	66	135	46	27	6	5	18	54	8	.261
Henry Workman	OF90,1B44	135	491	72	131	88	18	3	23	61	44	2	.267
Bob Cerv	OF89	94	349	49	106	49	10	13	14	5	71	13	.304
Bill Drescher	C93	110	289	31	77	35	14	1	5	53	24	1	.266
LeRoy Jarvis	C67	80	195	32	52	24	13	1	3	35	26	2	.267
Jim Gleeson	OF37	72	135	25	33	36	7	2	6	29	26	2	.244
Joe Polich	SS35,3B11	51	144	5	38	12	8	1	0	7	18	2	.264
Paul Hinrichs	P49	50	15	1	3	1	0	0	0	2	5	0	.200
Thomas Gorman	P45	46	19	0	2	0	0	0	0	1	9	0	.105
Malcolm Mick	1B31	38	118	24	36	15	2	2	1	19	9	2	.305
Leo Thomas	3B35	36	112	11	28	19	4	0	0	16	10	2	.250
Wallace Hood	P32	32	48	2	13	4	0	0	0	4	8	0	.271
Clarence Wotowicz	OF28,3B1	31	98	8	20	11	6	0	2	11	11	0	.204
Dain Clay	OF30	30	111	16	27	9	3	1	1	9	10	2	.243
Robert Keegan	P30	30	37	6	7	2	0	0	0	3	7	0	.189
Al Martin	2B29	29	118	15	33	10	6	2	4	6	11	2	.280
Lew Burdette	P27	29	40	5	6	4	0	0	0	10	10	0	.150
William Renna	OF23	27	79	6	16	7	4	1	1	7	13	0	.203
Frank Shea	P27	27	36	1	4	0	1	0	0	4	3	0	.111
John Mize	1B25	26	94	18	28	18	4	0	5	13	5	0	.298
David Madison	P24	25	51	5	7	2	0	0	0	2	7	0	.137
Arnold Landeck	P23	23	13	0	2	1	0	0	0	3	2	0	.154
Sidney Schacht	P17	18	41	2	8	6	2	2	0	4	18	0	.195
William Woop	P18	18	7	1	0	0	0	0	0	2	3	0	.000
Nicholas Witek	3B14	15	52	6	14	4	2	0	1	6	5	0	.269
Henry Foiles	C12	15	24	3	6	3	1	0	1	3	6	0	.250
Bill Virdon	OF11	14	41	3	14	3	3	0	0	0	3	0	.341
Ed Ford	P12	12	32	2	3	2	0	0	0	4	8	0	.094
George Prigge	SS,3B	9	27	1	6	1	1	0	0			0	.222
Al Pilarcik	OF	8	24	4	6	3	0	0	0			0	.250
Ted Atkinson	C	5	9	0	0	1	0	0	0			0	.000
Earl Wooten	OF	4	11	2	3	0	1	0	0			0	.273
Otis Strain	SS	4	10	2	2	0	0	0	0			1	.200
Robert Kline	PH,PR	2	1	0	0	0	0	0	0			0	.000
Herb Plews	3B	2	0	1	0	0	0	0	0			1	----
Harry Schaeffer	P1	1	1	0	1	1	0	0	0			0	1.000
Pete Gebrian	PR	1	0	0	0	0	0	0	0			0	----

PITCHERS	W	L	PCT	G	GS	CG	SH	IP	H	BB	SO	ERA
Lew Burdette	7	7	.500	27	18	9	0	139	150	52	77	4.79
Wallace Hood	7	16	.304	32	26	8	1	161	202	96	64	5.42
Ed Ford	6	3	.667	12	12	8	2	95	81	48	80	3.22
Paul Hinrichs	6	5	.545	49	4	0	0	96	112	57	62	5.53
Sidney Schacht	6	8	.429	17	17	8	2	117	102	46	62	3.38
Frank Shea	6	11	.353	27	19	4	0	116	132	65	58	6.28

KANSAS CITY (cont.)
Blues

PITCHERS	W	L	PCT	G	GS	CG	SH	IP	H	BB	SO	ERA
David Madison	6	15	.286	24	24	7	1	170	184	73	79	4.50
Robert Keegan	4	12	.250	30	19	6	1	127	152	61	62	5.81
Thomas Gorman	3	5	.375	45	3	1	0	97	101	55	66	5.01
Art Del Duca	1	0	1.000	4			0	9	9	4	5	6.00
Arnold Landeck	1	4	.200	23	3	0	0	60	80	24	24	5.40
William Woop	1	6	.143	18			0	43	45	46	24	8.16
Hugh Radcliffe	0	1	.000	2			0	2	4	4	1	18.00
Ervin Porterfield	0	2	.000	3			0	8	9	2	3	5.63
Duane Pilette	0	4	.000	4			0	28	37	9	8	7.07
John Fitzgerald	0	0	----	4			0	6	11	11	6	
Robert Curtis	0	0	----	3			0	8	6	10	10	
Eugene Olsen	0	0	----	2			0	3	3	1	1	0.00
Harry Schaeffer	0	0	----	1			0	1	3	1	0	40.29

MULTI-TEAM PLAYERS

BATTERS	POS-GAMES	TEAMS	GP	AB	R	H	BI	2B	3B	HR	BB	SO	SB	BA
Culley Rikard	OF97	KC-IND	115	308	45	87	41	11	2	3	81	22	2	.282
Boris Martin	C34,OF3	LOU-TOL	58	152	13	32	13	6	1	3	7	18	0	.211

TEAM BATTING

TEAMS	GP	AB	R	H	BI	2B	3B	HR	BB	SO	SB	BA
MINNEAPOLIS	155	5169	879	1411	823	221	46	176	688	710	34	.273
INDIANAPOLIS	153	5080	750	1414	695	250	61	114	573	690	41	.278
COLUMBUS	153	4910	665	1290	625	233	66	72	574	575	46	.263
ST. PAUL	152	4938	788	1288	715	195	57	114	720	717	138	.261
LOUISVILLE	153	5012	717	1312	670	219	53	75	616	620	39	.262
MILWAUKEE	154	5048	693	1335	622	225	40	123	532	622	34	.264
TOLEDO	152	4982	658	1255	598	220	26	119	550	717	37	.252
KANSAS CITY	156	4980	638	1294	576	197	42	91	506	604	59	.260
	614	40119	5788	10599	5324	1760	391	884	4759	5255	428	.264

1951
Willie and Mickey

Two young outfielders came rocketing through the American Association in 1951. One played for the Minneapolis Millers, while the other graced the roster of the Kansas City Blues. While both of these two were "can't miss" major league prospects, their paths took decidedly different trajectories. The name of the first outfielder was Willie Mays, and the name of the second was Mickey Mantle. Willie Mays was first signed by New York Giant scouts off the roster of the Negro National League's Birmingham club in 1950. After half a season tune-up in Trenton, Mays was deemed ready for the American Association. Unfortunately for the Association's pitchers, they were not ready for him. He slashed more than 50 hits in the first month of the season, while pushing his batting average near the stratospheric .500 level.

Mickey Mantle started his pro career with the New York Yankees in 1949. After fine seasons in Independence (1949) and Joplin (1950), Yankee management promoted Mantle to New York before the start of the 1951 season. Here, he did not fare as well. While mired in a deep slump, the young outfielder was sent to the Yankees' top farm team in Kansas City. As his poor batting continued, Mantle decided to call it quits. After a stern lecture by his father pertaining to the stark employment alternatives outside the game, he chose to give baseball another try. The decision was a wise one as Mantle immediately went on a tear. In his first game back, he connected for the cycle, while hitting an additional home run to boot. He continued to hit, and soon his homer level reached ten and his average climbed over .350.

On the field, the Milwaukee Brewers captured their first pennant in six years, outlasting St. Paul by nine games, while Kansas City and Louisville finished third and fourth. Defending champions Minneapolis dropped to fifth, with Toledo, Indianapolis and Columbus bringing up the rear. Despite his club's tailender status, Columbus player-manager Harry Walker won the batting title with a .393 mark, the second highest total in league history. Home run champion Harold Gilbert (29) played for Minneapolis, while RBI champ George Crowe (119) played for the pennant winning Brewers. On the pitching side, Crowe's teammate, Ernest Johnson won the ERA crown (2.62), while Kansas City pitcher Robert Wiesler struck out the most batters (162), and James Atkins of Louisville finished with the most wins (18).

After 35 games and sporting a .477 batting average, Willie Mays was promoted to the Giants. Later with his 11 home runs and .360 batting average, Mickey Mantle was called up by the Yankees. Although neither stayed long in the Association, the league certainly served as a launching pad for their Hall of Fame careers.

MILWAUKEE Brewers

| | 1st | 94-57 | .623 | | Charles Grimm |

BATTERS	POS-GAMES	GP	AB	R	H	BI	2B	3B	HR	BB	SO	SB	BA
George Crowe	1B150	150	557	105	189	119	41	7	24	85	61	2	.339
William Reed	2B127	129	469	60	146	55	30	4	1	52	29	4	.311
James Clarkson	SS73,3B,OF	97	283	52	97	49	12	4	5	43	29	6	.343
Bill Klaus	3B151	151	621	105	177	55	31	14	3	64	57	3	.285
James Basso	OF151	151	605	86	160	114	28	8	25	37	81	2	.264
Ben Thorpe	OF138	139	578	108	173	77	29	8	10	34	75	9	.299
Luis Olmo	OF82	82	312	38	87	52	12	2	8	17	32	0	.279
Al Unser	C115	122	393	57	115	62	14	1	17	44	48	1	.293
Robert Montag	OF52,1B1	86	195	35	50	34	9	1	9	34	34	1	.256
Johnny Logan	SS57	57	189	25	47	25	8	1	4	26	28	2	.249
Paul Burris	C46	48	129	19	33	12	3	0	1	21	12	0	.256
Virgil Jester	P47	47	31	0	4	0	1	0	0	1	13	0	.129
Murray Wall	P32	40	68	12	11	3	1	0	1	11	23	0	.162
Earl Wooten	OF25	39	43	4	10	5	2	1	1	4	2	0	.233
Gene Mauch	SS27,2B10,1B	37	109	30	33	16	2	0	1	26	10	2	.303
Robert Jaderlund	OF27	37	49	8	11	7	2	1	0	10	6	0	.224
Maynard Thiel	P36	36	52	3	11	3	0	0	0	0	8	0	.212
Charles Gorin	P32	33	62	7	19	14	2	0	1	4	13	0	.306
Ernest Johnson	P32	32	67	7	19	12	4	0	0	3	9	0	.284
Richard Hoover	P27	28	24	4	7	0	1	0	0	3	2	0	.292
Mark Christman	2B23,3B,1B	27	73	7	17	7	3	0	1	7	8	0	.233
Richard Donovan	P21	22	43	8	11	9	3	0	2	5	13	0	.256
Howie Moss	OF17	19	58	13	15	8	1	0	3	10	9	1	.259
Art Fowler	P17	17	24	2	2	2	1	0	0	2	4	0	.083
Emil Kush	P16	16	4	0	0	0	0	0	0	0	0	0	.000
Sidney Schacht	P14	14	28	1	6	0	0	0	0	0	9	0	.214
Eddie Mathews	3B12	12	9	2	3	5	0	0	1	2	3	0	.333
Jack Weisenburger	SS	8	3	3	0	1	0	0	0			0	.000
Ted Sepkowski	OF	7	11	1	2	1	0	0	0			0	.182
Len Pearson	1B	5	9	0	1	1	0	0	0			0	.111

PITCHERS		W	L	PCT	G	GS	CG	SH	IP	H	BB	SO	ERA
Ernest Johnson		15	4	.789	32	23	14	3	196	168	63	133	2.62
Murray Wall		15	5	.750	32	30	13	3	203	207	104	107	4.30
Maynard Thiel		14	9	.609	36	19	8	3	153	155	34	62	3.71
Virgil Jester		13	6	.684	47	1	0	0	115	107	38	49	3.21
Charles Gorin		12	9	.571	32	23	8	3	152	140	108	93	4.38
Richard Donovan		7	5	.583	21	16	10	1	129	124	55	88	3.28
Richard Hoover		5	4	.556	27	7	2	0	83	91	26	36	3.14
Sidney Schacht		4	1	.800	14	7	3	0	77	81	24	48	4.09
Art Fowler		4	7	.364	17	13	2	1	78	101	27	51	5.31
Hall		2	4	.333	9	9	3	0	63	83	36	37	4.29
Emil Kush		2	1	.667	16			0	32	42	16	10	6.47
Bob Chipman		1	0	1.000	1			0	7	1	6	5	0.00
Don Liddle		0	1	.000	4			0	6	10	4	4	9.00
Norman Roy		0	1	.000	1			0	3	7	1	0	12.00

ST. PAUL Saints

| | 2nd | 85-66 | .563 | -9 | Clay Hopper |

BATTERS	POS-GAMES	GP	AB	R	H	BI	2B	3B	HR	BB	SO	SB	BA
Danny Ozark	1B115	124	376	64	98	74	21	1	15	61	56	1	.261
Jack Cassini	2B117	130	463	92	141	50	29	0	8	64	48	34	.305
James Pendleton	SS143	143	564	116	170	79	18	13	21	44	81	14	.301
Don Hoak	3B110,SS,OF	126	366	60	94	34	10	4	5	68	48	4	.257
Frank Marchio	OF134	140	405	45	100	51	22	7	4	37	50	3	.247
Eric Tipton	OF121	132	385	52	106	81	26	6	11	89	48	9	.275
William Antonello	OF111	116	363	50	92	65	13	7	17	29	75	4	.253
Charles Thompson	C92	108	335	47	99	38	15	5	3	27	16	1	.296
Richard Whitman	OF95	97	334	47	104	57	21	6	3	41	28	4	.311
Al Brancato	3B40,2B37,1B4	88	264	32	68	41	8	0	8	33	20	1	.258
Richard Teed	C65	67	207	22	46	17	9	0	2	13	29	1	.222
Donald Nicholas	OF36	40	108	26	26	2	0	2	0	29	5	16	.241
Gaylord Lemish	P37	37	31	3	4	2	0	1	0	2	7	0	.129
John Van Cuyk	P36	37	22	0	3	0	1	0	0	4	15	0	.136
Al Epperly	P34	34	18	2	4	2	0	0	0	1	6	0	.222
Ezra McGlothin	P30	31	62	8	17	7	3	0	0	12	7	0	.274
Earl Mossor	P27	30	57	6	15	10	0	1	2	1	16	0	.263
William Samson	P29,OF1	30	41	4	6	2	2	0	0	2	4	0	.146
John Rutherford	P26	26	67	3	9	8	2	0	0	7	17	0	.134

ST. PAUL (cont.)
Saints

BATTERS	POS-GAMES	GP	AB	R	H	BI	2B	3B	HR	BB	SO	SB	BA
Richard Raklovits	3B13,SS	23	36	10	9	3	2	0	0	3	5	0	.250
Clem Labine	P20	21	39	3	9	2	2	0	0	1	15	0	.231
Jack Lindsey	SS,2B,3B	17	39	2	8	3	0	1	0	2	8	1	.205
Robert Bundy	3B,OF	17	38	5	5	0	0	0	0	4	1	1	.132
James Romano	P16	16	22	2	3	3	1	0	0	2	6	0	.136
Earl Naylor	OF2	13	16	0	2	0	0	0	0	1	1	1	.125
Kent Peterson	P12	12	12	1	2	1	0	0	0	2	3	0	.167
Joe Black	P9	10	20	4	5	2	0	0	1	2	10	0	.250
Mickey Livingstone	C	6	11	2	2	3	0	0	1			0	.182
Joe Torpey	2B	4	9	1	1	1	0	0	0			0	.111

PITCHERS		W	L	PCT	G	GS	CG	SH	IP	H	BB	SO	ERA
Ezra McGlothin		15	7	.682	30	24	15	2	195	184	69	91	3.78
John Rutherford		15	8	.652	26	24	14	0	190	194	53	72	2.94
Al Epperly		13	4	.765	34	1	0	0	71	65	23	33	3.80
Clem Labine		9	6	.600	20	15	7	3	117	104	42	63	2.62
Earl Mossor		9	10	.474	27	22	8	2	152	164	69	87	4.80
William Samson		8	9	.471	29	18	7	0	119	130	81	64	5.14
Gaylord Lemish		5	6	.455	37	6	2	1	111	124	58	41	5.11
Joe Black		4	3	.571	9	7	6	1	60	44	24	35	2.25
Marion Fricano		2	0	1.000	9			0	35	29	17	14	4.89
Kent Peterson		2	1	.667	12	8	1	0	46	52	32	26	6.07
James Romano		2	5	.286	16	13	4	1	73	73	50	25	5.79
John Van Cuyk		1	6	.143	36	10	0	0	94	116	46	53	6.22
Leon Griffeth		0	1	.000	4			0	3	8	1	1	18.00
Nick Andromidas		0	0	----	1			0	1	0	4	0	18.00

KANSAS CITY   3rd   81-70   .536   -13   George Selkirk
Blues

BATTERS	POS-GAMES	GP	AB	R	H	BI	2B	3B	HR	BB	SO	SB	BA
Don Bollweg	1B122	122	426	109	129	69	26	12	20	106	56	1	.303
Kal Segrist	2B74,SS38,OF15,3B,1B	129	468	80	136	58	26	4	17	72	66	1	.291
Robert Thomson	SS35	37	115	9	26	6	5	0	0	5	29	0	.226
Andy Carey	3B118	120	424	47	122	72	15	6	14	34	74	3	.288
Keith Thomas	OF114,1B11	138	471	59	133	81	24	6	14	60	62	0	.282
Robert Marquis	OF110	123	432	57	120	49	15	6	10	49	71	6	.278
Bob Cerv	OF107	109	425	85	146	108	22	21	28	40	79	4	.344
Clint Courtney	C91	103	343	34	101	35	14	2	8	34	15	1	.294
Eugene Markland	2B31,SS29,3B22	85	290	65	75	39	16	3	10	73	49	2	.259
Ray Partee	C60	69	190	28	46	24	9	2	3	25	25	0	.242
Bill Ramsey	OF36	45	88	17	17	4	5	0	0	20	16	0	.193
Jackie Jensen	OF41	42	160	23	42	26	4	1	9	20	22	2	.263
Bob Muncrief	P41	41	25	1	4	4	1	0	0	3	9	0	.160
Mickey Mantle	OF40	40	166	32	60	50	9	3	11	23	30	5	.361
Thomas Upton	SS34	34	129	11	30	8	4	2	0	5	21	0	.233
Ernest Nevel	P31	31	69	7	16	5	0	0	0	1	14	0	.232
Rex Jones	P27	30	58	4	10	5	1	0	0	3	20	0	.172
Kermit Wahl	3B12,SS,2B	28	109	18	30	9	5	0	0	13	11	0	.275
Cliff Melton	P25	26	38	2	7	2	0	0	0	5	13	0	.184
Robert Wiesler	P24	24	69	5	14	4	2	0	0	1	11	0	.203
Robert Ross	P18	24	24	6	3	2	0	0	0	1	7	0	.125
Carmine Meligano	P23	23	9	0	0	0	0	0	0	1	6	0	.000
Richard Carr	P13	22	28	2	8	5	2	0	0	6	4	0	.286
Hank Wyse	P21	22	24	3	4	1	0	0	0	2	3	0	.167
William Cope	2B15,SS	21	72	8	19	11	3	1	2	1	25	0	.264
Gerald Snyder	2B20	20	93	12	25	6	2	0	0	6	3	3	.269
Arnold Landeck	P16	17	23	4	5	1	0	0	1	5	2	0	.217
Ray Hamrick	SS,3B,2B	16	53	8	11	6	5	0	0	7	4	1	.208
Frank Logue	P16	16	11	2	1	0	0	0	0	3	6	0	.091
John Blanchard	OF10	14	41	7	11	4	1	1	0	3	3	0	.268
Robert O'Neal	C,1B	11	40	6	9	8	1	1	0	6	5	0	.225
Augie Bergamo	OF,1B	11	24	4	7	5	3	0	1	5	3	0	.292
Louis Sleater	P7	11	24	7	7	0	1	0	0	2	2	0	.292
Max Peterson	P10	10	3	0	1	0	0	0	0	1	1	0	.333
Clarence Wotowicz	1B,OF	9	29	4	7	7	3	0	1			0	.241
Henry Foiles	C	9	24	1	4	3	0	0	0			0	.167
Robert Keegan	P2	2	4	1	2	0	0	0	0			0	.500
Gus Trianos	C	2	4	0	0	0	0	0	0			0	.000

KANSAS CITY (cont.)
Blues

BATTERS	POS-GAMES	GP	AB	R	H	BI	2B	3B	HR	BB	SO	SB	BA
Al Sperenza	SS	2	1	0	0	0	0	0	0			0	.000
Tom McKelvey	C	1	3	1	1	0	0	0	0			0	.333
Robert Kline	SS	1	2	0	0	0	0	0	0			0	.000

PITCHERS		W	L	PCT	G	GS	CG	SH	IP	H	BB	SO	ERA
Ernest Nevel		14	11	.560	31	25	17	1	191	212	80	46	3.86
Robert Wiesler		10	9	.526	24	23	11	2	194	155	**143**	**162**	2.92
Cliff Melton		9	8	.529	25	18	4	1	113	142	49	47	5.02
Hank Wyse		7	5	.583	21	10	1	0	77	102	35	27	5.73
Rex Jones		7	6	.538	27	18	7	1	146	169	76	59	4.13
Bob Muncrief		5	6	.455	41	1	0	0	88	94	20	51	3.07
Robert Hogue		4	0	1.000	7			0	22	18	8	7	4.50
Louis Sleater		4	2	.667	7	7	5	1	54	50	27	28	4.50
Arnold Landeck		4	3	.571	16	8	3	0	76	84	24	27	4.86
Robert Ross		4	5	.444	18	10	4	1	72	78	47	41	4.25
Richard Carr		3	6	.333	13	13	5	0	70	72	52	29	3.86
Tom Morgan		2	1	.667	4			0	20	14	8	11	2.25
Frank Logue		2	2	.500	16			0	41	44	12	12	4.83
Ervin Porterfield		2	2	.500	8			0	29	37	14	19	4.66
Hugh Radcliffe		1	0	1.000	3			0	11	9	5	4	3.27
Robert Keegan		1	0	1.000	2			0	9	19	6	6	8.00
Carmine Meligano		1	2	.333	23			0	42	53	39	17	7.50
Thomas Gorman		0	1	.000	3			0	6	5	6	4	1.50
Joe Page		0	0	----	6			0	15	15	7	7	

LOUISVILLE   4th   80-73   .523   -15   Mike Higgins
Colonels

BATTERS	POS-GAMES	GP	AB	R	H	BI	2B	3B	HR	BB	SO	SB	BA
Norbert Zauchin	1B134	135	498	61	133	104	30	6	12	54	79	1	.267
Edward Lyons	2B97	102	383	61	96	67	18	2	10	54	37	1	.284
Allen Richter	SS129	129	511	107	164	57	28	4	0	81	35	2	.321
Ken Chapman	3B87	99	308	45	79	36	10	6·	2	63	20	0	.256
Taft Wright	OF113	129	439	74	147	115	34	4	15	64	16	1	.335
Tom O'Brien	OF100	110	361	55	100	61	21	2	5	55	37	0	.277
Robert Broome	OF79,1B10	99	338	61	96	67	18	2	10	54	37	1	.284
Robert Scherbath	C80,1B,3B	84	251	39	58	22	9	1	4	63	37	2	.231
Mel Hoderlein	3B54,2B44,SS27	111	407	59	127	40	15	2	5	50	25	8	.312
Tom Wright	OF71	72	262	38	74	45	12	5	2	42	26	0	.282
Karl Olson	OF61	63	228	35	73	31	6	2	5	17	31	1	.320
Len Okrie	C55	55	165	17	31	20	5	1	1	16	42	1	.188
Gordon Mueller	P45	45	24	1	4	1	0	0	0	2	3	0	.167
Charles Maxwell	OF40	40	153	21	39	17	7	3	4	26	24	1	.255
Dave Ferriss	P21,1B2	38	59	8	21	5	4	0	0	10	8	0	.356
James Atkins	P31	36	96	10	23	10	2	1	0	6	11	1	.240
Ted Lepcio	2B22,3B11	35	137	24	36	11	5	3	5	10	24	0	.263
Donald Asmanga	P25	29	35	4	7	1	1	0	0	2	3	0	.200
Harley Hisner	P24	24	36	3	6	0	1	0	0	5	12	0	.167
Tom Herrin	P16	22	27	7	7	3	3	0	0	1	7	0	.259
James McDonald	P19	19	51	8	9	5	0	0	0	7	12	0	.167
John Douglas	1B17	17	43	6	13	2	1	1	0	5	4	0	.302
Jim Piersall	OF15	17	42	8	13	2	0	2	0	5	5	0	.310
Leo Kiely	P15	16	45	5	12	3	0	0	1	0	5	0	.267
Bill Evans	P15	15	41	1	4	4	1	0	0	2	8	0	.098
Raymond Holton	3B11,C1	13	41	1	8	5	1	0	0	4	2	0	.195
William Kennedy	P13	13	30	4	5	1	1	0	0	5	10	0	.167
Alfred Evans	C10	11	39	6	13	7	2	0	1	7	5	0	.333
Robert Nelson	C10	11	37	2	6	3	1	0	0	2	3	0	.162
Jack Parks	C	4	12	1	2	0	0	0	0			0	.167
William Boyce	OF	3	4	0	0	0	0	0	0			0	.000
LeRoy Jones	C	2	5	0	0	1	0	0	0			0	.000
Robert DiPietro	PH	2	1	1	1	0	0	0	0			0	1.000

PITCHERS		W	L	PCT	G	GS	CG	SH	IP	H	BB	SO	ERA
James Atkins		**18**	9	.667	31	29	17	1	**210**	231	94	90	4.24
James McDonald		10	7	.588	19	19	12	0	144	139	50	51	3.50
Bill Evans		8	4	.667	15	14	8	2	103	102	42	57	3.67
Gordon Mueller		8	7	.533	45	2	1	0	99	86	52	53	3.64
Dave Ferriss		7	7	.500	21	18	11	1	120	145	40	25	5.25
Harley Hisner		7	13	.350	24	15	7	2	125	145	59	69	6.26

LOUISVILLE (cont.)
Colonels

PITCHERS	W	L	PCT	G	GS	CG	SH	IP	H	BB	SO	ERA
William Kennedy	6	2	.750	13	12	5	4	89	73	30	57	2.73
Tom Herrin	3	6	.333	16	14	3	0	91	98	57	35	4.55
Robert Austin	2	2	.500	7			0	29	28	17	12	4.34
Donald Asmanga	2	5	.286	25	8	4	0	92	82	64	52	4.30
George Susce	1	4	.200	8			0	41	40	26	11	4.83
Rollin Schuster	0	1	.000	7			0	15	18	10	18	6.60
Jim Suchecki	0	2	.000	5			0	22	31	17	15	7.36
Tom Casey	0	0	----	6			0	21	27	12	8	

MINNEAPOLIS　　　5th　　77-75　　.507　　-17.5　　Thomas Heath
Millers

BATTERS	POS-GAMES	GP	AB	R	H	BI	2B	3B	HR	BB	SO	SB	BA
Harold Gilbert	1B141,3B3	145	479	92	131	100	25	3	29	86	49	1	.273
Dave Williams	2B79	80	293	61	84	49	9	5	12	42	18	2	.287
Rudolph Rufer	SS137	137	557	91	130	45	18	8	1	56	85	54	.233
Ray Dandridge	3B103,SS2	107	423	59	137	61	24	1	8	29	18	1	.324
William Milne	OF122	131	463	87	139	68	26	9	9	75	44	13	.300
John Kropf	OF111	116	340	67	85	43	17	1	10	89	61	2	.250
Neill Sheridan	OF75	75	304	48	93	50	17	0	9	25	51	1	.306
Ray Katt	C112,1B2	117	354	56	109	57	27	0	11	43	44	0	.308
Robert Hofman	2B67	67	241	40	70	45	11	2	10	41	26	3	.290
Millard Howell	P29,OF3	58	83	14	28	27	4	0	7	8	6	0	.337
Michael Natisin	1B26	53	112	12	26	24	5	0	5	21	14	0	.232
Guilford Dickens	OF49,3B2	50	167	26	45	26	8	1	6	27	20	0	.269
Adrian Zabala	P49	50	64	7	24	12	5	0	1	1	12	0	.375
Dave Barnhill	P33	44	54	3	11	8	2	0	2	1	12	0	.204
Hoyt Wilhelm	P40	40	74	6	18	4	3	0	0	5	21	0	.243
Gail Henley	OF34	39	123	19	32	18	4	2	5	15	24	1	.260
Jake Early	C37	37	92	16	23	23	5	0	5	19	7	0	.250
Willie Mays	OF35	35	149	38	71	30	18	3	8	14	10	5	.477
Roy Weatherly	OF28	32	111	13	22	7	2	1	3	8	10	1	.198
Hugh Oser	P25	32	31	6	6	1	0	0	0	0	3	0	.194
Norman Fox	P30	31	38	4	3	2	2	0	0	4	13	0	.079
Frank Fanovich	P26	26	34	4	7	6	1	0	0	3	3	0	.206
Andy Tomasic	P21	23	32	3	6	4	0	0	2	3	9	0	.188
Walter Cox	P23	23	20	0	2	2	0	0	0	0	7	0	.100
Ed Sokol	C19	22	58	4	12	11	3	0	0	10	11	0	.207
Barney Martin	P17	20	9	1	1	0	0	0	0	0	5	0	.111
Roger Bowman	P12	16	31	2	4	2	1	0	0	0	10	1	.129
Art Wilson	SS,2B,3B,OF	17	59	12	23	13	2	1	2	13	8	0	.390
Henry Thompson	OF,3B,SS	14	53	18	18	13	2	0	7	8	8	5	.340
Harvey Gentry	OF10	10	22	3	8	3	1	0	0	4	2	1	.364
Carvel Rowell	3B1	5	5	0	1	1	0	0	0			0	.200

PITCHERS	W	L	PCT	G	GS	CG	SH	IP	H	BB	SO	ERA
Adrian Zabala	14	12	.538	49	16	4	0	177	198	60	76	3.97
Hoyt Wilhelm	11	14	.440	40	29	12	1	210	219	82	148	3.94
Millard Howell	9	9	.500	29	21	8	1	137	155	69	77	6.50
Hugh Oser	7	3	.700	25	10	4	1	92	109	56	28	5.58
Frank Fanovich	7	12	.368	26	14	4	1	114	114	76	86	5.53
Dave Barnhill	6	5	.545	33	7	2	0	105	96	47	59	4.46
Norman Fox	6	6	.500	30	18	4	0	123	137	114	61	5.41
Roger Bowman	5	3	.625	12	11	3	1	76	58	42	82	3.32
Barney Martin	4	1	.800	17			0	39	45	28	16	5.77
Walter Cox	3	1	.750	23	5	1	0	73	79	47	30	3.08
Andy Tomasic	3	5	.375	21	12	3	0	88	99	56	49	4.46
Ed Wright	2	0	1.000	8			0	30	41	17	4	5.70
Ike Pearson	0	1	.000	4			0	5	10	2	0	9.00
Cyril Buker	0	0	----	2			0	3	8	2	4	21.00

TOLEDO　　　6th　　70-82　　.481　　-24.5　　Jack Tighe
Mud Hens

BATTERS	POS-GAMES	GP	AB	R	H	BI	2B	3B	HR	BB	SO	SB	BA
Paul Campbell	1B110,OF10	134	471	77	141	58	25	4	12	35	35	2	.299
Al Federoff	2B99	106	387	53	106	33	11	5	3	43	18	7	.274
Alex DeLaGarza	SS84,P2,2B,3B	96	318	31	84	39	14	1	5	15	20	3	.264

TOLEDO (cont.)
Mud Hens

BATTERS	POS-GAMES	GP	AB	R	H	BI	2B	3B	HR	BB	SO	SB	BA
Bill Barnacle	3B109,OF27	140	502	72	139	60	21	5	9	68	47	4	.277
Don Lund	OF117	128	428	74	111	65	26	0	18	52	39	4	.259
Russ Sullivan	OF112	120	402	72	137	88	23	8	11	68	26	2	.341
Glenn McQuillen	OF92	114	340	46	93	44	15	4	6	30	30	3	.274
Ed Mordarski	C88	96	260	40	75	44	17	1	4	50	31	0	.288
Robert Morris	2B55,3B23	99	282	32	88	48	18	3	4	36	19	0	.312
Jack Conway	SS75	80	257	28	67	30	10	4	6	26	24	1	.261
Ralph Atkins	1B47	67	177	29	46	30	3	2	9	31	33	1	.260
George Lerchen	OF57	66	192	39	51	27	9	3	8	43	36	5	.266
Frank House	C61	64	185	15	43	19	10	1	1	27	17	0	.232
Ralph Poole	P53	53	29	0	3	1	1	0	0	3	6	0	.103
John Phillips	OF52	52	203	33	58	16	12	0	4	11	17	4	.286
Dwain Sloat	P42,1B1	51	30	6	11	5	3	1	0	1	5	0	.367
Milt Jordan	P45	45	45	2	3	2	0	0	0	2	17	0	.067
Harold Daugherty	3B22,SS	44	118	17	32	17	6	1	2	9	17	2	.271
Richard Marlowe	P39	39	63	3	5	2	0	0	0	6	27	0	.079
John Weiss	P32	32	38	1	5	1	0	0	0	1	11	0	.132
Wayne McLeland	P28	28	58	3	5	0	0	0	0	1	25	0	.086
Billy Hoeft	P27	27	57	7	7	2	0	1	0	6	17	0	.123
Ernest Funk	P23	24	30	2	3	2	0	0	0	3	2	0	.100
Pat Haggerty	OF12	21	43	12	17	5	2	0	1	5	2	1	.395
Don Griffin	C18	18	58	6	11	6	0	0	0	3	5	0	.190
Bill Connelly	P14	14	25	2	6	4	2	0	0	1	4	0	.240
Alex Nedelco	P10	10	4	0	1	0	0	0	0	0	2	0	.250
Ed Neville	P6	6	4	1	2	0	0	0	0			0	.500

PITCHERS		W	L	PCT	G	GS	CG	SH	IP	H	BB	SO	ERA
Ralph Poole		13	7	.650	53	9	3	0	114	144	46	42	5.21
Richard Marlowe		10	10	.500	39	26	10	0	197	208	78	83	4.34
Billy Hoeft		9	14	.391	27	26	12	1	164	171	85	124	5.43
Wayne McLeland		7	15	.318	28	24	11	2	182	175	65	103	3.76
Ernest Funk		6	8	.429	23	15	5	1	101	132	47	44	6.06
Milt Jordan		6	12	.333	45	16	5	1	160	168	78	73	4.56
John Weiss		5	2	.714	32	9	5	0	122	112	64	63	4.20
Dwain Sloat		5	3	.625	42	3	1	0	80	86	55	51	5.85
Bill Connelly		3	4	.429	14	12	0	0	69	79	46	50	6.13
Paul Foytack		3	5	.375	9	9	5	0	54	42	35	26	3.17
Ed Neville		2	0	1.000	6			0	15	19	7	6	4.80
Ken Fremming		1	1	.500	4			0	6	6	6	3	7.50
Alex Nedelco		0	1	.000	10			0	21	22	11	9	5.14
Alex DeLaGarza		0	0	----	2			0	3	2	0	5	0.00

INDIANAPOLIS   7th   68-84   .447   -26.5   Don Gutteridge
Indians

BATTERS	POS-GAMES	GP	AB	R	H	BI	2B	3B	HR	BB	SO	SB	BA
Ed Stevens	1B151	152	575	85	150	91	21	7	12	50	52	0	.261
John Merson	2B147	147	600	86	177	94	36	4	10	25	64	1	.295
Melvin Rue	SS67,3B5	72	216	30	61	13	12	1	0	32	18	1	.282
Froilan Fernandez	3B145,SS4	147	530	77	137	76	20	2	15	57	63	4	.258
Ted Beard	OF115	117	396	101	108	30	17	9	8	101	61	17	.273
Frank Kahn	OF103	111	408	54	120	89	20	3	18	31	50	1	.294
Dom Dallessandro	OF86	99	297	56	86	61	22	4	9	75	20	0	.290
James Mangan	C88	100	299	39	87	51	14	4	9	31	51	0	.291
Lloyd Gearhart	OF60,1B3	86	137	22	31	17	8	0	4	17	34	0	.226
Harry Fisher	P23	80	115	15	34	26	6	2	6	4	10	0	.296
Earl Turner	C75	78	256	30	69	33	9	3	10	18	41	0	.270
Forrest Main	P60	60	39	3	7	1	2	0	0	2	11	0	.179
Richard Cole	SS57	57	195	37	58	28	8	5	2	31	18	2	.297
Mizell Platt	OF48,3B1	57	150	18	37	16	10	1	2	12	24	1	.247
Royce Lint	P38	49	64	15	13	6	3	1	0	6	11	1	.203
Tom Saffell	OF40	42	150	29	48	14	5	0	1	19	19	10	.320
Inman Chambers	P34	41	13	3	4	0	0	0	0	0	5	0	.308
John Hutchings	P38	38	3	0	0	0	0	0	0	1	1	0	.000
Monty Basgall	SS31,3B,2B	37	106	15	27	13	5	1	1	15	11	0	.255
Ed McGhee	OF32	32	144	29	51	17	5	7	2	5	13	1	.354
John McCall	P28	29	66	7	17	8	4	1	0	5	15	0	.258
Joe Rowell	OF24,3B3	28	98	10	24	7	3	0	2	9	6	0	.245
Frank Papish	P25	28	54	3	5	3	0	0	1	2	12	0	.093
Fred Strobel	P28	28	29	2	2	1	0	0	0	2	10	0	.069

INDIANAPOLIS (cont.)
Indians

BATTERS	POS-GAMES	GP	AB	R	H	BI	2B	3B	HR	BB	SO	SB	BA
Joe Muir	P23	26	39	4	5	6	0	0	0	3	8	0	.128
Russ Peters	3B10,SS,2B	22	40	4	5	3	3	0	0	4	8	0	.125
Robert Curtis	P14	14	23	2	2	2	0	0	0	2	0	0	.087
James Clark	SS,2B	10	17	3	2	0	0	0	0	2	0	0	.118
Culley Rikard	PH	8	7	0	3	1	0	0	0			0	.429
Don Hedrick	SS	2	5	1	0	0	0	0	0			0	.000

PITCHERS		W	L	PCT	G	GS	CG	SH	IP	H	BB	SO	ERA
Forrest Main		12	13	.480	60	6	2	0	143	144	54	109	4.22
Royce Lint		11	11	.500	38	26	11	2	205	215	75	106	3.91
John McCall		10	9	.526	28	26	10	0	171	173	92	111	4.53
Frank Papish		9	12	.429	28	27	10	3	156	175	73	80	5.25
Joe Muir		7	5	.583	23	17	7	2	113	137	30	51	5.65
Harry Fisher		6	9	.400	23	18	7	0	131	149	68	60	5.15
John Hutchings		4	1	.800	38	0	0	0	55	66	26	21	5.07
Robert Curtis		3	8	.273	14	13	2	0	68	86	39	39	6.88
Inman Chambers		2	4	.333	34	1	0	0	79	104	32	20	4.33
Fred Strobel		2	8	.200	28	11	2	0	97	114	55	44	6.12
Paul LaPalme		1	1	.500	5			0	22	19	8	18	3.68
Elmer Riddle		1	2	.333	4			0	17	31	16	8	9.53
Stan Milankovich		0	1	.000	6			0	15	26	8	7	7.80
Paul Pettit		0	0	----	4			0	6	6	5	0	7.50

COLUMBUS   8th   53-101   .344   -42.5   Harry Walker
Red Birds

BATTERS	POS-GAMES	GP	AB	R	H	BI	2B	3B	HR	BB	SO	SB	BA
Maurice Mozzali	1B67,OF42	123	426	81	124	49	32	3	8	46	21	2	.291
Bernard Creger	2B71,SS2	84	294	31	71	17	11	0	1	17	25	3	.241
Fred McAllister	SS140	144	516	45	114	48	22	6	2	13	86	3	.221
Vern Benson	3B106,2B20,OF14,SS	138	467	95	144	89	25	6	18	111	51	2	.308
Rip Repulski	OF105	115	400	49	110	56	24	4	9	20	88	4	.275
Ellis Deal	OF104,P4	114	393	62	103	69	17	3	18	70	55	1	.262
Roy Broome	OF101	102	369	41	109	74	14	7	8	31	39	6	.295
Richard Morgan	C94	102	322	27	75	34	12	2	1	18	27	0	.233
Harry Walker	OF50,2B29,1B10,P2,SS	110	298	63	117	39	24	1	6	55	18	10	.393
Joe Aliperto	3B53,SS17,2B12	86	251	26	54	25	6	2	0	32	23	2	.215
Charles Kress	1B59	68	202	31	53	41	10	2	9	31	27	8	.262
Charles Marshall	C66	67	160	20	42	19	7	1	4	53	54	0	.263
Lee Peterson	P52	52	25	3	5	1	1	0	0	2	6	0	.200
Howard Phillips	2B37	42	145	23	34	7	6	0	2	24	28	0	.234
John Crimian	P36	36	10	1	2	3	1	0	0	0	3	0	.200
Mars Lewis	OF29,SS	35	120	7	28	7	2	1	0	4	14	0	.233
Edward Blake	P27,OF1	34	62	4	13	5	2	0	0	8	14	0	.210
Peter Mazar	P26	27	50	1	3	1	1	0	0	4	12	0	.060
Steve Bilko	1B21	26	74	13	21	6	2	0	1	12	18	0	.284
Hisel Patrick	P25	25	54	6	9	3	0	1	0	3	13	0	.167
Glen Moulder	P23	23	40	4	6	2	1	0	0	0	6	0	.150
Harvey Zernia	OF15,3B2	22	69	11	19	6	5	0	0	4	8	0	.275
Herb Moford	P16	17	18	3	3	1	0	0	0	2	7	0	.167
Elroy Joyce	P14	14	26	2	7	3	1	0	0	0	8	0	.268
David Thomas	P14	14	13	0	1	1	0	0	0	2	2	0	.077
George Copeland	P13	13	14	1	1	0	1	0	0	0	3	0	.071
Vince Moreci	OF10	12	31	6	9	5	0	0	2	7	6	1	.290
James Neufeldt	OF11	11	31	5	7	2	1	0	0	4	3	0	.226
Kurt Krieger	P7	11	20	1	4	2	1	1	0	0	5	0	.200
Sanford Silverstein	P11	11	14	0	1	0	0	0	0	0	7	0	.071
Elwood Clear	P11	11	3	1	1	0	0	0	0	3	2	0	.333
Maurice Garlock	P10	10	12	1	5	2	2	0	1	0	5	0	.417
Luther Phillips	C	8	28	4	7	3	1	1	0			0	.250
Neal Heartweck	PH	5	4	0	1	0	0	0	0			0	.250
Russ Kerns	C	2	3	0	0	0	0	0	0			0	.000

PITCHERS		W	L	PCT	G	GS	CG	SH	IP	H	BB	SO	ERA
Hisel Patrick		8	11	.421	25	22	8	0	149	165	89	76	5.86
Peter Mazar		7	12	.368	26	22	8	0	143	168	61	58	5.85
Ed Blake		7	15	.318	27	24	12	1	172	206	93	72	5.91
John Crimian		5	3	.625	36	0	0	0	58	64	30	40	3.41
Lee Peterson		4	4	.500	52	1	0	0	112	135	41	51	4.74
Luis Arroyo		3	2	.600	9			0	41	44	21	11	4.17

COLUMBUS (cont.)
Red Birds

PITCHERS	W	L	PCT	G	GS	CG	SH	IP	H	BB	SO	ERA
Elwood Joyce	3	9	.250	14	11	6	1	75	90	34	36	6.00
David Thomas	2	1	.667	14			0	42	64	23	7	7.29
George Copeland	2	3	.400	13	5	1	0	46	49	41	22	5.67
Cloyd Boyer	2	3	.400	5			0	40	29	22	44	2.03
Herb Moford	2	5	.286	16	9	0	0	63	69	57	17	7.43
Glen Moulder	2	12	.143	23	16	5	0	115	135	61	53	6.26
George Drees	1	0	1.000	7			0	27	36	17	10	7.00
Max Peterson	1	1	.500	10			0	27	25	16	8	4.00
John Grodzicki	1	1	.500	4			0	8	12	11	5	14.63
Maurice Garlock	1	2	.333	10			0	38	38	27	15	6.63
Ellis Deal	1	2	.333	4			0	22	25	12	9	6.95
Sanford Silverstein	1	4	.200	11			0	42	49	31	22	6.43
Kurt Krieger	1	5	.167	7			0	42	44	22	27	5.79
Don Kohler	0	1	.000	4			0	7	12	8	3	10.28
Robert Kerce	0	2	.000	4			0	18	20	10	5	6.00
Elwood Clear	0	4	.000	11			0	22	33	23	15	9.82
Harry Walker	0	0	----	2			0	3	6	1	1	

MULTI-TEAM PLAYERS

BATTERS	POS-GAMES	TEAMS	GP	AB	R	H	BI	2B	3B	HR	BB	SO	SB	BA
John Lucadello	3B47,2B9	TOL-MIN	74	173	34	43	25	11	1	2	62	25	0	.249
Mike Rocco	1B48	KC-SP	72	175	22	41	27	7	1	7	36	41	0	.234

TEAM BATTING

TEAMS	GP	AB	R	H	BI	2B	3B	HR	BB	SO	SB	BA
MILWAUKEE	151	5126	808	**1466**	752	243	52	120	553	637	33	**.286**
ST. PAUL	151	4872	728	1288	658	211	55	108	617	654	**94**	.264
KANSAS CITY	152	5099	777	1408	725	226	71	149	663	663	29	.276
LOUISVILLE	153	**5151**	782	1422	734	242	48	84	**726**	592	26	.276
MINNEAPOLIS	152	5056	**846**	1413	**784**	**253**	38	**154**	713	658	91	.279
TOLEDO	152	5036	704	1353	647	229	45	103	587	547	40	.269
INDIANAPOLIS	153	5088	752	1370	699	233	55	114	575	656	39	.269
COLUMBUS	**154**	5013	669	1315	625	232	43	90	581	707	42	.262
	609	40441	6066	11035	5624	1869	407	922	5015	5241	394	.273

1952
Era's End

With the changes in American entertainment choices (especially television) and accompanying trends, it was only a matter of time before the American Association would lose its immunity to franchise relocation. With dwindling attendance, it was too much to ask for exactly the same teams to remain forever in their founding cities. The first crack in the Association's stable structure appeared in a predictable place.

For several years, the Toledo Mud Hens had been hit hard in the box office, trailing the Association year after year with annual attendance totals under 100,000. As the 1952 season unfolded, their woes continued. Finally, enough was enough. On June 23, with Toledo mired in the financial cellar, the Mud Hens were transferred to Charleston, West Virginia, to close out the year.

The Milwaukee Brewers finished atop the heap in 1952, followed by Kansas City, St. Paul, Minneapolis, Louisville, Indianapolis, Columbus, and Toledo/Charleston. The league's highest average was posted by Dave Pope of Indianapolis (.352), while Bill Skowron of Kansas City hit the most home runs (31) and runs batted in (134). Pitching laurels went to Ed Erautt of Kansas City for wins (21) and to Don Liddle of Milwaukee for the lowest earned run average (2.70) and most strikeouts (159). After the season, a second crack appeared in the Association's facade of stability. For many years, several major league team owners had been striving to move their unprofitable franchises to greener pastures. These major league teams, mostly in dual-team cities such as St. Louis, Boston, and Philadelphia, had been hard pressed to keep them afloat. Minor league cities such as Milwaukee, Kansas City, or even on the West Coast in Los Angeles, were enticing targets.

As far back as 1941, the St. Louis Browns planned a move to Los Angeles. This was thwarted by the United States' entry into World War II. Later, the Browns sought a move to Milwaukee but were voted down. In early 1953, the owner of the Boston Braves sought a similar move. This time, the baseball owners said yes, and on March 18, 1953, the Boston Braves became the Milwaukee Braves, and the city joined the National League. Instantly, the American Association Milwaukee Brewers found themselves homeless, bumped out of the home they had enjoyed since 1902.

The first 50 years of the Association had been an era of uncommon franchise stability. Through thick and thin, prosperity and depression, the circuit had stuck together. But with the Braves' move to Milwaukee, a final and permanent wedge had been driven into the American Association's stability. This ended the Association's first era, and signalled the beginning of its next.

MILWAUKEE   1st   101-53   .656   Grimm-Walters -Smith
Brewers

BATTERS	POS-GAMES	GP	AB	R	H	BI	2B	3B	HR	BB	SO	SB	BA
Henry Ertman	1B120	127	433	75	126	76	20	2	17	49	55	2	.291
John Dittmer	2B57	57	222	40	79	55	14	2	8	19	14	1	.356
Gene Mauch	SS50,2B47,3B1	102	327	58	106	60	24	3	4	58	19	7	.324
Bill Klaus	3B126,SS17	143	585	94	173	74	33	7	7	44	61	6	.296
Bill Bruton	OF154	**154**	**650**	**130**	**211**	62	37	7	5	51	78	30	.325
Luis Marquez	OF125,3B9	136	521	100	180	99	38	10	14	51	91	24	.345
James Basso	OF59	59	239	31	58	34	10	1	3	9	29	0	.243
Dewey Williams	C80	84	272	33	80	36	14	3	1	39	49	3	.294
Al Unser	C80	84	263	36	68	29	10	5	9	27	31	0	.259
James Clarkson	SS48,3B19,2B2	74	242	49	77	68	14	2	12	56	27	10	.318
Robert Montag	OF35,1B11	69	162	37	34	24	3	5	8	28	49	6	.210
Tom Whisenant	OF56	68	180	30	46	25	8	3	2	28	38	5	.256
Wally Post	OF44	51	149	25	36	24	10	2	5	14	36	1	.242
William Reed	2B39	50	134	23	42	27	9	2	1	3	6	0	.313
Johnny Logan	SS42	42	146	20	44	27	8	2	6	17	7	0	.301
Murray Wall	P38	40	67	7	7	5	2	0	1	8	27	1	.104
Don Liddle	P34	34	67	12	13	6	1	0	1	9	20	0	.194
Maynard Thiel	P33	33	29	3	4	2	0	0	0	0	5	0	.138
George Estock	P31	31	21	2	3	2	0	0	0	0	6	0	.143
Don Conley	P20	29	65	8	22	8	3	0	0	4	21	0	.338
Bill Allen	P29	29	24	4	8	0	0	0	0	2	5	0	.333
George Crowe ·	1B27	27	94	19	33	29	8	1	6	20	15	1	.351
Richard Hoover	P24	25	43	3	10	4	1	0	0	1	6	0	.233
Roy Hartsfield	2B22	23	84	15	20	5	3	1	1	9	8	2	.238
Edward Blake	P21	21	47	4	12	7	3	0	0	6	6	0	.255
Virgil Jester	P19	19	28	4	4	3	4	0	0	1	8	0	.143
Richard Donovan	P16	18	33	6	10	4	2	0	1	5	14	0	.303
Don Schmidt	P12	12	3	0	0	0	0	0	0	0	0	0	.000
Chuck Tanner	OF	11	27	2	4	4	1	1	0	2	2	0	.194
Howard Anderson	P11	11	5	0	0	0	0	0	0	0	1	0	.000
Earl Wooten	OF	8	7	1	1	0	0	0	0	0		0	.143
John Kerr	SS	5	3	0	0	0	0	0	0	0		0	.000
Jerome Barinski	2B	3	8	0	1	1	0	0	0	0		0	.125
Jack Parks	C	3	3	1	0	0	0	0	0	0		0	.000

PITCHERS		W	L	PCT	G	GS	CG	SH	IP	H	BB	SO	ERA
Don Liddle		17	4	**.810**	34	24	12	**5**	197	179	68	**159**	**2.70**
Murray Wall		16	10	.645	38	26	15	1	203	206	81	92	4.08
Don Conley		11	4	.733	20	19	11	1	160	143	46	143	3.15
Ed Blake		10	3	.769	21	19	10	0	134	132	39	47	3.96
Virgil Jester		10	5	.667	19	9	4	0	84	91	32	28	4.50
Dick Hoover		10	5	.667	24	16	9	2	121	110	31	48	2.60
Bill Allen		8	3	.727	29	12	4	1	94	99	55	33	4.69
Maynard Thiel		8	6	.571	33	7	3	0	99	109	31	63	4.36
George Estock		6	3	.667	31	8	2	2	90	96	37	41	3.07
Richard Donovan		4	6	.400	16	12	4	0	91	111	43	36	4.55
Don Schmidt		1	1	.500	12			0	18	18	8	6	3.50
Howard Anderson		0	3	.000	11			0	26	32	13	13	5.54
Al Dumouchelle		0	0	----	3			0	4	5	2	0	0.00
Elmer Toth		0	0	----	1			0	1	3	0	1	9.00

KANSAS CITY   2nd   89-65   .578   -12   George Selkirk
Blues

BATTERS	POS-GAMES	GP	AB	R	H	BI	2B	3B	HR	BB	SO	SB	BA
Don Bollweg	1B124	126	464	108	151	81	27	14	23	96	64	10	.325
Kal Segrist	2B132,OF,3B	136	477	97	147	92	25	4	25	98	53	1	.308
Art Mazmanian	SS75,2B22	99	355	52	93	30	3	3	0	52	27	5	.262
Vic Power	3B65,OF55,1B16	140	550	95	182	109	**40**	**17**	16	33	28	10	.331
Bill Skowron	OF141	147	560	113	191	**134**	38	11	31	49	71	4	.341
William Renna	OF108	110	414	67	122	90	20	8	28	37	88	5	.295
Robert Marquis	OF89,1B2	97	354	62	87	32	18	6	10	50	37	13	.246
Mickey Owen	C81	94	291	27	69	39	12	1	3	23	28	1	.237
Kermit Wahl	SS60,3B30,2B2	97	331	70	100	43	21	1	5	55	38	2	.302
Roy Partee	C78	87	242	26	61	28	12	0	4	52	33	0	.252
Andy Carey	3B58,SS24	82	324	44	92	45	18	3	16	30	48	4	.284
Bob Cerv	OF59	60	219	39	65	48	13	6	12	24	27	3	.297
Rex Jones	P42	43	41	3	7	1	2	0	0	1	13	0	.171
David Jolly	P40	40	22	2	5	1	0	0	0	0	3	0	.227
Ed Erautt	P30	31	75	10	17	6	2	1	1	5	26	0	.227

KANSAS CITY (cont.)
Blues

BATTERS	POS-GAMES	GP	AB	R	H	BI	2B	3B	HR	BB	SO	SB	BA
Ed Cereghino	P28	28	69	9	14	10	2	0	2	5	23	0	.203
Art Schallock	P26	26	32	0	1	1	1	0	0	2	14	0	.031
Ernest Nevel	P22	22	40	1	6	4	1	1	0	5	16	0	.150
George Maier	P21	21	21	1	4	1	0	1	0	1	8	0	.190
Al Cicotte	P19	20	24	2	5	4	0	0	1	1	2	0	.208
Marshall Carlson	OF14	18	44	5	13	2	2	1	0	6	3	0	.295
Wallace Hood	P17	17	14	2	3	2	0	0	1	1	6	0	.214
Fenton Mole	1B15	15	56	8	14	9	1	1	4	9	8	0	.250
James Russell	P10	14	31	0	9	3	0	0	0	4	6	0	.290
Harry Schaeffer	P14	14	29	3	8	1	0	0	0	1	5	0	.276
Whitey Herzog	OF,1B	14	27	5	8	5	1	0	1	4	2	1	.296
Thomas Gorman	P13	13	30	3	3	0	0	0	0	2	13	0	.100
Robert O'Neal	C	13	29	4	5	4	0	1	0	7	4	0	.172
Frank Verdi	3B	12	13	6	6	1	0	0	0	4	2	1	.462
Gerald Snyder	3B	6	16	1	2	0	0	0	0			0	.125
Kent Kurtz	2B	6	6	1	1	0	0	0	0			0	.167
Marv Throneberry	1B	4	5	1	2	1	1	0	0			0	.400

PITCHERS		W	L	PCT	G	GS	CG	SH	IP	H	BB	SO	ERA
Ed Erautt		21	5	.808	30	28	20	2	210	189	57	104	3.00
Ed Cereghino		10	8	.556	28	27	11	2	184	165	80	85	4.16
Art Schallock		8	6	.571	26	13	5	2	105	109	52	64	5.49
Thomas Gorman		7	4	.636	13	11	7	0	86	93	22	43	3.66
Rex Jones		7	6	.538	42	1	0	0	122	119	55	58	3.61
Ernest Nevel		7	6	.538	22	16	7	2	114	140	33	37	4.66
David Jolly		6	1	.857	40	2	1	0	82	64	61	52	3.51
Harry Schaeffer		6	4	.600	14	11	4	0	82	79	39	51	2.74
James Russell		5	4	.556	10	10	5	1	69	70	39	48	4.70
Al Cicotte		4	7	.364	19	14	1	0	75	75	85	84	7.20
Grenkoski		3	5	.375	8	8	1	0	54	56	22	26	5.47
George Maier		2	4	.333	21	9	1	0	64	69	44	50	4.08
Wallace Hood		2	4	.333	17	3	0	0	46	49	35	13	5.48
Ruben Gomez		1	0	1.000	5			0	10	16	6	4	11.70
John Gray		0	1	.000	3			0	7	7	5	8	9.00
John Gages		0	0	----	2			0	6	6	6	4	
John Mackinson		0	0	----	2			0	3	8	0	2	
Jim Blackburn		0	0	----	2			0	3	1	7	0	

ST. PAUL   3rd   80-74   .519   -21   Clay Bryant
Saints

BATTERS	POS-GAMES	GP	AB	R	H	BI	2B	3B	HR	BB	SO	SB	BA
Danny Ozark	1B94,OF1	112	334	58	77	62	18	0	17	40	54	2	.231
Jack Cassini	2B126	133	504	108	155	37	23	4	3	59	53	35	.308
Russell Rose	SS151	153	513	62	116	59	10	3	7	60	72	8	.226
Robert Wilson	3B151,2B1	154	626	99	209	117	31	9	13	25	29	7	.334
Gino Cimoli	OF134	142	474	75	151	70	24	10	5	35	56	13	.319
Sandy Amoros	OF128	129	489	108	165	78	24	10	19	65	63	14	.337
Bill Sharman	OF118,3B1	137	411	63	121	77	16	4	16	29	32	2	.294
Frank Baldwin	C115	120	369	40	94	57	22	1	12	28	45	1	.255
Richard Whitman	OF112	116	415	58	138	83	27	5	6	44	24	5	.333
Bert Haas	1B67,OF2	89	255	43	64	33	12	2	4	31	14	5	.251
Wayne Terwilliger	2B27,SS,3B,OF	77	125	32	39	17	6	0	4	32	19	1	.312
Al Epperly	P57	57	10	1	2	0	0	0	0	0	3	0	.200
Ron Negray	P46	53	52	7	12	2	0	0	0	2	14	0	.231
Thaddeus Bosiack	C40	41	106	4	29	6	0	1	0	5	6	1	.274
Don Otten	P37	37	40	2	4	0	0	0	0	0	4	0	.100
Earl Mosser	P36	36	83	3	17	9	3	1	0	2	22	0	.205
Ezra McGlothin	P32	36	75	11	17	5	1	0	0	9	6	0	.227
Tom Lakos	P27	27	20	0	1	0	0	0	0	1	10	0	.050
Ray Cash	C23	23	66	7	14	12	0	1	4	6	10	0	.212
Mike Rocco	1B	23	26	3	6	9	1	2	1	9	2	0	.231
Eldred Byerly	P23	23	14	1	1	1	0	0	0	1	4	0	.071
Forrest Jacobs	2B15,SS1	17	56	13	13	5	4	1	0	10	2	2	.232
William Samson	P8	14	10	1	1	0	0	0	0	1	2	0	.100
Joe Baliga	P12	14	8	1	0	1	0	0	0	3	5	0	.000
Raymond Moore	P12	12	27	5	5	5	1	1	1	3	7	0	.185
William Glane	P11	12	13	1	3	0	1	0	0	1	2	0	.231
Frank Marchio	OF	11	29	4	8	4	1	1	0	3	3	0	.276
Galeard Wade	OF	9	12	4	2	1	1	0	0			0	.167
Earl Naylor	OF,P2	7	9	1	1	0	0	0	0			0	.111
Mervin Dornburg	C	5	13	2	4	1	1	0	0			0	.308

ST. PAUL (cont.)
Saints

BATTERS	POS-GAMES	GP	AB	R	H	BI	2B	3B	HR	BB	SO	SB	BA
Al Brancato	SS,3B	5	12	2	2	1	0	1	0			0	.167
Arnold Fischer	C	5	5	0	0	1	0	0	0			0	.000

PITCHERS		W	L	PCT	G	GS	CG	SH	IP	H	BB	SO	ERA
Earl Mossor		14	13	.519	36	30	11	2	226	241	105	145	3.94
Ezra McGlothin		13	14	.481	32	31	14	2	213	229	79	95	3.97
Ron Negray		11	7	.611	46	21	10	1	189	177	102	102	3.95
Al Epperly		9	4	.692	57	0	0	0	72	78	22	18	3.63
Don Otten		9	9	.500	37	12	4	1	126	143	59	44	4.86
Raymond Moore		4	4	.500	12	12	6	3	78	69	56	72	3.46
Ken Lehman		3	1	.750	4			0	24	21	8	21	3.75
Eldred Byerly		3	2	.600	23	2	0	0	61	63	21	30	3.54
William Glane		3	2	.600	11			0	33	37	26	23	9.55
Tom Lakos		1	1	.500	27	4	0	0	74	103	46	24	7.66
Pershing Mondorff		1	1	.500	6			0	9	15	1	4	9.00
Joe Baliga		1	2	.333	12			0	36	47	20	19	7.50
Rex Barney		0	1	.000	4			0	3	7	14	4	51.00
Earl Naylor		0	1	.000	2			0	7	5	3	2	5.14
Clem Labine		0	1	.000	2			0	14	11	11	5	5.14
William Samson		0	4	.000	8			0	33	30	23	16	5.45
Peter Nicolis		0	0	----	3			0	5	6	9	5	
Marion Fricano		0	0	----	2			0	6	12	2	2	6.00

MINNEAPOLIS   4th   79-75   .513   -22   Frank Genovese
Millers

BATTERS	POS-GAMES	GP	AB	R	H	BI	2B	3B	HR	BB	SO	SB	BA
Marv Blaylock	1B123,OF2	133	473	86	134	73	26	9	16	70	93	11	.283
Ron Samford	2B137,OF2	139	433	47	116	35	15	1	6	39	61	11	.268
Daryl Spencer	SS141	142	523	85	154	80	35	2	27	57	60	5	.294
Ray Dandridge	3B144	145	618	86	180	68	27	1	10	32	36	3	.291
Roy Broome	OF135	142	512	83	156	99	26	4	17	55	57	3	.305
Clint Hartung	OF94	105	368	64	123	93	20	5	27	27	90	1	.334
Bill Howerton	OF65	67	231	57	71	61	7	5	24	52	55	1	.307
Ray Katt	C116,1B2	123	448	57	136	68	24	1	15	33	58	0	.304
William Gardner	2B55,SS19,3B11,OF2	93	224	29	58	15	15	1	1	14	24	3	.259
John Harshman	P26,1B20	77	135	14	30	15	3	0	8	27	28	0	.222
Adrian Zabala	P69	69	48	4	8	1	0	0	0	2	9	0	.167
Jake Early	C48	63	146	24	43	28	5	1	8	27	26	1	.295
Charles Diering	OF50	55	177	34	46	16	10	2	4	37	23	4	.260
Bob Lennon	OF49	50	193	32	57	32	10	0	8	22	38	1	.295
Fred Gerken	OF28,1B17	50	164	3	45	24	5	3	6	24	19	2	.274
Elmer Corwin	P26	48	66	15	16	9	1	1	2	0	10	0	.242
Andy Tomasic	P35	35	34	4	10	10	3	0	2	1	7	0	.294
Richard Libby	P32	33	66	6	7	6	3	0	0	7	30	0	.106
Norman Fox	P31	31	54	4	8	3	2	0	1	4	19	0	.148
Raymond Berns	OF22	28	45	8	8	4	0	0	2	6	9	2	.178
Dick Wakefield	OF19	27	74	10	17	8	0	1	2	9	7	0	.230
Jake Schmitt	P25	25	44	4	13	1	0	0	0	2	6	0	.295
Harry Nicholas	P18	18	31	4	8	2	3	0	0	1	13	0	.258
Alex Konikowski	P15	15	33	1	4	1	0	0	0	0	15	0	.121
Mario Picone	P9	11	29	4	9	4	0	0	2	2	9	0	.310
Bill Barnacle	OF	10	17	0	2	1	0	0	0	0	2	0	.118

PITCHERS		W	L	PCT	G	GS	CG	SH	IP	H	BB	SO	ERA
Adrian Zabala		14	10	.583	69	1	0	0	139	138	59	65	2.98
Richard Libby		13	9	.591	32	25	9	1	186	185	79	78	4.06
Norm Fox		9	10	.474	31	29	10	1	161	150	100	75	4.30
Elmer Corwin		8	11	.421	26	25	7	1	159	166	111	133	5.04
Jake Schmitt		7	7	.500	25	18	6	1	119	129	67	39	4.54
Mario Picone		6	1	.857	9	9	7	0	73	60	25	40	3.33
Jack Harshman		6	7	.462	26	14	4	0	131	135	71	78	4.67
Harry Nicholas		4	3	.571	18	9	3	1	84	98	51	53	6.86
Andy Tomasic		4	4	.500	35	4	1	0	94	110	49	47	5.17
Alex Konikowski		3	8	.273	15	10	3	1	90	87	42	41	4.30
Roger Bowman		2	2	.500	6			0	37	31	12	15	4.62
Peter Burnside		0	1	.000	1			0	2	1	7	2	27.00
George Heller		0	0	----	7			0	8	8	12	7	

LOUISVILLE Colonels   5th   77-77   .500   -24   Mike Higgins

BATTERS	POS-GAMES	GP	AB	R	H	BI	2B	3B	HR	BB	SO	SB	BA
Charles Maxwell	1B88,OF49	135	500	104	141	85	25	13	21	102	101	3	.282
Edward Lyons	2B141,SS5	145	561	78	140	83	30	5	8	70	43	6	.250
Carl Peterson	SS139	139	533	94	144	61	27	7	3	78	53	10	.270
Ken Chapman	3B106,SS,2B,OF	125	390	54	105	66	17	3	5	86	30	4	.269
Tom Umphlett	OF124	124	518	75	144	80	24	9	8	48	42	6	.278
Taft Wright	OF112	126	426	62	126	84	14	4	11	66	18	2	.296
Robert DiPietro	OF61,3B16,2B7	85	260	35	71	39	4	2	4	47	17	3	.273
Alfred Evans	C89	93	300	37	77	39	7	3	4	43	42	0	.257
Harold Buckwalter	3B28,1B28	69	225	33	62	32	8	6	4	17	17	0	.276
Eugene Stephens	OF58	60	216	43	61	17	12	3	3	16	32	8	.282
Larry Isbell	C54,OF1	55	184	18	49	19	5	1	2	25	49	3	.266
Allen Van Alstyne	OF50	52	136	17	36	2	5	0	0	10	11	3	.265
Tom Herrin	P28	39	70	8	11	8	1	1	1	3	20	0	.157
Hershell Freeman	P38	39	22	0	2	1	0	0	0	0	7	0	.091
Dave Ferriss	P21	36	68	5	14	3	2	0	0	2	6	0	.206
Robert Broome	OF26	31	104	18	21	13	3	0	2	17	12	1	.202
Harry Taylor	P25	25	56	6	8	3	1	0	0	3	9	0	.143
Russ Kemmerer	P25	25	44	4	6	3	1	1	0	2	13	0	.136
Gary Killingsworth	3B17,1B7	24	94	3	21	9	1	0	0	3	10	0	.223
Alphens Curtis	P23	23	63	4	9	4	0	0	0	1	19	0	.143
Dick Gernert	1B18	19	73	17	23	16	7	0	4	11	8	0	.315
John Douglas	1B16	18	57	7	12	4	2	0	0	8	5	0	.211
Harley Hisner	P18	18	17	2	4	2	2	1	0	2	4	0	.235
Robert Austin	P17	17	20	0	1	0	0	0	0	1	2	0	.050
Len Okrie	C14,OF1	16	39	6	6	3	1	0	0	10	5	1	.154
Frank Baumann	P15	15	30	1	6	2	1	0	0	3	11	0	.200
Faye Throneberry	OF13	13	56	9	15	5	3	1	4	5	11	2	.268
Ken Aspromonte	SS,2B	12	29	5	7	1	1	0	0	2	5	1	.241
Ken Trinkle	P12	12	7	1	1	0	0	0	0	1	1	0	.143
Richard Brodowski	P10	11	38	6	11	9	2	1	0	2	2	0	.289
Archie Wilson	OF	11	29	2	3	0	0	1	0	2	6	0	.103
Ed Sadowski	C	7	16	1	4	5	0	0	0			0	.250
Ted Lepcio	PH	1	1	0	0	0	0	0	0			0	.000

PITCHERS		W	L	PCT	G	GS	CG	SH	IP	H	BB	SO	ERA
Tom Herrin		10	12	.455	28	26	16	2	191	190	94	78	4.15
Alphens Curtis		9	6	.600	23	23	10	2	161	138	110	111	4.14
Harry Taylor		9	10	.474	25	21	7	1	150	174	48	75	4.32
Hershell Freeman		8	7	.533	38	0	0	0	74	73	28	48	2.92
Richard Brodowski		7	1	.875	10	10	7	0	82	80	31	53	3.40
Dave Ferriss		7	5	.583	21	12	8	1	128	170	39	26	4.71
Russ Kemmerer		7	8	.467	25	16	6	1	126	155	62	69	5.43
Ken Holcombe		5	2	.714	9	9	4	3	63	57	12	30	3.86
Frank Baumann		4	6	.400	15	14	6	2	88	83	55	69	4.09
Ivan Delock		2	0	1.000	2			0	16	10	5	16	2.25
Ralph Brickner		2	2	.500	6			0	38	30	10	12	2.36
Cliff Coggin		2	2	.500	4			0	26	27	21	12	5.54
Ken Trinkle		2	3	.400	12			0	31	47	10	10	5.81
Robert Smith		1	0	1.000	2			0	12	17	6	7	6.00
Harley Hisner		1	3	.250	18	1	0	0	58	58	16	31	2.95
Bill Evans		1	3	.250	7			0	35	46	14	13	4.63
Robert Austin		0	7	.000	17	7	2	0	71	69	28	33	4.82

INDIANAPOLIS Indians   6th   75-79   .487   -26   Gene DesAutels

BATTERS	POS-GAMES	GP	AB	R	H	BI	2B	3B	HR	BB	SO	SB	BA
Herb Conyers	1B46	48	168	14	39	25	4	0	4	13	18	3	.232
Robert Wilson	2B117,SS,3B	126	454	67	122	36	15	1	1	51	43	7	.269
Harry Malmberg	SS151	152	550	85	158	60	18	7	1	82	38	5	.287
George Stirnweiss	3B65,2B27,SS,1B	97	320	62	76	39	9	7	7	80	53	3	.238
Milt Nielson	OF125	137	486	78	151	87	22	5	8	43	28	6	.311
David Pope	OF121	126	475	77	167	79	29	7	13	45	42	4	.352
Al Smith	OF80,3B59,SS,2B,P1	136	455	80	131	69	26	12	20	52	86	10	.288
Quincy Troupe	C72	84	205	39	53	40	7	2	8	57	32	0	.259
Lloyd Gearhart	OF62,1B30	113	270	47	76	60	11	1	12	28	44	2	.281
Jewett Baumer	3B49,2B24,1B19,SS1	96	302	51	91	36	18	2	3	51	48	8	.301
Eulas Hutson	OF47,3B3	64	152	20	45	23	6	6	2	20	22	0	.296
Joe Montaluo	C50	54	135	21	31	17	6	0	6	25	23	1	.230
Lloyd Dickey	P37	51	39	5	11	3	1	0	0	3	11	0	.282
Charles Sipple	P43	43	55	5	11	6	1	0	2	2	18	0	.200

INDIANAPOLIS (cont.)
Indians

BATTERS	POS-GAMES	GP	AB	R	H	BI	2B	3B	HR	BB	SO	SB	BA
Ray Narleski	P41	41	54	3	12	6	2	0	0	6	14	0	.222
Richard Kinaman	C38	40	108	17	28	19	3	1	6	16	12	0	.259
Bill Higdon	OF30	37	99	18	26	23	5	2	4	12	13	1	.263
George Zuverink	P37	37	59	4	11	3	2	0	0	3	12	0	.186
George Vico	1B34	34	119	19	33	20	2	0	5	12	12	3	.277
Bill Abernathie	P34	34	48	1	6	7	2	0	1	8	22	0	.125
Robert Kerrigan	P34	34	19	2	1	0	0	0	0	3	10	0	.053
Robert Chakales	P30	32	47	7	11	11	0	0	4	3	10	0	.234
James Fridley	OF28	29	102	19	24	14	5	1	1	15	12	2	.235
Earl Turner	C22	28	62	3	11	5	0	0	1	3	13	1	.177
Frank Papish	P23	23	25	3	3	2	2	0	0	2	9	0	.120
Ben Taylor	1B18	22	65	8	15	8	1	1	0	6	6	0	.231
Paul Lehner	OF15	22	59	6	12	8	4	0	1	8	5	0	.203
Frank Kalin	OF16,1B2	21	58	7	12	8	1	2	3	8	11	0	.207
William Tosheff	P12,1B3	17	20	4	6	1	3	0	0	1	5	0	.300
Luke Easter	1B14	14	50	13	17	12	2	0	0	10	7	1	.340
Herb Score	P12	12	23	1	5	3	1	0	0	1	8	0	.217
Dino Restelli	3B	5	4	2	1	1	0	0	1			0	.250
Melvin Rue	SS,3B	5	4	1	0	0	0	0	0			0	.000
Andy Phillip	1B	2	3	0	0	0	0	0	0			0	.000
Tom Dobkins	C1	1	3	0	0	1	0	0	0			0	.000
Gene DesAutels	C1	1	0	0	0	0	0	0	0			0	----

PITCHERS		W	L	PCT	G	GS	CG	SH	IP	H	BB	SO	ERA
George Zuverink		12	11	.522	37	19	12	2	168	185	49	70	3.75
Bill Abernathie		11	9	.550	34	21	7	0	164	182	62	51	5.27
Ray Narleski		11	15	.423	41	24	9	1	181	189	117	132	4.67
Robert Chakales		10	6	.625	30	16	4	0	125	147	72	69	5.18
Charles Sipple		9	5	.643	43	15	7	0	159	173	51	88	4.98
Lloyd Dickey		5	9	.357	37	18	5	1	117	134	52	56	4.38
Sam Jones		4	0	1.000	5			0	35	28	18	24	3.09
Frank Papish		4	7	.364	23	12	1	0	82	100	43	41	7.02
Robert Kerrigan		4	8	.333	34	9	2	0	96	122	40	47	5.63
John McCall		2	3	.400	7			0	28	34	22	9	6.11
Herb Score		2	5	.286	12	10	3	0	62	37	62	61	5.23
James Vitter		1	0	1.000	8			0	21	26	5	7	5.57
Ray Peters		0	1	.000	5			0	8	13	9	5	22.50
William Tosheff		0	0	----	12			0	42	56	27	12	
Charles Harris		0	0	----	6			0	9	13	5	4	4.00
Inman Chambers		0	0	----	5			0	12	12	8	1	4.50
Al Smith		0	0	----	1			0	2	3	1	0	12.00

COLUMBUS   7th   68-85   .444   -32.5   John Keane
Red Birds

BATTERS	POS-GAMES	GP	AB	R	H	BI	2B	3B	HR	BB	SO	SB	BA
Charles Kress	1B127	128	435	79	125	85	23	4	24	102	50	5	.287
Howard Phillips	2B136,SS1	140	475	56	129	55	20	13	4	60	68	4	.272
Walt Lammers	SS122,3B2	125	459	64	118	47	22	3	1	69	50	2	.257
Daniel Lynch	3B90,SS27,2B13	128	486	70	128	39	23	5	2	55	39	10	.263
Jay Van Noy	OF124	126	436	63	108	61	21	6	9	40	81	6	.248
James Neufeldt	OF104,3B27	137	421	62	110	34	15	5	3	35	56	10	.261
Russell Rae	OF89	104	292	33	63	31	8	3	5	29	39	1	.216
Richard Rand	C83	109	309	39	79	51	18	3	2	50	56	4	.256
Bill Sarni	C62,OF2	89	276	29	70	43	11	3	7	15	26	2	.254
Maurice Mozzali	OF51,1B24	81	225	41	71	27	13	5	2	28	14	2	.278
Russ Derry	OF63	72	223	40	71	55	13	1	18	32	33	3	.318
Vern Benson	3B31,OF29,1B2	58	213	31	51	30	11	0	4	36	28	2	.239
William Allen	P32	37	56	7	13	5	2	1	0	1	6	0	.232
Hisel Patrick	P36	36	39	1	6	4	0	0	0	2	5	0	.154
Harland Coffman	P29,OF1	36	37	3	12	3	1	2	1	4	14	0	.324
Floyd Milliere	P32	34	64	5	9	1	1	0	0	2	15	0	.141
Ralph Beard	P31	31	48	3	10	3	0	0	0	3	11	0	.208
Tom Keating	P29	29	29	0	3	1	0	0	0	3	14	0	.103
Stu Miller	P28	28	31	2	6	1	1	0	0	4	7	0	.194
Herb Mancini	3B,2B,SS	25	62	6	16	4	0	0	0	5	9	1	.161
Ed Ludwig	P25	25	27	0	6	3	1	0	0	3	11	0	.222
Dan Lewandowski	P21	21	12	0	1	0	0	0	0	0	5	0	.083
Everette Joyner	OF11	20	41	4	10	4	2	0	1	2	1	0	.244
Bill Killinger	OF16,3B1	19	53	8	22	9	5	0	0	9	5	0	.415
Kurt Krieger	P18	18	32	3	5	1	1	1	0	3	9	0	.156
Richard Morgan	C	17	41	1	10	6	1	1	0	0	5	0	.244

COLUMBUS (cont.)
Red Birds

BATTERS	POS-GAMES	GP	AB	R	H	BI	2B	3B	HR	BB	SO	SB	BA
Ralph Lageman	OF13	15	43	2	7	2	2	0	0	2	9	0	.163
J.C. Dunn	OF	15	25	4	3	1	0	0	0	4	4	0	.120
Ed Mickelson	1B	12	26	3	8	5	4	0	0	2	4	0	.308
Donald Spencer	3B	7	21	3	3	3	0	1	1			0	.143
David Johnson	OF	7	17	1	0	0	0	0	0			0	.000
Robert Moscrey	2B	6	1	4	0	0	0	0	0			0	.000

PITCHERS		W	L	PCT	G	GS	CG	SH	IP	H	BB	SO	ERA
Floyd Melliere		15	10	.600	32	25	14	2	180	221	60	64	4.60
Stu Miller		11	5	.688	28	13	5	4	119	113	38	82	2.34
Hisel Patrick		9	5	.643	36	11	2	0	125	117	77	73	4.90
William Allen		8	10	.444	32	19	6	2	148	155	85	101	4.99
Ralph Beard		8	11	.424	31	18	7	0	150	140	58	54	3.66
Ed Ludwig		6	7	.462	25	13	5	0	108	126	35	54	5.08
Tom Keating		3	9	.250	29	13	2	0	104	123	74	63	5.88
Kurt Krieger		3	9	.250	18	15	5	0	114	120	39	39	4.42
Willard Schmidt		2	1	.667	4			0	28	24	10	21	2.89
Dan Lewandowski		2	6	.250	21	7	0	0	53	67	19	17	5.94
Harland Coffman		1	8	.111	29	12	2	0	108	136	57	66	5.67
Lee Peterson		0	1	.000	7			0	11	7	1	2	0.82
Bob Tiefenauer		0	1	.000	2			0	10	16	5	3	4.50
Doug Clark		0	2	.000	3			0	6	6	6	2	15.00
George Eyrich		0	0	----	8			0	22	30	5	10	
Herb Mofor		0	0	----	4			0	10	10	9	4	1.80
Robert Bills		0	0	----	1			0	2	7	2	1	
David Manier		0	0	----	1			0	2	1	4	1	13.50
Roy Pounds		0	0	----	1			0	2	2	3	2	0.00

TOLEDO / CHARLESTON   8th   46-107   .301   -54.5   Rollie Hemsley
Mud Hens / Senators

BATTERS	POS-GAMES	GP	AB	R	H	BI	2B	3B	HR	BB	SO	SB	BA
Fred Taylor	1B100	103	357	27	81	45	13	3	5	31	36	1	.227
Leo Righetti	2B110,SS4	113	371	24	74	26	16	1	3	28	49	0	.199
Stan Rojek	SS124	125	496	57	122	20	12	4	0	34	13	3	.246
Ansel Moore	3B56,OF32,1B12	111	328	34	83	35	12	1	7	43	26	0	.253
Saturnino Escalera	OF142,1B1	148	530	73	132	39	22	6	4	57	58	15	.249
Babe Barna	OF103	122	345	53	99	72	21	2	14	67	44	1	.287
Lomax Davis	OF71	77	257	28	82	35	13	3	4	12	20	1	.319
Russ Kerns	C98	106	312	23	78	21	9	0	0	39	30	0	.250
Mylon Vukmire	3B38,2B32,SS8	73	243	28	57	29	13	2	3	41	43	4	.235
Rollie Hemsley	C38,1B,2B,3B,OF	52	145	7	31	11	6	1	0	8	6	0	.214
Bill Ramsey	OF41	51	124	28	26	20	2	0	3	23	17	0	.210
Harry Grubb	P41	42	42	4	6	0	1	0	0	2	13	0	.143
Willie Williams	3B28,SS,2B	36	128	16	30	14	3	2	2	8	10	0	.234
Robert Rhawn	3B32,2B2	36	123	10	33	16	5	2	2	3	13	0	.268
Bill Connelly	P32	34	54	7	10	3	2	0	0	5	15	0	.185
Bill Powell	P31	32	59	4	12	5	2	0	0	10	20	0	.203
Henry Behrman	P31	31	51	3	6	4	0	0	0	5	14	0	.118
Glenn McQuillen	OF24	29	77	12	20	10	4	2	1	7	8	0	.260
Clarence Beers	P27,C1	29	59	3	7	1	3	0	0	4	12	0	.119
Charles Embree	P28	28	40	4	6	5	1	0	0	5	9	0	.150
Jack Cerin	OF19,3B1	26	67	6	12	8	7	0	1	7	13	1	.179
Vance Carlson	P19,OF2	22	23	2	4	0	0	0	0	1	3	0	.174
Stan Spence	1B20	21	74	13	22	12	3	0	4	13	6	0	.297
Don Wheeler	C18	19	59	8	18	9	2	0	1	9	3	0	.305
Pedro Gomez	SS17,2B,3B	18	52	4	10	5	1	0	0	7	18	0	.192
Glen Moulder	P18	18	34	3	7	4	2	0	0	1	2	0	.206
Robert Kellogg	2B15	15	44	3	12	6	4	0	0	8	7	0	.273
Walter Novick	C12	14	37	1	6	3	1	0	0	3	5	0	.162
Clarence Zieser	P13	13	13	0	1	0	0	0	0	0	3	0	.077
Robert Van Eman	OF	12	25	3	7	3	2	0	0	3	3	0	.280
Bill Houtz	P10	10	19	1	2	3	0	0	0	1	4	0	.105
Ken Guettler	OF	8	23	4	6	4	1	0	2			0	.261
Herman Lewis	1B	7	21	3	6	1	1	0	0			0	.286
Harry Donabedian	3B	6	19	1	6	1	0	0	0			0	.316

PITCHERS		W	L	PCT	G	GS	CG	SH	IP	H	BB	SO	ERA
Bill Connelly		10	10	.500	32	23	10	0	168	147	87	117	3.38
Henry Behrman		7	**18**	.280	34	25	13	2	182	187	66	113	4.05

TOLEDO / CHARLESTON (cont.)
Mud Hens / Senators

PITCHERS	W	L	PCT	G	GS	CG	SH	IP	H	BB	SO	ERA
Charles Embree	6	10	.375	28	15	8	1	136	179	43	45	5.16
Bill Powell	5	15	.250	31	22	12	1	175	205	88	88	5.09
Clarence Beers	5	18	.217	27	25	10	2	174	222	34	60	4.47
Harry Grubb	4	9	.308	41	8	6	1	127	165	37	48	5.39
Bill Houtz	3	5	.375	10	9	4	0	61	70	40	36	5.61
Glen Moulder	3	13	.188	18	17	3	0	93	127	33	39	7.55
Clarence Zieser	2	2	.500	13			0	40	50	20	13	5.85
Ernest Bickhaus	1	1	.500	2			0	11	14	1	5	4.09
Charles Bowles	0	1	.000	2			0	2	9	8	0	58.50
Vance Carlson	0	5	.000	19	4	3	0	66	85	22	34	5.86
Garry Clarke	0	0	----	6			0	12	22	3	3	
Robert Penny	0	0	----	4			0	9	6	11	7	
Richard Murphy	0	0	----	4			0	5	3	8	3	
Alex Nedelco	0	0	----	3			0	5	6	7	0	

MULTI-TEAM PLAYERS

BATTERS	POS-GAMES	TEAMS	GP	AB	R	H	BI	2B	3B	HR	BB	SO	SB	BA
Dom Dallessandro	OF74,1B14	MIN-T/C	115	292	42	86	30	18	2	7	83	28	0	.295
Hugh Oser	O34	MIN-SP	35	58	3	6	1	0	0	0	1	19	0	.103

PITCHERS		TEAMS	W	L	PCT	G	GS	CG	SH	IP	H	BB	SO	ERA
Hugh Oser		MIN-SP	11	9	.550	34	22	10	1	173	176	98	80	4.21

TEAM BATTING

TEAMS	GP	AB	R	H	BI	2B	3B	HR	BB	SO	SB	BA
MILWAUKEE	154	5183	872	1512	801	280	59	112	560	737	99	.292
KANSAS CITY	154	5233	869	1499	829	260	82	183	661	718	61	.286
ST. PAUL	155	5267	815	1481	756	228	57	112	518	611	96	.281
MINNEAPOLIS	154	5287	811	1487	770	244	38	193	575	828	48	.281
LOUISVILLE	154	5255	767	1357	708	211	63	84	693	635	53	.258
INDIANAPOLIS	155	5134	794	1408	733	211	58	120	676	699	57	.274
COLUMBUS	153	5010	666	1269	616	219	57	84	613	693	52	.253
TOL/CHAR	153	4885	525	1179	485	198	30	58	556	560	26	.241
	616	41254	6119	11192	5698	1851	444	946	4852	5481	492	.271

Postlude
The Association Evolves

In the years following the breakup of the league's original structure, the American Association continued to be one of the top minor leagues of the land. Except for a six-year hiatus during the 1960s, it has continued strong to this day, showcasing quality baseball to the fans of America's heartland.

The eight original cities of the American Association have continued to enjoy baseball activity as well. Six of the cities no longer have ties to the Association as their baseball teams have moved to other leagues. But two of the eight still maintain franchises in the league.

The Columbus Red Birds stayed in the Association until the 1955 season, when the franchise moved to Omaha. After a brief interlude, Columbus received another team, this time in the International League. Aside from a six-year break in the 1970s, the International League is where the team from Columbus still plays.

The Kansas City Blues remained in the American Association through the 1954 season when they became the second league team to be bumped by a major league franchise. In 1955, the Kansas City franchise moved to Denver, while the Philadelphia Athletics moved to Kansas City where they remained until 1967. One year later, the expansion major league Kansas City Royals started up, the team that plays in the city today.

The Milwaukee Braves stayed put until the 1965 season, when they moved on to Atlanta. After a short time, another major league team moved in, this time honoring the city's Association roots by taking the name of the Milwaukee Brewers.

The Minneapolis Millers and St. Paul Saints remained in the American Association until the 1960 season when the American League's Washington Senators moved in and displaced them. The two teams were not replaced, as the league dropped to six members. The new major league team honored both cities by taking the name the Minnesota Twins.

The Toledo Mud Hens were not out of the Association for long, as in 1953, the uprooted Milwaukee franchise moved to Toledo for a few years. After the 1955 season, however, the franchise moved to Wichita. Ten years later, Toledo became the second Association city to join the International League, where they have continued to the present day.

The Indianapolis Indians and the Louisville Colonels are the only two teams still playing in the American Association. Louisville rejoined the league in 1982 after a twenty-year absence, broken up by a four-year fling in the International League

(1968–1972). Indianapolis, on the other hand, is the one true link to the Association's beginnings, as they have played in all years of the league's existence.

The American Association itself has maintained a strong presence for the past 45 years. As the original cities were whittled away, new strong cities such as Denver, Omaha, and Wichita took their places.

The league continued in an eight-team format until 1959, when it added a ninth and tenth team for two years. Following major league expansion in 1960, the league dropped to six teams for another two years. After the 1961 season, the League faced a dire predicament. Faced with the loss of a major affiliation with one of the members, the league decided to disband. And for six years, the American Associations lights were dark.

In 1969, the American Association was resurrected in the form of a new six-team league, expanding to eight teams in 1970. Since then, the American Association has remained a prosperous entity to the present day.

In looking at the story of the American Association, we are looking at a microcosm of the development of baseball from the turn of the century until now. In this space of time, the game of baseball has changed, developed, and grown into the game we know today. As we have seen, not all of the changes were good, as many were detrimental to the franchises and cities populating America's heartland. Despite these changes, the American Association has prospered, and should continue to do so for many years to come.

Selected Bibliography

BOOKS

Bauer, Carlos, editor. *The SABR Guide to Minor League Statistics*. Society for American Baseball Research, 1995.

Cramer, Richard Ben. *Ted Williams, The Seasons of the Kid*. New York: Prentice Hall, 1991.

Foster, John B. *A History of the National Association of Professional Base Ball Leagues*. National Association of Professional Base Ball Leagues, 1927.

Hano, Arnold. *Willie Mays*. New York: Grossett and Dunlap, 1966.

Johnson, Lloyd, editor. *The Encyclodepia of Minor League Baseball*. Durham: Baseball America, 1993.

____. *The Minor League Register*. Durham: Baseball America, 1994

Mayer, Ronald. *1937 Newark Bears*. East Hanover: Vantage Press, 1980.

Murdock, Eugene. *"Some Called Him Tarzan." Baseball Research Journal*, 1981. Society for American Baseball Research.

Nemec, David. *The Great American Baseball Team Book*. New York: Signet, 1992.

Obojski, Robert. *Bush Leagues*. New York: Macmillan, 1975.

Okkonen, Marc. *The Federal League of 1914–1915*. Society for American Baseball Research, 1989.

O'Neal, Bill. *The American Association*. Austin: Eakin Press, 1991.

Reddick, David B., and Rogers, Kim M. *The Magic of Indians Baseball: 1887–1987*. Indianapolis: Indians, Inc, 1988.

Seymour, Harold. *Baseball: The Golden Age*. New York: Oxford Univ. Press, 1971

Sullivan, Neil J. *The Minors*. New York: St. Martin's Press, 1991.

Thorn, John, and Palmer, Peter, editors. *Total Baseball IV*. New York: Viking, 1995.

Veeck, Bill. *Veeck—as in Wreck*. New York: G.P. Putnam's Sons, 1962.

GUIDES

American Association Sketch and Record Book, 1995
Reach's Official American Association Baseball Guide, 1903
Reach's Official Baseball Guide, 1903–1938
Spalding-Reach Official Baseball Guide, 1939–1941
Spalding's Official Baseball Guide, 1903–1938

Sporting News Baseball Guide and Record Book, 1942–1953
Supplemental American Association Statistics (unpublished), 1919–1952

NEWSPAPERS

The Sporting News, 1902–1953

Index

Aaron 115
Abbott, Fred 17, 30, 34, 40, 46, 50
Abbott, Spencer 158
Abernathie, Bill 359
Abernathy, Ted 264
Abernathy, Woody 300, 308, 309, 317, 326
Aberson, Cliff 341
Abrams, Cal 341
Abreu, Joe 272
Ackerman 116
Acosta 128
Acosta, Baldomero 87, 106, 112, 119, 130, 135, 142, 148, 149, 156, 168, 176
Acosta, Julio 282, 289, 297
Adair, James 208, 214, 220, 229, 235, 238, 245, 253
Adams 114
Adams 39
Adams, Charles 75, 88, 98
Adams, Earl 226
Adams, Elvin 255
Adams, K. 108
Adams, Spence 172
Adams, W. 108
Addis, Robert 324, 331, 338, 342
Aderholt, Morris 307
Adkins 207
Ahlf 246
Ahman 151
Ahnman, Ben 146
Aiken 20
Ainsmith, Ed 150, 156, 188
Aitchison, R. 89

Akers, Abe 7
Akers, Bill 195
Albertson, Robert 300
Albosta, Ed 319, 336
Albright, Hal 316
Albright, Jack 284, 306
Aldridge 81, 86
Aleno, Charles 270, 276, 311
Alexander 116, 117
Alexander, Dale 226, 227, 233
Alexander, Robert 335, 342
Alexander, Walt 82, 102, 123, 124
Aliperto, Joe 292, 352
Allaire, Robert 221, 228
Allemang 11, 19
Allen 105
Allen 53, 62, 75
Allen, Bill 355
Allen, H. 119
Allen, Horace 141, 149
Allen, Nick 122, 127, 134, 141, 150, 159, 166, 173, 215
Allen, William 359
Allison 70, 76, 82
Allison, Mack 138, 139
Alloway 12, 13
Almada, Mel 222
Alston, Walt 324, 331
Altenberg 95
Altizer, Dave 14, 50, 55, 56, 62, 68, 77, 80, 87, 94, 101
Altrock, Nick 7, 45, 50, 60, 63
Ambler, Wayne 270

Ambrose, Elmer 124, 136, 145, 167, 181, 192
American League 2
Ames, L. 116, 117, 120, 128
Amoros, Sandy 357
Ananicz, Thomas 268, 269, 292
Anderson 106, 128, 129, 146
Anderson, Alf 279
Anderson, Charles 293
Anderson, Ferrell 324, 331, 341
Anderson, George 94, 100, 109
Anderson, Harold 159, 166, 173, 179, 187, 195, 203, 211, 218, 226, 234, 317, 325, 334
Anderson, Henry 327, 334
Anderson, Howard 355
Anderson, John 138, 142, 148, 149, 156, 167, 171
Andres, Ernest 253, 261, 267, 308, 318
Andrews 14
Andrews, Hubert 326
Andrews, I. 259
Andrews, Nathan 226, 249, 255, 256, 262, 272
Andrews, Stan 280, 286
Andromidas, Nick 331, 341, 348
Angle, Jack 276
Angley, Tom 179, 192, 196, 206, 212, 218
Ankenman, Fred 226, 234, 238, 249